CONCORDIA COLLEGE LIBRARY
BRONXVILLE, N. Y. 10708

*THE CAMBRIDGE BIBLE
FOR SCHOOLS AND COLLEGES*

General Editor for the Old Testament:—
A. F. KIRKPATRICK, D.D.
DEAN OF ELY

THE
BOOK OF GENESIS

CAMBRIDGE UNIVERSITY PRESS
C. F. CLAY, Manager
LONDON : FETTER LANE, E.C.4

NEW YORK : THE MACMILLAN CO.
BOMBAY
CALCUTTA } MACMILLAN AND CO., LTD.
MADRAS
TORONTO : THE MACMILLAN CO.
OF CANADA, LTD.
TOKYO : MARUZEN-KABUSHIKI-KAISHA

ALL RIGHTS RESERVED

THE
BOOK OF GENESIS

In the Revised Version

With Introduction and Notes

by

HERBERT E. RYLE, D.D.

Dean of Westminster,
Sometime Bishop of Exeter, and of Winchester;
Fellow of the British Academy.

Cambridge:
at the University Press
1921

First Edition 1914
Reprinted 1921

*Printed in Great Britain
by Turnbull & Spears, Edinburgh*

PREFACE

BY THE
GENERAL EDITOR FOR THE OLD TESTAMENT

THE present General Editor for the Old Testament in the Cambridge Bible for Schools and Colleges desires to say that, in accordance with the policy of his predecessor the Bishop of Worcester, he does not hold himself responsible for the particular interpretations adopted or for the opinions expressed by the editors of the several Books, nor has he endeavoured to bring them into agreement with one another. It is inevitable that there should be differences of opinion in regard to many questions of criticism and interpretation, and it seems best that these differences should find free expression in different volumes. He has endeavoured to secure, as far as possible, that the general scope and character of the series should be observed, and that views which have a reasonable claim to consideration should not be ignored, but he has felt it best that the final responsibility should, in general, rest with the individual contributors.

A. F. KIRKPATRICK.

CAMBRIDGE.

PREFACE

AN apology is due for the long delay in the appearance of this volume. It is ten years since it was begun. But, as Bishop of Winchester from 1903 to 1911, I had little leisure except during the annual summer holiday for consecutive literary work. The shortcomings of the present book, of which I am only too conscious, are partly attributable to this cause.

I acknowledge with gratitude my obligations to the larger Commentaries of Dillmann, Driver, Gunkel, and Skinner, and to the smaller books of Spurrell and of Bennett. I should like especially to refer to the encouragement I received from my friend Dr Driver, whose loss all English-speaking Bible Students are deploring, and whose work on the Old Testament generally, and on Genesis and Exodus in particular, has so greatly promoted the cause of Sacred Study on lines of reverent criticism and simple faith. My old friend, the Dean of Ely, as General Editor of this Series, has helped me with many useful suggestions. It only remains for me to record my indebtedness to one who, when I was recovering from illness, added to other kindnesses that of copying out at dictation a very large portion of this little Commentary.

HERBERT E. RYLE.

THE DEANERY, WESTMINSTER,
Easter Eve, 1914.

CONTENTS

INTRODUCTION	PAGES
§ 1. Name	ix, x
§ 2. Contents	x—xiii
§ 3. Composition	xiv—xviii
§ 4. The Documents (J, E, P)	xviii—xxxi
§ 5. Literary Materials	xxxii—xxxviii
§ 6. Historical Value	xxxviii—xlv
§ 7. Religious Teaching	xlvi—liii
§ 8. Moral Difficulties	liii—lv
§ 9. The Names of God in the Book of Genesis	lvi—lxv
§ 10. Bibliography	lxv—lxvii
NOTE	lxviii
CHRONOLOGICAL NOTE	lxviii
TEXT AND NOTES	1—446

SPECIAL NOTES:

On the plural form of the word *Elohim*	23
On the Jewish Interpretation of I. 26	24
On the Sabbath	40 f.
On the Cosmogonies of Genesis	42—46
On the Rivers of Paradise	47
On the Fall	60—67
On the Antediluvian Patriarchs	88—92
On the Flood Narratives	115—122
On IX. 25—27	130
On the Genealogy of Shem	154

CONTENTS

SPECIAL NOTES—*continued*	PAGES
On Chapter XIV.	179—181
On Melchizedek	182—184
On the Sacrifice of Isaac	240—245
On the Name "Jacob"	272

APPENDICES:

A. Babylonian Myths of Creation	447
B. A Legend of Lamech	452
C. The Duplicate Account of the Flood	453
D. The Tel el-Amarna Tablets	458
E. The Israelites in Egypt	463

INDEX	478—483

MAPS:

Palestine	At End
Western Asia	,,

PLATES:

A diagram representing the Semitic conception of the Universe	To face p. 8
Assyrian Winged Bull	,, 59
Fragment of Cuneiform Tablet, belonging to the Deluge Series	,, 116
Khammurabi (? Amraphel), King of Babylon, receiving laws from Shamash, the Sun-god	,, 167
Egyptians measuring the wheat and depositing it in the granaries	,, 380
Marduk and Tiâmat	,, 449

INTRODUCTION

§ 1. Name.
§ 2. Contents.
§ 3. Composition.
§ 4. The Documents (J, E, P).
§ 5. Literary Materials.
§ 6. Historical Value.
§ 7. Religious Teaching.
§ 8. Moral Difficulties.
§ 9. The Names of God.
§ 10. Bibliography.

§ 1. *Name.*

"GENESIS" is the name of the first book in the English Bible, as also in the Latin Bible (or Vulgate) and in the Greek Old Testament (or Septuagint). The name is taken from the Greek rendering of the Hebrew word for "generations" in Gen. ii. 4, "This is the book of the generations (Heb. *tôledôth*, Gr. γενέσεως) of the heavens and the earth." In the Codex Alexandrinus (5th cent. A.D.) of the Greek Old Testament, Genesis has the title of ΓΕΝΕϹΙϹ ΚΟϹΜΟΥ, i.e. "The Origin of the World." The word "genesis," in the sense of "origins" or "beginnings,' has passed into familiar use in the English language.

In the Hebrew Bible the book is entitled B^e*rêshîth* (= "In the beginning") from the opening word of the first verse.

The Hebrew Bible is divided into "The Law," or *Tôrah*, "The Prophets," or *N^{e}bhîîm*, and "The Writings," or *K^{e}thûbîm* (Hagiographa). "The Law," or *Tôrah*, contains the first five books of our English Bible, "the Pentateuch," a title which also is of Greek origin (ἡ πεντάτευχος, sc. βίβλος) and means "the book of five volumes." Sometimes, (*a*) because "the first stage in the history of God's dealings with His chosen people ends with their settlement in the Promised Land, rather than with the death of Moses[1]," and (*b*) because the same documents can be traced from the beginning of Genesis to the end of Joshua, the first six books are treated as one work and spoken of as "the Hexateuch." *Berêshîth* is the first book of the *Tôrah*.

We do not know at what date the Jews divided up the *Tôrah*, or Pentateuch, into five books. The division is mentioned by Philo[2] and Josephus[3], and it may fairly be assumed to have suggested the division of the Psalter into five books. The division of "Genesis" was a very natural one. It was clearly marked off, by the nature of its contents, from the four books that follow. There is an appropriate break in the narrative at the death of Joseph, and before the birth of Moses.

§ 2. *Contents.*

(*a*) *Two main divisions.*

The Hexateuch, as has been said, "forms in itself a connected whole, and displays to us the origin, choice, and planting of the people of God, or the founding of the Israelitish theocracy[4]." The Book of Genesis contains, in outline, the preliminary materials of the sacred history, previous to the call of Moses. These preliminary materials fall into two easily recognized divisions: (1) the Primaeval History of Mankind (chaps. i.—xi.), and (2) the History of the Hebrew Patriarchs (chaps. xii.—l.).

These two divisions may, for clearness' sake, be subdivided as follows:

I. Primaeval History · Narratives respecting

   (i) The Origin of the World and of the Human Race (chaps. i.—v.).

   (ii) The Flood (chaps. vi.—ix.).

   (iii) The Primitive Races before the call of Abraham (chaps. x., xi.).

---

[1] Chapman's *Introd. to the Pent.*, p. 6.
[2] *De Abrahamo*, § 1, ii. 1.   [3] *Contr. Ap.* i. 8.
[4] Knobel, quoted in Dillmann's *Genesis*, vol. I. p. 3.

II. Patriarchal History: Narratives respecting
  (i) The Patriarch Abraham (chaps. xii. 1—xxv. 18).
  (ii) The Patriarchs Isaac and Jacob (chaps. xxv. 19—xxxvi. 43).
  (iii) The Patriarchs Joseph and his brethren (chaps. xxxvii.—l.).

(*b*) *Arrangement of material.*

The arrangement of the material explains the plan which is followed throughout the book. It is not a history of the world; but it is an introduction to the History of the Chosen People. In consequence, as each stage in the Primaeval and Patriarchal History is reached, the collateral material is disposed of, before the main thread is resumed. Thus (1) the origin of the Human Race having been described, the descendants of Adam through the Cainite families are mentioned (iv. 16—26), before the main narrative is resumed in the descendants of Seth (chap. v.). (2) After the story of the Flood, the descendants of Japheth and Ham are recorded (chap. x.), before the main subject of the book is approached through the family of Shem (xi. 10 ff.). (3) After the death of Abraham, the story of Isaac's sons is not commenced, until the descendants of Ishmael have been enumerated (xxv. 12—18). (4) The account of Joseph and his brethren is not commenced, until the genealogy of Esau (chap. xxxvi.) has disposed of the collateral branch. The plan of the book, therefore, is continually to concentrate attention upon the direct line of the ancestors of the Israelite people, tracing them back to the very beginnings of the Human Race.

It has sometimes been maintained that the best sub-division of the book is furnished by the formula "These are the generations," which is found eleven times in reference to (1) the heavens and the earth, ii. 4; (2) Adam, v. 1; (3) Noah, vi. 9; (4) the sons of Noah, x. 1; (5) Shem, xi. 10; (6) Terah, xi. 27; (7) Ishmael, xxv. 12; (8) Isaac, xxv. 19; (9) Esau, xxxvi. 1; (10) "Esau, the father of the Edomites in Mount Seir," xxxvi. 9; (11) Jacob, xxxvii. 2. But the repetition of this formula offers no real clue to the analysis of the whole book, though it reproduces the outline of the contents of one of its component documents (see below, p. xxviii).

(*c*) *Primaeval History.*

Chaps. i.—xi. The first main division of the Book of Genesis consists of a group of Narratives which furnishes answers to the instinctive questionings of mankind: How did the earth, the sea, the sky, and the heavenly bodies come into being? What was the origin of the vegetable world, and of the birds, fishes, reptiles and beasts? What was the origin of man? What was the beginning of sin and of death? What explanation can be given of the sufferings of child-birth and of the laboriousness of human life? How did the arts and industries take their rise? What caused the difference of languages, and the various types of races dispersed throughout the world? What, again, led to the Flood of which traditions were handed on from one generation to another?

These Narratives, though doubtless based upon the cosmogonies which had come down from remote Hebrew ancestors, are conspicuous for their beauty and simplicity. They do not affront us with the superstition, silliness, or coarseness, which are too often prominent in the literature of cosmogonies and mythologies.

The events recorded are evidently regarded as affecting the whole human race. The scenes are neither those of actual history, nor those of mere mythology. We come across a few survivals of an older mythological element, e.g. God speaks to the inhabitants of heaven (i. 26); the serpent speaks to Eve in human language (iii. 1—5); there is mention of the marriage of angels with the daughters of men (vi. 1—4). But these instances are very rare. The Narratives, while they preserve the outlines of earlier legends, have been adapted to the religious thought of the later Israelites. If, as is most probable, the primitive form in which they were current was polytheistic, practically every trace of polytheism has been removed. The Narratives are presented to us in such a manner as to convey in a fully developed stage the distinctive teaching of the Israelite Prophets.

(d) *Patriarchal History.*

Chaps. xii.—l. In the second main division of the book the Narratives belong to a different class. We pass from legends respecting the Origin of the World and of the Human Race to traditions respecting the earliest ancestors of the Israelite People. The portraits of individual personages are well and skilfully drawn. The scenes are laid in Palestine and Egypt, and the incidents, for the most part, are associated with well-known places, and are recounted with remarkable vividness of description.

The impression given of the religious life of the Patriarchs is that of the simple monotheistic worship of Jehovah. The power of Jehovah is felt in Egypt (xii. 17, xxxix. 1—5), in the Cities of the Plain (chap. xix.), in Gerar (chap. xxvi.), in Syria (xxxi. 24), no less than in Canaan. The idolatry of the heathen is scarcely referred to. The *teraphim*, stolen by Rachel from her father's house, and possibly included among "the strange gods," constitute almost the sole exception (xxxi. 19 and xxxv. 2—4).

The Patriarchal Narratives preserve to us traditions respecting, for the most part, domestic incidents in the lives of Abraham, Isaac, Jacob, and Joseph. Only in one passage (chap. xiv.), where "Amraphel" is very possibly Ḥammurabi, the famous Babylonian monarch, is any person mentioned whose name is found in the inscriptions of the contemporary ancient monuments.

In a word, the Patriarchal Narratives represent a group of Israelite traditions respecting remote ancestors, whose existence belonged to the twilight of history, anterior to the era of Moses and earlier than the beginnings of the Nation. The materials which are embodied in the Narratives are very various. But in this, as in the first division of the Book of Genesis, the contents have been brought into harmony with the religious thought of the worshipper of Jehovah.

§ 3. *Composition.*

On the origin and composition of the Pentateuch the reader is referred to Chapman's admirable *Introduction to the Pentateuch* (1911) in this series, Simpson's *Pentateuchal Criticism* (1914), the articles in Hastings' *Dictionary of the Bible*, and Black's *Encyclopaedia Biblica*, the *Oxford Hexateuch* (1900) by Estlin Carpenter and Battersby Harford, Driver's *Literature of the Old Testament* (9th ed. 1913), and G. B. Gray's *Critical Introd. to the O. T.* (1913).

The fact that the Pentateuch was known to the Jews as "The Law of Moses" (Luke xxiv. 44; Acts xxviii. 33), and was referred to as "Moses" (Acts xv. 21), was once regarded as a sufficient reason for assuming that Moses himself was the author. This view, however, is no longer tenable. That Moses himself did not write the Pentateuch, as we now have it, is one of the literary conclusions of Biblical Criticism upon which scholars are unanimous.

Here it must suffice to point out three important considerations:

1. The Book of Genesis contains a number of passages which imply that at the time of its composition the Israelites were in settled possession of the land of Canaan.

(*a*) "The Canaanite was then in the land" (xii. 6, xiii. 7) is an expression which compares the age of the Patriarchs when the Canaanites were in undisturbed occupation of the land, with the age of the writer, when the Israelites had become its undisputed masters.

(*b*) "To," or "Unto, this day" (xxii. 14, xxvi. 33, xxxv. 20)[1].

The names of places in Canaan are thus spoken of in accordance with the usage of Israelites who had long resided there;

---

[1] xxii. 14, And Abraham called the name of that place Jehovah-jireh: as it is said to this day, In the mount of the LORD, &c.

xxvi. 33, therefore the name of the city is Beer-sheba unto this day.

xxxv. 20, the same is the Pillar of Rachel's grave unto this day.

In these passages, "To," or "Unto, this day" could not have been used except by a person who was living in Palestine.

cf. Deut. ii. 22, iii. 14, x. 8, xxxiv. 6; Jos. iv. 9, v. 9, vii. 26, viii. 29, ix. 27, x. 27, xiii. 13, xiv. 14, xv. 63, xvi. 10.

(c) "And pursued as far as Dan" (xiv. 14). The town of Laish in the extreme N. of Palestine received the name of Dan, after it had been conquered by the Danites (Judg. xviii. 29).

(d) "Before there reigned a king over Israel" (xxxvi. 31), an expression which implies acquaintance with the monarchy as the recognized form of government in Israel, i.e. a date later than Saul.

(e) The Philistines, who, as is most probable, are identifiable with the *Purasati* of the Egyptian inscriptions, established themselves in the reign of Ramses II (1300—1224 B.C.) in the S.W. of Palestine. They were regarded by the Israelites (cf. Deut. ii. 23; Jer. xlvii. 4; Am. ix. 7) as invaders from Caphtor (=Crete). But the occurrence of their name in Gen. x. 14, xxi. 32, xxvi. 1, is an indication that the traditions embodied in our book have come down to us from a time when the Philistines were accepted as the inhabitants of S.W. Palestine.

(f) "He had wrought folly in Israel" (xxxiv. 7) is an expression which implies the existence of an ordered community of Israel (cf. Jos. vii. 15; Judg. xx. 6). "The land of the Hebrews" (xl. 15) is a phrase which would most naturally be used by a writer who regarded Canaan as the home of the Hebrew people. The fact that the "West" (e.g. in xii. 8) is denoted by the Hebrew word meaning "the sea," i.e. the Mediterranean, and "the South" by the word "Negeb" (e.g. xiii. 14, xxviii. 14), i.e. the country S. of Judah, implies a writer dwelling in Palestine.

(g) Abraham is described as a prophet, *nabî* (Gen. xx. 7). In 1 Sam. ix. 9, we are told that "he that is now called a Prophet, *nabî*, was beforetime called a Seer, *rô'eh*." The use of the word *nabî* is therefore more likely to be found in literature belonging to a time subsequent to, than to a time before, the age of Samuel.

2. The literary criticism of the Pentateuch shews that it is not like a modern book of history, written, from beginning

to end, by a single author, but that, on the contrary, it is of composite origin, being a compilation of no less than four distinct writings.

To a modern reader such an account will sound strange and improbable. He reads the books in English as continuous historical works. And so in a true sense they are. But they are not homogeneous. Hebrew scholarship can, with a great degree of certainty, discriminate between the different materials out of which the books were composed. It is not often realized that, in the Hebrew Bible, all the narrative books have been composed in this way. The Books of Judges, Samuel, Kings, Chronicles, Ezra and Nehemiah are compilations. The Pentateuch and Joshua are no exceptions to the general rule. They were built up out of previously existing materials. We must remember that there were no rights of Hebrew authorship. Writers made free use of earlier documents. They cut out and omitted: they expanded and amplified: they combined, adapted, and adjusted, according to the purpose which they had in view. See the examples of Hebrew and Semitic composite narrative given in Chapman's *Pentateuch*, Appendix vii., "Characteristics of Composite Documents."

Instead of the composite origin of Genesis and the rest of the Pentateuch being a thing improbable in itself, it is, on the contrary, if analogy be appealed to, most reasonable and probable. It corresponds with what we know of the formation of other books of the Bible, and with the literary practice unquestionably followed in other Hebrew and Semitic prose writings.

3. Moreover, the discovery that the Book of Genesis is not a homogeneous work, but a compilation of different writings, has been found to explain, most simply and satisfactorily, the numerous minor difficulties and discrepancies which catch the attention of every careful reader.

For instance, why should there be two accounts of the Creation, in the one of which man and woman are created after all the animals (i. 26), while, in the other, man is created before and woman after the animals (ii. 7, 18, 19, 22)? How is it that there are two versions of the number of the animals that went into the ark and of the duration of the Flood upon the earth (chaps. vi., vii.)? Is it not strange that the promise of a son to Sarah should be given twice over (xvii. 16—19 and xviii. 10 ff.)? that the name of Isaac should three times be accounted for by a mention of laughter (xvii. 17, xviii. 12, xxi. 6)? that a second blessing should be given by Isaac to Jacob in xxviii. 1 ff. without any reference to the blessing and the deceitful manner of obtaining it, just recorded in chap. xxvii.? How is it possible, after such passages as xvii. 17 and xviii. 11, 12, to account for the statement that, after Sarah's death, Abraham should beget a number of sons (xxv. 1 ff.)? Who does not realize that the passages relating to Sarah in xii. 11, xx. 2 ff. are out of harmony with the statement as to her age in xvii. 17? Does not the account of Isaac's failing powers in xxvii. 1, 2 appear incompatible with the mention of his having lived to the age of 180 years (xxxv. 28), i.e. for 100 years (cf. xxv. 26, xxvi. 34) after the marriage of Esau? How can we explain the mention of Rachel's death in xxxv. 19 and of her being alive in xxxvii. 10? How is it that immediately after the account of Benjamin's birth and Rachel's death near Bethlehem (xxxv. 18, 19), Benjamin's name is included among the sons of Jacob born to him in Paddan-aram (xxxv. 25, 26)? Why should Esau's wives have different names in xxvi. 34, xxviii. 9 and in xxxvi. 2, 3? How does it happen that we find varying explanations of the names Bethel (xxviii. 18, 19, xxxv. 14, 15), Beer-sheba (xxi. 31, xxvi. 33), Israel (xxxii. 28, xxxv. 10)? Is the description of Benjamin as a "child of his [Jacob's] old age, a little one" (xliv. 20) reconcilable with the statements as to the date of his birth (xxxv. 18, 23, 26), according to which he would have been not less than 20 years of age when he appeared before Joseph in Egypt (cf. xxxvii. 2, xli. 46, xlv. 6)?

These are examples of difficulties and discrepancies to be found in the story of Genesis. The list could easily be added to. They are not compatible with the theory of uniform, continuous, and homogeneous literary composition. On the hypothesis of a single author and a continuous work, they would denote an extraordinary lack of literary attention and care. But, on the supposition that in the same book there are woven together portions of different documents containing similar, but not in all respects identical, accounts of the same narratives, we have an explanation which satisfies the requirements of the problem. Ridicule used to be directed against the Bible on account of the presence of these difficulties and discrepancies. That ridicule is seen now to be misplaced. We are able to understand their nature and cause. The Book of Genesis is a compilation. The combination of different documents has led to the inclusion of divergent statements. Numerous in quantity, though trifling in importance, these inconsistencies survive as evidence of the literary process, through which the books of the Pentateuch passed before they were given their final shape.

§ 4. *The Documents* (J, E, P).

In 1753 Jean Astruc, a French physician, published anonymously at Brussels a book entitled *Conjectures sur les mémoires originaux dont il paroit que Moyse s'est servi pour composer le Livre de la Genèse*. He had been led to infer from the intermittent use of different names of God in Genesis that Moses had employed different documents in its composition. This was the beginning of systematic literary criticism upon the Pentateuch. Other scholars carried on the work. It was soon seen (1) that the use of the Divine Names was only one of many literary characteristics by which the different component documents were capable of being distinguished, (2) that the different sources of the Pentateuch, thus linguistically and stylistically determined, (*a*) correspond to different stages in the development of the religion of Israel, and (*b*) reflect the influence of different epochs in the nation's history. As the History of Pentateuchal criticism would carry us further afield than space will here allow, the student is referred to Chapman's *Introduction to the Pentateuch*, Driver's *Literature of the Old*

THE DOCUMENTS (J, E, P)

Testament, Carpenter and Harford's *Oxford Hexateuch*, D. C. Simpson's *Pentateuchal Criticism* (1914).

After a century and a half of minute and laborious research, scholars are now agreed that the books of the Pentateuch and of Joshua present to us a compilation of four distinct documents, to which the names have very generally been given of (1) J, because of its preference for the Name familiarly known in English as Jehovah (Heb. *Jahweh*), translated "LORD," (2) E, because of its preference for the Name *Elohim*="God," (3) D, the Deuteronomist, and (4) P, the Priestly Code. Of these four documents, three, J, E, and P, may clearly be identified in the Book of Genesis. The Deuteronomist, whose style and characteristics are so unmistakable in Deuteronomy and in certain passages of the Book of Joshua, has left little, if any, trace of influence upon Genesis (? xxvi. 5).

J, E, and P may, as a rule, be identified by the character of their contents and by distinctive features of language. But the Priestly Code (P) can be very much more easily distinguished from J and E than these can be distinguished from one another. In style and diction as well as in selection and treatment of subject-matter there is a much closer affinity between J and E, than between either of these and the Priestly Code. As compared with J and E, P is always recognizable. But it is frequently impossible to determine whether a passage has been derived from J or E.

The J Narratives.

The passages in Genesis which probably have been derived from J are as follows:

ii. 4^b—iv. 26, vi. 1—4, vii. 1—viii. 22 (partially), ix. 18—27, x. (partially), xi. 1—9, 28—30, xii. 1—4^a, 6—20, xiii. 1—5, 7—11^a, 12^b—18, xv. (partially), xvi. 1^b, 2, 4—14, xviii., xix. (exc. 29), xxi. (partially), xxii. 20—24, xxiv., xxv. 1—6, 11^b, 18, 21—26^a, 27—34, xxvi. 1—33, xxvii. 1—45, xxviii. 10—22 (partially), xxix.—xxx. (partially), xxxi. 1, 3, 36—50, xxxii. 3—xxxiii. 17, xxxiv. (partially), xxxv. 14, 16—22, xxxvi., xxxvii. (partially), xxxviii., xxxix., xli. (partially), xlii.—xliv., xlvi. 28—xlvii. 4, 6^b, 12—27^a, 29—31, xlix. 1—27, l. 1—11, 14.

A glance through this list will shew that J contained the greater number both of the Primaeval and of the Patriarchal Narratives. Many of them are masterpieces of Hebrew prose writing. The story is told with beauty, vividness, and brevity. The dialogue which is introduced, in e.g. chaps. iii., iv., xviii., xix., xxiv., xliii., xliv., adds a touch of brightness and life which it would be difficult to find surpassed in any literature.

The Narratives are pervaded with deep religious feeling. This is noticeable (a) in the account given of the beginnings of sin and crime (chaps. iii., iv.), the spread of evil (vi. 1—8, viii. 21), and the corruption of the people of the Plain (chap. xix.); and (b) in the emphasis laid upon the Divine call which caused Abraham to migrate into Canaan (xii. 1—3), and the Divine purpose of goodness and mercy expressed in the promises to the Patriarchs (xviii. 18, xxiv. 7, xxvi. 4, xxvii. 28, 29). "In order to illustrate the divine purposes of grace, as manifested in history, he introduces...prophetic glances into the future (Gen. iii. 15, v. 29, viii. 21, ix. 25—27, xii. 2, 3, xviii. 18, 19, xxviii. 14, Num. xxiv. 17, 18), as he also loves to point to the character of the nations or tribes as foreshadowed in their beginnings (Gen. ix. 22—24, xvi. 12, xix. 31—38, xxv. 21—28, xxxiv. 25—31, xxxv. 22, cf. xlix. 9 ff.)[1]."

In representations of the Deity, J makes use of simple anthropomorphic expressions, e.g. iii. 8 "the LORD God walking in the garden in the cool of the day," vi. 6 "it repented the LORD that he had made man," vii. 16 "the LORD shut him [Noah] in," viii. 21 "the LORD smelled the sweet savour," xi. 5 "the LORD came down to see the city and the tower, which the children of men builded," xviii. 1 "And the LORD appeared unto him [Abraham] by the oaks of Mamre, as he sat in the tent door in the heat of the day"; cf. xviii. 21, 33, xxxii. 24—30.

Characteristic as is the use of Jehovah [Jahweh] for the

---

[1] Dillmann in Driver's *L.O.T.*, p. 120.

name of God, Elohim (= God) is also found, e.g. in the colloquy between the serpent and the woman (iii. 1, 3, 5), and in the words of Eve (iv. 25) before "men began to call on Jehovah" (iv. 26); when a foreigner addresses an Israelite (xliii. 29), or when, as in xxxii. 28, 30 (Heb. 29, 31), xxxiii. 10, the use of Elohim seems intended to contrast the Divine with the human nature.

J traces back the religious institutions of Israel to the very earliest times, e.g. sacrifice (iv. 3), prayer to Jehovah (iv. 26), distinction of clean and unclean animals (vii. 2, viii. 20), altars (viii. 20, xii. 7, 8), enquiry of Jehovah (xxv. 22).

There is an especial fondness in J for the etymology of proper names: (1) Of persons, e.g. "woman" (ii. 23), Eve (iii. 20), Cain (iv. 1), Seth (iv. 25), Noah (v. 29), Peleg (x. 25), Ishmael (xvi. 11), Moab and Ammon (xix. 37, 38), Jacob and Esau = Edom (xxv. 25, 26, 30), the sons of Jacob (xxix. 31—xxx. 24), Israel (xxxii. 28), Benjamin (xxxv. 18), Perez (xxxviii. 29). (2) Of places, e.g. Babylon (xi. 9), Beer-lahai-roi (xvi. 14), Zoar (xix. 22), Esek, Sitnah and Rehoboth (wells) (xxvi. 20—22), Beer-sheba (xxvi. 33), Bethel (xxviii. 19), Galeed and Mizpah (xxxi. 48, 49), Peniel (xxxii. 30).

The diction of J abounds in striking and happy expressions, e.g. "to find favour (or grace) in the eyes of" (vi. 8, xviii. 3, xix. 19, xxx. 27, xxxii. 5), "to call by [R.V. "on," or "upon"] the name of the LORD" (iv. 26, xii. 8, xiii. 4, xxi. 33, xxvi. 25), and familiar phrases, e.g. "Behold now" (xii. 11, xvi. 2, xviii. 27, 31, xix. 2, 8, 19, xxvii. 2), "forasmuch as" (xviii. 5, xix. 8, xxxiii. 10, xxxviii. 26).

The E Narratives.

The passages generally assigned to E are as follows:

xx. 1—17, xxi. 6—32, xxii. 1—13, 19, xxvii. 1—45 (partially), xxviii. 10—22 (partially), xxix.—xxx. (partially), xxxi.—xxxii. 2 (partially), xxxiii. 19, 20, xxxiv. (partially), xxxv. 1—8, xxxvii. (partially), xl., xli. (partially), xlii. (partially), xlv., xlvi. 1—5, xlviii. 1, 2, 8—22, l. 15—22.

The extent of narrative covered by E is thus much more limited than that of J. Whether any portions of E (e.g. possibly in chap. xv.) are to be identified before chap. xx., is doubtful. But it may be assumed that E contained some account of the call of Abraham and of his migration into Canaan.

As compared with J, the narrative in E is less prominently marked by its religious thought. But it contains some of the most striking passages in the book, e.g. the story of the sacrifice of Isaac (chap. xxii.), and the bulk of the story of Joseph (chaps. xxxvii., xxxix.—l.).

Anthropomorphisms are not so prominent as in J. The revelation of the Divine Will is generally conveyed through a dream (xx. 3, 6, xxviii. 12, xxxi. 10, 24, xxxvii. 5—11, xl., xli., xlii. 9, xlvi. 2), or by an angel (xxi. 17, xxii. 11, xxviii. 12, xxxi. 11, xxxii. 1). Very interesting are the traditions of worship, e.g. the altar on Moriah (xxii. 9), and at Bethel (xxxv. 1, 3, 7), the pillar (*maṣṣêbah*), the vow, and "the tenth" at Bethel (xxviii. 18, 22), the *teraphim* of Laban stolen by Rachel (xxxi. 19, 20) and "the strange gods" (xxxv. 2). Abraham is called a "prophet" (xx. 7). Important personal details in the patriarchal story are preserved to us by E, e.g. the names of Deborah, Potiphar, Zaphenath-paneah, Asenath; also the mention of Jacob's purchase of land at Shechem (xxxiii. 18—20), his conquest of Shechem by arms (xlviii. 22), and many details of Egyptian life, e.g. xli. 14.

Characteristic of E is the preference for the use of the Divine Names Elohim (though Jehovah occurs, e.g. in xxii. 11, xxviii. 21), and Êl, used absolutely, xxxiii. 20, xxxv. 7, xlvi. 3.

There are also many phrases and words which are regarded by scholars as sound criteria for distinguishing the materials of E. But, as appears from the frequent occurrence of the word "partially" in the list of passages assigned above to E, it is often impossible to say for certain whether the tradition has been derived originally from J or E. For it seems to be the case both that passages derived from E were very commonly expanded by extracts from J, and that details of interest recorded in E were very commonly inserted into the Narrative of J.

THE DOCUMENTS (J, E, P)

The J and E Narratives.

(a) *Origin.*

Collections of popular narratives containing the early folklore of the Israelites were derived from, or based upon, oral tradition. This had been recited at festivals, treasured up in connexion with sacred spots, repeated over camp-fires, and declaimed at burial-places. Some of the narratives may soon have obtained a stereotyped form, others may long have been current in varying traditions. A certain number were early embodied in collections of songs, like the Book of the Wars of Jehovah, quoted in Num. xxi. 14, and the Book of Jashar, quoted in Jos. x. 12, 13 and 2 Sam. i. 18. All of them would, presumably, be circulated and known in different versions, before they were committed to writing.

The collections represented by J and E respectively had, probably, been only very gradually formed; and may each of them have been known in shorter and longer versions. It would be a mistake to regard either of them as the work of a single author, or as the composition of a single mind, or as the product of the generation in which they were committed to writing.

(b) *Locality.*

It has, on the whole, been deemed probable that J presents us with popular traditions current in the Southern Kingdom of Judah. In J, Abraham and, possibly, Jacob appear as living at Hebron: the story of Judah and Tamar seems to contain a tradition of S. Palestine tribal memories. In the Joseph narratives, Judah enjoys a position of eminence above his brethren. E, on the other hand, has been assigned to the Northern Kingdom. The sacred places of Bethel, Shechem, and Beer-sheba (a place of pilgrimage from the Northern Kingdom, Amos v. 5, viii. 14) are given great prominence. Abraham resides at Gerar and Beer-sheba, Jacob at Beer-sheba and Shechem. Joseph is the hero among his brethren; alone of Jacob's sons his body is to be carried out of Egypt (l. 25). Reuben, not Judah, takes the lead as the eldest-born. In E Hebron is not mentioned; and Central Palestine is Jacob's residence for a long time.

(c) Date.

At what date they were respectively committed to writing, can only be a subject of approximate conjecture. In the case of J, it has been pointed out (1) that the curse pronounced upon Canaan (ix. 25) would reflect popular feeling after, but not long after, the final reduction of the Canaanites to subjection (1 Kings ix. 20): (2) that the boundaries of the Promised Land, as defined in xv. 18, correspond with the boundaries of Solomon's kingdom in 1 Kings iv. 21; and (3) that the prediction of Edom's subjugation under Israel and of his ultimate recovery of liberty (xxv. 23, xxvii. 40) would hardly have been written before the time of Edom's successful revolt (2 Kings viii. 22). Obviously such a line of argument is not to be pressed.

In the case of E, it has been conjectured that the compact concluded between Jacob and Laban in the mountain of Gilead (xxxi. 23—55) may reflect the relations between Israel and Syria in the early part of the 8th cent. B.C.; and, on the hardly less precarious ground of xxxvii. 8 ("shalt thou indeed have dominion over us?"), it has been inferred that E was committed to writing at some time subsequent to the Disruption of the Kingdom.

Allusions in the early Hebrew Prophets to events recorded in the Pentateuch are exceedingly rare; and, when they occur, it is not easy to say whether they are based upon the written Narratives embodied in the Hebrew Bible, or upon similar, but not identical, oral tradition recording the same events: cf. Hos. ix. 10; Am. ii. 9; Mic. vi. 4, 5. Take, for instance, the passage in Hos. xii. 3, 4, "In the womb he [Jacob] took his brother by the heel...he had power over the angel and prevailed: he wept and made supplication unto him: he found him at Bethel, and there he spake with us... 12, Jacob fled into the field of Aram, and Israel served for a wife, and for a wife he kept *sheep.*" This shews close resemblances with xxv. 26, xxvii. 43, xxviii., xxix. 20, 30, xxxi. 41, xxxii. 24—32. But there is nothing in the text of Genesis corresponding to "he wept and made supplication unto him." The most that we are entitled to say is that the earlier prophets were acquainted with Narratives recorded by J and E, but, whether with the actual J and E documents incorporated in the Pentateuch, the evidence is insufficient to prove.

The *literary style* of J and E is of such perfection in its simplicity and vividness, that they clearly do not represent the beginnings, but rather the brightest and most finished specimens of Hebrew prose.

The *religious thought* both of J and E assumes the sole pre-eminence of the God of Israel. He is one Who reveals Himself in Haran, and Who protects the family of Abram in Egypt (xii. 1, 17). He protects Eliezer in his journey into Mesopotamia (chap. xxiv.) : He warns Laban on "the mountain of Gilead" (xxxi. 24) : He prospers Joseph in everything in the land of Egypt (xxxix. 3, 5). The intercession of Abraham on behalf of Sodom (xviii. 17—33) has been thought to reflect a somewhat later phase in the revision of the Patriarchal Narratives. But when Abraham appeals to Him as "judge of all the earth" (xviii. 17), his monotheist sentiment is in full harmony with the general teaching of J and E.

There is no expression of hostility to the religion of the native Canaanite, or to the religion of Egypt and Philistia. The closer relation with Shechemites is not opposed on the ground of religion (chap. xxxiv.): nor is the faith of Joseph an obstacle to his marriage with the daughter of the priest of On (xli. 45). Abraham, speaking of Gerar, is made to say, "Surely the fear of God is not in this place" (xx. 11). But God manifests Himself to Abimelech "in a dream of the night," and Abimelech replies, "Lord, wilt thou slay even a righteous nation?" (xx. 3, 4 E).

Once more, it cannot be said that the allusions to Assyria and Babylon in x. 9—12 (J), xi. 1—9 (J), xiv. 1 ff. imply any recognition of the menace to Israel which the great powers of the Euphrates valley subsequently became. If the rivalry of the Canaanite has disappeared, the dread of Assyria has not yet become real.

Abraham builds altars at Shechem, Bethel (xii. 7, 8 J), Hebron (xiii. 18 J and xv. 9, 10 J (E)), and Moriah(?) (xxii. 9 E). Jacob ets up a pillar at Bethel (xxviii. 18 E) and on the mountain of Gilead (xxxi. 45): he builds an altar at Bethel (xxxv. 3, 7 E) and at Beer-sheba (xlvi. 1 E). To the writer of the Priestly Code it seemed impossible that any sacrifices could have been offered before the Levitical Law was instituted, or were lawful except at the central sanctuary. But J and E represent the simpler traditions of the early monarchy. The erection of a pillar (*maṣṣêbah*), which is recorded of Jacob in xxviii. 18, xxxi. 13, 45, xxxv. 14 (cf. 1 Sam. vii. 12 ; 2 Sam. xviii. 18), is condemned as hateful to Jehovah in Deut. xvi. 22, cf. Mic. v. 13, in the later days of the monarchy.

The conclusion which has been reached by the most sober criticism of the Hexateuch is that the composition of J belongs probably to the ninth, and that of E to the early part of the eighth century B.C.

The P Narratives.

The passages in Genesis generally assigned to P are as ollows :

i. 1—ii. 4^a, v. 1—28, 30—32, vi. 9—22, vii. 6, 11, 13—16^a, 18—21, 24, viii. 1, 2^a, 3^b—5, 13^a, 14—19, ix. 1—17, 28, 29, x. 1—7, 20, 22, 23, 31, 32, xi. 10—26, 27, 31, 32, xii. 4^b, 5, xiii. 6, 11^b—12^a, xvi. 1^a, 3, 15, 16, xvii., xix. 29, xxi. 1^b, 2^b—5, xxiii., xxv. 7—11, 12—17, 19, 20, 26^b, xxvi. 34, 35, xxvii. 46—xxviii. 9, xxix. 24, 29, xxxi. 18^b, xxxiii. 18^a, xxxiv. (partially), xxxv. 9—13, 15, 22^b—29, xxxvi., xxxvii. 1, 2^a, xli. 46, xlvi. 6—27, xlvii. 5, 6^a, 7—11, 27^b, 28, xlviii. 3—6, 7 (?), xlix. 1^a, 28^b—33, l. 12, 13.

These passages shew that they belong to a continuous and systematic summary of the Primaeval and Patriarchal Periods. The Narrative itself is, for the most part, slender and jejune, except in connexion with important events and institutions in

THE DOCUMENTS (J, E, P)

the religion of Israel. In Genesis these are (1) the Creation and the Sabbath (i.—ii. 4ª), (2) the covenant of Noah (chap. ix.), (3) the institution of circumcision (chap. xvii.), (4) the purchase of Machpelah (chap. xxiii.).

The character of the contents and the style of the diction are so distinct that as a rule there is no difficulty in separating P from J and E throughout the Hexateuch. "Because of the precise assignment of dates and the systematic arrangement of material, this document practically forms a framework which binds together the component parts of the Hexateuch" (Chapman, p. 71). The main portion, which describes the legislation at Sinai (Ex. xxv.—Num. x.), is so largely occupied with Priestly functions, that the whole document is denoted by P, or PC, the Priestly Code.

Its contents are marked by *orderliness* of arrangement and by careful attention to *chronology*. Under the head of *orderliness* may be noted in Genesis (1) the sequence of the creative acts in the Six Days of Creation (chap. i.); (2) the arrangement of the genealogies in chap. v., where three verses are assigned to each name, and in xi. 10—26, where two verses are assigned to each name; (3) the details of the purchase of the cave of Machpelah in chap. xxiii.: and (4) the genealogy of the sons of Jacob (xxxv. 23—26, xlvi. 8—27).

Under the head of *chronology*, the system followed by P, however artificial, is methodical and continuous; we may note the mention of the day, month, and year of the Deluge (vii. 6, cf. viii. 4, 5, 13, 14); the ages of the descendants of Seth (chap. v.) and of Shem (xi. 10—26); and the ages of the Patriarchs and their wives (xii. 4ᵇ, xvi. 16, xvii. 1, 24, xxi. 5, xxiii. 1, xxv. 7, 17, 26, xxvi. 34, xxxv. 28, xxxvii. 2ª, xli. 46, xlvii. 9, 28).

The narrative, as a rule, is little more than is sufficient to trace the chronology of Israel from the earliest times. "The history," says Driver[1], "advances along a well-defined line, marked

---

[1] *L.O.T.*, p. 127.

by a gradually diminishing length of human life, by the revelation of God under three distinct names, *Elohim, El Shaddai,* and *Jehovah,* by the blessing of Adam and its characteristic conditions, and by the subsequent covenants with Noah, Abraham, and Israel, each with its special 'sign,' the rainbow, the rite of circumcision, and the Sabbath (Gen. ix. 12, 13, xvii. 11; Ex. xxxi. 13)."

The Name of God which is regularly used by the Priestly Document until Ex. vi. 2, is Elohim, not Jehovah. There are two exceptions in xvii. 1 and xxi. 1[b], where it is possible that the Names have been altered in transcription. There are four passages in which God makes Himself known to the Patriarchs, or in which they speak of Him, as *Êl Shaddai* (xvii. 1, xxviii. 3, xxxv. 11, xlviii. 3). It is only after the account of the communication of the Name Jehovah to Moses and the people (Ex. vi. 2 ff.) that that Name is regularly used in the Priestly Document.

P ignores the distinction between clean and unclean animals in the Story of the Flood, and does not record the offering of sacrifices before the institution of the Levitical system. In Genesis the only religious usages referred to are (1) the Sabbath (ii. 1—4[a]), (2) the prohibition to eat blood (ix. 4, 5), (3) the rite of circumcision (chap. xvii.).

In style there is a frequent *redundancy*, e.g. i. 27 "God created man in his own image, in the image of God created he him"; vi. 22 "Thus did Noah; according to all that God commanded him, so did he" (cf. Ex. xl. 16); ix. 9 "And I, behold, I establish my covenant with you...; 11 And I will establish my covenant with you...; 12 This is the token of the covenant which I make...; 13 I do set my bow in the cloud, and it shall be for a token of a covenant between me and the earth...; 16 And the bow shall be in the cloud...; 17 This is the token of the covenant which I have established...."

There are also *recurrent formulae* which form a noticeable feature in the style, e.g. "These are the generations of, &c." (see ii. 4[a], v. 1, vi. 9, &c.), "These are the sons of...after their families, after their tongues, in their lands, in their nations"

THE DOCUMENTS (J, E, P)

(x. 20, 31), "And these are the names of the sons of Ishmael" (xxv. 13), "And these are the names of the children of Israel" (xlvi. 8); cf. xxv. 16, xxxvi. 40.

A very large number of *words and phrases* peculiar to, or characteristic of P, have been collected (see the fifty "literary characteristics," with references, in Driver's *L.O.T.* (pp. 131—5)). As instances may be cited here the expressions for "to be gathered unto his people" (xxv. 8, 17, xxxv. 29, xlix. 29, cf. Num. xx. 24): "make or establish a covenant" (vi. 18, ix. 9, xvii. 2, cf. Ex. vi. 4): "male and female," *zâkâr un^eḳêbah* (i. 27, v. 2, vi. 19, vii. 3): "sojournings" (xvii. 8, xxviii. 4, xxxvi. 7, xlvii. 9, cf. Ex. vi. 4): "possession" (xvii. 8, xxiii. 4, 9, 20, xxxvi. 43, xlvii. 11, xlviii. 4, xlix. 30, l. 13): "be fruitful and multiply" (i. 22, 28, viii. 17, ix. 1, 7, xvii. 20, xxviii. 3, xxxv. 11, xlvii. 27, xlviii. 4): "the selfsame day" (vii. 13, xvii. 23, 26, cf. Ex. xii. 17).

"Israel" is not used by P as a name for Jacob. The Hittites are the *b'nê Ḥêth* ("children or sons of Heth") in P (xxiii. 3, 5, 7, 10, 16, xxv. 10, xxvii. 46), not "Ḥittîm" as in the other documents. Hebron appears as "Kiriath-Arba" (xxiii. 2, xxxv. 27, cf. Jos. xv. 13), Haran as "Paddan-aram" (xxv. 20, xxviii. 2, 5, 6, 7, xxxi. 18, xxxiii. 18, xxxv. 9, 26, xlvi. 15), not Aram-naharaim (J).

The recurrence of the distinctive phraseology and style of P, together with the distinctive treatment of the subject-matter, both in the Pentateuch and in the Book of Joshua, enables the Hebrew reader without difficulty to identify the materials of this document.[1]

The Process of Compilation or Redaction (R).

Those who were responsible for the work of compiling the Pentateuch and the Book of Joshua, desired to give an account of the people of Israel from the earliest times down to the conquest of Canaan and the death of Joshua. The first portion extended from the creation of the world down to the death of Joseph in the land of Egypt. The materials employed for this part of the compilation were, in all probability,

---

[1] On the date of P, see additional note on page lxvii.

(1) the J and E collections of traditions, and (2) the Priestly Code (P).

The methods adopted in the process of compilation were very various. Six, at least, may be recognized: i.e. (1) Verbatim extracts, (2) Abridgment and omission, (3) Duplication of narratives, (4) Conflation and combination, (5) Harmonizing, (6) Glosses.

1. Sometimes long extracts were transferred almost verbatim, as in the case of the account of the Creation (i. 1—ii. 4^a), the Genealogy of the Sethites (chap. v.), the Covenant of Noah (ix. 1—17), the Covenant of Circumcision (chap. xvii.), the purchase of Machpelah (chap. xxiii.), which are taken from P; and as in the case of the story of Eden (ii. 4^b—iv. 26), the story of Abraham at Mamre and the fate of Sodom (chaps. xviii., xix., except *v.* 28), the story of Abraham's servant and Rebekah (chap. xxiv.), the story of Tamar (chap. xxxviii.), which are taken from J.

2. Sometimes the account taken from one document is abridged, because a fuller narrative is preferred from another source. Thus the Cosmogony in J (ii. 4, 5) is fragmentary. The opening portion of it has evidently been omitted, because the previous section from P (i. 1—ii. 4^a) has been given the preference. The account of Abraham's death in J, in or after chap. xxiv. 1 ff., seems to have been omitted, because the account in P is to be inserted later on in chap. xxv. 7—11. Similarly the account, in J, of Isaac's death which is imminent in the story of xxvii. 41, is withheld, because of the insertion, in xxxv. 28, 29, of P's record of the event.

3. Sometimes parallel, but not necessarily identical, narratives are retained side by side. Thus J's account of the formation of man and the animals, in chap. ii., follows immediately upon P's story of Creation in chap. i. In J's account Rebekah persuades Jacob to flee to Haran in order to escape Esau's after-wrath (chap. xxvii.); but in P (xxviii. 1—9), Jacob departs with Isaac's blessing in order to seek for a wife from Rebekah's kindred. Again, in xlviii. 3—7 we have P's account of Jacob's

THE DOCUMENTS (J, E, P)

last words to Joseph, with special reference to Ephraim and Manasseh, which are immediately followed by the parallel account from JE (xlviii. 7—22) in which Israel (not Jacob) beholds Joseph's sons and enquires who they are, and blesses them. The combination of duplicate narratives may be illustrated also by the twofold explanation of the names Issachar, Zebulon and Joseph (xxx. 16—24).

4. Sometimes, when the narratives were identical in their main outlines, but differed in small details, the Compiler combined them, selecting first from one, and then from the other, the material most suitable for his purpose, and omitting or altering material that obviously was not harmonious. This is especially noticeable in the Deluge Narratives (chaps. vii., viii.), the Table of the Nations (chap. x.), the story of Jacob at Haran (chaps. xxx., xxxi.), and the story of Joseph (chaps. xxxix.—l.).

5. Sometimes, in order to remove an appearance of discrepancy, and to secure continuity between passages, editorial changes were introduced. Thus, in view of the change of the forms Abram and Sarai to Abraham and Sarah (related by P, in chap. xvii.), the names Abram and Sarai are used throughout the previous J, as well as P, portions of the narrative. The use of the double Name LORD God (Jehovah Elohim), in chaps. ii. and iii., is probably thus to be explained, as an addition by the compilers, in order to combine the Elohim of chap. i. (P) with the first mention of Jehovah in the following section. In xxxix. 1, the name of "Potiphar, an officer of Pharaoh's, the captain of the guard" is inserted in order to harmonize the account in J, in which Joseph's master is a nameless Egyptian, with that in E, in which Potiphar's name is given (xxxvii. 36).

6. Sometimes, explanatory notes or glosses, which may have come from a later hand, have been inserted into the text, as in xiv. 2, 3, 7, 8, xx. 18, xxxi. 47, xxxv. 6, 19.

§ 5. *Literary Materials.*

The very various materials embodied in JE and P in connexion with the main thread of personal narratives, relating to Adam, Noah, and the Patriarchs, Abraham, Isaac, Jacob and Joseph, can be classified under at least six groups: (1) primitive folk-lore: (2) local traditions: (3) tribal traditions: (4) national traditions: (5) songs: (6) genealogies.

1. *Primitive folk-lore.* The early stories respecting the Creation, the beginnings of the Human Race, and the Deluge, are probably ultimately to be traced back to the common stock of primitive Semitic folk-lore. Whether the people of Israel received them (*a*) through Canaanite channels, or (*b*) directly from Babylonian influence, or (*c*) from their own Hebrew ancestors long previous to immigration into Palestine, is a question which at present we lack the means of answering. Babylonian thought and culture pervaded W. Asia in the second millennium B.C. But the points of resemblance between the Babylonian and the Israelite cosmogonies are neither so numerous nor so close as to make it necessary to infer that the Hebrew stories were borrowed *immediately* from the Babylonian. The Canaanites, among whom the Israelites settled, must have had their own version of a cosmogony. That this was coloured by Babylonian influence would be a reasonable conjecture. Again, the ancestors of the Hebrew race in the valley of the Euphrates had their own primitive Semitic traditions, and these would have been influenced by contact with Assyrian and Babylonian religion.

These stories were originally myths[1], that is, poetical tales in

---

[1] See Kirkpatrick's *Divine Library of the O.T.*, Note C, on "Allegory and Myth," Westcott's *Hist. of Religious Thought in the West*, pp. 3 ff. Cf. Sprott's *Inspiration and the O.T.* (Cambridge), pp. 130 f. "The greatest difficulty presented to ordinary people by modern Criticism, viz. the alleged presence of *myth* and *legend* in the early Biblical records...is of course accentuated by our colloquial use of the word *myth* as a synonym for mere fiction....Without exception, unless

the imagery of which the primitive Semite found an explanation for the phenomena of nature, ascribing them to the action of supernatural beings. The myths were rooted in polytheism. The polytheistic element, in Genesis, has been entirely removed. The Biblical cosmogony gives us a representation of folk-lore, not in its early, crude and superstitious form, but as it was shaped and adapted to be the vehicle of religious thought, in accordance with the needs of a much later age, with the teaching of the Hebrew Prophets, and the monotheistic worship of Jehovah.

2. *Local traditions.* Many of the narratives in Genesis are associated with localities whose sanctity was traditionally connected by the Israelites with manifestations to the Patriarchs, e.g. Shechem (xii. 7), the oaks of Mamre (xiii. 18), Beer-lahai-roi (xvi. 14), Beer-sheba (xxvi. 23—25), Bethel (xxviii. 10—22), Mahanaim (xxxii. 1), Penuel (xxxii. 24—31). In some of these spots, stones, trees, and springs had been regarded from prehistoric times as tenanted by Divine beings. When the Israelites dispossessed the Canaanites, the sanctity of these places continued; and popular legend connected them with historic incidents in the lives of the Hebrew ancestors.

3. *Tribal traditions.* It can hardly be doubted that, under the guise of personal incidents, some of the Narratives of Genesis have preserved the recollection of events in the early history of Hebrew clans and tribes. One very possible example may

the Hebrew literature be an exception, the earliest literature of all peoples is mythical and legendary. Not until a comparatively late date does it reach the stage of matter-of-fact history....The myths of the world's childhood are not historically true: events did not happen so. In fact, a myth is but a parable—a story with a hidden meaning; with this difference that the mythic narrative presents itself not merely as the vehicle of the truth, but as being itself the truth; whereas in the parable, form and essence, husk and kernel, are consciously distinguished. The myth is the parable of the world's childhood; the parable is the myth of the world's maturity. The myth then contains no 'fact.' The legend, on the other hand, does contain 'facts'...but fact so modified and coloured by thought that it is always difficult, and not seldom impossible, to recover just what really happened. It thus belongs to a later stage in human development."

be found in the story of Dinah and the treacherous revenge taken by Simeon and Levi (chap. xxxiv.). It is possible that Dinah impersonates a weak Israelite tribe or clan, which was in danger of being absorbed among the native Canaanite clans, and that this peril brought about the savage attack by the two brother tribes. It is almost certain that the story of Tamar (chap. xxxviii.) turns upon the tribal history of Judah; and that, while accounting for the disappearance of the Hebrew clans of Er and Onan, it represents, under the symbolism of marriage relations, the building up of the tribe of Judah through fusion with local Canaanite clans.

Once more, the blessing of Jacob, conferred upon Ephraim and Manasseh (chap. xlviii. E), is evidently intended to ratify the position of the two most prominent tribes in the Northern Kingdom; while the words of the Blessing of Jacob in chap. xlix. reflect the history and geographical position of the tribes after the conquest of the land.

4. *National traditions.* What has been said about tribal history being impersonated in the Patriarchal Narratives, is clearly capable of extension to nations and peoples. The rivalry between Israel and Edom is prefigured in the antenatal struggle of Jacob and Esau (xxv. 23). The delimitation of the frontiers between Israel and Syria may be symbolized in the covenant between Jacob and Laban (xxxi. 44). It is, at least, a possible interpretation of the repulsive legend in chap. xix., respecting the origin of Moab and Ammon, that Israelite prejudice expressed itself in a story based upon the popular etymology of the two names. In the stories of Hagar and Ishmael, the presentation of traits of the Bedouin type is clearly not excluded: and, under the similitude of family relationship, the connexion of the Israelite people with their neighbours, Aramaean, Edomite, and Arabian, is illustrated in numerous passages, e.g. chaps. xi., xxii. 20—24, xxv. 1—6, 12—16, xxix., xxxvi.

5. *Songs.* The Book of Genesis contains several poetical pieces. It is very probable that many of the prose narratives

LITERARY MATERIALS xxxv

have been derived from earlier lyrical compositions, just as the Song of Deborah (Judg. v.) contained in poetry the record of a great national event which was afterwards related in prose (Judg. iv.). Popular song has often preceded prosaic narrative. In the other books of the Pentateuch we are familiar with the Song of Moses (Ex. xv.), the Songs of the Wars of the LORD and of the Well (Num. xxi. 14, 15, 17, 18), the Song of Triumph over the Defeat of Sihon (Num. xxi. 27—30), Balaam's Oracles (Num. xxiii. 7—10, 18—24, xxiv. 3—9, 15—24), the Song of Moses (Deut. xxxii.), and the Blessing of Moses (Deut. xxxiii.). In Genesis the following passages are genuine specimens of Hebrew poetry, and in style and language are quite distinct from the setting of prose narrative in which they are preserved:

(i) The Song of Lamech (iv. 23, 24), on the invention of weapons.

(ii) The Song of Lamech (v. 29), on the introduction of vine culture.

(iii) Noah's Oracle on his Sons (ix. 25—27).

(iv) The Oracle granted to Hagar (xvi. 11, 12).

(v) The Blessing on Rebekah, pronounced by her family (xxiv. 60).

(vi) The Oracle granted to Rebekah respecting her children (xxv. 23).

(vii) The Blessing of Isaac upon Jacob (xxvii. 27—29).

(viii) The Blessing of Isaac upon Esau (xxvii. 39, 40).

(ix) The Blessing of Jacob upon his sons (xlix. 2—27).

It may safely be assumed that these Songs were composed long before the time at which they were included in the J narrative of the Book of Genesis. The Blessing of Jacob seems to be a very early collection of Israelite Songs or poetical Oracles, having reference to the tribes after the settlement in Canaan (xlix. 13, 14); and it is possible that the allusion to "the sceptre of Judah" may indicate a period at which the kingdom was established at Jerusalem (xlix. 10).

6. *Genealogies*. At least *eight* Genealogies occur in the Book of Genesis. They constitute a remarkable feature in its

literary composition. They illustrate the diligent care with which the attempt was made to trace back not only Israel, but Israel's neighbours, into the remotest antiquity. The majority of the Genealogies belong to the statistics preserved in P.

The Priestly Document computes that the Exodus from Egypt occurred in the year 2666, and the Flood in the year 1656, after the Creation. It is in connexion with this chronology that the age of Noah, at the time of the Flood, is given with such minuteness (vii. 11); and that the ages of the Patriarchs are so carefully recorded. The narratives of J and E are not built upon this chronology, and in consequence their statements are often irreconcilable with those contained in the narrative of P.

(i) Genealogy from Adam to Noah (chap. v. P). It has been thought possible that the original source for the contents of this list is to be sought for in a version of Babylonian Tradition. Berossus, the Babylonian Chronicler (circ. 200 B.C.) commences his Babylonian dynasties with Alōrus, Alaparus, Amēlon, Ammĕnon, Megalarus, Daōnus, Evedorachus, Amempsinus, Otiartes, and Xisuthros. There are ten names, and the list closes with Xisuthros, the Babylonian Noah. The list in Gen. v. has ten names, and closes with that of Noah.

(ii) The Genealogy of the Sons of Noah (chaps. x., xi., P (J)).

The Genealogy of the Nations is derived from J as well as from P. The lists of names are of great interest and value. They must not be regarded as possessing any scientific value ethnographically. But they illustrate the political geography of the Hebrews, and embody a reminiscence of Israelite tradition upon the relative position of peoples known by name and repute.

(iii) The Genealogy of Terah (xi. 27—32) contains fragments from J and P, and, probably, portions of J's genealogy of Shem, resumed from x. 24—30. It has been thought to describe a tradition of early tribal relationships in the Terahite branch of the Hebrews, and to preserve the recollection of (*a*) the disappearance of the clan of Haran, (*b*) the survival of the clan of Lot, and (*c*) the amalgamation of the clan of Milcah with the native clans.

LITERARY MATERIALS

(iv) The Genealogy of Nahor (xxii. 20—24) is an ancient list preserved in J. The twelve tribes here named traced their ancestry back to Nahor. Probably the list belongs to a late revision of J. For, while, in chap. xxiv., Abraham's servant finds Nahor's grandchildren, Laban and Rebekah, fully grown, in this 22nd chapter Abraham receives the news of the birth of Nahor's children. The Genealogy contains an ethnographical record, not a personal history: and, accordingly, while the legitimate sons of Nahor (*vv.* 20—23) typify the true tribal stock, the sons of the concubine (*v.* 24) denote clans of mixed or inferior lineage.

(v) The Genealogy of Keturah (xxv. 1—6) contains a list of North Arabian tribes with whom the Israelites acknowledged a degree of kinship. They were, therefore, represented as the children of Abraham by a later marriage, after the death of Sarah. As in the case of the Genealogy of Nahor, the Genealogy of Keturah probably belongs to a late insertion into J. For the main narrative of J leaves no room for the mention of a second marriage of Abraham. The beginning of chap. xxiv. suggests that Abraham is conscious of his approaching end.

(vi) The Genealogy of Ishmael (xxv. 12—18) contains a list, from P, of the twelve traditional ancestors of the Ishmaelite tribes whose home was in the Syro-Arabian Desert.

(vii) The Edomite Genealogies (chap. xxxvi.) consist of (1) a list of the wives and children of Esau, *vv.* 1—5; (2) a list of Esau's descendants, *vv.* 9—14; (3) a list of Esau clans, *vv.* 15—19; (4) a list of Horite clans, *vv.* 20—30; (5) a list of Edomite kings, *vv.* 31—39; (6) a second list of Esau clans, *vv.* 40—43. This very valuable genealogy seems to contain an authentic record of Edomite tribal history, presumably derived from some Edomite source.

(viii) The Genealogy of Jacob's descendants (xlvi. 8—27 P) is a list which purports to contain the names of "the children of Israel, which came into Egypt, Jacob and his sons." But as it includes the names of Er and Onan (*v.* 12) who died in Canaan, and also the names of Joseph and his two sons

Manasseh and Ephraim (*v.* 20), who were already in Egypt when Jacob went down, the title of the list is evidently inexact.

§ 6. *Historical Value.*

A. *Gen.* i.—xi.

The first portion of the Book of Genesis deals with the Origin of the Universe and the Beginnings of the Human Race. These Narratives, from a modern point of view, are unscientific. There is nothing in them of which modern astronomy, geology, or biology can take account. Physical Science and the Biblical Cosmogony, in their description of natural phenomena, belong to two wholly diverse phases of thought.

The Biblical Narrative, under the symbolism of primitive folk-lore, represents, as in a series of parables, fundamental religious ideas respecting the beginning of things. It is neither history nor science. In the attempt to answer the instinctive questionings of mankind, it lifts the mind Godward. The mysteries of the Universe and the riddles of sin, suffering, and death receive their interpretation through the medium of stories which have come down from the intellectual childhood of the Semitic peoples.

No historic records of primitive man can be looked for. Before the ages of civilization, for thousands, perhaps for hundreds of thousands, of years, man, with the spark of Divine life implanted in him, slowly fought his way out of the condition of the savage. The earliest traces of Assyrian or Egyptian civilization, between six and ten thousand years before the Christian era, belong to a comparatively recent stage in the growth and spread of the human race. Any historic reminiscence of the Beginning is inconceivable.

The Legend of the Flood finds an echo in the early traditions of peoples in all parts of the world. It is evident, however, that the Biblical Narrative of the Flood stands in close relationship to the Babylonian. The earliest Babylonian accounts are based upon ancient records written many centuries before the days of Moses. While geological science has demonstrated that a

Flood has never simultaneously covered the whole surface of the globe, there is nothing improbable in the view that the Hebrew Narrative records a tradition of a vast and overwhelming Deluge in Mesopotamia, the memory of which is also contained in the inscriptions of Babylon.

The Israelite had no such conception as we possess of the physical laws of Nature. He was not interested, as we should say, in secondary causes. The science of the Israelite consisted in the recognition of the handiwork of the Creator. His knowledge of physical phenomena was knowledge of the Power and Presence of God. Accordingly, the Deluge, the earliest event of which a recollection is preserved in Babylonian and Hebrew legend, is related as a symbol of Divine judgement upon sin, and as a typical example of Divine deliverance: while the description of its physical characteristics follows the exaggerated account of popular tradition.

B. *Gen.* xii.—l.

When we turn to the Patriarchal Narratives, we pass into an entirely different atmosphere. Nevertheless, the Patriarchal Narratives are very different from those which describe the adventures of David or the rebellion of Absalom. We stand, as it were, on the threshold of the shrine of History. We have not yet passed through its doorway. A thousand years separate the age of David from that of Abraham.

It is evident that not all the contents of the Book of Genesis were intended to convey literal fact. Folk-lore is often expressed under the symbolism of personal relationship and domestic experiences. Many names, e.g. those of Midian, Aram, Amalek, are not those of individual personages, but of tribes and peoples. Stories which turn upon the popular etymology of proper names, e.g. Ishmael, Isaac, Issachar, cannot be regarded as on the same footing with the annals of history.

It is, however, otherwise with the great Patriarchs themselves. It is not too much to claim that the main personages who most vividly impressed themselves upon the popular recollection were actual historic characters. Their names, we may be sure, were not invented. That they are the names of real persons, and that round a nucleus of historic facts poetry and tradition collected and expanded popular legends, is the simplest and most probable explanation. The episodes with which these narratives are concerned are for the most part events and details of domestic life. There is a lack in them of contact with the larger history of the time. In consequence, in recent years, there has been a tendency to deny historic value to the Genesis story; and to account for the Patriarchs (a) either as impersonations of the people, (b) or as the survivals of the recollection of Canaanite deities, (c) or as astral emblems.

(a) It has been urged, for instance, that the departure of the Patriarch Abraham from Ur of the Chaldees, and from Haran, merely personifies a great migratory movement, and that the marriage of Jacob with Rachel and Leah symbolizes the reinforcement of the Hebrew stock from Aramaean tribes. In a certain number of instances this line of explanation will be found to throw an interesting additional light upon the narratives. But it does not admit of being generally applied. It fails to account for the main thread of personal incident. The intensely vivid portraiture of individual character looks as if it were drawn from the life, though viewed at a distance of time and through the haze of poetry and legend.

(b) The theory has been advanced that the names of the Patriarchs are the names of Canaanite deities, and that the Israelites passed from the stage of offering them worship to that of revering them as heroes and ancestors. It is quite possible that such names as Abram, or "lofty Father," and Sarah, or "Princess," were borne by Semitic deities. But this does not prove that the Israelites ever worshipped them, or that the names could not be borne by human beings. The fact that the names of Abiram, Abner, Samuel, and many other Israelites, were compounded with names of the Deity, and that "Isaac," "Jacob," "Joseph," were very possibly shortened forms of "Isaac-el," "Jacob-el," "Joseph-el" (cf. Ishma-el, Jeraḥme-el, &c.), in no way precludes us from regarding them as the names of historical personages. The suggestion that the "Fear of Isaac" (xxxi. 42, 53) denotes the "fear inspired by Isaac," i.e. the local deity of Beer-sheba, and not "the God whom Isaac the patriarch feared," is an example of the very precarious arguments by which this view has been supported. There is practically no support from Genesis itself for regarding the Patriarchs as degenerated objects of Divine worship. When Abraham at Mamre receives the three angelic visitants (chap. xviii.) or when Jacob wrestles with the angel at Penuel (chap. xxxii.), the early tradition depicts man in conscious communion with Deity. The tradition may contain more of symbolical instruction than of actual history. But it rests on the assumption that the Patriarchs were flesh and blood, and were neither Canaanite deities nor Hebrew demigods.

(*c*) Another line of interpretation, which looks for "astral motifs" in the Patriarchal Narratives, may be illustrated from the writings of the distinguished Assyriologist, Jeremias (*Old Test. in the Light of the Ancient East*, II. pp. 19, 20, Eng. Tr.): "The number 318 in Gen. xiv. 14...is the number of days in the lunar year when the moon is visible."..."'Twelve years they served Chedorlaomer, and in the thirteenth year they rebelled' (Gen. xiv. 4). This is distinctly a lunar number."..."The moon is 'the Wanderer.'...Abraham moved from East to West like the moon."..."Our Biblical story also recognizes the Tammuz-Ishtar motif. The journey of Abraham with his sister and wife (!) Sarah to Egypt is presented there as a journey into, and a rescue from the Underworld. As south, Egypt is the Underworld....When Ishtar, the primeval Mother, descends into the Underworld all fertility ceases....The chronicler hints this, Gen. xii. 7 : the house of Pharaoh was 'plagued' because of Sarah...sterility had come upon the women." Speculations, upon lines like these, will be more likely to excite our surprise at the ingenuity of their originators, than to impress us with confidence in their judgement.

While upholding the historical character of the Patriarchs, we must not be too sanguine in the expectation that the historical elements in early legend can easily be demonstrated. This is far from being the case. Fact, poetry, and symbolism are often inextricably intertwined. Let us recognize the fact that it is not possible to claim a high standard of historical accuracy for a narrative, the date of whose composition is separated by many centuries from the events which it records, and whose statements have not as yet been verified by contemporary evidence. Even the written traditions of Israel were liable to be modified, in a strange degree, by subsequent generations, as is evident by a comparison of the Books of Chronicles with the Books of Kings, or, still more, of the Book of Jubilees with the Book of Genesis. Oral tradition, however high the standard of its accuracy in the Semitic world, was not likely to be less susceptible to the influences affecting the transmission of narrative than was tradition embodied in writing. But while we are prepared to hear it alleged that "the basis of our belief in the historical character, e.g. of Abraham, is somewhat sentimental[1]," statements to the effect that Abraham "seems to have been created to connect together the peoples kindred to Israel in a genealogical system of relationship" must be described as purely speculative. The framework of literary style and of religious thought, in which the portraits of the Patriarchs are presented to us, is derived from the prophetic period. But there is no evidence to shew that the prophets or their contemporaries either created the names of the patriarchs, or invented the traditions respecting them. That which they inherited from their forefathers they reproduced, stripped of crudity and archaism, and arrayed in the perfect style of their prose narrative. This they presented to their countrymen, glowing with the life of that Revelation which raised the teaching of the Hebrew Prophets immeasurably above the level of contemporary Semitic thought.

---

[1] Prof. Curtiss, "Chronicles," p. 70, *Internat. Critical Commentary.*

HISTORICAL VALUE xliii

During the past forty years light has been shed by *archaeological research* upon the history of the world in the Patriarchal Period (2100—1400 B.C.). It has been shewn that the influence of Babylonian arms, culture, and worship had made itself felt throughout Western Asia as far as to the shores of the Mediterranean. It has been shewn that Egyptian kings exercised suzerainty over the provinces and cities of Canaan in the 15th century. It has been shewn that in the 15th and 14th centuries the peoples of Canaan, nominally subject to Egypt, were being hard pressed by the Hittites in the North and the Ḥabiri in the East. It has been shewn that the names of Jacob-el and Joseph-el occur among the names of places in Canaan conquered by Thothmes III, and recorded in his inscriptions on the Great Temple of Karnak; and that, in the time of Seti I, Aser appears as the name of a region subsequently occupied by the tribe of Asher. Whether the Ḥabiri, of the Tel el-Amarna Tablets, and the 'Apuriu of the Egyptian inscriptions of Ramses II and his successors, should be identified with the Hebrews, is still much disputed[1].

It is not easy, in our present incipient stage of knowledge, to see precisely in what way some of these new historical data are reconcilable with the Biblical account. We may look forward with confidence to receiving further light from the monuments. In the meantime it is advisable to abstain from hasty judgements.

The only incident in the Patriarchal Narratives, which puts us into touch with the history of the surrounding nations, is the rebellion of the Cities of the Plain and the punitive invasion by the allied armies under Chedorlaomer (chap. xiv.). It is quite possible that in Amraphel king of Shinar we may recognize Ḥammurabi, the historic founder of the Babylonian Empire. On this assumption the period of Abraham is roughly that of the century 2200—2100 B.C. Abraham has not yet been

[1] See Driver's *Schweich Lectures* (1909); Hogarth's *Authority and Archaeology* (1899); P. S. P. Handcock's *Latest Light on Bible Lands* (S.P.C.K., 1913). See Appendix D.

identified in the Babylonian inscriptions. It has, indeed, been claimed by Egyptologists that in the list of places, which Shishak (circ. 930 B.C.) records he has conquered in Palestine, there is one (No. 71—72) which has the Semitic title *ḥaḳal Abram*, "field of Abram." If this is substantiated, it may represent the earliest occurrence of the Patriarch's name in writing, i.e. about twelve hundred years after his death (Breasted's *Hist. of Anc. Eg.*, p. 363).

Even Joseph's name has not yet been found in the Egyptian monuments. There is no means of ascertaining, with any degree of confidence, under which king of Egypt Joseph rose to power. See Appendix E.

Accordingly, while future archaeological research may have many surprises in store for us, truth compels us to admit that up to the present no event recorded in the Patriarchal Narratives of Genesis has been found related in contemporary Monuments. Nor do the Patriarchal Narratives by themselves enable us to form any adequate impression of the political and social condition of Canaan and of its inhabitants during that period. Babylonian culture was predominant: Babylon and Egypt seem alternately to have ruled over Canaan: in the 16th and 15th centuries B.C. the chief towns of Canaan were held by Egyptian officials, and were paying tribute to the Egyptian kings. These are the historical features which archaeology has unexpectedly revealed, but of which, before recent archaeological discovery, no Biblical student could have had any conception from reading the Book of Genesis.

The fact seems to be that the historic traditions respecting the Hebrew Patriarchs, both as to language, social conditions, and religious thought, have come down to us in the garb, not of the period from which they first emanated, but of the period in which they were committed to writing. "The writers necessarily threw back their own modes of thought upon the earlier times of which they wrote[1]." It is this explanation, also, which

---

[1] Davidson, *O.T. Prophecy*, 314.

fully accounts for the occurrence of such apparent anachronisms as the mention of "Philistines" and of "Dan" (=Laish), and the use of such phrases as "folly in Israel," and "the land of the Hebrews" in the Patriarchal period (see above, p. xv).

Social customs in the East are little altered by the lapse of centuries. The scenes of Patriarchal life in Palestine and Syria may be witnessed every day by travellers of the 20th century A.D.

At the same time the student will do well very carefully to note the allusions to the semi-nomadic life of the Patriarchs. They were dwellers in tents, and their encampments were very often in the vicinity of wells and springs (xii. 8, xiii. 3, 18, xviii. 1, 2, 6, 9, 10, xxiv. 67, xxv. 27, xxvi. 25, xxxi. 25, 33, xxxiii. 19). Abram and Lot possess cattle and sheep in great abundance (xii. 16, xiii. 2, 5). Isaac has great possessions "of flocks and herds" (xxvi. 14). Jacob is a skilled shepherd (chap. xxx.). He leaves Haran with flocks, herds, and camels (xxxii. 7). Jacob's sons are shepherds (xxxvii. 2, 12—16), and the pasture-lands of Goshen are assigned to them as such (xlvi. 34, xlvii. 3). The regular Bedouin, roving on the frontiers of the desert, the warrior Ishmaels and Esaus, though of kindred origin, are different in character and pursuits (xxi. 20, xxxiii. 12—16).

On the other hand, Isaac grows corn in the land of the "Philistines" (xxvi. 12—14); Jacob receives from his father the blessing of a fruitful soil, with plenty of corn and wine (xxvii. 28); he has corn-fields in Haran (xxx. 14); and Joseph's dreams suggest a bringing-up in corn-growing land (xxxvii. 5, 6). In the Blessing of Judah the luxuriant growth of the vine is the pride of the tribe (xlix. 11). The mention of "houses" in connexion with the Patriarchs indicates how easily the narrative passes into the use of the terms belonging to a more settled condition of life (xv. 3, xxiv. 23, xxvii. 15, xxviii. 21, xxxiii. 17, xxxviii. 11).

§ 7. *Religious Teaching.*

The Book of Genesis, like the rest of the Pentateuch to which it forms the Introduction, is primarily a book of religious instruction (*Tôrah*). It traces back, to the earliest imaginable time, the relations of the People of Israel to their God. For this purpose the Narratives were collected, and to this purpose they were adapted. The main religious idea is this; that the God who made the Universe, created mankind, brought the Flood upon the world, and appointed the distribution of the Human Races, was the God of Israel, who in the remote ages called, chose, protected, and guided the ancestors of the Hebrew People.

"Creation" and "Election" are the aspects under which, in the Book of Genesis, the devout Israelite was taught the two primary lessons of his relation to God. In answer to the question "What am I?" he learned (1) that he was a member of the Human Race *Created* by the One God, and (2) that he was a member of the Family of Abraham *Chosen* by the One God.

The Narratives are recorded in language which never deviates from the pure monotheism of the Israelite prophets. (*a*) They have no taint of the idolatry of Canaan or of Egypt. (*b*) They carry with them no trace of the struggle with Baal worship. (*c*) They suggest no claim on the part of any God except Jehovah to be supreme in the world. The people of the land as impersonated in Melchizedek (chap. xiv.), Abimelech (chap. xx.), Pharaoh and Joseph's steward (chaps. xli. 38, 39, xliii. 23), are not wanting in the fear of the true God.

The supreme value of the Book of Genesis has always consisted in its religious message. Its influence has not resulted from perfection of scientific or historical accuracy, but from its power of presenting, through the medium of the people's traditions and folk-lore, the essential truths of the Revelation of the God of Israel. Like every other human medium, it was adapted to the age of its production. It was neither infallible nor perfect. But it was part of that inspired witness by which throughout the ages the Spirit of God has spoken to the spiritual nature of man with a voice adapted to his understanding. In every phase of Christian experience the Book of Genesis has been recognized as having borne a prominent part in the "Praeparatio Evangelica." The God of Abraham, Isaac, and Jacob is the One Supreme Divine Person, omnipotent in power, perfect in righteousness, infinite in wisdom. Whether in Canaan, in Egypt, or in Haran, His Will is sovereign and absolute. To the Canaanite King, Melchizedek, He is the Most High God (*Êl Elyon*): to the Hebrew Patriarchs, He is God Almighty (*Êl Shaddai*).

God, who "hath at the end of these days spoken unto us in his Son," "of old time spoke unto the fathers in the prophets by divers portions and in divers manners (πολυμέρως καὶ πολυτρόπως)" (Heb. i. 1). The Book of Genesis is one of those "divers manners." They were truly "prophets" to whom we owe it. They were inspired men, moved by the Holy Ghost (*a*) to collect, purge, and edit the primitive traditions of the race and the early legends of the people, and (*b*) thereby to interpret to their countrymen and to the world "divers" fragments and "portions" of the message of Divine Redemption. Human judgement stumbles at the thought that the first of the sacred writings of Israel to be set apart as "the oracles of God" should contain the initial stages of a national literature, i.e. legends and folk-lore. Our preconceptions make us slow to realize the meaning of the progressive character of Divine Revelation. Where law and prophecy, poetry and narrative have their share, legend and tradition are not wanting to complete the human element in the preparation for the coming of the Christ.

(1) *God.* In some of the Narratives preserved by the earlier traditions there are traces of the earlier and more anthropomorphic conception of the Almighty. Jehovah speaks as if apprehensive of the human race becoming too powerful (iii. 22, xi. 6); as if regretting the act of creation (vi. 6, 7); as if needing to be convinced of human wickedness (xi. 7), or of the corruptions

of Sodom (xviii. 20, 21). But these survivals of a more naïve treatment of the Divine Nature are only evidence of the fact that there has been growth and development in the religious thought of Israel.

The mention of the *teraphim* of Laban (xxxi. 19, 30—35) and of "the strange gods" in Jacob's household (xxxv. 1—4) acknowledges rather than condemns the usage of other peoples.

The God of Israel is the beneficent Creator of the Universe: His Word and Will are the only means by which created things are brought into existence (chaps. i., ii.). Their creation is in accordance with His moral purpose of goodness (i. 31). Matter is neither self-existent, nor inherently evil; what God creates, is "very good." From the first He maintains communion and intercourse with mankind. At every stage He communicates His Will to man, to Adam and Eve, to Cain, to Noah, to the Patriarchs, to Hagar, to Rebekah, to Pharaoh, &c. He hears their prayer (iv. 15, xv. 1—6, xxv. 22, 23, xxxii. 29, xlvi. 1—4). He makes covenants with them (ix. 1—17, xv. 18, xvii. 2 ff.). He overrules the wrong-doings and troubles of life to be the means of blessing (iii. 16, 17, xlv. 5, l. 20).

(2) *Man.* Man is made in the image of God (i. 27). His nature is twofold, partly material, partly spiritual (ii. 7). His life is designed for activity; he is the crowning point of creation; he is intended to exercise authority and to maintain order and control upon earth (i. 28, 29, ii. 15, 20). From the first he approaches God with sacrifice (iv. 3—5) and prayer (iv. 26).

(3) *Sin.* The Nature, not the Origin, of Sin is depicted in chap. iii. Temptation to sin comes from an external source (iii. 1—5). It is not in man, nor from God. It exalts personal desire against the knowledge of the Divine Will: it shews itself in distrust and self-will. Conscience is active in the wake of sin (chaps. iii., iv., xlii.).

There is no direct assertion of the hereditary transmission of sin. Perhaps it is implied in the fact that the story of the murder of Abel follows at once upon that of the expulsion from the Garden. The rapid spread of moral corruption occasions the Divine judgement of the Deluge (chaps. vi.—ix.), and in the overthrow of the Cities of the Plain (chap. xix.). There is no such thing as human immunity from sin. Even Abraham, the father of the faithful, is guilty of turpitude and cowardice (xii. 11—13, xx. 12). The character of Jacob is a medley of warm feeling, persevering energy, deceitfulness, and self-interestedness. Even in Joseph, before the discipline of suffering, there is a strain of vain-glory (xxxvii. 5—12).

(4) *Election.* The Call of Abraham is represented as the free expression of Divine Favour and Grace. It is not the reward of merit, nor the recognition of service. The human aspect is ignored. God's Voice is the test of obedience and of faith. Abraham's belief in Jehovah (xv. 6) precedes the covenant. He represents the ideal of righteousness, i.e. right relations with God (cf. Rom. iv. 9; Gal. iii. 6; James ii. 23). The command comes from God to Abraham to leave his home; and the promise is added of a blessing in the distant future. The promise has reference (1) to numberless descendants, (2) to the possession of Canaan, (3) to a source of benediction for all the dwellers on the earth (xii. 2, 3, xvii. 6—8, xviii. 18, xxviii. 13, 14, xxxv. 9—12). As interpreted in the Book of Genesis, Election implies no selfish enjoyment of prerogative, but a vocation to discipline, patience, and service. Its origin is God's call; its sphere is the service of man; its ratification is the covenant relation; the rite of circumcision is its sacrament; its reward is the revelation of the Divine Will. The Election of the individual leads up to the Election of the Nation, out of whose ranks and from whose country shall come the ultimate Blessing for all the families of the earth. The material blessings of long life, numerous descendants, and a fertile land, are the appointed symbols and pledges of the spiritual fulfilment of the Divine Promise, to which our Lord refers in the words, "Abraham rejoiced to see my day; and he saw it and was glad" (Joh. viii. 56). The Hebrew mind may have been deficient in speculative and philosophical ability. But it was intensely sensitive of religious impressions; and, while rejecting all external representations

of the Deity, could rest with quiet confidence in the absolute Power, Wisdom, and Goodness of His Personality (cf. xv. 6, xviii. 25, xxxv. 3, xlviii. 15).

(5) *The Messianic Hope.* The Divine Promises, in the Book of Genesis, cannot be said to indicate a belief in the coming of a *personal* Messiah. In Gen. iii. 15, the enmity between the Serpent and the Seed of the Woman symbolizes the antagonism between the human race and the forces of Evil. The passage predicts, that victory over the source of transgression will rest with man. It contains in germ the Gospel of Redemption for humanity. It is universal, not national, in its range of application. But it contains no announcement of a personal Redeemer.

The much controverted words, "Until Shiloh come" (xlix. 10), have very frequently been understood to predict the advent of a personal Messiah. But it is very improbable that "Shiloh" can bear the meaning of a proper name. Probably nothing more definitely Messianic is indicated than that the most sacred hopes of Israel were bound up with the future of the royal tribe of Judah. The promises made to Abraham and to Jacob included the kingship of their descendants (xvii. 5, 6, xxxv. 11); and the poetical prediction concerning "the sceptre of Judah" points forward, with the indefiniteness of an ancient oracle, to the expectation of an ideal, a Messianic, kingdom.

(6) *Love.* But, although the Book of Genesis contains but little that belongs to definitely Messianic predictions, its whole idea of the Divine Nature and of its relation towards mankind, whether expressed in Creation, or in Election, or in Discipline, is the same. It is that of love. Love first originates the object of benevolence; and then, by gradual and progressive revelation, seeks to raise, educate, and enlighten it, until the full communion between God and man can be established.

The assurance of the Divine Presence ("I am with thee," xxvi. 24, xxviii. 15, xxxi. 3; cf. v. 24, vi. 9, xxxix. 2, 21, xlviii. 15) is at every epoch conveyed to the servants of Jehovah.

"In the early stages of Bible history there was not a direct, immediate and adequate revelation of the true God, but an indirect and educational revelation of God, which was to the knowledge of God Himself as the shadow of blessings to come ...is to the glorious light of Christ[1]."

No account of the Book of Genesis would be adequate which omitted to notice the religious and moral teaching of its narratives. The great succession of scenes which pass before the reader's eyes is unrivalled in any literature for simplicity, vividness, moral force, and adaptability for purposes of instruction. Except the Parables of the Gospels, probably no stories have been so universally used as material for sacred lessons. When the Apostle speaks of the Scriptures being "profitable for teaching, for reproof, for correction, for instruction which is in righteousness" (2 Tim. iii. 16), his words are in a peculiar degree applicable to Genesis. Unless it be the Psalter, there is no book of the O.T. which has so deeply influenced the Christian consciousness as the Book of Genesis. It deals with the simplest and the profoundest thoughts in terms of everyday life. A child can grasp the outline of the story: the profoundest theologian is continually finding in it fresh depths of unexpected meaning.

It has ceased to be regarded, as once was the case, in the light of a text-book of secular science. It is more and more regarded as a treasury of religious truth. The stories of Adam and Eve, of Cain and Abel, of the Flood, of Abraham, of Sodom and Gomorrah, of Lot's Wife, of Jacob, were used by our Lord as parables, already known to His hearers, for the purpose of enforcing His instruction (Matt. xix. 4, 5, xxiii. 35, xxiv. 37; Luke xvii. 29, 32; John i. 51, viii. 56). St Paul continually employs the Genesis narratives as illustrations in theological argument. Abraham, Sarah and Hagar, Ishmael and Isaac, are to him impersonations of religious ideas (cf. Rom. iv. 3—18, ix. 7—13; Gal. iv. 22—30).

---

[1] Westphal, *The Law and the Prophets* (p. 18).

The Story of Paradise and the Story of Cain and Abel are passages in which nearly every verse is full of religious significance. The Flood Narrative which emphasizes the Divine hatred of sin and the purpose of salvation, prepares the way for the call of Man and the Chosen Family; while the Genealogy of the Races reminds us that the unknown peoples and dark ages of the world are included within the range of the Divine plan of Redemption[1].

In the Narratives of the Patriarchs the delineation of character is extraordinarily varied and lifelike. We are conscious that the view, e.g. of Ewald who regarded the Patriarchs as emblems or impersonations of the people, utterly fails to satisfy. Though they may not as yet be identified in the Monuments of antiquity, we feel that they have stepped straight out of the heart of the religious experience of the people.

We see in Abraham the type of unquestioning trust and obedience. He leaves all at the Divine call. His strong faith is put to the test by long waiting for the fulfilment of the Promise; and it is put to a yet more supreme test by a command which seems to revoke the Promises previously given (chap. xxii.). His character is depicted as magnanimous (chaps. xiii., xiv.), hospitable (xviii. 1—8), courteous (chap. xxiii.). He is the wise and thoughtful head of a great household (xviii. 19). He is not free from human weakness, he yields to ignoble cowardice (xii. 14—20, xx. 1—18); and yet he is admitted into terms of closest communion with Jehovah (xviii. 23—33). Isaac, the man of meek and yielding temperament, of obscure, retiring, perhaps self-indulgent habits, is none the less included in the privileges of personal relation with the God who reveals His will. Jacob, warm-hearted, calculating, self-seeking, persevering, is the type of character in which good and evil are strangely blended. In the turning-points of his life, he realizes (1) that there is communion between earth and heaven, (2) that, in spite of what he is, Jehovah has even sought him out and is ready to

---

[1] See the writer's *Early Narratives of Genesis* (Macmillan).

grant the Divine blessing on one who perseveres to sue for it. Joseph, high-minded, capable, faithful to his God in the hour of temptation, strong in family affection, ready to forgive, presents a noble type of virtue in high position. How lifelike also are the touches in the representation of the secondary characters! the jealousy of Sarah; the selfishness of Lot; the meanness of Laban; the generous, but shallow, impulsiveness of Esau. We see Rebekah as she hastens to give drink to the camels of Abraham's servant, and hurriedly plots to secure the blessing for her favourite son. We see Joseph's brethren now scheming for his death in the field of Dothan, and now conscience-stricken and bewildered in the house of the Egyptian lord.

§ 8. *Moral Difficulties.*

The Moral Difficulties which have been felt by readers of the Book of Genesis may be grouped under three heads.

(i) A rudimentary moral standard of life is presented in the Patriarchal Narratives. For instance, the substitution of Hagar for Sarah (chap. xvi.), the expulsion of Hagar (chap. xxi.), and the marriage of Jacob with two sisters (chap. xxix.), are incidents which, though they shock and offend our notions of morality, were in harmony with the ethical standard of early Israelite society. It is terrible to our ideas that Abraham should be ready to sacrifice his son (chap. xxii.), and that Reuben should offer his two sons as hostages to be slain (xlii. 37). But, according to the usages of ancient Semitic life, individual rights were entirely subordinated to those of "corporate responsibility[1]." Scripture enables us to recognize the law of growth in moral life. If so, we must be prepared to meet with its earlier as well as with its later stages. We must not expect from the picture which is given us of the Hebrew Patriarchs in Canaan the standard of morality represented in the Sermon upon the Mount.

---

[1] Robinson Wheeler's *Christian Doctrine of Man*, pp. 27—30.

(ii) The moral failures of the Patriarchs are recorded without any expression of censure. The repudiation of Sarah by Abraham at the courts of Pharaoh and of Abimelech (chaps. xii., xx.), and of Rebekah by Isaac at the court of Abimelech (chap. xxvi.); the drunkenness and incest of Lot (chap. xix. 30—38); the acts of deception practised by Jacob in order to obtain his father's blessing (chap. xxvii.), are episodes in which it is impossible to palliate or excuse the behaviour of the Patriarchs. And yet, it is objected, there is no word of disapproval on the part of the narrator. Is it, however, necessary that the moral should always be told at full length? The incidents tell their own story. Their narration is their condemnation. They illustrate the moral failures of the representative historic personages of primitive Israel. There is no claim of moral perfection made for them; there is nothing of the hero or demigod in their conduct. Abraham and Isaac are rebuked by heathen princes (xx. 9, xxvi. 10). Racial antipathy may be reflected in the story of the shameful origin of Moab and Ammon, but Jacob's deception is punished by twenty years' exile from his home, by the wiles of Laban, and by the treacherous conduct of his own children. In the millennium before Christ, deception and craftiness may conceivably have seemed to Orientals more humorous and less repellent than they do to us. But conscience always and unhesitatingly condemns such forms of evil. There is no room for the sophistry that, because the Patriarchs were the chosen servants of God, their bad actions have been condoned. Holy Scripture records without comment the sins of Abraham, Isaac, and Jacob, of King David, and of St Peter. The mere statement of moral lapse is enough: censure may be less eloquent than silence.

(iii) The representation of the Divine attributes sometimes tallies rather with the crude conceptions of paganism than with enlightened ideas of the God of Holiness. Allowance must be made for the progressive character of the Revelation granted to Israel. (*a*) The destruction of the world's inhabitants by the Deluge is described as a moral judgement for sin and wickedness.

MORAL DIFFICULTIES

The emphasis rests upon the sternness of the visitation. But the picture which it gives of the extermination of the human race rests on a primitive idea of the Deity, without mercy for the ignorant and without consideration for the innocent and the weak. (*b*) The Narratives of the Deluge and of the Tower of Babel preserve some features of the fierceness and wrath, which in the Old Testament belong to the earlier conceptions of the God of Israel. Similarly, God is represented as threatening Abimelech and all his people with death, because in ignorance and entire innocency of intention he has taken Abraham's wife (xx. 7). The purpose of the story is to emphasize the Divine favour which protected the Chosen Family from peril. But the words which threaten Abimelech reflect a "particularism" against which conscience protests. (*c*) When, however, in chap. xxii. 2, God is said to command Abraham to offer Isaac for a burnt offering, the difficulty is not simply to be met by admitting, that in early days the Israelites could think of their God as one who impersonated their own fierceness. The story presupposes a recognition of the practice of human sacrifice. The utterance of God symbolizes the impulse of conscience, stirring the religious feelings in Abraham. Could he make the same supreme sacrifice which the Canaanite peoples were willing to make to their gods? Could he trust a God who seemed to repudiate His own promise? This was the final test of the Patriarch's faith. The word of God, conveying so terrible a command, reflects indeed the moral standard of a time at which such sacrifices were thought compatible with true devotion. But the God of the Hebrews, who "proved" Abraham by the voice of conscience, no less definitively forbade the inhumanity of such offerings. He who was continually raising His people to a higher moral level, taught them "little by little" that God is love.

§ 9. *The Names of God in the Book of Genesis.*

The subject of the Divine Names as used in the Old Testament has been discussed in recent years by some of our ablest scholars. Students should consult Dr Driver's Excursus I (pp. 402—409) in his Commentary on *The Book of Genesis*, and his valuable note on Ex. iii. 14 (p. 40, *Cambridge Bible for Schools*); Prof. A. B. Davidson's *Theology of the O.T.* (1904), pp. 46, 54—58; Principal Skinner's discussion of the subject in "Genesis" (*Internat. Crit. Comm.*), pp. xxxv—xxxviii, and in his remarkable series of articles in the *Expositor*, April—Sept. 1913. There are also important articles in the chief Dictionaries, e.g. by Kautzsch, *Encycl. Bibl.*, *s.v.* "Names" (§§ 109—113), Kittel in the *Realencyklopädie*³, *s.v.* "Elohim" and "Jahve," Davidson in *D.B.* II. 199.

(i) *Elohim* (אֱלֹהִים) is the ordinary and regular Hebrew name for "God." Its origin and etymology are obscure. In its form it is a plural word, and yet, with only a few exceptions, it is used with verbs and adjectives in the singular. This usage is to be explained not as a relic of polytheism, but as an instance of the "plural of excellence" or "majesty" (Gesenius, *Heb. Gram.* § 124, g, E.T.), as in the case of *adonim* in Gen. xlii. 30, "the *lord* of the land." It must not be supposed that Elohim is always used of the God of Israel. It is used generically for "God"; and, moreover, is often found in the plural to denote the "gods" of the heathen. It may be assumed to be akin to *Él*, another Hebrew word for "God"; and is evidently closely related the Canaanitish *El*, the Assyrian *Ilu*, and the Arabian *Ilâh*. The conjecture that it denotes "strength" and "protecting power" is very probable, but cannot be regarded as certain.

In the Book of Genesis *Elohim* is used by itself for "God" 177 times. With a few exceptions, it is used by both E and P throughout Genesis and in the Exodus Narrative up to the passage in which the distinctive name "Jahweh" is revealed to Moses (Ex. iii. 13 ff. E: Ex. vi. 2 ff. J).

(ii) *Jahweh* (or *Yahveh*), "the LORD," is the distinctive name of the God of the Israelites. It is quite possible that its original pronunciation and etymology have been lost. While some have suggested that it is the causative form of the verb meaning "to fall," and thus denotes "the feller" or "destroyer," others regard it as the causative of the verb meaning "to become," and hence understand it to mean "the creator." But we know that Hebrew proper names may originally have had a different pronunciation from that which popular etymology has made familiar. The origin of the name may, therefore, be irrecoverable. We have, however, the popular explanation which is preserved to us in the Book of Exodus, where God, revealing Himself to Moses, says in the first person "I will be that I will be" (*'Ehyeh 'ăsher ehyeh*). The meaning of the Name, expressed, as proper names so frequently were, by the 3rd pers. sing. of the Imperfect tense (Heb.) of a verb (e.g. Isaac, Ishmael, Jerahmeel), would be "He will be." The rendering of the Eng. vers. "I am that I am," fails to give the full sense of the verb, and suggests an idea of abstract metaphysical existence which is foreign to Hebrew thought. "He will be" expresses the promise of a permanent relation with the Israelite people: it implies the presence and protection, the loving care and Divine guidance, which they will receive from Him who made Himself known to them.

The pronunciation "Jehovah" is unquestionably wrong. It is attributed to Petrus Galatinus, confessor of Leo X, in 1518. It unites the vowels of the word meaning "Lord," *adonai* (אֲדֹנָי), with the consonants of the Sacred Name, the Tetragrammaton JHVH (יהוה). And although, in consequence of four centuries of Christian use, the name "Jehovah" enjoys a peculiar sanctity, it is etymologically a "mongrel word." There is no doubt, of course, that the Jews, owing to a superstitious dread of pronouncing the Sacred Name, had given to it the vowels of "Adonai" at the time when the vowel points were introduced into the Hebrew MSS. (7th—9th cent. A.D.). Accordingly, in public reading, "Yahveh," as we may pronounce it, was pronounced "Adonai," and translated by the LXX as κύριος. But traces of the original pronunciation survive in proper names, and in Greek it is found transliterated as ιαβέ and ιαώ.

According to P and E, the Name was not known until it was revealed to Moses. But in J it is used in Genesis from the very first. In the Paradise section (ii. 4ᵇ—iii. 24) we find *Jahweh Elohim*, an unusual combination due probably to the editorial insertion of *Elohim*, in order to preserve the continuity with the previous section (i. 1—ii. 4ᵃ) in which "Elohim" alone is used. But after chap. iii. "Jahweh" is regularly used by J: and in iv. 26 it is expressly said, "Then began men to call upon the name of the LORD (Jahweh)." Evidently in the J Narratives, it was assumed that "Jahweh" was from the first the Proper Name of God.

It is, however, important to realize that Jahweh and Elohim are not synonymous. "Jahweh is Elohim in relation to Israel." Just as Chemosh was God in Ammon, so Jahweh was God in Israel: and it is probable that a long interval elapsed, before the Israelites realized the truth that not only was Jahweh the God of Israel, but that the God of Israel alone was the God, *ha-Elohim*. The Monotheism of the Jew represents the growth of centuries. It was preceded by the period of monolatry, when the Israelite recognized the existence of many "gods" (*elohim*), but worshipped only One, the Elohim of Israel, whose appellation was Jahweh.

In recent years it has been contended that Jahweh was the name of a deity which is to be found in certain Babylonian compound proper names, e.g. *Ja-a-ve-ilu*. It is possible that *Jahu* may have been the name of a West Semitic deity. But in the O.T. its earliest occurrence is in the proper names Jochebed, the mother of Moses (Ex. vi. 20), and Joshua, his successor.

(iii) *Êl* (אל) is another generic name for "God" in Hebrew. It appears in most of the other Semitic languages, e.g. Babylonian, Phoenician, Aramaic and Arabic. Its origin and etymology are lost in obscurity. How it is connected with Elohim (sing. Eloah) is a doubtful point. Some scholars have

THE NAMES OF GOD

derived it from roots denoting "strength" or "leadership": but all such derivations are conjectural. It is found in the Book of Genesis on a few occasions by itself, e.g. xvi. 13, xxviii. 3, xxxi. 13, xxxiii. 20, xxxv. 1, 3, 7, xlix. 25. But it is also frequently found in conjunction with some descriptive epithet or substantive. (1) *Êl Elyon*, "the most high God," may have had been an ancient Canaanite name for the Deity (xiv. 18). The Phoenicians had a god Ἐλιοῦν καλούμενος Ὕψιστος (Euseb. *Praep. Ev.* i. 10, 11, 12), cf. Ps. lxxviii. 35. (2) *Êl Shaddai* (see below). (3) *Êl 'Olam*, "the God of everlasting" (xxi. 43). (4) *Êl Rᵒi*, "the God of seeing" (xvi. 13). (5) *Êl Beth-el*, "the God of Bethel" (xxxi. 13, xxxv. 7).

(iv) *Shaddai* (שַׁדַּי). This name for "God" is generally found combined with *Êl*; but in poetry it is found alone. It occurs in Genesis xvii. 1 ("I am *Êl Shaddai*" addressed to Abraham), xxxv. 11 ("I am *Êl Shaddai*," addressed to Jacob), xxviii. 3 and xlviii. 3 (*Êl Shaddai*, spoken of by Isaac and Jacob): see also xlix. 25. According to P, while Elohim was the name of God regularly employed, *Êl Shaddai* was the Name revealed to the Patriarchs and used by them (see Exod. vi. 2).

The name is obscure in origin and meaning. It is rendered "Almighty"; and the conjectural derivations, from words denoting "wasting" and "mountain," are most precarious. In the LXX it is rendered θεός, κύριος, and παντοκράτωρ. It appears in compound names in Num. i. 6, 12 "Zuri-shaddai" = "Shaddai is my rock," and "Ammi-shaddai" = "Shaddai is my kinsman." It is probable that Shaddai is an ancient Divine appellative meaning "omnipotence," which was traditionally associated with the early revelation granted to the Hebrew ancestors. It is very noticeable that in the poetical book of Job the name "Shaddai" occurs no less than 41 times. See also Num. xxiv. 4, 16; Ruth i. 20, 21; Ps. lxviii. 14, xci. 1; Isai. xiii. 6; Ez. i. 24; Joel i. 15.

On other titles ("the Fear of Isaac," "the Mighty One of Jacob," and "the Stone of Israel"), see notes on xxxi. 42, 53; xlix. 24.

TABLE OF PASSAGES IN GENESIS IN WHICH THE CHIEF PROPER NAMES OF GOD OCCUR

E CHAP. I.	1, 2, 3, 4², 5, 6, 7, 8, 9, 10², 11, 12, 14, 16, 17, 18, 20, 21², 22, 24, 25², 26, 27², 28², 29, 31
J	
E CHAP. II.	2, 3²
J (E)	4, 5, 7, 8, 9, 15, 16, 18, 19, 21, 22
E CHAP. III.	1, 3, 5²
J (E)	1 8², 9, 13, 14, 21, 22, 23
E CHAP. IV.	25 V. 1², 22, 24²
J	1, 3, 4, 6, 9, 13, 15², 16 26 29
E CHAP. VI. 2, 4	9, 11, 12, 13, 22 9, 16, VIII. 1², 15
J	3 5, 6, 7, 8 VII. 1 16 20, 21²
E CHAP. IX. 1, 6, 8, 12, 16, 17	26 X. 9², XI. 5, 6, 8, 9², XII. 1, 4, 7², 8², 17
J	27
E CHAP. XIII.	4, 10², 13, 14, 18
Êl Elyon	22, XV. 1, 2 (*Adônai J.*), 4, 6, 7, 8 (*Adônai J.*), 18
E CHAP. XVI.	XIV. 18, 19, 20, 22
J	2, 5, 7, 9, 10, 11², 13, XVII. 1 3, 7, 8, 9, 15, 18, 19, 22, 23 XVIII. 1, 13, 14, 17, 19²
Êl	13
Êl Sh.	1

THE NAMES OF GOD

E	CHAP. XVIII. (cont.)	29^2, XX. 3, 6, 11, 13, 17^2
J		20, 22, 26, 33, XIX. 13^2, 14, 16, 24^2, 27 18
E	CHAP. XXI.	2, 4, 6, 12, 17^3, 19, 20, 22, 23 XXIII. 6
J		1^2 XXII. 1, 3, 8, 9 12
El 'Olam		33 11 14^2, 15, 16
E		33
J	CHAP. XXIV.	1, 3, 7, 12, 21, 26, 27^2, 31, 35, 40, 42, 44, 48^2, 50, 51, 52, 56, XXV. 21^2, 22, 25
E		28 (ha-E), XXVIII. 4, 12, 17, 20, 22
J	CHAP. XXVI. 2, 12, 22, 24, 25, 28, 29, XXVII. 7, 20, 27 13^2, 16 21
El		19
El Sh.		3
E		XXX. 2, 6, 8, 17, 18, 20, 22^2, 23
J	CHAP. XXIX. 31, 32, 33, 35 24, 27, 30
E	CHAP. XXXI. 7, 9, 11 (ha-E), 16^2, 24, 42 50, XXXII. 1, 2 28, 30
J		3 49 9
El		13
E	CHAP. XXXIII. 5, 10, 11 XXXV. 1, 5, 7, 7 (ha-E), 9, 10, 11, 13, 15
J		XXXVIII. 7^2, 10
El		20 1, 3, 7
El Sh.		11

E	CHAP. XXXIX. 2, 3², 5², 21, 23²	
J	9	XL. 8, XLI. 16, 25 (ha-E), 28 (ha-E), 32² (ha-E), 38, 39, 51, 52
E	CHAP. XLII. 18 (ha-E), 28, XLIII.	
J		29, XLIV. 16 (ha-E), XLV. 5, 7, 8 (ha-E), 9
Êl Sh.	14	
E	CHAP. XLVI. 2, 3, XLVIII.	
J	9, 11, 15² (ha-E), 20, 21	XLIX. 18
Êl Sh.	3	25
Êl		25
E	CHAP. L. 19, 20, 24, 25	
J		

In this Table, E = *Elohim* = God, J (E) = *Jahveh Elohim* = the LORD God, J = *Jahveh* = the LORD, Êl Sh. = *Êl Shaddai* = God Almighty. *Elohim* is only recorded in cases where it is used *absolutely*, i.e. as a Proper Name. In cases where it is used *generically*, or *in the construct state*, e.g. "my God," or "the God of Abraham," i.e. not as a Proper Name, *Elohim* is not recorded in the above Table. The references are to the English Bible (not the Hebrew).

(In Gen. vi. 5, "God" in the A.V. is a mistake for "LORD" (*Jahveh*); in xx. 4, "LORD" in some reprints of the A.V. is a mistake for "Lord" (*Adônai*); in xviii. 27, 30, 31, 32, "Lord" is '*Adônai*; in xxx. 8, "mighty wrestlings" is in Heb. "wrestlings of God"; in xliv. 7, 17, where the English rendering is "God forbid," there is no Name of God in the Hebrew.)

THE NAMES OF GOD

The renderings of the Hebrew by the LXX shew as we might have expected, that in a translation the tendency to substitute one Sacred Name for another is very strong, and that a Greek scribe prefers the usual Greek word for "God," ὁ θεός, to the Hebraic title κύριος. The suggestion that the Hebrew text is so corrupt that no reliance can be placed upon its use of the Divine Names, and that, therefore, the Documentary analysis of the Pentateuch falls to the ground, can only be ascribed to an entire misapprehension of Pentateuchal Criticism. It is a mistake to suppose that "the employment of various designations for God" is regarded by critics as "sufficient evidence for the assumption that different documents were employed in the compilation of the Pentateuch." Pentateuchal Criticism is based, not on a single point of evidence, but on a wide range of inductive reasoning, dealing with (1) the evidence of words and phrases, (2) the literary evidence of style, selection, and treatment of material, (3) the historical evidence supplied by the allusions to different stages in the growth of Israelite religion and worship. The distinctness of origin of (a) JE, (b) D, and (c) P may be treated as having been finally established as the result, not of a single brilliant guess, but of a long, minute, and scientific process of literary criticism. It is true that the first clue to the Documentary analysis of the Pentateuch was supplied by the observation of the manner in which the Hebrew Names of God were distributed throughout Genesis. But it was soon realized that there were numerous other characteristic differences between the component Documents. "If P had used *Yahweh* in Genesis, as he does after Ex. vi. 2, the grounds for the separation of P from JE would have been substantially not less strong than they are now....In view of the smaller number of criteria distinguishing J and E the varying use of the Divine names is of relatively greater importance for the analysis of JE than it is for the separation of JE from P; but there are many cases in which it is not the only criterion on which critics rely for the purpose" (Driver, *Genesis*, Addenda II., p. xliv).

With regard to the Hebrew text, the general agreement of the Samaritan Version in the use of the Divine Names shews that in Palestine there was no serious change, and certainly no arbitrary change, in their transcription, from a time not improbably previous to the LXX translation. The LXX MSS. are full of variations. In the rendering of the Sacred Names, the Greek translator would not attach the significance to the difference between θεός and κύριος ($\overline{\theta c}$, $\overline{\kappa c}$) which the Hebrew discerned between Elohim and Jahweh. The Greek copyist would prefer the use of ὁ θεός. Habit, as well as feelings of reverence, would lead to the substitution of ὁ θεός or κύριος ὁ θεός for the Hebraic ὁ κύριος. The tendency, therefore, both in the translation and in the transcription of the Greek Version, would not be on the side of scrupulous avoidance of alteration.

The substitution of one Divine Name for another in a translation, e.g. in the A.V.'s mistake of "God" for "LORD" (Gen. vi. 5), will, generally, be a matter of small moment. But in the transmission of the original Hebrew text, certainly from the 2nd cent. A.D., a painful care, almost amounting to superstition, has been shewn by Hebrew copyists. The LXX contains valuable material for the textual criticism of the O.T. But in the Hebrew of Genesis the number of doubtful readings is very small, and the superiority of the Greek translation (if the original Greek text is obtainable) over the Hebrew text, in such a matter as the readings for the Divine Names, could not, with any regard for accuracy of statement, be asserted as a general principle. Nor, indeed, except at the most in one or two instances, could it reasonably be claimed in connexion with the reading of the Sacred Names. The mere occurrence of variants in the LXX, or other versions, is no evidence that they represent a more original reading than that of the Massoretic, or official Hebrew text. And where the Sacred Names occur, the presumption is in favour of the greater scrupulousness, care, and avoidance of variation, on the part of the Hebrew copyist than of the Greek transcriber or translator.

The LXX variations, as Dr Skinner[1] has pointed out, would, at the most, only throw doubt upon "three-sixteenths of the whole number" of the occurrences of the Divine Names in Genesis. And, even in this small proportion of cases, there are very few, if any instances, where the Greek variation from the Heb. text of the Divine Name is not to be ascribed rather to loose inaccurate renderings than to any superiority of reading.

For a full and exhaustive enquiry into the whole subject, which is too technical to be pursued here, see Dr Skinner's valuable articles in the *Expositor*, April—September, 1913, entitled "The Divine Names in Genesis"; Driver's *Genesis*, Addenda II. (1910); *L. O. T.* Addenda, pp. xxvi—xxxiii (1913); D. C. Simpson's *Pentateuchal Criticism* (1914), which in an Appendix discusses B. D. A. Troelstra's *The Name of God in the Pentateuch*; and, on the other side, Wiener's *Essays on Pentateuchal Criticism* (1909), and Dahse's *Text-Kritische Materialien zur Hexateuchfrage* (1912).

§ 10. *Bibliography.*

(*a*) Commentaries:

The Book of Genesis, by S. R. Driver, D.D. (Westminster Commentaries), 8th ed., 1911 (London).

A Critical and Exegetical Commentary on Genesis, by John Skinner, D.D. (International Critical Commentary), 1910 (Edinburgh).

Genesis Critically and Exegetically Expounded, by Dr A. Dillmann (Eng. Trans.), 1897.

Genesis übersetzt u. erklärt, von D. Hermann Gunkel, 3te Aufl., 1910 (Göttingen)

Genesis (The Century Bible), by W. H. Bennett, D.D. (Edinburgh).

The Book of Genesis (The Expositor's Bible), by Marcus Dods, D.D., 1890 (Edinburgh).

The Book of Genesis, by G. Woosung Wade, D.D., 1896.

---

[1] *Expositor*, Sept. 1912, p. 272.

The Early Traditions of Genesis, by A. R. Gordon, D.Litt., 1907 (Edinburgh).

The Early Narratives of Genesis, by Herbert E. Ryle, D.D., 3rd ed., 1904 (London).

Genesis, erklärt von D. Holzinger (Kurzer Hand-Commentar A.T.), 1898 (Freiburg).

Die Genesis übersetzt u. erklärt, von D. Otto Pröcksch, 1913 (Leipzig).

A New Commentary on Genesis, by Franz Delitzsch, D.D. (Eng. Trans.), 1888.

Notes on the Text of the Book of Genesis, by G. J. Spurrell, M.A., 1896 (Oxford).

The Speaker's Commentary, vol. I., pt 1 (1876)

(b) Introductions

Driver, *Introduction to the Literature of the Old Testament*, 9th ed. (1913).

Driver, *Exodus* (1911).

Chapman, *Introduction to the Pentateuch* (1911).

Carpenter and Harford, *The Composition of the Hexateuch* (1902).

G. Buchanan Gray, *A Critical Introduction to the O.T.* (1913).

D. G. Simpson, *Pentateuchal Criticism* (1914).

W. R. Smith, *Old Testament in the Jewish Church*, 2nd ed. (1892).

(c) Archaeology

J. H. Breasted, *History of the Ancient Egyptians* (1908).

Flinders Petrie, *History of Egypt*, vols. I. and II.

D. G. Hogarth, *Authority and Archaeology* (1899).

Driver, *Schweich Lectures* (1908), on "Modern Research as illustrating the Bible" (1909).

P. S. P. Handcock's *Latest Light on Bible Lands* (S.P.C.K.), 1913.

C. I. Ball, *Light from the East* (1899).

Alfred Jeremias, *Old Testament in the Light of the East*, 2 vols. (Eng. Trans.) (1911).

A. H. Sayce, *The "Higher Criticism" and the Verdict of the Monuments* (1894).

A. H. Sayce, *The Early History of the Hebrews* (1897).

L. W. King, *The Seven Tablets of Creation* (1902).

Morris Jastrow, Jr, *The Religion of Babylonia and Assyria* (1898).

Hugo Gressmann, *Altorientalische Texte u. Bilder z. A. T.*, 2 Bde (1909).

(*d*) Dictionaries :
Hastings, *Dictionary of the Bible*, 5 vols. (1898—1904).
Hastings, *Dictionary of the Bible*, 1 vol. (1909).
Cheyne and Black, *Encyclopaedia Biblica*, 4 vols. (1903).

Additional note on the date of P (page xxix).

The date of P is probably best assigned to the 6th or 5th century B.C. It embraces materials derived from an earlier period. Doubtless, also, it contains additions which were made to it subsequently. The authorship of it should not be ascribed to any individual ; but rather to a school of priestly writers. Their literary activity belongs to the interval of time between the Captivity and the Age of Nehemiah. Some have conjectured that Ezra, the priest, himself was largely responsible for its final acceptance by the people and its incorporation with JE and D.[1]

[1] See Chapman's *Introduction to the Pentateuch*, pp. 184 f.

NOTE

The letters on the margin (J, E, P, R) indicate the sources of which the text appears to be composed.

In citations, the letters [a] and [b] denote the first and second parts of the verse cited.

In the transliteration of Hebrew words, it has been usual to adopt the following equivalents:

'=א, '=ע, ḥ=ח, ḳ=ק, ṣ=צ;

but this has not been done in the case of familiar names.

CHRONOLOGICAL NOTE

Babylonian and Egyptian civilization before 5000 B.C.:

Ḥammurabi, 6th king of First Dynasty of Babylon } 2130—2088 B.C. (Ungnad) / 1958—1916 B.C. (Meyer)

Expulsion of Hyksos from Egypt } 1587 B.C. (Petrie) / 1580 B.C. (Breasted)

Tel el-Amarna Correspondence:

Burnaburiash, king of Babylon } 1399—1365 B.C. (Ungnad) / 1382—1358 B.C. (Meyer)

Amenophis IV (Khu-n'aten) } 1383—1365 B.C. (Petrie) / 1375—1358 B.C. (Breasted)

Ramses II, probably Pharaoh of Oppression } 1300—1234 B.C. (Petrie) / 1292—1225 B.C. (Breasted)

Merenptah, probably Pharaoh of Exodus } 1234—1214 B.C. (Petrie) / 1225—1215 B.C. (Breasted)

THE FIRST BOOK OF MOSES,

COMMONLY CALLED

GENESIS

IN the beginning God created the heaven and the earth. 1 P
And the earth was waste and void; and darkness was 2

CHAPTER I. 1—II. 4ᵃ (P). THE CREATION NARRATIVE.

1—5. THE BEGINNING OF ALL THINGS, AND THE FIRST CREATION DAY.

1. *In the beginning*] B'rêshîth: LXX ἐν ἀρχῇ: Lat. *in principio*. This opening word expresses the idea of the earliest time imaginable. It contains no allusion to any philosophical conception of "eternity." The language used in the account of Creation is neither that of abstract speculation nor of exact science, but of simple, concrete, and unscientific narrative.

The opening words of St John's Gospel (ἐν ἀρχῇ ἦν ὁ λόγος, i. 1) are based upon this clause. But, whereas St John refers to the Word's eternal pre-existence before time, the Hebrew writer simply speaks of "the beginning" of the universe as the historic origin of time and space.

In the Hebrew Bible the book of Genesis is called "B'rêshîth," deriving its title from this first word.

God] *Elohim* : LXX ὁ Θεός: Lat. *Deus*. See Introduction on "The Names of God." The narrative begins with a statement assuming the Existence of the Deity. It is not a matter for discussion, argument, or doubt. The Israelite Cosmogony differs in this respect from that of the Babylonians, Phoenicians, Egyptians, &c. The Cosmogonies of the ancients were wont to be preceded by Theogonies. The existence and nativities of the creating divinities were accounted for in mythologies which were often highly complicated, and not seldom grotesque. The Hebrew narrator, by beginning with the Creation, emphasizes his entire freedom from, and exclusion of, polytheistic thought. If Polytheism had existed in the earliest Hebrew times, it had been abandoned in the growing light of the Israelite religion. "God" is infinite; He was before all time: "In the beginning God created." Upon the subject of the Divine Existence prior to "the beginning" the writer does not presume to speculate. That Israelite imagination did not wholly avoid the subject, we know from Job xxviii. 25—28, Prov. viii. 22—30, Wisd. ix. 9, Ecclus. xxiv. 9.

Concerning the Israelite conception of God (*Elohim*), we learn (1) from the present verse, that He (i) is a Person, and (ii) exists from all eternity; (2) from the whole passage, i. 1—ii. 4^a, that He is (i) supreme in power, and (ii) perfect in wisdom and goodness. The attribute of power is shewn in creative omnipotence; that of wisdom in the orderly sequence of creation; that of goodness in the benevolent purpose which directed its successive phases.

created] The word so rendered (*bârâ*, LXX ἐποίησεν, Lat. *creavit*) is used especially of the acts of God, in doing, or calling into existence, something new or marvellous: cf. Ex. xxxiv. 10, "I will do marvels such as have not been wrought (Heb. created) in all the earth": Ps. li. 10, "Create in me a clean heart." In the present section it occurs again in connexion with (1) the creation of living organisms (ver. 21); (2) the creation of man (ver. 27); (3) the creation of the whole universe (ii. 3, 4). It is used in Ps. cxlviii. 5, "He commanded, and they were created," where the reference is to this section.

A different word, "made" (*'âsâh*), is used in connexion with the "firmament" (ver. 7), the heavenly bodies (ver. 16), the terrestrial animals (ver. 25).

It is, however, a mistake to suppose that the word *bârâ* necessarily means "to create out of nothing."

the heaven and the earth] These words express the Hebrew conception of the created universe. They do not denote, as has of late been suggested, "matter" in the mass, or in the rough. They embrace sky, earth, and ocean: cf. xiv. 19, 22, xxiv. 3; Dt. iii. 24.

Attention should be called to an alternative rendering of this verse, preferred by many eminent commentators. It turns upon the grammatical point that the first word of the verse, "*B'rêshîth*," means literally "In beginning," not "In the beginning," which would be "*Bârêshîth*." Consequently, it is contended that "*B'rêshîth*," being grammatically in "the construct state," should be translated "In the beginning of," or "In the beginning when"; and not, as if in "the absolute state," "In *the* beginning." If this contention, i.e. that *b'rêshîth* is in the construct state, be correct, verse 1 will be the protasis; verse 2 will be a parenthesis; verse 3 will be the apodosis: "In the beginning *when* God created the heaven and the earth (now the earth was waste, &c.…upon the face of the waters), *then* God said, 'Let there be light.'"

In comparison with our familiar translation (in both R.V. and A.V.) the alternative rendering seems to present the serious disadvantage of opening the book with a long, cumbrous, and involved sentence. The reply, that the second creation narrative (ii. 4^b—7) opens with a similarly long sentence, hardly meets the objection. The opening words of the whole book can hardly be compared with the opening words of a subsequent section.

The simplicity and dignity of the short opening sentence in the familiar translation impress themselves upon every reader. The author of the Fourth Gospel was evidently conscious of it.

The force of the grammatical objection is weakened by the parallel case of the anarthrous use of *b'rēshîth* in Is. xlvi. 10. It is doubtful whether *rēshîth* is found with the article. In the present instance, it may be pleaded that the absence of the article lends a significant indefiniteness. The rendering of the LXX, ἐν ἀρχῇ ἐποίησεν ὁ θεὸς τὸν οὐρανὸν καὶ τὴν γῆν, which supports the anarthrous *b'rēshîth* (ἐν ἀρχῇ, not ἐν τῇ ἀρχῇ), was evidently the traditional rendering of the Jews in at least the third century B.C. The rendering of the Targum of Onkelos, "In the first times" (*b'qadmîn*), supports it in the second century A.D.

2. *And the earth,* &c.] Notice, in the present verse, (1) that "darkness" exists which God is not said to have made: (2) that "waters" exist before the formation of the seas: (3) that "the spirit of God" is mentioned, without explanation of its nature or origin, as "brooding upon the face of the waters." The whole picture is vague and obscure, because the touches, by which it is conveyed, are left unexplained. The old monstrous and grotesque figures with which primitive Semitic, and possibly primitive Hebrew, imagination sought to fill up the void of the unimaginable past, have been left out. The gap which they filled is not wholly supplied. The description is brief and condensed. But, even making allowance for the brevity of the narrative, we are conscious of the presence of features in it, which represent the dim and cancelled outlines of an earlier mythological story. The thought of the Israelite reader is elevated to a higher religious plane in this simple and stately account.

the earth] i.e. the materials out of which the universe is formed. We are not told what the origin of these materials was, or whether God had created them. God is not here spoken of as creating the universe out of nothing, but rather as creating it out of a watery chaos: cf. Wisd. **xi.** 18. That which is affirmed in Heb. xi. 3, i.e. that God did not make "that which is seen out of things which do appear," is not asserted in this verse, though it is implied in the general representation of God's omnipotence and His solitary personal action.

was] The simplest description of what "existed" before the first day of Creation. To translate "became," or "came into being," in order to import into the verse an allusion to the nebular hypothesis for the origin of the solar system, is an expedient not to be entertained by any scholarly interpreter. It has, however, found favour in some quarters. Apologists have been known to appeal to this verse as demonstrating that the Bible contains anticipations of the latest discoveries in Natural Science, as if the Hebrew auxiliary denoted the process of gradual evolution out of nebulous gas.

The theory, however, would never have been thought of except for the well-meaning, but mistaken, purpose of defending the honour of

Holy Scripture on the supposition that it must contain perfection of instruction upon all matters of scientific knowledge.

It is sufficient to remind the reader that the ancients were entirely ignorant of the Copernican theory of the solar system; and, *ex hypothesi*, could not have comprehended Laplace's nebular theory.

It violates every canon of interpretation to assume that simple words, like "earth," "darkness," "water," &c., were intended to convey to the Israelite reader not the meanings which the Hebrew equivalents everywhere else conveyed, but those which could only be understood after the scientific discoveries of the nineteenth century had transformed men's conception of the universe.

Equally arbitrary is the explanation of this verse, that it is intended to summarize the period, or periods, of catastrophe which, according to some writers, preceded the present geological condition of our planet. Geology is a modern science. The view which regarded the geological history of the globe as a succession of gigantic catastrophes is now very generally abandoned. The theory, that the earth has reached its present condition through gradual changes which have taken place during an enormous span of time (the uniformitarian theory), has now received the general adherence of geologists. (Cf. Sir Arch. Geikie, Art. "Geology," *Encyc. Brit.*)

On the other hand, the Hebrew conception of the Creation in this chapter is in agreement with a fundamental principle of scientific thought. It recognizes in Nature an orderly progress from the simple into the complex, from the lower into the higher. Evolution, in the modern acceptance of the word, would have been unintelligible. But the ideas of order and progress, which it endorses and illustrates, are dominant in the present description. See Special Note, pp. 45 f.

waste and void] A.V. "without form and void." The Heb. *tôhû va-bhôhû* is untranslateable. The LXX, ἀόρατος καὶ ἀκατασκεύαστος, "invisible and unformed," fails to give the meaning. The Latin, *inanis et vacua*, is closer to the original. The alliteration of the Heb. words cannot be reproduced in English: "void and vacancy" would partially represent the sense and the sound.

tôhû in Isai. xlv. 18, where there is a reference to the Creation Narrative, seems to denote "waste" or "vacancy"; while *bôhû* = "emptiness," "void," occurs elsewhere only in Isai. xxxiv. 11, Jer. iv. 23, with a reference to the present passage. Conceivably, the words may contain some similarity to primitive names, which had become obsolete, but which had been used to personify the conditions of chaos out of which the universe was formed. We may, at least, in connexion with this suggestion, compare the Phoenician Βαύυ = Night, the Mother of Chaos, and the Gnostic technical terms Βύθος and Χαός, designating primaeval matter.

darkness] The existence of "darkness" is here assumed. It is not said to have been created. "Light," not "darkness," has its origin in the creative act of God.

For another conception, cf. Isai. xlv. 7, "I form the light, and create darkness."

upon the face of the deep: and the spirit of God ¹moved P

¹ Or, *was brooding upon*

the deep] Heb. *t'hôm*, LXX ἀβύσσον, Lat. *abyssi*. This word is generally used in the O.T. for the "Ocean," which, according to Hebrew ideas, both encircled the world, and occupied the vast hollows beneath the earth: cf. Gen. xlix. 25. It is used like a proper name, without the article; and is very probably Babylonian in origin. In the present verse it denotes the chaotic watery waste destined on the Second Day to be confined within certain definite limits. It is conceivable that in primitive Hebrew mythology this *t'hôm*, or "abyss," fulfilled the same part as the somewhat similar Babylonian *Tiamtu*, or *Tiamath*, "the Goddess of the Great Deep," with a dragon's body, whose destruction preceded the creative deeds of the Babylonian Supreme God, Marduk, or Merodach. Marduk slew the dragon, clave its body in two parts, and made the heaven of one portion, and the earth of the other. See Appendix A.

The Hebrew notion that, before the Creation, the universe was enveloped in the waters of the great deep is possibly referred to in Ps. civ. 6, "Thou coveredst it [the earth] with the deep as with a vesture," cf. Ps. xxxiii. 7.

the spirit of God] Nothing could more effectually distinguish the Hebrew Narrative of the Creation from the representations of primitive mythology than the use of this simple and lofty expression for the mysterious, unseen, and irresistible presence and operation of the Divine Being. It is the "breath" of God which alone imparts light to darkness and the principle of life to inert matter.

The student should be warned against identifying this expression with the Holy Spirit in the Christian doctrine of the Blessed Trinity. We must not look for the distinctive teaching of the Christian Revelation in the pages of the O.T.

The word for "wind," Heb. *ruah*, Gr. πνεῦμα, Lat. *spiritus*, was accepted as the most suitable term to express the invisible agency of God. In consequence, it is sometimes difficult to decide whether the word is used literally in its meaning of "wind" or "breath," or metaphorically in its meaning of "spirit" as the symbol of the invisible operation and influence of the Almighty. An instance of this ambiguity occurs in our Lord's words in John iii. 8, "The wind (πνεῦμα) bloweth (marg. 'The Spirit breatheth') where it listeth, &c....so is every one that is born of the Spirit (πνεῦμα)." Similarly, whereas the Targum of Onkelos probably rendered our clause by "wind from the LORD blew upon the face of the waters," the Targum of Palestine renders "the Spirit of mercies from the LORD breathed upon the face of the waters."

moved upon the face of the waters] The rendering of the margin, *was brooding upon*, furnishes the picture of a bird spreading its wings over its nest: it also reproduces the meaning of the participle of the

P 3 upon the face of the waters. And God said, Let there be

Hebrew verb, which implies continuousness in the action. For the use of the same unusual Hebrew word, cf. Deut. xxxii. 11, "As an eagle that stirreth up her nest, That *fluttereth* over her young, He spread abroad his wings, He took them, He bare them on his pinions."

By the selection of this word the writer conveys the thought that the continuous, fostering care of the Almighty was given to the welter of primaeval chaos no less than to the orderly successive phenomena of the universe.

Milton employs this metaphor in two well-known passages.

> Thou from the first
> Wast present, and, with mighty wings outspread,
> Dove-like sat'st brooding on the vast Abyss,
> And mad'st it pregnant...
> —*Par. Lost*, i. 19.

> ...Matter unformed and void. Darkness profound
> Covered the Abyss; but on the watery calm
> His brooding wings the Spirit of God outspread,
> And vital virtue infused, and vital warmth,
> Throughout the fluid mass....
> —vii. 234.

It may, indeed, be questioned whether, if the word is intended to denote the action of a bird, it should not be rendered "was fluttering," or "was hovering," rather than "was brooding." Motion seems to be implied: and the simile is not so much that of a bird sitting upon its nest as that of a bird hovering with outstretched wings over the young ones in the nest. The choice of the word, with its allusion to bird life, has been thought to contain an intentional reference to primitive mythologies, e.g. Phoenician, Egyptian, according to which the universe was hatched by a female deity out of the primaeval egg of Chaos.

3. THE FIRST DAY.

3. *And God said*] Observe here that the spoken Word is the only means employed throughout the six days' Creation, cf. Ps. xxxiii. 6, 9, "By the word of the LORD were the heavens made....For he spake, and it was done; he commanded, and it stood fast." Creation by a word combines the idea of perfect facility with that of absolute power.

It is only through the Revelation of the N.T. that we learn to identify the work of Creation with the operation of the Personal Word (John i. 3): "All things were made through him (ὁ Λόγος); and without him was not anything made that hath been made," cf. Col. i. 16, "For in him [the Son] were all things created...all things have been created through him, and unto him." Heb. i. 2, "through whom [his Son] also he made the worlds."

Let there be light] This command, in the Hebrew, consists of two

light: and there was light. And God saw the light, that it 4 P
was good: and God divided the light from the darkness.
And God called the light Day, and the darkness he called 5
Night. And there was evening and there was morning,
one day.

short words, *y'hi 'ôr*. Light is the first created thing, that upon which
depends all life and growth known to us on earth.

For "light" as the symbol of the Divine Presence in the Revelation
of the N.T., cf. John i. 4, "in him was life; and the life was the light
of men," cf. *v.* 9, and viii. 12, "I am the light of the world."

and there was light] Literally, "and light came into existence."
Apparently the primitive conception of the Hebrews was that light and
darkness were separate things, incomprehensible indeed, but independent
of the sun, cf. Job xxvi. 10, xxxviii. 19, "where is the way to the
dwelling of light, and as for darkness, where is the place thereof?"
The unscientific notions of the Israelite have received in regard to
light an unexpected illustration from modern discovery; but we must
be careful not to suppose that there is any resemblance between the
Hebrew picture of the creation of light, and modern theories respecting
light and the ether of infinite space. The Hebrew view of the universe was (cf. *vv.* 6—8) extremely limited; the modern scientific view
of the universe is practically infinite in its capacity for development,
and is continually being enlarged. There is little room for comparison
between them.

4. *And God...good*] This phrase is repeated (*vv.* 10, 12, 18, 21,
25, and in slightly amplified form, *v.* 31) at each successive creative act,
except on the second day (*v.* 8, where see note). The purpose of this
sentence is to express (1) that the phenomena of the natural world, in
their respective provinces, fulfil the will of the Creator, (2) that what is
in accordance with His will is "good" in His sight.

and God divided...darkness] By this simple and concrete expression
it is implied, that God assigned their own places to "light" and "darkness" respectively, and that, before the moment of separation, the light
had been confused and entangled in the darkness. The two elements
were now divided, and apportioned to different dwelling places, cf. Job
xxxviii. 19 quoted above.

5. *And God called...*] That God should give names to things is to
our minds a strange and almost unintelligible thought. To the Hebrews,
on the contrary, it seemed a natural feature of the story. To them the
Hebrew language was that in which the Divine Will was expressed;
and, to their minds, the Hebrew name and the thing which it designated
had been rendered inseparable by Divine Decree on the day of its
creation.

Observe that the names "Day" and "Night" are given to "light"
and "darkness," although the heavenly bodies are not made until the
fourth day.

and there was...] The "day" with the Hebrews began in the evening.

P 6 And God said, Let there be a ¹firmament in the midst of

¹ Heb. *expanse*.

It was reckoned from 6 p.m. to 6 p.m. The Israelite writer, therefore, in speaking of the days of Creation, describes them as ordinary days with their succession of evening and morning. There is no need to suppose, as some have done, that the "evening" in this verse refers to the pre-existent darkness of *v.* 2, and that "morning" denotes the period of light before the creative work of the second day. In the mention of the days, the Hebrew story of Creation is perfectly simple and natural. With childlike faith, it told how the Creator completed His work in a time corresponding to six earthly days, each consisting of evening and morning. The hallowing of the seventh day, in chap. ii. 2, 3, presupposes the literal character of the previous six days.

Suggestions have frequently been made in the course of the last half century, that each of the six days is to be understood as a period of indefinite duration. But it is important to remember that the facts, with which modern science has familiarized us, respecting the antiquity of the earth, as shewn by geology, and our solar system, as shewn by astronomy, were wholly unknown until quite recent times. We must be careful, therefore, not to read back such notions into the minds of the writer and of those for whom he wrote this chapter. The assumption that the inspired record must be literally accurate has led to much misinterpretation of Scripture as well as to great mental confusion and religious distress.

The difficulties, which have been felt with regard to the mention of "days," have arisen from the natural wish to reconcile the plain and childlike language of ancient unscientific Semitic story, which accounted for the origin of the world, with the abstruse and dazzling discoveries of modern Physical Science. The two must be kept absolutely distinct.

one day] So the Hebrew, not "the first day"; but "one day," LXX ἡμέρα μία, Lat. *dies unus*.

6—8. THE FIRMAMENT OF THE HEAVEN.

6. *Let there be...waters*] The work of the "second day" is the creation of the so-called "firmament" of heaven. The Hebrews had no conception of an infinite ethereal space. The vault of heaven was to them a solid arched, or vaulted, structure, resting upon the pillars of the earth (Job xxvi. 11). On the top of this dome were the reservoirs of "the waters above the heaven," which supplied the rain and the dew. Beneath the earth were other reservoirs of waters, which were the sources of the seas, lakes, rivers and springs. After the creation of light the next creative act was, according to the Hebrew cosmogony, the division of the primaeval watery abyss, by means of a solid partition, which is here denoted by the word rendered "firmament." The waters are above it and below it.

a firmament] This word reproduces the Lat. *firmamentum*; LXX

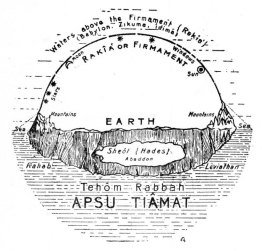

A diagram representing the Semitic conception of the Universe.

From Dr Hastings' *Dictionary of the Bible*, by kind permission of Messrs T. & T. Clark.

the waters, and let it divide the waters from the waters. And God made the firmament, and divided the waters 7 which were under the firmament from the waters which were above the firmament: and it was so. And God 8 called the firmament Heaven. And there was evening and there was morning, a second day.

And God said, Let the waters under the heaven be 9

στερέωμα. The Hebrew *râqîa* denotes (see *Heb. Lex.*) "extended surface, (solid) expanse" (as if *beaten out*; cf. Job xxxvii. 18). For the verb *raq'a=beat*, or *spread*, *out*, cf. Ex. xxxix. 3, Num. xvii. 4, Jer. x. 4, Ezek. i. 22, "and over the head of the living creatures there was the likeness of a *firmament*...stretched forth over their heads above." Compare Job xxxvii. 18, "canst thou with him *spread out* (*tarqi'a*) the sky which is strong as a molten mirror?" See Ps. xix. 1, cl. 1, Dan. xii. 3, where "firmament"=sky.

For the solidity of the heaven according to this conception, cf. Amos ix. 6, "it is he that buildeth his chambers in the heaven, and hath founded his vault upon the earth." The fall of rain was regarded as the act of God in opening the sluices of heaven, cf. Gen. vii. 11, 2 Kings vii. 2, 19, Ps. lxxviii. 23, cxlviii. 4, "ye waters that be above the heavens."

The LXX adds at the end of this verse, "and it was so." This formula, which appears in *vv.* 11, 15 and 24, in each case after the words of Divine fiat, seems more suitable here than at the close of *v.* 7, as in the Hebrew text.

7. *and it was so*] This formula is here out of place. See previous note.

8. *God called the firmament Heaven*] It is clear therefore that what the Hebrews meant by "Heaven," was neither the clouds and mist, nor the empty space of the sky. It was a solid arch, to which, as we shall see in *v.* 14, the luminaries of the sky could be attached.

At the close of the description of the work on the other days, we find the formula "And God saw that it was good" (*vv.* 10, 12, 18, 21, 25, 31). The omission of it here, at the close of the second day, is probably due to textual error.

LXX adds after the word "Heaven," "and God saw that it was good." It is more probable that the words have fallen out accidentally from the Hebrew text, than that the formula was intentionally omitted because, "the waters under the firmament" not having yet received their place, the Divine work upon the waters of the deep was regarded as still incomplete.

9—13. THE THIRD DAY—TWO CREATIVE ACTS. (1) THE SEPARATION OF SEA AND EARTH (*vv.* 9, 10). (2) THE CREATION OF THE VEGETABLE WORLD (*vv.* 11—13).

9. *Let the waters...appear*] In this verse the dry land is rendered

P gathered together unto one place, and let the dry land 10 appear: and it was so. And God called the dry land

visible by the removal of the waters, that were under the Heaven, into their special place. The account reads as if the Earth had existed previously, but had been submerged in the water. It is not stated that God made the earth at this juncture; but only that He now caused it to become visible. The description of the formation of the earth, like other details of the old Hebrew cosmogony, has been omitted either for the sake of brevity, or in order to free the account from materials which were out of harmony with its general religious teaching.

unto one place] According to the Hebrew conception the Earth was supposed to have a flat surface, surrounded on all sides by the ocean; while the ocean was connected by subterranean channels with vast reservoirs of water that lay under the earth and fed the springs and rivers. Cf. Ps. xxiv. 2, "for he hath founded it (the world) upon the seas, and established it upon the floods"; cxxxix. 9, "if I take the wings of the morning, and dwell in the uttermost parts of the sea." In the story of the Flood we read that "all the fountains of the great deep" (Gen. vii. 11 P) were broken up.

Instead of "place," the LXX reads "gathering," συναγωγήν, the word which is reproduced in the familiar term "synagogue." It has been suggested that this may very possibly represent the original reading; and that, at any rate, the less usual word מִקְוֶה, *miqveh* = "gathering," was more likely to be altered in transcription into the common word מָקוֹם, *maqom* = "place," than *vice versa*. On the other hand, the word מִקְוֶה, *miqveh*, occurs in the following verse (v. 10), "the *gathering together* of the waters" (τὰ συστέματα τῶν ὑδάτων), in a slightly different sense, and a copyist may have introduced the word here by accident and given rise to the LXX rendering.

the dry land] That is, the surface, or crust, as it would now be called, of the earth, consisting of soil, sand, and rock. Christian tradition, until the beginning of the 19th or the end of the 18th century, was satisfied that the Hebrew narrative, attributing the origin of the earth's crust to the work of a single day, adequately met the requirements of terrestrial phenomena, and did justice to the conception of Divine omnipotence. The rise of the science of Geology, in the last century and a half, has totally transformed educated opinion. It is recognized that the Hebrew cosmogony is devoid of scientific value (see p. 4). Geologists are agreed that the cooling process, by which the surface of the glowing and molten body of our planet came to be sufficiently solidified to support the weight of vast seas, must have extended over long ages to be reckoned by millions and millions of years. The subsequent geological ages, Palaeozoic, Mesozoic, Cainozoic, and Quaternary, which account for the gradual formation of the rocks as we know them, have been demonstrated to have covered a similarly stupendous length of time. The thicknesses of the successive geological

GENESIS I. 10—13

Earth; and the gathering together of the waters called he
Seas: and God saw that it was good. And God said, Let
the earth put forth grass, herb yielding seed, *and* fruit tree
bearing fruit after its kind, wherein is the seed thereof,
upon the earth: and it was so. And the earth brought
forth grass, herb yielding seed after its kind, and tree
bearing fruit, wherein is the seed thereof, after its kind:
and God saw that it was good. And there was evening
and there was morning, a third day.

P

11

12

13

strata furnish the means of estimating the relative durations of the periods. The infinite tracts of time and space, which modern science has in an increasing degree revealed to be in relation to one supreme and all embracing harmony, testify to the omnipotence of the Divine Will and Wisdom even more impressively than did the brief and intermittent acts of Creative Power, which in the legends of the ancient world accounted for the origin of earth and sea and stars.

The LXX adds at the end of the verse, "And the water that was under the heaven was gathered together into their gatherings (συναγωγὰς αὐτῶν), and the dry land appeared," which looks like a gloss. But αὐτῶν implies a Heb. original (i.e. the plural form הַמַּיִם, "the waters," not the sing. τὸ ὕδωρ).

11. *Let the earth...grass*] The creation of the vegetable world follows naturally and logically upon the emergence of the earth out of the waters. The most common and beautiful thing in nature, in the East, is the instantaneous appearance of fresh green blade and shoot, after the rain has fallen upon some parched and apparently lifeless soil. This phenomenon suitably marks the commencement of organic life in the Hebrew cosmogony.

It is doubtful whether we should distinguish in this verse three, or two, types of vegetation. Assuming that the former is to be preferred, we may distinguish (1) the grasses, (2) the herbs, (3) the trees. According to another view, the main class of vegetation ("grass") is described under two heads, (1) the herbs, (2) the fruit-trees.

This classification of the vegetable world into three (or two) orders marks the beginnings of what we call botany. The "herb" and the "fruit-tree" are described in popular language, according to the mode of their propagation by seed or fruit.

after its kind] The word is collective, and the phrase means according to their various species. Cf. *vv.* 21, 25; vi. 20 (P).

We should notice the emphasis that is here laid upon the fact that both the main orders of the vegetable kingdom and their subdivisions have their origin in the Divine command. The food of the Oriental is almost entirely vegetable.

P 14 And God said, Let there be lights in the firmament of the heaven to divide the day from the night; and let

14—19. Fourth Day. The Creation of the Heavenly Bodies.

Observe that the creation of the "lights" in the heaven on the fourth day corresponds to the creation of "light" on the first day. If we divide the six days into two groups of three, there are in each group four creative acts, and at the head of each group is the creation of light in *two* different forms, (1) elemental, (2) sidereal.

14. *Let there be lights*] The word rendered "lights" (LXX φωστῆρες: Lat. *luminaria*) denotes a thing, or body, carrying light; cf. Ps. lxxiv. 16, "The day is thine, the night also is thine: Thou hast prepared the light (Heb. *luminary*) and the sun"; Ezek. xxxii. 8, "All the bright lights of heaven."

It has seemed strange to some that the creation of the heavenly bodies should follow after that of the vegetable world, whose life, according to our notions, is dependent on the light of the sun. But, beside the artificial arrangement (according to which the creation of "the lights" of the sky on the fourth day corresponds to the creation of "the light" on the first day), it is probable that, in the ascending scale from vegetable organisms to animal life, the "lights," i.e. the sun, moon, and stars, with their mysterious movements and changing, yet ordered, paths in the sky, seemed to be endowed with a vital activity, which, if inferior to that of the animals, yet was far surpassing that of the plants.

Described in terms of astronomy, the account here given of the origin and functions of the heavenly bodies is, what is called, "geocentric," that is, it supposes the earth to be the centre of the system. It conceives the sun, moon and stars to be much smaller bodies of varied light-giving capacity, formed for purposes of use to the dwellers upon earth, and attached to the roof of heaven at no very great altitude above the flat earth.

Primitive and childlike will this Hebrew view seem now to us who inherit the privilege of the continually advancing discoveries of astronomical science since the days of Copernicus, Galileo, and Newton. But we shall do well to recollect, that the statement in these verses respecting the origin, nature, and function of the heavenly bodies, stands on an immensely higher level of reasonable and dignified intelligence, than the notions of other peoples in the ancient world, who identified the heavenly bodies with gods, or semi-divine beings, exercising a benevolent or malevolent potency over the affairs of men and women, countries, and nations. The Hebrew account is simple almost to baldness, but it is an account which harmonizes with the fear and worship of the one God of Israel. There is neither idolatry nor superstition in it. It gives no loophole for the follies or fears of astrology, which even down to modern times has been known to enslave the reason of Christian minds.

GENESIS I. 14—16

them be for signs, and for seasons, and for days and years: 15
and let them be for lights in the firmament of the heaven
to give light upon the earth: and it was so. And God 16
made the two great lights; the greater light to rule the day,
and the lesser light to rule the night: *he made* the stars also.

P

God is described as calling into existence the heavenly bodies for three distinct purposes: (1) to divide between day and night; (2) to determine periods of time, days, months, years, seasons, festivals, &c.; (3) to give light upon earth, providing by day for the growth, health, and strength of living organisms, and by night for the guidance of the wayfarer and the mariner.

for signs, and for seasons] Literally, "for signs and for fixed times."

The seasons of the year were indicated by the position of the sun, moon, and stars; the "signs" probably have special reference to the constellations, and especially to what are called "the constellations of the Zodiac"—a knowledge of which was from a very early time possessed by the Babylonians. Comets, eclipses, shooting-stars, &c. would also be included among the "signs" of the sky.

The "fixed times" probably denote the periods of the year for agricultural and rural occupations, together with their festivals. Days of festivals were determined by particular moons, or by the rising of particular stars. Cf. Job xxxviii. 32, "Canst thou lead forth the Mazzaroth (signs of the Zodiac) *in their season*?"

16. *And God made*, &c.] The work of creation on the fourth day is twofold. In verse 16 God is said to make the sun, the moon, and the stars; in verse 17 He is said to set them in their place.

It is noticeable that, although the "greater" and the "lesser lights" are here mentioned, the names of "sun" and "moon" are omitted: possibly in order to avoid reference by name to heavenly bodies whose worship was a source of idolatrous superstition, from the peril of which Israel was not free.

to rule] This expression assigns to the sun and moon a kind of quasi-personal dominion over the realms of day and night. Cf. Job xxxviii. 33, "Knowest thou the ordinances of the heavens? Canst thou establish the dominion thereof in the earth?" Possibly the expression "rule" may be a survival of an earlier stage in the Hebrew cosmogony, in which the sun and moon received some kind of personification. At least, the word is noticeable in a context singularly free from metaphor.

he made *the stars also*] A translation must fail to do justice to the abruptness of the original, which literally runs, "and the stars." The brevity of this clause, together with the absence of any further definition of the function of "the stars" as distinguished from "the greater lights," is very noteworthy. It may possibly indicate a necessary abbreviation, in order to remove some older features of the cosmogony which conflicted with the pure monotheism of Israel.

P 17 And God set them in the firmament of the heaven to give
18 light upon the earth, and to rule over the day and over the
night, and to divide the light from the darkness: and God
19 saw that it was good. And there was evening and there
was morning, a fourth day.
20 And God said, Let the waters ¹bring forth abundantly

¹ Heb. *swarm with swarms of living creatures.*

17. *And God set them*] Having made the heavenly bodies (as in
v. 16) God is now said to "set," that is, to place (LXX ἔθετο, Lat.
posuit), them in "the firmament of heaven." They are located in the
firm structure which stood as a dome, or convex roof, over the surface
of the earth; see note *v.* 6; cf. Pliny II. 106, *sidera coelo adfixa*. No
mention is here added of the movements of the heavenly bodies; nor
is any explanation given, in this condensed narrative, of the way in
which the luminaries placed in the firmament were nevertheless apparently possessed with mysterious powers of movement; cf. Job xxxviii.
32. They occupied certain positions, and moved upon certain paths,
appointed them by God; and, like the sea, they were not able to pass
the bounds set them.

20—23. The Fifth Day. The Creation of Water Animals and Flying Animals.

20. *Let the waters...life*] The rendering, "bring forth abundantly
the moving creature that hath life," fails to give the full meaning of
the original. Literally, the words mean "let the waters swarm
swarms, even living soul": and the purpose of the command is that
the waters are to teem with myriads of living animals. Hence the
R.V. margin, "swarm with swarms of living creatures" is closer to
the original; but it fails to reproduce the phrase "living soul," in
apposition to the word translated "swarms." No translation is satisfactory which fails to give prominence to the thought, that the waters
are to teem with things endowed with a wondrous new gift, the active
principle of animal life, which the Hebrews called *nephesh*, and which
is nearly represented by the Greek ψυχή. We might, therefore, translate "let the waters swarm with swarms of creatures, even with countless things which have life."

That there should ever be any difficulty in deciding whether an
organism belonged to the vegetable or to the animal kingdom would
never have occurred to an ancient writer.

The rendering "the moving creature" went wrong in following the
ancient versions, which supposed that the word rendered in the margin,
"swarm," denoted only "creeping things" or "reptiles." LXX ἑρπετὰ
ψυχῶν ζωσῶν. Lat. *reptile animae viventis*. This gives an entirely

GENESIS I. 20, 21

the moving creature that hath life, and let fowl fly above P
the earth ¹in the open firmament of heaven. And God 21
created the great sea-monsters, and every living creature

¹ Heb. *on the face of the expanse of the heaven.*

false impression. The command is for the creation of all sorts of water animals.

and let fowl fly] Rather, "and let winged things fly." The command includes all creatures with wings, e.g. bats, butterflies, beetles, insects, as well as birds.

in the open firmament of heaven] This rendering scarcely reproduces the sense of the Hebrew words, which literally mean "in the face of," or "over against, the firmament of heaven." The idea is that winged things are to fly "above" the earth, and "in front of" the vault of heaven. The R.V. margin, *on the face of the expanse of the heaven*, is cumbrous and obscure. The meaning seems to be that the flight of winged things shall be in mid air, "in front," as it were, of the solid "firmament of heaven," which was not remote. The winged creatures would continually be visible against the sky.

21. *And God created*] Observe the use of the word "create" (Heb. *bârâ*). It signalizes a new departure of the Divine work, when the principle of animal life (*nephesh*) is first communicated on earth, and living animals are formed: cf. note on *v.* 1.

The writer does not directly speak of fish; but the water animals are described under two main classes, which would include all marine and fresh-water creatures.

the great sea-monsters] Better, "the great monsters." The word in the Hebrew is applied to monsters, or creatures of strange and monstrous size, such as occur in mythological and poetical pictures, e.g. the Dragon, Behemoth, and Leviathan; cf. Ps. lxxiv. 13, cxlviii. 7, Is. xxvii., li. 9. It was also used of the crocodile (cf. Ezek. xxix. 3), and of snakes (Ex. vii. 9). The Hebrew did not know of the megatherium, ichthyosaurus, iguanodon, &c. But the expression here used is singularly appropriate to them.

The translation of the A.V., "great whales," was based upon the versions LXX τὰ κήτη τὰ μεγάλα, Vulg. *cete grandia*; but the word is used of any animals of vast size. Moreover, there is no probability that the warm-blooded marine animal, which we call a "whale," was known to the Israelites.

every living creature] Literally, "and all the living soul that moveth with which the waters swarmed." This is the second main class of water animals, viz. all the things in which is the principle of animal life, and with which the waters teem. They are further described by their motion, "that moveth." The Hebrew word denotes the gliding, swift movement of the fish for which there is no adequate English equivalent.

The LXX, πᾶσαν ψυχὴν ζῴων ἑρπετῶν, gives too restricted a sense

P that moveth, which the waters brought forth abundantly, after their kinds, and every winged fowl after its kind: and
22 God saw that it was good. And God blessed them, saying, Be fruitful, and multiply, and fill the waters in the seas,
23 and let fowl multiply in the earth. And there was evening and there was morning, a fifth day.
24 And God said, Let the earth bring forth the living

and suggests only lizards and reptiles: while the Vulg. *omnem animam viventem atque motabilem*, like the R.V., is too general.

which...brought forth abundantly] Better, "with which the waters teemed" or "swarmed."

after their kinds] Cf. vv. 11, 12; the expression has reference to the great variety of species of water animals.

and every winged fowl] or "and every winged flying thing": LXX πᾶν πετεινὸν πτερωτόν. The actual word "bird" is not used, doubtless intentionally, in order that the class may comprehend as many varieties as possible of winged creatures.

The assignment of the creation of birds and fishes to the second day after that of vegetation is probably due to the view that an ascending scale of vitality is represented by plants, heavenly bodies, fish, and birds. Clearly the Israelite drew a very sharp line of distinction between the vegetable and the animal world. Modern science has shewn how infinitely fine is this line; and geology has shewn that, in the earliest rock formations which contain fossils, it is difficult to decide whether vegetable or animal life recedes into the most distant antiquity.

22. *God blessed them*] With the creation of the living animals of the water and the air is introduced the mention of a new Divine act, that of blessing. It is connected with the gift of life (see note on *v.* 21). The animal world differs from the vegetable world in its distinctive principle of life. The animals possess powers, instincts, and energies which are to be exercised, and on the exercise of which God gives His blessing. He has placed them in conditions favourable to their development and multiplication. Modern science, especially as represented by the honoured names of Darwin and Lyell, has shewn in what wonderful and varied ways the blessing of God has attended both the multiplication of animal life and the adaptation of the animals to their surroundings.

24—31. SIXTH DAY: (*a*) CREATION OF THE LAND ANIMALS (*vv.* 24, 25);
(*b*) CREATION OF MAN (*vv.* 26—30);
(*c*) THE END OF THE CREATION (*v.* 31).

24. *Let the earth*, &c.] The work of the sixth, like that of the third, day is twofold. Furthermore, the creation of the land animals on the

GENESIS I. 24, 25

creature after its kind, cattle, and creeping thing, and P
beast of the earth after its kind: and it was so. And 25
God made the beast of the earth after its kind, and the
cattle after their kind, and every thing that creepeth upon
the ground after its kind: and God saw that it was good.

sixth day seems to correspond to the creation of the earth on the third day.

The creation of the land animals immediately precedes that of mankind. It is implied that they are closer both in structure and in intelligence to the human race than the animals of the water and air. On the other hand, the words "let the earth bring forth" (the same phrase as is used in v. 11 of the creation of the vegetable world) emphasize the difference in origin between the land animals ("let the earth bring forth") and mankind, who are described (vv. 26, 27) as, in a special manner, "created" by God Himself.

the living creature] viz. "living soul," as above (vv. 20, 21). Here the words are used especially of the land animals. To speak of animals having "a soul" is strange to modern ears. But it was not so to the Israelites, who realized, perhaps better than we do, man's kinship with the animal world, in virtue of that principle of *nephesh*, the mystery of life, which is shared by the animals and human beings.

after its kind] viz. the various species of the animals about to be mentioned.

cattle, and creeping thing, and beast of the earth] This is a rough threefold classification of the animals dwelling on the earth: (1) "the cattle" (Heb. *behêmah*, LXX τετράποδα (="quadrupeds"), Lat. *jumenta* (="cattle")), under which head are here probably classed all the domestic animals, e.g. oxen, sheep, horses, asses, camels, as in Jonah iv. 11. Here it seems to be implied that the domestic animals were tame originally, and not through association with mankind. (2) "creeping things"; LXX ἑρπετά, Lat. *reptilia*. In this class seem to be included not only snakes and lizards, but also the smaller animals, generally, and the insect world. (3) "the beasts of the earth"; LXX θηρία τῆς γῆς, Lat. *bestias terrae*, viz. the wild beasts, strictly so called, as distinguished from the domestic animals.

25. *And God made*] Notice the word "made," Lat. *fecit*, not "created"; cf. vv. 7, 16.

and God saw that it was good] It is noticeable that the blessing, which followed these words after the creation of the water animals and the birds (v. 22), is here omitted. Either the blessing was allowed to drop out, in order that the description of the sixth day might not become too long in comparison with that of the previous five days; or the blessing so fully pronounced upon man in vv. 28—30 may be considered to embrace also the living creatures created on the same sixth day.

GENESIS I. 26

P 26 And God said, Let us make man in our image, after our

26—30. *Let us make*, &c.] The creation of man, although taking place on the same day with that of the land animals, is a completely separate creative act. It constitutes the climax and the crown of Creation. It is, therefore, described with especial fulness and solemnity. There is no formula, "let there be man," or "let the earth bring forth man," as in the case of the previous creative acts. We observe, (1) *firstly*, that God prefaces the creation of man with a declaration concerning (*a*) the Divine purpose; (*b*) man's future nature; (*c*) his sphere of authority and influence (v. 26); (2) *secondly*, that in a direct and special manner God creates man, in His own image, both male and female (v. 27); (3) *thirdly*, that He both blesses them, and intrusts them with duties and powers upon the earth (v. 28); (4) *fourthly*, that He makes provision for their food and sustenance (v. 29), as well as for that of the lower animals.

26. *Let us make*] LXX ποιήσωμεν, Lat. *faciamus*. The use of the 1st pers. plur. is a well-known *crux* of interpretation. How are we to explain its occurrence in the utterance of the Almighty? The only other passages in which it is found are (1) Gen. iii. 22, "And the LORD God said, Behold, the man is become as one of *us*"; (2) Gen. xi. 7, "Go to, and *let us go down*, and there confound their language"; (3) Isai. vi. 8, "And I heard the voice of the LORD, saying, Whom shall I send, and who will go for *us*?" Very different explanations have been given.

i. Until recently, the traditional Christian interpretation has seen in the 1st pers. plur. a reference to the Three Persons of the Blessed Trinity. The requirements of a sound historical exegesis render this view untenable: for it would read into the Book of Genesis the religious teaching which is based upon the Revelation of the New Testament.

ii. It has been regarded as a survival of polytheism, and has been compared with "Elohim," a plural word for "God" which some regard as a relic of polytheism. But "Elohim, in the present context, is always combined with a verb in the singular. Why should "said" be in the singular, if "let *us*" indicates the plurality of Gods? Again, any departure from the strictest monotheism is unthinkable in the writing of the Priestly Code. The explanation may safely be dismissed as improbable in the extreme.

iii. It has been explained as the plural of Majesty. It is pointed out that the commands and rescripts of royal personages are conveyed in the 1st pers. plur.; and reference is made, in support of this view, to Ezra iv. 18, 1 Macc. x. 19, xi. 31. It may be allowed that the view is tenable; but the examples adduced are drawn from a very late period of Biblical literature, and, as an explanation, it appears to be little in harmony with the directness and simplicity of the passage.

iv. It has been explained as the "plural of the fulness of attributes and powers." It is pointed out that not only is the word for God

(*Elohim*) plural in form, but also the words for "Lord" (*Adon*) and "Master" (*Ba'al*) are often used in the plural of a single person. "It might well be that, on a solemn occasion like this, when God is represented as about to create a being in His own image, and to impart to him a share in that fulness of sovereign prerogatives possessed by Himself, He should adopt this unusual and significant mode of expression" (Driver, *in loc.*). It may, however, be questioned whether the passage in Gen. xi. 7 satisfies the exacting requirements of this finely described test. Again, while "the plural of plenitude" in a substantive or adjective is unquestioned, it may be doubted, whether we should be right to explain the 1st pers. plur. of a verb on the ground that the speaker is one to whom the plural of the fulness of power can justly be attributed.

v. It has been explained as the plural of Deliberation. It has been truly remarked that there is more solemnity and dignity in the words, "Let us make man in our own image," than would have been conveyed in the words, "Let me (or, I will) make man in my own image." The entire simplicity of this explanation tends to recommend it.

vi. It was the old Jewish explanation that God is here addressing the inhabitants of heaven. In the thought of the devout Israelite, God was One, but not isolated. He was surrounded by the heavenly host (1 Kings xxii. 19); attended by the Seraphim (Is. vi. 1—6); holding His court with "the sons of God" (Job i. 6, ii. 1). We are told in a poetical account of the Creation, that when the foundations of the earth were laid, "all the sons of God shouted for joy," Job xxxviii. 7 (cf. Ps. xxix. 1, lxxxix. 7, ciii. 19—22). It is claimed that, at the climax of the work of Creation, when man is about to be formed, the Almighty admits into the confidence of his Divine Purpose the angelic beings whose nature, in part, man will be privileged to share (Ps. viii. 4, 5, cf. Heb. ii. 7). At the risk of appearing fanciful, we may remind the reader that the birth of the Second Adam was announced by "the angel," and "there was with the angel a multitude of the heavenly host praising God" (Luke ii. 13).

It has been objected against this view (1) that the Priestly Narrator nowhere mentions angels, and (2) that the explanation tends to detract from the dignity of man's creation. But (1) angels are not here mentioned; and if the plur. indicates their presence in attendance upon the Almighty, the picture which it suggests is in harmony with the religious thought of the Israelites; and (2) the work of creating man is neither delegated to, nor shared with, others. God "created man in his own image" (*v.* 27); but, before creating him, He had associated with Himself all those who, through participation in image and likeness with Himself, would henceforth be allied to man.

The two last explanations appear to be the most probable.

man] Heb. *âdâm*. This, the first mention of "man" in Holy Scripture, is spoken by God. It denotes "mankind" generally. Note the plural "they" in the next sentence. On "Adam" as a personal name, see note on ii. 7.

in our image, after our likeness] LXX reads "and after our likeness."

P likeness: and let them have dominion over the fish of the sea, and over the fowl of the air, and over the cattle, and over all the earth, and over every creeping thing that 27 creepeth upon the earth. And God created man in his own image, in the image of God created he him; male and 28 female created he them. And God blessed them: and God

Some distinction must clearly be drawn between "image" (Heb. *ṣelem*; LXX εἰκών; Lat. *imago*) and "likeness" (Heb. *d'mûth*; LXX ὁμοίωσις; Lat. *similitudo*). The former is more permanent, the latter more fleeting. But the distinction cannot be pressed. In v. 1 we read "in the likeness (*d'mûth*) of God made he him," and v. 3, "And he (Adam) begat a son in his own likeness, after his own image." The most we can say is that "image" suggests reproduction in form and substance, physical or spiritual: and "likeness" gives the idea of resemblance and outward similarity. The words contain a truth which was wont to be exaggerated by Jewish and Patristic commentators. Man's *nature* is made "in the image of God"; he possesses divine qualities indestructible and inalienable, which no animal possessed. He is made "after the likeness of God"; his *character* is potentially divine. He is capable of approaching, or receding from, the "likeness" of God. The resemblance can never be perfect: but it can increase, and it can diminish.

The view that there is any reference to the conception of an outward resemblance, in shape or form, to the Hebrew idea of the Personal Deity is wholly improbable, and is contrary to the spirit and teaching of the religion of Israel.

and let them have dominion, &c.] As this dominion is promised to man in virtue of his creation in God's image, this sentence will helpfully shew that man's superiority arises, not from physical strength, but through the equipment of his higher nature.

and over all the earth] It seems strange that mention of "the earth" should be interposed between two of the four classes of animals, "the cattle" and "every creeping thing," over which man should rule. There can hardly be any doubt that the text, which is that also of the LXX and the Latin, has suffered from an early omission. We should read, with the Syriac Peshitto, "over all the beasts of the earth." The addition of the words "beasts of," in the sense of "the wild beasts of," will complete the classification of living creatures, as (1) fish, (2) birds, (3) domestic animals, (4) wild beasts, (5) creeping things. This enumeration reproduces the animals previously mentioned (*vv*. 20—25).

27. The reiteration of the principal words in the clauses of this verse has something of the rhythm of poetry. Repetition and love of detail are characteristics of the Priestly Code. "Created," cf. *vv.* 1, 21 (see notes).

male and female] The distinction of the sexes, which is here given, has been omitted, probably for brevity's sake, in the mention of the animals.

When, in view of the discoveries of the science of Anthropology, the

GENESIS I. 28, 29

said unto them, Be fruitful, and multiply, and replenish   P
the earth, and subdue it; and have dominion over the fish
of the sea, and over the fowl of the air, and over every
living thing that [1]moveth upon the earth. And God said, 29
Behold, I have given you every herb yielding seed, which
is upon the face of all the earth, and every tree, in the
which is the fruit of a tree yielding seed; to you it shall

[1] Or, *creepeth*

question is asked whether there was one original pair of human beings, or whether each of the different races, Caucasian, Mongolian, Negro, Red Indian, Australian, &c., originated from one pair, or from groups of pairs, we must answer that such questions do not come within the horizon of thought in our passage. They are to be solved not by Revelation in Holy Scripture, but by the exercise of the gifts of patient enquiry, accurate observation, and sound reasoning. The Hebrew writer has in view a population drawn from a single stock. His account of the origin of Man, applicable to one race, is symbolical of all, if a plurality of origin is to be assumed.

28. THE BLESSING AND THE COMMAND.

28. *replenish*] The word is the same as that used in *v.* 22 of the fishes, "be fruitful, and multiply, and *fill* the waters."

and subdue it] A strong word, denoting subjugation to power. Man's authority over the creatures of the earth confers upon him responsibility for the exercise of his powers. Supremacy over the fishes, the birds, and the beasts, will require courage, forethought, skill, observation, and judgement. The blessing, therefore, of "fruitfulness" is incomplete, until reinforced by the commission so to exercise the faculties as to ensure intellectual growth. In this connexion, compare Ray Lankester ("Rede Lecture, 1905"), "What we call the will or volition of Man... has become a power in nature, an *imperium in imperio*, which has profoundly modified not only Man's own history, but that of the whole living world, and the face of the planet on which he lives."

29. PROVISION OF FOOD.

In this verse God gives food to mankind consisting of the seed-bearing herbs and the fruit of trees. By comparison with ix. 3, we see that the writer believed that, until after the Flood, mankind subsisted upon a purely vegetable diet. It may be asked how, if this were the case, man had the opportunity of exercising his dominion over fish, birds, and beasts: if he did not wish to eat them, neither would he wish to kill them. The truth seems to be that, according to the P version of Hebrew tradition, the first generations of mankind were intended to live, without bloodshed or violence, in an ideal condition, like that predicted by Isaiah (xi. 6—9),

P 30 be for meat: and to every beast of the earth, and to every fowl of the air, and to every thing that creepeth upon the earth, wherein there is [1]life, *I have given* every green herb
31 for meat: and it was so. And God saw every thing that he had made, and, behold, it was very good. And there was evening and there was morning, the sixth day.

[1] Heb. *a living soul.*

"they shall not hurt nor destroy in all my holy mountain." The prophet's words, "a little child shall lead them," imply a dominion over the animal world which does not rest upon force.

30. *to every beast of the earth*] God ordains that the wild beasts, the birds, and all living creatures, shall have the leaves for their food. The words, "every green herb," would be more literally "all the green, or verdure, of the herbs." A distinction is, therefore, drawn between the food ordained for mankind and the food ordained for the animals. Man is to have the herb bearing seed and the fruit of the trees (*v.* 29): the animals are to feed on the grass and the leaves.

for meat] This expression, here and in the previous verse, is liable to be misunderstood by English readers. The Hebrew means "for food." The word "meat" is an old English term for "food." Cf. St Luke xxiv. 41 A.V. "He said unto them, Have ye here any meat?" R.V. "Have ye here anything to eat?"

It may be asked whether we are to understand that, according to Gen. i., the nature of animals was different at the first from what it became afterwards, and that they did not prey upon one another. The reply is that this was evidently the belief of the Israelite, as represented in this chapter. Like other features of the picture, it is childlike and idealized. Palaeontology has demonstrated, that, from the earliest geological period at which animal life can be shewn to have existed, the animals preyed upon one another. From the earliest days of animal life nature has been "red in tooth and claw."

31. *and, behold, it was very good*] The work of the six days' Creation having been completed, God, as it were, contemplates the universe both in its details and in its entirety. That which He saw to be "good," on each separate day, was but a fragment; that which He sees to be "very good," on the sixth day, is the vast ordered whole, in which the separate parts are combined. The Divine approval of the material universe constitutes one of the most instructive traits of the Hebrew cosmogony. According to it, matter is not something hostile to God, independent of Him, or inherently evil, but made by Him, ordered by Him, good in itself, and good in its relation to the purpose and plan of the Creator. The adjective "good" should not therefore be limited in meaning to the sense of "suitable," or "fitting." There is nothing "evil" in the Divinely-created universe: it is "very good" (LXX καλὰ λίαν: Lat. *valde bona*).

SPECIAL NOTE A, ON I. 26.

Professor Davidson, On the plural form of the word Elohim.

"The plural form of the word *Elohim* might be supposed to have some bearing on the question of unity. And, indeed, by many it has been supposed to bear testimony to the plurality of gods originally worshipped among the Semitic peoples; and by others, who seem to consider the name Elohim part of God's revelation of Himself, to the plurality of persons in the Godhead. The real force of the plural termination...is not easy, indeed, to discover. But a few facts may lead us near it. In Ethiopic the name of God is *Amlāk*, a plural form also of a root allied to *melek*—a *king*. All Shemitic languages use the plural as a means of heightening the idea of the singular; the precise kind of heightening has to be inferred from the word. Thus *water*—מַיִם—is plural, from the fluidity and multiplicity of its parts; the *heavens*—שָׁמַיִם—from their extension. Of a different kind is the plural of *adon—lord*, in Hebrew, which takes plural suffixes except in the first person singular. Of this kind, too, is the plural of *Baal*, even in the sense of *owner*, as when Isaiah uses the phrase אֲבֻם בְּעָלָיו (i. 3). Of the same kind, also, is the plural *teraphim, penates*, consisting of a single *image*. And of this kind probably is the plural *Elohim*—a plural not numerical, but simply enhancive of the idea of *might*. Thus among the Israelites the *might* who was God was not an ordinary might, but one peculiar, lofty, unique. Though the word be plural, in the earliest written Hebrew its predicate is almost universally singular. Only when used of the gods of the nations is it construed with a plural verb; or, sometimes, when the reference is to the general idea of the Godhead. This use with a singular predicate or epithet seems to show that the plural form is not a reminiscence of a former Polytheism. The plural expressed a *plenitude of might*. And as there seems no trace of a Polytheism in the name, neither can it with any probability be supposed to express a plurality of persons in the Godhead. For it cannot be shown that the word is itself part of God's revelation; it is a word of natural growth adopted into revelation, like other words of the Hebrew language. And the usage in the words *baal, adon, rab*, and such like, similar to it in meaning, leads us to suppose that the plural is not numerical, as if *mights*, but merely intensifying the idea of might. Nor can it be shown to be probable that the doctrine of a plurality of persons should have been taught early in the history of revelation. What the proneness of mankind to idolatry rendered imperative above all and first of all, was strenuous teaching of the Divine Unity." Davidson's *Theology of the O.T.* pp. 99, 100 (T. and T. Clark).

P **2** And the heaven and the earth were finished, and all the
2 host of them. And on the seventh day God finished his

SPECIAL NOTE B.

Note on the Jewish Interpretation of i. 26.

(a) Targum of Pseudo-Jonathan, "And the Lord said to the angels who ministered before Him, who had been created in the second day of the creation of the world, Let us make man in Our image, in Our likeness."

(b) *Pesikta* 34ᵃ (ed. Buber), "God took counsel with the ministering angels, and said unto them, Let us make, &c."

(c) Philo (i. 556, ed. Mangey), "The Father of the Universe discourses to His own Hosts" (ταῖς ἑαυτοῦ δυνάμεσιν).

(d) Rashi, Commentary.

Humilitatem Sancti illius Benedicti hinc discimus, quoniam homo ad similitudinem angelorum creatus fuit et illi erga eum invidia incitati fuerunt, idcirco Deus cum illis consultavit....Etiamsi angeli non opem tulerint ei Deo in illius creatione...non omittit tamen Scriptura, quominus doceat morem hominum modumque humilitatis, ut nimirum is, qui major est, consultet et facultatem impetret a minore, quod si scripsisset Moses faciam hominem, non docuisset nos, quod Deus locutus sit cum domo judicii sui; sed cum seipso; responsionem vero Epicuraeis opponendam scripsit Moses in latere ejus, "et creavit," inquiens, hominem; non vero scripsit: "et creaverunt."

Ed. Breithaupt, i. pp. 15, 17.

CH. II. 1—4ᵃ. THE SEVENTH DAY: (a) THE CESSATION FROM WORK; (b) THE HALLOWING OF THE DAY.

1. *were finished*] In these verses the repetition of the words "finish," "work," "seventh day," "made," is probably intended to heighten the solemnity connected with the seventh day; see also note on i. 27, and Introduction, on the characteristics of P.

and all the host of them] The word "host" is noteworthy. The Hebrew is *ṣâbâ*, "army," the plural of which is the word "Sabaoth" (= *ṣ'bâôth* = "hosts") familiar to us in the Te Deum. Here, as applied to the countless forces of the universe, its use is metaphorical. In the ancient world a great army represented the ideal of an organized multitude: and the designation of "host" (*ṣâbâ*) is often given in the O.T. to the heavenly bodies (e.g. 2 Kings xvii. 16). The LXX ὁ κόσμος αὐτῶν, = "their order, beauty, or array," is reproduced in the Lat. *ornatus eorum* = "their splendour," missing the significance of the original. Upon this error of the Vulgate St Thomas Aquinas based his division of the works of Creation into "*opera distinctionis*" and "*opera ornatus.*"

2. *on the seventh day*] Some misunderstanding arose in very early times in consequence of these words. Jealous for the sanctity of the

work which he had made; and he rested on the seventh P
day from all his work which he had made. And God 3
blessed the seventh day, and hallowed it: because that in

Sabbath, men said, "No, not on the seventh day, but on the sixth day, God finished the work of creation." So we find "on the sixth day" is the reading of the Samaritan, the LXX, and the Syriac Peshitto. The mistake was not unnatural: it was not perceived that the conclusion of work was identical with the cessation from work. God wrought no work on the seventh day; therefore, it is said, He brought His work to an end on the seventh day. The reading, "on the sixth day," may be dismissed as an erroneous correction made in the interests of keeping the Sabbath. All reference to the sixth day was concluded in ch. i. 31.

his work] LXX τὰ ἔργα αὐτοῦ, "his works." The same Hebrew word as in the Fourth Commandment, Ex. xx. 9, "all thy work"; it denotes not so much the "result" of labour, as its "process," or "occupation." Driver renders by "business."

rested] LXX κατέπαυσε = "ceased," Lat. *requierit*. Heb. *shâbath* has strictly the sense of "ceasing," or "desisting." It is this thought rather than that of "resting" after labour, which is here prominent. Elsewhere, the idea that God rested on the seventh day, is more directly expressed, e.g. Ex. xxxi. 17, "And on the seventh day he (the LORD) rested (*shâbath*, 'desisted'), and was refreshed." The idea of "cessation" from the employment of the six days suggested the conception of "rest," which is mentioned, both in Ex. xx. 11 and xxxi. 17, as the sanction for the observance of the Sabbath. Rest in the best sense is not idleness, but alteration in the direction of activity.

3. *And God blessed the seventh day*] It was the belief of the devout Israelite that in some mysterious way God at the beginning conferred His special favour upon the seventh day. The writer does not in this passage mention the name "Sabbath," but the reference to the Israelite Sabbath is indisputable. A play on the word "Sabbath" is evidently intended by the use of the word *shâbath*. The Hebrew cosmogony traced back the observance of the Sabbath to the Divine example on the seventh day of the creative week. Whether its observance was followed by the Israelites before the time of Moses, has been much disputed. No reference to it occurs in the Patriarchal narratives: but the intervals of seven days occurring in the story of the Flood (vii. 10, viii. 10, 12 J) may indicate the belief in the primitive recognition of the "week" as a sacred division of time. The reference to the Sabbath in Ex. xvi. 23 ff. has led many commentators to suppose that the opening word ("Remember") of the Fourth Commandment assumes the primitive recognition of the institution. See Special Note.

hallowed] viz. separated from common and profane usage. LXX ἡγίασεν: Lat. *sanctificavit*. This is the first mention of the idea of

P   it he rested from all his work which God had created and
made.

4   These are the generations of the heaven and of the earth

holiness, which in Holy Scripture occupies such an important place in the description of religious worship and godly life.

We may be unable fully to discern what was intended by the writer, when he spoke of God "hallowing" or "making separate" the seventh day. But it conveys to us the thought that God from the first, set His seal upon "time" as well as His blessing upon matter; and this consecration of the seventh day should serve as the continual reminder that as "the earth is the Lord's and the fulness thereof," so time is of the LORD and the opportunities thereof. The Sabbath is the sacrament of time: its rest is the symbol of the consecration of work. The worship of the Creator made a demand for the consecration of time as well as of place. Notice the absence of the formula, "There was evening and there was morning, the seventh day." This omission led some to suppose that the seventh, or rest, day of God is not yet ended; and that, when the work of Creation was finished, there began on the seventh day the different task of the maintenance of the universe. But it seems more probable that by the reference to the seventh day in *v.* 2, and by the blessing of the seventh day in *v.* 3, the writer intended that the seven days should be regarded as completed, and as presenting the Divine type for every week of seven days. After the seventh day came another phase of Divine activity, the unceasing operation of Divine laws. The Immanence of Creative Love and Wisdom needs to be acknowledged no less than their Transcendence; cf., especially, John v. 17, "My Father worketh even until now, and I work." In that conception of Divine work, there is no room for the thought of cessation.

4ᵃ. *These are the generations...created*] These words, as they stand here, seem to form a summary of the *preceding* account of the Creation. Elsewhere, however, the phrase "These are the generations, &c." is the formula employed in P as a heading, title, or superscription, to introduce the passage that *follows*. Cf. v. 1, "The generations of Adam," vi. 9 (Noah), x. 1 (The Sons of Noah), xi. 10 (Shem), 27 (Terah), xxv. 12 (Ishmael). The conjecture has been made that the formula "These are the generations, &c." originally stood at the beginning of ch. i., and was transferred to its present place, either, in order that the book might begin with the word *b'rêshîth* (= "In the beginning"), or to obtain a sentence which would serve both as an epitome of the opening section and as a link with the one that follows.

generations] Heb. *tô-l'-dôth* = "successions by descent," usually meaning "the chronicles," or "genealogies," of persons and families, is here metaphorically applied to "the heaven and the earth" in the sense of the "history" of their origin and their offspring. LXX, therefore, gives an explanatory rendering, αὕτη ἡ βίβλος γενέσεως οὐρανοῦ καὶ γῆς.

It is quite a different word from that found, e.g. in xv. 16, "in the fourth *generation*" (Heb. *dôr*, LXX γενέα).

when they were created, | in the day that ¹the LORD God   PJ

¹ Heb. *Jehovah*, as in other places where LORD is put in capitals.

created] This word closes the first section of the book, and there should be a full stop after it. The next section, giving another narrative, that of the creation of man and of Paradise, opens with the words "In the day that."

The first section has been derived from the materials of the Priestly Code (P), the second is from the Prophetic Writing (J). The styles which characterize the two sources offer a marked contrast.

CH. II. 4ᵇ—III. 24 (J). THE STORY OF PARADISE: I. THE CREATION OF MAN (ii. 4ᵇ—25). II. THE FALL OF MAN (iii. 1—24).

I. The Creation of Man (ii. 4ᵇ—25).
    4ᵇ—7.   The Creation of Man.
    8—9.   The Garden in Eden.
    10—14.   Its geographical situation.
    15—17.   The Trees of Life and of the Knowledge of good and evil.
    18—20.   The Creation of the Animals.
    21—25.   The Creation of Woman.

In this passage the compiler has had before him another account of the Creation. The earliest part dealing with the formation of the earth, the heavens, and the seas, he has omitted. The account in the previous chapter was evidently deemed to be sufficient. The description, however, of the origin of man and woman and of the animals is quite different from that given in ch. i. The narrative goes into greater details; and events are described in a different order. It cannot escape the reader's notice that, whereas in ch. i. all the living creatures are created before man and woman, in ch. ii. man is first created (*vv.* 6, 7), the animals are created afterwards as companions to him (*vv.* 18—20), and that woman, last of all, is created out of his rib to be his wife (*vv.* 21—25). The picture, therefore, presented in this chapter comes from a different source from that in ch. i.; and the fact is shewn not only by the variety in the treatment of the subject matter, but also by the unmistakable variety in the style and vocabulary. Some of the more noteworthy instances will be commented upon.

4ᵇ—7. THE CREATION OF MAN.

4. *in the day that*] There is no allusion here to the Days of Creation. It is simply the vivid Hebrew idiom for "at the time when."

the LORD God] The Hebrew words "Jahveh Elohim" are used in this section for the Almighty. On the Sacred Names, see Introduction. The use of JHVH, the Name of the God of Israel (Ex. iii.) which the Jews in reverence forbore to pronounce, and which received, in the 16th century, the wholly erroneous pronunciation of "Jehovah," is one of the

GENESIS II. 4, 5

J 5 made earth and heaven. And no plant of the field was yet in the earth, and no herb of the field had yet sprung

characteristics of the writing of J. In the previous section, i. 1—ii. 4ᵃ, the Sacred Name is "Elohim"="God"; and the use of "Elohim" is prevalent in the P Narratives of Gen. In the present section, ii. 4ᵇ—iii. 25, the Sacred Name is a combination of *Jahveh* and *Elohim*, i.e. Jehovah (=LORD) and "God." In the next section, the story of Cain and Abel, Jehovah alone is used; throughout the rest of Genesis we find either Jehovah or Elohim alone. The combination of the two Sacred Names is elsewhere of exceedingly rare occurrence. How to account for it in the present passage, is a problem to which no certain answer can be given. The theory that "God" (Elohim) is used for the God of Nature, and LORD (Jehovah) for the God of Revelation, is unsupported by the facts: e.g. "God" (Elohim) is the name used of the Deity in ch. xvii. at the establishment of the covenant of circumcision: the LORD (Jahveh) is the name used at the destruction of the cities of the Plain (xix. 1—28, see note on xix. 29). There seems no reason to assign any doctrinal ground for the exceptional usage.

It should most probably be attributed to the handiwork of the compiler. On the first occasion in which the sacred title of the God of Israel was used, he wished to emphasize the fact that Jehovah and the Elohim of Creation were one and the same.

Another suggestion has been made, that the Paradise Narrative was current in two versions, in one of which the Sacred Name was *Jahveh*, in the other *Elohim*, and that the compiler who was acquainted with both versions left a trace of the fact in the combined names. But the compiler has not resorted to any such expedient elsewhere.

earth and heaven] An unusual order of words, found only in Ps. cxlviii. 13.

5. *And no plant, &c.*] If, as is possible, *vv.* 5 and 6 are a parenthesis, then *v.* 7 carries on the sentence of *v.* 4ᵇ. The whole sentence would then run, "At the time when Jehovah Elohim made earth and heaven (there was as yet no plant of the field...face of the ground), Jehovah Elohim formed man." But this arrangement is too cumbrous to be probable. Moreover, the state of things described in *vv.* 5 and 6 is evidently one of considerable duration; it intervenes between the making of the earth and the heavens (*v.* 4ᵇ) and the formation of man (*v.* 7). It is better to regard *v.* 5 as the apodosis to *v.* 4ᵇ, "At the time when Jehovah Elohim made, &c., (5) there was as yet no plant, &c., (6) but a mist (or, flood) used to come up, &c."

plant of the field...herb of the field] The word "plant" is the same in the original as that rendered "shrub" in Gen. xxi. 15, the stunted growth of the desert under which Hagar cast her child, and "bushes" in Job xxx. 4, 7. The "herb" is the vegetation useful for food and requiring cultivation. There was no "plant" or "bush," because the LORD God had not yet caused it to rain: there was no "herb," because there was no man to prepare the ground. In the

up: for the LORD God had not caused it to rain upon the
earth, and there was not a man to till the ground; but 6
there went up a mist from the earth, and watered the whole
face of the ground. And the LORD God formed man of 7
the dust of the ground, and breathed into his nostrils the

absence of rain and of tillage there was no vegetation. The ground originally was desert, without tree, bush, or grass.

6. *there went up*] or "there used to go up," i.e. periodically. The frequentative idea of the verb is given in the LXX ἀνέβαινεν, Lat. *ascendebat*.

a mist] Heb. *'êd*, a word found elsewhere in the O.T. only in Job xxxvi. 27, where it is rendered "vapour." Here the meaning is not certain: the versions (LXX πηγή: Lat. *fons*: Targum "cloud") reflect the doubt. The English versions follow the Targum. Recently, Assyriologists have compared the Babylonian *êdû*, meaning a "flood" or "overflowing." It is possible that the rendering "spring" or "stream" may be more accurate than "mist"; that in Job xxxvi. 27 *'êd* may denote the "source" of the waters above the heavens; and that here it may refer to the hidden source of the rivers of the world. No account is given of the origin of rain.

watered] Literally, "gave to drink"; an expression better suited to a "stream" than to a "mist": cf. v. 10, where it is used of a river. "The ground," the face of which was watered by it, was "the cultivable soil" (*adâmah*).

7. *formed*] A different word from that used in i. 1 and 27, "created," or in i. 26, "made." The metaphor is that of the potter shaping and moulding the clay, LXX ἔπλασεν, Lat. *formavit*. As applied to the Creator, the metaphor is a favourite one; cf. Isai. xlv. 9, Jer. xviii. 1—5, Wisd. xv. 7, Rom. ix. 20—24.

See Browning's *Rabbi Ben Ezra*, "Aye, note that Potter's wheel, That metaphor, &c."

man] Heb. *âdâm*. Man was popularly thought to be so called because taken from the *adâmah*, "the cultivated ground," to which he is to return at death (iii. 19), and which he is to cultivate during life (iii. 23). It is impossible in English to give any equivalent to this play upon the names for "man" and "ground."

In this verse and elsewhere, where the Heb. *âdâm* (=man) occurs with the def. article (*hâ-âdâm*), there is no reference to the proper name "Adam." See note on *v.* 16.

of the dust of the ground] These words describe the Hebrew belief concerning the physical structure of man. It was seen that after death the bodily frame was reduced, by dissolution, into dust: it was, therefore, assumed that that frame had at the first been built up by God out of dust. For other passages illustrating this belief, cf. Gen. iii. 19, xviii. 27, Ps. xc. 3, civ. 29, 1 Cor. xv. 47. We find the same idea in the Babylonian myth, where man is made out of earth mingled with the

J 8 breath of life; and man became a living soul. And the
Lord God planted a garden eastward, in Eden; and there

blood of the God Marduk[1], and in the Greek myth of Prometheus and Pandora.

breathed...life] The preceding clause having explained man's bodily structure, the present one explains the origin of his life. His life is not the product of his body, but the gift of God's breath or spirit.

At death the breath (*ruah*) left man's body; hence it was assumed, that, at the first, the mystery of life had been imparted to man by the breath (*ruah*) of God Himself. Through life, man became "a living soul," (*nephesh*), and, as "a living soul," shared his life with the animals. But man alone received his life from "the breath of God." It is this breathing (*n'shâmâh*) of life (LXX πνοὴ ζωῆς: Lat. *spiraculum vitae*) which imparts to man that which is distinctive of his higher principle of being, as compared with the existence of the animals, cf. *v.* 19. It would seem from Job xxxiv. 14, 15 that one phase of Hebrew belief was (1) that at death the flesh of man turned again unto dust; (2) that God took back unto Himself His breath (*ruah*) which He had given; (3) that the *nephesh*, or soul, departed into the *Sheol*, the region of the dead.

For the picture here given of vitality imparted to man by the breath breathed by God into man's nostrils, cf. Job xxvii. 3, "The spirit (or breath) of God is in my nostrils."

We should compare the expression "breathed into" with the words in St John's Gospel xx. 22. There the symbolical act of our Lord derives significance from this verse. Christ who is "the New Man," Himself imparts the life-giving Spirit; "He breathed on them, and saith unto them, Receive ye the Holy Spirit."

8—9. The Garden in Eden.

8. *a garden*] More strictly "an enclosure." LXX παράδεισον, Lat. *paradisum*, a word borrowed from the Persian, and meaning "a park-like enclosure." Its use here has given rise to the Christian metaphorical use of the word "Paradise." "The word is of Iranian origin. In Avesta it is *pairi-daêza* 'encircling wall' (*Vend.* iii. 18). It passed into Neo-Babylonian, Aramaic, post-Exilic Hebrew, Neo-Hebrew, Armenian, Persian, Kurdish, Greek, and Arabic as a word for a park or splendid garden. In the O.T. it is found in Neh. ii. 8, Cant. iv. 13, Eccles. ii. 5" (*Encycl. Rel. and Eth.* vol. II. p. 705).

eastward] The point of view is not that of the Babylonian, but of the Israelite, who regarded the East, and, in particular, Babylonia, as the cradle of man's earliest civilization. Notice here the quite general description of the site of the "garden." For its more minute definition, see *vv.* 10—15. LXX κατὰ ἀνατολάς: Vulg. *a principio*. The Hebrew, when speaking or writing, is mentally facing East. "Eastward" is the same as "on the side fronting you."

in Eden] Eden is not the name of the "garden," but of the country

---
[1] See Appendix A.

GENESIS II. 8, 9

he put the man whom he had formed. And out of the 9
ground made the LORD God to grow every tree that is
pleasant to the sight, and good for food; the tree of life

or district in which Jehovah planted his "garden." *Eden* in Hebrew means "delight," or "happiness"; and the Israelite naturally associated this meaning of the word "Eden" with the dwelling place of the first man and woman, because this auspicious name seemed appropriate to the Garden of Jehovah. Hence we find the Garden of God spoken of as the place of fertility, beauty, and delight, Isa. li. 3, Ezek. xxviii. 13, xxxi. 8, 9, xxxvi. 35, Joel ii. 3.

"In Eden"; so, rightly, LXX ἐν Ἐδέμ. The Lat. "voluptatis," = "of pleasure," represents a popular misapprehension, not recognizing it as a proper name.

Assyriologists point out that the Assyrian word *edinnu*, meaning "a plain" or "steppe," was applied to the Euphrates Valley. They suggest that the "garden" lay in this region. The Hebrew narrative, however, evidently contemplates a fruitful enclosure, not a plain: the name "Eden" is chosen because of its auspicious meaning in Hebrew, while the fact that in sound it reproduced the Babylonian designation of a remote Eastern, or Mesopotamian, region, made it appear all the more appropriate.

9. *And out of the ground,* &c.] The characteristic feature of the "garden," or "enclosure," is not its flowers, but its trees. This is evident, also, from the traditional belief as to the Garden, which is reproduced in Ezek. xxxi. 8, 9. To the Oriental, the large well-grown tree was an especial object of reverence ("pleasant to the sight"): and man was to live on the fruit of the trees ("good for food"). It is implied that the trees of the "garden," like the man who is put into it, were from the first fully grown.

the tree of life] There are two wonder-working trees in the "garden." One is called "the tree of life," whose fruit imparts immortality to those who eat it (cf. iii. 22—24): the other is called the "tree of the knowledge of good and evil," whose fruit conveys moral discernment. These gifts of knowledge and of immortality are the special prerogatives of Jehovah (iii. 5, 22).

The mention of the two trees in this verse comes in a little abruptly. "The tree of life" is spoken of as "in the midst of the garden"; "the tree of knowledge" is then mentioned, but without any description of its position. In *v.* 17 the LORD God forbids the man to eat of "the tree of knowledge"; but does not mention "the tree of life." In iii. 3 the woman refers to "the tree which is in the midst of the garden," as if there was only one tree that had been forbidden to them, and *v.* 5 shews it is "the tree of knowledge." It is probable that we have here the trace of some little confusion between two Hebrew traditions about the sacred trees. The mention of "the tree of life" has here, and in iii. 22, 24, been added to that of "the tree of knowledge." At any

J also in the midst of the garden, and the tree of the know-
10 ledge of good and evil. And a river went out of Eden to
water the garden; and from thence it was parted, and

rate, in this verse, "the tree of life" is given the place belonging to
"the tree of knowledge" which is "in the midst of the garden." The
story of the Temptation and the Fall turns on the tradition, according
to which there was one tree, that "of the knowledge of good and evil,"
"in the midst of the garden." The expression "tree of life" was
used as a common metaphor of health and fruitfulness in Hebrew
language, cf. Prov. iii. 18, "She (Wisdom) is a tree of life"; xi. 30,
"the fruit of the righteous is a tree of life."

the tree of the knowledge of good and evil] What is signified by this
is doubtful. Some say it is the knowledge which infancy lacks and
experience acquires, cf. Deut. i. 39, "Your children which this day
have no knowledge of good or of evil." Judging by the context we
should rather identify it with moral judgement: the fruit produces the
exercise of conscience, which is accompanied by the realization of evil,
though not necessarily by the forfeiture of innocence. See Special Note
on Chap. iii.

Palms as sacred trees are frequent objects of representation in Assyrian
and Babylonian art.

On the possible connexion of "the tree of the knowledge of good and
evil" with the date palm, see Barton's *Semitic Origins*, pp. 93—95.

10—14. A Geographical Description of the Garden.

This is very probably a later insertion. It interrupts the sequence of
thought.

10. *And a river went out*] The description of the river in this verse
is as follows: (1) it took its rise in the land of Eden; (2) it flowed
through the garden, and irrigated it; (3) after passing through the
garden, it separated into four branches, or, as they are here called,
"heads."

to water] The same word as in v. 6, "a mist...*watered* the whole
face of the ground."

The account which follows (11—14) is irreconcilable with scientific
geography. But the locality of a garden planted by the Lord God,
containing two wonder-working trees, is evidently not to be looked for
on maps. In the description of the four rivers, we must remember that
the Israelites possessed only a very vague knowledge of distant lands.
They depended upon the reports of travellers who possessed no means
of accurate survey. Mediaeval maps often present the most fantastic
and arbitrary arrangement of rivers and seas to meet the conjectures of
the cartographist. We need not be surprised, if the early traditions of
the Hebrews claimed that the four greatest known rivers of the world
had branched off from the parent stream, which, rising in Eden, had
passed through the garden of the Lord God. The four rivers here

GENESIS II. 10—13

became four heads. The name of the first is Pishon: that 11 J
is it which compasseth the whole land of Havilah, where
there is gold; and the gold of that land is good: there is 12
bdellium and the ¹onyx stone. And the name of the 13
second river is Gihon: the same is it that compasseth the

¹ Or, *beryl*

mentioned are referred to in the order of Pishon, Tigris, Euphrates, and Gihon in Ecclus. xxiv. 25—27.

"Alexander the Great believed he had found the sources of the Nile in the Indus, because of the crocodiles and beans he saw there (Arrian, vi. i. 2 ff.; Str. xv. i. 25)...Pausanias records the tradition that 'the same Nile is the river Euphrates, which was lost in a lake, and re-emerged as the Nile in the remote part of Ethiopia'" (Gordon, p. 278). When such views of geography were held by the most enlightened Greeks, we need wonder at nothing in the primitive traditions of Palestine.

11. *Pishon*] The name of this river does not occur elsewhere in the Bible except in Ecclus. xxiv. 25. What river was intended, we can only conjecture, (*a*) from the description of its course, and (*b*) from the names of the rivers with which it is classed, two being the Tigris and the Euphrates. It is described as "compassing," that is, encircling, "the whole land of Havilah." The identification of Havilah is much controverted. In the present day scholars are of opinion that the name probably denotes a region either in N.E., or in S., Arabia. It is mentioned again in Gen. x. 7, 29, xxv. 18, passages in which Arabia seems to be indicated. Havilah is further called a land "where there is gold." Arabia, in ancient times, was famous for its gold.

The river which would encircle Havilah is, therefore, quite probably rightly identified by P. Haupt, the Assyriologist, with the Persian Gulf and the sea that surrounded Arabia, on the east.

Josephus identifies it with the "Indus."

12. *bdellium*] LXX ἄνθραξ: Lat. *bdellium*. In Numb. xi. 7, "manna" is compared with "bdellium"; where the LXX gives κρύσταλλος. Possibly it may be identified with an aromatic transparent resin, obtained from balsam (*balsamodendron mukul*), and found in Arabia as well as in India, Bactria and Africa. The Hebrew name *b'dôlah* is probably a foreign word. Another rendering, "pearls" (which are abundantly found in the Persian Gulf), would be more poetical, and possibly more appropriate for comparison with "manna": but we can only conjecture.

the onyx stone] or *beryl*. Hebrew *Shoham* mentioned elsewhere, Ex. xxv. 7, Job xxviii. 16. A precious stone is clearly intended; possibly = "carbuncle." Assyriologists have identified it with an Assyrian word *Samdu*; but what *Samdu* was, is not known. Sayce conjectures "turquoise"; Haupt "pearl."

13. *Gihon*] This river is not mentioned again by the same name in

GENESIS II. 13, 14

J 14 whole land of Cush. And the name of the third river is
¹Hiddekel: that is it which goeth ²in front of Assyria. And

¹ That is, *Tigris*.   ² Or, *toward the east of*

the Bible, except in Ecclus. xxiv. 27. The student will be careful not to confound it with the Gihon of 1 Kings i. 33, a spring in the neighbourhood of Jerusalem. It is here described as encircling "the whole land of Cush." "Cush" in the Bible generally denotes Ethiopia (but cf. Gen. x. 8 note); and by Ethiopia would be signified Nubia, the Soudan, and Upper Egypt, a great tract of country watered by the Nile, cf. Isa. xviii. 1. Hence, though the description "that compasseth the whole land of Cush" is fanciful, it seems very probable that the Gihon here means the Nile. The Nile is generally called in the Bible $y^{e}or$ (cf. Gen. xli. 1), and sometimes *Shihor* (cf. Isa. xxiii. 3, Jer. ii. 18). See note xli. 1. For Cushites in David's time, cf. 2 Sam. xviii. 21.

14. *Hiddekel*] Tigris. The Assyrian name is "Idiklat," or "Diklat," the old Persian "Tigra," whence the Greek "Tigris" (modern *Digle*). It is mentioned in the Bible elsewhere only in Dan. x. 4 and Ecclus. xxiv. 25. This famous river rises not far from the source of the Euphrates, and flows at first east from Diarbekr and unites with the Bohtan Tsckai, after which it flows south-east. It approaches the Euphrates at Bagdad, but continues a separate course until it unites at Korna with that river, and enters the Persian Gulf as the *Schatt-el-Arab*. In earlier times the two rivers entered the sea at different points. The Tigris was so called from an old Persian word meaning "arrow," and probably because of its swiftness.

in front of Assyria] The Hebrew expression rendered "in front of" generally denotes "to the east of," cf. *v.* 8, iv. 16, xii. 8 notes. The Hebrew standpoint is always that of a person facing east. That which is in front is east: towards his right hand is the south, towards his left the north, at his back the west. It is objected that Assyria was a country, through which the Tigris flowed, and that, as Assyrian territory lay on the east as well as the west bank of the Tigris, it would not be correct to describe the Tigris as "that which goeth towards the east of Assyria." Hence Sayce conjectures that we should here understand, not the country "Assyria," but the country's old capital "Asshur" which gave its name to the country, and which lay on the west bank of the Tigris. But Asshur, the city, is not mentioned elsewhere in the Bible; presumably, therefore, it was little known to the Hebrews, and was not likely to be mentioned in a geographical description. On the other hand, "Asshur" is the regular Hebrew designation of the country "Assyria"[1]; the mention here of "Assyria" is parallel to that of "Cush" in the preceding verse. There seems no sufficient reason for doubting that the name "Asshur" is here used, in its usual Biblical application, for the land of Assyria. If so, the geographical description of the Tigris may not be strictly accurate.

[1] See x. 22. The "Asshur" of Ezek. xxvii. 23 is mentioned with "Sheba...and Chilmad."

the fourth river is Euphrates. And the LORD God took 15 J
the man, and put him into the garden of Eden to dress it
and to keep it. And the LORD God commanded the man, 16
saying, Of every tree of the garden thou mayest freely eat:
but of the tree of the knowledge of good and evil, thou 17
shalt not eat of it: for in the day that thou eatest thereof
thou shalt surely die.

Considering its remoteness from Palestine, this need not surprise us, especially in a writing dating from a period previous to the active Assyrian interference in the course of Israelite affairs.

Euphrates] Heb. *Prath*. Assyrian "Puratu," old Persian *Ufrâtū*, whence the Greek and Latin "Euphrates." The Euphrates rises in the mountains near Erzerum, and, after following a tortuous course through the Taurus Mts., flows first in a southerly, and then, from Balis, in a S.E. direction, uniting with the Tigris before entering the Persian Gulf.

The Israelites seem to have regarded the Euphrates as "*the* river par excellence." Hence "the River," as a proper name, in Ex. xxiii. 31, 1 Kings iv. 21, 24, Ps. lxxii. 8, lxxx. 11, Isai. viii. 7, Zech. ix. 10.

15. This verse resumes the subject matter of *v.* 9, which has been interrupted by the description of the rivers.

to dress it and to keep it] The LORD God puts man into the garden for a life, not of indolence, but of labour. "To dress it," that is to cultivate the soil, tend and prune the trees: "to keep it," that is to defend it from depredation by animals, or from the evils arising from unchecked luxuriance. In other words, he is given, from the first, his work to do, by which he is (1) to improve his surroundings, (2) to provide for the necessities of life, (3) to protect from waste or loss that which is committed to his care. This work will exact abundant physical effort; it will exercise his powers of observation and judgement; it will furnish him with food for his body, and with thought for his mind.

Notice, that the garden requires to be dressed and kept; it is not a place of spontaneous perfection. Man in the garden is to work, to take trouble, to practise forethought, to exercise solicitude and sympathy for the objects of his toil. "Paradise" is not a place for indolence and self-indulgence.

16. Here, as in i. 29, man receives a command to eat the fruit of the trees: but this command is to receive one special limitation.

"man," LXX Ἀδάμ = "Adam," as a proper name, wrongly: see on *v.* 7.

17. *of the tree of the knowledge of good and evil*] See above, on *v.* 9. Here only one tree is mentioned, as in iii. 3; and it seems not unlikely that the mention of "the tree of life" did not belong to the main original version of the story, but was derived from a separate source.

thou shalt not eat of it] In this prohibition man is apprised of another element in the discipline to which he is subjected in the garden

J 18 And the Lord God said, It is not good that the man should be alone; I will make him an help ¹meet for him.

¹ Or, *answering to*

of the Lord God. In *v.* 15 it is his physical and intellectual powers which are to be exercised : in this verse he receives warning of a moral discipline. His moral being is to be tested by a simple injunction for which no reason is assigned. No hardship is imposed: but a limitation to self-gratification is required. He who makes the requisition has given freely the enjoyment of everything beside. Man's character is to be tested in the simplest manner. Will he shew obedience to the Divine will and trust in the Divine goodness?

in the day that...die] Literally, in the day that Adam ate of the fruit, he did not die. This is one of the minor inconsistencies in the story which are not explained for us. Either we are to assume that, in some fuller version of it, the Lord God was described as "repenting" of the sentence of immediate death, as changing His mind and sparing man in His mercy : or the words "in the day, &c." are to be regarded as metaphorical, and the doom, "thou shalt surely die," merely means "thou shalt become mortal."

We must not infer from this verse that the Lord God was considered to have made man other than mortal. It is clear from iii. 22, that man was created a mortal being. Perhaps, in one version of the story, he was intended to eat of the tree of life "and live for ever."

18—25. The Creation of Animals and of Woman.

18. *It is not good*, &c.] Man is created a social animal. His full powers cannot be developed by physical and mental work alone; nor his moral being by self-discipline in solitude. His faculties and his character require to be expanded and beautified by the duties of domestic and social life, as a member of a family, as a friend, as a fellow-worker, as a citizen. To be alone is not "good"; it does not promote his fullest life, or his best service.

an help meet for him] "meet": or *answering to*. The word "meet" means "suitable," or "adapted to." The Lord God will make for man a "help" corresponding to his moral and intellectual nature, supplying what he needs, the counterpart of his being.

"Help meet," which has become a recognized English word, fails to give the full sense of this passage from which it is derived. Man will find help from that which is in harmony with his own nature, and, therefore, able adequately to sympathise with him in thought and interests. It is not identity, but harmony, of character which is suggested. The word "help" in the Hebrew is '*ézer*, the same as is found in Ebenezer (1 Sam. vii. 12): LXX βοηθόν: Lat. *adjutorium*.

"Meet for him" is lit. "as over against him." LXX κατ' αὐτόν, Vulg. *simile sibi*.

Observe that the versions have "let *us* make," LXX ποιήσωμεν, Lat. *faciamus*, in imitation of i. 26, but inaccurately.

And out of the ground the LORD God formed every beast 19 J
of the field, and every fowl of the air; and brought them
unto the man to see what he would call them: and whatsoever the man called every living creature, that was the
name thereof. And the man gave names to all cattle, and 20
to the fowl of the air, and to every beast of the field; but
for ¹man there was not found an help meet for him. And 21

¹ Or, *Adam*

19. *And out of the ground*] The animals *also* (LXX adds ἔτι; so also Sam.) are "formed," or "moulded," out of the ground, like man: see *v.* 7. They are brought into man's presence to see whether they could be the needed help to him. Only the beasts of the field and the birds are mentioned in this account.

to see what he would call them] The names which man will give them will determine their use and position in reference to man's own nature. Their names would reflect the impression produced on the man's mind. A "name," in the estimation of the Hebrew, conveyed the idea of personality and character. It was more than a mere label. The animals, in this account, are created after man, and in definite relation to him; an entirely different representation from that in ch. i.

20. *the man gave names*] We have here the exercise of man's powers of discrimination and classification. This is the birth of science. Man's first use of speech is in the naming of animals. The names describe their character or appearance. From the instance given in *v.* 23 of a name thus applied, it is clear that primaeval man was supposed to speak in the Hebrew language.

but for man] From this clause it appears, as indeed is shewn by *vv.* 18, 19, that the animals on being formed were brought to the man, in order that, if it were possible, some amongst them might be the help that his nature needed. The passage implies that the nature of the animals had a kinship with that of man; but, while full of sympathy with the animal world, it implies that companionship, in the truest sense, was not to be found by man in creatures destitute of the higher prerogatives of human nature. "An help meet for man" must be on a level with him in feeling, in intellect, and reason.

for man] Not, as R.V. marg., *for Adam*. We should undoubtedly here read "for the man" (*lâ'âdâm*) in accordance with the general usage in this section. The LXX introduces the proper name at *v.* 16, Lat. Vulg. at *v.* 19: both ignore the definite article here and in *vv.* 21, 22, 23.

21—22. THE CREATION OF WOMAN.

The description in these verses is remarkable for its delicacy and beauty. Nothing could be more clear than that we are dealing with the poetry of symbolism, not with the record of literal fact.

J the LORD God caused a deep sleep to fall upon the man, and he slept; and he took one of his ribs, and closed up
22 the flesh instead thereof: and the rib, which the LORD God had taken from the man, ¹made he a woman, and brought
23 her unto the man. And the man said, This is now bone of my bones, and flesh of my flesh: she shall be called

¹ Heb. *builded he into*.

21. *deep sleep*] The word is used in Gen. xv. 12, 1 Sam. xxvi. 12, Isai. xxix. 10, indicating a mysterious heavy sleep sent by God. Heb. *tardēmah*, LXX ἔκστασις, Lat. *sopor*. The mystery of Divine working is thus hidden from man's perceptions.

one of his ribs] Symbolizing the closeness and intimacy of the relation between the sexes. Woman, formed from the side of man, is to be the "help meet for him." As his own flesh, he is to watch over and protect the woman. The story is a parable interpreting the instinct of love.

It is man's description, respecting the origin of woman, as of one made for man, after man, and subordinate to him. The "rib" is mentioned presumably, because "ribs" are comparatively numerous, and it was thought that one could be spared without structural loss.

22. *made he*] Heb. "builded He," so LXX ᾠκοδόμησεν, Lat. *aedificavit*: a different word from that in vv. 7—19.

23. *This is now*, &c.] The exclamation of joy and wonder is expressed in the rhythmical language of poetry. It is as if the man, after passing in review the animals, recognizes instantaneously in woman the fulfilment of his hope. "This is now" is equivalent to "here at last"; the German "Diese endlich."

bone of my bones] A strong metaphorical phrase to denote that the woman is different from all the animals, and is absolutely one with the man. For similar expressions used of near relationship, compare xxix. 14, xxxvii. 27; Jud. ix. 2; 2 Sam. v. 1, xix. 12, 13; 1 Chron. xi. 1. This proverbial expression may have furnished the symbolism of the story.

she shall be called, &c.] The marg. by pointing out that the Hebrew for "woman" is *Isshah*, and for "man" *Ish*, shews the resemblance in the sound of the two words. This is fairly reproduced in the English words "Woman" and "Man"; and in Luther's rendering "Männin" and "Mann." The LXX is unable to reproduce it. The Latin attempts it with questionable success, *haec vocabitur virago, quoniam de viro sumpta est*.

Instead of "from man," *mē-ish*, LXX and Targ. read "from her husband" = *mē-ishâh*, which adds to the resemblance in sound.

As a matter of philology the derivation is inaccurate. Probably *Isshah* is derived from a different root, *anash*. But nearly all these popular derivations of words prove to be inaccurate when judged by scientific etymology. They are based upon the assonance, or obvious resemblance

¹Woman, because she was taken out of ²Man. Therefore 24 J
shall a man leave his father and his mother, and shall cleave
unto his wife: and they shall be one flesh. And they were 25
both naked, the man and his wife, and were not ashamed.

¹ Heb. *Isshah*.   ² Heb. *Ish*.

in sound; and this, while it cannot fail to catch the ear and cling to the recollection of the people, is notoriously to be distrusted for supplying the real derivation.

24. *Therefore shall a man*, &c.] This verse contains the comment which the narrator makes upon the words of the man in *v.* 23. The word "therefore" introduces his inference. As in x. 9, xxvi. 33, xxxii. 32, a sentence beginning with "therefore" supplies the application, or relation, of the ancient narrative to later times. It is the man who is to leave "father and mother," not "the woman." Some compare the story in Judg. xv. 1, where the woman remains with her family or clan, and Samson comes to live with her. This feature has been thought to illustrate the primitive usage of "the matriarchate." But it is unlikely that the Hebrew narrative would contain a reference to such conditions.

Instead of "shall leave," the full force of the tense in the Hebrew would be given by "doth leave" and "cleaveth." The sanctity of marital relations is thus referred back to the very birthday of human society, being based on a principle laid down before the Fall.

The relation of the man to his wife is proclaimed to be closer than that to his father and mother. By the words, "shall cleave unto his wife...one flesh," is asserted the sanctity of marriage. Polygamy is not definitely excluded; but the principle of monogamy seems to be implied in the words "cleave" and "shall be one flesh": and this principle is upheld by the prophets as the ideal of marriage, in their representation of the relation of Jehovah and Israel under the metaphor of the married state.

This is the classical passage dealing with marriage to which our LORD appeals, Matt. xix. 4—6, Mark x. 6—8, in His argument against divorce.

St Paul quotes it in 1 Cor. vi. 16, in condemnation of unchastity, and in Eph. v. 31, when describing the ideal relationships of Christ and His Church.

and they shall be one flesh] Lit., as LXX καὶ ἔσονται οἱ δύο εἰς σάρκα μίαν, Lat. *erunt duo in carne una*, where the addition of "the two" is supported by the Syriac Peshitto, the Targum of Pseudo-Jonathan, and the quotations in the N.T., Matt. xix. 5; Mark x. 8; 1 Cor. vi. 16.

25. This verse by one simple illustration describes the condition of the man and the woman in the garden. It is not that of moral perfection, but that of the innocence and ignorance of childhood. The untried innocence of the child does not possess the sense of shame: the depravity of vice forfeits it. The sense of shame is the shadow which temptation to sin throws across the pathway of purity.

NOTE ON THE SABBATH

In connexion with the Institution of the Sabbath recorded in Gen. ii. 1—3 the following points deserve to be noticed.

1. The writer gives the reason for the sanctity among the Hebrews of the Seventh Day, or Sabbath. As, in chap. xvii., he supplies an answer to the question: What is the origin of the Hebrew sacred rite of circumcision? so, here, he gives an answer to the question: What is the origin of the observance of the Sabbath?

2. Whereas the Hebrew rite of circumcision is described as having its origin in the command of God delivered to Abraham, the Father of the Chosen People, the origin of the Sabbath is treated as more ancient and uniquely sacred. As an institution, it follows at once upon the work of Creation. Whatever its import, therefore, may be, it is regarded by the writer as universal in its application. The Divine rest from Creation, like the Divine work of Creation, was a pledge of Divine Love, not to the Jew only, but to the whole world.

3. From the first, God is said to have "blessed" and "sanctified" the seventh day. In other words, he invested the seventh day with the quality of highest value and advantage to those who observed it; stamped its observance with the seal of Divine approbation; and "set it apart," as distinct from the other six days, for sacred purposes.

4. The account of the origin of the Sabbath, given in this passage, is followed in the legislation, Ex. xxxi. 17 (P), and seems to have supplied the appendix to the primitive form of the Fourth Commandment as found in the Decalogue of Exodus (xx. 11).

In the Deuteronomic Decalogue (Dt. v. 12—15) the observance of the Sabbath is enjoined, without any reference to the days of Creation, but with an appendix explaining its humanitarian purpose. "And thou shalt remember that thou wast a bondman in the land of Egypt, and the LORD thy God brought thee out thence by a mighty hand and by a stretched out arm: therefore the LORD thy God commanded thee to keep the sabbath day."

A similar explanation for the observance of the Sabbath is found in the so-called Book of the Covenant (Ex. xx. 22—xxiii. 33 E), which contains the earliest collection of Hebrew laws: "Six days thou shalt do thy work, and on the seventh day thou shalt rest: that thine ox and thine ass may have rest, and the son of thy handmaid, and the stranger, may be refreshed" (Ex. xxiii. 12). In the old ritual laws of Ex. xxxiv. 10—28, the observance of the seventh day is commanded as a duty with which no pressure of field labour is to interfere: "Six days thou shalt work, but on the seventh day thou shalt rest; in plowing time and in harvest thou shalt rest" (*v.* 21).

What relation exists between the Hebrew institution of the Sabbath and Babylonian usage is a question which has been much discussed in recent years. It has sometimes been too hastily assumed that the Hebrew

GENESIS II.

ordinance has been directly imported from Babylonia. For a full discussion, see Driver (*D.B.* s.v. Sabbath); Gordon, *Early Traditions of Genesis*, pp. 216—223; the Commentaries by Driver and Skinner; Meinhold, *Sabbath u. Woche im A.T.* The following points may here be noticed:

(*a*) The Assyrian word *shabattu* appears in a cuneiform syllabary (II Rawlinson 32, 16 a, b) with the equivalent *ûm nûḥ libbi* (*ilâni*), i.e. "day of resting (satisfying or appeasing) the heart of the gods."

(*b*) In a tablet, discovered in 1904 by Pinches, the word *shapattu* appears to have been applied to the 15th day, or full-moon day, of the month (*P.S.B.A.* xxvi. 51 ff.).

(*c*) There is evidence which shews that the 7th, 14th, 21st and 28th days, and also the 19th (i.e. the 49th = 7 × 7th, from the commencement of the preceding month) were in certain, if not in all, of the Babylonian months, regarded as "unlucky" days. The following quotation is from a calendar of the intercalated month of Elul. "On the 7th day, supplication to Marduk and Sarpanitum, a favourable day (*sc.* may it be). An evil day. The shepherd of many nations is not to eat meat roasted by the fire, or any food prepared by the fire. The clothes of his body he is not to change, fine dress (?) he is not to put on. Sacrifices he is not to bring, nor is the king to ride in his chariot. He is not to hold court, nor is the priest to seek an oracle for him in the holy of holies. The physician is not to be brought to the sick room. The day is not suitable for invoking curses. At night, in the presence of Marduk and Ishtar, the king is to bring his gift. Then he is to offer sacrifices so that his prayer may be acceptable" (M. Jastrow's *Religion of Babylonia and Assyria*, pp. 376, 377).

(*d*) It is only on the side of prohibition that we can here see any resemblance between the Babylonian treatment of the seventh day and the Hebrew Sabbath of every seventh day. Of course it is possible that if the use of the Babylonian word *shapattu* for "full-moon" day is sustained, it may be a survival of Semitic lunar sacred days, the observance of which, though dropped by Babylonian usage, was retained by Hebrew legislation and given a new religious significance.

(*e*) In the pre-exilic writings of the O.T. (2 Kings iv. 23; Is. i. 13; Hos. ii. 11; Amos viii. 5) we notice the joint mention of the New Moon and the Sabbath as sacred festivals observed by the people; but the conjecture of Meinhold, that the Sabbath was originally the Hebrew name of the Full Moon Festival, seems very improbable. That there is some underlying connexion between the Babylonian *shabattu* and the Hebrew *shabbath* is highly probable. At present, there is no evidence to shew that the Hebrew usage is borrowed from Babylonian. Nor does the language of the post-exilic writers suggest that the Hebrew observance of the Sabbath was one which they associated with Babylonian religion.

NOTE ON THE COSMOGONIES OF GENESIS

The Book of Genesis contains *two* Cosmogonies: (1) the earlier and simpler one, that of ii. 4^b—25 J, (2) the later and more systematic one, that of i. 1—ii. 4^a P.

(1) The distinctive features of the earlier one suggest a scene familiar to dwellers in the desert. The earth is barren and dry: there is as yet no rain to make it fruitful, no man to till it (*v.* 5). A stream[1] issues "from the earth"; it irrigates "the whole face of the ground" (*v.* 6). Jehovah forms "man" out of the dust, and breathes life into him (*v.* 7). He causes him to dwell in a garden of rich soil and fruitful trees (*vv.* 8—17). He forms "the beasts of the field" and "the fowls of the air" to be man's companions (*vv.* 18—20). But they give no true companionship: and Jehovah, casting "man" into a deep sleep, takes out of him a rib, and forms "woman" to be man's companion (*vv.* 21—25).

The process of formation is orderly: (1) dry earth, (2) water, (3) man, (4) vegetation, (5) animals, (6) woman. Jehovah is the maker of all. Man is, in all, the object of Jehovah's care and solicitude. The scene of the garden is that of an oasis teeming with life and vegetation.

(2) The later and more elaborate Cosmogony (i. 1—ii. 4^a) is, undoubtedly, ultimately derived from the alluvial region of Babylonia. At the first, there is a primordial watery chaos, over which "broods" the quickening "spirit of God" (*v.* 2). Then ensue six days of Creation. On the first, God creates the light, causing day and night (*v.* 3). On the second, He "makes" the "firmament," or solid expanse of heaven, which parts asunder the waters above and the waters below (*v.* 7). On the third day, God collects the lower waters into seas, and makes the earth appear, and clothes it with vegetation (*vv.* 9—13). On the fourth day, He makes the sun, moon, and stars; and "sets" them in the "firmament," to rule over the day and the night (*vv.* 14—19). On the fifth day, He causes the water and the air to bring forth water-animals and winged things (*vv.* 20—23). On the sixth day, God "makes" the animals of the earth; and, finally, "creates" man, "male and female," "in the image of God" (*vv.* 24—31).

In this Cosmogony there are certain points of resemblance to the Babylonian Cosmogony contained in the *Seven Tables of Creation*, in which Marduk, the god of light, overthrows Tiamat, the dragon-goddess of the watery chaos, sets up the luminaries of heaven, and makes man[2]. The following table, taken from Gordon's *Early Traditions of Genesis* (p. 51), will shew all the chief points of resemblance, and will also make it clear that the Biblical story is not a mere reproduction of the Babylonian myth.

Gen. i.	Seven Tables.
i. The emergence of light (*vv.* 3 f.).	i. The appearance of Marduk, god of light (ii. 97).

[1] "Stream": R.V. "mist." See note *in loc.*

[2] See Appendix A.

GENESIS II.

Gen. i.	Seven Tables.
ii. The division of primaeval chaos into heaven and earth (vv. 6 ff.).	ii. The splitting in two of Tiamat, to form heaven and earth (iv. 135 ff.; cf. Berosus)[1].
iii. The growth of herbs and trees from earth (vv. 11 f.).	iii. The setting up of the sun, moon, and stars in heaven, as images of the great gods, to "rule" the day and night, and determine the seasons (v. 1 ff.).
iv. The placing of the sun, moon, and stars in the firmament of heaven, to "rule" the day and night, and to serve as "signs" of seasons, &c. (vv. 14 ff.).	iv. The creation of plants (not found in our present text, but evidently an original element of the Epos—prob. in Tab. v., after the setting up of the heavenly bodies) (cf. vii. 1 f., 21 ff.).
v. The creation of the animals (vv. 20 ff.).	v. Creation of the animals (also missing from our present text, but authenticated by Berosus—its place also, probably, in Tab. v., after creation of plants).
vi. The creation of man in God's image (vv. 26 ff.).	vi. Creation of man from Marduk's blood mixed with earth (Tab. vi. 5 ff.; cf. vii. 29, and Berosus).

It will be observed that, except for the exchange in the position of the creation of the plant world and the heavenly bodies, the same general order is followed. In the details of the account, the division of the waters above and below the firmament seems to correspond closely to the cleaving of Tiamat into two pieces, to form the heaven and the earth; and the setting of the heavenly bodies as "signs," for the determining of seasons, days, and years, and for ruling the day and night, presents a feature of striking similarity to the Babylonian story.

The Genesis Cosmogony has dispensed with the grotesque and often unlovely and confusing details of the Babylonian mythology. For example, whereas man is made out of the compound of Marduk's blood and the dust of the earth, the truth, which underlies this crude representation, is stated by the Hebrew writer in the simple words, "And God said, Let us make man in our image, after our likeness" (i. 26).

The two main ideas that run through this Hebrew Cosmogony are:

(1) God is the One Almighty Creative Power; whether calling into being light (v. 3), the firmament (vv. 6, 7), the heavenly bodies (vv. 16, 17), and man (v. 27), or causing vegetation to come forth from the earth (vv. 11, 12), fish from the water (vv. 20, 21), animals from the earth (vv. 24, 25).

[1] See Appendix A.

(2) The sequence in the creative acts is an orderly ascent from one stage to another, progressing from amorphous chaos to man as the crown of creation. At first, there is darkness and watery mass. Light displaces darkness; a solid dome of heaven separates the waters; the waters are collected; earth emerges, and out of the earth vegetation; the heavenly bodies are bearers of light; the waters and the air produce their living creatures; and, lastly, the earth produces the beasts; and, to crown the whole work, God creates man.

It is progress from chaos to order; from elemental to complex; from inorganic to organic; from lifeless matter to vegetable; from vegetable to animal, and, finally, to human life.

THE SIX DAYS.

The most distinctive feature in the Hebrew Cosmogony of Gen. i. 1—ii. 4ª is the scheme of *Six Days Creation*. The orderly arrangement of chronological material is characteristic of the style of P. The stages of the Divine Creative work lent themselves to be distributed over Six Days. But, according to the religious thought of the devout Israelite, the Seventh Day must from the first have been a day of rest, and the Divine example alone could have communicated to the observance of the Sabbath its supreme seal of sanctity.

It is noteworthy that the only two passages in the Old Testament in which reference is made to the "six days work" of Creation, are Ex. xx. 11 and xxxi. 17, both of which are probably based upon P's narrative. (See Commentaries by McNeile and Driver, *in loc.*) The Six Days Creation, followed by the Seventh Day of Rest, are distinctively Israelite and not Babylonian features. There is nothing corresponding to them in the Babylonian myth. The *Seven Tables of Creation* are not arranged in any sequence of days.

The Creative works of the Six Days have been classified in different ways.

(1) Thomas Aquinas divided them into *three "opera distinctionis"* and *three "opera ornatus."*

Opera distinctionis.	*Opera ornatus.*
1st Day. Light.	4th Day. Heavenly Bodies.
2nd Day. The Firmament.	5th Day. Fishes and Birds.
3rd Day. Sea, Land, and Vegetation.	6th Day. Cattle, Beasts, and Man.

(2) Many modern scholars, e.g. Wellhausen and Gunkel, suggest that the Cosmogony originally told of *eight* creative works, and that these have been arranged in P's scheme of "six days":

Elements.	*Inhabitants.*
1. Light.	5. Luminaries.
2. Heaven.	6. Fishes.
3. Sea.	7. Birds.
4. Vegetation.	8. Animals and Man.

(3) The endeavour to find any exact symmetry of parallelism between the works of the first three days and the works of the second three days must be abandoned. Roughly speaking, it may suffice to say, to quote Driver, that "the first three days are days of preparation, the next three are days of accomplishment." But the following facts are noteworthy. (*a*) Each group of three days contains four creative acts: (*b*) the third day, in each group, has two creative acts assigned to it: (*c*) the creation of light on the first day has corresponding to it on the fourth day the creation of the "light-bearers," or heavenly bodies: (*d*) the separation of the waters, on the second day, by the making of the firmament, seems to correspond with the creation, on the fifth, of the creatures of the sea and of the fowls "that fly above the earth in the open firmament of heaven" (*v.* 20): (*e*) whereas, on the third day, the dry land appears, and vegetable life is made, it is on the sixth day that the animals of the earth, and man, are created; while the herbs, grasses, and fruits of the third day's creation are the appointed food (*v.* 30), both of animals and of mankind.

1st Day. Light.	4th Day. Heavenly Bodies.
2nd Day. The Firmament, separating between the waters above and below.	5th Day. Fowls of the Air, and Water Animals.
3rd Day. (*a*) Formation of the Sea and the Earth, and (*b*) of the Vegetable World.	6th Day. (*a*) Animals of the Earth, (*b*) Mankind.

THE COSMOGONIES AND SCIENCE AND RELIGION.

Every Cosmogony expresses, under the form of imagery, the childlike answers of a people in its earliest phases of civilization to the questionings of the human mind as to the origin of the world and of life. No Cosmogony, therefore, can be expected to give any but naïve, crude, and simple explanations of the deep mysteries of the universe.

The Biblical Cosmogonies only differ from other Cosmogonies in this respect. They reproduce the early beliefs of the Israelite people respecting the Origin of the World and of the Human Race in the form of narrative which, however simple and childlike, is devoid of any taint of polytheism or degrading superstition, and is capable of conveying the profoundest truths respecting God, the Universe, and Mankind.

Unquestionably, they present to us the physical science of their age. And, by comparison with other Cosmogonies, the statement, contained in the first two chapters of Genesis, surpasses in dignity, lucidity, and simplicity that which is to be found in any other ancient literature. It is no exaggeration to say that the picture, which the first chapter of Genesis presents of the orderly progress out of primordial chaos, and of the successive stages in the creation of vegetation, fishes, birds, mammals, and man, is unrivalled for its combination of simplicity, grandeur, and truth. It contains, in principle, though, of course, without exactitude in detail, the thought which is contained in the modern idea of evolution.

Judged by the standards of modern knowledge, the Cosmogonies of Genesis are wholly defective. They present to us pictures, accounting for the origin of things, which vividly corresponded with the Semitic thought of their age and country, but which from the point of view of science are devoid of any value.

For instance, in Gen. ii., the formation of man out of the dust of the earth, and of woman out of man's rib, is the symbolism of primitive legend, not actual fact.

In Gen. i., the conception of the universe, as in the O.T. generally, is geocentric. The sun, moon and stars are formed after the earth, and attached to the "firmament." The "firmament" of the heaven is a solid dome above which are vast reservoirs of water. The vegetation of the earth appears before the formation of the sun. "Six Days" account for the origin of the whole universe. Two days are assigned for the formation of all forms of animal life and of mankind.

These are ideas which, however beautifully expressed, belong to the childhood of the enquiring thought of mankind. They have had their value in helping to supply the science of the Christian world in pre-scientific days. In this respect they have served their time. We derive our knowledge of the structure of the globe, of the universe, of the stars, of the succession of animal life, of the antiquity of man, not from these two chapters of Genesis, but from the continually progressive teaching of modern science. Modern science is based upon the skilled and minute observations of men of genius and highly trained intellect. The astronomical discoveries of Copernicus, Galileo, and Newton, reinforced by the philosophical teaching of Bacon's *Novum Organon*, have revolutionized the natural sciences. The pre-Copernican conception of the universe has passed for ever away.

It is to be remembered that to the Israelite writers "the realm of natural sciences," as we call them, had no existence. The universe had come into being by the Will of God. The phenomena of Nature were the manifestations of His handiwork. God was the immediate fashioner of all from the beginning. The religion of Jehovah had chased away the Nature Deities of the heathen nations. The Spirit of God is the source of all life: every law of Nature is the direct fulfilment of Divine command. To the Israelite writer "religion" and "science" are one. The gaps in human knowledge are filled up with the poetry of primitive imagination; but this is never allowed to conflict with the pure monotheism of Israel. Neither the world, nor any creature, nor the heavenly bodies, are identified with the Divine Being. Nothing in the universe has any existence save through the Will of God. There is no independent, no hostile, deity. God has willed and made all; and, therefore, He is able to pronounce all to be "very good." The Hebrew Cosmogonies testify to a God who is not only omnipotent, but whose works proclaim His praise as the God of order, of progress, and of love.

NOTE ON THE RIVERS OF PARADISE

Gen. ii. 11—14.

The mention of the four rivers of Paradise has given rise to many endeavours to localize the site. A famous pamphlet by Prof. F. Delitzsch, entitled *Wo lag das Paradies?* (= *What was the site of Paradise?*), 1881, gave an immense impulse to the enquiry.

1. Delitzsch himself ingeniously identifies Pishon with the Pallakopas, a canal on the W. bank of the Euphrates, flowing into the Persian Gulf, and Gihon with the modern *Shaṭṭ-en-Nil*, a canal from the E. bank of the Euphrates, near Babylon, and returning to the Euphrates over against Ur. Hiddekel and Euphrates will then be the lower portions of the Tigris and the Euphrates; Havilah part of the desert W. of the Euphrates; Cush the name for that region in Babylonia, which gave its name to the Kassite dynasty. According to this theory, Eden is the *plain* (*edinu*) between the Tigris and the Euphrates, and the *river* in v. 10 is the Euphrates. It seems, however, fatal to this ingenious view that

(*a*) it identifies the river of *v*. 11 with one of the four heads into which it divides itself:

(*b*) "the whole land of Havilah" must be intended to denote something much more extensive than the small district enclosed by the Pallakopas canal: while the canal *Shaṭṭ-en-Nil* could never be described as encircling the land of Cush:

(*c*) "in front of Assyria" is a description of the Tigris to the N. of Babylonia, and is unsuitable to the region near Babylon where the two rivers approach most closely to each other.

2. Sayce, in *H. C. M.* 95 ff., proposes that the garden of Eden is to be identified with the sacred garden of Ea at Eridu, once the seaport of Chaldaea on the Persian Gulf; and the river which waters it (*v*. 11), with the Persian Gulf, while the four rivers are the Euphrates, the Tigris, the Pallakopas (= Pison), the Choaspes (modern *Kerkha*) = Gihon, their waters entering the Persian Gulf by separate mouths. The Persian Gulf was sometimes designated in the Babylonian language *Nâr Marratum* ("Bitter River"). It is an objection that the Biblical account makes the one river divide up into four, while this theory makes four rivers flow into one.

3. With this view should be associated that of Hommel (*A.H.T.* 314 ff.), who identifies Eden with the "garden" at Eridu, the river of *v*. 11 with the Persian Gulf, and the three rivers Pishon, Gihon and Hiddekel with three *wādis* in N. Arabia.

4. Haupt, quoted in Driver, supposes the common source of the four rivers to have been an imaginary lake in N. Mesopotamia. The Pishon is the Persian Gulf encircling Havilah, or Arabia; the Gihon is the *Karun*, supposed to flow eventually through Cush and become the Nile; while the Tigris and the Euphrates entered, by separate mouths, the marshes, beyond which was the Persian Gulf.

J 3 Now the serpent was more subtil than any beast of the

5. Skinner suggests (p. 64) that the Hebrew geographer, who was himself only acquainted with the two great Mesopotamian rivers, the Tigris and the Euphrates, added to them the names of two others, the Pishon and the Gihon, by which he intended the two mysterious rivers of the Indian world, the Indus and the Ganges.

Delitzsch and Dillmann identify the Pishon with the Indus, and the Gihon with the Nile. "But if the biblical narrator believed the Nile to rise with Euphrates and Tigris, it is extremely likely that he regarded its upper waters as the Indus, as Alexander the Great did in his time; and we might then fall back on the old identification of Pishon with the Ganges" (Skinner).

6. Two of the rivers are the Tigris and the Euphrates, which were known to flow from a remote Northern region into Mesopotamia. The tradition supposed this Northern region to contain also the sources of two other rivers which rivalled the Tigris and the Euphrates. One of them, according to the vague notions of ancient geography, somehow encircled Havilah (= Arabia), while the other watered the region of Cush (= Soudan).

7. The well-known names embodied in this strange piece of ancient geography make it very improbable that any mythological or astrological explanation can meet the requirements of the problem.

Ch. III. (J.) The Story of Paradise (cont.): II. The Fall of Man (1—24).

1—5.	The Temptation.
6—8.	The Fall.
9—13.	The Enquiry.
14—19.	The Sentence.
20—21.	Man's Clothing.
22—24.	The Expulsion from the Garden.

1. *Now the serpent*] The abrupt mention of the serpent is characteristic of this narrative. Vivid and picturesque as it is, the story leaves many things omitted and unexplained. The present verse is an illustration. It makes no mention of time; whether the interval between the Creation and the Fall was one of days, months, or years, is not stated. The serpent is brought upon the scene without explanation, though he is gifted with speech and is able, by means of knowledge superior to that of the woman, to tell her what will be the results of eating of the forbidden fruit; cf. *v.* 5 with *v.* 22.

Ch. iii., though one of the same group of narratives as ch. ii. 4b—25, has no appearance of being the immediate continuance of ch. ii., but rather of being a distinct and independent story. The connecting link is the mention of the tree "in the midst of the garden."

The serpent is (1) one of "the beasts of the field" (cf. ii. 19), "formed out of the ground"; (2) more "subtle" than any of them;

GENESIS III. 1—3

field which the LORD God had made. And he said unto the woman, Yea, hath God said, Ye shall not eat of ¹any tree of the garden? And the woman said unto the serpent, 2 Of the fruit of the trees of the garden we may eat: but of 3 the fruit of the tree which is in the midst of the garden,

¹ Or, *all the trees*

(3) not identified with a spirit, or any personal power, of evil. For this development of the narrative, belonging to a late period of Jewish literature, cf. Wisdom ii. 23, "by envy of the devil death entered into the world," Rev. xx. 2, "the dragon, the old serpent, which is the Devil and Satan."

more subtil] i.e. more sly, clever, and mischievous. For the wisdom of the serpent, cf. the proverbial expression quoted by our LORD, "Be ye wise (φρόνιμοι) as serpents," Matt. x. 16. Here the LXX has ὁ δὲ ὄφις ἦν φρονιμώτατος πάντων τῶν θηρίων.

Yea, hath God said] The serpent, in order to secure success, addresses the woman, who (*a*) was the weaker, (*b*) was apparently alone, and (*c*) had not herself received the Divine command respecting the fruit of the tree (ii. 16).

Observe that in the serpent's mouth the general name, "God" (*Elohim*), is used, and not the sacred name "Jehovah" (LORD), and that the woman replying takes up the serpent's words.

The method which the serpent adopts is insidious. He knows the prohibition; he feigns ignorance, and asks to be instructed. The question suggests a doubt of Divine goodness. It takes the tone of indignant surprise at the injustice and harshness of a prohibition which had forbidden the man and the woman to eat of any tree of the garden. Such a suggestion, however easily refuted, might instil into the mind of the unsuspicious woman a grain of doubt, whether even any limitation was consonant with perfect justice and kindness. Compare the first temptation: "If thou art the Son of God," Matt. iv., Luke iv. 3.

The versions, misunderstanding the Hebrew particles, give a slightly different turn to the serpent's question: LXX τί ὅτι, Lat. *cur*, making the serpent ask, not as to the fact, but as to the reason of the prohibition.

2. *the woman*, &c.] The woman is quick to correct the error into which she fancies the serpent has fallen, and to defend the generosity of the LORD.

3. *of the fruit of the tree*, &c.] The woman speaks of only one tree, and that one is in the midst of the garden. She does not mention it by name. In ii. 9, where two trees are mentioned, the one which is described as "in the midst of the garden" is the tree of life. Here the woman speaks of the tree, which is "in the midst of the garden," as the tree of knowledge.

J God hath said, Ye shall not eat of it, neither shall ye touch
4 it, lest ye die. And the serpent said unto the woman, Ye
5 shall not surely die: for God doth know that in the day ye
eat thereof, then your eyes shall be opened, and ye shall be
6 as ¹God, knowing good and evil. And when the woman

¹ Or, *gods*

neither shall ye touch it] This is an addition to the prohibition contained in ii. 17, either an element omitted in the previous chapter, or an exaggeration expressive of the woman's eagerness.

4. *Ye shall not surely die*] The words are very emphatic, "by no means shall ye die." The serpent directly contradicts the statement of the penalty of death, and thus craftily removes the cause for fear, before dwelling upon the advantages to be obtained from defiance of the Divine decree.

5. *for God doth know*, &c.] Having denied the fact of the penalty, the serpent proceeds to suggest that there is an unjust motive for the threat. It is not, he says, for the good of the man and the woman, but in order to exclude them from their privilege and right. No reason had been assigned: the serpent suggests one, that of jealous fear, lest men should be as God. According to the story, there is a half-truth in each utterance of the tempter: (1) "Ye shall not surely die"; and it is true that the penalty of ii. 17 was not literally carried out. The man did not die *in the day* that he ate of the fruit: (2) "in the day ye eat thereof your eyes shall be opened"; the prediction is verified in *v.* 7: (3) "Ye shall be as God, knowing good and evil": the prediction is confirmed by the words of Jehovah Himself, *v.* 22, "Behold the man is become as one of us, to know good and evil." These three assertions, the denial of penalty, the promise of knowledge, and the prospect of independence, therefore, are not lies capable of direct refutation, but half-truths requiring explanation.

your eyes shall be opened] An expression denoting the sudden acquisition of discernment to apprehend that which before had been hidden from ordinary sight. Cf. xxi. 19; 1 Sam. xiv. 29; 2 Kings vi. 17.

as God] or *as gods*. Both translations are possible, as in the Hebrew the word for God, *Elohim*, is plural; and consequently it is sometimes impossible to say whether "a god," or "gods," is the right translation: e.g. 1 Sam. xxviii. 13, "and the woman said unto Saul, I see a god (or 'gods') coming up out of the earth." In favour of the plural "gods" is the expression in *v.* 22, "the man is become as one of *us*." The word "Elohim" may be used of the Heavenly Beings, "Sons of God," who living in the presence of God are spoken of as sharers in His Divinity; see note on i. 26. But as the purpose of the serpent is to implant distrust of, and disaffection towards, the LORD who had made the man and woman, the singular, "as God," is to be preferred.

saw that the tree was good for food, and that it was a delight to the eyes, and that the tree was ¹to be desired to make one wise, she took of the fruit thereof, and did eat; and she gave also unto her husband with her, and he did eat. And the eyes of them both were opened, and they 7

¹ Or, *desirable to look upon*

6—8. THE FALL.

The serpent here disappears from the story, except for the mention of him in the woman's words of excuse (*v.* 13), and in the Divine sentence upon him (*vv.* 14, 15). He did not tell the woman to eat the fruit. The temptation which is most dangerous is rarely the most direct. The soul, which has once yielded to the temptation to distrust the goodness of God, may be left to itself to disobey Him, and, in the conflict between pleasure and the service of God, will prefer its own way. Disobedience to God is the assertion of self-will, and "sin is lawlessness" (ἀνομία), 1 John iii. 4.

6. *And when the woman*] The woman's attention has been drawn to the tree. She finds that the serpent's suggestion, based on the mysterious properties of the fruit and on the supposition of Jehovah's jealousy and unkindness, is reinforced by the attractive appearance of the fruit. Probably good to taste, evidently fair to look on, and alleged to contain the secret of wisdom, the sight of the fruit stimulates desire, and this being no longer resisted by a loyal love of God obtains the mastery; cf. Jas. i. 14, 15, "Each man is tempted when he is drawn away by his own lust, and enticed. Then the lust, when it hath conceived, beareth sin: and the sin, when it is fullgrown, bringeth forth death."

to be desired to make one wise] or rather, "to be desired, in order to be wise." The same word in the Hebrew as in Ps. ii. 10, "now therefore be wise, O ye kings." The R.V. marg., "desirable to look upon," gives a rendering of the Hebrew word which is not supported by its use elsewhere in the Bible, though found with this sense in late Hebrew, and in this verse supported by the versions, LXX ὡραῖον τοῦ κατανοῆσαι, Vulg. *aspectu delectabile*, and the Syriac Peshitto.

and she gave also] The story is so condensed that we are left in ignorance, whether the man yielded as easily to the woman as she had to the serpent. The fact that the woman "fell" first, before the man, was presumably a point upon which stress was laid in the Rabbinic teaching, to which St Paul alludes in 1 Tim. ii. 14, "and Adam was not beguiled, but the woman being beguiled hath fallen into transgression."

7. *And the eyes*, &c.] The serpent's promise is fulfilled; their eyes having been opened, they have forfeited the state of innocence of which nakedness was symbolical, cf. ii. 25. The knowledge to which

J knew that they were naked; and they sewed fig leaves 8 together, and made themselves ¹aprons. And they heard the ²voice of the Lord God walking in the garden in the ³cool of the day: and the man and his wife hid themselves from the presence of the Lord God amongst the trees of 9 the garden. And the Lord God called unto the man, and 10 said unto him, Where art thou? And he said, I heard thy ²voice in the garden, and I was afraid, because I was naked;

¹ Or, *girdles* ² Or, *sound* ³ Heb. *wind*.

they have attained is neither that of happiness, of wisdom, nor power, but that of the consciousness of sin and of its conflict with the Will of God.

fig leaves] These leaves would be chosen because of their size. The fig tree is said to be indigenous in Palestine, but not in Babylonia. If so, it is an indirect proof that our version of the story is genuinely Israelite. "Fig leaves are thick, palmately lobed, and often a span or more across" (Hastings' D.B., *s. v.*).

aprons] Better, as R.V. marg., *girdles*: LXX περιζώματα, Lat. *perizomata*.

The rendering "breeches," which appeared in the Genevan Bible (1560), caused that version to be popularly known as "the breeches Bible."

8. *the voice*] Better, as R.V. marg., *sound*. The man and woman are represented as hearing the sound of God's footsteps in the garden.

in the cool of the day] Lit. "in the wind of the day"; that is, at the time of day when, in the East, a cool wind springs up, and people leave their houses. LXX τὸ δειλινόν, Vulg. *ad auram post meridiem*.

hid themselves] Evidently it had hitherto been their custom to go with Jehovah when He "walked in the garden." Now conscience makes cowards of them; and, like children who had done wrong, they hide themselves "in medio ligni Paradisi" (Vulg.).

9—13. The Enquiry.

The certainty of tone with which the following questions are put indicates either perfect knowledge or accurate perception, and reduces the guilty man to a speedy confession. The questions are put, not to obtain information, but to give opportunity for self-examination and acknowledgment of guilt. The endeavour of the man and woman to put the blame on others is a lifelike trait.

9. *Where art thou?*] The Lord does not abandon, He seeks, the guilty. The question is one which the voice of conscience puts to every man who thinks that he can hide his sin from God's sight.

10. *heard...afraid...hid*] The man has not courage to tell the whole

GENESIS III. 10—14

and I hid myself. And he said, Who told thee that thou 11 J
wast naked? Hast thou eaten of the tree, whereof I commanded thee that thou shouldest not eat? And the man 12
said, The woman whom thou gavest to be with me, she
gave me of the tree, and I did eat. And the LORD God 13
said unto the woman, What is this thou hast done? And
the woman said, The serpent beguiled me, and I did eat.
And the LORD God said unto the serpent, Because thou 14
hast done this, cursed art thou ¹above all cattle, and ¹above

¹ Or, *from among*

truth. Fear suppresses that part of the truth which love should have avowed. To hide from God's presence is the instinct of guilt; it is the converse of "to seek His face."

11. *Who told thee*, &c.?] To this question no answer is expected. The knowledge could only come in one way. The sense of shame implies contact with sin.

Hast thou eaten, &c.?] An opportunity is given for a full confession of disobedience and for the expression of contrition.

12. *The woman*, &c.] The man, unable to deny the charge, seeks to excuse himself by laying the blame primarily on the woman, and secondarily on Jehovah Himself, for having given him the woman as his companion. Guilt makes the man first a coward, and then insolent.

13. *The serpent beguiled me*] The woman, in answer to the direct and piercing question, lays the blame upon the serpent. For the word "beguiled," cf. 2 Cor. xi. 3. See St Paul's use of the passage in 1 Tim. ii. 14.

The serpent is not interrogated. Perhaps, as some suggest, because "being an animal it is not morally responsible: but it is punished here as the representative of evil thoughts and suggestions" (Driver). Others have surmised that, as some features of the story have disappeared in the condensed version that has come down to us, the question put to the serpent and his answers may have seemed less suitable for preservation.

The interrogation is over: it has been admitted, (1) that the man and the woman had eaten the fruit: (2) that the woman had given it the man: (3) that the serpent had beguiled her. The evil has been traced back from the man to the woman, from the woman to the serpent: there is no enquiry into the origin of the evil. Judgement is now delivered in the reverse order, beginning with the serpent, and concluding with the man on whom the chief responsibility rests; for he had enjoyed direct converse with the LORD, and had received the charge of the garden.

14—19. THE SENTENCE.

14. *cursed art thou*] The word "cursed" is only used in addressing the serpent, as the originator of the temptation, and in reference to

GENESIS III. 14, 15

J every beast of the field; upon thy belly shalt thou go, and
15 dust shalt thou eat all the days of thy life: and I will put
enmity between thee and the woman, and between thy

"the ground" as the sphere of man's penalty (*v.* 17). Jehovah does
not pronounce a curse either upon the man or upon the woman.

above] Better, as R.V. marg., *from among*. Taken from among
the other animals, the domestic cattle and the wild beasts, the serpent
alone receives the curse. So LXX ἀπό, Vulg. "inter." An objection
to the rendering "above" is, that it would imply a curse of some sort
upon all animals, and a special one upon the serpent.

upon thy belly, &c.] It appears from this sentence that the story
considered the serpent to have been originally different in appearance
and mode of progression. Its crawling movement on the ground and
the apparent necessity for its swallowing dust are regarded as the results
of the curse pronounced in the garden.

Prostrate, no longer erect, and feeding on the dust which man shakes
off from his foot, the serpent-race typified the insidious character of the
power of evil, to which the upright walk of man was the typical
contrast.

all the days of thy life] Not the individual serpent, but the whole
serpent-race. These words, together with the details of the curse,
conclusively shew that Jehovah is addressing an animal, and not the
spirit of evil.

15. *and I will put enmity*] The first meaning of this sentence
refers to the instinctive antipathy of mankind towards the serpent,
and the frequently deadly character of the wounds inflicted by serpents
upon human beings.

But this explanation does not exhaust the full meaning of the verse.
The narrator tells the story, not in the spirit of a compiler of folk-lore,
but with the purpose of embodying in it the truths of religion. The
hostility between the serpent and the woman, between the serpent's
seed and the woman's seed, typifies the unending conflict between all
that represents the forces of evil on the one hand, and all that represents
the true and high destiny of mankind on the other. Upon this
antagonism Jehovah has, as it were, set His seal from the very beginning. He has ordained it. There must be war between every form
of evil and the children of man. This verse has been called the Protevangelium. There is no prediction of a personal victor, or even of an
ultimate victory. Commentators used to see in the words, "thou shalt
bruise his heel," a prediction of the sufferings and crucifixion of our
Lord, as "the seed" of the woman; and in the words, "it shall bruise
thy head," the victory of the Crucified and Risen Son of Man over the
forces of sin and death. We are not justified in going to the full length
of this interpretation. The victory of the Cross contains, in its fullest
expression, the fulfilment of the conflict, which God here proclaims
between Mankind and the symbol of Evil, and in which He Himself

seed and her seed: it shall ¹bruise thy head, and thou shalt ¹bruise his heel. Unto the woman he said, I will greatly multiply thy sorrow and thy conception; in sorrow thou

¹ Or, *lie in wait for*

espouses the cause of man. The Conflict and the Victory are oracularly announced. But there is no prediction of the Personal Messiah.

enmity] An unusual word in the Hebrew, occurring elsewhere in O.T. only in Num. xxxv. 21, 22, Ezek. xxv. 15, xxxv. 5. LXX ἔχθραν, Lat. *inimicitias*. It denotes the "blood-feud" between the man and the serpent-race.

bruise] The Hebrew word rendered "bruise" is the same in both clauses. Suitable as it is in its application to the "crushing" of a serpent's head beneath a man's foot, it is unsuitable as applied to the serpent's attack upon the man's heel. Accordingly some scholars prefer the rendering "aim at," from a word of a similar root meaning to "pant" or "pant after." So the R.V. marg. *lie in wait for* (which, however, the root can hardly mean). The LXX has *watch*, τήρησει and τήρησεις, probably with the same idea. Vulg. has *conteret* = "shall bruise," in the first clause; *insidiaberis* = "shalt lie in wait for," in the second clause. It has been conjectured that the root *shûph* = "bruise," may have had some special secondary meaning in which it was used of the serpent's bite.

The Vulgate *ipsa conteret caput tuum* is noticeable. By an error, it rendered the Heb. masc. pronoun ("he" = LXX αὐτός) by the feminine pronoun "ipsa," ascribing to the woman herself, not to her seed, the crushing of the serpent's head. The feminine pronoun has given rise to some singular instances of exegesis in honour of the Blessed Virgin Mary.

16. *I will greatly multiply*] The sentence upon the woman deals with the two aspects of the married woman's life, as wife and as mother. The story explains the pains of child-bearing as the penalty for the Fall. The possession of children is the Eastern woman's strongest passion. The sentence upon the woman gratifies her desire, but crosses it with sorrow. The penalty brings also its blessing; and the blessing its discipline.

thy sorrow] Better, as Driver, "thy pain," as the word, elsewhere used only in *vv.* 17, 29, is evidently not restricted to mental distress.

thy conception] Lat. *conceptus tuos*. But LXX τὸν στεναγμόν σου = "thy groaning," according to a reading which differs by a very slight change in two Hebrew letters. This is preferred by some commentators, who represent that in the Israelite world a numerous family was regarded as a sign of God's blessing, and not in the light of a penalty. But the change is needless. The sentence both upon the man and upon the woman is not so much punitive as disciplinary. The woman's vocation to motherhood was her highest privilege and most intense happiness. The pains and disabilities of child-bearing, which darken

J shalt bring forth children; and thy desire shall be to thy
17 husband, and he shall rule over thee. And unto Adam he
said, Because thou hast hearkened unto the voice of thy
wife, and hast eaten of the tree, of which I commanded
thee, saying, Thou shalt not eat of it: cursed is the ground
for thy sake; in ¹toil shalt thou eat of it all the days of thy
18 life; thorns also and thistles shall it bring forth to thee;
19 and thou shalt eat the herb of the field; in the sweat of

¹ Or, *sorrow*

the mystery of many a woman's life, are declared to be the reminder that pain is part of God's ordinance in the world, and that, in the human race, suffering enters largely into the shadow of sin.

in sorrow] viz. "in pain" as above.

thy desire, &c.] LXX ἡ ἀποστροφή σου, i.e. "thy turning or inclination," with a very slight change of one letter in the Hebrew. But, again, there is no need to alter the reading. The two clauses present the antithesis of woman's love and man's lordship. Doubtless, there is a reference to the never ending romance of daily life, presented by the passionate attachment of a wife to her husband, however domineering, unsympathetic, or selfish he may be. But the primary reference will be to the condition of subservience which woman occupied, and still occupies, in the East; and to the position of man, as head of the family, and carrying the responsibility, as well as the authority, of "rule."

This is emphasized in the Latin *sub viri potestate eris*.

17. *cursed is the ground*] The man is addressed as one who in the future is to be dependent upon the soil for the means of subsistence. Not man, but the ground for man's sake, is accursed. Its fruitfulness is withheld, in order that man may realize the penalties of sin through the pains of laborious toil. The sentence, which reverses the blessing of ii. 15, befalls the whole earth.

in toil] R.V. marg. "sorrow." But see note on *v.* 16.

18. *thorns also*, &c.] These are not new products of the soil because of sin, but are typical of that which the earth brings forth of itself, and of ground neglected or rendered fallow by man's indolence. Left to itself, the soil produces weeds which must be removed. Man is to live upon that which he laboriously sows and plants and cultivates.

thistles] Elsewhere only in Hos. x. 8.

the herb of the field] It is here ordained that man shall eat "the herb of the field," requiring laborious cultivation. This is a change from the diet of fruit assigned to him in ii. 16 (J). The passage assumes that agriculture was man's first industry. Anthropology tells a different story; but the Hebrew belief is a recognition of the fact that agriculture was essential to the life of dwellers in Palestine.

19. *in the sweat of thy face*] As in the sentence upon the woman,

GENESIS III. 19—21

thy face shalt thou eat bread, till thou return unto the ground; for out of it wast thou taken: for dust thou art, and unto dust shalt thou return. And the man called his wife's name ¹Eve; because she was the mother of all living. And the LORD God made for Adam and for his wife coats of skins, and clothed them.

J

20

21

¹ Heb. *Havvah*, that is, *Living*, or, *Life*.

so here, in the sentence upon the man, suffering is not punitive, but disciplinary, being associated with his highest vocation. The necessity of labour has proved man's greatest blessing; it has evoked the qualities which are distinctively most noble, and has been the cause of all progress and improvement.

till thou return, &c.] Man's work is to continue to the end. Old age has its own scope for activities. Physical robustness is not the only measure of responsibility or efficiency.

dust thou art, &c.] See note on *v*. 7. Jehovah does not slay man at once; He is merciful, and relaxes His first decree. Man is not to enjoy earthly immortality: but he shall live until "the breath of God" is taken from him, and he becomes dust again.

20—21. These two verses are a parenthesis interrupting the thread of the narrative. Probably they contain materials current in some other thread of tradition, and inserted here at the close of the judicial sentence.

20. *Eve*] Heb. *Ḥavvah*, that is, *Living*, or *Life*. The man is represented as calling his wife by this name, because she was the mother of the whole human race. The word is evidently of great antiquity; for it is not found with this spelling in Biblical Hebrew, but in the form of *ḥayyah*. The sound of the name "Havvah" (Eve) was sufficiently close to that of the root meaning "Life" (*ḥay*) to suggest connexion. Whether *ḥavvah* was an old form, or a name taken over from the primitive people of Palestine, we have no means of deciding.

21. *coats of skins*] in reference to *v*. 7. The sense of shame is the result of the knowledge of evil.

The present verse gives the traditional explanation of the origin of clothes. The word "coats" hardly represents the Hebrew so well as LXX χιτῶνας, and Lat. "tunicas," cf. 2 Kings i. 8, Heb. xi. 37. The Heb. *kʼthôneth* (=χιτών) was a kind of shirt without sleeves, reaching down to the knees.

The first mention of death among animals is implied in this provision for man's clothing. Does it contain an allusion to the otherwise unrecorded institution of sacrifice?

The Divine sentence of punishment is thus followed at once by a Divine act of pity, as if to certify that chastisement is inflicted not in anger, but in affection.

J 22   And the LORD God said, Behold, the man is become as one of us, to know good and evil; and now, lest he put forth his hand, and take also of the tree of life, and eat, and
23 live for ever: therefore the LORD God sent him forth from the garden of Eden, to till the ground from whence he was
24 taken.   So he drove out the man; and he placed at the east of the garden of Eden the Cherubim, and the flame of

22—24. THE EXPULSION FROM THE GARDEN.

22. *as one of us*] It is not stated to whom Jehovah addresses these words. Two explanations are possible. Either (1) He speaks to the Heavenly Beings by whom the throne of God was believed to be surrounded. See notes on i. 26 and iii. 5, vi. 1, xi. 7. "As one of us" will then mean, not "like unto Jehovah personally," but "like to the dwellers in Heaven," who are in the possession of "the knowledge of the distinction between good and evil." Or (2) the words are used in the language of deliberation, and represent the LORD moved, as it were, by apprehension or displeasure, because the eating of the Tree of Knowledge had conferred upon man an attribute to which he was not entitled.

According to either line of explanation, the sentence is one which is most easily understood as one of the few survivals of the earlier myth form of narrative.

The Targum of Onkelos, to avoid the phrase "as one of us," renders "is become one from himself."

and now, lest, &c.] Man must be prevented from eating of the Tree of Life, and so obtaining another prerogative of Divinity, that of immortality. Man is created mortal. Immortality, obtained by disobedience and lived in sin, is not according to Jehovah's will.

The verse contains a survival of the naïve trait in the primitive story, which represented Jehovah as jealous of the possible encroachment by man upon the prerogatives of Divinity. The serpent had referred to this (*v.* 5); and it appears again in xi. 5.

23. *sent him forth,* &c.] Man is dismissed from the garden with the duty imposed upon him to till the ground. Agriculture is here treated as the earliest human industry. See note on *v.* 18.

24. *So he drove out*] The expulsion from the garden is repeated in this verse in stronger terms. In *v.* 23, it was "sent him forth" (LXX ἐξαπέστειλεν, Lat. *emisit*): here, it is "drove out" (LXX ἐξέβαλε, Lat. *ejecit*). Though there is a repetition which may possibly imply different narratives combined together, the milder tone of *v.* 23 is connected with the description of man's vocation to work, the sterner tone of *v.* 24 expresses the exclusion of sinful beings from the privileges of the Divine presence.

at the east] Implying that the entrance was on the east side. Man

Assyrian Winged Bull.

GENESIS III. 24

a sword which turned every way, to keep the way of the   J
tree of life.

is driven out eastward, in accordance with the prevalent belief that the cradle of human civilization was to be sought for in the east.

the Cherubim] Mentioned here without explanation, as if their character must be well known to the readers. The O.T. contains two representations of the Cherubim: (1) they are beings who uphold the throne of God, cf. 1 Sam. iv. 4, 2 Sam. vi. 2, 2 Kings xix. 15, Ps. lxxx. 2, xcix. 1; possibly, in this aspect, they were originally the personification of the thunder clouds, cf. Ps. xviii. 10, "And he (Jehovah), rode upon a cherub, and did fly," where the passage is describing the Majesty of Jehovah in the thunderstorm: (2) they are symbols of the Divine Presence, e.g. two small golden cherubim upon the Ark of the Covenant, Ex. xxv. 18 ff.; two large-winged creatures made of olive wood, sheltering the Ark in the Holy of Holies, 1 Kings vi. 23. They were represented in the works of sacred art in the Tabernacle, Ex. xxv. 18 ff.: and on the walls and furniture of the Temple, 1 Kings vi. 29, 35, vii. 29, 36, cf. Ezek. xli. 18 ff.

The description of the four living creatures in Ezek. i. 5 ff., and x. 20 ff., gives us the Prophet's conception of the Cherubim, each one with four faces (of a man, a lion, an ox, and an eagle), and each one with four wings. But in Ezek. xli. 18, 19 the Cherubim have two faces, one of a man, and one of a lion. It is natural to compare the Assyrian composite figures, winged bulls, and lions with men's heads, and the Greek γρύψ, or "gryphon." In the present passage, the Cherubim are placed as sentinels at the approach to the Tree of Life, and, therefore, we are probably intended to understand that they stood, one on either side of the entrance to the garden, like the two winged figures at the entrance of an Assyrian temple. They are emblematical of the presence of the Almighty: they are the guardians of His abode.

the flame of a sword] It is not usually noticed that we have in these words a protection for the Tree of Life quite distinct from the Cherubim. The hasty reader supposes that the "sword" is a weapon carried by the Cherubim. In pictures, the sword with the flame turning every way is put into the hand of a watching Angel. But this misrepresents the language of the original Hebrew, which states that God placed, at the east of the garden, not only the Cherubim, but also "the flame of a sword which turned every way." What the writer intended to convey we can only conjecture. Very probably it was a representation of the lightnings which went forth from the Divine Presence, and were symbolical of unapproachable purity and might.

The student should refer to the description of the Cherub, in Ezek. xxviii. 11—19, and note particularly the words, *v.* 13, "thou wast in Eden, the garden of God," *v.* 14, "thou wast the anointed Cherub that covereth: and I set thee, so that thou wast upon the holy mountain of God; thou hast walked up and down in the midst of the stones of fire." (See Davidson's Notes, *in loc.* in *Cambridge Bible*.)

The LXX τὴν φλογίνην ῥομφαίαν τὴν στρεφομένην, and Lat. *flammeum gladium atque versatilem*, give a good rendering of the original.

to keep the way of the tree of life] That is to "keep," or "protect," "the way that led to the tree of life," so that man should not set foot upon it.

In the N.T. "the tree of life" is mentioned Rev. ii. 7, "to him that overcometh, to him will I give to eat of the tree of life, which is in the Paradise of God," cf. xxii. 2.

NOTE ON THE FALL

I. The following illustrations of the Story of the Fall are from Jeremias (*O.T. in the Light of the Ancient East*, E.T.).

(*a*) In *Mexican* mythology the first woman is called "the woman with the serpent," or "the woman of our flesh," and she has twin sons.... In the same way the *Indians* have a divine first mother of the race of man, who dwells in Paradise (the Indian Meru). Also in the beginning the evil demon Mahishasura fought with the serpent, trod upon and cut off his head; a victory to be repeated at the end of the world, when Brahma will give back to Indra the rulership over all....The *Chinese* have a myth according to which Fo-hi, the first man, discovered the wisdom of Yang and Yin, masculine and feminine principle (heaven and earth)....A dragon rose from the deep and taught him. "The woman," it is said in an explanatory gloss, "is the first source and the root of all evil" (p. 231).

(*b*) *Legend of Eabani.* The [Babylonian] epic of Gilgamesh tells about a friend of the hero, reminiscent of Pan and Priapus, Eabani, whose whole body was covered with hair. He is the creation of Aruru when she "broke off clay" and "made an image of Anu." He is a being of a gigantic strength. "With the gazelles he eats green plants, with the cattle he satisfies himself (?) with drink, with the fish (properly *crowd*) he is happy in the water. He spoils the hunting of the 'hunter.' Out of love to the animals he destroys snares and nets (?), so that the wild beasts escape. Then by the craft of the hunter, who feared him, a woman is brought to him, who seduces him, and keeps him from his companions the beasts, for six days and seven nights. When he came back, all beasts of the field fled from him. Then Eabani followed the woman, and let himself be led into the city of Erech. In the following passages of the epic the woman appears as the cause of his troubles and sorrows. A later passage records that Eabani cursed her. The First Man is not in question here, but a certain relationship of idea in this description to the story of the happy primeval state of Adam must be granted" (p. 232 f.).

(*c*) *Legend of Adapa.* Adapa, the son of Êa, was one day fishing when "the south wind suddenly overturned his boat and he fell into the sea. Adapa in revenge broke the wings of the south wind (the bird

Zu), so that he could not fly for seven days. Anu, God of Heaven, called him to account, saying, 'No mercy!' but at the prayer of Tammuz and Gishzida, Watchers of the Gate, Anu softened his anger, and commanded that a banquet should be prepared, and a festival garment presented to him, and oil for his anointing: garment and oil he accepted, but food and drink he refused. Êa had warned him: 'When thou appearest before Anu, they will offer thee food of Death: eat not thereof! Water of Death will they offer thee: drink not thereof! They will present thee with a garment: put it on! They will offer thee oil: anoint thyself with it!' But, behold, it was Bread of Life and Water of Life! Anu breaks forth in wonder. Upon the man who has been permitted by his creator to gaze into the secrets of heaven and earth..., he (Anu) has desired to bestow also immortality. And by the envy of the God the man has been deceived" (p. 183 f.).

Jastrow remarks upon this legend: "Adam, it will be recalled, after eating of the fruit of the tree of knowledge, makes a garment for himself. There can be no doubt that there is a close connection between this tradition and the feature in the Adapa legend, where Adapa, who has been shown the 'secrets of heaven and earth,'—that is, has acquired knowledge—is commanded by Êa to put on the garment that is offered him. The anointing oneself with oil, though an essential part of the toilet in the ancient and modern Orient, was discarded in the Hebrew tale as a superfluous feature. The idea conveyed by the use of oil was the same as the one indicated in clothing one's nakedness. Both are symbols of civilization which man is permitted to attain, but his development stops there. He cannot secure eternal life" (*Religion of B. and A.*, p. 552 f.).

In this legend, the man Adapa who has acquired "knowledge," is prevented by the deceit of Êa, the creator of man, from acquiring immortality. There is therefore a striking parallelism of idea with the narrative of Gen. iii., but there is no resemblance in its general features.

Hitherto there has not been discovered any Babylonian story of the Fall. But, when we observe the occurrence of such features as "the garden," "the tree of life," "the serpent," "the Cherubim," it is clear that the symbolism employed is that which is quite common in the records and representations of Assyrian and Babylonian myths.

II. The Story of the Fall does not offer an explanation for the origin of sin. But (1) it gives a description of the first sin; and (2) it presents an explanation of (*a*) the sense of shame (*v.* 7), (*b*) the toil of man (*vv.* 17—19), (*c*) the birth-pangs of woman (*v.* 16), (*d*) the use of clothing (*v.* 21). Whether it offers an explanation of the origin of death, is doubtful. The penalty of death, threatened in ii. 17, was not carried out. In iii. 19 it is assumed that man will die, if he does not eat of the tree of life. He is not, therefore, created immortal; yet immortality is not impossible for him.

The story turns upon man's eating of the fruit of the tree of knowledge of good and evil. What is this "knowledge of good and evil"?

Four answers have been given. (1) Initiation into the mysteries of magical knowledge. (2) Transition to the physical maturity of which the sense of shame is the natural symptom (iii. 7). (3) Acquisition of the knowledge of the secrets of nature and the gifts of civilization, e.g. clothing (iii. 21), arts, industries, &c. (iv. 17 ff.). (4) Arrival at the moral sense of discernment between right and wrong.

Of these, (1) the first may at once be dismissed as quite alien to the general tenour of the story.

(2) The second emphasizes one feature in the story (iii. 7, 10, 21), the sense of shame on account of nakedness. But this new consciousness of sex is only one symptom of the results of disobedience. As an explanation, though possibly adequate for some earlier version of the story, it fails to satisfy the requirements of its present religious character.

(3) The third explanation goes further. It supposes that the knowledge is of that type which afterwards characterizes the descendants of Cain (iv. 17 ff.). It implies the expansion of culture with deliberate defiance of God's will. It means, then, simply the intellectual knowledge of "everything," or, in the Babylonian phrase, of the "secrets of heaven and earth." Cf. Jastrow, p. 553 *n*.

(4) The fourth explanation has been objected to on the ground that God could not originally have wished to exclude man from the power of discerning between good and evil. Notwithstanding, it seems to be the one most in harmony with the general religious character of the story, which turns upon the act of disobedience to God's command, and upon the assertion of man's will against the Divine. It may, of course, fairly be asked whether the fact of prohibition did not assume the existence of a consciousness of the difference between right and wrong. We need not expect the story to be psychologically scientific. But the prohibition was laid down in man's condition of existence previous to temptation. It was possible to receive a Divine command without realizing the moral effect of disobedience. The idea of violating that command had not presented itself before the Serpent suggested it. Conscience was not created, but its faculties were instantaneously aroused into activity, by disobedience. "It is not the thought of the opposition and difference between good and evil..., but it is the *experience of evil*, that knowledge of good and evil which arises from man having taken evil into his very being, which brings death with it. Man, therefore, ought to know evil only as a possibility that he has overcome; he ought only *to see* the forbidden fruit; but if he *eats* it, his death is in the act." (Martensen, *Christian Dogmatics*, p. 156.)

III. (*a*) It does not appear that the Story of the Fall is elsewhere alluded to in the Old Testament. The passages in Job xxxi. 33, "If like Adam I covered my transgressions," Hos. vi. 7, "But they like Adam have transgressed the covenant," are doubtful exceptions. But, in all probability, in both cases the rendering of *adam*, not as a proper name, but as "man" or "men," is to be preferred. There is, indeed, a reference to the "garden of Eden" tradition in

GENESIS III.

Ezek. xxviii.[1] But there is no instance, either in the prophetical or sapiential writings, in which the Story of the Fall is made the basis for instruction upon the subject of sin and its consequences. "The Old Testament," as Mr Tennant says[2], "supplies no trace of the existence, among the sacred writers, of any *interpretation* of the Fall-story comparable to the later doctrine of the Fall." At the same time, there is no ancient literature comparable to the writings of the O.T. for the deep consciousness of the sinfulness of man in God's sight.

The later Jewish literature shews how prominently the subject of the first sin and of man's depravity entered into the thought and discussions of the Jews in the last century B.C. and in the first century A.D.

(*b*) The most notable of the passages referring to the Fall, which illustrate the theology of St Paul, are as follows:

Rom. v. 12—14, "Therefore, as through one man sin entered into the world, and death through sin; and so death passed unto all men, for that all sinned:—for until the law sin was in the world, but sin is not imputed when there is no law. Nevertheless death reigned from Adam until Moses, even over them that had not sinned after the likeness of Adam's transgression, who is a figure of him that was to come." *v*. 18, "For as through the one man's disobedience the many were made sinners, even so through the obedience of the one shall the many be made righteous." 1 Cor. xv. 21—22, "For since by man came death, by man came also the resurrection of the dead. For as in Adam all die, so also in Christ shall all be made alive." 2 Cor. xi. 3, "The serpent beguiled Eve in his craftiness." 1 Tim. ii. 14, "Adam was not beguiled, but the woman being beguiled hath fallen into transgression."

In Romans v. and 1 Cor. xv. St Paul compares the consequences of the Fall of Adam with the consequences of the redemptive work of Christ. Adam's Fall brought with it sin and death: Christ's justifying Act brought righteousness and life. The effects of Adam's sin were transmitted to his descendants. Sin, the tendency to sin, and death, became in consequence universal. But the effect of Adam's Fall has been cancelled by the work of Grace, by the Death and Resurrection of Christ.

For a full discussion of St Paul's treatment of the Fall, see Sanday and Headlam's *Commentary on the Epistle to the Romans* (chap. v.), Bishop Gore's *Lectures on the Romans* (vol. 1. pp. 185 ff.), Thackeray's *St Paul and Jewish Thought* (chap. ii.), Tennant's *The Fall and Original Sin* (chap. xi.), Bernard's article *Fall* in Hastings' D.B. (vol. 1.).

(*c*) The following passages, quoted from Charles' *Apocrypha*, will illustrate Jewish religious thought upon the subject of the Fall and its consequences:

Wisd. ii. 23, 24, "Because God created man for incorruption, and made him an image of his own proper being; But by the envy of the

---

[1] Mic. vii. 17, "to lick the dust like a serpent," is an illustration of Gen. iii. 14 rather than an allusion to the story.
[2] *The Fall and Original Sin*, p. 93.

devil death entered into the world, and they that belong to his realm experience it."

Ecclus. xxv. 24, "From a woman did sin originate, and because of her we must all die."

4 Ezra iii. 7, "And to him [Adam] thou commandedst only one observance of thine, but he transgressed it. Forthwith thou appointedst death for him and for his generations."

4 Ezra iii. 21, "For the first Adam, clothing himself with the evil heart, transgressed and was overcome; and likewise also all who were born of him. Thus the infirmity became inveterate; the Law indeed was in the heart of the people, but (in conjunction) with the evil germ; so what was good departed." Cf. iv. 30, 31.

4 Ezra vii. 118, "O thou Adam, what hast thou done! For though it was thou that sinned, the fall was not thine alone, but ours also who are thy descendants!"

2 Baruch xvii. 2, 3, "For what did it profit Adam that he lived nine hundred and thirty years, and transgressed that which he was commanded? Therefore the multitude of time that he lived did not profit him, but brought death, and cut off the years of those who were born from him."

2 Baruch xxiii. 4, "When Adam sinned and death was decreed against those who should be born."

2 Baruch xlviii. 42, "O Adam, what hast thou done to all those who are born from thee? And what will be said to the first Eve who hearkened to the Serpent?"

2 Baruch liv. 15, 19, "Though Adam first sinned and brought untimely death upon all, yet of those who were born from him each one of them has prepared for his own soul torment to come....Adam is therefore not the cause, save only of his own soul, But each of us has been the Adam of his own soul."

2 Baruch lvi. 6, "For when he [Adam] transgressed, untimely death came into being."

It will be observed that in some of these passages, e.g. 2 Baruch liv. 15, 19, the spiritual consequences of Adam's Fall are in the main limited to Adam himself. Jewish thought was not agreed upon the question whether all men inherited from Adam a tendency to sin, or whether each man enjoyed freedom of choice and responsibility. Both views could be supported from St Paul's words, "Through the disobedience of the one the many were made sinners," "And so death passed unto all men, for that all sinned."

(d) The teaching of the Talmud is summed up by Weber: "Free will remained to man after the Fall. There is such a thing as transmission of guilt, but not a transmission of sin (*es gibt eine Erbschuld, aber keine Erbsünde*); the fall of Adam occasioned death to the whole race, but not sinfulness in the sense of a necessity to sin. Sin is the result of the decision of each individual; as experience shows it is universal, but in itself even after the Fall it was not absolutely necessary" (quoted by Thackeray, *ut supra*, p. 38). Compare the Midrash Bemidbar Rabba, chap. xiii.: "When Adam transgressed the command of the Holy One, and ate of the tree, the Holy One demanded of him penitence, thereby revealing to him the means of freedom (i.e. from the result of his sin), but Adam would not show penitence."

(*e*) Christian doctrine has been much influenced by the teaching of the Fall. But it is not too much to say that speculation upon Original Sin and the effects of the Fall of Adam has too often been carried into subtleties that have no warrant either in Holy Scripture or in reason. "Speaking broadly, the Greek view was simply that 'the original righteousness' of the race was lost; the effect of Adam's sin was a *privatio*, an impoverishment of human nature which left the power of the will unimpaired. But the Latin writers who followed Augustine took a darker view of the consequences of the Fall. It is for them a *depravatio naturae*; the human will is disabled; there is left a bias towards evil which can be conquered only by grace." (Bernard, art. *Fall*, D.B.)

According to St Augustine, Adam's sin was the abandonment of God, and his punishment was abandonment by God. Adam forfeited the *adjutorium* of grace. His will was no longer capable of good. In virtue of the "corporate personality" of Adam, all in Adam sinned voluntarily in him. All shared his guilt. This idea of the whole race being tainted with Adam's act of sin, rests partly upon the exaggerated emphasis laid upon the Roman legal phrase of "imputation," partly upon the mistranslation, "in quo," of St Paul's words ἐφ' ᾧ πάντες ἥμαρτον, as if it were "in whom all sinned," instead of "in that all sinned."

The Fathers very generally held that original righteousness, which combined natural innocence and the grace of God granted to Adam, was lost at the Fall: and that man, therefore, lost primaeval innocence and the Divine Spirit simultaneously.

(*f*) Thomas Aquinas went still further in the systematization of the doctrine. Mr Wheeler Robinson gives the following summary: "The immediate result of the Fall was the loss of man's original righteousness, that is, of the harmonious inter-relation of his nature, through the complete withdrawal of the gift of grace and the decrease of his inclination to virtue (I. b, Q. lxxxv. 1). The disorder of his nature, when uncontrolled by grace, shews itself materially in *concupiscentia* and formally in the want of original righteousness (I. b, Q. lxxxii. 3), these two elements constituting the 'original sin' which passed to Adam's descendants with the accompanying 'guilt' (I. b, lxxxi. 3)…. all men are one, through the common nature they receive from Adam. As in the individual the will moves the several members, so in the race the will of Adam moves those sprung from him" (I. b, lxxxi. 1). (*The Christian Doctrine of Man*, p. 206 f.)

The Council of Trent, *Sessio Quinta* §§ 2, 3, June 17, 1546, in the "Decree concerning Original Sin," laid down the following dogma: "If any one asserts that the prevarication of Adam injured himself alone, and not his posterity; and that the holiness and justice, received of God, which he lost, he lost for himself alone, and not for us also;

or that he, being defiled by the sin of disobedience, has only transfused death and pains of the body into the human race, but not sin also, which is the death of the soul; let him be anathema: whereas he contradicts the apostle who says: *By one man sin entered into the world, and by sin death, and so death passed upon all men, in whom* (in quo) *all have sinned*"..." this sin of Adam,—which in its origin is one, and being transfused into all by propagation, not by imitation, is in each one as his own...." (Schaff's *Creeds of the Gr. and Lat. Churches*, p. 85.)

(*g*) XXXIX Articles. "Original sin standeth not in the following of Adam (as the Pelagians do vainly talk), but it is the fault and corruption (*vitium et depravatio*) of the nature of every man, that naturally is engendered of the offspring of Adam, whereby man is very far gone (*quam longissime distet*) from original righteousness, and is of his own nature inclined to do evil, so that the flesh lusteth always contrary to the spirit, and therefore in every person born into this world, it deserveth God's wrath and damnation. And this infection (*depravatio*) of nature doth remain, yea in them that are regenerated (*in renatis*)...." (Art. ix. *Of original or Birth Sin.*)

"The condition of man after the fall of Adam (*post lapsum Adae*) is such that he cannot turn and prepare himself by his own natural strength and good works, to faith and calling upon God...." (Art. x. *Free Will.*)

For a valuable series of discussions, in which traditional Christian doctrine respecting "Original Sin" and the "Fall of Adam" is criticized, see *The Origin and Propagation of Sin* (1909), *The Sources of the Doctrines of the Fall and Original Sin* (1903), *The Concept of Sin* (1912) by the Rev. F. R. Tennant, D.D., B.Sc., Cambridge University Press.

The problem has very largely been modified by modern enquiry, both as regards the origin of the race and the character of the Scripture narrative. Christian doctrine is no longer fettered by the methods of the Schoolmen. Modern philosophy of religion, assisted by the newer studies of sociology, anthropology, and comparative religion, is beginning to revise our conceptions both of personality and of sin. It is inevitable, that, in the larger horizon which has opened up, the attempt should be made to restate Christian thought in reference to the nature of "sin," of "guilt," and of "personal freedom."

In conclusion, the following extract from Sanday and Headlam's Note on Rom. v. 12—21 (p. 146 f.) will repay the student's careful consideration:

"The tendency to sin is present in every man who is born into the world. But the tendency does not become actual sin until it takes effect in defiance of an express command, in deliberate disregard of a known distinction between right and wrong. How men came to be possessed of such a command, by what process they arrived at the conscious distinction of right and wrong, we can but vaguely speculate. Whatever it was, we may be sure that it could not have been presented to the imagination of primitive peoples otherwise than in such simple

And the man knew Eve his wife; and she conceived, 4 J

forms as the narrative assumes in the Book of Genesis. The really essential truths all come out in that narrative—the recognition of the Divine Will, the act of disobedience to the Will so recognised, the perpetuation of the tendency to such disobedience; and we may add perhaps, though here we get into a region of surmises, the connexion between moral evil and physical decay, for the surest pledge of immortality is the relation of the highest part of us, the soul, through righteousness to God. These salient principles, which may have been due in fact to a process of gradual accretion through long periods, are naturally and inevitably summed up as a group of single incidents. Their essential character is not altered, and in the interpretation of primitive beliefs we may safely remember that 'a thousand years in the sight of God are but as one day.' We who believe in Providence and who believe in the active influence of the Spirit of God upon man, may well also believe that the tentative gropings of the primaeval savage were assisted and guided and so led up to definite issues, to which he himself perhaps at the time could hardly give a name but which he learnt to call 'sin' and 'disobedience,' and the tendency to which later ages also saw to have been handed on from generation to generation in a way which we now describe as 'heredity.' It would be absurd to expect the language of modern science in the prophet who first incorporated the traditions of his race in the Sacred Books of the Hebrews. He uses the only kind of language available to his own intelligence and that of his contemporaries. But if the language which he does use is from that point of view abundantly justified, then the application which St Paul makes of it is equally justified. He, too, expresses truth through symbols, and in the days when men can dispense with symbols his teaching may be obsolete, but not before."

CH. IV. 1—16. THE NARRATIVE OF CAIN AND ABEL. (J.)

The vivid interest, which this section inspires, sometimes causes it to be forgotten that we have here the only tradition relating to the family life of Adam and Eve.

The narrative, as we have it, is evidently intended to describe the spread of sin, its hereditary character, and its issue in violent deeds and death. It is conceivable that J preserved other ancient narratives in which the Hebrew folk-lore recounted the sayings and doings of the first family and their descendants. They might have answered the questions which the gaps in the present narrative inevitably raise; e.g. what was the origin of sacrifice (*v.* 3)? why was Cain's sacrifice rejected (*v.* 5)? whose vengeance did Cain fear (*v.* 14)? did Cain confess his deed to his parents? who was Cain's wife (*v.* 17)? who lived in the city which Cain built (*v.* 17)? As it is, such questions are incapable of being answered, except by conjecture. Only such portions of the Hebrew folk-lore have been incorporated from the J source of narrative as seemed likely to serve the religious purpose of the book.

J and bare Cain, and said, I have ¹gotten a man with *the*

¹ Heb. *kanah*, to get.

Our curiosity remains unsatisfied. The narratives, more especially in the early part of Genesis, obviously make no claim to be regarded as complete. They are brief, disjointed, and fragmentary excerpts from Hebrew tradition, recording the popular belief respecting the infancy of the human race.

In its original setting, the narrative of Cain and Abel may have been intended to give an account of the first murder, and to supply the origin of blood-revenge. At any rate, the absence of any reference to Adam and Eve between *v.* 2 and *v.* 24 is very noticeable.

1, 2. The birth of Cain and Abel.
3—7. The sacrifices of Cain and Abel: Abel's accepted, Cain's rejected: Cain's anger; Jehovah's remonstrance.
8—15. Cain's murder of Abel: the curse of Jehovah: Cain's fear, and the sign of Jehovah for his protection.
16. Cain an exile.

1. *Cain...gotten*] Heb. *kanah*, to get. The word "Cain" does not mean "gotten"; but Eve's joyful utterance gives a popular etymology, which derived the proper name from the verb whose pronunciation it resembled. The word "Cain" (*Ḳayin*) means in Hebrew "a lance"; and by some the name is interpreted to mean "a smith." Its relation to Tubal-Cain "the artificer" is doubtful (see *v.* 24). That the name is to be identified with that of the nomad tribe of the "Kenites" (cf. Num. xxiv. 22, Judg. iv. 11) is a view which has been strongly maintained by some scholars. But the evidence seems to be very slight. The Kenites were not traditionally hostile to Israel, and did not play any important part in the history of the people so far as is known. The fact that the name appears in another form, "Kenan," in the genealogy (chap. v. 9—14) should warn us against hasty identifications. Pronunciation notoriously suffers through transmission, and spelling of proper names is wont to be adapted to the sound of more familiar words.

Eve gives her child its name as in *v.* 24. It has been pointed out that elsewhere, where the mother is mentioned in J and E, she gives the name, cf. xxix. 32—35, xxx. 1—24 (but see iv. 26, v. 29, xxv. 25); whereas, in P, the father gives the name, cf. xxi. 3. That the mother should name the child, has been considered to be a survival of a primitive "matriarchal" phase of society: see note on ii. 24. But the inference is very doubtful.

I have gotten a man with the LORD] Literally,"I acquired (or, have acquired) man, even Jahveh." Eve's four words in the Hebrew (*ḳānîthî îsh eth-Yahveh*) are as obscure as any oracle.

(i) The difficulty was felt at a very early time, and is reflected in the versions LXX διὰ τοῦ θεοῦ, Lat. *per Deum*, in which, as R.V., the particle *êth* is rendered as a preposition in the sense of "in conjunction with," and so "with the help of," "by the means of."

help of the LORD. And again she bare his brother Abel. 2 J

König, who holds an eminent position both as a commentator and as a Hebrew grammarian and lexicographer, has recently strongly defended the rendering of *êth* as a preposition meaning "with," in the sense here given by the English version "with the help of" (see *Z.A.T.W.* 1912, Pt I, pp. 22 ff.). The words will then express the thanksgiving of Eve on her safe deliverance of a child. It is a pledge of Divine favour. Child-birth has been "with the help of the LORD."

(ii) The Targum of Onkelos reads *mê-êth* = "from" (instead of *êth* = "with"), and so gets rid of the difficulty: "I have gotten a man from Jehovah," i.e. as a gift from the LORD. But this is so easy an alteration that it looks like a correction, and can scarcely be regarded as the original text. *Praestat lectio difficilior.*

(iii) According to the traditional Patristic and mediaeval interpretation, the sentence admitted of a literal rendering in a Messianic sense: "I have gotten a man, even Jehovah," i.e. "In the birth of a child I have gotten one in whom I foresee the Incarnation of the LORD." But, apart from the inadmissibility of this N.T. thought, it is surely impossible that the Messianic hope should thus be associated with the name of Cain. The Targum of Palestine, however, has "I have acquired a man, the Angel of the LORD."

(iv) Another direction of thought is given by the proposed alternative rendering: "I obtained as a husband (i.e. in my husband) Jehovah," in other words, I discern that in marriage is a Divine Gift. Perhaps the Targum of Palestine meant this, "I obtained as a husband the Angel of the LORD": my husband is the expression to me of the Divine good-will which I have received. The objection, however, to this interpretation is that it is the reverse of simple and natural. It makes Eve's words go back to marriage relations, instead of to the birth of her child.

(v) Conjectural emendations have been numerous, and ingenious. Thus, at one time, Gunkel conjectured *ethavveh* for *eth-Yahveh*, i.e. "I have gotten a son that I longed for"; the unusual word *ethavveh* accounted, in his opinion, for the easier reading *eth-Yahveh*. But in his last edition (1908) the conjecture does not appear.

2. *Abel*] Heb. *Hebel* = "breath," or "vapour," a name suggestive of fleeting life, cf. Job vii. 16. No better explanation of the name is given. Assyriologists have suggested that the name reproduces the Assyrian *aplu* = "a son." But it is doubtful whether the resemblance is anything more than accidental. At any rate, no Babylonian version of this narrative has yet come to light. More probable is the suggestion that "Hebel" might represent a form of "Jabal," as the keeper of sheep (cf. *v.* 20). As in the case of Cain (see above), the original form and significance of proper names preserved in primitive folk-lore must be extremely uncertain. In the course of the transmission and repetition of the narrative, less known names would continually be altered to forms which would suggest familiar ideas.

J   And Abel was a keeper of sheep, but Cain was a tiller of
3 the ground. And in process of time it came to pass, that
Cain brought of the fruit of the ground an offering unto the
4 LORD. And Abel, he also brought of the firstlings of his
flock and of the fat thereof. And the LORD had respect
5 unto Abel and to his offering: but unto Cain and to his

keeper of sheep] Abel is here mentioned first, as the representative of pastoral life. Cain follows the agricultural life, which was commanded for Adam in iii. 17, 23. The calling of Abel is one for which the Israelites had a special fondness. The metaphors taken from the shepherd and the sheep are among the most frequent and the most striking in Holy Scripture.

3. *in process of time*] Lit. "at the end of days," a phrase for a period of quite indefinite length; LXX μεθ' ἡμέρας; Lat. *post multos dies*.

of the fruit of the ground] Probably the best, or the earliest, of the fruit, corresponding to the "firstlings" in Abel's offering. Cf. Num. xviii. 12, "All the best (Heb. *fat*) of the oil, and all the best (Heb. *fat*) of the vintage, and of the corn."

an offering] Heb. *minhah*, lit. a "gift" or a "present," as in xxxii. 13, when Jacob sends "a *present* for Esau his brother," and in xliii. 11, where he says unto his sons, "carry the man down a *present*." The word is used especially for "a gift" made to God; and with that sense, especially in P and Ezek., of the "meal offering," cf. Lev. ii., vi. 7—10. Here it is used of "offerings to God" generally, both of animals and of the fruits of the earth.

This is the first mention of sacrifice in Scripture. Its origin is not explained, nor is an altar mentioned. Man is assumed to be by nature endowed with religious instincts, and capable of holding converse with God. Worship was man's mode of approach to the Deity; and sacrifice was its outward expression. The purpose of the offering was (1) propitiatory, to win favour, or to avert displeasure; and (2) eucharistic, in expression of gratitude for blessings on home or industry. It was deemed wrong to approach God with empty hands, that is, without an offering or gift, Ex. xxiii. 15, xxv. 30.

4. *the firstlings*] i.e. "the firstborn," regarded as the best and choicest, cf. Ex. xxxiv. 19; Num. xviii. 17; Prov. iii. 9.

the fat] i.e. the fatty portions, which were regarded as choicest for the purpose of a banquet (cf. 1 Sam. ii. 16), or for burning in sacrifice, Is. i. 11, "the fat of fed beasts."

had respect unto] i.e. looked with favour upon. In the two passages which it is natural to quote in illustration of this expression, Num. xvi. 15, "Respect not thou their offering," and Amos v. 22, "Neither will I regard the peace-offerings," the Hebrew has a different verb, but the Latin renders, as here, by *respicere*.

How the favourable regard was expressed we are not told. See note on the next verse.

offering he had not respect. And Cain was very wroth, J

5. *but unto Cain*] In what way the Divine displeasure was conveyed is not recorded. The suggestion that fire from heaven consumed the offering of Abel, but left that of Cain untouched, is a pure conjecture based upon the group of passages in the O.T., in which the fire from God attested the approval of the sacrifice, Lev. ix. 24; Judg. vi. 21, xiii. 19, 20; 1 Kings xviii. 38; 1 Chr. xxi. 26; 2 Chr. vii. 1; 2 Macc. ii. 10, 11.

It is a serious omission, also, that we are left to conjecture the reason for the favour shewn to Abel and withheld from Cain. We can hardly doubt, that in the original form of the story the reason was stated; and, if so, that the reason represented in the folk-lore of Israel would not have been in harmony with the religious teaching of the book.

Taking, therefore, the omission of the reason in conjunction with the language of *vv.* 6, 7, and with the general religious purport of the context, we should probably be right in inferring that the passage, as it stands, intends to ascribe the difference in the acceptability of the two offerings to the difference in the spirit with which they had been made. Jehovah looked at the heart (cf. 1 Sam. xvi. 7). Thus the first mention of worship in Holy Scripture seems to emphasize the fundamental truth that the worth of worship lies in the spirit of the worshipper, cf. John iv. 24, "God is spirit; and they that worship him must worship in spirit and truth." This is the thought of Heb. xi. 4, "By faith Abel offered unto God a more excellent sacrifice than Cain....God bearing witness in respect of his gifts."

The following conjectures have at different times been put forward to explain the preference of Jehovah:

(*a*) It has been suggested that Abel's offering was preferred, because it consisted of flesh, and that Cain's was rejected, because it consisted of vegetable produce. Each man offered of the fruits of his work and calling. Did the original story contain a condemnation of the agricultural as compared with the pastoral calling? But Adam was commanded to till the ground (ii. 15, iii. 19).

(*b*) The old Jewish explanation was that Cain had failed to perform the proper ritual of his offering, and therefore incurred the Divine displeasure: see note on the LXX of *v.* 7. But, again, if so, it has to be assumed that Divine directions upon the ritual of service had previously been communicated to man.

(*c*) The common Christian explanation that Cain's sacrifice, being "without shedding of blood" (Heb. ix. 22, cf. Lev. xvii. 11), could not find acceptance, equally assumes that the right kind of sacrifice had previously been Divinely instituted, and that Cain's rejection was, therefore, due to the wilful violation of a positive command as well as to the infringement of sacrificial rule.

In the silence of the narrative respecting the origin of the institution of sacrifice, these conjectures are merely guess-work, and must be considered more or less fanciful.

GENESIS IV. 5—7

J 6 and his countenance fell. And the LORD said unto Cain, Why art thou wroth? and why is thy countenance fallen? 7 If thou doest well, [1]shalt thou not be accepted? and if thou doest not well, sin coucheth at the door: and unto thee

---

[1] Or, *shall it not be lifted up?*

his countenance fell] A picture true to nature and more familiar than easy to express in any other words.

The passage illustrates the progress of sin in Cain's heart. Firstly, disappointment and wounded pride, aggravated by envy of his brother, lead to anger; secondly, anger unrestrained, and brooding sullenly over an imaginary wrong, rouses the spirit of revenge; thirdly, revenge seeks an outlet in passion, and vents itself in violence and murder.

6. *And the LORD said*, &c.] Whether Jehovah appeared in a visible form, or spoke to Cain in a dream or vision, is not recorded. The importance of the interrogation lies in the fact, that Jehovah mercifully intervenes to arrest the progress of evil thoughts, by simple words demanding self-examination.

7. *If thou doest well*, &c.] A verse well known for its difficulties. The rendering in the marg. "shall it not be lifted up?" should be followed. Literally the first clause runs thus: "Is there not, if thou doest well, to lift up?" The infinitive "to lift up" must be taken as an infinitival substantive = "a lifting up," with reference, in all probability, to the previous phrase, "the falling" of Cain's countenance. The meaning then is, "If thou doest well, and makest thy offering with a pure and right motive, thy face, instead of falling, shall be lifted up in happiness." This, on the whole, seems better than the alternative rendering "is there not forgiveness?" The word "to lift up" admits of the meaning "to forgive," but is hardly likely to be used in this sense without an object, and before any mention of sin has been made.

sin coucheth] The meaning is, "and, if thou doest not well and cherishest evil in thy heart, then, remember, sin, like a savage wild beast, is lying in ambush ready to spring out upon you."

"Sin" is here mentioned for the first time. *Hattâ'th* has a varied significance, and might here mean either "guilt," or "punishment," or "the active principle of sin." And in view of the personification in the next clause, this last meaning is here to be preferred.

The Hebrew text of *v.* 7 is probably corrupt.

The LXX took the first clause to refer to a ritual inaccuracy in sacrifice, and mistranslated the words "sin coucheth," failing to perceive the metaphor: οὐκ, ἐὰν ὀρθῶς προσενέγκῃς, ὀρθῶς δὲ μὴ διέλῃς, ἥμαρτες; ἡσύχασον. "If thou madest thine offering rightly, but didst not rightly divide it, didst thou not sin? hold thy peace." In other words: "you broke the ritual rules of offering; you have no right to complain."

The Latin reads: *Nonne, si bene egeris, recipies? sin autem male,*

¹shall be his desire, and thou shalt rule over him. And 8 J
Cain ²told Abel his brother. And it came to pass, when

¹ Or, *is its desire, but thou shouldest rule over it*   ² Heb. *said unto*. Many ancient authorities have, *said unto Abel his brother, Let us go into the field.*

statim in foribus peccatum aderit; sed sub te erit appetitus ejus, et tu dominaberis illius.

shall be his desire, &c.] Better, as marg., "is its desire, but thou shouldest rule over it." Evil, like a savage animal, is ravening for thee; but thou hast strength, if thou hast the will, to overcome it. The alternative rendering of the text, "his desire...over him," introduces the idea of one brother's authority over the other, which seems foreign to the context.

The metaphor of sin as a wild beast ready at any moment to spring upon, and get the mastery of, the man who will not make the effort to do what he knows to be right, embodies deep spiritual truth. The evil passions, always ready to take advantage of the will that refuses to hear the voice of the better self, have often in literature been likened to a wild beast, cf. Tennyson's *In Memoriam*, Canto 118:

" Arise and fly
The reeling Faun, the sensual feast;
Move upward, working out the beast,
And let the ape and tiger die";

and George Meredith's expression: "The unfailing, aboriginal, democratic, old monster, that waits to pull us down" (*Diana of the Crossways*, p. 14, edit. 1892).

his desire...rule over] The phrase is identical with that in iii. 16, but obviously the words have a different signification suitable to the context. That these words should refer to the younger brother is the interpretation of the text (R.V.), to which no exception can be taken on lexical or grammatical grounds. But the relation of a younger to an elder brother is not that which is likely to be described in this way. It is better to refer the phrase to the personification of sin, over which Cain can, if he will, obtain the mastery.

8. *told*] Heb. *said unto*, which is the only possible meaning of the original. The rendering "told" implies that Cain repeated to Abel, his brother, the words spoken to him by Jehovah. But this is not the meaning of the original, which is, "Cain said unto Abel his brother"; some words, which are wanting in the Hebrew text, either having been intentionally omitted by the compiler, or accidentally dropped by carelessness in transcription. As the R.V. margin states, "many ancient authorities [Sam., LXX, Syr. Pesh., and Ps. Jon.] read *said unto Abel his brother, Let us go into the field*"; LXX, διέλθωμεν εἰς τὸ πεδίον; Lat. *egrediamur foras*. This addition has all the appearance of an insertion, supplied to fill up an obvious gap, and borrowed from the next verse. Gunkel proposes to read, instead of

J they were in the field, that Cain rose up against Abel his
9 brother, and slew him. And the LORD said unto Cain,
Where is Abel thy brother? And he said, I know not: am
10 I my brother's keeper? And he said, What hast thou done?
the voice of thy brother's blood crieth unto me from the

"and said" (*vayyômer*), "and was bitter" (*vayyêmer*), i.e. "and made a quarrel." Here, as in the preceding verse, we have probably an instance of a very early disturbance of the text.

Possibly, the words spoken by Cain to his brother Abel contained some allusion which seemed wanting in the right spirit towards the faith and worship of the God of Israel, and were omitted without other words being substituted.

the field] i.e. having left the sacred place, shrine or altar, where they had offered their sacrifices. An allusion to such a spot might well have been omitted as unsuitable.

rose up] preliminary to assault: see Judg. viii. 21; 2 Sam. ii. 14; 2 Kings iii. 24.

9. *And the LORD said*, &c.] The condensed narrative does not say whether Cain tried to conceal the body of Abel, or had fled at once from the spot. Apparently Jehovah speaks to him suddenly, when at a distance from the scene of the murder. The process of interrogation may be compared with that in iii. 9—13.

I know not: am I my brother's keeper?] Cain's reply consists of (*a*) a statement which is a falsehood; and (*b*) a question which is defiance. "Keeper," perhaps with reference, in a mocking tone, to Abel's occupation as a keeper of sheep. "Am I the keeper's keeper?"

The first words of the first murderer renounce the obligations of brotherhood. The rejection of the family bond is the negation of love; it is the spirit of murder; cf. 1 John iii. 12, 15.

10. *What hast thou done?*] The same question as that put to Eve (iii. 13). This question has been put by the voice of conscience to every murderer since Cain; it had a special force in reference to the first man done to death by his brother.

the voice of thy brother's blood] Probably it would be more accurate to translate, as Driver, "Hark! thy brother's blood, &c." The word "blood" in the Hebrew is plural, and the word "crieth" is in the plural agreeing with it. The Hebrew for "voice" (*kôl*) should similarly be rendered "Hark!," instead of "noise," in Isa. xiii. 4, and instead of "the voice of," in Isa. lii. 8; see Heb. Lexicon.

The Hebrew idea was that blood shed, for which there was no avenger, cried to Jehovah for vengeance against the murderer. Jehovah has learned of Abel's murder from the cry of his blood spilt upon the ground. Another Hebrew belief was that, if only the blood were covered with earth, it would be silent. Cf. Job xvi. 18, "Oh! earth, cover not thou my blood and let my cry have no resting-place";

ground. And now cursed art thou from the ground, which 11 J
hath opened her mouth to receive thy brother's blood from
thy hand; when thou tillest the ground, it shall not hence- 12
forth yield unto thee her strength; a fugitive and a wanderer

Isa. xxvi. 21, "The earth also shall disclose her blood, and shall no more cover her slain"; Ezek. xxiv. 7. To this ancient supposition there is an allusion in Heb. xii. 24, "the blood of sprinkling that speaketh better than that of Abel."

"In the picturesque legend of the Arabs, there rose from the blood (or bones) of the slain man the 'death-owl,' which shrieked, 'Give me to drink,' until it was appeased by the blood of vengeance." (Gordon's *Early Traditions of Genesis*, p. 203.)

11. *from the ground*] The meaning is not quite obvious. Probably, we should not understand, that the curse is to come from the ground upon Cain, but that Cain is driven by Jehovah's curse from the ground. The emphasis is on "the ground" (*hâ-adâmâh*). It is the *ground* which Cain tilled, the *ground* whose fruits he offered, and the *ground* which he has caused to drink human blood. From this *ground* he is now driven by a curse. For pollution of the land by bloodshed cf. Num. xxxv. 33, "So ye shall not pollute the land wherein ye are: for blood, it polluteth the land: and no expiation can be made for the land, for the blood that is shed therein, but by the blood of him that shed it."

On blood-revenge, cf. Robertson Smith, *Kinship and Marriage*, pp. 25—27.

12. *when thou tillest*, &c.] The meaning is, that when, or if, after this curse, Cain continues to till the ground, the ground will refuse to give a return for his labour. Therefore, he will not be able to live on the cultivated ground. He must leave it and wander forth.

her strength] That is, "her fruits." So the Vulg. "fructus suos." The word "strength" is used in this sense for the produce of the soil in Job xxxi. 39, "If I have eaten the fruits (marg. Heb. *strength*) thereof (i.e. of the land) without money."

a fugitive and a wanderer] The alliteration of the two words in the original (*n‘â vâ-nâd*) is difficult to reproduce in English. The word for "a fugitive" means "one who staggers, or reels," from weakness, faintness, or weariness.

"Weary and wandering," or "staggering and straying" would be attempts at reproducing the original. The LXX στένων καὶ τρέμων = "groaning and trembling," is more of a comment than a translation; and the Lat. "vagus et profugus," like the English version, is inexact.

Two points are to be noticed in this sentence upon Cain:

(1) He is sent forth from the cultivated soil: in other words, he is banished into the desert. He is to lead the life, neither of the shepherd, nor of the tiller of the soil, but of the roaming Bedouin of the desert.

(2) His wandering is not the result of a guilty conscience, but of a

J 13 shalt thou be in the earth. And Cain said unto the LORD,
14 ¹My punishment is greater ²than I can bear. Behold, thou
hast driven me out this day from the face of the ground;
and from thy face shall I be hid; and I shall be a fugitive
and a wanderer in the earth; and it shall come to pass,
15 that whosoever findeth me shall slay me. And the LORD

¹ Or, *Mine iniquity* ² Or, *than can be forgiven*

Divine sentence. It is his penalty to lead the nomad life of the desert, homeless and insecure and restless. Whereas Adam was banished from the garden to till the soil (iii. 17), now that soil is to refuse its fruits to Cain, and he must fly into the desert.

13. *And Cain said*] The bitter cry of Cain is not that of repentance for his sin, but of entreaty for the mitigation of his doom.

My punishment] Better than marg. *mine iniquity*. The Hebrew word is used to denote both guilt and its penalty, and consequently is sometimes ambiguous, e.g. 1 Sam. xxviii. 10, "And Saul sware to her by the LORD, saying, As the LORD liveth, there shall be no punishment happen to thee (marg. *guilt come upon thee*) for this thing." In our verse the rendering "punishment" is to be preferred. Cain in *v.* 14 is thinking of his sentence, not of his sin.

than I can bear] The rendering of the margin, *than can be forgiven*, which is that of the versions, though possible, is not to be preferred. It has sometimes been advocated on the ground that the "iniquity" of Cain was typical of the sin "that is unto death" (1 John v. 16), and that cannot be forgiven (St Mark iii. 29). LXX μείζων ἡ αἰτία μου τοῦ ἀφεθῆναί με. Lat. *major est iniquitas mea quam ut veniam merear*. Similarly Targum of Onkelos: cf. Ps. xxxviii. 4, "As an heavy burden, they [mine iniquities] are too heavy for me."

14. *Behold, thou hast*, &c.] Cain accepts Jehovah's sentence as a banishment from the cultivated ground. "And from thy face shall I be hid," Cain recognizes that banishment from the land, in which Jehovah's presence was manifested, implied expulsion from Jehovah's presence. In the desert to which he was to flee, Jehovah would not be found: Cain would be hidden from His face. The early Israelites believed that, if a man was driven from the land in which Jehovah was worshipped, he was no longer in the presence of Jehovah, but of other gods. Thus David says, 1 Sam. xxvi. 19, "they have driven me out this day that I should not cleave unto the inheritance of the LORD, saying, Go, serve other gods." The desert to which Cain would be driven was a region believed to be haunted by the demon Azazel (Lev. xvi. 8) and dangerous spirits.

whosoever findeth me, &c.] Of whom was Cain afraid? Different answers have been given. 1. The wild beasts (Josephus). 2. A pre-Adamite race of man. 3. Other sons of Adam. 4. It has been suggested that the present story formed part of a tradition originally referring to a later time, when the earth was numerously inhabited,

said unto him, Therefore whosoever slayeth Cain, vengeance J
shall be taken on him sevenfold. And the LORD appointed
a sign for Cain, lest any finding him should smite him.

and has been adapted, on account of its moral significance, to the story of the first family. But it is unreasonable to expect from the detached narratives of early folk-lore the logical completeness of history. Cain's words are rightly understood as a reference to the custom of blood-revenge, which went back to the remotest prehistoric age. The cultivated land was regarded as the region in which there prevailed social order and regard for life; but in the desert there would be none of the restrictions which regulated the existence of settled communities.

In the desert Cain, as the murderer, would be destitute of the protection of Jehovah. He would have no rights of kinship: anyone might slay him with impunity. He would find no friendly tribe; he would be an outlaw.

15. *Therefore*] i.e. on account of Cain's entreaty, Jehovah's mercy is shewn to the first murderer. Cain has no friend: Jehovah, by an act of benevolence and authority, will protect him, and undertake his cause even in the desert.

A slight variation in text accounts for LXX οὐχ οὕτως, Lat. *Nequaquam ita fiet*.

vengeance...sevenfold] i.e. if Cain were killed, seven deaths would be exacted in retaliation; the murderer and six of his family would forfeit their lives, cf. 2 Sam. xxi. 8. The words of Jehovah are noticeable, because (1) they emphasize the corporate responsibility of family life, which so often meets us in the O.T.; and (2) they recognize, but regulate, blood-revenge, as a disciplinary primaeval custom of Semitic life. This Oriental custom, while recognized in the O.T. as part of Israelite institutions, is continually being restricted by the operation of the spirit of love, gradually revealed by prophet and by law, in the religion of Jehovah.

the LORD appointed a sign for Cain] The popular expression "the brand of Cain," in the sense of "the sign of a murderer," arises from a complete misunderstanding of this passage. The object of the sign was to protect Cain. It was a warning that should prevent the avenger of blood from slaying him. Even in the desert Jehovah would be Cain's champion. We have no means of knowing what the sign was. The words imply that some visible mark, or badge, was set upon Cain's person. If so, it may have some analogy to the totem mark of savage tribes. "There seems little doubt, that the sign which Jahveh gave to Cain...was a tattoo mark, probably on his forehead (cf. Ezek. ix. 4, 6), to show all men that Cain was under His protection, and thus to save his life. In all probability the mark was the 'sign of Jahveh,' the *tav* (Ezek. ix. 4, 6)—which was once doubtless worn quite openly by His devotees, and only afterwards degenerated into a superstition." (Gordon, *Early Traditions of Genesis*, p. 211.)

J 16 And Cain went out from the presence of the LORD, and
17 dwelt in the land of ¹Nod, ²on the east of Eden. And
Cain knew his wife; and she conceived, and bare Enoch:
and he builded a city, and called the name of the city, after

¹ That is, *Wandering*.   ² Or, *in front of*

16. *from the presence of*] Cf. 14, "from thy face." Cain going out "from the presence of" Jehovah, quits the land in which that presence was revealed. Jonah in fleeing from Palestine fled "from the presence of the LORD" (Jonah i. 3).

in the land of Nod] That is, *Wandering*, cf. the word "wanderer" (*nâd*) in *vv*. 12 and 14. This region cannot be identified; it serves as a vague designation for all the country in the unknown East, which was thought to be inhabited only by nomads.

on the east of] This rendering, like the Lat. *ad orientalem plagam*, is preferable to that of the marg. *in front of* (LXX κατέναντι). See notes on ii. 14 and iii. 24.

17—24. THE DESCENDANTS OF CAIN: THE GENEALOGY OF THE CAINITES. (J.)

See the Special Note on "the Antediluvian Patriarchs," pp. 88 ff. The traditions preserved in this section probably belong to a different J source from that of the verses immediately preceding. This will explain how it is that Cain, who has just been condemned to a nomad life and has withdrawn into the land of "Wandering" (Nod), is in *v.* 17 described as the founder of a city, and as the ancestor of men who originated the industries and callings of civilization.

17. *his wife*] On the question, Who was Cain's wife? see note at the beginning of the chapter. If the narrative be homogeneous, she must have been either a daughter of Eve, or of a family of whose contemporaneous origin and existence this narrative in Genesis gives no account. But the compilation of our primitive story from different sources necessarily leaves many questions unanswered. No attempt is made to remove this and similar obvious inconsistencies.

Enoch] Heb. *Ḥănôkh* = "dedication": the same name occurs in *v.* 18; see note. It is also the name of a Midianite clan, xxv. 4; 1 Chron. i. 33; and of a Reubenite clan, xlvi. 9; Ex. vi. 14.

builded a city] It seems strange that we should have the mention of a city at a time when the inhabitants of the world were so few. But the purpose of this section is evidently to trace back to the Cainites, in the antediluvian period, the origin of early institutions. To the Hebrew the "city," that is to say, a town community, represented the nucleus of civilized life, and hence the building of a city is ascribed to the father of the line from which emanated the various callings of civilization. It is needless to say that this tradition is devoid of scientific value for any

the name of his son, Enoch. And unto Enoch was born 18 J
Irad: and Irad begat Mehujael: and Mehujael begat
Methushael: and Methushael begat Lamech. And Lamech 19
took unto him two wives: the name of the one was Adah, and
the name of the other Zillah. And Adah bare Jabal: he 20

enquiry into the progress of civilization in prehistoric times. Its interest lies in the record of the belief, that urban life could be dated back into the most primitive age. The site of the city is not indicated.

18. *And unto Enoch*, &c.] The genealogy of Cain is a framework of names, each of which may have been connected with traditions that either had been forgotten, or were not deemed suitable for preservation in this context. It is a mistake, into which some commentators have been betrayed, to endeavour to extract meanings from the proper names of the antediluvian patriarchs. It is very doubtful, whether the original names would have conveyed the same thoughts which their later Hebraized pronunciation has suggested to devout, but fanciful, imagination. The facts of history are not to be spelt out from the obscure etymology of primaeval proper names. These well-meaning endeavours have sometimes been based on the assumption that Hebrew was the original language.

The most that can be said is that these names preserve the recollection of legendary persons, and that they have received a Hebraized form which rendered them easier of pronunciation and facilitated a symbolical interpretation.

Irad] The name occurs in 1 Chron. iv. 18; see note on Jared, v. 16.

Mehujael] Cf. Mahalalel, v. 12. If a Hebrew word, it may mean "blotted out by God." Cf. vi. 7, where "destroy" is in the marg. *blot out*.

The LXX Μαιηλ must have read *Mahyiel* = "God maketh me to live."

Methushael] Cf. Methuselah, v. 21. Assyriologists say that the name means "Man of God," and is the same as *Mutu-sha-ili*.

19. *Lamech*] The seventh of the Cainite line has three sons, as Noah, the tenth of the Sethite line, has three sons.

two wives] Lamech is the first recorded instance of polygamy. The custom, prevalent in patriarchal times and in the days of the kings (e.g. David, Solomon), was recognized in the Law of the Pentateuch and placed under restrictions, Deut. xxi. 13—30, Levit. xviii. 6—20.

On the ideal of monogamy, from which Israel fell far short, see note on ii. 24. Lamech, the Cainite, is its first transgressor.

Adah] The name appears in xxxvi. 2 as that of one of Esau's wives. If of Hebrew origin, possibly connected with the word meaning "adornment," but also possibly derived from a root = "brightness," found in Arabic and Assyrian, and, if so, may mean "the dawn."

Zillah] Probably from the Heb. *ṣēl* = "shade" or "shadows,"

GENESIS IV. 20—23

J was the father of such as dwell in tents and *have* cattle.
21 And his brother's name was Jubal: he was the father of all
22 such as handle the harp and pipe. And Zillah, she also
bare Tubal-cain, ¹the forger of every cutting instrument of
²brass and iron: and the sister of Tubal-cain was Naamah.
23 And Lamech said unto his wives:

¹ Or, *an instructor of every artificer*   ² Or, *copper* and so elsewhere.

implying "comfort" and "coolness" in the glare of a day in the desert.

20. *Jabal*] The meaning of this name is doubtful. Dillmann conjectures "a wanderer." Jabal, like Abel (see note on *v.* 2), is a founder of the shepherd's and herdsman's life.

father of] i.e. the founder, or originator, of nomad life. To the Hebrews, to live in tents was the alternative to life in the village or the town. It is strange to find that tent life is here placed later than the building of a town (*v.* 17).

such as dwell in tents, &c.] Literally, "such as dwell in tents and cattle"; i.e. those who wander about, occupied in the care of flocks and herds, and pitching their camps at different places. The eldest brother represents the Bedouin chieftain, the second brother represents the arts of primitive pastoral life, the third brother represents the most necessary industry.

21. *Jubal*] The originator of musical instruments. Music is thus regarded as the most ancient art. For the name, compare the word "Jubilee"; *yôbêl* is "the ram's horn."

harp and pipe] i.e. the simplest of stringed and wind instruments used by shepherds. LXX ψαλτήριον καὶ κιθάραν: Lat. *cithara et organo*.

22. *Tubal-cain*] The double name is strange, and presumably means "Tubal of the family of Cain." Tubal is traditionally supposed to have given his name to the people mentioned in x. 2 (see note). "Tubal" in Ezek. xxvii. 13, xxxii. 26, xxxviii. 2, xxxix. 1 is associated with Javan and Meshech as a community whose traffic included "vessels of brass." The Assyrian inscriptions record a people called "Tabal," apparently living to the S.E. of the Black Sea.

the forger] Heb. "the sharpener." The expression is intended to denote the first smelter of metals. LXX τὸν Θόβελ, καὶ ἦν σφυροκόπος χαλκεὺς χαλκοῦ καὶ σιδήρου. Lat. *Tubalcain qui fuit malleator et faber in cuncta opera aeris et ferri*.

The R.V. marg.=A.V. "an instructor of every artificer," is a conjectural rendering of an obscure passage, and does not follow the original.

22. *brass*] Better than *copper*. The metal, like the Gr. χαλκός, was probably our "bronze," for which "brass" was the equivalent in all early English literature. "Brass" is an alloy of copper and zinc;

GENESIS IV. 23

Adah and Zillah, hear my voice;   J
Ye wives of Lamech, hearken unto my speech :
For [1] I have slain a man [2] for wounding me,

[1] Or, *I will slay*
[2] Or, *to my wounding, and a young man to my hurt*

"bronze" of copper and tin. Copper-mining (not "brass") is referred to in Deut. viii. 9; Job xxviii. 2. Our English word "bronze" is derived from "Brundusium."

It should be noticed here (1) that Hebrew tradition realizes how important an epoch in the progress of civilization is marked by the discovery of the use of metals; (2) that in this verse the mention of bronze precedes that of iron; (3) that no knowledge is shewn of a stone age, which archaeology has demonstrated to have preceded.

Naamah] meaning "pleasant." The mention of her name, concerning whom nothing else is recorded, implies the existence of legends or traditions which have disappeared. Perhaps she symbolized luxury, as Jubal symbolized art and Tubal-Cain industry. The juxtaposition of Naamah and Tubal-Cain reminds us of Venus and Vulcan, more especially as Naamah is said to have been the Phoenician title of the Semitic goddess Istar. It is the name borne by the mother of Rehoboam, an Ammonitess (1 Kings xiv. 31).

23, 24. The Song of the Sword. These verses are written in a poetical style, with the parallelism of clauses characteristic of Hebrew poetry. It is the first instance of Hebrew poetical composition in the Bible[1]. It contains (1) the address of Lamech to his wives; (2) the announcement of a recent exploit; (3) the boast of confidence and security against injury or insult. It is generally supposed that Lamech's Song is intended to represent his exultation after the invention of metal weapons by his son Tubal-Cain. The new possession inspired primitive man with confidence and eagerness for savage retaliation.

The substance of line (or *stichos*) 1 is repeated in line (or *stichos*) 2: "Adah and Zillah" correspond to "Ye wives of Lamech," and "Hear my voice" to "Hearken unto my speech."

In line (or *stichos*) 3, the word "I have slain" gives the note to the whole distich; but "a man for wounding me" is repeated in greater detail in line (or *stichos*) 4, "a young man for bruising me." Line (or *stichos*) 5 mentions the traditional vengeance promised for Cain; line (or *stichos*) 6 boasts of a vengeance tenfold greater than this for Lamech.

23. *a man for wounding me*] Lamech boasts that he has slain a man who had wounded him and a young man who had bruised him. Whether "a man" and "a young man" are the same person, or whether they mean a man and his son, cannot be decided. Lamech has exacted the vengeance of death for the insult of a blow[2].

It is, however, possible that the poem only describes an imaginary

[1] See G. Adam Smith's *Early Poetry of Israel*, p. 21 (Schweich Lectures, 1910).
[2] See for an explanation by Jewish tradition Appendix B.

J   And a young man for bruising me:
24   If Cain shall be avenged sevenfold,
            Truly Lamech seventy and sevenfold.
25 And Adam knew his wife again; and she bare a son, and called his name [1]Seth: For, *said she*, God [2]hath appointed
26 me another seed instead of Abel; for Cain slew him. And to Seth, to him also there was born a son; and he called

       [1] Heb. *Sheth*.   [2] Heb. *shath*.

instance in which Lamech had retaliated in self-defence, and boasts that with the assistance of metal weapons Lamech's capacity for revenge is increased elevenfold.

24. *seventy and sevenfold*] Cf. *v.* 15. Lamech boasts that seventy and seven deaths should be the penalty of revenge if he were slain.

The first note of warfare is sounded in this fierce exultation in a deed which has exceeded the limits of self-defence and passed into the region of the blood-feud. The possession of new weapons and the lust of revenge are here recorded as the typical elements of the war spirit. "Although, technically, the law of Vengeance was satisfied by a 'life for a life,' yet in practice the avenging of blood was often carried to the utmost length of ruthless ferocity. For one life many were taken, the murderer and his kinsfolk together." (Gordon, *Early Traditions of Genesis*, p. 204.)

25, 26. THE LINE OF SETH.

These two verses begin the line of Seth which is parallel to that of Cain. The more complete genealogy, found in ch. v., comes from a different source (P). But it is not unlikely that they are derived from the same materials as the previous section.

25. *called his name*] Here, as in *v.* 1 (see note), the mother gives the name.

God] Elohim (not Jehovah, as in *v.* 1), probably because of *v.* 26.

hath appointed] Heb. *shath*. As was pointed out in the note on *v.* 1, the resemblance to a Hebrew word in the sound of a proper name does not supply its strict etymology. The name "Seth" (*shêth*) = "setting" or "slip," resembles in sound the Hebrew verb for "appointed" or "set" (*shâth*), and it is to this assonance that Eve's words refer.

It is an instance of a play on a word, viz. paronomasia, of which there are many cases in the O.T. But assonance is a delusive element in etymology.

another seed] We are not to infer that no other children were born to Eve, but that Seth was "appointed" to take the place of Abel, and his seed to form a righteous counterpart to the unholy seed of Cain. In Ecclus. xlix. 16 Seth is united with Shem as "glorified among men."

his name Enosh: then began men to call upon the name of   J
the LORD.

This is the book of the generations of Adam. In the 5   P

26. *Enosh*] This word, used in Hebrew poetry, means "man," and is thus to be compared with Adam.

then began men] In the Hebrew it is impersonal, "then was a beginning made." The origin of Jehovah worship is here connected with the line of Seth, and is probably intended to be contrasted with the origin of secular callings in the line of Cain.

to call upon] "Properly, as always, *to call with*, i.e. to use the name in invocations, in the manner of ancient cults, especially at times of sacrifice; cf. xii. 8, xiii. 4, xxi. 33, xxvi. 25." (Driver.)

the name of the LORD] i.e. the name of Jehovah. This statement by J, who uses this title by preference, is in conflict with the statement that the name was first revealed to Moses (E), (P), Ex. iii. 14, vi. 2. But in view not only of this text, but also of recent cuneiform decipherments, shewing the probability that a form of the name was known in Babylonia before the time of Moses, it is not unreasonable to suppose that the name belongs, as the tradition of J evidently taught, to prehistoric antiquity.

CH. V. THE DESCENDANTS OF SETH. (P.)

On the Cainites and Sethites, see note at the close of the chapter. In iv. 25, 26 a commencement was made of the Sethite genealogy taken from J. In ch. v. a fresh start is made, and the line of Seth is traced from Adam to Noah. The genealogy is taken from a different source, which is clearly P. (*a*) The contents of *vv*. 1—3 refer back to i. 26—28; (*b*) the "generations" (*tôl'dôth*) of *v*. 1 is the expression employed by P as the superscription of successive sections in his narrative (see note on ii. 4); (*c*) the name Seth in *v*. 3 is given by Adam; according to J (iv. 25) it was given by Eve; (*d*) the formal and systematic description of the patriarchs, consisting of (1) their names, (2) their age at the birth of their firstborn, (3) the length of their life, corresponds with the characteristics of P's literary style and his fondness for statistics. With the exception of *v*. 29, the whole of the chapter may be regarded as the writing of P and the continuation of i. 1 to ii. 4ª.

1. *This is the book*, &c.] The word rendered "book" (Heb. *sêpher*) is used of any written document. Our word "book" gives rather too much the meaning of a piece of literature. The word is often used in a much more general sense, e.g. Isa. l. 1, "where is the bill (Heb. *sêpher*) of your mother's divorcement?" Jer. xxxii. 10, "and I subscribed the deed (Heb. *sêpher*), and sealed it"; 2 Sam. xi. 14, "David wrote a letter (Heb. *sêpher*) to Joab." Here it is equivalent to "a written list."

the generations] See note on ii. 4, "The generations of Adam," i.e.

P day that God created man, in the likeness of God made
2 he him; male and female created he them; and blessed
them, and called their name ¹Adam, in the day when they
3 were created. And Adam lived an hundred and thirty
years, and begat *a son* in his own likeness, after his image;
4 and called his name Seth: and the days of Adam after he
begat Seth were eight hundred years: and he begat sons
5 and daughters. And all the days that Adam lived were
nine hundred and thirty years: and he died.

6 And Seth lived an hundred and five years, and begat
7 Enosh: and Seth lived after he begat Enosh eight hundred
8 and seven years, and begat sons and daughters: and all the
days of Seth were nine hundred and twelve years: and he
died.

9
10 And Enosh lived ninety years, and begat Kenan: and

¹ Or, *Man*

the genealogy from Adam to Noah. LXX γενέσεως, Vulg. "generationis," regarded the Hebrew word as singular.

Adam] The proper name, *Adam*, not *ha-adam*="the man" or "mankind."

God created man] The words "God" (*Elohim*), "created" (*bara*), "in the likeness," reproduce the distinctive language of i. 26—28.

2. *male and female*, &c.] This clause is repeated from i. 27.

blessed them] From i. 27. The words of the command, "be fruitful and multiply," &c., which accompanied the blessing, are not repeated; they are implied in the genealogy that follows.

called their name Adam] Better than marg. "called their name Man." That God gave the name "man" (Heb. *adam*) is not recorded in ch. i. The proper name is probably here intended; but, if so, we should read "*his* name," as the LXX, τὸ ὄνομα αὐτοῦ.

3. *in his own likeness, after his image*] Cf. i. 26. Man was made *in* God's image, *after* His likeness; he begets a son, *in* his own likeness, *after* his image. Many Heb. MSS., however, only read "in his image." On the words "image" and "likeness," see note on i. 26. The phrase here is evidently intended to shew that the elements of resemblance to the Divine image, which at the first were implanted in man's nature, were communicated from father to son.

That the priestly document contained any tradition respecting the Fall, or the murder of Abel, seems improbable.

Seth] See note on iv. 25. The father here gives the name; the mother's name is not mentioned in this genealogy.

6. *Enosh*] See note on iv. 26.

9. *Kenan*] The first syllable of this name is the same in Hebrew

Enosh lived after he begat Kenan eight hundred and fifteen years, and begat sons and daughters: and all the days of Enosh were nine hundred and five years: and he died.

And Kenan lived seventy years, and begat Mahalalel: and Kenan lived after he begat Mahalalel eight hundred and forty years, and begat sons and daughters: and all the days of Kenan were nine hundred and ten years: and he died.

And Mahalalel lived sixty and five years, and begat Jared: and Mahalalel lived after he begat Jared eight hundred and thirty years, and begat sons and daughters: and all the days of Mahalalel were eight hundred ninety and five years: and he died.

And Jared lived an hundred sixty and two years, and begat Enoch: and Jared lived after he begat Enoch eight hundred years, and begat sons and daughters: and all the days of Jared were nine hundred sixty and two years: and he died.

And Enoch lived sixty and five years, and begat Methuselah: and Enoch walked with God after he begat

as the name "Cain," and it is presumably akin in meaning as well as in form (see note on iv. 1).

12. *Mahalalel*] As a Hebrew name this would mean "the praise of God"; but see note on the etymology of proper names in prehistoric times, iv. 17. For Mahalalel the versions give a different form. LXX Μαλελεήλ; Vulg. "Malaleel."

15. *Jared*] Heb. *Yared* = "a going down." Cf. Jordan (Heb. *Yardên*) = "the going down, or descending, river" (?). The Book of Jubilees, written in the latter part of the second century B.C., made use of this Hebrew etymology of the name, when "the sons of God saw the daughters of men," &c., vi. 2. To suppose that it denotes "descent," in the sense of "deterioration," is very far fetched.

18. *Enoch*] Heb. *Ḥanôkh*; cf. iv. 17. Enoch and Mahalalel are here transposed.

21. *Methuselah*] Possibly = "the man of Shelah"; and, if so, Shelah may indicate the name of a deity; cf. Methushael (iv. 18) = "the man of God."

22. *walked with God*] The phrase here, as in *v.* 24, used of Enoch, has passed into common use to express intimacy of communion with God. It denotes more than either standing in His presence, or walking

P Methuselah three hundred years, and begat sons and
23 daughters: and all the days of Enoch were three hundred
24 sixty and five years: and Enoch walked with God: and
he was not; for God took him.

before Him (vi. 9, xvii. 1), or following after Him. It combines the
ideas of fellowship and progress. It is the picture of one who has
God with him in all the various scenes of life.

The audacity of the metaphor caused the LXX to render it by a
paraphrase; εὐηρέστησε δὲ Ἐνὼχ τῷ θεῷ = "and Enoch was well pleasing
unto God," which is quoted in Heb. xi. 5. For other paraphrases, see
Targ. Onkelos, "walked in the fear of God"; Targ. Palestine, "served
in the truth before the Lord."

23. *and all the days*, &c.] Concerning Enoch the following points
deserve attention: (1) He is the seventh in the genealogy, cf. Jude 14;
(2) by comparison with the lives of his fathers and descendants, the
length of his life is immensely curtailed; (3) the number of his years
agrees with the number of days in the solar year; (4) owing to the
closeness of his walk with God he was believed to have been "translated" into Heaven. With this summary must be compared the
account of the *seventh* king in the antediluvian Babylonian Dynasty,
Enmeduranki by name, who received revelations from the Sun-god
Samas, and was the builder of the town of Sippar, which was dedicated
to the Sun-god.

24. *and he was not*] For this expression used to denote an un-
accountable disappearance, cf. Gen. xlii. 13, 36; 1 Kings xx. 40. In
order to make it quite clear that the words did not imply death, LXX
renders οὐχ εὑρίσκετο; Vulg. "non apparuit."

The shortness of his life as compared with the other patriarchs might
have been regarded as a proof of Divine displeasure, if the next sentence
had not been added to explain the circumstance.

for God took him] "Took," or "received," him, i.e. into His own
abode, without death: cf. "he shall receive me" (Ps. xlix. 15). Sam.
"the Angel took him"; LXX μετέθηκε = "translated"; Lat. *tulit*;
Targ. Onkelos, "for the Lord had made him to die." Our word
"translated" has passed into general use from this passage and from
the allusion to it in Heb. xi. 5, "By faith Enoch was *translated* (Lat.
translatus est) that he should not see death, and he was not found,
because God translated him." For the only other instance in the O.T.
of a Saint's "translation," see the story of Elijah (2 Kings ii.). In the
early Babylonian traditions, Xisuthros, the hero of the Babylonian
Deluge story, is "translated" after the Deluge, that he may dwell
among the gods.

Late Jewish tradition was very busy with the story of Enoch. Enoch
was supposed to have received Divine revelation concerning "all
mysteries," and to have recorded them in writing in apocalyptic books.
This current belief concerning Enoch, as the repository and the recorder

GENESIS V. 25—29

And Methuselah lived an hundred eighty and seven years, and begat Lamech: and Methuselah lived after he begat Lamech seven hundred eighty and two years, and begat sons and daughters: and all the days of Methuselah were nine hundred sixty and nine years: and he died. 25 P
26
27

And Lamech lived an hundred eighty and two years, and begat a son: and he called his name Noah, | saying, This same shall ¹comfort us for our work and for the toil of our hands, ²because of the ground which the LORD hath cursed. | 28
29 J

¹ Heb. *nahem*, to comfort.   ² Or, which cometh *from the ground*

of the mysteries of the universe, gave rise to the writing of the extant apocalyptic work, "The Book of Enoch," composed in the second century B.C.

The devout Israelite was able to believe that they who *walked* with God would somehow be *taken* by God; cf. Ps. lxxiii. 24, "Thou shalt guide me with thy counsel, and afterward *take* me to glory." In an age which had no conception of a general resurrection there was faith in God's power and a trust in fellowship with Him.

25. *Methuselah*] According to the Hebrew text and the Samaritan version, Methuselah lived the longest of all the patriarchs, and, according to their figures, his death at the age of 969 years occurred in the year of the Flood.

29. *saying, This same shall comfort us*, &c.] It is generally supposed that this verse, containing a poetical couplet which is intended to explain the name of Noah, has been inserted from the same source of tradition (J) as iv. 25, 26. Certainly, (*a*) the saying interrupts the bare list of names and years; (*b*) it contains a reference to the curse pronounced upon the soil, iii. 17; (*c*) it recurs to the use of the sacred name "Jehovah" ("Jahveh"), whereas "God" ("Elohim") has been used in *vv.* 1, 22 and 24.

comfort] Heb. *nahem*, "to comfort," "relieve." The name "Noah," however, is not derived from *nahem*, but there is a play on the general similarity of sound. The LXX renders "gives us rest."

for our work] The word "for" is in the Heb. "from," and the meaning is that Noah will comfort his fellow-creatures and give them relief and refreshment "from" their toil.

because of the ground] Better, as R.V. marg., "which cometh *from the ground*." This clause is in prose, following two metrical clauses.

In what way did the tradition connect the name of Noah with "comfort" as regards work upon the ground? According to the Hebrew figures in this chapter, Lamech, Noah's father, must have died either before or in the Flood. It is conceivable that the saying recorded in this verse is taken from a group of Israelite traditions which contained no account of the Flood, and only associated the name of Noah

P 30 And Lamech lived after he begat Noah five hundred ninety
31 and five years, and begat sons and daughters: and all the days of Lamech were seven hundred seventy and seven years: and he died.
32 And Noah was five hundred years old: and Noah begat Shem, Ham, and Japheth.

with the work of an husbandman and with the first planting of a vineyard (ix. 20).

31. *and all the days of Lamech*] Lamech's life of 770 years was shorter than Methuselah's by 192 years. His death occurred five years before the Flood. In the Samaritan text the date of his death coincided with the year of the Flood.

32. *And Noah was*, &c.] Noah is thus represented as much older, when he begets his children, than were the other patriarchs, when children were born to them. A hundred years is the interval of time between the birth of Noah's sons and the Deluge (vii. 6).

Compare the mention of three sons born to Lamech, the last name in the Cainite genealogy (iv. 20—24).

NOTE ON THE ANTEDILUVIAN PATRIARCHS

According to chap. v. (P), the interval of time between the work of Creation (i. 1—ii. 4ª) and the visitation of the Flood (vi. 9 ff.) is occupied by a list of ten Patriarchs.

The chronological scheme of P, according to the Hebrew text, makes this period to consist of 1656 years (in the Samaritan text, it is 1307 years; in the LXX, 2242). The description given of the ten Patriarchs is precise and formal. It is limited in each case to the bare formulae narrating facts respecting (i) the age of the Patriarch at the birth of his firstborn, (ii) the number of his remaining years, and the fact that he was the father of other children, (iii) his age at the time of his death.

The account which is thus given furnishes an explanation of the great population of the earth which is overthrown in the Flood. The chapter, however, contains no mention of the growing wickedness of the race. And it does not appear that P takes any account of the Narrative of the Fall (chap. iii. J). Budde, indeed (*Urgesch.* 93—103), contends that the names of the Patriarchs are intended to symbolize the condition of their age, the names Jared (=*descent*), Methuselah (=*the man of the weapon*, or *the man of violence*) denoting its deterioration.

The ten names represented the history of the human race before the Flood. The distribution of these ten names over the period of 1656 years implies a minute and elaborate calculation by the chronologists and chroniclers, whose work has been employed in P.

I. *Ten Babylonian Kings.*

It is impossible to resist the conclusion that there is some sort of connexion between the ten Antediluvian Patriarchs of Gen. v. and the

GENESIS V.

ten kings before the Flood in the Babylonian Legends. The names of the ten kings are as follows:

(A. According to Berossus.)

1. Alôrus.
2. Alaparos.
3. Amêlôn.
4. Ammenôn.
5. Megalâros.
6. Daônos.
7. Euedôrachos.
8. Amempsinos.
9. Ôtiartes.
10. Xisûthros.

(B. According to cuneiform inscriptions.)

1. Arûru.
2. Alapapa.
3. Amêlu (=Man, ?=Enosh).
4. Ummanu (=Master-craftsman, ?=Kenan).
7. Enmeduranki (?=Enoch).
8. Amel-Sin (=Man of the god Sin, ?=Methuselah).
9. Ubara-Jutu.
10. Ḥasisatra (?=Noah).

In this list there may possibly be discerned some points of correspondence with the Hebrew. (*a*) In No. 3 Amelu (=Man) may be translated in Enosh=Man. (*b*) In (4) Ummanu (=Workman), in Kenan; and in (8) Amel-Sin (Man of Sin), in Methuselah (=Man of Shelah). (*c*) No. 7, Enmeduranki (king of Sippar, the city of the Sun-god, Shamash), who was the friend of the gods Ramman and Shamash, looks as if he must stand in some close relation to Enoch, whose life was 365 years and who walked with God. (*d*) The 10th in the list, Xisuthros or Ḥasisatra, the Ut-napishtim of the Epic, is the hero of the Babylonian Flood, and corresponds to Noah in the Hebrew list.

In the Babylonian list, the ten kings are assigned a period of 432,000 years.

II. *Sethite and Cainite Genealogies.*

It is important to compare the two lists of the Sethite (P) and Cainite (J) Genealogies.

Sethite (chap. v.).
1. Adam
2. Seth
3. Enosh
4. Kenan
5. Mahalalel
6. Jared
7. Enoch
8. Methuselah
9. Lamech
10. Noah

Shem, Ham, Japheth.

Cainite (chap. iv. 17—24).
1. Adam
2. Cain
3. Enoch
4. Irad
5. Mehujael
6. Methushael
7. Lamech

Jabal, Jubal, Tubal-Cain.

(*a*) The general resemblance in the names is very striking. (*b*) One list contains the perfect number *ten*, the other the perfect number *seven*. (*c*) Each list concludes in a family of *three* sons. We have to deal

GENESIS V.

either with two variants of the same tradition; or with two distinct traditions, in which the same stock of primitive legendary names is found very closely repeated.

III. *Different Chronologies.*

The Chronology of the Antediluvian Patriarchs varies in the three principal sources for the text, (1) the Massoretic (Hebrew), (2) the Samaritan, (3) the Septuagint. They are presented in the following Table.

	Massoretic Text			Samaritan			LXX			Year (Anno Mundi) of Death		
	Firstborn	Remainder	Total	Firstborn	Remainder	Total	Firstborn	Remainder	Total	Mass. Text	Samaritan	LXX
1. Adam	130	800	930	130	800	930	230	700	930	930	930	9
2. Seth	105	807	912	105	807	912	205	707	912	1042	1042	11
3. Enosh	90	815	905	90	815	905	190	715	905	1140	1140	13
4. Kenan	70	840	910	70	840	910	170	740	910	1235	1235	15
5. Mahalalel ...	65	830	895	65	830	895	165	730	895	1290	1290	16
6. Jered	162	800	962	62	785	847	62	785	847	1422	1307	19
7. Enoch	65	300	365	65	300	365	165	200	365	987	887	14
8. Methuselah...	187	782	969	67	653	720	167*	802*	969	1656	1307	22
9. Lamech	182	595	777	53	600	653	188	565	753	1651	1307	22
10. Noah	500			500			500					
Till the Flood	100			100			100					
Year of the Flood	1656			1307			2242					

* LXX Cod. Alexandrinus and other MSS. have 187 : 782.

These different figures are not due to errors in the text. They seem to arise from the adoption of differing systems for the calculation of the chronology.

It has commonly been supposed that the Hebrew figures (1656) are part of a scheme which calculated 2666 years to have been the interval between the Creation and the Exodus, and that 2666 years represented *two-thirds* of a cycle of 4000 years.

The 2666 years are computed as follows:

  1656 Creation to Flood
   290 Flood to birth of Abraham
   100 To birth of Isaac (xxi. 5)
    60 To birth of Jacob (xxv. 26)
   130 To Jacob's descent into Egypt (xlvii. 9—28)
   430 Sojourn in Egypt (Ex. xii. 40)

2666

The Samaritan figure of 1307 is part of a system which calculated 3007 years to intervene between the Creation and the entrance into Canaan. The calculation was as follows:

Creation to Flood	= 1307 years
Flood to birth of Abraham	= 940 ,,
Birth of Abraham to descent into Egypt	= 290 ,,
Sojourn in Egypt	= 430 ,,
Wandering in Wilderness	= 40 ,,
	3007 years

Skinner (*in loc.*) points out, that, if the calculation be made in round numbers = 3000, the entire period may then be divided into three decreasing periods of 1300, 940, 760 years, of which the second exceeds the third by 180 years, and the first exceeds the second by *twice* 180 years (2×180) = 360 years.

The LXX figure of 2240 is the equivalent of the Samaritan calculation from the Creation to the Flood (1300 years) + the Samaritan calculation from the Flood to the birth of Abraham (940 years). But whether this be the result of accident or design, it is impossible to say.

IV. *Longevity of Patriarchs.*

The Hebrew tradition evidently assumed that human vitality, in the era immediately following upon the Creation, was at its highest point, and that, in consequence, immense longevity was to be expected in the lives of the Antediluvian Patriarchs.

The immense duration of life assigned to these ten Patriarchs has always been the occasion of difficulty. Attempts have been made to explain away the figures. (*a*) It has been suggested that the names of the Patriarchs represent dynasties. But the mention of the first-born and of other children obviously refers to personal history. Nor does the transference of these enormous figures to the duration of dynasties greatly diminish the improbability of their literal historicity. (*b*) It has been suggested that the Hebrew word for "year" (*shânah*) is used in this chapter to denote a shorter period of time. But this arbitrary solution is devoid of any evidence in its favour. Familiar Hebrew words, like "years" in this chapter, or like "day" in chapter i., must not be supposed, because of our difficulties in interpretation, to require new meanings.

There is no reason not to interpret the statements respecting the longevity of the ten Antediluvian Patriarchs quite literally. The account of them belongs to the domain of primitive tradition. It would be strange, if the primitive unverifiable tradition were not accompanied by the exaggerations which popular legend weaves around prehistoric names.

It is instructive to compare the ages of the Antediluvian and Post-diluvian Patriarchs with those of the famous Israelites of more historic times.

Adam, the first of the Antediluvians, lived	930 years
Seth, the second of the Antediluvians, lived	912 ,,
Noah, the tenth of the Antediluvians, lived	950 ,,
Shem, the first of the Post-diluvians, lived	600 ,,
Arpachshad, the second of the Post-diluvians, lived	408 ,,
Terah, the tenth of the Post-diluvians, lived	205 ,,

Abraham lived	175 years		
Isaac ,,	180 ,,		
Jacob ,,	147 ,,		
Joseph ,,	110 ,,		
Moses ,,	120 ,,		
Joshua ,,	110 ,,		

David reigned	40 years		
Solomon reigned	40 ,,		
Rehoboam lived	58 ,,	(2 Chr. xii. 13)	
Hezekiah ,,	54 ,,	(2 Chr. xxix. 1)	
Manasseh ,,	67 ,,	(2 Chr. xxxiii. 1)	

It is clear that this descending scale, in the duration of life, corresponds to the stages of transition from legend to history.

There is no evidence to shew that the earlier phases of civilization were more favourable to longevity than the later.

CH. VI. 1—IX. 29. THE DELUGE.

1—4. *The sons of God and the daughters of men*] This short strange passage serves as a kind of Preface to the Narrative of the Deluge. There is nothing to be found quite like it elsewhere in the O.T. It obviously is not a continuation of the previous chapter; and, except for a possible, though most disputable, allusion in the mention of the 120 years (*v.* 3), its contents do not presuppose the catastrophe of the Flood. In all probability, we should be right in regarding these four verses as a fragment from some quite independent source of early Hebrew tradition, most certainly distinct from the regular materials represented in J and P.

The mention of the marriages between "the sons of God" and "the daughters of men" is clearly a survival of early Hebrew mythology. It accounted for the existence of an Israelite tradition respecting a primitive race of giants. There are traces, in the literature of other countries, of a similar belief in fabulous giants, or semi-divine heroes, who lived in a far-remote age of antiquity.

The tradition preserved in this brief fragment is condensed, and the language is not free from obscurity. There are, however, allusions in other parts of the O.T. (see note on *v.* 4) to the race of giants which was believed not to have been extinct at the time of the occupation of Palestine by the Israelite tribes. Such a belief was incompatible with the tradition that all the primaeval dwellers in the world, except Noah and his family, perished in the waters of the Flood (vii. 21—23). If,

And it came to pass, when men began to multiply on the 6 J
face of the ground, and daughters were born unto them,
that the sons of God saw the daughters of men that they 2

therefore, the impious unions of angels with the daughters of men were
considered to account for the existence of a giant human race surviving
in later times, the tradition which recorded them must have been quite
distinct from, and independent of, the tradition of a universal Flood.

As an isolated survival of Hebrew mythology, it furnishes an instructive reminder, that the popular ideas of Israel concerning primaeval
times may be presumed, at least originally, to have resembled those of
other nations. They were pervaded by fanciful and legendary elements.
We must realize that the spiritual teaching of the religion of Jehovah
was responsible for an extensive purgation of the traditions which
described the beginnings of the world and of the Israelite people.
Polytheistic and unedifying materials were most successfully excluded
in the compilation of the Hebrew sacred books. The result is simple,
dignified, and elevating. We have in these four verses a glimpse of
the material which for the most part was rigorously discarded.

1. *men*] Heb. *ha-adam*, i.e. "the man." It is not the proper
name "Adam"; nor is it "the man" as an individual as in iii. 24, iv.
1: but "the man" collectively, in the sense of "the human race,"
LXX οἱ ἄνθρωποι. This use of the word is different from anything in
the Paradise Narrative: see v. 1.

began to multiply] No account is taken of (*a*) the description of the
growth of the population, and of (*b*) the genealogies of Cainites and
Sethites, which have occupied chaps. iv. 17—25, and v.

2. *that the sons of God*, &c.] This is one of the most disputed
passages in the book. But the difficulty, in a great measure, disappears,
if it is frankly recognized, that the verse must be allowed to have its
literal meaning. According to the legend which it preserves, intermarriages took place between Heavenly Beings and mortal women.

Commentators have often shrunk from the admission that this piece
of mythology could have a place in the Hebrew Scriptures. Accordingly, very fanciful explanations have sometimes found favour; e.g.
(*a*) "the sons of God" are the men of the upper classes, "the daughters
of men" are "the women of the lower classes"; (*b*) "the sons of God"
are "the sons of the god-fearing," "the daughters of men" are "the
daughters of the impious"; (*c*) "the sons of God" are "the descendants of Seth," "the daughters of men" are "the women of the
Cainite race."

Such interpretations may be dismissed as arbitrary and non-natural:
and they furnish no explanation of the inference in *v*. 4, that a race of
giants or heroes was the progeny of these marriages.

the sons of God] Heb. *B'nê Elohim*, "sons of Elohim," i.e.
beings partaking of the Divine nature. It has been pointed out above
(see note on i. 26), that the Israelites believed the Almighty to be
surrounded by a court of beings who were subordinate to Him in

GENESIS VI. 2, 3

J were fair; and they took them wives of all that they chose.
3 And the LORD said, My spirit shall not ¹strive with man

¹ Or, *rule in* Or, according to many ancient versions, *abide in*

authority, office, and rank: their dwelling-place was in Heaven; their duty was to perform the tasks appointed them by the Almighty. They were "angels" or "messengers," Heb. *mal'âkhîm*, Gr. ἄγγελοι. The sons of God are mentioned in Job i. 6, ii. 1, xxxviii. 7, Ps. xxix. 1, lxxxix. 1, Dan. iii. 25, 28.

The expression must be judged in accordance with Hebrew, not English, idiom. "The sons of the prophets" (1 Kings xx. 35: cf. Amos vii. 14) are persons who belong to the guild of the prophets, members, as we should say, of the prophet's calling. No family relationship is implied. Similarly "the sons of God" are not "sons of gods," in the sense of being their children, but "sons of Elohim" in the sense of belonging to the class of super-natural, or heavenly, beings.

There is no reference, on the one hand, to Oriental speculations respecting emanations from the Deity; nor to actual sonship, or generation. The description is quite general. Nowhere do we find in the O.T. mention of the "sons of Jehovah" instead of the "sons of Elohim."

of all that they chose] i.e. whomsoever they chose. The sons of God are represented as being irresistible. The sons of men could offer no effective opposition. The marriages, contracted in this way, are evidently implied to be wrong, and the result of mere unbridled passion. The men were powerless to defend their women folk.

In the later days of Judaism, this passage became the source of the strange legends respecting "fallen angels," of which we find traces in the N.T.: 2 Pet. ii. 4, "for if God spared not angels when they sinned, but cast them down to Hell"; Jude 6, "angels which kept not their own principality, but left their proper habitation"; and in the Book of Enoch.

There is no trace, however, in the Book of Genesis of any tradition respecting either the fall, or the rebellion, of members of the angel-host. Unquestionably English ideas are profoundly affected by the influence of Milton's *Paradise Lost*, and by the vague impression that a great and noble religious poem must have been founded upon literal facts.

3. *And the LORD said*] It is not evident in this verse, why the LORD should pass a sentence of condemnation upon man. In the two preceding verses, it is not man, but "the sons of God," whose depravity has been described. Perhaps, however, the object of the words is, in view of the mixed marriages, to impose a more restricted limit upon the duration of human life. Man is warned, as in iv. 22, that on earth he has no immortality. The warning is administered to the progeny of the sons of God and the daughters of men no less than to the children of men generally.

for ever, ¹for that he also is flesh: ²yet shall his days be an hundred and twenty years. The ³Nephilim were in the

¹ Or, *in their going astray they are flesh*   ² Or, *therefore*   ³ Or, *giants* See Num. xiii. 33.

Following this line of interpretation, we obtain some clue to the meaning of a most obscure verse. Its obscurities, indeed, are such that it may well be the case, that the original text has suffered corruption in the early stages of its transmission.

1. The R.V. text may be paraphrased: "My spirit shall not for ever be contending with man; seeing that he also is carnally minded. His days are numbered: but I will not at once consume him. There shall yet be an interval of 120 years, before I bring upon mankind the catastrophe of the Deluge." The objections to this are numerous: (*a*) the rendering "strive" is exceedingly doubtful; (*b*) the idea of the spirit of Jehovah striving with men is unsuitable; (*c*) the rendering, "for that he also, &c." represents a Hebrew idiom found nowhere else in the Pentateuch, while the word "also" has no logical connexion; (*d*) the mention of "his days" being 120 years despite the Flood is, to say the least, strange—Noah is expressly stated in P to be 500 years old at the birth of his sons (*v*. 32), and 600 years old when he entered the ark (vii. 6); (*e*) "flesh" is used in its metaphorical, not in its literal, sense.

2. R.V. marg. *rule in*. Better, according to many ancient versions, *abide in...in their going astray they are flesh*. The following paraphrase may be given: "the Spirit which I have implanted in man is not to abide in him for ever. (Still he shall not be judged too severely.) In their continual going astray men shew that they are frail flesh. Mortal life, therefore, shall be limited to 120 years (no admixture of the heavenly strain shall avail for the greater prolongation of life)."

It is objected that the lives of the patriarchs in P exceed this limit. But the passage is evidently an independent fragment from J. And it is a more serious objection that the words of the verse, taken literally, make no clear allusion to the illicit marriages, and are applicable to mankind generally.

4. *The Nephilim*] i.e. *giants*. It is natural to refer to Num. xiii. 33, "And there we saw the Nephilim (Or, *giants*), the sons of Anak, which come of the Nephilim; and we were in our own sight as grasshoppers, and so we were in their sight." The tradition that the Nephilim existed at the time of the Exodus was therefore quite strongly held. The precise meaning of the name has been lost. The passage in Numbers shews clearly that it denoted men of gigantic stature. The etymology very probably goes back to primitive times; and its origin is lost with the dialects that disappeared when the Israelites finally occupied Palestine. It was natural to connect the word with the Hebrew *naphal*, "to fall"; hence arose the renderings of Aquila, οἱ ἐπιπίπτοντες, "the assailants," and of Symmachus, οἱ βιαῖοι, "the

J earth in those days, and also after that, when the sons of God came in unto the daughters of men, and they bare children to them: the same were the mighty men which 5 were of old, the men of renown. And the LORD saw that

violent," while among Patristic commentators the word was connected with "the fallen angels." But these are merely guesses; and we must be content to leave the etymology of "the Nephilim," like that of "the Rephaim" and "the Anakim," unexplained.

and also after that] These words are introduced very awkwardly; and were very probably added as a gloss, in order to shew that the Nephilim existed not only in primitive ages, but also at the time of the Exodus from Egypt, as would be implied by Num. xiii. 33. The continuance of the Nephilim in later times seems to contradict the account of the destruction of all the dwellers on the earth by the Flood. This contradiction is to be explained on the supposition, mentioned above, that the present passage is a fragment of a tradition in which the Flood was not recorded.

the mighty men, &c.] That is to say, "the well-known giants of old-world time," familiar personages in Israelite folk-lore. To this class belong such names as "Nimrod," x. 8, and "Og," Deut. iii. 11.

the men of renown] Literally, "the men of name," as in Num. xvi. 2, "men of renown," Lat. *viri famosi*, viz. famous for deeds of prowess and audacity.

VI. 5—IX. 17. THE FLOOD. (J and P.)

Here follows the Hebrew narrative of the Flood. The Flood is the one great event in the history of the world, which in the Hebrew narrative emerges out of the obscurity between the creation of man and the period of the patriarchs. It marks the close of the first era of the human race. According to the story in Genesis, it was a judgement for the depravity of mankind.

It marks also the beginning of a new era in the history of mankind. This has its origin in the mercy of God, who, in recognition of the righteousness of Noah, preserves him and his family in the general overthrow. This is a symbol of salvation. The new age opens with the renewal of promises to man, and with a covenant entailing new obligations on man's part, in return for the assurance of Divine protection.

On the relation of the Genesis narrative to the Babylonian and other accounts of the Flood, see Special Note.

The present narrative is woven together out of the two distinct Israelite traditions, J and P: see Introduction. This compositeness of structure in the Flood narrative is quite unmistakable[1]. It accounts for the (*a*) repetitions, (*b*) discrepancies, (*c*) intermittent use of special words and phrases, inexplicable on the assumption of a continuous

[1] See Appendix C.

GENESIS VI. 97

homogeneous narrative. Under the head of (*a*) "repetitions," notice the duplicated account of the growing corruption of mankind in vi. 5—8 (J), and in vi. 9—12 (P); of the entrance of Noah and his family into the ark vii. 7 (J) and vii. 13 (P); of the rising of the waters of the Flood vii. 17 (J) and vii. 18, 19 (P); of the end of all living creatures vii. 21 (P) and vii. 22, 23 (J); and of God's promise to Noah in viii. 15—19 (P) and viii. 20—22 (J).

Under the head of (*b*) "discrepancies," notice that, in P, Noah takes one pair of every kind of animal into the ark (vi. 19, 20, and vii. 15, 16), while, in J, Noah is commanded to take seven pairs of every clean animal and one pair of every unclean animal into the ark (vii. 2, 3); again, in P, the Flood is brought about through the outburst of the waters from the great deep both from beneath the earth and from above the firmament (vii. 11, viii. 2); while, in J, it is produced by the rain (vii. 12, viii. 2). According to P, the Flood was in progress for 150 days (vii. 24, viii. 3), while according to J the rain lasted for 40 days (vii. 12); in J the waters were subsiding for 14 or 21 days (viii. 10, 12), and in P the earth was dry after a year and 10 days (viii. 14).

Under the head of (*c*), the following are examples of distinctive phraseology:

P	J
"God" (*Elohim*), vi. 9, 11, 12, 13, 22, vii. 16ᵃ, viii. 1, 15.	"the LORD" (Jehovah), vii. 1, 5, 16ᵇ, viii. 20, 21.
"male and female" (*zâkâr un'kê-bâh*), vi. 19, vii. 9, 16.	"the male and his female" (*ish v'ishto*), vii. 2.
"destroy" (*shâhath*), vi. 13, 17.	"destroy" (*mâhâh*), vi. 7, vii. 4, 23.
"all flesh," vi. 12, 13, 17, vii. 21.	"every living thing," vii. 4, 23.
"breath (*ruah*) of life," vii. 15.	"breath of (*nishmath*) the spirit of (*ruah*) life," vii. 22.
"die" (*gâv'â*), vii. 21.	"die" (*mûth*), vii. 22.
"waters prevailed" (*gâbâr*), vii. 18, 19, 24.	"waters increased" (*râbâh*), vii. 17ᵇ.
"waters abated" (*hâsêr*), viii. 3ᵇ, 5.	"waters abated" (*qâlal*), viii. 8.

Also characteristic of P is the minute description of the ark and its dimensions (vi. 14—16), the varieties of animals (vi. 20), the Flood's depth (vii. 20), and the members of Noah's family (vii. 13, viii. 15, 18); while, in J, Divine action is described in anthropomorphic terms (e.g. vi. 6, vii. 16, viii. 21), and vivid details of narrative are introduced (viii. 6—12).

Roughly speaking the portions derived from P consist of vi. 9—22, vii. 6, 11, 13—16ᵃ, 18—21, 24, viii. 1, 2ᵃ, 3ᵇ—5, 13ᵃ, 14—19, ix. 1—17: the remainder of the narrative is derived from the J tradition, with here and there a few alterations for the purpose of harmonizing the two sources of narrative. The process of harmonizing was not difficult: for both narratives agreed in their main outlines, and differed only in the treatment of details.

J the wickedness of man was great in the earth, and that every imagination of the thoughts of his heart was only 6 evil continually. And it repented the LORD that he had made man on the earth, and it grieved him at his heart.

5—8. Introduction to the story of the Flood from J: Jehovah sees the sinfulness of man and resolves to annihilate the race.

5. *of man*] Literally, "the man," *ha-adam*, used generically, as in *v.* 1.

"The unity of the race is a consistent doctrine of the O.T. It was הָאָדָם, *man*, when created as a single individual. It spread over the earth, and was still הָאָדָם, *man*. It was כָּל־בָּשָׂר, 'all flesh,' that had corrupted its way before the Flood. Mankind is, as a whole, corrupt; and, corresponding to this, each individual is unclean.... Probably the O.T. does not go the length of offering any rationale of the fact that each individual is sinful, beyond connecting him with a sinful whole." (Davidson, *Theology of the O.T.* pp. 218, 219.)

every imagination of the thoughts of his heart] An elaborate description. The word rendered "imagination" means "form," "formation," or "shape," and, as applied to the region of thought, denotes "an idea," or "the concept of thought," *cogitatio*, cf. viii. 21.

continually] Literally, "all the day." Man's sinfulness is thus described as universal and unintermittent. The beginnings of "sin" are seen in the picture of the Fall, chap. iii., its propagation in the murderous act of Cain, chap. iv.; we have reached in this passage its complete and unrestrained expansion.

The LXX translating the word for "imagination" as a verb, gives καὶ πᾶς τις διανοεῖται ἐν τῇ καρδίᾳ αὐτοῦ ἐπιμελῶς ἐπὶ τὰ πονηρὰ πάσας τὰς ἡμέρας, Lat. *quod...cuncta cogitatio cordis intenta esset ad malum omni tempore*.

6. *And it repented the LORD...grieved him at his heart*] This is a strong instance of what is called anthropomorphism, an expression descriptive of human emotion or action ascribed to Jehovah (e.g. iii. 8, vii. 16, viii. 21). Such expressions have often given rise to superficial criticisms, depreciatory of Holy Scripture, on the part both of those who are ignorant of Oriental literature, and of those who assume that the Books of Holy Scripture must be free from the literary characteristics of the writers' age and nationality. In this verse Jehovah is represented as intensely grieved at the frustration of His purposes for the human race. The description is given in the childlike simplicity of the language of an early age: compare Gen. xi. 5, 6, xviii. 21.

In other passages, e.g. Num. xxiii. 19, 1 Sam. xv. 29, it is asserted that Jehovah is not, like man, capable of repentance. There are two representations in Holy Scripture of the Divine Nature: one, which, as here, makes the Divine Purpose fluctuate, in reflexion, as it were, of man's changing experiences; the other, which depicts the Divine Purpose as uniform, changeless, and unvarying, cf. James i. 17.

And the LORD said, I will ¹destroy man whom I have 7 J
created from the face of the ground; both man, and beast,
and creeping thing, and fowl of the air; for it repenteth me
that I have made them. But Noah found grace in the eyes 8
of the LORD.

These are the generations of Noah. Noah was a righteous 9 P

¹ Heb. *blot out*.

It was the dread of any expression being liable to the suspicion of
irreverence towards the Almighty, which led to the strange renderings
of this verse by the later Jews. Thus, LXX renders "repented" by
ἐνεθυμήθη = "considered," and "grieved" by διενοήθη = "purposed,"
while the Targum of Onkelos renders the second clause "and spake
by his word to break their strength according to his will," and Pseudo-
Jonathan, "and disputed with his word concerning them." The object
of such paraphrases is to avoid anthropomorphism. The LXX also
avoids the expression of repentance as applied to God in Ex. xxxii. 12.

The Latin rendering is quite free from any such shrinking, and is
noteworthy: *poenituit eum et tactus dolore cordis intrinsecus*.

7. *destroy*] R.V. marg. Heb. *blot out*. LXX ἀπαλείψω, Lat. *delebo*.
A characteristic word in J, cf. vii. 4, 23; and different from the word
for "destroy" in v. 13. (LXX καταφθείρω, Lat. *disperdam*.)

both man, and beast, &c.] No reference is here made to any preservation of life.

8. *But Noah*] The sudden introduction of Noah's name implies
that there had been some previous account, in J, describing the contrast of Noah's virtue with the sinfulness of his contemporaries. In the
composite narrative of Genesis many features have necessarily disappeared in the process of combining the different traditions. Possibly,
the passage at the beginning of this chapter (*vv.* 1 to 4) was substituted
for one that had introduced the mention of Noah's piety in contrast
with the wickedness of man.

found grace] This familiar expression occurs here for the first time
in the Bible. For the expression "find grace" cf. xix. 19, xxxii. 5,
xxxiii. 8, 10, 15. The rendering "grace" is sometimes altered to
"favour," cf. xviii. 3, xxx. 27. It is implied that the "favour" which
Noah "finds" in the eyes of Jehovah is based on moral grounds. The
phrase, common in J, is not found in E or P.

9—12. The introduction to the Story of the Flood in P. Observe
that, whereas J begins with the corruption of the human race, and
closes with the mention of Noah, P begins with the mention of Noah
and continues with the corruption of the human race.

9. *These are the generations*, &c.] The heading, or superscription
of a new section in the narrative of P; cf. ii. 4, v. 1.

a righteous man] The word "righteous" (*ṣaddîq*), which occupies
such an important place in Biblical Theology, occurs here for the first

P man, and ¹perfect in his generations: Noah walked with
10 God. And Noah begat three sons, Shem, Ham, and
11 Japheth. And the earth was corrupt before God, and the
12 earth was filled with violence. And God saw the earth,
and, behold, it was corrupt; for all flesh had corrupted his
way upon the earth.
13 And God said unto Noah, The end of all flesh is come

¹ Or, *blameless*

time. The sense of "rectitude," or "uprightness," may be derived from a root-idea of "straightness." It is used of Noah again in vii. 1: in Ezek. xiv. 14, 20 Noah is mentioned, with Daniel and Job, as pre-eminent for "righteousness." Cf. also Ecclus. xliv. 17, "Noah was found perfect and righteous; in the season of wrath he was taken in exchange for the world," and 2 Pet. ii. 5, "Noah...a preacher of righteousness."

perfect] R.V. marg. *blameless*. Heb. *tâmîm*. The word "perfect" (LXX τέλειος, Lat. *perfectus*) means "without flaw." As a ritual term used of an animal for sacrifice, "perfect" would mean "free from blemish." Transferred to morals, it denotes "integrity," as in the account of Job (Job i. 1).

in his generations] viz. amongst the people of his own generation, a different word in the Heb. from the one used in "these are the generations." It denotes the members of one family, dwelling together, e.g. grandfather, father, son.

walked with God] See note on v. 22—24. The account of Noah as "righteous," "perfect," and "walking with God," embraces three aspects of the good and devout character, justice, purity, holiness.

10. *And Noah begat*] See v. 32.

11. *corrupt*] The full strength of the word would rather be given by "corrupted." LXX ἐφθάρη, Lat. *corrupta est*, "was marred, ruined." "Before God," i.e. according to the standard of His judgement. "God" is here *ha-Elohim*, i.e. *the* God, *the* Elohim, absolutely.

violence] The particular form of wickedness represented by this word, here and in *v.* 13, is doubtless meant to be impious insolence and active disregard of all law of right and wrong. LXX ἀδικίας and Lat. *iniquitate* miss the specific thought of "violence."

12. *all flesh*] Used here for "all the human race." The phrase, which is found 13 times in the Story of the Flood, is a characteristic of P.

had corrupted his way] This expression seems to be used with the object of shewing that man was a free agent, and that his corruption was not the result of blind fate, or of any external malign influence.

13—17. NOAH IS COMMANDED TO BUILD THE ARK.

13. *is come before me*] viz. mentally. The intention to destroy all flesh has entered the mind of God.

GENESIS VI. 13—16

before me; for the earth is filled with violence through them; and, behold, I will destroy them with the earth. Make thee an ark of gopher wood; ¹rooms shalt thou 14 make in the ark, and shalt pitch it within and without with pitch. And this is how thou shalt make it: the length 15 of the ark three hundred cubits, the breadth of it fifty cubits, and the height of it thirty cubits. A ²light shalt 16

¹ Heb. *nests*.   ² Or, *roof*

14. *an ark*] The word here used, *têbâh*, is only found in this passage and in Ex. ii. 3—5. It is of foreign origin; according to some, an Egyptian word; according to others, derived from the Assyrian. LXX κιβωτός, Lat. *arca*, which our translators adopted and transliterated. The "ark" of the Covenant (e.g. Ex. xxv. 10) is another Heb. word, *'arôn*, but unfortunately rendered also by LXX κιβωτός, Lat. *arca*.

gopher wood] A word only used here. "Gopher" is said to be a resinous coniferous tree, possibly the "cypress" (*cuparissus*), to which word it may be akin.

The versions, not realizing that it was a botanical description, made wild guesses at the meaning. Thus LXX ἐκ ξύλων τετραγώνων = "of squared beams": so, Vet. Lat. *ligna quadrata*, Vulg. *ligna laevigata*.

rooms] The meaning is obvious. The interior of the ark was to consist of cabins, or cubicles. The sentence would be rendered literally, "nests shalt thou make the ark." Vulg. *mansiunculas*.

pitch] Heb. *kopher*, a word only found here in the Bible, and its resemblance in pronunciation to "gopher" (see above), is, to say the least, strange. The Assyrian word for bitumen is *kupru*, and that word is used in the Babylonian account, in which the hero of the Flood is made to say, "Six *sars* of bitumen (*kupru*) I spread over it for caulking." The word suggests (1) that there is some connexion of the Hebrew story with the Babylonian version, (2) that the region was the Euphrates Valley in which bitumen was freely obtainable. The word in Ex. ii. 3 is not *kopher*, but *khêmar*, which is also found in Gen. xi. 3, xiv. 10.

15. The dimensions of the ark, as here given, are somewhat smaller than in the Assyrian account. Assuming that a cubit measured 1½ feet, the ark was 450 ft. long, 75 ft. broad, and 45 ft. high. It will be noticed that the breadth is exactly one-sixth, and the height exactly one-tenth, of the length. In the Assyrian account we miss these proportions. The length is not given, but the height and breadth are the same, viz. 120 cubits, or 180 ft., broad and high. Berossus, the Greek writer of Babylonian traditions, records that the ship of the Flood was 5 stadia (about ⅔ of a mile) long, and 2 stadia (about ¼ mile) broad.

16. *A light*] Perhaps better than *a roof*. The word so rendered (*ṣôhar*) only occurs here in the singular: in the dual it is the regular Heb.

P thou make to the ark, and to a cubit shalt thou finish it ¹upward; and the door of the ark shalt thou set in the side thereof; with lower, second, and third stories shalt 17 thou make it. And I, behold, I do bring the flood of waters upon the earth, to destroy all flesh, wherein is the breath of life, from under heaven; every thing that is in

¹ Or, *from above*

word for "noonday." Accepting the rendering which connects it with "light," we should probably be right in conjecturing that it means here "a window," or "opening," beneath the over-hanging eaves of the roof on both sides of the ark. So Latin, *fenestram*. In the Babylonian version, a window is mentioned. Others, connecting the word with an Arabic form, render it by *roof*, deeming that the roof, being of such importance to the inmates, could not have been omitted in the description. LXX ἐπισυνάγων is unintelligible, but possibly gives the idea of the converging sides of the covering.

and to a cubit, &c.] This clause is very difficult. (*a*) The commonest opinion is that, if the reference be to a window, it was to be a cubit high, running round the ark. This, however, would have been a mere slit, and practically inadequate for purposes of light and air. Perhaps it may mean the distance of a cubit from the top of the window to the roof. (*b*) The idea that it represented a little square window in Noah's own cell is fanciful. (*c*) If the word rendered "light" denoted the roof, the cubit "upward," or "from above," might indicate the amount of slope, which, however, would be extremely small. An allusion to the "window" is the most probable explanation. The opening would have run all round the ship, with the necessary intervals of beams and supports. The description must not be judged by modern standards either of ship-building or of hygiene. It is more or less imaginative.

upward] The rendering of the margin, *from above*, gives a more intelligible meaning.

Gunkel, who considers that the text is corrupt, makes the strange conjectural emendation, "and on a hinge shalt thou make it revolve."

the door] Cf. vii. 16.

stories] The Babylonian account is more elaborate: "Then I built 6 decks in it so that it was divided into 7 stories. The interior (of each storey) I divided into 9 compartments."

17. *And I, behold, I*] The emphasis on the 1st person seems to bring out the thought of the necessity of this act of universal destruction brought upon the world by its Creator.

the flood] Heb. *mabbûl*, a word used only of the Deluge in this passage (vi.—ix.) and in Ps. xxix. 10, where "the flood of waters" fails to give the meaning, which is "the Deluge (the *mabbûl*) of waters."

all flesh] See *v.* 12. Here, however, it denotes the animals as well as mankind.

the breath of life] Lit. "the spirit (*ruaḥ*, LXX πνεῦμα) of life," a

GENESIS VI. 17—20

the earth shall die. But I will establish my covenant with **18** P
thee; and thou shalt come into the ark, thou, and thy sons,
and thy wife, and thy sons' wives with thee. And of every **19**
living thing of all flesh, two of every sort shalt thou bring
into the ark, to keep them alive with thee; they shall be
male and female. Of the fowl after their kind, and of the **20**
cattle after their kind, of every creeping thing of the ground

different phrase from that in ii. 7, "the breath (*nishmath*) of life" (J).
Noah is commanded to enter the ark, taking with him his own family
and two of *all* the animals. The Priestly Writer could not endorse the
idea that the distinction between "clean" and "unclean" was known
before the days of Moses. In J, however (vii. 2, 3), it is assumed that
this distinction was primaeval (see note).

18. *I will establish my covenant*] We have here the first mention
of a covenant relation between God and man. In the writing of P
great stress is laid upon the covenant with Noah, here and in ix. 8—17,
and with the patriarchs, e.g. in xvii. 2—14. The word "covenant" (*b'rîth*,
LXX διαθήκη, Lat. *foedus*) plays an important part in O.T. theology.
Its place here in relation to the manifestation of sin on the one
side, and of Divine salvation on the other, is typical of its permanent
significance in the history of the Chosen People. It is this relationship
of covenant (διαθήκη) which is renewed by our Lord and ratified at
the institution of the Lord's Supper, Matt. xxvi. 28. A covenant
means an agreement, or compact between two parties, for the observance
of which promises and pledges are given. Cf. on ix. 7.

thou, and thy sons, &c.] This is the redundant style of P, cf.
vii. 13, viii. 16, 18.

19. *two of every sort*] Observe that here one pair of every kind of
living creature is to be brought into the ark.

"Male and female," as in i. 27 (P). A different phrase is used in
vii. 2 (J), where see note.

20. *Of the fowl*, &c.] The order in which the animals are here
mentioned is deserving of notice; first the fowls, then the cattle, and
finally the creeping things. What is the reason of this order? Probably
the order of the account of the Creation in chap. i. is followed, where
the creation of the fowls is recorded in *vv.* 20—23, and of the cattle
and creeping things in *v.* 24. The same order is maintained in i. 26.

kind] The same word as in i. 12 (P).

cattle] as in i. 24, denoting domestic animals generally. The only
group of animals mentioned in i. 21 and 24, which is here omitted, is
"the beast of the earth," i.e. "the wild beast." Is this intentional?
The LXX adds, after "every creeping thing," καὶ ἀπὸ πάντων τῶν θηρίων
= "and of every wild beast."

creeping thing] See note on i. 24. The exact phrase "everything
that creepeth upon the ground after its kind" is reproduced from i. 25.

P after its kind, two of every sort shall come unto thee, to
21 keep them alive. And take thou unto thee of all food that
is eaten, and gather it to thee; and it shall be for food for
22 thee, and for them. Thus did Noah; according to all that
God commanded him, so did he.

J 7 And the LORD said unto Noah, Come thou and all thy
house into the ark; for thee have I seen righteous before
2 me in this generation. Of every clean beast thou shalt
take to thee seven and seven, the male and his female;

21. *of all food that is eaten*] Presumably vegetables, cereals, and fruit. Cf. i. 29.

22. *Thus did Noah*] Lit. "and Noah did (it)." The words of this verse are characteristic of the style of P. We find the same formula in Ex. vii. 6, xii. 28, 50, xxxix. 32, 43, xl. 16, all belonging to P.

CH. VII. 1—5.

The account, from J, of the command to enter the ark. The chief difference, between the J and P versions, lies in the number of the animals which Noah is to take into the ark. According to J, Noah is to take seven pairs of every clean animal and two pairs of the unclean; according to P he is to take in with him one pair of every kind of creature living upon earth.

1. *And the LORD*] The command of Jehovah. See vi. 13, "And God said unto Noah."

and all thy house] A more brief description of Noah's family than in vi. 18. We should observe here the first mention of a man's "house," in the sense of a household, or family. The identification of a man with his family, whether for punishment or for deliverance, is a feature in the ethics of O.T. religion.

for thee] viz. thee alone.

righteous...generation] See notes on vi. 9 and 11.

2. *Of every clean beast*] The distinction is here made between the clean and the unclean animals. Categories of both kinds, according to the Levitical Law, are found in Lev. xi. and Deut. xiv. 3—20. In the account given by P (vi. 19) no allusion is made to this distinction. According to P, the distinctions of clean and unclean were for the first time laid down in the Mosaic legislation, and could not, therefore, be recognized as existing in the primaeval or patriarchal age. According to J, the distinction existed in pre-Mosaic times, and was to be presupposed as having existed side by side with the institution of sacrifice.

seven and seven, the male and his female] By this is meant seven pairs. "The male and his female," i.e. "each and his mate," *îsh v'ishtô*, seems to make this clear. But some consider seven clean animals, and not seven pairs of clean animals, are intended. The words and of the beasts that are not clean two, the male and his female; of the fowl also of the air, seven and seven, male and female: to keep seed alive upon the face of all the earth. For yet seven days, and I will cause it to rain upon the earth forty days and forty nights; and every living thing that I have made will I ¹destroy from off the face of the ground. And Noah did according unto all that the LORD commanded him.

And Noah was six hundred years old when the flood

¹ Heb. *blot out*.

"the male and his female" are different from those rendered "male and female," *zākār un'ķēbah*, i. 27, vi. 19, vii. 3, 9, 16.

The reason why so many more clean animals than unclean are required is, presumably, because they would be wanted (*a*) for food, (*b*) for sacrifice, and (*c*) for domestic purposes.

There is no reason to assume that the J tradition of the narrative shared the opinion of the P tradition, that before the Flood man subsisted on vegetable diet (see i. 29, vi. 20, ix. 2, 3).

3. *the fowl*] Apparently, according to the Hebrew text, all the birds were regarded as clean. Possibly, however, the omission of the distinction between clean and unclean birds is due to the condensed form of the narrative. LXX reads "of fowl also of the air that are clean, seven and seven, male and female," and of "fowl that are not clean, two and two, male and female."

And it is very possible that this last clause has been dropped, through the common error of homoeoteleuton on the part of a scribe.

to keep seed alive] viz. "to maintain life," and "to propagate the species," literally, "to make seed to live." The ideas are combined of continuance by breeding and of preservation from destruction: LXX διαθρέψαι σπέρμα gives the one; the Lat. *ut salvetur semen*, the other.

4. *seven days*] Note the period of seven days, the same interval as occurs again, in the J narrative, in viii. 10, 12.

forty days and forty nights] The duration of the Flood is here announced. Cf. *v.* 12 and viii. 6. In the Babylonian version the rain lasts for six days.

every living thing] or rather, "every existing thing." A peculiar word in the Heb. occurring only here and Deut. xi. 6. (LXX ἀνάστεμα, Lat. *substantiam*.) It is, therefore, different from the expression "living thing," which is used by P in vi. 19, viii. 1, 17, 21.

destroy] Heb. *blot out*, so also *v.* 23 (J): see note on vi. 7.

6—9. A description of the entrance into the ark, with evident editorial adaptations to harmonize vi. 19 and vii. 2 and 15.

6 (P). *six hundred years old*] P gives Noah's age at the time of the Flood. In v. 32 he was said to be 500 years old before "he begat Shem, Ham, and Japheth": see also *v.* 11.

106   GENESIS VII. 6—11

PJ(R) 7 of waters was upon the earth. | And Noah went in, and
his sons, and his wife, and his sons' wives with him, into
8 the ark, because of the waters of the flood. Of clean
beasts, and of beasts that are not clean, and of fowls,
9 and of every thing that creepeth upon the ground, there
went in two and two unto Noah into the ark, male and
10 female, as God commanded Noah. And it came to pass
after the seven days, that the waters of the flood were
P 11 upon the earth. | In the six hundredth year of Noah's life,
in the second month, on the seventeenth day of the month,

7 (partly J). *Noah went in*] This account, which anticipates *v.* 13 (P), is probably from J, with editorial adaptations to avoid clashing with P.

8. *and of fowls*] There is no mention of a distinction between clean and not clean in the birds and the creeping things, see note on *v.* 3. The mention of a distinction between "clean" and "unclean" beasts (*behêmah*, "cattle" or "domestic animals" of vi. 20) is certainly a later insertion by the compiler. The account in vi. 19, 20 (P) does not recognize the distinction of clean and unclean.

9. *two and two*] Apparently these words are introduced in order to harmonize the account in this verse with the command in vi. 19, and with the description in vii. 15. There is no mention of the admission of seven, or of seven pairs, of "clean" animals.

male and female] The same phrase as in *v.* 3, vi. 19: cf. i. 27. It is not the expression of *v.* 2, "the male and his female" (see note). The compiler is following P, who gives one pair of each kind.

God] Elohim. So LXX ὁ Θεός; but the LXX text is not uniform. Cod. E and other MSS. κύριος; Lat. *Dominus*, and the Samaritan version, and the Targum, represent a text which read "Jehovah." The work of the compiler, which is obvious in these verses, has left the reading in doubt.

VII. 10—VIII. 14. THE ACCOUNT OF THE FLOOD, COMPILED FROM J AND P.

10. *after the seven days*] The seven days mentioned in *v.* 4, the period during which Noah and his family were in the ark, before the commencement of the Flood. The arrangements necessary for the inmates of the ark required time. Moreover, throughout the Genesis story, a period of probation and patience precedes the fulfilment of the Divine word.

11. *the second month, on the seventeenth day*] P gives, according to its fondness for statistics, the exact date in years, months, and days. Cf. Ex. xii. 41 (P). The months and days apparently are reckoned on the assumption that Noah was born on the first day of the year,

GENESIS VII. 11, 12

on the same day were all the fountains of the great deep P
broken up, and the windows of heaven were opened. | And 12 J
the rain was upon the earth forty days and forty nights. |

600 years previously. LXX here, and in viii. 4, reads "twenty-seventh
day," because of viii. 14.

the second month] According to Josephus (*Ant.* I. 3, 3), this second
month was Marchesvan, equivalent to our November, the beginning
of the season of rain in Palestine. The account is, therefore, well
adapted to Israelite presuppositions. But, on the supposition that
Abib, or April, was reckoned as the first month, the Flood would have
begun in May, the month in which the Tigris and the Euphrates are
liable to be flooded through the melting of the snows in the mountains.
It is doubtful whether Tisri (= October) or Abib is here regarded as the
first month of the year.

the fountains of the great deep] The origin of the Flood, according
to P, was not merely rain. The Israelites believed that beneath the
surface of the earth were accumulated enormous reservoirs of water, to
supply, through channels or fissures, the seas, lakes, and rivers. This
accumulation of water is poetically described as "the deep that coucheth
beneath" (Gen. xlix. 25), and "the great deep" (Ps. xxxvi. 6; Isa.
li. 10; Amos vii. 4). Here it is supposed that the channels, or, as the
account calls them, "the fountains of the great deep," were violently
rent asunder, "broken up," whereupon the subterranean waters swept
out in portentous volume and violence over the surface of the earth.

the great deep] On the "deep" (*tehom*), here called "great," see
note on i. 2.

the windows of heaven] The other source of the Deluge is here
given. Above the solid firmament (see note on i. 6) were stored the
masses of water which supplied the rainfall of the earth. Now "the
sluices of heaven" (cf. 2 Kings vii. 2, 19; Mal. iii. 10) and "the
windows on high" (cf. Isa. xxiv. 18) are thrown open, and the water
descends in unrestrained mass. For this description of the waters
above and below, cf. Prov. viii. 27—29; Job xxxviii. 16. LXX οἱ
καταρράκται τοῦ οὐρανοῦ, Lat. *cataractae coeli*. Aquila and Symmachus
αἱ θυρίδες.

12 (J). *the rain*] In this verse the cause of the Flood and its duration are given by J. Its cause, torrents of rain, the Heb. word denoting
something much stronger than ordinary rain. Its duration, forty days
and forty nights, as in *v.* 4.

13—16ᵃ (P). THE ENTRANCE INTO THE ARK, ACCORDING TO P.

The repetition of what has already been narrated in *vv.* 7—9 can
hardly fail to strike the reader; and, without our recognition of the
composite elements which are here interwoven, it would be unintelligible.

P 13 In the selfsame day entered Noah, and Shem, and Ham, and Japheth, the sons of Noah, and Noah's wife, and the 14 three wives of his sons with them, into the ark; they, and every beast after its kind, and all the cattle after their kind, and every creeping thing that creepeth upon the earth after its kind, and every fowl after its kind, every bird of every 15 ¹sort. And they went in unto Noah into the ark, two and 16 two of all flesh wherein is the breath of life. And they that went in, went in male and female of all flesh, as God com-
J(R) 17 manded him : | and the LORD shut him in. | And the flood
J was forty days upon the earth; | and the waters increased, and bare up the ark, and it was lift up above the earth. |
P 18 And the waters prevailed, and increased greatly upon the

¹ Heb. *wing*.

13. *In the selfsame day*] Observe that P represents the Flood as ommencing on the same day (cf. *v.* 11) that Noah entered the ark. There is no account taken here of the interval of seven days, mentioned by J in *vv.* 4 and 10, preceding the catastrophe. For the expression "selfsame day," a characteristic of P, cf. xvii. 23, 26; Ex. xii. 17, 41, 51. Lat. *in articulo diei illius*.

with them] LXX and Peshitto Syriac, "with him," as in viii. 16, 18.
14. *kind*] See note on i. 12 and vi. 20.
of every sort] Heb. *wing*. Literally, "every bird, every wing," i.e. all sorts of birds. The clause is wanting in the LXX. Some scholars prefer the rendering, "every bird, every winged thing," so that the phrase should include all winged animals, insects as well as birds.

Notice in this verse the comprehensive description of the animal world; "beast"=wild animals, "cattle"=domestic animals, "creeping things," "fowls," "winged things of all sorts," as in i. 21, 24, 25, 26.
15. *all flesh...breath of life*] See note on vi. 17.
two and two] See note on vi. 19, 20. LXX adds "male and female."
16 (P). *as God commanded him*] This is evidently P's account: notice the use of *Elohim*, and the phrase itself, cf. vi. 22, vii. 5, 9.

(J) *and the LORD shut him in*] Notice the introduction of Jehovah. These words are evidently from J, and probably originally concluded the previous account of Noah's entry into the ark (*vv.* 7—9) before the seven days mentioned in *v.* 10, and before the rain (*v.* 12).

On the anthropomorphism of this action, see note on vi. 6; and compare iii. 8, xi. 5.
17 (R). *forty days*] Cf. *v.* 12, where the rain lasts for 40 days and 40 nights. Here it is the duration of the Flood.
18 (P). *the waters prevailed*] The description given in *v.* 17 of the

earth; and the ark went upon the face of the waters. And 19 P
the waters prevailed exceedingly upon the earth; and all
the high mountains that were under the whole heaven were
covered. Fifteen cubits upward did the waters prevail; 20
and the mountains were covered. And all flesh died that 21
moved upon the earth, both fowl, and cattle, and beast,
and every ¹creeping thing that creepeth upon the earth,
and every man : | all in whose nostrils was the breath of 22 J
the spirit of life, of all that was in the dry land, died.

¹ Or, *swarming thing that swarmeth*

rising waters and of the floating ark is here repeated, in order to introduce the record of the more elaborate details contained in *vv.* 19, 20.

19. *all the high mountains*] The account, given by P, describes the covering of the mountains of the whole earth by the waters of the Deluge. It is this hyperbolical description which has naturally seized upon the imagination of readers. It is not necessary to enlarge upon the physical impossibility of such an event. If the literal interpretation were adopted, the waters would have submerged not only the mountains of Western Asia and of Europe, but also the Andes and the Himalayas. Water at that height would have been ice: organic life would have been impossible. Geology has shewn that no such universal Deluge has ever occurred. The accumulation of the vast amount of water represented in such a scene and encompassing the whole globe is beyond the range of physical possibility.

Popular imagination working upon the tradition of a vast inundation in the Euphrates Valley lent itself to exaggeration.

20. *Fifteen cubits*] P describes a depth of water of 15 cubits (=22 feet) above the mountains. Why should 15 cubits be mentioned? Very possibly, because the height of the ark was 30 cubits (vi. 15), and the ark was considered to be submerged for half its depth. It would thus just touch the top of "the mountains of Ararat" (viii. 4).

21 (P). *And all flesh died*] Cf. vi. 17. P here describes the death by drowning of all living creatures.

creeping thing] Literally, as marg., *swarming thing that swarmeth.* See note on i. 20. The word used is characteristic of P.

22 (J). *all*] The account in this and the following verse gives J's description of the destruction of all life. The repetition is obvious.

in whose nostrils, &c.] The expression is evidently based upon the words in ii. 7, "breathed into his nostrils the breath of life." But "the breath of life" of that passage is combined here with "the spirit of life" which we find in vi. 17, vii. 15 (P). The one is a phrase characteristic of J, the other of P. The combination is not found elsewhere. Possibly the word "spirit" has been introduced by the compiler or by a copyist.

in the dry land] as if to emphasize the thought that the marine

J 23 ¹And every living thing was ²destroyed which was upon the face of the ground, both man, and cattle, and creeping thing, and fowl of the heaven; and they were ²destroyed from the earth: and Noah only was left, and they that were
P 24 with him in the ark. | And the waters prevailed upon the earth an hundred and fifty days.
8 And God remembered Noah, and every living thing, and all the cattle that were with him in the ark: and God made a wind to pass over the earth, and the waters assuaged;
2 the fountains also of the deep and the windows of heaven
J were stopped, | and the rain from heaven was restrained;
3 and the waters returned from off the earth continually: |
P and after the end of an hundred and fifty days the waters

---

¹ Or, *And he destroyed every living thing*
² Heb. *blotted out*.

animals survived. The word in the Heb. rendered "the dry land" is different from that so rendered in i. 9 (P).

23 (J). *was destroyed...were destroyed*] The better reading is that rendered in the R.V. marg., *and he destroyed every living thing*. For the word "destroyed," Heb. *blotted out*, see vi. 7, vii. 4.

24 (P). *an hundred and fifty days*] The duration of the Flood, corresponding to the 40 days of J in *v.* 12. According to P, the rising of the waters, described in *vv.* 18—20, continued or "prevailed" for 150 days, after which the waters began to fall: see viii. 3ᵇ, 4ᵃ.

CH. VIII. 1—14. THE DIMINUTION OF THE WATERS.

1 (P). *God remembered*] The same expression occurs in xix. 29, xxx. 22. It is a form of anthropomorphism which is not infrequent in the O.T. and which is in continual use in the language of devotion.

and all the cattle] LXX adds "And all the fowls and all the creeping things." For the expression of pity for the brute beasts, cf. "and also much cattle," in Jonah iv. 11.

God made a wind to pass] The wind was to drive the waters back into their channels, and to dry up the ground. Cf. the action of the wind in Ex. xiv. 21.

2ᵃ (P). *the fountains, &c.*] The first clause in this verse describes the closing of the sources of the Flood mentioned in vii. 11 (P).

2ᵇ, 3ᵃ (J). *and the rain...continually*] This is the duplicate account from J, in whose version the rain for 40 days was the cause of the Flood (vii. 12).

3ᵇ (P). *after the end, &c.*] The 150 days are those mentioned in vii. 24.

decreased. And the ark rested in the seventh month, on 4 P
the seventeenth day of the month, upon the mountains of
Ararat. And the waters decreased continually until the 5
tenth month: in the tenth month, on the first day of the
month, were the tops of the mountains seen. | And it came 6 J
to pass at the end of forty days, that Noah opened the
window of the ark which he had made: and he sent forth 7
a raven, and it went forth to and fro, until the waters were

4. *the seventh month*, &c.] The Flood had begun on the 17th day of the 2nd month (see vii. 11): the highest point of the Flood is reached on the 17th day of the 7th month. Five months have elapsed. Probably the 150 days were reckoned as five months of 30 days each.

the mountains of Ararat] Ararat is not a mountain, but a district mentioned in Isa. xxxvii. 38; Jer. li. 27. It is the country which appears in the Assyrian inscriptions as "Urartu." It lies between the river Araxes and Lake Van. It comprises a large portion of Armenia. There were high mountains in Ararat; and the loftiest among them, called in the present day Mount Ararat, is over 16,000 ft. high.

Assuming that the tradition referred to this mountain as the highest known, and that the water was said to have covered it by 15 cubits (vii. 20), the very existence of mountains of the altitude of Mount Everest (31,000 ft. high) was not contemplated. It is more probable that a well-known name like Ararat was accepted, in the Hebrew version of the story, for some similarly-sounding, but less familiar, name of hills in the neighbourhood of the Tigris.

5 (P). *the tenth month*] Another date is here given. The tops of other mountains were visible on the 1st day of the 10th month. Reckoning 30 days for a month, we thus have an interval of 73 days between the grounding of the ark upon the mountains of Ararat and the visibility of the other mountains.

tops of the mountains] This detail in the narrative suggests that Ararat was thought to be a lonely peak towering above all the neighbouring mountains.

6—12. THE STORY OF THE RAVEN AND THE DOVE. (J.)

6. *at the end of forty days*] The forty days mentioned in vii. 4, 12.

the window] LXX θυρίδα, Lat. *fenestram*. This was not mentioned by P in the description of the ark in chap. vi. The word used here is the ordinary equivalent for a window (*ḥallôn*), and is different from the "light" (*ṣohar*) mentioned in vi. 16.

7. *a raven*] The Heb. and LXX give the definite article, "the raven," which some have explained as the only male raven in the ark. But the article is idiomatically generic; cf. *v.* 8, Gesenius, *Heb. Gr.* 126, § 4. The Israelite story records the sending, first of a raven, and then, on two successive occasions, of a dove. The Babylonian account records

J 8 dried up from off the earth. And he sent forth a dove from him, to see if the waters were abated from off the 9 face of the ground; but the dove found no rest for the sole of her foot, and she returned unto him to the ark, for the waters were on the face of the whole earth: and he put forth his hand, and took her, and brought her in unto him 10 into the ark. And he stayed yet other seven days; and 11 again he sent forth the dove out of the ark; and the dove came in to him at eventide; and, lo, in her mouth ¹an olive leaf pluckt off: so Noah knew that the waters were abated 12 from off the earth. And he stayed yet other seven days; and sent forth the dove; and she returned not again unto

¹ Or, *a fresh olive leaf*

the sending first of a dove, which returned; then of a swallow, which returned; and lastly of a raven, which turned not back.

Noah, stranded with the ark on the highest point, is unable to see anything around or below him.

went forth to and fro] Presumably it was preying upon floating carcases. The "to and fro" suggests the picture of its flitting backwards and forwards, near the ark.

8. *a dove*] The definite article is used also here, though there would have been seven pairs of doves. From the opening clause of *v.* 10, we may conclude that the narrative here was originally fuller, and that this verse must have begun "and he stayed seven days."

9. *no rest*] Compare the Babylonian description, "the dove went to and fro; as there was no resting-place, it turned back." Clearly the account in these verses implies that only water was visible: it represents an earlier stage than that in *v.* 5 (P).

put forth his hand] The description is one of great beauty and simplicity. The dove trusted Noah: the ark was its only home. The dove was only for a short time absent from the ark.

10. *yet other seven days*] See note on *v.* 8. The word "other" shews that an interval of seven days has already been mentioned. The importance of the period of seven days seems to receive emphasis from this passage, as well as from vii. 4, 10.

11. *at eventide*] i.e. at the time when the dove would return to roost; implying a long absence from the ark.

an olive leaf pluckt off] Better, as R.V. marg., *a fresh olive leaf*. This would shew two things, (1) that the waters had sunk to a level at which the olive would grow, and (2) that life had revived upon the earth. The scene has universally been accepted as symbolical of reconciliation and peace. It finds no counterpart in the Babylonian story. The olive would be the most familiar tree to the dweller in Palestine.

LXX φύλλον ἐλαίας κάρφος, Lat. *ramum olivae virentibus foliis*.

him any more. | And it came to pass in the six hundred 13 P
and first year, in the first month, the first day of the month,
the waters were dried up from off the earth: | and Noah   J
removed the covering of the ark, and looked, and, behold,
the face of the ground was dried. | And in the second 14 P
month, on the seven and twentieth day of the month, was
the earth dry.

And God spake unto Noah, saying, Go forth of the ark, 15
thou, and thy wife, and thy sons, and thy sons' wives with 16
thee. Bring forth with thee every living thing that is with 17
thee of all flesh, both fowl, and cattle, and every creeping
thing that creepeth upon the earth; that they may breed

---

13 (P). *And it came to pass...earth*] The disappearance of the
waters is dated by P as coinciding with the 1st day of the 1st month
of Noah's 601st year. The 1st month would be Tisri, corresponding
to our October. See note on vii. 11. Those who assume a reference to
the later Heb. reckoning, which was identical with that of the Babylonian
calendar, suppose the 1st month to be that of Abib, in the spring time,
when the rainy season ended.

(J) *and Noah removed*] LXX ἀπεκάλυψε τὴν στέγην τῆς κιβωτοῦ,
Lat. *aperiens tectum arcae*.

the covering of the ark] The literal rendering of the Heb. But what
it was, and how it was removed, we are not told. The details of the
structure of the ark, according to J, were probably left out, in order to
make way for the description of P in vi. 14—16.

14 (P). *And in the second month*] We have here the last date in the
Flood story. The earth is dry on the 27th day of the 2nd month in
the 2nd year. The Flood had begun on the 17th day of the 2nd month in
the previous year (vii. 11). From first to last we have here a period of one
year and 10 days. It has been pointed out that a lunar year consists of
354 days; and that one lunar year and 11 days is exactly a solar year of
365 days. This may be merely a coincidence; and in calculating the
months we reckon them as solar months of 30 days each.

The LXX in vii. 11 dated the commencement of the Flood from the
27th day of the 2nd month of the 1st year; and, therefore, assigns
an exact year to its duration.

dry] Note the successive stages in P: *v.* 5 waters decreased, tops
of mountains visible; *v.* 13 waters gone; *v.* 14 soil dry.

**15—19. NOAH IS COMMANDED TO LEAVE THE ARK, AND TO
REPLENISH THE EARTH. (P.)**

17. *that they may breed abundantly*] The same word as in i. 20,
"let the waters bring forth abundantly" (see note). Cf. ix. 7.

P abundantly in the earth, and be fruitful, and multiply upon
18 the earth. And Noah went forth, and his sons, and his
19 wife, and his sons' wives with him: every beast, every
creeping thing, and every fowl, whatsoever moveth upon
the earth, after their families, went forth out of the ark. |
J 20 And Noah builded an altar unto the LORD; and took of
every clean beast, and of every clean fowl, and offered
21 burnt offerings on the altar. And the LORD smelled the

be fruitful, and multiply] as in i. 22, 24—28. The repetition of the Creation command marks the beginning of a new era in the history of the world. The fuller blessing, according to P, is given in chap. ix. (*vv.* 1—7). For the detailed enumeration in *vv.* 18, 19, cf. vii. 13, 14 P.

19. *after their families*] A phrase characteristic of P. Cf. x. 5, 20, 31, xxxvi. 40. It is in accordance with P's fondness for method and order that, in his description, the animals are made to leave the ark "after their families"; they had entered it "after their kind" (vii. 14 P).

20—22. NOAH'S BURNT-OFFERING AND JEHOVAH'S ACCEPTANCE OF IT. (J.)

20. *builded an altar unto the LORD*] It will be noticed that, in this account by J, the first thing that Noah does, on leaving the ark, is to build an altar, and to offer sacrifice. In J's estimation sacrifice was primitive, and not merely Mosaic, in origin. See note on vii. 2.

In P there is no mention of "altar" or "sacrifice" before the institution of the Levitical system in the wilderness.

of every clean beast, and of every clean fowl] The clean animals were used for sacrifice. Cf. vii. 2. Observe the mention of "clean fowl," implying the distinction between clean and unclean fowl. This distinction was not observed in vii. 3, 8. The number of "clean" animals, seven pairs of each, in the ark, according to J, would allow for the offering of sacrifice.

In the Babylonian account, also, sacrifices were at once offered to the gods on quitting the ark.

and offered burnt offerings] The word for "burnt offering" is *'ôlâh*, which is derived from a verb meaning "to go up." A burnt-offering, or *'ôlâh*, was the sacrifice which "went up" to God, being different from other sacrifices, because the whole of it was consumed in the fire of the altar. The offerer of an *'ôlâh* ate nothing of the sacrifice; nor did the priest. It was in an especial sense a propitiatory offering: compare David's offering in 2 Sam. xxiv. 25. The *'ôlâh* is different from the *minḥah* of iv. 3. LXX renders εἰς ὁλοκάρπωσιν, Lat. *holocausta*.

21. *smelled the sweet savour*] A very strong anthropomorphism which only occurs here. "Sweet savour" is a technical expression in the

GENESIS VIII. 21, 22

sweet savour; and the LORD said in his heart, I will not again curse the ground any more for man's [1]sake, for that the imagination of man's heart is evil from his youth; neither will I again smite any more every thing living, as I have done. While the earth remaineth, seedtime and 22 harvest, and cold and heat, and summer and winter, and

[1] Or, *sake; for the*

language of Levitical sacrifice. Cf. Lev. i. 9, 13, 17. Literally, it meant "the smell of complacence" or "satisfaction," with the idea of restfulness and calm produced. "Sweet savour" is, therefore, somewhat of a paraphrase based on the LXX ὀσμὴ εὐωδίας, Lat. *odor suavitatis*.

The technical term is employed to express that the offering is acceptable to God. The heart of the offerer is acceptable (the converse of iv. 5). See the use made of the phrase "sweet savour" by St Paul in 2 Cor. ii. 15, 16.

The Babylonian version describes how "the gods smelt the goodly savour of the sacrifice, and swarmed like flies over the sacrificer."

in his heart] Lit. "to his heart" = "to himself," an anthropomorphism similar to that in vi. 6. LXX, in order to avoid the term, renders by διανοηθείς; Targum of Onkelos, "by his word."

curse] i.e. do injury to by a sentence, or decree, of evil.

for man's sake, for that] Better, as R.V. marg., *sake; for the*. The difference of the two renderings is obvious: (*a*) that of the text gives the reason for which God's curse had been inflicted upon the ground, i.e. man's sinfulness: (*b*) that of the margin gives the reason why God will not *again* curse the ground, i.e. man is essentially sinful; he must not be expected to be otherwise. Perhaps the rendering of the margin which emphasizes the element of mercy is in better harmony with the context. The sentence already pronounced upon the earth in iii. 17 (cf. iv. 11, 12) had rendered life arduous and distressing.

the imagination of man's heart] Cf. vi. 5.

22. *While the earth remaineth*] Observe the poetical character of this verse. The four pairs of words are recorded with an impressive and rhythmical dignity.

NOTE ON THE FLOOD NARRATIVE

I. "The original Babylonian Flood story is often treated as purely mythical, spun out of light (Usener, *Die Sintflutsagen*, pp. 185 ff.), moon (Böklen, *Archiv f. Religionswissenschaft*, vi. p. 5 f.), astral (Jensen, *Gilgamesh Epos in der Weltgeschichte*, i. *passim*), or other motives. There is certainly a large mythical element in the tale (e.g. the actions of the different gods). But the personal and local names (Ut-napishtim, Shurippak, Nizir), and the nautical descriptions and details, would argue for a certain basis in fact. There seems no real reason to doubt that the story has grown up around the tradition of some great inundation, perhaps accompanied by a cyclonic storm, that overwhelmed the city of Shurippak (cf. Ed. Süss, *Das Antlitz der Erde*, i. 25 ff. *ap.* Andrée, *Die Flutsagen*, pp. 11 ff.), only a few persons escaping on an ark resembling the pitch-covered barges still seen in use on the Euphrates (cf. Lady Anne Blount, *Bedouin Tribes of the Euphrates*, i. 166). In an alluvial land like Babylonia, such catastrophes were only too liable to occur. Thus Strabo tells of a great rising of the sea in Egypt, near Pelusium, in his own day, which overflowed the land, 'and converted Mt Casius into an island, so that a journey from Casius into Phoenicia might have been taken by water' (I. iii. 17). Andrée quotes records of many similar destructive catastrophes in more recent times (*op. cit.* pp. 143 ff.)." (Gordon's *Early Traditions of Genesis*, p. 193, *n.* 1.)

II. The following brilliant and rapid summary of the Babylonian Flood story is taken from Skinner (p. 175).

"Of the Babylonian story the most complete version is contained in the eleventh Tablet of the Gilgamesh Epic [discovered by G. Smith, in 1872, among the ruins of Asshur-banipal's library; published 1873—4; and often translated since]. Gilgamesh has arrived at the Isles of the Blessed to inquire of his ancestor Utnapishtim how he had been received into the society of the gods. The answer is the long and exceedingly graphic description of the Flood which occupies the bulk of the Tablet. The hero relates how, while he dwelt at Shurippak on the Euphrates, it was resolved by the gods in council to send the Flood (*abûbu*) on the earth. Êa, who had been present at the council, resolved to save his favourite Utnapishtim; and contrived without overt breach of confidence to convey to him a warning of the impending danger, commanding him to build a ship (*elippu*) of definite dimensions for the saving of his life. The 'superlatively clever one' (*Atra-ḥasis*, a name of Utnapishtim) understood the message and promised to obey; and was furnished with a misleading pretext to offer his fellow-citizens for his extraordinary proceedings. The account of the building of the ship (ll. 48 ff.) is even more obscure than Gen. vi. 14—16: it is enough to say that it was divided into compartments and was freely smeared with bitumen. The lading of the vessel, and the embarking of the family and dependants of Utnapishtim (including artizans), with domestic and wild animals, are then described (ll. 81 ff.); and last of all, in the evening, on the appearance of a sign predicted by Shamash the sun-god, Utnapishtim himself enters the ship, shuts his door, and hands over the command to the steersman, Puzur-Bel (ll. 90 ff.). On the following morning the storm (magnificently described in ll. 97 ff.) broke; and it raged for six days and nights, till all mankind were destroyed, and the very gods fled to the heaven of Anu and 'cowered in terror like a dog.'"

Photo Mansell & Co.

Fragment of Cuneiform Tablet, belonging to the Deluge Series.

(British Museum.)

GENESIS VIII.

"When the seventh day came, the hurricane, the Flood, the battle-storm was stilled,
Which had fought like a (host?) of men.
The sea became calm, the tempest was still, the Flood ceased.
When I saw the day, no voice was heard,
And the whole of mankind was turned to clay.
When the daylight came, I prayed,
I opened a window, and the light fell on my face,
I knelt, I sat and wept.
On my nostrils my tears ran down.
I looked on the spaces in the realm of the sea;
After twelve double-hours an island stood out.
At Nizir the ship had arrived.
The mountain of Nizir stayed the ship..." (ll. 130—142).

This brings us to the incident of the birds (ll. 146—155):

"When the seventh day [i.e. from the landing] came
I brought out a dove and let it go.
The dove went forth and came back:
Because it had not whereon to stand it returned.
I brought forth a swallow and let it go.
The swallow went forth and came back:
Because it had not whereon to stand it returned.
I brought forth a raven and let it go.
The raven went forth and saw the decrease of the waters,
It ate, it... it croaked, but returned not again."

On this Utnapishtim released all the animals; and leaving the ship, offered a sacrifice:

"The gods smelt the savour,
The gods smelt the goodly savour,
The gods gathered like flies over the sacrificer" (ll. 160 ff.).

The deities then began to quarrel, Ishtar and Êa reproaching Bel for his thoughtlessness in destroying mankind indiscriminately, and Bel accusing Êa of having connived at the escape of Utnapishtim. Finally Bel is appeased; and entering the ship blesses the hero and his wife:

"'Formerly Utnapishtim was a man;
But now shall Utnapishtim and his wife be like to us the gods:
Utnapishtim shall dwell far hence at the mouth of the streams.'
Then they took me, and far away at the mouth of the streams
they made me dwell" (ll. 202 ff.).

"Two fragments of another recension of the Flood-legend, in which the hero is regularly named Atra-ḥasis, have also been deciphered. One of them, being dated in the reign of Ammizaduga (c. 1980) is important as proving that this recension had been reduced to writing at so early a time; but it is too mutilated to add anything substantial to our knowledge of the history of the tradition.... The other is a mere scrap of twelve lines, containing Ea's instructions to Atra-hasis regarding the building and entering of the ark and the latter's promise to comply.... The extracts from Berossus preserved by Eus. present the Babylonian history in a form substantially agreeing with that of the Gilgamesh Tablets, though with some important variations in detail, see Euseb. *Chron.* i."

III. The points of resemblance between the Babylonian and the Hebrew Flood narratives are unmistakable. In both the Flood is a visitation sent in Divine anger. In both, a favoured person receives a Divine warning and is commanded beforehand to construct a ship. In both, precise instructions are given as to the dimensions of the ship, and as to its being covered with bitumen. In both, the whole human race is destroyed in the waters. In both, the entry of the man and his family into the ship, and the shutting of the door, are mentioned. In both, there is an episode with birds. In both, after the waters have abated, the ship has grounded on a mountain. In both, after leaving the ship, the man offers sacrifice. In both, the Divine anger is appeased, and a blessing is pronounced upon the survivors.

This correspondence is too general to be the result of accident. The accounts differ as to details of time, the number and order of the birds, and the sign of the rainbow. These are details; but, as details, are sufficient to shew that the Biblical narratives are not simply reproduced from the Tablets recording the Gilgamesh Epos.

The Babylonian story, in one of its versions, was committed to writing about 2000 B.C. The Flood narrative, therefore, was current among the people of Babylonia and Mesopotamia before the migration of Abraham. Through what process it passed into the literature of the Israelites, can only be a matter of conjecture. Was it the result of early Babylonian influence and civilization in Canaan absorbed by the Israelite invaders? Was it the result of the early Hebrew forefathers having migrated from Mesopotamia into Canaan, carrying their folk-lore with them? Was it the result of Babylonian thought and religion, subsequently encroaching far and wide, and penetrating into Western Asia?

Whatever the process was, the narrative of the Flood is preserved to us, in two Hebrew versions, entirely divergent from the Babylonian in religious spirit, literary style, and character.

(*a*) *Religious spirit.* The change from the quarrelsome, deceitful, vindictive pack of Babylonian deities to the One Supreme and Righteous God of the Hebrews imparts strength, dignity, and purity to the narrative.

(*b*) *Literary style.* The diffuse and poetical descriptions of the Babylonian epic have made way for the direct, simple, and terse account in Hebrew prose.

(*c*) *Character.* The purpose of the Hebrew story is a moral one, to emphasize (1) the corruption of the human race through sin, (2) the Divine anger and disappointment because of man's sinfulness, (3) the Divine favour and goodness towards the one righteous person, (4) the classical example of salvation, and (5) the Divine promise of future mercy. The Babylonian story is part of an elaborate series of legendary stories, relating to the gods of Babylonia and their dealings with one another and with mankind. It is devoid of any uniform or exalted purpose: it is lacking in reverence and restraint. "The Biblical story of the Deluge possesses an intrinsic power, even to the present day, to awaken the conscience of the world, and the Biblical chronicler wrote it with this educational and moral end in view. Of this end there is no trace in the extra-Biblical records of the Deluge." (Jeremias, *O.T. in the Light of the E.* i. 274.)

IV. Other Flood stories are very numerous, and are found among the early legends of races all over the world. Andrée reckoned up eighty-five, of which he considered forty-three to be original, and twenty-six to be derived from the Babylonian (*Die Flutsagen ethnographisch betrachtet*, 1891). But with the increasing study of anthropology the number is likely to be enlarged. The fact that, according to Andrée, they had not been found in Arabia, North and Central Asia, China and Japan, Europe (except Greece) and Africa, shews that too much ought not to be made of the so-called universality of the legend. Interesting Flood myths are reported from N. American, Mexican, and Polynesian races.

1. A Flood story may refer to a catastrophe overwhelming the primitive dwelling-place of mankind, from which it radiated into the different races of the world. But, *ex hypothesi*, this would have been an event long previous to any civilized memorials of human history.

2. A Flood story may represent the influence upon crude and savage minds, in comparatively recent times, of the Babylonian tradition or of Christian teaching.

3. A Flood story may embody the recollection of a great local cataclysm, preserved in the folk-lore of the country.

The following are examples of other Flood stories:

1. Egyptian. Egypt was long supposed to have no Flood tradition. Naville (P.S.B.A., 1904, pp. 251—257, 287—294) has recently published the following from a text of the Book of the Dead: "And further I (the god Tum) am going to deface all I have done; this earth will become water (or an ocean) through an inundation, as it was at the beginning" (quoted by Skinner, p. 175).

2. Syrian. "The wickedness of men became so great that they had to be destroyed. Then the fountains of the earth and the floodgates of the heaven were opened, the sea rose ever higher, the whole earth was covered with water and all men went under. Only the pious Deucalion (Xisuthros) was rescued, by hiding himself with his wives and children in a great chest 'which he possessed.' When he entered, there came in also, in pairs, every kind of four-footed thing, serpents, and whatever else lives upon the earth. He took them all in, and God caused great friendship to be amongst them. At last the water ran away through a small cleft in the earth. Deucalion opened the chest, built altars, and founded over the cleft in the earth the holy temple of the goddess" (Pseudo-Lucian, *De dea Syria*, § 12).

3. Phrygian. Coins of Apameia, of the time of Augustus, "show

two scenes of the Deluge. On the right is the chest upon waves of water, with a man and woman raising themselves out of it, and upon the open lid of it a dove sitting, whilst a second (!) dove with a branch flies towards it from the left. On the left stand the same figures...with the right hand raised in prayer....The name Noah [on the chest] rests upon Jewish (or Christian) influence."

4. Greek. Apollodorus i. 712 ff. "Zeus wished to destroy the generation of mankind...but by the counsel of Prometheus, Deucalion made a chest, put food therein, and entered it with his wife Pyrrha. A few saved themselves by flight to the mountains. After nine days and nights Deucalion landed upon Parnassus. He came forth and offered a sacrifice to Zeus. Zeus permitting him to express a wish, he prayed for mankind; and they arise by his throwing over his head 'the bones of the mother,' that is, the stones of the mountain which are changed into men."

5. Indian. The Brahmana "of the hundred paths" relates: "There came into the hands of Manu, the first man and son of the God of the sun, whilst he was washing, a fish who said to him: 'Take care of me and I will save you.' 'From what wilt thou save me?' 'A flood will carry away all this creation, I will save thee from that.' Manu took care of the fish, which grew strong. When it had become a great fish, he put it into the sea. But first of all it said: 'In such and such a year the flood will come, so thou mayest prepare thyself a ship and turn (in spirit) to me: when the flood rises thou shalt enter the ship, and I will save thee.' Manu built the ship, entered it at the appointed time, and bound the rope to the horn of the fish, who had come back and was swimming near. Thereupon it (the fish) hurried away to the mountain in the north, then when the waters sank, the ship rested upon it....The flood had carried away every creature, only Manu remained. He lived in prayer and fasting, desirous of descendants. He offered sacrifice, and from this there arose a woman. Manu said to her: 'Who art thou?' 'Thy daughter.' 'How art thou my daughter, fair one?' 'From those sacrificial gifts hast thou begotten me....Turn to me when thou offerest sacrifice: then shalt thou become rich in children and in cattle....Through her he begot this generation which is now called the generation of Manu. Whatever blessing he desired from her that he received."

(For the above, see Jeremias, *O.T. in the Light of the East*, i. 254—257.)

CH. IX. 1—17 (P). THE CONCLUSION OF THE FLOOD STORY ACCORDING TO P.

The passage falls into two sections: (*a*) 1—7, (*b*) 8—17.

(*a*) 1—7. The blessing pronounced upon Noah and his family: man's prerogatives are enlarged; but two prohibitions are imposed: (i) of eating blood, (ii) of manslaughter.

day and night shall not cease. | And God blessed Noah 9 J P
and his sons, and said unto them, Be fruitful, and multiply,
and replenish the earth. And the fear of you and the 2
dread of you shall be upon every beast of the earth, and
upon every fowl of the air; with all wherewith the ground
¹teemeth, and all the fishes of the sea, into your hand are
they delivered. Every moving thing that liveth shall be 3
food for you; as the green herb have I given you all. But 4

¹ Or, *creepeth*

> (*b*) 8—17. God establishes a covenant with Noah and his descendants, according to which He will never again destroy the inhabitants of the world, and in token of which He appoints the rainbow to be the perpetual symbol of Divine mercy.

Section (*b*) stands in immediate relation to the Flood story, and corresponds to J's account of the Divine promise never again to curse the ground (viii. 21).

1. *And God blessed*, &c.] The substance of this verse is a repetition of i. 28. Another chapter in history is begun. As in chap. i., after the Creation, a single pair confronted the whole earth and its animal world, so here, the single family of Noah is to "replenish the earth," and receives a special blessing, the assurance of Divine favour.

his sons...] The females are not mentioned, but, as often in the O.T., the wives are included in the mention of the husbands: cf. the Sethite Genealogy in chap. v.

2. *the fear of you and the dread of you*] This is a new feature in God's ordering of the world. Hitherto (i. 28) man had received the command (1) to replenish the earth, (2) to subdue it, (3) to have dominion over the animals. Now, however, a new stage is reached. Man hereafter is invested with the right to take the life of animals for food. The animals, therefore, are in a new measure placed at the mercy of man; and "the fear and the dread" of him are associated with man's fresh prerogatives.

teemeth] R.V. marg. *creepeth*, as in i. 29, 30 (P).

into your hand...delivered] i.e. placed at the mercy of you who now have absolute power. Cf. Deut. xix. 12, "deliver him into the hand of the avenger of blood, that he may die."

3. *Every moving thing*] P assumes here that all animals are capable of furnishing food for man, and that there is no distinction between "clean" and "unclean" in the pre-Mosaic dispensation.

as the green herb] See note on i. 30. As, at the Creation, God said of the whole vegetable world, that it should be man's food ("to you it shall be for meat," i. 29), so, now, He declares that the whole animal world shall be food for man. As He gave the vegetable, so now He gives the animal, life to man. But this gift is accompanied with two prohibitions.

P flesh with the life thereof, *which is* the blood thereof, shall
5 ye not eat. And surely your blood, *the blood* of your lives, will I require; at the hand of every beast will I require it:

4. *But flesh with the life thereof, which is the blood thereof*] Man's privilege is attended, first, with a strict ritual prohibition. The words might be more literally rendered thus, "nevertheless flesh with its vital principle (or 'soul'), which is its blood, ye shall not eat." The Israelites regarded the blood as in a mysterious way the vehicle of the soul, or vital principle (*nephesh*), of the flesh (Lev. xvii. 11). The blood was always offered in sacrifice to God as the most sacred part of the victim, the symbol of its life. The prohibition to eat flesh, with the blood in it, formed one of the strictest rules of Israelite and Jewish life. As the institution of the Sabbath was associated with the age of the Creation, so the prohibition of blood-eating was associated with the age of Noah. In other words, its primitive character was shewn by its traditional origin, being regarded as antecedent even to the Call of Abraham. The infringement of the regulation betokens savage impiety (1 Sam. xiv. 32—34), or contamination with idolatrous abominations (Ezek. xxxiii. 25). In Acts xv. 29 to abstain from blood and from things strangled was absolutely necessary for the purpose of holding together the Jewish and Gentile members of the new Christian community[1]. In our own time the Jews observe this regulation with strictness, and the Jewish butcher follows special rules in order that the meat may be entirely freed from blood ("Kosher Meat").

The passages in the Law bearing upon this important regulation are Lev. xvii. 10—14, Deut. xii. 16, 23.

5. *your blood*] The second prohibition is that of manslaughter. The thought of human bloodshed is naturally suggested by the subject of the slaying of animals. Man's life is sacred. Neither man nor beast is to take it.

the blood of your lives] A difficult expression. Literally, "for," or "according to, your souls," i.e. the blood of a person for the life of each person, "blood for blood," "life for life," will God require (as *v.* 6). That "the blood of your souls" means "the blood of your own selves," as distinguished from "the blood of the animals," is another explanation, but not so probable.

But either of these renderings is to be preferred to that of Tuch, "for the protection of your lives."

will I require] This thought that God Himself "will require it," in the case of human bloodshed, appears in Ps. ix. 12, "he that maketh inquisition for blood remembereth them," and Ps. x. 13, "wherefore doth the wicked contemn God, and say in his heart, Thou wilt not require it." See also Gen. xlii. 22, "behold, his blood is required."

---

[1] But καὶ πνικτῶν is possibly here a gloss; and, if so, the gloss is a tribute to the usage. See Kirsopp Lake, *The Earlier Epp. of St Paul.*

GENESIS IX. 5—7

and at the hand of man, even at the hand of every man's brother, will I require the life of man. Whoso sheddeth man's blood, by man shall his blood be shed; for in the image of God made he man. And you, be ye fruitful, and multiply; bring forth abundantly in the earth, and multiply therein.

P

6

7

of every beast] e.g. in Ex. xxi. 28, 29, the ox that gores a person to death is to be stoned.

at the hand of every man's brother] "Brother" here denotes the brotherhood of humanity, not of a particular family. He who slays a man slays his own "brother," although technically there is no relationship.

the life of man] i.e. "the *nephesh*, or vital principle, of man." In the first clause God had said He would "require" the blood: here He says He will "require" the life. In *v.* 4 "the life" is "the blood."

6. *Whoso sheddeth man's blood*, &c.] In the first clause of this verse the principle is laid down, that murder is to be punished with death. Blood for blood and life for life is to be the penalty (cf. ver. 5). The sanctity of human life is thus protected by Divine sanction. The custom of blood-revenge (cf. iv. 10—15), which has entered so largely into the social conditions of Semitic life, whether civilized or barbarous, is here stated in its simplest terms. The murderer's life is "required."

The sentence reads like a line of poetry, *Shôphêk dām hā-ādām Bā-ādām dāmô yis-shāphêk*. LXX seems to have misread *bā-ādām* (="by man"), rendering ἀντὶ τοῦ αἵματος αὐτοῦ="for his blood" (? *b'dāmô*): while in the Latin it is omitted altogether.

for in the image of God, &c.] This clause contains the foundation-principle for the tremendous sentence just promulgated. Man is different from the animals. God made him expressly "in His own image" (see note on i. 27). Violence done to human personality constitutes an outrage against the Divine. Man is to discern in his neighbour "the image of God," and to honour it as the symbol of Divine origin and human brotherhood. As that "image" is not physical (for God is spirit), nor moral (for man is sinful), it must denote man's higher nature, expressed by his self-consciousness, freedom of will, reason, affection, &c.

The prohibitions of blood eating and of murder form two of the so-called "commandments of Noah" which were held by the Rabbis of the Jewish synagogue to have been Divinely imposed upon mankind before the days of Abraham; and were, therefore, in theory required from Gentiles living among the Israelites and from Gentiles who attached themselves to the Jewish community.

The "commandments of Noah" are seven—the prohibitions of (1) disobedience, (2) idolatry, (3) blasphemy, (4) adultery, (5) theft, (6) murder, and (7) the eating of blood.

P 8 And God spake unto Noah, and to his sons with him,
9 saying, And I, behold, I establish my covenant with you,
10 and with your seed after you; and with every living creature that is with you, the fowl, the cattle, and every beast of the earth with you; of all that go out of the ark, even every
11 beast of the earth. And I will establish my covenant with you; neither shall all flesh be cut off any more by the waters of the flood; neither shall there any more be a flood to destroy the
12 earth. And God said, This is the token of the covenant which

8—17b. THE COVENANT WITH NOAH.

9. *I, behold, I*] Cf. vi. 17, "I, behold, I do bring the flood of waters." The same personal emphasis is expressed in proclaiming the mercy of the covenant as previously in the sentence of doom.

establish my covenant] See vi. 18. The Pentateuch mentions three covenants between God and man: (1) with Noah, and its token is the rainbow; (2) with Abraham, xv. and xvii., and its token is circumcision, chap. xvii.; (3) with the people of Israel at Mt Sinai, and its tokens are "the blood of the covenant," the Tabernacle, and the Levitical system (Ex. xxiv., xxv.).

In a covenant between God and man, God makes the promise and lays down the conditions. Man accepts the terms unconditionally, while God "establishes," or ratifies, them.

There is no equality of relationship as in a covenant agreement between men. Man is pledged to obedience on the strength of God's promise of blessing. An outward sign is the "sacrament" of the relation.

10. *and with every living creature*] The Heb. for "creature" is *nephesh*, cf. i. 20. God's covenant with the creatures, as well as with mankind, suggests the thought of the interdependence between the animal world and the human race. Goodness and kindness towards man involve a corresponding blessing upon the animal world. Love is all-pervasive.

11. *a flood to destroy the earth*] The promise here given, that there shall never more be a flood, is appealed to by the prophet in Isa. liv. 9, 10, "for this is as the waters of Noah unto me: for as I have sworn that the waters of Noah should no more go over the earth, so have I sworn that I would not be wroth with thee...for the mountains shall depart and the hills be removed; but my kindness shall not depart from thee, neither shall my covenant of peace be removed, saith the LORD that hath mercy on thee."

12. THE TOKEN OF THE COVENANT.

The word "token," Heb. *ôth*, is the same as that rendered "sign" in iv. 15, "and the LORD appointed a sign for Cain." The "token" is

I make between me and you and every living creature that is with you, for perpetual generations: ¹I do set my bow in the cloud, and it shall be for a token of a covenant between me and the earth. And it shall come to pass, when I bring a cloud over the earth, that the bow shall be seen in the cloud, and I will remember my covenant,

¹ Or, *I have set*

the outward and visible sign of the covenant relation. Its outwardness serves to remind man, whose spiritual adherence will become weak without something visible as the pledge of the inner and spiritual bond.

13. *I do set my bow in the cloud*] Better, as marg., *I have set*. The Hebrew would literally be rendered "I do give," or "have given."

The language is capable of two interpretations:

(1) "I do now, and have just for the first time, set the rainbow in the sky, that mankind may hereafter have a token of the covenant between us."

(2) "I have appointed my bow, which you and mankind have often seen in the heavens, that henceforth it may be for a token of the covenant between us."

The former seems preferable. Hebrew legend explains thus the origin of the rainbow. Of course, it must have been visible from the first, being dependent upon the refraction of the light from the particles of water. The words "my bow" imply either that the bow was a familiar object, or that it was God's gift. The giving of a "token" is not necessarily equivalent to the creation of a feature in nature (cf. iv. 15). Nevertheless, the simplicity of the language favours the most literal interpretation; and the promise in *vv.* 14, 15 suggests that the rainbow was a new phenomenon.

14. *that the bow shall be seen*] This should be rendered "and the bow is seen." The promise is not that the bow shall be seen whenever God sends clouds over the earth, but that, whenever He sends clouds and His bow is visible, then He will remember the covenant.

It is possible that this beautiful employment of the rainbow symbol may be the adaptation of a still earlier semi-mythological conception, according to which the God of Israel is represented in poetry as a warrior armed with bow and arrow (the lightnings are His arrows, cf. Ps. vii. 12, 13; Hab. iii. 9—11); when His anger had passed, He hung His bow in the clouds. The rainbow does not, however, appear frequently in the imagery of Jewish poetry. In Ezek. i. 28, and in Rev. iv. 3, x. 1, it is mentioned in connexion with the appearances of Divine glory. As a feature in nature, it is referred to in Ecclus. xliii. 12, l. 7.

15. *and I will*] This should be rendered "that I will." It forms the apodosis to the words in 14, "and it shall come to pass when."

P	which is between me and you and every living creature of all flesh; and the waters shall no more become a flood to
16	destroy all flesh. And the bow shall be in the cloud; and I will look upon it, that I may remember the everlasting covenant between God and every living creature of all flesh
17	that is upon the earth. And God said unto Noah, This is the token of the covenant which I have established between me and all flesh that is upon the earth.
J 18	And the sons of Noah, that went forth of the ark, were Shem, and Ham, and Japheth: and Ham is the father of
19	Canaan. These three were the sons of Noah: and of these was the whole earth overspread.
20	And Noah began to be an husbandman, and planted a

16. *remember*] Used of God, cf. viii. 1. Here it suggests that the primitive tradition implied that God might forget, if it were not for "the bow." The word "remember" may be anthropomorphic; but in the later stage of the tradition, as in this passage, the rainbow is the "sign" or "reminder" for man, not for God.

the everlasting covenant] See xvii. 7, 13, 19; Ex. xxxi. 16; Lev. xxiv. 8; Num. xviii. 19, xxv. 13, a phrase used by P. Heb. *b'rîth 'ôlâm*, LXX διαθήκη αἰώνιος, Lat. *foedus sempiternum*.

17. *This is the token*, &c.] This verse, according to the style of P, reiterates the substance of 11—13.

18—27. NOAH, AS THE VINE-DRESSER, AND HIS THREE SONS. (J.)

In this section the narrative, which begins at v. 20, is introduced by the two connecting verses 18, 19, which either conclude J's account of the Flood, or are an editorial insertion by the compiler.

(*a*) 18, 19 Noah and his family leave the ark: (*b*) 20—24 Noah plants a vineyard, drinks wine, becomes intoxicated, is observed and ridiculed by Ham, but Shem and Japheth shew respect: (*c*) 25—27 the curse of Noah on Canaan, the blessing on Shem and Japheth.

18. *the sons of Noah*] The names of Noah's sons have already frequently been given in the P narrative (v. 32, vi. 10, vii. 13).

Ham is the father of Canaan] This note has in all probability been inserted by the compiler, with reference to the section vv. 20—27 and the curse pronounced upon Canaan (vv. 25 and 27).

20. *And Noah began to be an husbandman*] This expression is an extremely awkward rendering of the strange Hebrew, which is literally "And Noah began man of the soil and planted," &c. Better, "And Noah the husbandman began and planted a vineyard," i.e. was the first to do so.

"The husbandman," lit. "man of the soil," LXX ἄνθρωπος γεωργὸς

vineyard: and he drank of the wine, and was drunken; 21 J
and he was uncovered within his tent. And Ham, the 22
father of Canaan, saw the nakedness of his father, and
told his two brethren without. And Shem and Japheth 23
took a garment, and laid it upon both their shoulders, and
went backward, and covered the nakedness of their father;
and their faces were backward, and they saw not their
father's nakedness. And Noah awoke from his wine, and 24
knew what his ¹youngest son had done unto him. And he 25
said,

¹ Or, *younger*

γῆs. This description of Noah introduces him in a new capacity. The present section seems to be taken from a distinct tradition concerning the primaeval time, in which Noah appears as the founder of agriculture and of vine cultivation.

21. *and he drank*] The representation is that of the man who first made wine out of grapes, and drinking of it in ignorance was overcome by its potency. No blame is attached to him.

22. *Ham, the father of*] Words probably inserted by the compiler (R). If so, in the original narrative there stood in this verse simply the name of "Canaan," "and Canaan saw the nakedness." Otherwise the curse pronounced upon Canaan, instead of upon Ham, in *v.* 25, is unintelligible (see note).

According to this view, the old tradition, from which these verses are derived, regarded "Canaan," and not "Ham," as the brother of Shem and Japheth.

23. *a garment*] Heb. *simlah*, LXX ἱμάτιον, Lat. *pallium*: the large upper garment which was also used as a covering by night, as appears from Ex. xxii. 26; Deut. xxiv. 13. The conduct of Shem and Japheth, in its regard for their father's honour, is contrasted with the levity and want of delicacy displayed by their brother.

24. *his youngest son*] The rendering of the R.V. marg. and of the A.V., *younger* (so LXX ὁ νεώτερος, Lat. *minor*), is not permissible. The Hebrew word, where there is a comparison between more than two persons, means "the youngest," as in the story of David (1 Sam. xvi. 11, xvii. 14). The difficulty, which has led to the rendering of the R.V. marg. and the A.V., arises from the fact that in the order of Noah's sons given by J in *v.* 18, and by P in v. 32, vi. 10, vii. 13, and x. 1, Japheth is mentioned third, and was therefore considered to be the youngest. If, however, as seems probable, we are here dealing with a distinct tradition, in which the third and youngest son was Canaan, the difficulty caused by the words, "his youngest son," taken in conjunction with the curse pronounced upon Canaan (Ham not being mentioned), will disappear.

Origen, in order to escape the difficulty, suggested that Canaan, the

J   Cursed be Canaan;
A servant of servants shall he be unto his brethren.

youngest son of Ham (x. 6), saw his grandfather, Noah, lying exposed, and reported it to his father, Ham; and this theory has found favour with many. But, at the best, it is an ingenious gloss; it is not in the text, but an addition to it.

had done] Nothing is told of the youngest son's misconduct. So far as our text goes, he had merely reported to his brothers their father's shameful condition. These words, however, suggest that the narrative in *v.* 22 has for good reasons been abbreviated or modified.

25. *And he said*] Noah's utterance of a curse upon Canaan and of a blessing upon Shem and Japheth is expressed in poetical terms. The solemn words of a father, as the head of his house, concerning his sons, partook of the character of prophecy, and were expressed in brief oracular sentences. Cf. in the story of Jacob chs. xxvii. and xlviii. and xlix.

Cursed be Canaan] Three times over, in these verses, is the curse repeated against Canaan, while a blessing is pronounced upon Shem and Japheth. It is difficult to resist the conclusion that Canaan here stands on a level with Shem and Japheth, and that he is regarded as Noah's third son; as, indeed, is expressly indicated by the mention of "his brethren" (*vv.* 22, 25). The explanation that the wrong-doing of "Ham" is punished by the curse levelled at Canaan, a son of Ham, seems most improbable; but this is the only explanation which the words of the text in *v.* 22, making "Ham, the father of Canaan," the offender, will admit. The mention of "Ham" in that verse is almost certainly a late insertion for harmonizing purposes.

A servant of servants] i.e. the meanest of servants, the slave of slaves. Lat. *servus servorum*. For this method of expressing the superlative, cf. "the Holy of holies," i.e. the innermost Sanctuary (Ex. xxvi. 33); "prince of the princes" (Numb. iii. 32); "God of gods, Lord of lords" (Deut. x. 17; Ps. cxxxvi. 2, 3); "Song of Songs," i.e. the fairest of songs (Cant. i. 1); "the King of kings," i.e. the Omnipotent (Ezek. xxvi. 7).

unto his brethren] Canaan is to be the slave of Shem and Japheth. The oracle predicts the subjugation of the Canaanites to the Israelites, and forecasts their inability to resist the power of Japheth. The precise manner in which the subjection of Canaan to Japheth was historically realized must be left uncertain. There is no suggestion of a whole race doomed to a condition of slavery. The application of this clause to the African races is an error of interpretation. Doubtless the power of the Japhetic races was from time to time successfully asserted against the Phoenicians. Japheth represents the races of the West and North.

If Canaan be not here regarded as the brother of Shem and Japheth, it must be assumed that the punishment of Ham is to be inflicted upon his son, Canaan. This is the usual explanation; but it breaks down

And he said,   26 J
> Blessed be the LORD, the God of Shem;
> And let Canaan be ¹his servant.
> God enlarge Japheth,   27
> And ²let him dwell in the tents of Shem;

     ¹ Or, *their*   ² Or, *he shall*

in view of the fact that all the names are used symbolically and representatively, and the oracle has reference, in each case, not to the individuals, but to their descendants. Hence there would be no point in singling out a son of the real offender, instead of indicating the offender himself.

26. *Blessed be the LORD, the God of Shem*] The blessing invoked, not upon Shem himself, but upon Jehovah the God of Shem, is intended to convey the thought that herein will lie the true welfare of the descendants of Shem. The point of this oracle is, of course, dependent on the fact that Shem is to be the ancestor of Israel. The blessing here invoked has reference only to the Hebrews whose God is Jehovah. They are the favoured ones: the God of Redemption will manifest Himself in them. After "Cursed be Canaan," we should expect to read "Blessed of Jehovah be Shem." But there hardly seems to be sufficient reason for regarding the text as corrupt. Graetz, who is followed by Gunkel, with a slight alteration of the text, viz. by the transposition of two consonants and by a different reading of the vowels (which of course did not appear in early Hebrew writing), reads, "bless, oh! Jehovah, the tents of Shem" (אהלי שם for אלהי שם), so that "the tents of Shem" should end this line as well as line 2 in the next verse.

his servant] The translation of the margin, *their*, is to be preferred. The word in the Hebrew is a poetical form of the plural pronoun; and here the reference is to Canaan's brethren.

27. *God*] The blessing on Japheth is introduced with the name not of "Jehovah," but of "Elohim." Jehovah is the God who reveals Himself through the descendants of Shem. The blessing of Japheth shall come from God; but Japheth will not know God by His name Jehovah.

enlarge] The word in the Hebrew, *yapht*, is employed on account of its resemblance in sound to the name of Japheth. The blessing means, "May God extend the rule of Japheth," i.e. may the meaning of his name be realized in the extension of his power!

let him dwell] Better than *he shall*. The "he" in this clause is not God, but Japheth. The clause contains the prayer that Japheth may ever continue on terms of peace with Shem, and that his descendants, dwelling as guests among the Israelites, may partake of their privileges. That "to dwell in the tents of Shem" should mean "to dispossess the Shemites and occupy their homes" (following the

> J And let Canaan be ¹his servant
> P 28 And Noah lived after the flood three hundred and fifty
> 29 years. And all the days of Noah were nine hundred and
> fifty years: and he died.

¹ Or, *their*

analogy of the phrase in Ps. lxxviii. 55), is an explanation quite unsuited to a clause of blessing.

The conjecture that "Shem" in this verse is not a proper name, but is the Hebrew word meaning "name" or "renown" (as in vi. 4), so that the meaning is "and let him dwell in the tents of renown," would hardly have been suggested, unless the clause had been one of some obscurity.

his] Better, as R.V. marg., *their*. See note on *v.* 26.

28 (P). *And Noah lived*] This and the following verses are the conclusion of P's account of the Deluge. In contents and character they belong to the genealogy of the Sethite patriarchs in ch. v.

SPECIAL NOTE ON IX. 25—27.

There is much uncertainty as to the period of history to which the Song, or Oracle, of Noah may be considered to refer. In all probability, the question must be left undecided.

1. It has been understood to refer to the times of David. Shem, i.e. the Israelites, have subjugated Canaan. Japheth, i.e. the Philistines, coming from the West, have first inflicted defeat upon the Canaanites, and then occupied the S.W. portion of the country of Palestine. But is it possible that an Israelite poet would have spoken so favourably of the Philistines, and have described their arrival under the simile of Japheth dwelling in the tents of Shem?

2. It has been understood to refer to the times either of Solomon or of Ahab. Shem, i.e. the Israelites, have subjugated Canaan, and have entered into terms of friendship with Japheth, i.e. the Phoenician king of Tyre. It is obviously an objection that, in Gen. x. 15, the Phoenicians are ranked among the sons of Canaan. Moreover, it is hardly probable that the devout Israelite would offer to the worshippers of Baal a welcome into the tents of the servants of Jehovah.

3. It has been conjectured (by Gunkel) that the poem has reference to the great racial movements of the second millennium B.C., and that Canaan may represent the earliest Semitic immigrants into Palestine; Shem, the invading races of Aramaeans and Hebrews; Japheth, the northern nations, and, in particular, the Hittites. It may be doubted, whether the migratory invasion of Aramaean and Hebrew peoples would ever have been comprehended by an Israelite singer under the single symbolic name of Shem; and, also, whether he would have regarded any other peoples besides Israel as belonging to Jehovah.

Again, if so wide a designation be assigned to Shem, the prayer that Japheth may "dwell in the tents of Shem" becomes unintelligible.

4. It has been conjectured, by Bertholet, that the Song has reference to a late period; that Shem represents the post-exilic Jews; Canaan, the heathen dwellers in Palestine and Phoenicia; Japheth, the Greeks under Alexander, who conquered and subjugated Phoenicia, and received a welcome from the Jews of Jerusalem. But this, beside other improbabilities, assumes too late a date for the composition of the Song.

5. It is better, for the present, to leave our judgement in suspense. But, in all probability, we should be right in supposing that under "Jehovah, the God of Shem," is contained a reference to the people of Israel; and that in the denunciation of Canaan, "A servant of servants shall he be unto his brethren," is implied a time when the subjugation of the Canaanites was not yet complete; when they were still formidable; and when the support of Japheth (unknown peoples (?) in the north) was likely to prove a welcome assistance, though only of a temporary nature, to Israel.

The period, then, might conceivably be not long after the settlement of the tribes of Israel in the land of Canaan.

It only remains to point out the importance of this poetical Oracle in the literature of the Old Testament. (1) It treats of the movements of the nations as ordered and guided by Jehovah. It may thus be described as possibly the first product of Israelite prophecy. (2) In its attitude of generous trust towards Japheth, it is an early example of the spirit of tolerance towards the stranger, which in later Judaism was almost lost in narrow exclusiveness[1].

CH. X.

1 (P).	The Generations of the Sons of Noah.	
2—5 (P).	The Sons of Japheth.	
6, 7, and 20 (P).	The Sons of Ham.	
8—19, and 21 (J).	Nimrod, Babylon, and Assyria: Egypt and Canaan.	
22—31 (P).	The Sons of Shem.	

The names of Noah's sons only occur in Genesis and in the parallel genealogical list in 1 Chron. i. The distribution of the races of the earth between their descendants necessarily results from the record, in vii. 21, of the destruction of all flesh in the Flood.

As will be seen from the names contained in this list, they represent not a formal genealogy, but a table of the principal races and peoples known to the Israelites. They are arranged, as if they were members of families intimately related to one another. This, however, represents the common attitude of the ancient world in explaining the

---

[1] I am indebted to the discussion of this Song in G. Adam Smith's *Schweich Lectures*, 1910, pp. 46—49.

GENESIS X. 1—3

P 10 Now these are the generations of the sons of Noah, Shem Ham and Japheth: and unto them were sons born after the flood.

2 The sons of Japheth; Gomer, and Magog, and Madai, 3 and Javan, and Tubal, and Meshech, and Tiras. And the

complexity of tribes and peoples, out of which nations had arisen. We may compare early Greek and Roman accounts of the origin of the inhabitants of Greece and Italy in prehistoric times. The names are some of them racial, and some of them geographical. The attempts at identification are precarious, and cannot often be relied upon.

Observe that the order of the sons of Noah is here reversed. Thus the family of Shem is the last to be enumerated, leading up to the Narratives of the Patriarchs (chaps. xii.—l.).

1. *Now these are the generations*] The title of a new section in P; see note on ii. 4.

2. *The sons of Japheth*] These are names of peoples who for the most part seem to have dwelt in remote northern and western regions in Asia Minor.

Gomer] Mentioned also in Ezek. xxxviii. 6. Probably the people dwelling in the region of Pontus in Asia Minor, and called by the Greeks Cimmerians (Κιμμέριοι). Cf. 1 Chron. i. 5, 6.

Magog] appears as the name of a country in Ezek. xxxviii. 2, and of a northern people in Ezek. xxxix. 6, generally identified with the Scythians. Sayce conjectures that Magog is for "Mat-Gog"="land of Gog." The allusions to Gog and Magog in Rev. xx. 8 are based upon the prophetic passages in Ezek. xxxviii. and xxxix.

Madai] Almost certainly "the land of the Medes." The people of Media are referred to in the Assyrian inscriptions as "Madai" in the 9th century B.C. In the history of Israel they are first mentioned in 2 Kings xvii. 6. Cf. Isa. xiii. 17 and xxi. 2; 1 Chron. i. 5.

Javan] This is the Hebrew name for "the Greeks." The Ionians were the Greeks of Asia Minor and of the islands of the Ægean Sea, who were first known to the peoples of Western Asia. They were called in Assyrian *Javanu*. For other passages in which the Greeks are mentioned in the O.T., cf. Isa. lxvi. 19; Ezek. xxvii. 13, 19; Dan. viii. 21, x. 20; Joel iii. 6; Zech. ix. 13.

Tubal...Meshech] These two names are mentioned, along with Javan, in Ezek. xxvii. 13, xxxix. 1. They have been identified with peoples in N.E. Asia Minor, Tibarenians and Moschians.

In Isa. lxvi. 19 Tubal is classed with Javan and "the isles afar off." In Ps. cxx. 5, "Meshech" is used as the name of a barbarous and remote people, "Woe is me that I sojourn in Meshech."

Tiras] Identified by Josephus (*Ant.* I. 6) with the Thracians, but now more frequently with a race of sea pirates of the Ægean Sea called Τυρσηνοί. Another conjecture is Tarsus; another, Tarshish; cf. 1 Chron. i. 6.

sons of Gomer; Ashkenaz, and ¹Riphath, and Togarmah. And the sons of Javan; Elishah, and Tarshish, Kittim, and ²Dodanim. Of these were the ³isles of the nations divided

¹ In 1 Chr. i. 6, *Diphath.* ² In 1 Chr. i. 7, *Rodanim.*
³ Or, *coastlands*

3. *Ashkenaz*] Mentioned in Jer. li. 27 along with Ararat; and now generally identified with the region of Armenia. It is worth noticing that the mediaeval Jews explained this name as denoting Germany. Thus the Ashkenazim are the German Jews.

Riphath] In 1 Chron. i. 6 the name appears as "Diphath." The letters, R (ר) and D (ד), are very similar in Hebrew. Cf. "Dodanim" for "Rodanim," *v.* 4. Josephus identified "Riphath" with the Paphlagonians. The name is now unknown.

Togarmah] Mentioned also in Ezek. xxvii. 14, with Javan, Tubal and Meshech; and in Ezek. xxxviii. 6, with Gomer, and generally identified with the western part of Armenia. Cf. 1 Chron. i. 6.

4. *the sons of Javan*] The names here mentioned are evidently geographical. Javan's sons are well-known Greek colonies and settlements or communities. This example will serve to illustrate the composition of the genealogical list.

Elishah] Mentioned in Ezek. xxvii. 7 as a place from which there was a trade in purple. Josephus identified it with the Æolians. Other conjectures have been Hellas, Elis, Sicily, and Carthage. Possibly, it is Alasa, the modern Cyprus.

Tarshish] Probably the ancient commercial town of Tartessus, at the mouth of the river Guadalquivir. It is classed with the isles in Ps. lxxii. 10, Isa. lx. 9. Its trade is mentioned in Ezek. xxvii. 12. On "the ships of Tarshish" in King Solomon's time, see 1 Kings x. 22, xxii. 48. There were Greek settlements at Tartessus. Cf. Herodotus, I. 163.

Kittim] Usually identified with Cyprus and its inhabitants. The chief town was Κίτιον, the modern *Larnaca*, and was probably occupied at an early time by Greek-speaking people. The name "Kittim" became transferred from Cyprus to other islands. Cf. Jer. ii. 10; Ezek. xxvii. 6.

Dodanim] In 1 Chron. i. 7, *Rodanim.* The LXX and Sam. agree with 1 Chron. i. 7; and this reading is generally preferred, Rodanim being identified with the island of Rhodes. In Ezek. xxvii. 15, "the men of Dedan" similarly appear in LXX as ῥόδιοι, i.e. the Rhodians trafficking with the city of Tyre.

5. *Of these,* &c.] It is probable that the text in this verse has suffered. As in *v.* 20 we find "these are the sons of Ham" and in *v.* 31 "these are the sons of Shem," so we should expect in this verse "these are the sons of Japheth." We should, therefore, probably put a full stop after the word "divided," and insert: "These are the sons of Japheth." This will improve the sense; for (1) the words "of these"

P in their lands, every one after his tongue; after their families, in their nations.

6 And the sons of Ham; Cush, and Mizraim, and Put,
7 and Canaan. And the sons of Cush; Seba, and Havilah,

cannot refer generally to the contents of *vv.* 2 and 3, but only to the contents of *v.* 4; (2) while the expression "the isles were divided in their lands" is intolerably harsh. "Of these" should be taken to refer to "the sons of Javan" only. From them the Greek settlements branched off in all directions among the islands and the coastlands, i.e. "the isles of the nations." After this piece of information the genealogist summarizes the foregoing list, "These are the sons of Japheth in their lands, every one after his tongue," &c.

isles] Better, as R.V. marg., *coastlands*. Cf. Isa. xi. 11; Jer. ii. 10; Ezek. xxvii. 6.

6—20. The Sons of Ham.

6. The races described as "the sons of Ham" are first traced in the most southerly regions. If the name has any connexion with *Kamt*, the native name of Egypt, it is noticeable that it is here applied to the parent stock of peoples, not only in Egypt, but also in South Arabia, Phoenicia, and Syria. "Ham" is used as a synonym for Egypt in Ps. lxxviii. 51, cv. 23, 27, cvi. 22.

Cush] A name of frequent occurrence in the O.T. for Ethiopia and the Ethiopians, i.e. the country and the people between Egypt and Abyssinia; the "Kas," or "Kes," of the Egyptian inscriptions. Cf. on ii. 13.

Mizraim] The regular Hebrew name for Egypt. Cf. the Assyrian *Muṣur*. The termination "-*aim*" denotes the dual number; and hence it has been supposed that "Mizraim" means the two "Mizrs," i.e. Upper and Lower Egypt. But we cannot rely on this for certain. "Mizraim" is the Hebrew name for Egypt without necessarily containing an allusion to this geographical division. It is best not to press the grammatical meaning that may be claimed to underlie the popular pronunciation of a geographical name; cf. Ephraim, Naharaim, Jerusalaim (=Jerusalem).

Put] Mentioned also in Ezek. xxvii. 10, xxxviii. 5; Jer. xlvi. 9; Nahum iii. 9. In these passages "Put" is mentioned together with the composite materials of an Egyptian mercenary army. It is generally identified with the Libyans. Pliny mentions a river "Fut" in Libya. In Nahum iii. 9 Put is associated with the "Lubim," and with Ethiopia and Egypt. *Punt* occurs in Egyptian inscriptions for the African "littoral" of the Red Sea.

Canaan] This is the land of Phoenicia, probably in its widest sense, like *Kinaḥi* in the Tel-el-Amarna tablets (1400 B.C.). The Canaanites were Semites, and spoke a language which closely resembled Hebrew, and was more akin to Aramaean and Assyrian than

and Sabtah, and Raamah, and Sabteca: and the sons of   P
Raamah; Sheba, and Dedan. | And Cush begat Nimrod: 8   J

Egyptian. Canaan was possibly associated by Israelite tradition with Egypt on account of the general similarity of its culture. Perhaps the Israelites, who regarded the Egyptians and the Canaanites as their two racial foes, and as the two corrupters of their faith, classed them together for that reason among "the sons of Ham."

7. *And the sons of Cush*] The names given in this verse are usually identified with the names of tribes, or places, on the African coast, or on the opposite shores of Arabia.

Seba] Cf. Ps. lxxii. 10; Isa. xliii. 3, xlv. 14, where it is named with Egypt and Cush; identified by Josephus (*Ant. Jud.* II. 10, § 2) with "Meroë"; but now generally supposed to denote tribes on the coast of the Red Sea in the neighbourhood of Massowah.

Havilah] The name occurs again in *v.* 29 among "the sons of Joktan"; possibly a branch of the same Arabian tribe which had settled on the African coast. See also ii. 11, xxv. 18.

Raamah] Mentioned also in Ezek. xxvii. 22 for its trade with Tyre, and with Sheba.

Sabtah...Sabteca] Unknown.

Sheba] Also in *v.* 28, among "the sons of Joktan," and in xxv. 3, among "the sons of Keturah." The trade of this people and their dependencies consisted especially of spices, precious stones, and gold (Ezek. xxvii. 22). The occurrence of the name of "Sheba" here among the sons of Ham, and in *v.* 28 among the sons of Shem, illustrates the difficulty of identification.

Dedan] Mentioned also in xxv. 3; apparently an Arabian tribe, bordering on Edom (Ezek. xxv. 13), and occasionally brought into contact with Israel through trade. Cf. Isa. xxi. 13; Jer. xxv. 23; Ezek. xxvii. 20.

8—19 (J). NIMROD, ASSYRIA AND BABYLON: CANAAN AND EGYPT.

8—12 (J). Nimrod.

8. *Cush begat Nimrod*] In connexion with the "sons of Cush" we have here an Israelite tradition that the foundation of the Assyrian and Babylonian empires was due to "a son of Cush," named Nimrod. What, if any, was deemed to be the connexion between Cush, and the origin of Babylon and Nineveh, is not related. At least, the explanation which has been hazarded, that some prehistoric Ethiopian monarch, having invaded and conquered Western Asia, founded the great cities of the Euphrates Valley, has not hitherto received confirmation.

Modern scholars call attention to the prominence of a people designated as the Cossaeans, Κοσσαῖοι, Assyr. *Kashu*, in Babylonian history. They were predominant in Babylonia between 1800 and 1200 B.C. It is suggested that the early Israelite tradition identified

J 9 he began to be a mighty one in the earth. He was a
mighty hunter before the LORD: wherefore it is said, Like
10 Nimrod a mighty hunter before the LORD. And the beginning of his kingdom was Babel, and Erech, and Accad,

the name of this people with the similarly sounding name of the African Cush, and that, in the halo of romance and legend encircling the name of Nimrod, the Ethiopian origin of the founder of Babylon presented no serious difficulty.

Nimrod] Mentioned elsewhere in 1 Chron. i. 10, Micah v. 6. Here he is described under two aspects: (1) as a mighty hunter, (2) as king of Babylonia, and founder of the chief cities in Assyria.

Assyriologists have been inclined to identify Nimrod with the mythical Babylonian hero, Gilgames, the hunter and lion-slayer, represented in Babylonian art as throttling, or gripping, a wild animal. No similarity in the name has yet been ascertained. Jeremias suggests that Nimrod is the Hebrew pronunciation of *Nâmir-Uddu* = "shining light." Another conjecture would identify him with the Cassite, or Cossaean, king *Nazi-maruttash* (circ. 1350 B.C.): but, if so, Israelite tradition seems to have transferred the name of a comparatively recent king (more recent than the patriarchs) into the ages of legendary obscurity.

began to be a mighty one] A strange expression. The word "began" should be connected with "the beginning of his kingdom" in v. 10. "He was the first great monarch." Compare "began to be an husbandman" (ix. 20).

9. *a mighty hunter before the LORD*] The phrase "before the LORD" is merely descriptive of magnitude, cf. xxiii. 6, "a great prince" (Heb. *a prince of God*), Jonah iii. 3, "Nineveh was an exceeding great city" (Heb. *a city great unto God*). But it is possible that the expression is traceable to some primitive traditions respecting the hunting exploits of Nimrod, and the favour shewn to him by his God.

The popularity of hunting scenes in Assyrian art may have led to a general impression that the founders of the Assyrian and Babylonian kingdoms were famous huntsmen.

It is noteworthy that in later times Nimrod was identified with Orion, both as a hunter and as a constellation. Hence some have fancifully explained these words to mean "a hunter in heaven."

wherefore it is said] The quotation of a proverb: Nimrod's name became proverbial for a great hunter.

10. *the beginning of his kingdom*] Nimrod is represented, not as the founder of the Babylonian cities, but as their king. His four cities are enumerated:

1. *Babel*, i.e. Babylon, as the Hebrew is rendered in the Greek: Assyrian *Babilu*, possibly = "the gate of God." This was the capital of the Babylonian empire from the time of Hammurabi who founded that empire, circ. 2130 B.C.

2. *Erech*, the *Uruk* of the inscriptions. LXX Ὀρέχ, the modern

and Calneh, in the land of Shinar. Out of that land ¹he 11
went forth into Assyria, and builded Nineveh, and Rehoboth-Ir, and Calah, and Resen between Nineveh and Calah 12

¹ Or, *went forth Asshur*

Warka, was the principal seat of the Babylonian deities Anu and Istar, and the scene of the exploits of the mythical hero Gilgames.

3. *Accad*, the *Agade* of the inscriptions, the chief town in ancient northern Babylonia, and the capital of Sargon the First, one of the earliest Babylonian kings.

4. *Calneh*, of doubtful identification; not to be identified with the Syrian town Calneh (Amos vi. 2). Jensen conjectures that there is an error of one Hebrew letter, and that we should read for Calneh *Cullaba*, an important town in Babylonia. Another conjecture is *Nippur*.

in the land of Shinar] i.e. in Babylonia, which comprised both northern Babylonia or Accad, and southern Babylonia or Sumer.

11. *Out of that land*, &c.] This verse preserves an historical tradition: (1) that the cities of Assyria were of later origin than those of Babylonia; (2) that they owed their existence to the development of the Babylonian power in a northerly direction; whether by conquest or by colonization we cannot tell.

into Assyria] or "Asshur." There is no difference in the Hebrew between the name of the country and that of its first capital (see ii. 14). The city Asshur was distant about 300 miles from Babylon.

The rendering of the R.V. marg.=A.V. *went forth Asshur* has no probability, though it has the support of LXX, Vulg., and Targ. Onk.

Nineveh] Assyr. *Nina*, the modern *Kouyunjik*, situated on the left bank of the Tigris, opposite to the modern *Mosul*. Nineveh was the capital of Assyria in its most famous period, but it was not until about 1000 B.C. that it became the royal residence of Assyrian monarchs. Nothing historical is known of its earliest days.

Rehoboth-Ir] Possibly to be identified, as some Assyriologists suggest, with *Rêbit Nina*, on the site of the modern *Mosul*, over against Nineveh.

Calah] The modern *Kellach*, at the confluence of the upper Zab and the Tigris, some 20 miles N. of Nineveh. It stands on the ruined mounds of *Nimrud*. The capital of Assyria was transferred by Shalmaneser I, circ. 1300 B.C., from Asshur to Calah.

12. *Resen*] Not yet identified; but conjectured to lie among the mounds which conceal ruins between Nineveh and Nimrud.

(*the same is the great city*)] This is a note added by the compiler; or, possibly, as Skinner suggests, a gloss, referring to Nineveh, which is misplaced.

13—19 (J). The descendants of Mizraim (Egypt), *vv.* 13, 14; and of Canaan (Phoenicia), *vv.* 15—19. The names of tribes (the plural termination *-im*) in *vv.* 13 and 14, and of peoples (*vv.* 16—19), seem to imply a different source of tradition from that in *vv.* 2—7.

GENESIS X. 12—14

J 13 (the same is the great city). And Mizraim begat Ludim,
14 and Anamim, and Lehabim, and Naphtuhim, and Pathrusim, and Casluhim (whence went forth ¹the Philistines), and Caphtorim.

¹ Heb. *Pelishtim*.

13. *Mizraim*] In *v.* 6, "the sons of Ham" are Cush, Mizraim, Put, and Canaan. The "sons of Cush" were given in *v.* 7. In *vv.* 13, 14 the genealogy is continued with the "sons of Mizraim." The intervening passage (*vv.* 8—12) has been a parenthesis. The names here mentioned are probably tribes on the borders of Egypt.

Ludim] Mentioned also in Jer. xlvi. 9; presumably the same as Lud in Isa. lxvi. 19; Ezek. xxvii. 10, xxx. 5.

the Anamim] W. Max Müller suggests that these are the *Kinamim* who dwelt in the largest and southernmost oasis, designated in the Egyptian inscriptions *K'n'mt*. Very strange is the reading of the LXX Αἰνεμετιείμ. Cf. 1 Chron. i. 11.

Lehabim] Possibly the same as the "Libyans," who appear as Lubim in 2 Chron. xii. 3, xvi. 8; Dan. xi. 43; Nahum iii. 9. The Libyans were the African tribes west of Cyrene.

Naphtuhim] The Egyptologist Erman suggests that this name is the corruption of the word *P-t-mhi*, the Egyptian designation for the dwellers in the north, i.e. the Delta of Egypt (*Z. A. T. W.* 1890, pp. 118, 119).

Another suggestion is that it represents the name of the third great oasis, between Ammon and *K'n'mt*, bearing the name of Ferâfia. Cf. 1 Chron. i. 11.

14. *Pathrusim*] Clearly to be identified with Upper Egypt, "the southlanders." "The land of the midday," Egyptian *Ptrsi*, is the Pathros of Isa. xi. 11; Jer. xliv. 1, 15; Ezek. xxix. 14, xxx. 14.

Casluhim] Not known; LXX Χασμωνιείμ, which has caused Max Müller to conjecture *Nasamonim*, a tribe in the vicinity of the great oasis of Ammon. Cf. 1 Chron. i. 12.

(*whence went forth the Philistines*), *and Caphtorim*] The parenthetical clause within the brackets seems to be out of place. According to Deut. ii. 23, Jer. xlvii. 4, Amos ix. 7 the Philistines came out of Caphtor. Accordingly, we may conjecture the clause originally stood after the word "Caphtorim," and has been accidentally transposed. On the other hand, this explanation seems so obvious, that some scholars consider that the clause "whence...the Philistines" is in its right place, but that the words "and Caphtorim" are only a gloss on the mention of "the Philistines."

the Philistines] Heb. *Pelishtim*, identified by many Assyriologists with the *Purasati*, a predatory horde which established itself in the 13th century B.C. in the south of Phoenicia. On the origin of the Philistines, see Macalister's *Excavations at Gezer* (Pal. Ex. Fund, 1912).

Caphtorim] The people of Caphtor which has commonly been identified

And Canaan begat Zidon his firstborn, and Heth; and 15
the Jebusite, and the Amorite, and the Girgashite; and the 16
Hivite, and the Arkite, and the Sinite; and the Arvadite, 17 18
and the Zemarite, and the Hamathite: and afterward were

with Crete. The only traces of real artistic work found at Gezer by Macalister were Minoan in character.

15. *Canaan*] Observe that we pass from Cush and Mizraim to Canaan, the fourth son of Ham; omitting Put, the third son in *v.* 6.

Zidon his firstborn] "Firstborn"; i.e. the capital, and most ancient city, of the Phoenicians. The Phoenicians called themselves Zidonians, and were so called by the Israelites. Cf. 1 Kings xvi. 31. Zidon probably means "fish-town."

Heth] i.e. the Hittites called by the Egyptians "Khêta," and by the Assyrians "Khatti." It is more than doubtful whether the Hittites had any connexion with the Phoenicians. Their language has not yet (1913) been deciphered. The Hittite empire appears to have lasted from 1800 B.C. to 700 B.C. Carchemish on the Euphrates was for a time their capital. They made their influence felt throughout Syria and Asia Minor. Their famous collision with Egypt occurred in the reign of Rameses III, about 1180 B.C. The mention of Heth as the "son of Canaan" is probably to be understood as indicating the presence of a large number of Hittite dwellers in Phoenicia and Palestine. There are traces of these elsewhere in O.T., e.g. ch. xxiii.; Num. xiii. 29; Judg. i. 26; 1 Kings x. 29; 2 Kings vii. 6. The supremacy of the Hittites throughout Syria and Canaan belongs to the period shortly after the age represented by the Tel-el-Amarna tablets (1400 B.C.).

16. *the Jebusite*] The Canaanite tribe dwelling in Jerusalem and its neighbourhood: cf. Josh. xv. 63; Judg. i. 21; 2 Sam. v. 6.

the Amorite] In the Tel-el-Amarna tablets the name *Amurru* is given to the dwellers in the north of Canaan in distinction from the *Kinaḥi*, the dwellers in southern Canaan. Later on, the name Amorite seems to have been used by the Assyrians to designate Palestine. In the O.T. the original inhabitants of Canaan are sometimes called by this name; e.g. Judg. i. 34—36; Amos ii. 9. See Driver, *Schweich Lectures*, p. 36.

the Girgashite] Mentioned e.g. xv. 21, Deut. vii. 1, with the other dwellers in Canaan, but their locality is not indicated.

17. *the Hivite*] The Hivites, dwellers in the country about Gibeon (Josh. ix. 7) and Sichem (Gen. xxxiv. 2); while Josh. xi. 3 and Judg. iii. 3 speak of the Hivites as dwelling near Mount Hermon and Mount Lebanon, though in neither passage is the reading (?Hittites) certain.

the Arkite] A Phoenician tribe represented by the modern *Tell Arḳa*, some 80 miles north of Zidon, and not far from Tripolis.

the Sinite] Jerome mentions a town *Sini* near Arka.

18. *the Arvadite*] Arvad, a famous maritime town, the modern *Ruwâd* on an island 100 miles north of Zidon; cf. Ezek. xxvii. 8, 11.

J 19 the families of the Canaanite spread abroad. And the border of the Canaanite was from Zidon, as thou goest toward Gerar, unto Gaza; as thou goest toward Sodom and Gomorrah and Admah and Zeboiim, unto Lasha. |
P 20 These are the sons of Ham, after their families, after their tongues, in their lands, in their nations.

the Zemarite] The dwellers in Simyra, modern *Sumra*, a few miles south of *Ruwâd*. It appears in the Tel-el-Amarna Letters as Zumur.

the Hamathite] The dwellers in Hamath, modern *Ḥama*, the famous ancient town to the extreme north of Canaan, on the Orontes, and the capital of a small kingdom overthrown by Sargon. Cf. Num. xxxiv. 8; 2 Kings xviii. 34; Amos vi. 14.

and afterward] It has been conjectured that this clause followed originally upon the mention of "Zidon his firstborn and Heth," ver. 15, and that the intervening passage (*vv.* 16, 17, 18ᵃ) is a later addition. The clause leads up to the description, in ver. 19, of the subsequent boundaries of Canaan. The writer implies that the "families of the Canaanite," who were driven out by the Israelites, were themselves not the original inhabitants.

In favour of 16—18ᵃ being a gloss, note (1) the change from the proper names, "Zidon" and "Heth," to the appellatives, "the Jebusite," "the Amorite," &c.: (2) the delimitation of "the Canaanite" in *v.* 19 excluding the Arkite, Sinite, Arvadite, Zemarite, and Hamathite, who in *vv.* 16 and 17 are included in the "sons of Canaan."

19. *And the border of the Canaanite*] This verse describes the geographical limits of the extension of the Canaanite peoples in a southerly direction, with Zidon as the starting-point in the north. As the limit on the south-west, we have "toward Gerar unto Gaza," and on the south-east "toward Sodom and Gomorrah, &c. unto Lasha." This would represent a triangle, having Zidon on the north, with Gaza and Lasha on the south-west and south-east. The description is not free from obscurity. "Toward Gerar unto Gaza" is hardly a natural definition; since Gaza lies to the north of Gerar.

"Lasha," or, as we should read it, "Lesha," was identified by Jerome with "Callirrhoe" on the east side of the Dead Sea; but, as the name does not occur elsewhere, this is only a traditional conjecture. Kittel (*Biblia Hebraica*) identifies it with "Bela," or "Zoar" (xiv. 2) which is mentioned together with the four "cities of the plain."

For "Lasha," Wellhausen conjectures "unto Laish" in the north-east of Palestine, which would give a fourth geographical limit of the Canaanite border, and alter the scheme of delimitation from a triangular to a four-sided area of country.

20. *These are the sons of Ham* (P), &c.] Cf. ver. 31; and the note on ver. 5.

The synonyms here given are characteristic of P's fondness for redundancy and repetition.

GENESIS X. 21—23

And unto Shem, the father of all the children of Eber, ¹the elder brother of Japheth, to him also were children born. | The sons of Shem; Elam, and Asshur, and Arpachshad, and Lud, and Aram. And the sons of Aram; Uz, 21 J

22 P

23

¹ Or, *the brother of Japheth the elder*

21—31. THE SONS OF SHEM (J and P).

21. *And unto Shem*, &c.] The brief account in this verse is from J.

the father of all the children of Eber] This is the point in the description of Shem which would seem most honourable to Israelite readers. The names "Eber" and "Hebrew" are almost identical in the Hebrew language. "Eber" was accepted as the ancestor of the Hebrew-speaking peoples. In the widest sense of the word, "Hebrews" are a group of Semitic peoples who issued from the Arabian Peninsula. They are included among the descendants of Joktan and Peleg, as well as of Terah. For the ordinary derivation of the word "Hebrew," as="the man from the further side" of the river, see *v.* 24 and xiv. 13. The term "Hebrew" is racial, "Israelite" national; though ultimately used as synonyms.

the elder brother of Japheth] These words seem to be inserted, in order to remind the reader that Shem, though here mentioned last, was the eldest of Noah's sons. The rendering of R.V. marg., *the brother of Japheth the elder*, is very improbable.

22. *The sons of Shem*] This is the account by P, corresponding to the previous mention of "the sons of Japheth," *v.* 2, and "the sons of Ham," *v.* 6.

Elam] The name of a people and a country east of the Tigris and north of the Persian Gulf. The Elamites were at one time supreme in Western Asia (see note on xiv. 1). They do not appear to have been a Semitic race; but the place of Elam in this verse probably indicates the easternmost people with which the descendants of Shem were brought into contact.

Asshur] See note on *v.* 11. The Assyrians were the most powerful of the Semitic peoples.

Arpachshad] This name used to be identified with Ἀρραπαχῖτις, a mountainous region north of Assyria, but this does not explain the two final syllables in which we naturally recognize *Chesed*, or the *Chasdim*, viz.=the "Chaldeans," a people dwelling in the south of Babylonia. Sayce explains the word to mean "the wall of Chesed," i.e. "the fortress-protected country of the Chaldeans." Cheyne thinks that the name in this passage and elsewhere is an erroneous fusion of two names, "Arpach" and "Chesed." (*Z.A.T.W.* 1897, p. 190.)

Lud] Presumably the Lydians of Asia Minor, though it is difficult to explain why they should be here associated with the "sons of Shem."

Aram] The people inhabiting the whole country north-east of

P J 24 and Hul, and Gether, and Mash. | And Arpachshad [1]begat
25 Shelah; and Shelah begat Eber. And unto Eber were born
two sons: the name of the one was [2]Peleg; for in his days
was the earth divided; and his brother's name was Joktan.

[1] The Sept. reads, *begat Cainan, and Cainan begat Shelah*.
[2] That is, *Division*.

Palestine, the northern region of the Euphrates Valley (*Aram-Naharaim*) and the country of Syria proper (*Aram-Dammesek*).

The people denoted by Aram were destined to exercise a great influence throughout Western Asia. The Aramaean language gradually prevailed over the other Semitic dialects, and before the Christian era it had displaced even the Hebrew language among the Jews. The Aramaic tongue spoken by our Lord and the Apostles was like the language in which portions of the books of Ezra and Daniel were written.

23. *the sons of Aram*] These names convey nothing to us, though presumably they possessed importance in the geography of the Hebrews.

Uz] The country of Job: see Job i. 1. Generally considered to have been in the south of Palestine. The name occurs again in another genealogy, xxii. 21, xxxvi. 28; cf. Jer. xxv. 20. In Lam. iv. 21, Uz is associated with Edom. These references however do not suit "a son of Aram."

Mash] In the parallel passage (1 Chron. i. 17) = Meshech.

24—30 (J). GENEALOGY OF SHEM.

A section from J, who speaks not of peoples, but of individuals of the heroic age. See xi. 10—19 (P) for a duplicate mention of "Arpachshad, ...Peleg."

24. *begat Shelah*] R.V. marg. "The Sept. reads *begat Cainan, and Cainan begat Shelah*." This addition is followed in Luke iii. 36.

Eber] See note on *v.* 21. Eber is evidently the most important name in this genealogy. As the grandson of Arpachshad, his name stands geographically in some kind of connexion with Elam, Asshur, Arpachshad and Aram. *Ēber* in the Hebrew means "on the other side of." The ancestors of Israel are described as those who "dwelt of old time beyond the River" (*ēber ha-nâhâr* = "on the other side of the Euphrates river"). See Josh. xxiv. 2.

25. *Peleg*] R.V. marg. That is, *Division*. His descendants are not recorded. In xi. 18—23 (P) Peleg is the father of Reu, the father of Serug, the father of Nahor. Eber's two sons, Peleg and Joktan, apparently represent the two divisions of Shemites, Peleg the northern or Mesopotamian, Joktan the southern or Arabian.

was the earth divided] The reference is generally assumed to be to the division, or dispersion, of the peoples at the tower of Babel, the words being an anticipation of the story in xi. 1—9. "The earth" will then mean "the inhabitants of the earth," as in xi. 1 and xix. 31.

And Joktan begat Almodad, and Sheleph, and Hazarma- 26 J
veth, and Jerah; and Hadoram, and Uzal, and Diklah; 27
and ¹Obal, and Abimael, and Sheba; and Ophir, and 28
Havilah, and Jobab: all these were the sons of Joktan. 29

¹ In 1 Chr. i. 22, *Ebal*.

Sayce, on the strength of *palgu* being Assyrian for "canal," would conjecture "the division of the earth" to signify the introduction of a system of canals into Babylonia during the reign of Hammurabi.

Perhaps, however, the name Peleg may indicate the historic "severance" of the northern Shemites from their southern brethren.

Joktan] The genealogy of Eber's elder son, Peleg, is here omitted, evidently because the compiler is giving the descendants of Peleg in xi. 18 from P; in which passage Joktan's name is not mentioned.

The thirteen sons of Joktan probably represent tribes in Arabia. The division of the population into tribes, continually warring with each other, has always been a feature of the Arabian Peninsula.

Dillmann suggests that one name has been interpolated; and that, as in the case of Israel, the number of tribes was originally twelve. Obal's name is omitted in some MSS. of LXX.

Most of their names have been, with more or less reason, identified with places in Arabia, for details of which the student should consult the dictionaries.

Sheleph] The name of a tribe, or region, in the *Yemen*, or southern Arabia.

26. *Hazarmaveth*] This name is very probably reproduced in the district of S.E. Arabia called the *Ḥadramaut*.

27. *Uzal*] Mentioned in Ezek. xxvii. 19, cf. R.V. marg., as a place from which iron was brought. Traditionally the old name of *Sana* the chief town of Yemen.

28. *Obal*] In 1 Chr. i. 22 *Ebal*, where LXX Cod. B omits. Here several MSS. of the LXX omit the name.

Sheba] See also ver. 7: presumably the Sabeans of south-west Arabia whose extant inscriptions shew that at one time they must have been a prosperous and civilized community. For the Queen of Sheba, see 1 Kings x.

For its exports of frankincense cf. Isa. lx. 6, Jer. vi. 20. Its merchandise is mentioned in Job vi. 19, Ezek. xxvii. 22, Ps. lxxii. 10.

29. *Ophir*] Famous for its trade in the days of Solomon, 1 Kings ix. 28, x. 11, xxii. 48, and for its gold of especial purity. Cf. Job xxii. 24, xxviii. 16; Ps. xlv. 9; Isa. xiii. 12. Its locality has been much disputed; it has been identified, at different times, with regions in India, East Africa, and the south coast of Arabia. In the present context it is evidently connected with Arabia.

Havilah] See ii. 11 and xxv. 18. Possibly a district in north-east Arabia.

J 30 And their dwelling was from Mesha, as thou goest toward
P 31 Sephar, the ¹mountain of the east. | These are the sons of
Shem, after their families, after their tongues, in their lands, after their nations.

32 These are the families of the sons of Noah, after their generations, in their nations: and of these were the nations divided in the earth after the flood.

¹ Or, *hill country*

30. *Mesha*] Dillmann conjectures "Massa" (xxv. 14), a north Arabian tribe. This is not improbable, if this verse delimits the geographical borders of "the sons of Joktan."

Sephar] Probably the same as *Daphar*, a town on the south coast of Arabia.

the mountain of the east] Better, as marg., *the hill country*. Probably the famous frankincense mountain in south Arabia, with Daphar as its furthest point, was reputed the southern limit of "the sons of Joktan."

31. *These are*, &c.] Cf. *vv*. 5, 20.

32. *of these were the nations divided*] Cf. *v*. 1, ix. 19. The word rendered "divided" is different from that in ver. 25, but is the same as that which is found in ver. 5. Looking back we can discern the object of the compiler in demonstrating (1) the unity of the race through Noah; (2) the origin of the peoples through his sons; (3) the origin of Israel through Shem and Eber.

CH. XI. 1—9. THE STORY OF THE TOWER OF BABEL. (J.)

The story of the Tower of Babel, contained in this short passage, preserves the recollection of a strange Israelite piece of folk-lore. No trace of this narrative has with any certainty, up to the present time, been discovered in the cuneiform inscriptions. Nor is this altogether surprising. The story connects the famous capital of Babylonia (Babel =Babylon) with an enterprise which is described as so colossal in its insolent impiety as to necessitate the personal interposition of the Almighty, Jehovah Himself. The success of the enterprise is frustrated by the simple exercise of the Divine Will; and the result is that the human race, which before had possessed one language, became in an instant subdivided into different communities by diversity of speech. The strangeness and the simplicity of the story inevitably seize upon the imagination. That it is devoid of any foundation in history or science hardly requires to be stated. So far as concerns the diversity of languages, science shews no tendency to favour the hypothesis, either of Babylonia having been the point of dispersion for the languages of the world, or, indeed, of the languages of the world having had any single common origin. Even the hopeful attempt in the 19th century to

And the whole earth was of one ¹language and of one 11 J

¹ Heb. *lip*.

reduce the languages of the world to three great families, or groups of dialects, each characterized by distinctive features of word formation and grammar, has in recent years been abandoned. The recognition of the existence of a far larger number of independent languages than before was supposed possible has shewn that the problem is one of immense complexity. We are led to suspect that the mystery of the origin of distinct languages belongs to the dim obscurity of the infancy of the human race, an infinitely remote and prehistoric age.

With this conclusion the account in the Book of Genesis stands in some measure of agreement. The story of the Tower of Babel is suddenly interposed between the genealogies which lead up to the birth of Abram. Though it supplies a theory which would account for the dispersion of the peoples of the world, it is evident that the Hebrews themselves did not regard the story as satisfying the problem. The tenth chapter of Genesis had already recorded the standard Hebrew tradition. It attributed the peopling of the world and the diversity of languages (*vv.* 5, 20, 31) to the dispersion of the descendants of the three sons of Noah. This was the working hypothesis, if we may so call it, of Israelite tradition in explaining the origin of the races. The present story by the suddenness of its introduction, the vagueness of its details, and the abruptness with which it breaks off, as well as by its startling anthropomorphic features, reminds us of the parenthesis in vi. 1—4. It reads like a fragment of an independent primitive tradition. It possessed an interest which justified its preservation, even though its details were hardly reconcilable with the narratives in ix. and x. It preserved a legend which (1) accounted for the diversity of race by the diversity of language; (2) attributed the diversity of language, with its attendant train of evils (misunderstanding, discord, hostility, and war), to the punishment or curse inflicted upon an impious race by a Divine decree; (3) associated with Babylon, the most ancient centre of civilization and town-life, the insolent impiety of a generation that sought to scale Heaven; (4) recorded the impression produced on the minds of the early Hebrews by the sight of the towers, *Ziggurats*, or temples which rose in many towns of Assyria and Babylonia to an immense height, and of which the meaning was unknown to nomad tribesmen or to wayfaring foreigners.

1. *the whole earth*] i.e. the inhabitants of the whole earth, as in x. 25.

one language...one speech] An expressive phrase, denoting that the generations of primitive man, being of one stock, continued to speak one common language. The Jewish tradition, which was followed by Christian tradition, as represented by Patristic, mediaeval, and many modern writers, assumed that Hebrew was the primitive language. This, however, was an assumption resting on no more satisfactory

J 2 ¹speech. And it came to pass, as they journeyed ²east, that they found a plain in the land of Shinar; and they dwelt 3 there. And they said one to another, Go to, let us make brick, and burn them throughly. And they had brick for 4 stone, and ³slime had they for mortar. And they said, Go to, let us build us a city, and a tower, whose top *may reach*

¹ Heb. *words*.   ² Or, *in the east*   ³ That is, *bitumen*.

foundation than (1) the proper names of the early Genesis narratives, and (2) the supposition that the language of the Chosen People was sacred and therefore aboriginal. The whole theory has been disproved by the scientific comparative study of languages, and of Hebrew and the cognate Semitic languages in particular.

2. *as they journeyed*] We are not told who are here spoken of, nor whence they come. This is an indication that this passage (1—9) is derived from an independent tradition distinct from the thread of the foregoing narrative. Like iv. 17—24, and vi. 1—4, it is probably a fragment of tradition which had no knowledge of the story of the Flood, or of the dispersion of the peoples through the sons of Noah.

journeyed] A word denoting the progress of nomads from one place of encampment to another.

east] Better, as marg., *in the east*. The Hebrew word means literally "from the east," as also LXX ἀπὸ ἀνατολῶν, and Lat. *de oriente*, and here probably signifies "in the east," i.e. on the east side from the writer's point of view. Some translate "eastward," as in xiii. 11, where Lot, on leaving Abram, is described as journeying "eastward." But, as we do not know who are referred to, or where they started from, the uncertainty as to the rendering remains.

a plain in the land of Shinar] For Shinar, probably denoting the ancient Babylonia, "Sumer and Akkad," see x. 10. The word "plain" (*biḳ'ah*) means the wide open expanse of a river valley. Here it is used of the Euphrates Valley. The expression, "found a plain in the land of Shinar," does not suggest close knowledge of Babylonia; but rather the general terms of popular and defective information respecting a distant country. Babylonia is one vast plain.

3. *brick for stone*, &c.] For a description of building with bricks held together with bitumen in Babylonia, see Herodotus, I. 179. The writer here is evidently more familiar with building in stone and mortar than in brick and bitumen: another indication that the story is Israelite in origin.

slime] That is, *bitumen*, LXX ἄσφαλτος, Lat. *bitumen*. The Hebrew word *ḥêmar* is found here and in xiv. 10, Ex. ii. 3. The word for bitumen or pitch used in vi. 14 (*kopher*) resembles the Assyrian; and the fact that it is not used here tells for the Israelite character of the story.

4. *a city, and a tower*] The story seems to suggest that in the

GENESIS XI. 4, 5

into heaven, and let us make us a name; lest we be scattered J
abroad upon the face of the whole earth. And the LORD 5
came down to see the city and the tower, which the children

abandonment of tent for city life these primitive people were disobeying the Divine command.

whose top may reach *unto heaven*] Lit. "its top in heaven." Probably the words are intended quite literally to suggest the endeavour to "reach unto" Heaven, which was regarded as a solid vault. As the highest stage in an Assyrian or Babylonian pyramid, *Ziggurat*, was surmounted by a shrine of the deity, there is perhaps more meaning and less fancifulness in these words than has often been suspected.

It is natural to compare the later Greek legend of the giants who sought to scale Olympus and to dethrone Zeus. But there is no indication of warlike defiance.

The famous tower at Borsippa, on the left bank of the Euphrates, whose ruins now go by the name of Birs Nimrud, was a temple dedicated to Bel-Nebo, and rose in seven tiers or stages, representing the seven planets. This building, having fallen into ruins, was restored by Nebuchadnezzar. A similar building, *E-sagil*, dedicated to Bel Merodach, the patron god of the city, must have been one of the most enormous structures of ancient Babylon. The fame of temple towers or pyramids, *Ziggurats*, of this description was doubtless widely current throughout Western Asia, and may have given rise to strange legends concerning their erection in primitive times.

let us make us a name] i.e. make ourselves renowned. Cf. Isa. lxiii. 12, "to make himself an everlasting name"; 2 Sam. vii. 23, "to make him a name." For the Heb. *shêm* = "name" in the sense of "renown," ch. vi. 4, "the men of renown"; Isai. lv. 13, "it shall be to the LORD for a name." Some scholars prefer to render *shêm* by "monument," or "memorial," as possibly in 2 Sam. viii. 13. Old Jewish commentators thought it might refer to Shem, or even to the sacred name of the Almighty!

lest we be scattered abroad] The tower was to be visible to the whole world, and make its builders famous for ever. The tower and the city would be a conspicuous place for purposes of concentration and defence. It was apparently (see *v.* 6) the LORD's Will that the people should scatter over the world. The people resolved upon a project which would frustrate the Divine purpose, gratify their own ambition, and protect them as far as possible against punishment. Distance and isolation meant danger.

5. *And the LORD came down to see*] Not a figurative, poetical, expression, as in Isai. lxiv. 1, but a strong and naïve anthropomorphism. The early religious traditions of Israel represent the Almighty in terms which to our minds appear almost profane, but which in the infancy of religious thought presented ideas of the Deity in the simplest and most vivid manner. Here, as in xviii. 21, God is described as descending to

J 6 of men builded. And the LORD said, Behold, they are o*
people, and they have all one language; and this is wh*
they begin to do: and now nothing will be withholden fro*
7 them, which they purpose to do. Go to, let us go dow*
and there confound their language, that they may not und*
8 stand one another's speech. So the LORD scattered the*
abroad from thence upon the face of all the earth: a*
9 they left off to build the city. Therefore was the name
it called Babel; because the LORD did there ¹confound t*

¹ Heb. *balal*, to confound.

the earth, in order to see what was not wholly visible to Him in t*
heavens.

6. *And the LORD said*] The account, in this and the following ver*
is evidently condensed. In *v*. 5 Jehovah is represented as comi*
down on earth, in order to see more closely, and on the spot to form*
better judgement. This He has done; He has returned to heaven, a*
now, in *v*. 6, announces what He has seen. In *v*. 7 He proposes *
descend a second time and inflict punishment.

one people...one language] This is evidently contrary to the intenti*
of the Deity who desires the whole earth to be populated.

nothing will be withholden from them] i.e. they will be baulked in *
enterprise. If they mount up to heaven, their arrogance will ma*
them endeavour to rival God Himself. It is the same kind of app*
hension as in iii. 22.

7. *Go to, let us go down*] For 1st pers. plur. see notes on i. 26, iii.*
22. Jehovah is represented probably as enthroned above the heav*
and either as addressing the powers of heaven, "the sons of Elohi*
who attend Him and minister to Him (cf. Job i. 6), or as announci*
His purpose in the deliberative 1st pers. plur.

8. *scattered them abroad*] The general result is stated; the mea*
by which the sentence was carried out are not related. Josephus reco*
a tradition that the Tower was overthrown by a mighty wind.

9. *Therefore was the name of it called Babel*] Babel is the regu*
Hebrew form of the name Babylon, see x. 10. The etymology h*
given is popular; cf. xvi. 14, xix. 22 (J). Like most popular etym*
logies, it rests on a resemblance of sound, and has no claim to scient*
accuracy. "Babel" is not a Hebrew name from *balal* = "to confound*
but very probably an Assyrian name meaning the "Gate of Go*
Bab-ilu.

confound] Heb. *balal* = "to confound," the same word as in *v*.
To the Hebrew the sound of the name Babel suggested "confusio*
"Babel" is regarded as a contraction from a form *Balbêl* (wh*
does not exist in Hebrew, but occurs in Aramaic) = "Confusion":
LXX Σύγχυσις. This derivation, so derogatory to the great Babylon*

language of all the earth: and from thence did the LORD   J
scatter them abroad upon the face of all the earth.

These are the generations of Shem. Shem was an 10 P
hundred years old, and begat Arpachshad two years after
the flood: and Shem lived after he begat Arpachshad five 11
hundred years, and begat sons and daughters.
And Arpachshad lived five and thirty years, and begat 12
Shelah: and Arpachshad lived after he begat Shelah four 13
hundred and three years, and begat sons and daughters.

capital, could hardly have been drawn from any Babylonian source.
The story (if, as in *vv.* 2, 3, 4, it shews acquaintance with Babylonia)
has clearly come down to us through a channel which regarded Babylon
as a foreigner and a foe.

10—26. THE GENEALOGY OF THE PATRIARCHS FROM SHEM TO ABRAM. (P.)

This genealogical table is taken from P. It resembles the table in chap. v. (1) in the manner of the enumeration of years, (*a*) at the birth of the firstborn, (*b*) at the patriarch's death: (2) in the general length of the list, nine (or, including Cainan, ten) generations: (3) in the last name, Terah, being represented, like Noah, as the father of three sons.

The gradual diminution in the duration of life from Shem (600 years) and Arpachshad (438 years) to Nahor (148 years) should be noticed. See Special Note on the Longevity of the Patriarchs, p. 91 f.

The period from the Flood to the birth of Abram covers 290 years. In LXX the period is given as 1070, in the Samaritan text as 940. See Note on the Genealogy of Shem, p. 154.

The names Arpachshad, Shelah, Eber, and Peleg coincide with those in x. 22, 24, 25 (J).

10. *These are the generations*] The heading of a new section in P: see ii. 4ᵃ.

Arpachshad] See note on x. 22, where Arpachshad is the third son of Shem. Possibly Babylonia, or a locality in it, was regarded as the primitive home of Abram's ancestors.

after the flood] Shem (see v. 32 and vii. 6) was a hundred years old when the Flood began.

11. *five hundred years*] According to this chronology Shem would have outlived Abram.

12. *Shelah*] LXX inserts "Cainan" before "Shelah"; and states that "Cainan lived 130 years, and begat Shelah, and lived after he begat Shelah 330 years."

The additional name of Cainan equalizes the list of names with that

P 14 And Shelah lived thirty years, and begat Eber: and
   15 Shelah lived after he begat Eber four hundred and three
       years, and begat sons and daughters.

   16 And Eber lived four and thirty years, and begat Peleg:
   17 and Eber lived after he begat Peleg four hundred and thirty
       years, and begat sons and daughters.

   18 And Peleg lived thirty years, and begat Reu: and Peleg
   19 lived after he begat Reu two hundred and nine years, and
       begat sons and daughters.

   20 And Reu lived two and thirty years, and begat Serug:
   21 and Reu lived after he begat Serug two hundred and seven
       years, and begat sons and daughters.

   22 And Serug lived thirty years, and begat Nahor: and
   23 Serug lived after he begat Nahor two hundred years, and
       begat sons and daughters.

   24 And Nahor lived nine and twenty years, and begat
   25 Terah: and Nahor lived after he begat Terah an hundred
       and nineteen years, and begat sons and daughters.

   26 And Terah lived seventy years, and begat Abram, Nahor,
       and Haran.

in chap. v. But it is also omitted in the parallel list of 1 Chron. i. 24. And it is suspicious that the figures are the same as those of Shelah (in the LXX).

14. *Eber*] See note on x. 24. Here, as in that passage, the context suggests that a name meaning "the other side" or "across," is most naturally applicable to a country on the east side of the river Euphrates.

16. *Peleg*] See note on x. 25.

The geographer Kiepert compares a place Φαλιγά at the junction of the tributary Habor with the river Euphrates.

19. *Reu*] Whether this is the name of a place or a tribe seems quite uncertain. Observe the sudden decline in the length of Peleg's life, and in that of his descendants, as compared with his predecessors. In the approach to historic times the figures become more normal.

20. *Serug*] The name of a town and region near Haran in Mesopotamia in the land of the upper Euphrates.

22. *Nahor*] The name here of Abram's grandfather, as also, in v. 26, of Abram's brother (cf. xxii. 20, Jos. xxiv. 2). Very similar personal names are found in early Assyrian business documents.

24. *Terah*] The father of Abram. The name has not yet been clearly identified with any locality, or tribe.

26. *seventy years*] The birth of Terah's firstborn is postponed for

Now these are the generations of Terah. Terah begat 27 P
Abram, Nahor, and Haran; and Haran begat Lot. | And 28 J
Haran died in the presence of his father Terah in the land
of his nativity, in Ur of the Chaldees. And Abram and 29

a period twice as long as in the case of the other patriarchs since
Shem. Shem was 100 years old when he begat Arpachshad (*v.* 10).
This greater duration of time is connected with the features of faith and
discipline attaching to the careers of the greater personages in the
Israelite ancestry.

Abram] According to the Hebrew tradition, the name means
"the father (*ab*) is exalted (*ram*)." It might also mean "Ram
(=Ramman) is father." Compare, in the one case, Jehoram (=Jah
is exalted); in the other, Abijah (=Jah is father). See note on xvii. 5.

Nahor] See on *v.* 22.

Haran] This name has by some scholars been derived from the
Heb. *har* = "a mountain," and explained as meaning "Highlanders."
"Beth-haran" is the name of a town built by the "children of Gad"
(Num. xxxii. 36) and mentioned along with "Beth-Nimrah." Possibly,
therefore, Haran was also the name of a local deity.

27—32. THE SONS OF TERAH. (J and P.)

27. *Now these are,* &c.] The story of Abram commences here
with the heading of a section from P. Cf. xxv. 19, "And these are
the generations of Isaac."

Haran begat Lot] Lot the nephew of Abram, and the traditional
ancestor of the peoples east of the Dead Sea. It is natural to suppose
that the name has some affinity with that of "Lotan," a Horite family
or tribe (xxxvi. 20, 29).

28. This and the following verse are taken from J, and commence
the personal history of the patriarch.

Haran died] This may indicate a tradition that the hill people, or
families who joined the main body of the Terahites, lost their separate
existence and became completely merged in the house of Terah.

The grave of Haran was shewn in the days of Josephus (*Ant.*
I. 151).

in the presence of his father] i.e. while his father Terah was still
alive.

in the land of his nativity] To these words is appended the explanation, "in Ur of the Chaldees," very possibly added as a gloss
by a later hand, as in xv. 7. Abram in xxiv. 4, 7, 10 refers to Haran,
or *Aram naharaim*, as the land of his nativity; and that region is
generally treated as the home of the ancestors of the Israelites. It
is clear, however, that, beside the tradition which ascribed the origin
of Israel to Mesopotamia, there was also another which derived them
ultimately from S. Babylonia. See *v.* 31.

J   Nahor took them wives: the name of Abram's wife was
Sarai; and the name of Nahor's wife, Milcah, the daughter
of Haran, the father of Milcah, and the father of Iscah.
P 30 And Sarai was barren; she had no child. | And Terah took
    31 Abram his son, and Lot the son of Haran, his son's son,
and Sarai his daughter in law, his son Abram's wife; and
they went forth with them from Ur of the Chaldees, to go

29. *Sarai*] Abram's wife was, according to xx. 12, his half-sister, i.e. a daughter of Terah by another wife. Milcah, Nahor's wife, is Nahor's niece. Whether in these marriages we have to deal with the actual details of relationship permitted in nomadic life, or whether we have presented to us, under the imagery of matrimony, the fusion of families or tribes in the main community, is a question which we are not able through lack of evidence to answer. The blending of personal and tribal history produces a result, in which it is impossible to be sure of disentangling the separate elements.

"Sarai" is believed to be an archaic form of "Sarah" = "princess": cf. xvii. 15.

The fact that *Sarratu* (= "princess") was a title of the moon-goddess, consort of Sin, and *Malkatu* (= "queen"), a title of Istar, among the deities worshipped in Harran, raises questions with regard to the origin of the Hebrew proper names, Sarah and Milcah.

For Milcah cf. xxii. 20, 23; xxiv. 15, 24, 47. "Iscah," otherwise unknown: by some identified with Sarai; by others as Lot's wife.

31, 32. THE MIGRATION OF TERAH TO HARAN, AND HIS DEATH. (P.)

31. *they went forth with them*] The words, as they stand, are meaningless. The Syriac reads "and he went forth with them." Better as LXX, Sam. and Lat. "and he brought them forth," which only requires the omission of one letter. Another conjectural emendation is "and they went forth with him."

No reason for the migration is here assigned. Later tradition attributed it to religious causes. Cf. Judith v. 6—9, "This people are descended of the Chaldeans. And they departed from the way of their parents, and worshipped the God of heaven, the God whom they knew: and they cast them out from the face of their gods, and they fled into Mesopotamia, and sojourned there many days. And their God commanded them to depart from the place where they sojourned."

Ur of the Chaldees] Heb. *Ur Kasdim*. "Ur" is the *Uru* of the inscriptions denoting a town and region. The town is generally believed to have been discovered in the mounds of the modern

into the land of Canaan; and they came unto Haran, and P
dwelt there. And the days of Terah were two hundred and 32
five years: and Terah died in Haran.

El-Muḳayyar in S. Babylonia, on the right bank of the Euphrates, more than 100 miles S.E. of Babylon. It was the principal seat of the worship of the moon-god, Sin, in S. Babylonia. Its position enhanced its importance in early times. It stood on the main route between Arabia and Syria; and the river Euphrates in those days must have flowed close to its walls. "Kasdim" = "of the Chaldees," has been added (evidently for purposes of distinction from other similar names), here and in *v*. 28, xv. 7; Neh. ix. 7; Judith v. 6. The Chaldeans, who dwelt in the south of Babylonia, became predominant in the 7th century B.C.; but their name does not appear in the inscriptions until long after the time of Abram.

'Or being the Hebrew word for "light," the rendering "in the fire of the Chaldees" (Jerome, *Quaest., ad loc., in igne Chaldaeorum*) gave rise to fantastic legends, which related how Haran perished in, and how Abram was ordered by Nimrod to be cast into, the furnace.

Haran] LXX Χαρράν, Gr. Κάρραι, Lat. *Carrhae*, where Crassus fell in battle with the Parthians. The name of a town distant 550 miles N., or N.W. from Ur; and one of the principal towns in Mesopotamia, situate on the left bank of the river *Belikh*, 70 miles N. from its confluence with the Euphrates on its eastern bank. The name is spelt differently from the Haran of *vv*. 26 and 27. It would be better to pronounce it "Ḥarran," like the Assyrian *Ḥarranu*, meaning "a road." The name implies its strategical importance as the converging point of the commercial routes from Babylon in the south, Nineveh in the east, and Damascus in the west.

Ḥarran, like Ur, was a centre of the worship of the moon-god, Sin. The two traditions, which derive Abram from Ur and from Haran, unite in connecting his home with a shrine of the moon-god, the one in Babylonia, the other in Mesopotamia.

The journey to Canaan from Ur would describe, by the ordinary caravan route, a great curve passing through Babylon N.W. to Ḥarran; thence 60 miles westward to Carchemish on the Euphrates; from Carchemish S.W. to Damascus, and from Damascus south into the land of Canaan. This curve is necessitated by the great desert which separates the river system of the Tigris and Euphrates from the hill country to the east of the Dead Sea and the Jordan.

32. *two hundred and five years*] For this figure the Samaritan version gives 145, obviously in order to make the year of Abram's departure from Haran (when Abram was 75 years old; see xii. 4) coincide with the year of Terah's death, since Abram was born (*v*. 26) in Terah's 70th year. It is this tradition which is followed by Stephen, Acts vii. 4.

NOTE ON THE GENEALOGY OF SHEM

Name	Massoretic Text			Samaritan Text			Septuagint Text			Book of Jubilees
	1st Son	After	Total	1st Son	After	Total	1st Son	After	Total	1st Son
1. Shem	100	500	600	100	500	600	100	500	600	102 ?
2. Arpachshad ...	35	403	438	135	303	438	135	430	565	66 ?
[Cainan]............	...	...	...	...	...	...	130	330	460	57
3. Shelah	30	403	433	130	303	433	130	330	460	71
4. Eber	34	430	464	134	270	404	134	370	504	64
5. Peleg	30	209	239	130	109	239	130 (L. 134)	209	339	61
6. Reu	32	207	239	132	107	239	132	207	339	59
7. Serug	30	200	230	130	100	230	130	200	330	57
8. Nahor............	29	119	148	79	69	148	79	129 (L. 125)	208	62
9. Terah	70	135	205	70	75	145	70	135	205	70
	390			1040			1170 (L. 1174)			669
From Flood to Birth of Abram	290			940			1070			567

In this Table it is possible to follow the different chronologies of the Massoretic, Samaritan, and Septuagint Text (L=Lucian).

(*a*) The Samaritan Text (except in the case of Shem, Nahor, and Terah) adds 100 years to the ages at the birth of the firstborn: in the case of Nahor, it adds 50.

The Septuagint Text does the same.

(*b*) The Samaritan Text (except in the case of Shem, Eber, Nahor, and Terah) deducts 100 years from the ages subsequent to the birth of the firstborn; in the case of Eber it deducts 160 years; in the case of Nahor it deducts 50 years; in the case of Terah it deducts 60 years.

The Septuagint Text adds in the case of Arpachshad 27 years; and of Nahor 10 years; and deducts in the case of Shelah 73 years, and of Eber 60 years.

(*c*) In chap. xi. only nine generations are recorded, as against ten in chap. v. The Septuagint, by inserting Cainan, secures the number *ten*.

(*d*) It will be noticed that the ages of the Shemite Patriarchs become greatly diminished in duration after Eber.

(*e*) The difficulty, occasioned by xi. 32 (Terah's death in Haran

Now the LORD said unto Abram, Get thee out of thy 12 J
country, and from thy kindred, and from thy father's house,
unto the land that I will shew thee: and I will make of 2
thee a great nation, and I will bless thee, and make thy
name great; and be thou a blessing: and I will bless them 3

at the age of 205), and by xii. 4 (Abram's departure from Haran at the age of 75, when Terah was 145 years old (cf. xi. 26)), is obviated in the Samaritan Text, according to which Terah died at the age of 145, the year of Abram's departure.

CH. XII. 1—9. 1—4ª (J); 4ᵇ, 5 (P). THE FIRST PROMISE: AND THE MIGRATION OF ABRAM INTO CANAAN.

This passage is from J, with the exception of 4ᵇ and 5 (P).

1. *Now the LORD said*] Lit. "and Jehovah said." The narrative opens with characteristic simplicity, and with the abruptness possibly indicating its selection from a group of similar traditions.

the LORD said] Here, as elsewhere, we must not suppose that "the word of Jehovah" was accompanied either by any external manifestation, or by an audible sound. God in old times "hath spoken unto the fathers" even as He speaks now to those who hear His voice, "in divers manners" (Heb. i. 1).

out of thy country...kindred...father's house] See xxiv. 7. The threefold tie of land, people, and home, is to be severed. Abram is to lay the foundations of the Chosen People independently of any obligation or favour due to local environment or personal association. He is to rely only on his God. Thus the first trial of the patriarch's faith requires him, (*a*) to renounce the certainties of the past: (*b*) to face the uncertainties of the future: (*c*) to look for and to follow the direction of Jehovah's will. Cf. Heb. xi. 8, "by faith Abraham, when he was called, obeyed to go out...and he went out, not knowing whither he went."

the land that I will shew thee] The country is not designated by name: an additional test of faith.

2. The promise, (1) of national greatness, (2) of personal privilege, embraces a double relation, to the world and to the individual.

a great nation] This thought stands in the forefront. The personal aspect of the promise made to Abram is from the first merged in the thought of its historic influence throughout the ages.

I will bless thee] The experience of happiness in the personal relation to Jehovah is to be the pledge of the ultimate fulfilment of blessing to the world.

make thy name great] Contrast xi. 4. The blessing of Abram, in its spiritual influence upon the world, will be of more enduring renown than any of the material forces of the world.

be thou a blessing] i.e. one who impersonates true felicity; cf. Zech.

156 GENESIS XII. 3, 4

J that bless thee, and him that curseth thee will I curse: and
4 in thee shall all the families of the earth be blessed. So
Abram went, as the LORD had spoken unto him; and Lot
P went with him: | and Abram was seventy and five years old

viii. 13. Not a source, but a type, of blessing, to be pronounced upon others. The imperative expresses a consequence which is intended (Gesenius, *Heb. Gr.* § 110. 1) = "so that thou shalt be a blessing." By a slight alteration of the pointing, Giesebrecht reads "and it (the name) shall be a blessing." For the "curse" of the primaeval age (iii. 13, iv. 11, v. 29, ix. 25 (J)) is substituted the "blessing" of the Chosen Family.

3. *and I will bless*, &c.] The blessing which Abram receives from God is to be a source of good to his friends and of evil to his foes. Observe the delicacy with which the recipients of the blessing are expressed in the plural; but of the curse in the singular ("him that curseth will I curse"). It is assumed that his friends are numerous and his foes few.

curse] Cf. xxvii. 29, "Cursed be every one that curseth thee."

in thee shall all the families of the earth, &c.] These words can be understood in two ways, according as the verb is rendered (*a*) passively, (*b*) reflexively. (*a*) "On account of thee the whole world shall be blessed." In Abram is impersonated a blessing that shall become universal. The directly Messianic application of this rendering is obvious. (*b*) "In thy name all the families of the earth will find the true formula of benediction." The blessing of Abram shall pass into a universal proverb. All will regard it as the best object of human wishes to participate in the happiness of Abram. The rendering would then be, "shall bless themselves." Cf. xlviii. 20. This rendering is probably supported by xxii. 18, xxvi. 4; Ps. lxxii. 17. Like the alternative rendering, it admits of a Messianic application in the universal recognition of the place of Abram in the Divine scheme of Redemption.

In this passage, the thought which was faintly foreshadowed in the prediction of (1) the conflict between man and the power of evil in iii. 15, and of (2) the privilege of the family of Shem in ix. 26, becomes more definite in (3) the selection of the patriarchal family as the channel of universal blessing.

4[b] (P). *and Abram was seventy and five years old*] Comparing this statement with xi. 26, we gather Abram left Haran when Terah was 145 years old. In xi. 32, Terah lived to an age of 205. If so, he lived for 60 years after Abram's departure. We should, however, naturally infer both from this verse, and from xi. 32, that Terah died before Abram left Haran. We must conclude, either, that the text of the figures in xi. 32 is erroneous, and should be 145; or, that Abram was born 60 years after Nahor and Haran (xi. 26); or, that divergent strata of tradition have been incorporated in the narrative.

The connexion of the ancestry of Israel with the Aramaeans is elsewhere indicated in chap. xxiv., xxviii. 1—xxxii. 2, and Deut. xxvi. 5.

when he departed out of Haran. And Abram took Sarai 5 P
his wife, and Lot his brother's son, and all their substance
that they had gathered, and the souls that they had gotten
in Haran; and they went forth to go into the land of
Canaan; and into the land of Canaan they came. | And 6 J
Abram passed through the land unto the place of Shechem,
unto the ¹oak of Moreh. And the Canaanite was then in the

¹ Or, *terebinth*

5. *substance*] or *goods*. A characteristic word in P (cf. xiii. 6, xxxi. 18, xxxvi. 7, xlvi. 6).

souls] i.e. the slaves and retainers. The movement of Abram out of Haran was evidently on the scale of a large migration, such as was not infrequent among the nomad peoples of Western Asia.

into the land of Canaan] The journey from Haran to Canaan would entail (1) the crossing of the river Euphrates, (2) the traversing of Hamath and Syria, (3) the entrance into N. Palestine. On an ancient tradition that, on the way, Abram conquered Damascus, see Josephus who quotes Nicolaus of Damascus: "Abraham reigned in Damascus, having come with an army from the country beyond Babylon, called the land of the Chaldaeans."

6. *the place of Shechem*] The word "place" is here probably used in the special sense of "sacred place" or "shrine," as also possibly in xxii. 4, xxviii. 11 and 16; Josh. v. 15; Jer. vii. 12. It does not mean the "site" of what was afterwards known as Shechem.

Shechem (modern *Nablus*), one of the most ancient and important towns in the central hill country of Palestine, at the foot of Mt Gerizim, in a fair and fertile valley on the road leading northward from Bethel. For other passages in which Shechem plays an important part, cf. xxxiv.; Jud. ix.; 1 Kings xii. 25. On the meaning of Shechem = a "shoulder" or "ridge," see note on xlviii. 22.

unto the oak of Moreh] Better, as marg., *terebinth*. The terebinth, or turpentine tree, is said at a distance to resemble the oak, but botanically it is of a different species; it does not grow in clumps. It is found in the S. and E. of Palestine in warm and sheltered spots; it often attains very considerable dimensions.

Moreh] Cf. Deut. xi. 30; Jud. vii. 1. In all probability Moreh is not a proper name, but the participle of the verb meaning to "teach" or "instruct," whence comes also the substantive *Torah*, "law" or "instruction." Probably we have here an example of one of the sacred trees under which, in primitive times, a priest, or seer, gave oracles and returned answers to devout questioners. If so, this terebinth may have been the famous tree mentioned elsewhere in connexion with Shechem: cf. xxxv. 4, Josh. xxiv. 26, and perhaps Jud. ix. 37. "The terebinth of Moreh" will then mean "The terebinth of the oracle, or of the soothsayer."

And the Canaanite was then in the land] i.e. long before the conquest

158 GENESIS XII. 6—9

J 7 land. And the LORD appeared unto Abram, and said, Unto thy seed will I give this land: and there builded he
8 an altar unto the LORD, who appeared unto him. And he removed from thence unto the mountain on the east of Beth-el, and pitched his tent, having Beth-el on the west, and Ai on the east: and there he builded an altar unto the
9 LORD, and called upon the name of the LORD. And Abram journeyed, going on still toward the ¹South.

¹ Heb. *Negeb*, the southern tract of Judah.

of Palestine. This clause reminds the reader, that the land promised to the seed of Abram was "then" in the possession of the Canaanites. It was not to be taken by merely encamping in it. Perhaps, also, the clause refers to the sacred tree. Abram recognized the sanctity of the spot in the old religious customs of the Canaanites; and here Jehovah manifested Himself. As the Canaanite was to yield to Israel, so the Canaanite religion was to make way for a higher Revelation. The reverence and awe of the unseen Deity were not to be banished, but to be purified and elevated for a higher worship.

7. *And the LORD appeared*] The first mention of a Theophany in the patriarchal narrative. What form it took, and in what way it was connected with the "sacred tree" or the altar, is not related.

Unto thy seed will I give this land] The continuance of the Divine promise. In vv. 2 and 3 we had the blessing of the people and the patriarch, in general terms. In this verse, immediately after the mention of the Canaanite occupation, possession of "this land" is promised to the descendants of Abram. This verse lays the foundation of the imperishable devotion of "the seed of Abram" to the Land of Promise.

builded he an altar] Cf. viii. 20. The building of an altar which implies the rite of sacrifice is mentioned in connexion with the promises and appearances of God, cf. 8, xiii. 18, xxxiii. 20, xxxv. 1, 7.

Sacrifice was the expression of the patriarch's dependence on, communion with, and devotion to, Jehovah.

8. *Beth-el on the west, and Ai on the east*] For Bethel, see note on xxviii. 12. For Ai, see Josh. vii. 2—5. The situation of Abram's tent between Bethel and Ai must have commanded a view of the valley of the Jordan and of the Dead Sea, with the mountains of Moab. "Beth-el," or "House of God," was probably also an ancient shrine, the modern *Bêtîn*, 9½ miles N. of Jerusalem.

on the west] The Heb. word for "the west" means literally "the sea," i.e. the Mediterranean Sea. Such an expression for a point of the compass could only have been used by a people who had long been resident in the country.

called upon the name] See note on iv. 26, i.e. he worshipped, using in his invocation the name "Jehovah." The Name is the symbol of the Divine attributes.

9. *toward the South*] Heb. *Negeb*, the southern tract of Judah.

And there was a famine in the land: and Abram went 10 J

Negeb means "the dry land," "the land of thin soil." It was applied especially to the country in the southernmost region of Canaan, described in Josh. xv. 21—32, and spoken of in Num. xiii. 17, 22, 26. The Israelite, dwelling in Palestine, was accustomed to speak of the south as the "negeb" quarter, just as he spoke of the west as the "sea" quarter, of the compass. The R.V. prints the word "South" with a capital, when it denotes the region between Hebron and the wilderness. It is found in the form *Ngb* in an Egyptian writing of the reign of Thothmes III (1479—1447 B.C.) as a name for S. Palestine (Müller's *Asien u. Europa*, p. 148).

XII. 10—XIII. 2. ABRAM IN EGYPT. (J.)

The narrative in this section should be compared with the similar ones in xx., xxvi. It is repellent to our sense of honour, chivalry, and purity. It is true that Abram's cowardice is reproved, and that the action of the Egyptian Pharaoh is represented in a more favourable light. On the other hand, Abram, though dismissed from the court, leaves Egypt enriched with great spoil. By a subterfuge he had hoped to save his own life at the cost of his wife's honour. His cowardly deceit is detected: and his life is not imperilled. Sarai's honour is spared; and the patriarch withdraws immensely enriched in possessions. This story, doubtless, would not have appeared so sordid to the ancient Israelite as it does to us. Perhaps the cunning, the detection, and the increase of wealth, may have commended the story to the Israelite of old times. Its popularity must account for its re-appearance in xx., xxvi.

It would be gratifying, if, in this story and in its variants, we were warranted in recognizing under an allegorical form the peril, to which nomad tribes of the Hebrew stock were exposed, of being absorbed among the inhabitants of a civilized community. Such a tribal misadventure might well be commemorated under the imagery of such a story. It is more probable, however, that the story illustrates the Divine protection over the patriarch amid the dangers of a foreign country. God's goodness, not Abram's merit, averts the peril.

In the present sequence of patriarchal narratives, this section shews how the fulfilment of the Divine promise is first imperilled through the patriarch's own failure in courage and faith. The very qualities for which he is renowned, are lacking in the hour of temptation. God's goodness and grace alone rescue him and his wife. A heathen king of Egypt upholds the universal law of virtue more successfully than the servant of Jehovah. The story reveals that Jehovah causes His will to be felt in Egypt no less than in Palestine. But the moral of the story does not satisfy any Christian standard in its representation either of Jehovah or of the patriarch. The knowledge of God is progressive.

10. *a famine in the land*] Cf. xxvi. 1, xlii. 1. The failure of crops in Palestine and the adjacent countries, owing to defective rainfall,

J down into Egypt to sojourn there; for the famine was sore
11 in the land. And it came to pass, when he was come near
to enter into Egypt, that he said unto Sarai his wife, Behold
12 now, I know that thou art a fair woman to look upon: and
it shall come to pass, when the Egyptians shall see thee,
that they shall say, This is his wife: and they will kill me,
13 but they will save thee alive. Say, I pray thee, thou art
my sister: that it may be well with me for thy sake, and
14 that my soul may live because of thee. And it came to
pass, that, when Abram was come into Egypt, the Egyptians
15 beheld the woman that she was very fair. And the princes
of Pharaoh saw her, and praised her to Pharaoh: and the
16 woman was taken into Pharaoh's house. And he entreated

often compelled the inhabitants to "go down" into Egypt, where the crops were not dependent on rainfall. They were wont to "sojourn" (i.e. to reside temporarily) there, until the scarcity was passed.

11. *thou art a fair woman*] According to xvii. 17 (P), Sarai was 10 years younger than Abram; and from xii. 4 (P) Abram was at least 75 when he entered Egypt, and Sarai, therefore, 65. This kind of difficulty has led to explanations of a somewhat undignified character. The true explanation is that the ages of the patriarchs which belong to the brief and statistical narrative of P have no place in the narrative of J, in which Sarai is beautiful and childless (xi. 30).

13. *my sister*] i.e. half-sister. Cf. xi. 29, xx. 12.

my soul] A vivid way of expressing the personal pronoun, cf. xxvii. 4, 19, 25.

15. *the princes of Pharaoh*] i.e. the chief officers at the court of the king of Egypt. Pharaoh is not a proper name, but the title of the Egyptian king. It is the Hebrew way of transliterating the Egyptian royal title *Per'o*, "the Great House," which was transferred from the dwelling to the dynasty of the sovereign. It is often compared with "the Sublime Porte." As the king's title, it is no more distinctive than "King," or "Tsar," or "Sultan." There is nothing in this passage to shew which Egyptian king is intended, or at what place he held his court. If Abram was a contemporary of Hammurabi (see note on xiv.), the Pharaoh of this chapter may have belonged to the 12th or 13th dynasty of Egypt.

All kings of Egypt mentioned in the O.T. (except Shishak, 1 Kings xiv. 25, and So, 2 Kings xvii. 4) are designated Pharaoh.

into Pharaoh's house] i.e. into the harem, or women's quarter of the king's palace. The verse illustrates the manner in which the courtiers of an Eastern monarch sought to win royal favour by recommending to his notice beautiful women who might be added to his harem. Cf. the story of the Book of Esther.

GENESIS XII. 16—18

Abram well for her sake: and he had sheep, and oxen, and J
he-asses, and menservants, and maidservants, and she-asses,
and camels. And the LORD plagued Pharaoh and his house 17
with great plagues because of Sarai Abram's wife. And 18
Pharaoh called Abram, and said, What is this that thou

The story is much abbreviated: but it is implied that Sarai consented to sacrifice her honour for her husband's life. We must remember that in the ethics of the O.T. woman is regarded in a less honourable light than man. The idea of a man sacrificing himself to save a woman's honour belongs almost entirely to the Christian age.

16. *entreated*] Old Eng. word for "treated," or "used." The manner in which Abram received and retained these extensive gifts implies his consent to Sarai's position at the court. Abram's acceptance of the purchase-money was his ratification of the transaction. If it struck the Hebrew mind as clever, it seems to us only base and despicable.

sheep, and oxen, &c.] This list represents the principal possessions of a nomad chieftain. The following points should be noticed: (*a*) menservants and maidservants (i.e. male and female slaves) are placed between the animals, either by mistake of a copyist, or being regarded as the chattels of the household, cf. xxiv. 35; (*b*) the mention of camels has been criticized as an anachronism, because the camel is not represented in the Egyptian inscriptions before the Persian period. But, whether used or not by the ancient Egyptians, the camel was certainly employed both by traders and nomads in Western Asia, and in the tradition, whether correctly or not, would be considered to be obtainable; (*c*) the horse is omitted; and the omission has been considered a sign of ignorance of Egyptian life. But the horse never appears among the possessions of the patriarchs, e.g. xxiv. 35, xxx. 43, and its use is condemned in Deut. xvii. 16; (*d*) the order of the items in the list may possibly denote their relative values, the camel being the most precious.

17. *plagued...with great plagues*] The words in the original run: "and Jehovah struck Pharaoh with great strokes, and his house." The words "and his house" have all the appearance of being a later explanatory addition. The "great strokes" or "plagues" must have been some kind of epidemic (cf. xx. 17; 1 Chron. xvi. 21; Ps. cv. 14), the cause of which could not be understood. Pharaoh and his house are guiltless; Abram and Sarai are deceitful and cowardly; Jehovah smites the Egyptian, in order to protect the patriarch and his wife. This representation of the Deity illustrates the immature stage of religious development presented by some of the early Israelite traditions.

18. *Pharaoh called Abram*] How Pharaoh discovered the truth is not recorded in our condensed version. All other explanations of the epidemic failing, possibly the wise men and magicians connected it with the presence of a foreigner in the palace serving Jehovah, and with the indignation of the offended local deities.

GENESIS

GENESIS XII. 18—XIII. 2

J hast done unto me? why didst thou not tell me that she
19 was thy wife? Why saidst thou, She is my sister? so that
I took her to be my wife: now therefore behold thy wife,
20 take her, and go thy way. And Pharaoh gave men charge
concerning him: and they brought him on the way, and his
wife, and all that he had.

13 And Abram went up out of Egypt, he, and his wife, and
2 all that he had, and Lot with him, into the South. And
Abram was very rich in cattle, in silver, and in gold.

19. *take her, and go thy way*] Pharaoh, justly incensed with Abram, dismisses him with sternness and abruptness.

20. *they brought him on the way*] i.e. they escorted him to the frontier, treating with respect and honour a man of wealth and substance, and a foreigner whose God had been a protection to himself and a peril to the Egyptian royal family. Abram apparently retained the wealth that he had procured on false pretences. For the word rendered "bring on the way," in the sense of "escort," cf. xviii. 16, xxxi. 27 ("sent away").

On this narrative, see the remarks of J. G. Frazer in *Psyche's Task*, p. 40, "among many savage races breaches of the marriage laws are believed to draw down on the community public calamities of the most serious character...in particular they are thought to blast the fruits of the earth through excessive rain or excessive drought. Traces of similar beliefs may perhaps be detected among the civilised races of antiquity." Frazer quotes, in illustration, Job xxxi. 11 *sq.*, and the two narratives of Gen. xii. 10—20 and xx. 1—18. "These narratives," he says, "seem to imply that adultery, even when it is committed in ignorance, is a cause of plague and especially of sterility among women."

CH. XIII. THE SEPARATION OF ABRAM AND LOT.
(J; P, *vv.* 6, 11b, 12a.)

1. *went up out of Egypt*] Cf. xii. 10, "went down into Egypt." Egypt is always regarded as the low-lying country; and Palestine as the high ground.

Lot with him] Lot was not mentioned in the previous chapter, but it is here implied that Lot had been with Abram in Egypt.

into the South] i.e. into the Negeb: see note on xii. 9. This is a good illustration of the meaning of Negeb. Abram's journey from Egypt into the Negeb was by a route leading N.E. The English reader, not understanding the technical meaning of "the South," might suppose that Abram's journey from Egypt into "the South" would have led in the direction of the Soudan.

2. *cattle...silver...gold*] Abram's wealth described in an ascending scale of value. Cf. xii. 16, xxiv. 35.

GENESIS XIII. 3—9

And he went on his journeys from the South even to 3 J
Beth-el, unto the place where his tent had been at the
beginning, between Beth-el and Ai; unto the place of the 4
altar, which he had made there at the first: and there
Abram called on the name of the LORD. And Lot also, 5
which went with Abram, had flocks, and herds, and tents. |
And the land was not able to bear them, that they might 6 P
dwell together: for their substance was great, so that they
could not dwell together. | And there was a strife between 7 J
the herdmen of Abram's cattle and the herdmen of Lot's
cattle: and the Canaanite and the Perizzite dwelled then
in the land. And Abram said unto Lot, Let there be no 8
strife, I pray thee, between me and thee, and between my
herdmen and thy herdmen: for we are brethren. Is not 9

on his journeys] i.e. by successive encampments.

the place...his tent] See xii. 8; to which passage also the phrases "at the beginning," and "at the first" (*vv.* 3, 4) refer.

5. *And Lot also*] This verse, describing the wealth of Lot, is intended, with *v.* 2, to prepare for the account of the separation of Abram from Lot. Lot's wealth consists only of flocks and herds and tents.

6. *And the land*, &c.] The account, according to P, of the reason for Lot's separation. The flocks and herds of the two chieftains when combined were so numerous, that there was not pasturage enough to feed them. Cf. a similar reason, in P's narrative, for the separation of Jacob and Esau, xxxvi. 7. The word "substance" is characteristic of P. Cf. xii. 5.

7. *And there was a strife*] The account according to J of the reason for the separation. Disputes were constantly arising between the herdsmen of the two caravans. For other examples of such causes of friction among shepherds and herdsmen, see xxi. 24—32, xxvi. 15—33.

and the Canaanite and the Perizzite] Cf. xii. 6. The introduction of this clause is probably intended to emphasize the danger of dissensions between the Hebrew camps at a time when the native inhabitants, jealous of the wealth of the strangers, might be glad of a pretext for attacking them singly. "The Canaanite" is the indigenous inhabitant (x. 15, 19, xii. 6) in J.

The Perizzite is mentioned with the Canaanite in xxxiv. 30, Jud. i. 4, 5, and in the lists of the nations, e.g. xv. 20, 21. In Josh. xvii. 15 the Perizzites are named with the Rephaim; and in Josh. xxiv. 11 with the Amorites. There is no means of determining where they dwelt. Some have supposed that the Perizzites meant the peasantry, or dwellers in villages and unwalled towns, as distinct from the Canaanites who dwelt in walled cities: and that the name is connected with the word *perazi*, used in Deut. iii. 5 and 1 Sam. vi. 18.

8. *for we are brethren*] i.e. kinsmen; Abram being Lot's uncle.

J the whole land before thee? separate thyself, I pray thee, from me: if *thou wilt take* the left hand, then I will go to the right; or if *thou take* the right hand, then I will go 10 to the left. And Lot lifted up his eyes, and beheld all the ¹Plain of Jordan, that it was well watered every where, before the LORD destroyed Sodom and Gomorrah, like the garden of the LORD, like the land of Egypt, as thou goest

¹ Or, *Circle*

Cf. xiv. 14, "and when Abram heard that his brother (i.e. Lot) was taken captive."

Abram, as the elder, takes the lead in the conference: his proposal is made with generosity and dignity. Lot, though the younger, is to have his choice.

9. *the whole land,* &c.] Abram's offer is made with the elaborate profuseness and courtesy characteristic of an Oriental bargain: cf. xxiii. 11—16; 2 Sam. xxiv. 21—24.

10. *And Lot lifted up his eyes*] The spot near Bethel, from which the view described in this verse can be obtained, is easily identified. Travellers speak in glowing terms of the scene commanded by this piece of high ground.

all the Plain (R.V. marg. *Circle*) *of Jordan*] The word *kikkar*, a "round," or "circle" (Skinner renders "Oval"), was applied by the Israelites to the broader portion of the level country on either side of the river Jordan, extending northwards as far as the river Jabbok, and southwards, originally, according to the tradition, to the supposed site of the submerged cities of the Plain at the lower end of the Dead Sea. Cf. xix. 24—29; 2 Sam. xviii. 23; 1 Kings vii. 46. The *kikkar* is specially mentioned in connexion with Jericho in Deut. xxxiv. 3; Neh. iii. 22, xii. 28. The present passage suggests, that the narrative emanated from a source, according to which the formation of the Dead Sea was subsequent to the destruction of the cities of the Plain (xix.), and that its bed had previously been a fertile agricultural region.

well watered] The basin of the Jordan is famous for its fertility. The climate is tropical, and the soil is watered by the Jordan and its tributaries.

before the LORD destroyed, &c.] The writer pictures this scene of fertility extending itself to the southern extremity of the Dead Sea, before the catastrophe described in xix. 24—29.

like the garden of the LORD] "The garden of Jehovah" is the garden of Eden (chap. ii.; cf. Isai. li. 3), the ideal of beauty and fertility. "Like the land of Egypt"; the writer adds a second simile. "The land of Egypt" was well known for the richness of its soil and for the abundance of its irrigation. The two similes, following in succession, have been thought to overload the sentence, but are not, on that account, to be regarded as glosses.

as thou goest unto Zoar] Zoar, a town situated probably in the S.E.

unto Zoar. So Lot chose him all the Plain of Jordan; and 11 J
Lot journeyed east: | and they separated themselves the one   P
from the other. Abram dwelled in the land of Canaan, 12
and Lot dwelled in the cities of the Plain, | and moved his   J
tent as far as Sodom. Now the men of Sodom were 13
wicked and sinners against the LORD exceedingly. And 14
the LORD said unto Abram, after that Lot was separated
from him, Lift up now thine eyes, and look from the place
where thou art, northward and southward and eastward and
westward: for all the land which thou seest, to thee will I 15
give it, and to thy seed for ever. And I will make thy seed 16

of the Dead Sea (cf. xix. 22): and hence this clause, as it stands, must
be connected with "the Plain of Jordan, that it was well watered
every where," the intervening clauses being parenthetical.

Another reading, "Zoan," found in the Syriac Peshitto, would
connect the clause with the mention of Egypt, by specifying the fertile
district of the famous city of Tanis on the east of the Nile Delta.

11. *So Lot chose*] This verse points onward both to the catastrophe
in xix. and to the dwelling-place of the Moabites and Ammonites.
Lot's selection (*a*) disregarded the rights of Abram his senior; (*b*) was
based on the material attractions of the country; (*c*) ignored the characteristics of the people of the land (*v.* 13). Its importance lay in its
symbolical resignation of any claim upon the land of Palestine by the
Moabites and Ammonites.

and Lot journeyed east] This is the account according to J. The
next two clauses are from P: they repeat the same thought and interrupt the sentence. The words in *v.* 12 "and moved his tent as far as
Sodom" continue the sentence "journeyed east," and follow very
awkwardly after the words "dwelled in the cities of the Plain." This
is a rare instance of unskilful combination of the two *strata* of tradition.

13 (J). *the men of Sodom*] The mention of the wickedness of the
people is here emphasized in reference to (*a*) the selfish choice of
Lot (*v.* 11); (*b*) the coming story of the overthrow of the cities of the
Plain (xix.); (*c*) the immediate assurance to Abram of Jehovah's blessing
outweighing all earthly privileges.

sinners against the LORD] i.e. by immorality, not idolatry. Jehovah's
supremacy over the heathen world is here implied, as in xii. 10—20
in connexion with Egypt, and in x. 10 in the mention of Nimrod.

14—17 (J). The promise of the land to Abram and his seed (xii. 7)
is renewed with more minute description, (*a*) as to the extent of the
country (*vv.* 14, 15); (*b*) as to the infinite number of his descendants
(*v.* 16).

14. *northward and southward*, &c.] The promise here includes, in
the future possession of Israel, the land which Lot had chosen for himself.

15. *to thee will I give it, and to thy seed for ever*] The gift to

J as the dust of the earth: so that if a man can number the dust of the earth, then shall thy seed also be numbered. 17 Arise, walk through the land in the length of it and in the 18 breadth of it; for unto thee will I give it. And Abram moved his tent, and came and dwelt by the [1]oaks of Mamre, which are in Hebron, and built there an altar unto the LORD.

[1] Or, *terebinths*

Abram is one of promise and prediction. The gift to his "seed" was to be fulfilled in history. If the words "for ever" are to have their fullest meaning, the land is a pledge symbolic of God's mercy and goodness towards the people. Their expansion and discipline will be in Palestine. The land and the people will be identified.

16. *as the dust of the earth*] For this simile cf. xxviii. 14, which is also from J. Abram's descendants are elsewhere compared in number to the stars, xv. 5, xxii. 17, xxvi. 4; and to the sand which is upon the seashore, xxii. 17, xxxii. 12.

17. *Arise, walk*] Abram is told to go up and down in the land of promise, and thus to view by faith the possession which his descendants will connect with the promise made to him.

18. *the oaks of Mamre*] Better, as R.V. marg., *terebinths*. Cf. xiv. 13, xviii. 1. Probably the sacred trees of the Canaanite sanctuary at Hebron. Josephus (*Ant.* I. x. § 4 and *B.J.* IV. ix. § 7) mentions the oak tree (δρύς) of Hebron. The so-called oak of Abraham, 3 miles N.W. of Hebron, was shattered by a storm in the winter of 1888—9. The tree was said to be six or seven hundred years old. In xiv. 24 Mamre is the name of a local chieftain allied with Abram. Here, and in xxiii. 17, 19, xxv. 9, xlix. 30, l. 13, it is the name of a place near Hebron.

in Hebron] The famous city of Judah; cf. xxiii. 2. From its connexion with Abram it derives its modern name *El Ḥalil*, "the friend," an abbreviation of *Ḥalil er-raḥman*, "the friend of the Merciful One," i.e. God," the designation of Abram. Cf. Isa. xli. 8; Jas. ii. 23. It stands 3000 ft. above the sea, at the junction of the main roads, from Gaza in the W., from Egypt in the S.W., from the Red Sea on the S.E., and from Jerusalem, 19 miles away, on the N.

CH. XIV. (*origin uncertain*).

1—12.   I.   THE CAMPAIGN OF CHEDORLAOMER KING OF ELAM AND THREE VASSAL KINGS AGAINST THE FIVE REBELLIOUS KINGS OF THE PLAIN, WHO ARE DEFEATED AND THEIR CITIES LOOTED; LOT MADE PRISONER.

13—16.   II.   ABRAM'S VICTORIOUS PURSUIT OF CHEDORLAOMER AND RESCUE OF LOT.

17—24.   III.   ABRAM, THE KING OF SODOM, AND MELCHIZEDEK.

This chapter presents us with the picture of Abram in the character of a warrior—vigorous, resourceful, successful, and magnanimous. On

Photo Mansell & Co.

Khammurabi (? Amraphel), King of Babylon, receiving laws from Shamash, the Sun-god.

A relief on the upper part of the basalt *stele* on which is inscribed in cuneiform characters the famous Code of Laws.

And it came to pass in the days of Amraphel king of **14** (?) Shinar, Arioch king of Ellasar, Chedorlaomer king of Elam, and Tidal king of ¹Goiim, that they made war with Bera **2**

¹ Or, *nations*

the historical background of the narrative, see the Special Note. The story is somewhat abruptly introduced. The mention of Lot who is dwelling in Sodom forms the chief point of contact with the previous narrative. There are numerous features in the account which seem to indicate its derivation from an entirely distinct source of tradition.

1—12. THE CAMPAIGN.

1. *And it came to pass in the days of*] The opening formula of a new Hebrew section. Cf. Ruth i. 1; 2 Sam. xxi. 1; Esther i. 1; Isa. vii. 1.

Amraphel] King of Shinar, very generally accepted as the Hebrew reproduction of the name *Hammurabi*, king of Babylonia about 2150 B.C. (?). On the assumption of this identification it has been conjectured that the last syllable of the name should be "-i" instead of "-el," i.e. Amraphi. For Shinar, see note on x. 10 and xi. 2.

Hammurabi is famous as the king who finally freed his kingdom from the yoke of the Elamites, who united northern and southern Babylonia under one rule, and extended his conquests as far west as Palestine. Many cuneiform documents, belonging to his reign and referring to his government, have been discovered and deciphered, most remarkable and important of all being his Code of Laws[1].

Arioch king of Ellasar] Possibly the same as *Rim-sin* who is said to be referred to in an ancient Sumerian record as *Eri-Aku*, son of *Kudur-Mabug*, king of Larsa, and a contemporary of Hammurabi. Ellasar is clearly the Babylonian town *Larsa*, which is identified with the ruins of the modern *Senkereh* on the E. bank of the Euphrates in S. Babylonia.

We meet with the name of Arioch in a Babylonian court-official (Dan. ii. 15); and as a "king of the Elymaeans," a vassal of Nebuchadnezzar (Judith i. 6).

Chedorlaomer] King of Elam. The name has not hitherto been identified in the history of Western Asia. In its formation, however, it is genuinely Elamite, i.e. *Kudur* = "servant," and *Lagamar* = an Elamite deity. The supremacy of Elam over all that region of Western Asia about the time of Hammurabi is attested by the ancient documents. For Elam, see note on x. 22. It is the country called in the Assyrian *Elamtu*, and in the Greek *Elymais*, north of the Persian Gulf and east of the Lower Tigris. Its capital was Susa, which appears in the classical form of Susiana. On the overthrow of Elam by the Persians, see Jer. xlix. 34—39.

Tidal king of Goiim] The attempts which have been made to

[1] Discovered in Dec. 1901 and Jan. 1902 by M. Le Morgan at Susa. See Driver's *Exodus*, Appendix III.

(?) king of Sodom, and with Birsha king of Gomorrah, Shinab king of Admah, and Shemeber king of Zeboiim, and the
3 king of Bela (the same is Zoar). All these ¹joined together

¹ Or, *joined themselves together against*

identify Tidal have not yet been successful. But there is no reason to suppose that it is a fictitious name; and future research may bring his name to light. *Goiim* is the regular Hebrew word for "nations," and therefore seems to be very improbable as the name of a country or city. It may have been substituted by a Hebrew copyist for some unfamiliar proper name resembling it in pronunciation, or in shape of letters. Thus Sir Henry Rawlinson's conjecture of *Gutim* has very generally found favour. The *Guti* were a people often mentioned in the inscriptions, living in the region of Kurdistan. Sayce suggests that Goiim may be correct as the Hebrew translation of the Assyrian *Ummanmanda*, the peoples, or nomad hordes, that constantly swept through those regions.

2. *that they made war*] This anticipates and summarizes the contents of *vv.* 5—10. As Hammurabi, the conqueror of Elam and founder of the Babylonian kingdom, terms himself king of *Amurru* = Amorites, or northern Palestine, there is nothing unhistorical in the representation of an invasion of this region by the Elamite suzerain.

Bera...Birsha] The kings of the cities of the Plain mentioned in this verse are not otherwise known. Identifications with the Arabic *Bari* and *Birshi*, and with the Babylonian *Sinabu*, have been conjectured. The five cities here named, sometimes (e.g. Wisd. x. 6) called the Pentapolis, were, according to the tradition, situated at the southern end of the Dead Sea, and, with the exception of Zoar, were overwhelmed in the catastrophe of chap. xix. Each city has its king, as was the case with the cities of Canaan, according to the Book of Joshua and the Tel-el-Amarna tablets.

It is noteworthy that Bera and Birsha can, in the Hebrew letters, denote "with evil" and "with wickedness" respectively.

The LXX (Cod. A) reads "Balla" for "Bera," and "Sennaar" for "Shinab."

Admah, and...Zeboiim] These towns are mentioned in Deut. xxix. 23 and Hosea xi. 8 as having been overthrown in the great catastrophe described in chap. xix.

the king of Bela] The only king whose name is not given. The omission favours the accuracy of the list. The name "Bela," meaning "destruction," conceivably contains a local allusion. It has been suggested that we should read "Bela, king of Zoar." The reader, in reviewing these two verses, will be struck with the fact that Chedorlaomer, king of Elam, whose name is mentioned first in the list of *v.* 9, and who is evidently the supreme sovereign in *vv.* 4 and 5, stands third in the list in *v.* 1. It is not easy to find an explanation. Some scholars suggest that the names are arranged in the order of their

in the vale of Siddim (the same is the Salt Sea). Twelve **4** (?)
years they served Chedorlaomer, and in the thirteenth year
they rebelled. And in the fourteenth year came Chedor- **5**
laomer, and the kings that were with him, and smote the

nearness to Palestine! Others, by a slight emendation of the text, reading the final "1" in "Amraphel" as a preposition, render as follows: "in the days of Amraph, when Arioch king of Ellasar was king over Shinar, then Chedorlaomer king of Elam and Tidal king of Goiim made war with, &c." But the mention of the four kings in *v.* 9, where their order is different, does not favour the conjecture.

3. *All these*] Probably the kings mentioned in *v.* 2, i.e. the five local subject princes. That there should be any doubt whether "all these" refers to the four kings of the east, or to the five kings of the west, is an example of the unskilful style in which this section is written.

joined together] The five local kings combined: "the vale of Siddim" was their rallying place. But as "the vale of Siddim" was their own country, the wording is awkward. Hence some prefer R.V. marg. "joined themselves together against," with a change of subject; i.e. the kings of the E. combined and marched against the kings of the W. But the change of subject, interrupting *vv.* 2 and 4, is surely too harsh.

the vale of Siddim] Not mentioned elsewhere; but traditionally identified with the Dead Sea, beneath whose waters the "cities of the Plain" were believed by the Israelites to lie engulfed. The suggestion of Renan to read *Shêdim* ("demons"), a word occurring in Deut. xxxii, 17, Ps. cvi. 37, is ingenious, but lacks support from any other passage mentioning the Dead Sea. LXX τὴν φάραγγα τὴν ἁλυκήν="the salt valley," Lat. *vallem silvestrem.*

the Salt Sea] An explanatory note, like the reference to Zoar, in the previous verse. "The Salt Sea" is the commonest name in the O.T. for "the Dead Sea": e.g. Num. xxxiv. 3, 12; Josh. xv. 2, 5. Another name by which it is called is "the sea of the Arabah," Deut. iii. 17, Josh. iii. 16, xii. 3, where "the Salt Sea" is added as an explanation. In Ezek. xlvii. 18, Joel ii. 20, it is called "the eastern sea." Josephus calls it "the sea of Asphalt"; and in the Jewish Talmud it appears as "the sea of Sodom," or "the salt sea." The intense saltness of its waters and its deposits of salt have given rise to its name. Nothing lives in its waters. The name "Dead Sea" goes back to the time of Jerome, 6th cent. A.D.

4. *they served*] The five kings "served," i.e. were vassals, and paid tribute to, the king of Elam who was their over-lord.

rebelled] Probably by omitting to pay tribute or to send gifts, as they had done for 12 years. The distance from southern Palestine to Elam was great. The five kings were doubtless petty princes, who took part in a wide-spread rebellion. Perhaps they took advantage of

(?) Rephaim in Ashteroth-karnaim, and the Zuzim in Ham,

the decline of the power of Elam, and of the growth of the power of Babylonia. This is a justifiable conjecture if "Amraphel" be the same as Hammurabi. For Hammurabi threw off the yoke of Elam, united Babylonia, and founded the Dynasty of Babylon.

Compare the description in 2 Kings xxiv. 1, "Jehoiakim became his [Nebuchadnezzar's] servant three years; then he turned, and rebelled against him."

5. *came Chedorlaomer*] The king of Elam was strong enough to deal vigorously with the rebellion in his western dependencies. This and the two following verses describe the punitive expedition, with which Chedorlaomer and his vassal kings crushed the rebellion. Whether the kings led their forces in person, we are not able to say for certain. The description leaves it to be inferred. The Oriental style of chronicle identified successful generals with the name of the king who sent them on their campaign.

The march of the punitive expedition must have been across the Euphrates at Carchemish, and then southward past Damascus. It overthrew the Rephaim, Zuzim, Emim, and Horites who, apparently, were peoples on the east side of Jordan, involved in the rebellion. The southernmost point of the march was reached at the head of the Gulf of Akabah. As it commanded an important trade route, it may have formed the chief objective of the march. Returning from that point, the expedition struck at the Amalekites in the wilderness to the south of Palestine, and then attacked the joint forces of the five cities of the Plain and overthrew them in the valley of Siddim.

the Rephaim] or "sons of the Rapha." The name given to the aborigines of Canaan, giant survivors of whom are mentioned in 2 Sam. xxi. 16—22. The name is specially applied, in Deut. iii. 11, to Og, the king of Bashan, whose territory corresponded with the country spoken of in this verse.

Ashteroth-karnaim] Generally identified with *Tell-'Ashtara*, in the plateau of Bashan, about 20 miles east of the sea of Galilee. *Karnaim* means "the two horns"; and the full name will therefore probably mean "the two-horned Astarte," who, as the Goddess of the Moon, was represented with two horns. "Astarte of horns was that immemorial fortress and sanctuary which lay out upon the great plateau of Bashan towards Damascus; so obvious and cardinal a site that it appears in the sacred history both in the earliest recorded campaign in Abraham's time and in one of the latest under the Maccabees. Gen. xiv. 5; 1 Macc. v. 26, 43" (G. Adam Smith, *The Twelve Prophets*, vol. I. p. 176.)

the Zuzim] Possibly the same as "the Zamzummim," mentioned in Deut. ii. 20 as the aborigines who were dispossessed by the Ammonites.

in Ham] Ham has been conjecturally identified with the old name of the Ammonite capital, mentioned in 2 Sam. xii. 26, *Rabbath Ammon*.

and the Emim in ¹Shaveh-kiriathaim, and the Horites in 6 (?)
their mount Seir, unto El-paran, which is by the wilderness.
And they returned, and came to En-mishpat (the same is 7
Kadesh), and smote all the ²country of the Amalekites, and
also the Amorites, that dwelt in Hazazon-tamar. And there 8

¹ Or, *the plain of Kiriathaim*   ² Heb. *field*.

the Emim] Mentioned in Deut. ii. 10 as the name of the aborigines, "a people great and many and tall, as the Anakim," dispossessed by the Moabites. The name means probably "the terrible ones."

in Shaveh-kiriathaim] or *the plain of Kiriathaim*. In Num. xxxii. 37 and Josh. xiii. 19 *Kiriathaim* is a town in Reuben: in Jer. xlviii. 23 in Moab. It is generally identified with *Kureyat*, about 10 miles east of the Dead Sea and north of the river Arnon.

6. *the Horites*] Mentioned also in xxxvi. 20, 21, 30, and in Deut. ii. 12, 22, where they are described as having been dispossessed of the country of Seir, the hill country between the Dead Sea and the Gulf of Elath, by the Edomites. They have been thought to represent primitive "cave-dwellers," of whom traces have been discovered by Macalister at Gezer.

unto El-paran] Generally identified with the town of *Elath*, the well-known port at the head of the Gulf of Akabah; which is sometimes called the "Aelanitic Gulf" from the name *Ailana* given to *Elath* in classical writings. The town may have derived its name from great palm trees in the neighbourhood (*El* = "a great tree").

the wilderness] The Wilderness of Paran (cf. xxi. 21) between the Gulf of Akabah and the borders of Egypt.

7. *En-mishpat*] i.e. "the Spring of Judgement." A spring of water at which there would be a sanctuary, whose priest gave oracles and decided disputes; known in the Israelite history as "Kadesh-barnea," or, as here, "Kadesh." It has been identified in modern times with a spring and oasis, called *Ain-Kadish*, in the desert to the south of Beer-sheba. This was the spot at which the Israelite tribes concentrated after quitting the neighbourhood of Sinai: cf. Num. xxi. 16; Deut. i. 46.

the country] Heb. *field*: LXX and Syr. "princes of" (reading *sârê* for *s'dêh*).

the Amalekites] The nomad peoples of the desert who opposed the Israelite march (Ex. xvii.); and were overthrown by Saul (1 Sam. xv.) in the wilderness south of Canaan.

the Amorites, that dwelt in Hazazon-tamar] The Canaanite people dwelling at Engedi (see 2 Chron. xx. 2) among the rocks on the west shore of the Dead Sea. It has also been conjecturally identified with the Tamar of Ezek. xlvii. 19, xlviii. 28, a town on the S.W. of the Dead Sea. The name *Hazazon-tamar* has been explained to mean "the cutting of palms." The name has been thought to be preserved in the *Wady Hasasa*, not far from *Ain-gidi*.

(?) went out the king of Sodom, and the king of Gomorrah, and the king of Admah, and the king of Zeboiim, and the king of Bela (the same is Zoar); and they set the battle in 9 array against them in the vale of Siddim; against Chedorlaomer king of Elam, and Tidal king of Goiim, and Amraphel king of Shinar, and Arioch king of Ellasar; four kings 10 against the five. Now the vale of Siddim was full of ¹slime pits; and the kings of Sodom and Gomorrah fled, and they fell there, and they that remained fled to the mountain. 11 And they took all the goods of Sodom and Gomorrah, and 12 all their victuals, and went their way. And they took Lot, Abram's brother's son, who dwelt in Sodom, and his goods,

¹ That is, *bitumen pits*.

9. *four kings against the five*] After *v.* 8 we should expect the "five kings against the four." Notice the impressive repetition of the names of the kings, and the variation in the order of the names of the eastern kings, Chedorlaomer coming first, as the over-lord against whom the rebellion had been made.

The description of the battle itself has most unfortunately not been preserved.

10. *full of slime pits*] i.e. bitumen pits. Bitumen, or asphalt, is found in the neighbourhood of the Dead Sea. Josephus speaks of the bitumen floating upon the surface of its waters. Here we are to suppose that the bitumen came out of large holes or pits in the earth, into which the confederates fell in their flight.

"Full of slime pits." The Hebrew idiom gives *be'erôth be'erôth hêmar*, "pits, pits of bitumen"="all bitumen pits." Cf. 2 Kings iii. 16, "trenches, trenches"="nothing but trenches."

The narrative is so fragmentary, or condensed, that only the rout is recorded.

they fell] Referring to the fugitive troops generally. The king of Sodom appears again in *v.* 17. It is implied that those who fell into the pits were lost.

to the mountain] i.e. to the mountains of Moab, the chain of hills on the east side of the Dead Sea.

11. *they took*] The subject is abruptly transferred to the victorious army. The account of the fall of the towns is omitted.

Sodom and Gomorrah] Mentioned perhaps as the chief towns; the three others are passed over in silence. The victorious troops did not wait; but after inflicting punishment hurried off, like a predatory horde, with their booty.

12. *Lot, Abram's brother's son*] Notice this minute description of Lot and the mention of his residence in Sodom, as if chap. xiii. had not immediately preceded. In *vv.* 14 and 16, Lot is spoken of as Abram's brother.

and departed. And there came one that had escaped, and 13 (?)
told Abram the Hebrew: now he dwelt by the ¹oaks of
Mamre the Amorite, brother of Eshcol, and brother of Aner;
and these were confederate with Abram. And when Abram 14
heard that his brother was taken captive, he led forth his

¹ Or, terebinths

13—16. ABRAM'S VICTORY.

13. *Abram the Hebrew*] Abram is described, as Lot in the previous verse, as if mentioned for the first time: an indication of the independent origin of the narrative.

The name "Hebrew" here occurs for the first time in Scripture. It is a title used of Israelites, either by foreigners, or in speaking of them to foreigners, or in contrast with foreigners. The word was popularly explained as a patronymic meaning "descendant of Eber," see notes on x. 24, xi. 14. Its formation, from the root *'br*, suggests that it means "one who has come from the other side," probably, of the river Euphrates, cf. Josh. xxiv. 2. The LXX renders here ὁ περάτης, Lat. *transeuphratensis*.

It is sometimes claimed that the name is identical with that of the *Ḥabiri*, a nomad, restless people, mentioned in the Tel-el-Amarna tablets as making war upon the Canaanite towns and communities (circ. 1400). The name *Ḥabiri* is akin to *Hebron*, and may denote "the confederates." The identification of *'Ibri* = "Hebrew" with *Ḥabiri* would require a change of the first consonant, and an alteration of root meaning¹.

the oaks of Mamre] Better, terebinths. See note on xiii. 18. Mamre, though probably the name of a place, is here personified in its occupant. But there is no indication in xiii. 18 that "the oaks of Mamre" were called by the name of a local chieftain.

Eshcol] The well-known name, meaning "a bunch of grapes," given to a valley near Hebron (cf. Num. xiii. 23), is here transferred to a person.

Aner] has not been identified as a place near Hebron, but appears as the name of a town in 1 Chron. vi. 70.

confederate with Abram] Lit. "lords of the covenant of Abram," i.e. allies with him by mutual compact, like Abimelech the Philistine, xxi. 22, 23, 32, xxvi. 28—31.

14. *And when Abram heard*] It is implied that, if Lot had not been taken prisoner, Abram would not have stirred either to attack the invader or to assist the native kings. But, as a dweller at Hebron, he was within sight of "the land of the Plain," cf. xix. 28; and must have been well aware of Chedorlaomer's punitive expedition against the kings of the Plain.

his brother] i.e. kinsman: see note on xiii. 8.

led forth] Lit. "emptied out," or "unsheathed," used of arrows from

¹ See Appendix D.

GENESIS XIV. 14, 15

(?) trained men, born in his house, three hundred and eighteen,
15 and pursued as far as Dan. And he divided himself against them by night, he and his servants, and smote them, and pursued them unto Hobah, which is on the ¹left hand of

¹ Or, *north*

a quiver, or of a sword from a sheath. Driver gives the meaning "drew out rapidly and in full numbers." The LXX ἠρίθμησεν, "counted" or "mustered," Lat. *numeravit*, following probably a reading which is also found in the Samaritan version.

his trained men, born in his house] i.e. his most faithful retainers, the slaves (*a*) born in his household, as distinguished from those obtained by purchase; (*b*) specially exercised in the use of arms.

three hundred and eighteen] This exact figure seems strange. The old Jewish commentators explained it by pointing out that the numerical value of the Heb. letters of the name "Eliezer," Abram's steward (xv. 2), was 318. In modern times Winckler has found some supporters for the astronomical explanation, that the moon is visible for 318 days in the year; and that the number of Abram's retainers must, therefore, indicate that the story of Abram is blended with a lunar myth. The two explanations possess a certain kind of resemblance in their ingenuity and their improbability.

Dan] The pursuit of Abram enabled him to overtake the booty-laden army at Laish (Josh. xix. 47), on the north frontier of Canaan. Laish received the name of Dan after its conquest by a band of Danites, as recorded in Jud. xviii. The mention of Dan, therefore, is, strictly speaking, an anachronism, though quite intelligible. That Abram should overtake and smite his enemy at the furthest northern limit of the future Israelite country, is a feature in the story not without symbolical significance.

But, if Abram with a small force had to pursue the enemy the whole length of Palestine, the retiring army, though burdened with spoil, must have marched at a high rate of speed. Again, Dan would not be on the high road to Damascus; it lay too far to the left.

15. *divided himself against them by night*] Abram divides his forces into three bands, and from three different quarters delivers a simultaneous night attack. The same manoeuvre was adopted by Gideon (Jud. vii. 20—22), when a small force similarly routed a large army. Cf. 1 Sam. xi. 11. The surprise was complete. Chedorlaomer's panic-stricken troops are chased for over 100 miles, and all the prisoners and booty recovered.

There is no mention of Abram's confederates (see *vv.* 13 and 24). The credit of the victories lies with Abram and his household force.

unto Hobah] Probably a place about 50 miles north of Damascus. Skinner rightly points out that "it is idle to pretend that Abram's victory was merely a surprise attack on the rearguard, and the recovery

Damascus. And he brought back all the goods, and also 16 (?)
brought again his brother Lot, and his goods, and the
women also, and the people. And the king of Sodom 17
went out to meet him, after his return from the slaughter of
Chedorlaomer and the kings that were with him, at the vale
of Shaveh (the same is the King's Vale). And Melchizedek 18
king of Salem brought forth bread and wine: and he was

of part of the booty. A pursuit carried so far implies the rout of the main body of the enemy" (p. 267).

which is on the left hand of Damascus] For "left hand," R.V. marg. has *north*. An Israelite always spoke as if he were facing eastward; and the north is, therefore, on his left hand; cf. ii. 24.

Damascus, the capital of Syria (Heb. *Dammések*=Assyr. *Dimashḳi*, =*Dimashḳ esh-Shâm*, i.e. "Damascus of Syria"), a famous city, mentioned in Egyptian inscriptions as early as the 16th century. On the fable of Abram's capture of it, see note on xii. 5.

17. *the king of Sodom*] See note on *v.* 10. The writer evidently assumes that this is the same king who had fallen in "the slime pits"; for only the king who had lost property and wealth, but saved his life, could suggest to Abram that the latter should keep the booty.

from the slaughter of Chedorlaomer] Lit. "from the smiting of." We need not suppose that Chedorlaomer and his vassal kings were personally involved in the overthrow.

the vale of Shaveh (the same is the King's Vale)] "The King's Vale" is mentioned in 2 Sam. xviii. 18 as the site of the monument raised by Absalom, and was supposed in the days of Josephus to be two "stadia" from Jerusalem (*Ant.* VII. 10, 3). The word *Shaveh* means "a plain," cf. *v.* 5.

The meeting of the king of Sodom with Abram is here strangely interrupted by the story of the appearance of Melchizedek, and is resumed at *v.* 21.

18—20. ABRAM AND MELCHIZEDEK.

18. *Melchizedek king of Salem*] The name Melchizedek was considered by the Jews to mean "the king of righteousness" (Heb. vii. 2), or "my king" (*malchi*) "is righteousness" (*zedek*). The name should be compared with that of Adoni-zedek (Josh. x. 1). It appears most probable that Zedek was the name of a Canaanite deity, and that the names Adoni-zedek, Melchizedek, meant "my Lord is Zedek," "my king is Zedek," just as Adonijah, Malchijah, meant "my Lord is Jah" and "my king is Jah."

Salem] In all probability to be identified with Jerusalem, as evidently by the writer of the Epistle to the Hebrews (Heb. vii. 1, 2). The objection, that Jerusalem was too far south for the present incident, is of no value. The objection that in Judg. xix. 10 the ancient name of Jerusalem was "Jebus" is not conclusive. "Jebus," as a name, seems

(?) 19 priest of ¹God Most High.   And he blessed him, and said,

¹ Heb. *El Elyon*.

only to have been inferred from the Jebusites. See Driver, *H.D.B.*, s.v. "Jebus"; G. A. Smith, *Jerusalem*, I. 266. The following points deserve consideration: (*a*) In the Tel-el-Amarna tablets Jerusalem appears with the name *Uru-salim*. (*b*) Salem is the poetical, or archaic, name for Jerusalem, in Ps. lxxvi. 2. (*c*) Melchizedek is compared to the king of Zion in Ps. cx. 4. (*d*) Abram's paying of tithe to Melchizedek gains greatly in symbolical significance, if Salem is the same as Jerusalem. (*e*) The tradition of this identification is favoured by Josephus (*Ant.* I. 10, 2) and the Targums.

The alternative suggestion, made by Jerome, that Salem is the place mentioned in John iii. 23, in the Jordan Valley, seems very improbable. On the other hand, if Salem be Jerusalem, it is the only mention of Jerusalem in the Pentateuch.

brought forth bread and wine] As a friendly king, Melchizedek provides food and drink for the returning victor, and, as a priest, gives to him his blessing. In the mention of bread and wine there is no idea of religious offerings. It is the gift of food to weary and famished soldiers. Jewish commentators have regarded these gifts as symbolizing the shew-bread and the drink-offering: Christian exegesis has often associated them with the Bread and Wine of the Eucharist. But the bread and wine are not offered to God; they are given to Abram as a token of good-will and as a means of refreshment. There is nothing sacrificial in the gift.

he was priest of God Most High] Melchizedek was not only king (*melek*) of Salem, but also a priest (*kohen*). The combination of the priestly with the kingly functions was common in the East; though amongst the Israelites it is not found until the Maccabean period.

This is the first mention of a priest in Holy Scripture. It is clearly intended that Melchizedek should impersonate pure Monotheism.

Melchizedek is *a*, not *the* priest of "God Most High" (Heb. *El Elyon*). Some have thought that *El Elyon* denotes here the name of an ancient Canaanite deity, and quote, in favour of this view, the statement of Philo of Byblus (Euseb. *Prep. Ev.* i. 10) that there was a Phoenician divinity Ἐλιοῦν καλούμενος Ὕψιστος = "Elyon called Most High." But *El* in the O.T. is one of the most common names of God, especially frequent in poetical and archaic usage. It is often combined with some qualifying epithet denoting an attribute, e.g. xvii. 1, "God Almighty" = *El Shaddai*: xxi. 33, "the Everlasting God" = *El 'olām*: Ex. xx. 5, "a jealous God" = *El kanna*. Again *Elyon*, "Most High," is an epithet often applied to Jehovah, e.g. Num. xxiv. 16; and combined with *El*, Ps. lxxviii. 35. Melchizedek seems, therefore, to be regarded by the writer as a priest of God Almighty, the God of the Universe. The fuller knowledge of God as Jehovah, the God of Revelation, was the privilege of Abram and his descendants. The conception of Melchizedek as the representative of a primitive phase of

GENESIS XIV. 19, 20

Blessed be Abram of ¹God Most High, ²possessor of heaven and earth: and blessed be ¹God Most High, which hath delivered thine enemies into thy hand. And he gave him 20

¹ Heb. *El Elyon*.   ² Or, *maker*

Natural Religion, in the Canaan of 2000 B.C., idealizes his figure. Very probably, in the scene before us, his interposition will best be interpreted symbolically. Josephus (*Ant.* xv. 6, 2) mentions that the Maccabee princes assumed the title of High Priest "of God Most High." Cf. *Assumption of Moses*, vi. 1, "There shall be raised up unto them kings bearing rule, and they shall call themselves priests of the Most High God."

19. *he blessed him*] Melchizedek, as a priest, blessed Abram for his courageous and chivalrous action. A stranger in the land, he had come to the rescue of its people.

of God Most High] i.e. by God Most High. The blessing of *El Elyon* is invoked by Melchizedek upon Abram, the servant of Jehovah.

possessor of heaven and earth] R.V. marg. *maker*. The word is poetical. It expresses the ideas of making, producing, creating, as in Deut. xxxii. 6, Ps. cxxxix. 13, Prov. viii. 22. It is more often used for "acquiring" (cf. iv. 1), a sense which would not here be applicable. In Isai. i. 3, it is found, as here, with the meaning of "owner."

20. *blessed be God Most High*] = "praised be *El Elyon*." The verb has a different sense when applied to the Deity from what it has when applied to man. To "bless God" means devoutly to acknowledge, that He has been the source of goodness which demands man's thankfulness and praise. Melchizedek blesses the God, whose priest he is, for the great victory which his God has granted Abram.

And he gave him a tenth of all] Note once more a change of subject. It is Abram who gives Melchizedek a tenth part "of all," i.e. the spoil; not of his own property, as he was at a distance from home, and was only in light marching order. The custom of paying a tithe, or tenth part, to the priesthood, or to the sanctuary, was very general in ancient times. Traces of it are found in Assyria and Babylonia. It prevailed among the Greeks. For the custom in Israel, see note on xxviii. 22. Abram, the father of the Israelite people, performs symbolically an action which recognizes for future time their obligation to the sanctuary of Jerusalem.

The two statements that Melchizedek, king of Salem and priest of God Most High, (1) blessed Abram, (2) received tithes from Abram, led to the figurative employment of Melchizedek in Ps. cx. 4 as the ideal of a priest-king appointed by God to rule over the kingdom of Judah; and in Heb. v. 9, vii. 4, as the type of the great kingly High Priest, raised above the Aaronic priesthood, at once king and priest receiving tithe from Abram, who impersonated the people and religion of Israel. See Special Note.

(?) 21 a tenth of all. And the king of Sodom said unto Abram,
22 Give me the persons, and take the goods to thyself. And
Abram said to the king of Sodom, I have lift up mine hand
unto the LORD, ¹God Most High, ²possessor of heaven and
23 earth, that I will not take a thread nor a shoelatchet nor
aught that is thine, lest thou shouldest say, I have made
24 Abram rich: ³save only that which the young men have
eaten, and the portion of the men which went with me;
Aner, Eshcol, and Mamre, let them take their portion.

¹ Heb. *El Elyon*. ² Or, *maker*
³ Or, let there be *nothing for me; only that &c.*

21. *the king of Sodom*] This verse resumes the narrative of *v.* 17. The incident of Melchizedek is parenthetical.

22. *I have lift up mine hand*] i.e. I have sworn, taken an oath with a gesture, symbolizing the appeal to God. Cf. Deut. xxxii. 40; Dan. xii. 7.

the LORD, *God Most High*] i.e. *Jehovah El Elyon*. The LXX and Syriac Peshitto omit "Jehovah." The Sam. reads *ha-Elohim* for "Jehovah." Abram takes his oath in the name of the God of Melchizedek whom a later scribe probably identified with Jehovah.

23. *a thread...a shoelatchet*] Not the most trifling thing, not even the lace for a sandal, will Abram take. The fact that Abram has already (*v.* 20) given to Melchizedek a tithe of all the spoil, strictly speaking, conflicts with his refusal, in this verse, to take any share of the spoil. Probably this discrepancy is an indication that the episode of Melchizedek (*vv.* 18—20) has been introduced from a distinct source of tradition.

lest thou shouldest say, &c.] Abram emphasizes the fact, (1) that he did not make war in order to make himself richer or stronger: (2) that he and his household are not going to be beholden to the king of Sodom and the people of the Plain. What he had done, was not for gain, but for the safety of his relative Lot. Contrast, however, Abraham's acceptance of gifts, in xii. 16, xx. 14—16, under different cumstances.

24. *save only that*] Better, as R.V. marg., "let there be *nothing for me; only that*, &c." The expression here used occurs again in xli. 16. It might be expressed in colloquial language: "nothing at all, please, so far as I am concerned." Abram goes on to specify the two necessary exceptions, (1) a claim for the rations of his 318 followers: (2) a claim that an equitable share in the spoil should be assigned to his three confederates, mentioned in *v.* 13, who, we here learn for the first time, had joined in the dangers of the enterprise. According to the rights of war, all the booty belonged to Abram: and he magnanimously renounces his claim.

SPECIAL NOTE ON CHAPTER XIV.

The precise amount of historical value to be assigned to the contents of this chapter has in recent years been much disputed. Archaeology, as Skinner says (p. 276), has proved "that the general setting of the story is consistent with the political situation in the East as disclosed by the monuments; and that it contains data which cannot possibly be the fabrications of an unhistorical age."

I. *Possible Historical Situation.* The following is a brief summary of the historical facts which are possibly involved in the account of the Eastern kings mentioned in this chapter: "Under the early kings of the first dynasty of Babylon, the Elamites had invaded Southern Babylonia, and possibly the invasion was the immediate cause of Terah's migration northwards. At the time of Khammurabi, Kudur-Mabug was the governor of Emutbal, while his son, Rîm-Sin, ruled over Larsa and Ur. Chedorlaomer, whether identical (?) with Kudur-Mabug, or his over-lord, might thus not unnaturally have obliged Amraphel (Khammurabi) to accompany him to battle (Gen. xiv. 1—2). During the latter part of his reign, however, Khammurabi threw off the Elamite yoke, and also defeated Rîm-Sin (who succeeded his brother Arad-Sin as ruler over Larsa) and established his supremacy over Babylonia as well as over the land of Amurru (i.e. Canaan)[1]."

II. *Possible Date.* The date assigned by Ungnad (Gressmann's *Texte u. Bilder* (1909), i. 103) to the reign of Khammurabi is 2130—2088. Driver (in his *Addenda*, p. xxxix. n. 3) mentions that Khammurabi "lived, according to Nabuna'id (559—539 B.C.), 700 years before Burnaburiash (1399—1365 B.C.), i.e. c. 2100 B.C."

No trace has yet been found in the inscriptions of this particular expedition in which the Elamite king Chedorlaomer, attended by his vassal kings of Babylonia, Larsa, and Goiim, invaded the country E. of the Jordan, in order to punish a rebellion. It may be prudent, until further evidence is forthcoming, to suspend our judgement upon the identification of the names of the four kings of the East. The distinguished Assyriologist, Johns, after an investigation of the whole subject, raised a warning voice ten years ago. "The cuneiform originals suggested for the names in Gen. xiv. are therefore only ingenious conjectures. They may all be right, but as yet not one is proved" (*Expositor*, Oct. 1903, p. 286).

III. *Literary Character.* The chapter differs in style from the three main literary sources of Genesis, J, E, and P. The special use of the words rendered "goods" (*vv.* 11, 12, 16, 21), "persons" (*v.* 21), "born in his house" (*v.* 14, cf. xvii. 12 P), which are characteristic of P, is insufficient for any general inference.

The mention of Lot in *v.* 12 as "Abram's brother's son" may possibly be a gloss. But the unique description of Abram in *v.* 13

---
[1] Handcock, *Latest Light on Bible Lands*, p. 59. S.P.C.K., 1913.

as "the Hebrew," as if his name were here freshly introduced, is certainly surprising. It cannot, however, be claimed that the chapter is a mere isolated fragment. It presupposes the residence of Lot in the region of Sodom and Gomorrah (xiii. 10—11 J). It assumes the residence of Abram by "the oaks (or, terebinths) of Mamre" (xiii. 18 J; cf. xiv. 13), although it identifies Mamre and Eshcol, with the names of persons and not of places.

The unskilfulness of the literary style is in marked contrast to that which is prevalent throughout the rest of the book. The following examples are noteworthy in this short passage. (1) The grammatical structure of *vv.* 1 and 2 is strangely cumbrous: "And it came to pass in the days of [four kings], that they made war." (2) Chedorlaomer, king of Elam, who, as appears from *vv.* 9 and 17, was the over-lord and leader of the expedition, is mentioned third in the list of the four kings in *v.* 1. (3) In *v.* 3 it is uncertain which kings are spoken of, and the contents of the verse anticipate *v.* 8. (4) It is implied in *v.* 10 that the king of Sodom perished; in *v.* 17 the king of Sodom meets Abram on his return from his victory. (5) The incident of Melchizedek (*vv.* 18—20) interrupts the account of the meeting of the king of Sodom with Abram (*vv.* 17, 21). (6) In *v.* 20 "he gave him a tenth of all," if, as has generally been supposed, Abram is the giver and Melchizedek the recipient, there is an abrupt change of subject. But the grammatical uncertainty has led some to suppose that Melchizedek paid tithes to Abram!

IV. *Geographical Notes.* In the geographical allusions, archaic names are for the most part employed.

(*a*) *v.* 2, "Bela (the same is Zoar)." It is implied that the city whose name was altered to Zoar (xix.) had previously been called Bela.

(*b*) *v.* 3, "the vale of Siddim (the same is the Salt Sea)." This name for the Dead Sea is only found in this passage. It assumes that four cities out of the five (i.e. Sodom, Gomorrah, Admah, and Zeboiim) were overwhelmed at the time of the catastrophe described in chap. xix.

(*c*) *vv.* 4, 5, "the Rephaim...the Zuzim...the Emim...the Horites" are mentioned in Deut. ii. 10—12, 20, 21 as the names of the aborigines subsequently dispossessed by Moab, Ammon, and Edom. The Rephaim, or sons of Rapha, were a legendary race of "giants."

(*d*) *v.* 7, "En-mishpat (the same is Kadesh)." Kadesh was the scene of the Israelite encampment in the wilderness; where Moses obtained water for the people by striking the rock (Num. xx. 1—13). If the name En-mishpat (a Well of Judgement) was an older title, it implied the existence of water there before the name of "The Waters of Meribah" had been given to the spring.

(*e*) *v.* 7, "the Amalekites and the Amorites." The mention of the Amorites along with the Amalekites who were a wandering race in the south of Canaan, is inexact. "Amorite" is sometimes used in E for "Canaanite." The "Amurru" of the Tel-el-Amarna tablets were in N. Palestine.

(*f*) *v.* 14, "as far as Dan." The writer, instead of using the archaic name Laish or Leshem, employs the name which could only have come into use after the capture of the town by the Danites, recorded in Judg. xviii. 29.

(*g*) *v.* 17, "the vale of Shaveh (the same is the King's Vale)." "Shaveh" is here used as a proper name; but, as in *v.* 5, it is usually a word meaning "a plain." The King's Vale, if we may judge from 2 Sam. xviii. 18, was in the vicinity of Jerusalem.

(*h*) *v.* 18, "king of Salem." See note. In view of the archaic names employed in the context, it is most natural to assume that "Jerusalem" is intended; and that the writer deliberately avoided the familiar name of the city. On the other hand, "The Samaritans identified the city of Salem with their sanctuary on Mount Gerizim (see LXX, Gen. xxxiii. 18; comp. Eusebius, *Praeparatio Evangelica* ix. 17)[1]."

V. *Origin of Tradition obscure.* Whatever its source may have been, the story stands by itself. It represents one of many legends which were current respecting the patriarch. Whether the framework in which it now stands be derived from a very early document or from some later collection of traditions (*Midrash*), it is impossible to decide.

That Abram should suddenly figure in events of the greater world's history, that he should appear as a warrior and inflict defeat upon the armies of four Eastern kings, produces an impression widely different from that which is forthcoming from the rest of the patriarchal narrative. But, making allowance for the tendency of traditions to magnify the deeds of the national hero, we need not pass any hasty verdict against the general trustworthiness of the story.

It is true that, according to the Hebrew tradition, the five kings of Sodom, Gomorrah, Admah, Zeboiim, and Bela, must have been petty princes of towns lying quite close together in a small inconsiderable district of S.E. Canaan; and that an expedition against them by their over-lord, the king of Elam, and his vassals would, on the face of it, have been most improbable. But we must remember that, if we might assume a wide-spread rebellion, or refusal to pay tribute, on the part of the Western Provinces belonging to the Elamite Empire, the punitive expedition, according to the Hebrew local legends, would have been reputed to be more especially directed against the Canaanite rebellious kings. As to the improbability of the route, or of the strategy, it is unreasonable to expect minute accuracy from a narrative reproducing archaic conditions, in reference to an almost prehistoric event. Proper names, when unfamiliar, are liable to undergo assimilation to more familiar ones. The heroic deeds of the hero become exaggerated: the greatness of his victories is enhanced by lapse of time.

If we may judge from geological evidence, there is no probability in the supposition that in the time of Abram the Dead Sea submerged a fertile district and overwhelmed populous cities. Hence it is not unlikely that the tradition of the Five Cities "in the vale of Siddim" may have received an erroneous identification as to their site and names.

[1] Kohler, art. "Melchizedek," *Jewish Encyclopaedia*.

SPECIAL NOTE ON MELCHIZEDEK

I. *Its significance.* The episode of Melchizedek (xiv. 18—20) is one of the most interesting in the Book of Genesis. Its extreme brevity heightens the sense of mystery in which it is involved. It may be taken for granted that the incident is introduced on account of its profound religious significance. It describes the meeting between the Priest-King of "the Most High God" of the Human Race and the Father of the Chosen People, the Servant of Jehovah, the God of the new Revelation. The moment chosen for this meeting is instructive. Abram, the Hebrew stranger, is returning from victory over the foes of the land: Melchizedek, the Canaanite Priest-King, has had no part in the campaign. Abram represents the new spiritual force that has entered the world's history: Melchizedek represents the ideal of the permanent communion of mankind with God. The new family and the new nation, through whom that communion is ultimately to be perfected, render their homage to the representative of the Universal and the Omnipotent.

To the Israelite reader Jerusalem was the centre of pure religion and spiritual aspirations. Abram, impersonating the people of which he was to be the founder, receives from Melchizedek, the Priest-King of Jerusalem (Salem), not riches, nor offers of reward and possessions, but firstly bread and wine, sustenance and refreshment, and secondly his blessing, in the name of the Most High God, upon the servant of Jehovah. Abram, in his turn, renders tithe to Melchizedek, typifying thereby the obligation of every true son of Abram to recognize the full claims of the spiritual life upon his loyal service.

II. *Details for study.* 1. The Name. Though originally the name may have meant "Zedek is king," it suggested to Israelite readers or hearers "the king of righteousness," cf. Heb. vii. 2, or "righteous king," cf. Joseph. *B. J.* vi. 10, Μελχ. ὁ τῇ πατρίᾳ γλώσσῃ κληθεὶς βασιλεὺς δίκαιος. For the Messianic significance of which, cf. Ps. xlv. 4 ff.; Jer. xxiii. 6, xxxiii. 15, 16; Dan. ix. 24; Mal. iv. 2.

2. His Royal Office. He is King of Salem; and, while this title denoted to the Israelite the personal character of "a king of peace" (cf. Heb. vii. 2), it can scarcely be doubted that in the identification of Salem with Jerusalem (cf. Ps. lxxvi. 2; Joseph. *Ant.* I. 180) lies the peculiar typical significance of the event. The name of the city in the Tel-el-Amarna tablets (circ. 1400) is *Urusalim*: the king of Jerusalem in Jos. x. 1 is Adoni-zedek.

3. His Priestly Office. He is Priest as well as king. He is Priest of the Most High God, the Creator of Heaven and Earth, who is identified, according to the text of *v.* 22, by Abram with Jehovah. There is no suggestion of anything evil, impure, or polluting, in the worship of which Melchizedek, a native Canaanite, is a priest. Abram treats him as the official representative of the true God. It was not until the age of the Maccabees that the High Priest was also king.

4. **His Blessing.** As the representative of the true God, Melchizedek invokes upon Abram a message of Divine blessing. He blesses God; the victory of Abram over his foes is a ground for grateful praise. He presents the patriarch with bread and wine as the pledge of good-will and as an expression of honour and gratitude.

5. He receives tithe from Abram, cf. Heb. vii. 7—10. The receiver is greater than the giver of tithe. The impersonator of the ideal worship at Jerusalem receives tithe from the father and founder of the Israelite people.

6. Melchizedek disappears from the page of history as suddenly as he appears. Nothing is recorded of his family or lineage, of his life or actions. He "stands unique and isolated both in his person and in his history...his life has no recorded beginning or close" (Westcott, *Ep. Hebrews*, p. 172). It is not the man Melchizedek, but the Scripture portrait of Melchizedek in Gen. xiv., which causes the writer of the Epistle to the Hebrews to designate him as "without father, without mother, without genealogy, having neither beginning of days, nor end of life."

7. The Messianic passage in Ps. cx. 4 (quoted in Heb. v. 6, vii. 17, 21), "Thou art a priest after the order (or, manner) of Melchizedek," seems to mean that the Messiah is not a priest of the tribe of Levi, or of the family of Aaron, but, like the Priest-King of Jerusalem in the story of Abram, is, according to a more primitive conception of priesthood, the king of a kingdom of priests (cf. Ex. xix. 6).

8. Melchizedek is not mentioned in the Apocryphal Books. There is a *lacuna* in the Book of Jubilees at this passage (xiii. 25). Abram has evidently made his offering of tithe; and the next words are "...for Abram, and for his seed, a tenth of the first-fruits to the Lord, and the Lord ordained it as an ordinance for ever that they should give it to the priests who served before Him, that they should possess it for ever. And to this law there is no limit of days; for He hath ordained it for the generations for ever that they should give to the Lord the tenth of everything, of the seed and of the wine and of the oil and of the cattle and of the sheep. And He gave it unto His priests to eat and to drink with joy before Him" (Charles' *Apocrypha and Pseudepigrapha*, vol. II. p. 33).

9. The writer of the Epistle to the Hebrews regards Melchizedek as the type of Christ; as (*a*) King of Righteousness; (*b*) King of Peace; (*c*) Priest, not of the line of Levi or Aaron; (*d*) greater than Abraham, receiving tithes from him; (*e*) eternal. See chap. vii. with Westcott's notes.

10. Philo allegorizes the person of Melchizedek, who, he considers, represents the priesthood of "right reason," offering to the soul the sustenance of gladness and joy in the thoughts of absolute truth (*Leg. Allegor.* iii. § 25).

11. Clement of Alexandria (*Strom.* iv. 25) regards the offerings of bread and wine as typical of the Eucharist, adding, "And Melchizedek is interpreted 'righteous King'; and the name is a synonym for righteousness and peace": cf. *Strom.* ii. 5, "He (the Saviour) is

Melchizedek, 'the king of peace,' the most fit of all to head the race of men."

12. Jerome (Ep. lxxiii. *ad Evangelum*), summarizing opinions about Melchizedek, mentions that Origen and Didymus held him to have been an Angel; many others thought he was a Canaanite prince, exercising priestly offices, like "Abel, Enoch, Noah, Job"; the Jews very commonly identified him with Shem. Again, it appears to have been held by some writers, that Melchizedek was a manifestation of the Son; by others, that he was an appearance of the Holy Spirit (cf. *Quaest. ex V. et N. Test. Augustini Opera*, tom. iii. App. § cix.: ed. Migne, *P. L.* 35, p. 2329).

13. Westcott (*Ep. to the Hebrews*, p. 203) gives an account of the interesting legend respecting Melchizedek preserved in "the Book of Adam." "To him (Melchizedek) and Shem...the charge was given to bear the body of Adam to Calvary, and to place it there where in after time the Incarnate Word should suffer, so that the blood of the Saviour might fall on the skull of the Protoplast. In the fulfilment of this mission Melchizedek built an altar of twelve stones, typical of the twelve apostles, by the spot where Adam was laid, and offered upon it, by the direction of an angel, bread and wine 'as a symbol of the sacrifice which Christ should make' in due time. When the mission was accomplished, Shem returned to his old home, but Melchizedek, divinely appointed to this priesthood, continued to serve God with prayer and fasting at the holy place, arrayed in a robe of fire. So afterwards when Abraham came to the neighbourhood he communicated to him also 'the holy Mysteries,' the symbolical Eucharist."

14. That the episode of Melchizedek has been introduced from a distinct source of tradition is very probable. (*a*) It interrupts the narrative in *v.* 17, which is continued in *v.* 21. (*b*) Its contents are not in harmony with the context. In *v.* 22, Abram refuses to take anything from the spoil: in *v.* 20, Abram is said to give Melchizedek "a tenth of all." If "a tenth of all" refers to the spoil, it contradicts *v.* 22: if it refers to "all" his own property, then it assumes for Abram quite different surroundings from those of the story in chap. xiv. No late tradition of Abram is likely to have represented him as offering a tithe "of all" to a Canaanite king. But the short passage may illustrate a large class of traditions, religious and symbolical in character, which in early days had collected round the name of the patriarch. Ps. cx. 4 is evidently based upon the present passage.

CH. XV. THE COVENANT WITH ABRAM. (J, E.)

This chapter contains at least two slightly different narratives, which dealing with the same subject have been blended together. Thus *vv.* 1 and 5 speak of Abram in sleep, at night time, when the stars are visible: in *vv.* 12 and 17 we read of the sun going down, and afterwards, when the sun had set, of its becoming dark. In *v.* 6, Abram's faith is singled out for especial commendation. In *v.* 8, Abram, in

After these things the word of the LORD came unto 15 E Abram in a vision, saying, Fear not, Abram: I am thy shield, ¹*and* thy exceeding great reward. And Abram said, 2 O Lord ²GOD, what wilt thou give me, seeing I ³go

¹ Or, *thy reward shall be exceeding great* other places where GOD is put in capitals.
² Heb. *Jehovah*, as in
³ Or, *go hence*

distress and doubt, asks for a sign. In *vv.* 13—16, is recorded an explicit promise of the occupation of the land of the Amorite. In *vv.* 17, 18, the covenant is made, with a brief sentence containing a promise of the land. The probability is that we have here a combination of the two threads of prophetic narrative, which have been distinguished by scholars as (E) Elohist, or Ephraimite, and (J) Jehovist, or Judean. See Introduction.

1—6. THE PROMISE OF AN HEIR.

1. *After these things*] A vague note of time. Cf. xxii. 1, 20; xl. 1; xlviii. 1.

the word of the LORD] i.e. the word of Jehovah, as in *v.* 4. This is a technical expression in the O.T. for a Divine revelation to a prophet. It occurs nowhere else in the Pentateuch. It suggests the prophetic character of Abram, and should be compared with xx. 7 (E), where Abram is spoken of as a prophet.

in a vision] Evidently, as is shewn by *v.* 5, the vision occurs in a dream, or in the condition described in Num. xxiv. 3, 4; cf. Job iv. 13, "in thoughts from the visions of the night, when deep sleep falleth on men."

Fear not] The situation requiring this particular encouragement is not described. Abram, alone, childless, surrounded with foreigners, is not a coward, but is tempted, at times of depression, to fear that there is to be no fulfilment of the promise.

thy shield] A poetical simile of frequent occurrence, e.g. Deut. xxxiii. 29; Ps. iii. 3; Prov. ii. 7, "He is a shield to them that walk in integrity"; xxx. 5, "He is a shield unto them that trust in him."

and thy exceeding great reward] So the Lat. *et merces tua magna nimis*. But R.V. marg. *thy reward shall be exceeding great* is preferable. So the LXX. That for which Abram shall be rewarded is his trust.

2. *Lord GOD*] GOD = Heb. *Jehovah*, as in other places where it is put in capitals. "Adonai Jehovah": this combination of sacred names occurs only here, *v.* 8, and Deut. iii. 24, ix. 26, in the Pentateuch. It is, however, not uncommon in the prophetical writings; and is especially frequent in Ezekiel. The Hebrew student will notice that the sacred name JHVH receives here the vowel points

186   GENESIS XV. 2—5

E   childless, and he that shall be possessor of my house is
J 3 ¹Dammesek Eliezer? | And Abram said, Behold, to me
    thou hast given no seed: and, lo, one born in my house
  4 is mine heir. And, behold, the word of the LORD came
    unto him, saying, This man shall not be thine heir; but he
    that shall come forth out of thine own bowels shall be thine
E 5 heir. | And he brought him forth abroad, and said, Look

¹ The Chaldee and Syriac have, *Eliezer the Damascene.*

"*e*" "*o*" "*i*" of *Elohim*, because the word "Adonai," whose pronunciation it generally receives, immediately precedes it. Where the full word "Adonai" precedes JHVH, the Jewish scribes, in order to prevent profane repetition of the word "Adonai," punctuate and pronounce JHVH as if it were "Elohim"; hence they would read here *Adonai Elohim*, not *Adonai Adonai.*

seeing I go childless] R.V. marg. *go hence.* LXX ἀπολύομαι, Lat. *ego vadam.* "I go" is generally understood to mean here, "I depart this life." Cf. "Lord, now lettest thou thy servant depart," Luke ii. 29 (νῦν ἀπολύεις τὸν δοῦλόν σου, δέσποτα). But it might mean, "I take my ordinary path in life, childless."

The misfortune of having no children was acutely felt by the Israelite: see Num. xxvii. 4, "Why should the name of our father be taken away from among his family, because he had no son?"

possessor of my house] i.e. my heir.

The conclusion of this verse, in the original, gives no sense. The R.V. probably furnishes the general meaning. The confusion is apparent in LXX, ὁ δὲ υἱὸς Μάσεκ τῆς οἰκογενοῦς μου, οὗτος Δαμασκὸς Ἐλιέζερ = "And the son of Masek, my slave born in the house, this is Damascus Eliezer."

Dammesek Eliezer] R.V. marg., Targum of Onkelos, and Syriac, have *Eliezer the Damascene.* The text is corrupt. Literally the sentence runs: "and the son of the possession of my house is Damascus Eliezer." *Dammesek* is the usual Hebrew word for "Damascus." Attempts to restore the text have not been successful.

Ball conjectures, "And he who will possess my house is a Damascene, Eliezer." Eliezer is probably the same as the faithful servant of Abram mentioned in xxiv. 2, where the name is not given. The possible reference to Damascus in this verse gave rise to the traditions connecting Abram with the conquest of Damascus; see Josephus (*Ant.* I. 7, 2), quoting Nicolaus of Damascus, who wrote in the days of Herod the Great; cf. note on xii. 5.

3. *one born in my house*] The childless master of the house is here represented as likely to be succeeded by a member of his household. Lot is ignored. For the favourable position of a trusted slave in an Israelite household, cf. xxiv.; 1 Sam. ix. 3—8, 22; 1 Chron. ii. 34 ff.; Prov. xvii. 2.

now toward heaven, and tell the stars, if thou be able to   E
tell them: and he said unto him, So shall thy seed be. |
And he believed in the LORD; and he counted it to him 6 J
for righteousness.   And he said unto him, I am the LORD 7

5. *tell the stars*] i.e. count. A proverbial expression for the infinite and innumerable, as in xxii. 17, xxvi. 4.

The word "tell" is Old English for "count," as in Ps. xxii. 17, "I may tell all my bones"; Ps. xlviii. 12, "tell the towers thereof"; Jer. xxxiii. 13, "and in the cities of Judah shall the flocks again pass under the hands of him that telleth them." Cf. "And every shepherd tells his tale Under the hawthorn in the dale" (Milton, *L'Allegro*, 67, 68).

6. *he believed in the LORD*] Abram believed (1) in God's protection (*v.* 1), (2) in the fulfilment of the promise of a son (*v.* 4), and (3) of innumerable descendants (*v.* 5). It is this trust to which St Paul refers (Rom. iv. 18), "who in hope believed against hope, to the end that he might become a father of many nations, according to that which had been spoken, So shall thy seed be."

"Believed in," i.e. "believed," "trusted," as with the same Hebrew construction, Ex. xiv. 31, Jonah iii. 5.

In the Ep. to the Hebrews (xi. 8, 17) Abram's faith is not illustrated from this passage, but from his leaving his country (chap. xii.) and from his sacrifice of his son (xxii.).

and he counted it to him for righteousness] A short pregnant sentence of abstract religious thought. The word "righteousness" ($ṣ^ed\hat{a}q\hat{a}h$) occurs here for the first time in Scripture. It denotes the qualities of the man who is "righteous," or "right with God" (see note on $ṣadd\hat{i}q$, vii. 1). To the Israelite, "righteousness" implied the perfect obedience of the law. The writer records that, at a time when there was no law, Jehovah reckoned the faith of Abram, shewn in simple trust and obedience, as equivalent to the subsequent technical fulfilment of legal righteousness. The trustful surrender to the loving will of God is represented, in this typical instance of the father of the Israelite people, as, in Divine estimation, the foundation of true religion.

For the phrase, cf. the reference to Phinehas, Ps. cvi. 31, "and that was counted unto him for righteousness."

For the argument based by St Paul on this verse in connexion with the doctrine of the justification by faith, see Rom. iv. 1—25; Gal. iii. 6: cf. Jas. ii. 23.

7—19. THE RATIFICATION OF THE PROMISE BY A SOLEMN COVENANT.

The occasion of the covenant is distinct from that described in *vv.* 1—6; but the connexion of thought is obvious. It is the man of faith who has the privilege of vision and is admitted into direct covenant relation with his God.

GENESIS XV. 7—11

J that brought thee out of Ur of the Chaldees, to give thee
8 this land to inherit it. And he said, O Lord GOD, whereby
9 shall I know that I shall inherit it? And he said unto him,
Take me an heifer of three years old, and a she-goat of
three years old, and a ram of three years old, and a turtle
10 dove, and a young pigeon. And he took him all these, and
divided them in the midst, and laid each half over against
11 the other: but the birds divided he not. And the birds of
prey came down upon the carcases, and Abram drove them

7. *out of Ur of the Chaldees*] Possibly a later gloss: see note on xi. 31, xii. 1. Cf. Neh. ix. 7, 8.

8. *whereby shall I know*] Abram requests a sign to assure him of the fulfilment of the promise: cf. the action of Gideon, Judg. vi. 17, and of Hezekiah, 2 Kings xx. 8. On "Lord GOD," see note on *v.* 2.

9. *Take me an heifer*, &c.] The sign to Abram is the sign of the covenant, of which the ceremonial is here described. This ceremonial is evidently of great antiquity. The writer, perhaps, intends to refer the origin of the institution to the time of Abram and to this occasion. The ceremony is as follows: (1) Animals permitted for sacrifice are selected. (2) They are killed, and their carcases divided. (3) The divided portions are placed in two rows over against each other. (4) The contracting parties pass between the rows, invoking, as they do so, an imprecation upon any violator of the covenant, that he should in like manner be cut asunder.

It is this ceremonial which causes the making of a covenant to be expressed by words meaning "to cut," e.g. Heb. *karath b'rîth*, Lat. *foedus icere*, Gr. ὅρκια τέμνειν.

The details of the ceremony probably differed slightly from age to age. The origin of some old customs is lost in obscurity. Why, for instance, are the animals mentioned to be three years old? is it because they are to be full grown? (Cf. 1 Sam. i. 24, R.V. marg.) Why are the birds not to be divided like the beasts? These are questions of a technical ritual character to which at present we can give no answer.

The most interesting Scriptural illustration of covenant ceremonial is afforded by Jer. xxxiv. 18, "the covenant which they made before me, when they cut the calf in twain and passed between the parts thereof."

11. *And the birds of prey*, &c.] The birds of prey, regarded as unclean, swooping down threatened to carry off the pieces of flesh. This would have interrupted the ceremony with an evil omen, polluted the sacrifice, and impaired the covenant. Abram drives away the birds of ill omen. In the context, these birds evidently symbolized the Egyptians, who threatened, by enslaving Israel in Egypt, to frustrate the fulfilment of the Divine promise to the seed of Abram. The chasing away of the birds typified the surmounting of all obstacles.

away. And when the sun was going down, a deep sleep 12 J
fell upon Abram ; and, lo, an horror of great darkness fell
upon him. And he said unto Abram, Know of a surety 13
that thy seed shall be a stranger in a land that is not theirs,
and shall serve them; and they shall afflict them four hundred years; and also that nation, whom they shall serve, 14
will I judge: and afterward shall they come out with great
substance. But thou shalt go to thy fathers in peace; thou 15
shalt be buried in a good old age. And in the fourth 16

The LXX συνεκάθισεν αὐτοῖς = "he sat with them" for "he drove
them away" (reading *vay-yêsheb ittâm* for *vay-yassêb ôthâm*) is a
strange example of the mistakes arising from Hebrew writing without
vowel points.

12. *a deep sleep*] See note on the same word in ii. 21. LXX
ἔκστασις.

an horror of great darkness fell] Lit. "an horror, even great darkness was falling." A vivid description of the sensation of terror, preliminary to the revelation he was to receive.

13. *a stranger*] The word used (*gêr*) (LXX πάροικος) means more
than a "sojourner" (cf. xxiii. 4, Ex. ii. 22).

A stranger (*gêr*) is properly a guest residing in another country, whose
rights are in a sense protected. He may be merely a temporary sojourner
(*tôshâb*). But as a "stranger" (*gêr*) he has a recognized *status* in the
community. As a "sojourner" (*tôshâb*), he has none; he is a mere
social "bird of passage." The difference is that between a "resident
foreigner" and "a foreign visitor."

and shall serve them; and they shall afflict them] The personal
pronouns in English are ambiguous. There is a change of subject.
Israel shall be slaves to the people of a land that is not theirs, i.e. to
the Egyptians; and the Egyptians shall afflict them. The LXX δουλώ-
σουσιν, "they, i.e. the Egyptians, shall make bondmen of them, i.e. the
Israelites," gives a different turn to the first clause, and avoids the
interchange of subject and object: cf. the quotation in Acts vii. 6.

four hundred years] See note on *v*. 16. The figure agrees in round
numbers with the number of 430 years assigned, in Ex. xii. 40, to
the sojourning of Israel in Egypt. Cf. Acts vii. 6; Gal. iii. 17.

14. *will I judge*] Referring to the plagues of Egypt.

with great substance] See Ex. xii. 35, 36; Ps. cv. 37.

15. *go to thy fathers*] i.e. depart in death to join thy forefathers in
the place of departed spirits, i.e. *Sheôl*. Cf. xlvii. 30, "when I sleep
with my fathers"; xlix. 33, "was gathered unto his people."

a good old age] See for the fulfilment of this promise, xxv. 7, 8. To
live to a good old age and to depart this life in peace, was, as is
shewn in the typical lives of the patriarchs, regarded as the reward
of true piety. Cf. Job v. 26, "Thou shalt come to thy grave in

J generation they shall come hither again: for the iniquity of
17 the Amorite is not yet full. And it came to pass, that, when the sun went down, and it was dark, behold a smoking furnace, and a flaming torch that passed between
18 these pieces. In that day the LORD made a covenant with Abram, saying, Unto thy seed have I given this land, from the river of Egypt unto the great river, the river Euphrates:

a full age, like as a shock of corn cometh in in its season"; Prov. ix. 11, x. 27.

16. *in the fourth generation*] This agrees with the genealogy in Ex. vi. 16—20, where the generations are: (1) Levi, (2) Kohath, (3) Amram, (4) Moses. If the fourth generation is to be harmonized with the 400 years in v. 13, a generation must have been computed as 100 years. Isaac was born in Abram's 100th year. But it may be doubted, whether the mention of "the fourth generation" comes from the same hand as "the 400 years" in v. 13.

for the iniquity of the Amorite] The idea is that the wickedness of the people of Canaan must reach a certain degree, before the Divine penalty can be inflicted. The postponement of the penalty, which indicates Divine forbearance, means also a terrible, but gradual, accumulation of guilt. For the iniquity of the Amorites, cf. xiii. 13, Lev. xviii. 24—30, Deut. ix. 5. On the Amorite, see x. 16.

17. *a smoking furnace*] The sign of the covenant is given in the appearance of a kiln, from which issued smoke and a blazing torch; and this passed through the two rows of the divided carcases. The figure described as a "smoking furnace" (*tannur*) was that of a clay-constructed kiln, or furnace, such as is used for baking purposes by the Fellaheen. It is the $κλίβανος$ = "oven," of Matt. vi. 30. For the fire and smoke as a symbol of the Theophany, see Ex. xiii. 21, xix. 18, xxiv. 17.

18. *the LORD made a covenant*] A covenant, or compact, as between man and man, is necessarily impossible between God and man. God in His mercy gives the promise; man in his weakness acknowledges his willingness to obey. For the other covenants in the Pentateuch cf. ix., xvii.; Ex. xxiv. The origin of *b'rîth* = "covenant," is uncertain. Some suggest *barah* = "eat," in the sense of a "solemn meal." See note on v. 9.

The fate of the victims was supposed to be invoked upon the head of the party who broke the covenant. Cf. Livy, I. 24, *tum illo die, Juppiter, populum Romanum sic ferito, ut ego hunc porcum hic hodie feriam, tantoque magis ferito quanto magis potes pollesque.* The idea of Robertson Smith that the two parties to the covenant, standing between the pieces, partook of the mystical life of the victim (*Relig. of Semites*, p. 480) remains doubtful.

from the river of Egypt] The *n'har Mizraim* is clearly the Nile.

the Kenite, and the Kenizzite, and the Kadmonite, and 19 J
the Hittite, and the Perizzite, and the Rephaim, and the 20
Amorite, and the Canaanite, and the Girgashite, and the 21
Jebusite.

The ideal boundaries of the future territory of Israel are here stated in hyperbolical fashion, as extending from the Nile to the Euphrates: so Jos. xiii. 3, 1 Chron. xiii. 5. The Eastern, i.e. the Pelusiac, arm of the Nile is meant.

"The River of Egypt" is to be distinguished from "the Brook of Egypt," *naḥal Mizraim*, Num. xxxiv. 5, Josh. xv. 4, 47, the *Rhinocolura*, the modern *Wady-el-Arish*, a watercourse on the extreme S.W. of Palestine, on the confines of Egyptian territory.

unto the great river, the river Euphrates] Cf. Deut. i. 7, xi. 24. It was probably only in the days of Solomon that this picture of Israelite greatness was ever approximately realized; see 1 Kings iv. 21, Ps. lxxx. 11.

19—21. The names of the ten peoples to be driven out by the Israelites. For other lists of these, cf. Ex. iii. 8, 17, xiii. 5, xxiii. 23, xxxiv. 11; Deut. vii. 1, xx. 17. Here only, are ten names given; usually only five or six are mentioned. The Kenite, the Kenizzite, the Kadmonite, the Perizzite, and the Rephaim, seem here to be added to make up the full list.

These verses and *v.* 18 are attributed by many scholars to a Deuteronomic editor.

19. *the Kenite*] Dwellers in the S. of Canaan, connected with the Amalekites and noted for their subsequent friendly relations with Israel. Cf. Num. xxiv. 20, 21; Judg. iv. 17; 1 Sam. xv. 6.

the Kenizzite] Also a people on the Edomite border of Canaan; cf. Kenaz, xxxvi. 11. Caleb, the head of the tribe of Judah, was a Kenizzite, Num. xxxii. 12, Josh. xiv. 6. Hence the Kenizzites were probably a south Palestinian clan absorbed into the tribe of Judah.

the Kadmonite] Probably dwellers on the eastern desert frontier of Canaan. Compare "the children of the east" (*b'nê ḳedem*) in xxix. 1.

20. *the Hittite*] See note on x. 15. Probably indicating the presence of Hittite settlements in Canaan—bands who had roamed southward from the great Hittite kingdom of the north.

the Perizzite, and the Rephaim] See notes on xiii. 7, xiv. 5.

21. *the Amorite, &c.*] See x. 15, 16.

CH. XVI. THE BIRTH OF ISHMAEL.

The narrative in this chapter contains Israelite traditions respecting the birth, name, and dwelling-place of Ishmael.

(*a*) It explains how the Israelites acknowledged the Ishmaelites to be an older branch of their own stock, dwelling on their southern borders.

P J 16 Now Sarai Abram's wife bare him no children: | and she
had an handmaid, an Egyptian, whose name was Hagar.
2 And Sarai said unto Abram, Behold now, the Lord hath
restrained me from bearing; go in, I pray thee, unto my
handmaid; it may be that I shall ¹obtain children by her.

¹ Heb. *be builded by her.*

(*b*) It illustrates how they regarded them as inferior in dignity of descent, and as degraded by an Egyptian connexion.

Verses 1ᵃ, 3, 15, 16 are from P, while *vv.* 9, 10, 11 have been attributed to an editorial insertion. The remainder is from J.

1—6. Hagar and her Flight into the Desert. (J, P.)

1. *handmaid*] or "maidservant," as in xii. 16. The wife generally had a female slave, who was her own property, and not under the husband's control: see xxix. 24, 29; xxx. 3—7, 9, 12.

an Egyptian] It is natural to connect Hagar's Egyptian origin with the sojourn in Egypt mentioned in chap. xii., or with the journeys in the Negeb (xii. 9, xiii. 1).

The theory that the "Egypt" (*Miṣraim*) of which Hagar was a native was the land of a N. Arabian tribe (*Muṣri*) has been suggested by Winckler on account of the mention of *Muṣri* in N. Arabia in the cuneiform inscriptions. His theory supposes that the *Muṣri* of N. Arabia was at an early time confounded by the Israelites with the more famous, but similarly sounding, *Miṣri*, "an inhabitant of Egypt." But, in view of the continual intercourse between Palestine and Egypt, as shewn by the Tel-el-Amarna tablets, the theory is improbable, and uncalled for. Egypt, at an early period, embraced the Sinaitic peninsula.

Hagar] The name "Hagar" is associated with that of wandering Arab tribes, called the Hagrites, 1 Chron. v. 10, 19, 20, xxvii. 31, with which should be compared the Hagarenes of Ps. lxxxiii. 6, "the tents of Edom, and the Ishmaelites; Moab, and the Hagarenes."

Whether the story of Hagar, in this chapter, in any way bears upon the meaning of her name, is more than we can say for certain. But, in Arabic, *hagara*="to flee," and the well-known word *hegira*, the epoch of Mohammed, is his "flight" from Mecca.

2. *it may be that I shall obtain children by her*] Heb. lit. *be builded by her*; the same expression occurs in xxx. 3; the idea is that of the building up of a house (cf. Ruth iv. 11, Deut. xxv. 9). The suggestion which Sarai here makes, may be illustrated from xxx. 3, 4, 9. Childlessness was, and still is, in the East, a great reproach (cf. 1 Sam. i. 2—20). It was the custom also in Babylonia, as is shewn by the Code of Hammurabi, that "if a man's wife was childless, he was allowed to take a concubine and bring her into his house, but he was not to place her upon an equal footing with the wife. Or, the wife

And Abram hearkened to the voice of Sarai. | And Sarai 3 JP
Abram's wife took Hagar the Egyptian, her handmaid, after
Abram had dwelt ten years in the land of Canaan, and gave
her to Abram her husband to be his wife. | And he went in 4 J
unto Hagar, and she conceived: and when she saw that she
had conceived, her mistress was despised in her eyes. And 5
Sarai said unto Abram, My wrong be upon thee: I gave
my handmaid into thy bosom; and when she saw that she
had conceived, I was despised in her eyes: the LORD judge
between me and thee. But Abram said unto Sarai, Behold, 6
thy maid is in thy hand; do to her that which is good in
thine eyes. And Sarai dealt hardly with her, and she fled

might give her husband a maidservant (*amtu*), and, if she brought up
children, he was forbidden to take in addition a concubine" (S. A. Cook,
The Laws of Moses and the Code of Hammurabi, p. 111).

by her] By the adoption of Hagar's children as her own.

3. *And Sarai Abram's wife*] This verse is P's duplicate version
of *vv.* 1, 2, adding the number of years that Abram had dwelt in
Canaan.

4. *was despised in her eyes*] Compare the story in 1 Sam. i., where
the two wives are both "free," and one is childless. Here the "free"
wife, the mistress (*gebéreth*), gives her own maidservant (*âmâh*) to her
husband; and is then jealous for her own dignity.

5. *My wrong*] i.e. may the wrong done to me be visited on thee!
Sarai's passionate and unjust complaint is the utterance of jealousy.
Abram is not to blame for the step which she herself had recommended
in accordance with the custom of the age. The possibility, that in these
cases the position of the mistress might be compromised by the insolence of the handmaid, formed the subject of special provision in the
Code of Hammurabi. "Branding was the punishment inflicted upon the
owner's handmaid who arrogantly set herself on an equality with her
mistress" (§ 146: see S. A. Cook, p. 160).

LXX ἀδικοῦμαι ἐκ σοῦ, Lat. *inique agis contra me*.

judge between me and thee] Cf. xxxi. 53; 1 Sam. xxiv. 12. The
latter passage adds "and the LORD avenge me of thee." The "judgement" of the LORD may be the source of punishment: see note on xv. 14.

6. *in thy hand*] Abram replies, with forbearance, that Hagar is
under Sarai's authority. Whether this is a formal transference of Hagar
back into the power of Sarai, after she had become, as a concubine, the
property of Abram, is not explained.

dealt hardly] The same word as that rendered "afflict" (xv. 13).
Here it evidently means "persecute," "ill-treat."

fled] The character of Hagar is depicted as high-spirited and
courageous, as well as independent. There is no evidence that her
conduct was insolent.

J 7 from her face. And the angel of the LORD found her by a fountain of water in the wilderness, by the fountain in the
8 way to Shur. And he said, Hagar, Sarai's handmaid, whence camest thou? and whither goest thou? And she said, I
9 flee from the face of my mistress Sarai. And the angel of the LORD said unto her, Return to thy mistress, and submit
10 thyself under her hands. And the angel of the LORD said unto her, I will greatly multiply thy seed, that it shall not
11 be numbered for multitude. And the angel of the LORD said unto her, Behold, thou art with child, and shalt bear a son; and thou shalt call his name [1]Ishmael, because the

[1] That is, *God heareth.*

7—14. HAGAR AND THE ANGEL AT THE WELL.

7. *the angel of the LORD*] The Angel, i.e. messenger, of Jehovah is the personification of Jehovah. Observe that in verse 10 He identifies Himself with Jehovah, expressing in the first person sing. what He will do (cf. xxi. 18, xxii. 15—18).

In all probability, in the development of religious thought, the Angel of Jehovah marks an intermediate stage between the simple anthropomorphisms of Gen. iii., xi. and xviii., and the later, more spiritual and abstract, conception of the Divine Being.

a fountain of water] i.e. a spring of water, which in the desert would mean an oasis towards which tracks would converge. See xxiv. 13.

in the way to Shur] Probably, on the main trade route leading to her own country of Egypt. "Shur," mentioned also in xx. 1 and xxv. 18, has not been identified. It seems to mean "a wall"; and very probably was the name given to some spot on the line of the Egyptian frontier fortifications on the north-east, not far from the present Suez Canal. Possibly = the modern *Tell abû-Sêpheh*, 20 miles S. of Port Said.

9. *And the angel of the LORD said*] Notice the triple repetition of these sayings of the Angel in *vv*. 9, 10, 11, containing in *v*. 9 the injunction to return and submit, in *v*. 10 the promise of a multitude of descendants, and in *vv*. 11 and 12 the name and character of her future son. Verses 9 and 10 both begin with the same words as *v*. 11, and probably are editorial additions from different versions of the story.

10. *I will greatly multiply*] The Angel of Jehovah expresses in the 1st person the promise of that which Jehovah will perform; as in xxi. 18, xxii. 15—18, xxxi. 13.

11. *thou shalt call his name Ishmael*] That is, *God heareth*. The name is to be given by the mother. Cf. note on iv. 1, 25. The name "Ishmael" may mean either "God hears," or "may God hear." See also xxi. 17. The reason for the name is explained by the words, "because the LORD hath heard (*shâma‘*) thy affliction."

GENESIS XVI. 11—13

LORD hath heard thy affliction. And he shall be *as* a wild- 12 J
ass among men; his hand *shall be* against every man, and
every man's hand against him; and he shall dwell ¹in the
presence of all his brethren. And she called the name of 13
the LORD that spake unto her, ²Thou art ³a God that seeth:
for she said, Have I even here looked after him that seeth

¹ Or, *over against* Or, *to the east of* ² Or, *Thou God seest me*
³ Heb. *El roi*, that is, *God of seeing.*

heard thy affliction] See note on *v.* 6. The expression means that
Jehovah has either heard of the persecution Hagar has received, or,
more probably, has heard the prayer uttered by her in her affliction
(*v.* 6). Cf. Ex. ii. 24, iv. 31.

12. **as *a wild-ass among men*]** Lit. "a wild-ass of a man." This
description of Ishmael vividly portrays the characteristics of his
descendants. The wild ass, for which see Job xxxix. 5—8, Hos.
viii. 9, is the typically untameable, strong, free, roaming, suspicious,
and untrustworthy animal, living wild in the desert, far from the haunts
of men.

in the presence of all his brethren] R.V. marg. *over against*. Cf.
xxv. 18. "Brethren": see notes on xiii. 8, xiv. 14. While "in the
presence," or "in the face of" all his brethren, might legitimately be
rendered "to the east of" the Israelites, the east was scarcely the
quarter in which the Ishmaelites were chiefly found. A better explanation gives to the words the meaning of a foe, dwelling close at hand and
"over against" his brethren, ever ready to attack and raid their territory.

13. *the LORD that spake unto her*] These words definitely identify
the Angel with a manifestation of the Almighty; see *v.* 7.

Thou art a God that seeth] LXX Σὺ ὁ Θεὸς ὁ ἐφιδών με, Lat. *Tu
Deus qui vidisti me*. Hagar designates the Divine Person who had
spoken to her, by the name *Êl*, with the epithet, or attribute, of
"Vision": see note on xiv. 18. She says, "Thou art *Êl roi*," i.e.
"a God of Seeing," or "of Vision." The familiar rendering, "Thou
God seest me," is, with our present text, incorrect.

Have I even here looked after him that seeth me] According to this
rendering, the emphasis is on the words "even here." The meaning
is, "have I, even here, in the wilderness, met God? and, though
I knew Him not, yet, after He had gone, I perceived that it was He."
The awkwardness of the phrase, "after him," is obvious. The difficulty of the passage was realized at a very early time: LXX καὶ γὰρ
ἐνώπιον εἶδον ὀφθέντα μοι, Lat. *profecto hic vidi posteriora videntis me*
(explaining the clause from Ex. xxxiii. 23).

On the assumption that the text is corrupt, Wellhausen conjectures
"have I seen [God, and remained alive] after [my] vision," reading
Elohim for *halôm*, and inserting *va-ehi*. This gives a good sense;

J 14 me? Wherefore the well was called ¹Beer-lahai-roi; behold,
P 15 it is between Kadesh and Bered. | And Hagar bare Abram
a son: and Abram called the name of his son, which Hagar
16 bare, Ishmael. And Abram was fourscore and six years
old, when Hagar bare Ishmael to Abram.
17 And when Abram was ninety years old and nine, the

¹ That is, *The well of the living one who seeth me*.

but is rendered doubtful by the alteration of the unusual word *halôm* (= "even hither").

Similarly, Ball conjectures "Have I even seen God, and survived?" (*S.B.O.T.*) It may be assumed that Hagar's utterance denoted joy and thankfulness for having seen Jehovah, and for having lived afterwards. Cf. xxxii. 30; Ex. iii. 6, xix. 21; Judg. xiii. 22; 1 Sam. vi. 19.

14. *Beer-lahai-roi*] The R.V. marg. *the well of the living one who seeth me* is an impossible translation of the text. Another rendering is, "Well of the Seeing alive," i.e. "Where one sees God and remains alive." The popular belief was, that he who saw God would die. See previous note.

Probably the name *Beer-lahai-roi* was explained by a popular etymology which connected its pronunciation with the sound of the Hebrew words *hai* = "living" and *roi* = "vision." A well, or spring, in a desert was generally deemed by the early nomad peoples to be frequented by a Divine presence.

between Kadesh and Bered] For Kadesh, see note on xiv. 7. Bered has not been identified. Hagar's well is commonly supposed to be the same as *Ain Muweileh*, a spot where there are springs, S. of Beersheba, and on the caravan road to Egypt.

15, 16. THE BIRTH OF ISHMAEL. (P.)

These verses are from P, and are inserted in place of J's account of the birth of Ishmael.

15. *Abram called...Ishmael*] See note on *v.* 11. The father here gives the name as usually in P: see notes on iv. 1, 17, 25, v. 3.

16. *fourscore and six years old*] An instance of P's careful computation of chronology. Compare the statements in *v.* 3 and xii. 4 with the years given here.

CH. XVII. THE INSTITUTION OF THE RITE OF CIRCUMCISION. (P.)

1— 8. The Covenant with Abram.
9—14. Circumcision the Token of the Covenant.
15—22. The Promise to Sarai.
23—27. Abraham circumcises his household.

The whole of this chapter is from P.

1. *ninety years old and nine*] There has been an interval of 13 years since the birth of Ishmael in xvi. 16.

LORD appeared to Abram, and said unto him, I am ¹God P
Almighty; walk before me, and be thou perfect. And I 2

¹ Heb. *El Shaddai*.

the LORD] "Jehovah," used here in P, probably, for the special purpose of connecting the covenant of Abram with Him whose full name was revealed to Moses, Ex. vi. 3. Or, as not infrequently must have happened, one sacred name has been substituted for another by editor or copyist.

Elsewhere in this chapter (*vv.* 3, 7, 8, 9, 18, 19, 22, 23) *Elohim* occurs, as usual in P's narrative.

I am God Almighty] Heb. *Êl Shaddai*. Notice the opening formula, "I am," used in this manifestation. Cf. xxxv. 11.

The name *Êl Shaddai* is that by which, according to Ex. vi. 3 (P), God "appeared" in the patriarchal age, and before the revelation to Moses of the name Jehovah (JHVH=Jahveh). This title *Êl Shaddai* occurs in xxviii. 3, xxxv. 11, xliii. 14, xlviii. 3 (cf. xlix. 25; Num. xxiv. 4, 16). *Shaddai* alone occurs frequently (31 times) in the Book of Job; in prose it is usually found with *Êl* = "God Almighty."

The derivation of the word Shaddai has hitherto baffled enquiry. (1) The old Rabbinic explanation, that it consisted of two combined words (*sh-*, and *dai*) meaning "one who is All-sufficient," is quite impossible; but it accounts for the rendering of Aquila and Symmachus ὁ ἱκανός. (2) It has been derived from a root (*shdd*) meaning "to destroy," which may be illustrated from Isai. xiii. 6, Joel i. 15. (3) Another suggestion connects it with *shêdim* = "demons"; see note on xiv. 3. (4) Others conjecture a derivation giving it the meaning of "the storm God." (5) LXX renders, in Pent., by ὁ θεός μου, Vulg. "omnipotens." The word is an ancient epithet of unknown origin, whose general meaning is that of irresistible power.

For *Êl* with *Shaddai*, see note on xiv. 18.

English readers will recollect the use of the name "Shaddai" in John Bunyan's *Holy War*.

The word appears in the compound proper names "Zurishaddai" (Num. i. 6, ii. 12), "Ammishaddai" (Num. ii. 25).

walk before me] For this word "walk," see v. 22, 24; vi. 9. Here it is the "walk," not "with," but "in the presence of." The idea is that of the progress in personal life and conduct in the continual realization of God's presence. In P there is no supposition of any code of law before the time of Moses. The rite of circumcision, whose observance is commanded in this chapter, the prohibition against eating blood given in chap. ix. 4, and the implied recognition of the Sabbath (ii. 1), are the only external observances of the patriarchal age recognized in P. Here the command, "walk before me," is simply that of living a good life in the sight of God. This is "to be well pleasing in his sight": hence LXX renders εὐαρέστει.

The substance of the command is expressed in xviii. 19, "keep the

P will make my covenant between me and thee, and will
3 multiply thee exceedingly. And Abram fell on his face:
4 and God talked with him, saying, As for me, behold, my
covenant is with thee, and thou shalt be the father of a
5 multitude of nations. Neither shall thy name any more be
called Abram, but thy name shall be Abraham; for the
6 father of a multitude of nations have I made thee. And I
will make thee exceeding fruitful, and I will make nations
7 of thee, and kings shall come out of thee. And I will

way of the Lord, to do justice and judgement"; Deut. x. 12, "to fear the Lord thy God, to walk in all his ways, and to love him, and to serve the Lord thy God"; Micah vi. 8, "to do justly and to love mercy, and to walk humbly with thy God."

be thou perfect] See note on vi. 9. Cf. Job i. 1, 8; Luke i. 6.

2. *And I will make my covenant*] See note on xv. 9, 18. The words of this verse imply no knowledge of the covenant described in chap. xv. The covenant has yet to be made. P's account of the covenant is different from that of J; and, the two traditions being distinct, there is no allusion here to the previous narrative.

fell on his face] The prostration of humility and reverence, as in *v.* 17. Cf. Num. xiv. 5.

4. *father of a multitude of nations*] "Multitude," *hamôn* = "tumult." LXX πολλῶν ἐθνῶν.

5. *Abram*] The shorter form is here used for the last time. Except in Genesis, it only occurs in 1 Chron. i. 27, Neh. ix. 7.

thy name shall be Abraham] The change from "Abram" to "Abraham" is associated with the covenant promise that the patriarch shall be "the father of a multitude of nations" (*'ab hamôn gôyyîm*). As in many other instances, we have here a resemblance through assonance, and not a real derivation of a proper name. There is no such word as *raham* meaning "a multitude." "Abraham" and "Abram" have, until recently, been regarded as forms of the same name, "Abiram," which meant "exalted father," or "the father is Ram," i.e. "the exalted one." But the longer name has been found in several Babylonian monuments belonging to the reign of Ammi-zaduga, who was tenth in the dynasty founded by Hammurabi. According to the distinguished Assyriologist, Ungnad, the Babylonian pronunciation was *Abaram*, and the meaning "He loves the father."

a multitude of nations] The promise of the covenant in P contemplates not only the nation of Israel (as J, xii. 2, xviii. 18, and E, xlvi. 3), but also the kindred nations of Edom and Ishmael.

6. *kings shall come out of thee*] Cf. *v.* 16 and xxxv. 11 (P). The promise contains a reference to the Israelite monarchy. This is recognized as overruled by God (cf. 1 Sam. xi., xii.) to be the

establish my covenant between me and thee and thy seed after thee throughout their generations for an everlasting covenant, to be a God unto thee and to thy seed after thee. And I will give unto thee, and to thy seed after thee, the 8 land of thy sojournings, all the land of Canaan, for an everlasting possession; and I will be their God. And God said 9 unto Abraham, And as for thee, thou shalt keep my covenant, thou, and thy seed after thee throughout their generations. This is my covenant, which ye shall keep, between 10 me and you and thy seed after thee; every male among you shall be circumcised. And ye shall be circumcised 11

means of the people's blessing and expansion. Cf. Num. xxiv. 14, 17—19.

With the "kings" of Israel, compare the "princes" of "Ishmael" (*v.* 20) and "the dukes of Edom" (xxxvi. 40).

7. *for an everlasting covenant*] Cf. 13, 19. LXX εἰς διαθήκην αἰώνιον. The relationship is to be one transcending the limits of time. The covenant is to be "established," cf. vi. 18, ix. 9. The idea is slightly different from that of the covenant being "made," xv. 18. There the phrase refers back to the solemnity of ancient binding institutions; here it points forward to the permanence of a new and enduring relationship. God undertakes to be the God of Abraham and of his descendants. He will take care of them as His own, and they on their side will obey and serve Him as His people. Cf. Ex. vi. 7; Deut. xxvi. 17.

8. *the land of thy sojournings*] This is explained to be "all the land of Canaan." The word "sojournings" denotes "residences of a stranger" (cf. xv. 13). The stranger (*gêr*) has no fixed possession in a land. The land where he has been a stranger is now promised to become his settled possession. The promise, therefore, reverses Abraham's present position. The land will be no longer one of "sojournings" (*megûrîm*), but a "possession" (*aḥuzzah*). Cf. xxviii. 4, xxxvi. 7, xxxvii. 1, xlvii. 9; Ex. vi. 4 (all in the P narrative). For "everlasting possession," see xlviii. 4 (P).

9—14. CIRCUMCISION THE TOKEN OF THE COVENANT.

9. *thou shalt keep*] "Keep" in the sense of "observe": the reverse is to "break" (*v.* 14) the covenant. Notice the sing. "thou," and the plur. "ye shall keep" in *v.* 10; cf. the interchange of plur. and sing. in *vv.* 11, 12, 13.

10. *shall be circumcised*] The rite of circumcision, which is here given as the symbol of the covenant with Abraham and his seed, was no new institution. In Abraham's time it was already a well-known

P in the flesh of your foreskin; and it shall be a token of
12 a covenant betwixt me and you. And he that is eight

practice. It is adopted as the sign of the covenant, and consecrated to be the abiding pledge and witness of the relationship between the God who revealed Himself to Abraham and the people of which Abraham was the founder.

Circumcision is found to have been practised among the peoples of Africa at a very early time. In Egypt records of the practice are said to go back to an age many centuries previous to the time of Abraham. From Egypt it is said to have been transmitted into Phoenicia and Syria (see Herodotus, II. 114). From the present account it is clear that the Israelites believed the institution to have had its origin in the patriarchal era. We learn from Jer. ix. 25, 26 that it was practised by Edomites, Ammonites, and Moabites, as well as by Egyptians and Israelites.

The custom is prevalent in very different parts of the world. For instance, it is found in S. Africa and in Madagascar.

It very possibly has some connexion with the cuttings and tattooings by which the savage avowed his relationship to the Deity of his tribe, and hoped to secure his favour by wearing his sign. Hence it took rank with the distinctive badges of a tribe or people.

Recent investigation has not tended to support the theory that circumcision has any connexion with primitive child sacrifice; nor, again, that it took its origin from hygienic motives. Apparently, it represents the dedication of the manhood of the people to God. In the history of Israel, it has survived as the symbol of the people belonging to Jehovah through His special election. Its significance in Israel is something quite distinct from that in other circumcised peoples. This corporeal sacrament remained to the Israelite, when every other tie of religion or race had been severed.

For its renewal (*a*) in the time of Moses, (*b*) in the time of Joshua, see Ex. iv. 25; Josh. v. 2. In both of these passages the use of a stone, or flint, instrument possibly represents the survival of the rite from an age of remotest antiquity, before the introduction of metal.

For circumcision as an honourable badge, the absence of which would be regarded as a reproach in Egypt, see Josh. v. 7—9. The alleged omission of the Philistines to practise this rite (Jud. xiv. 3; 1 Sam. xxxi. 4; 2 Sam. i. 20) may possibly be due to their foreign origin.

11. *a token*] i.e. an outward sign. Cf. the rainbow which was the token of the covenant of Noah, ix. 12, 13.

12. *he that is eight days old*] The performance of the rite at this early age is distinctive of the Israelite usage. Cf. xxi. 4; Lev. xii. 3; Luke i. 59, ii. 21; Phil. iii. 5. The operation at this exceedingly early age (see note on *v*. 25) is probably for the purpose (1) of including all males, (2) of coinciding with the first period of the mother's uncleanness, Lev. xii. 2, 3, (3) of inflicting the smallest degree of suffering.

days old shall be circumcised among you, every male throughout your generations, he that is born in the house, or bought with money of any stranger, which is not of thy seed. He that is born in thy house, and he that is bought 13 with thy money, must needs be circumcised: and my covenant shall be in your flesh for an everlasting covenant. And the uncircumcised male who is not circumcised in the 14 flesh of his foreskin, that soul shall be cut off from his people; he hath broken my covenant.

And God said unto Abraham, As for Sarai thy wife, thou 15 shalt not call her name Sarai, but ¹Sarah shall her name be. And I will bless her, and moreover I will give thee a son of 16 her: yea, I will bless her, and she shall be *a mother of nations*; kings of peoples shall be of her. Then Abraham 17

¹ That is, *Princess*.

every male] The important principle is here laid down that the rite is to be required of every male member of the household. All slaves are to be circumcised, both those "born in the house" (cf. xiv. 14), and those "bought with money" (cf. Ex. xii. 44). It was thus that the first principles of charity were interwoven with the foundation of the Chosen People. The privileges of the covenant relation are at once extended beyond the literal seed of Abraham.

14. *shall be cut off*] The penalty of being "cut off" is frequently mentioned in P. It does not appear certain, (1) whether the penalty is to be inflicted by God or by man; (2) whether, if it be the infliction of a judicial punishment by man, it denotes capital punishment, or expulsion from the ranks of the community. The formula has probably been transmitted from a very early period; and the lapse of time led to change in practice. Thus, in Ex. xxxi. 13, 14, the penalty of death is inflicted by the people: see Num. xv. 32—36. But, in Lev. xvii. 10, xx. 3, the sentence is pronounced by God, "I will cut him off."

from his people] Lit. "from his peoples," a phrase used by P, which seems to denote "father's kin," and evidently possessed a special technical meaning of clanship. See note on xxv. 8.

15—22. THE PROMISE TO SARAI.

15. *Sarah shall her name be*] That is, *Princess*. The name "Sarai" (LXX Σάρα) is altered to "Sarah" (LXX Σάρρα). The name "Sarah" is the feminine form of the Heb. *Sar*, "a prince." Other explanations which give the meaning "the contentious one," or "the merry one," are improbable. "Sarai" may possibly have been an older form of "Sarah." It cannot mean, as used to be asserted, "*my* princess."

16. *nations...kings of peoples*] See note on *v.* 6.

P fell upon his face, and laughed, and said in his heart, Shall a child be born unto him that is an hundred years old? and 18 shall Sarah, that is ninety years old, bear? And Abraham said unto God, Oh that Ishmael might live before thee! 19 And God said, Nay, but Sarah thy wife shall bear thee a son; and thou shalt call his name ¹Isaac: and I will establish my covenant with him for an everlasting covenant for 20 his seed after him. And as for Ishmael, I have heard thee: behold, I have blessed him, and will make him fruitful, and

¹ From the Heb. word meaning *to laugh*.

17. *fell upon his face*] See *v.* 3.
laughed] The incredulous laughter of Abraham here, according to P, should be compared with that of Sarah, in xviii. 12, according to J, as a play upon the name "Isaac" and its meaning of "laughter."

Along with the incredulity must be reckoned the joy of the assurance that the promise of a son should be fulfilled. The joy of that hope, and of its significance to the whole world, is the subject of the allusion in John viii. 56, "Your father Abraham rejoiced to see my day, and he saw it and was glad."

ninety years old] The age of Sarah, nine years younger (cf. *v.* 24) than Abraham.

18. *said unto God*] The previous verse contained what Abraham "said in his heart." Aloud he expresses his incredulity in a more reverent manner, shewing that his hope of descendants rested upon Ishmael.

might live before thee] i.e. that his life might be blessed by God's special protection.

19. *Sarah thy wife*] God's answer in this verse is made to the utterance of Abraham's heart (*v.* 17), and not of his lips (*v.* 18).

thou shalt call his name Isaac] R.V. marg. "From the Heb. word meaning *to laugh*." See xxi. 3. The name Isaac is here, and in xviii. and xxi., associated with "laughter." The word "he laughed," used in *v.* 17, has the same root letters (*ṣḥq*) as the name "Isaac." The name "laughter" will thus commemorate the involuntary doubt of Abraham (*v.* 17) to which St Paul refers (Ro. iv. 19), "without being weakened in faith he considered his own body now as good as dead (he being about a hundred years old) and the deadness of Sarah's womb."

Note that the father is commanded to give the name; see note on *v.* 3 (P).

20. *as for Ishmael, I have heard thee*] This verse contains the reply to Abraham's spoken words in *v.* 18. "I have heard thee" contains a reference to the meaning of the name "Ishmael"="God hears." See note on xvi. 11.

will multiply him exceedingly; twelve princes shall he P
beget, and I will make him a great nation. But my 21
covenant will I establish with Isaac, which Sarah shall bear
unto thee at this set time in the next year. And he left off 22
talking with him, and God went up from Abraham. And 23
Abraham took Ishmael his son, and all that were born in
his house, and all that were bought with his money, every
male among the men of Abraham's house, and circumcised
the flesh of their foreskin in the selfsame day, as God had
said unto him. And Abraham was ninety years old and 24
nine, when he was circumcised in the flesh of his foreskin.
And Ishmael his son was thirteen years old, when he was 25
circumcised in the flesh of his foreskin. In the selfsame 26
day was Abraham circumcised, and Ishmael his son. And 27
all the men of his house, those born in the house, and those
bought with money of the stranger, were circumcised with
him.

twelve princes] Recorded in xxv. 13—16. As in the family of Israel, so also in that of Ishmael, the number "twelve" symbolizes the distribution and organization of a people under responsible leaders, and represents ancient usage.

22. *God went up*] This expression, which occurs also in xxxv. 13 (P), means that God returned to His dwelling-place, which the Israelite believed to be above the Heavens.

23—27. ABRAHAM CIRCUMCISES HIS HOUSEHOLD.

23. *And Abraham took*, &c.] This verse repeats the directions contained in *vv.* 11—13.

in the selfsame day] As in *v.* 26: see note on vii. 13. The expression is characteristic of P. The performance of this rite upon all the males of Abraham's household, consisting of several hundred (cf. xiv. 14), in one day is hardly to be understood literally. The narrative is more concerned with the thought of the symbolism of a ritual precept, than with its literal practicability. The operation for full-grown males is a serious one, and not unattended with risk, cf. xxxiv.

25. *Ishmael...thirteen years old*] The mention of Ishmael and of his age, is of interest; for it implies (1) the fact that the Ishmaelite people practised circumcision; (2) the possible reminiscence of a variant custom by which it was performed at the age of thirteen years, instead of eight days, as in Israel, *v.* 12. The modern Arabian use is said to be much later in life than that of the Jews, and in some cases corresponds with the age of Ishmael. A boy at 13 was regarded as

J 18 And the LORD appeared unto him by the ¹oaks of Mamre,
2 as he sat in the tent door in the heat of the day; and he lift up his eyes and looked, and, lo, three men stood over against him: and when he saw them, he ran to meet them from the tent door, and bowed himself to the earth, and

¹ Or, *terebinths*

on the threshold of manhood. Origen (Euseb. *Praep. Evang.* VI. 11) and Ambrose (*de Abrah.* II. 348) mention fourteen as the age for the practice of the rite among the Egyptians.

CHS. XVIII., XIX.   THE DESTRUCTION OF SODOM AND GOMORRAH (J).

xviii. 1—15.   Visit of three Angels to Abraham, and the promise of a son to Sarah.
        16—33. Colloquy of Jehovah with Abraham; Jehovah's purpose to overthrow Sodom and Gomorrah and the intercession of Abraham.
xix.   1—23.   Visit of two Angels to Lot in Sodom, and the escape of Lot to Zoar.
        24—28. The destruction of Sodom and Gomorrah and the cities of the Plain.
        30—38. The origin of the Moabites and Ammonites.

With the exception of xix. 29, which is from P, the whole of this remarkable section is from J. Few passages in the O.T. narrative can rival it in simplicity, vividness, and grace of style.

The interposition of this section tends to heighten the expectancy with which the reader awaits the fulfilment of the promise; and to augment the impression of the Divine favour and esteem in which the patriarch is held.

1—15. VISIT OF THREE ANGELS TO ABRAHAM, AND THE PROMISE OF A SON TO SARAH (J).

1. *the* LORD *appeared*] The personal Theophany of Jehovah (cf. xvi. 13) was evidently at first not recognized by Abraham.

the oaks of Mamre] Better, as R.V. marg., *terebinths*. See note on xiii. 18. Mamre is here the name of a place, not of a chieftain (xiv. 24).

in the heat of the day] i.e. at noontide, as in 2 Sam. iv. 5. Cf. 1 Sam. xi. 9, "by the time the sun is hot"; Neh. vii. 3. For "the cool of the day," see iii. 8.

2. *lo, three men*] The sudden appearance of the three men before the tent is especially recorded. Their approach had not been observed. As in the case of xxxii. 24, Josh. v. 13, Jud. xiii. 10, 11, the angelic visitants are not distinguishable from ordinary men.

bowed himself to the earth] Cf. xix. 1, xxiii. 7, xxxiii. 3, xlii. 6; the regular gesture of salutation towards those of higher rank.

said, ¹My lord, if now I have found favour in thy sight, 3
pass not away, I pray thee, from thy servant: let now a 4
little water be fetched, and wash your feet, and rest yourselves under the tree: and I will fetch a morsel of bread, 5
and comfort ye your heart; after that ye shall pass on:

¹ Or, *O Lord*

3. *My lord*] R.V. marg. *O Lord*. The Heb. word so rendered has received three different translations.

(1) "O Lord," as in *vv.* 27, 30—32, *Adonâi*, addressed to God. So the Massoretic Heb. text, adding the word "holy," as a note, to safeguard the meaning and the pronunciation.

(2) "my lords," *adonâi*, as if Abraham addressed his three visitors together: compare the plural in *vv.* 4, 5.

(3) "my lord" (with change of vocalization), *adônî* (cf. xxiii. 6, 11). The sing. is used in *v.* 3 ("*thy* servant"). This third rendering seems the most probable: (*a*) there is no sign of Abraham's recognizing the real character of the strangers; (*b*) it would seem probable that he instinctively recognized one of them as the superior in position, though he does not perceive in him the manifestation of Jehovah until after *v.* 15.

4. *wash your feet*] Abraham's offer of hospitable welcome is said to be a faithful representation of the reception of a traveller by an Eastern sheikh. Here we have its various aspects of (1) the courteous greeting; (2) the feet washing; (3) the repast and personal attendance by the host; (4) the escort on the road at departure.

The washing of the feet is necessary for comfort as well as cleanliness in the East where sandals are worn. Cf. xix. 2, xxiv. 32, xliii. 24; Luke vii. 44; John xiii. 14.

rest yourselves under the tree] Abraham invites them to recline in the shade, while the meal is made ready. It does not necessarily indicate the posture at the meal. Judging from 1 Sam. ix. 22, xx. 5, 1 Kings xiii. 20, a sitting posture was usual among the Israelites. Probably we should understand that, in this scene, as in xxvii. 19, Jud. xix. 6, those who ate were seated on the ground, the food being placed in front of them.

5. *a morsel of bread*] Cf. Judg. xix. 5. With true Oriental subserviency of speech Abraham gives this description of the generous entertainment which he intends to provide. For this modesty of speech as a formula of courtesy, cf. xiii. 9, xxiii. 11; 2 Sam. xxiv. 22, 23.

comfort ye your heart] As in Jud. xix. 5, 8; lit. "support your heart," Lat. *confortate cor vestrum*. The English word "comfort," derived from the Lat., originally had the meaning of "strengthen." The Heb. word here used is found in Ps. civ. 15, "bread that strengtheneth man's heart."

J ¹forasmuch as ye are come to your servant. And they said, 6 So do, as thou hast said. And Abraham hastened into the tent unto Sarah, and said, Make ready quickly three 7 measures of fine meal, knead it, and make cakes. And Abraham ran unto the herd, and fetched a calf tender and good, and gave it unto the servant; and he hasted to dress 8 it. And he took butter, and milk, and the calf which he had dressed, and set it before them; and he stood by them 9 under the tree, and they did eat. And they said unto him, Where is Sarah thy wife? And he said, Behold, in the

¹ Or, *for therefore*

forasmuch as] Marg. *for therefore*: cf. xix. 8, xxxiii. 10 (J). Abraham graciously assumes that the strangers have only honoured him with a visit, in order to allow him to provide for their refreshment and entertainment on their journey.

6. *into the tent unto Sarah*] Sarah does not appear before the strangers. She is occupied with the baking. Abraham and his servant are responsible for the selection and killing of a calf, the cooking of the meat, and the procuring of butter and milk from the herd. A meal in which meat is provided is a rarity in a Bedouin's life, and is the sign of the offering of hospitality.

three measures of fine meal] A "measure" is a *seah*, or one-third of an *ephah*. The amount, therefore, represented by three *seahs* was one *ephah*. It is the same quantity mentioned by our Lord in Matt. xiii. 33, "the kingdom of heaven is like unto leaven, which a woman took, and hid in three measures of meal." The *seah* contained nearly a peck and a half.

fine meal] Two words are here used, *ḳemaḥ* and *sôleth*, meaning "meal," "fine flour."

cakes] These would be baked on flat hot stones placed in the clay oven, or in the hot ashes which were sometimes heaped up over them; hence LXX ἐγκρυφίαι, Lat. *panes subcinericii*. Cf. 1 Kings xix. 6.

7. *fetched a calf*] We must remember that meat is rarely eaten by the tent-dwelling nomads. The killing of an animal for a repast indicated a desire to do special honour to a guest.

8. *butter, and milk*] Butter (*ḥem'ah*, LXX βούτυρον) is not what we should call butter, but rather "curds," mentioned here and Judg. v. 25, as a cool and refreshing delicacy to be offered to a guest. It is called in the East *leben*. It is probably this which we find so often mentioned with honey, e.g. 2 Sam. xvii. 29; Isa. vii. 22. The milk (*ḥâlâb*) would be the fresh milk of sheep or goats.

they did eat] The manifestation of the Deity is here, as in xix. 3, associated with a meal. Cf. Exod. xxiv. 11; Judg. vi. 19, 20. God's Presence may bless the simplest duties of home life.

9. *Sarah thy wife*] The knowledge of his wife's name must have

tent. And he said, I will certainly return unto thee when 10 J
the season ¹cometh round; and, lo, Sarah thy wife shall
have a son. And Sarah heard in the tent door, which was
behind him. Now Abraham and Sarah were old, *and* well 11
stricken in age; it had ceased to be with Sarah after the
manner of women. And Sarah laughed within herself, 12
saying, After I am waxed old shall I have pleasure, my
lord being old also? And the LORD said unto Abraham, 13
Wherefore did Sarah laugh, saying, Shall I of a surety bear
a child, which am old? Is any thing too ²hard for the 14
LORD? At the set time I will return unto thee, when the

¹ Heb. *liveth*, or, *reviveth*.   ² Or, *wonderful*

caused Abraham surprise, and gives perhaps the first indication of his
guests' real character.

10. *I will certainly*] A first hint of Divine knowledge of the
parents' grief over their childlessness.

when the season cometh round] R.V. marg. Heb. *liveth*, or, *reviveth*.
A strange phrase, probably meaning "at this time a year hence," as in
xvii. 21. Cf. 2 Kings iv. 16, 17, LXX κατὰ τὸν καιρὸν τοῦτον εἰς ὥρας,
Lat. *tempore isto, vita comite*. Skinner conjectures, with a slight
alteration of the vowel points, "according to the time of a pregnant
woman," on the ground that the Heb. word for "liveth" means in
modern Heb. "a woman in child-birth."

Sarah...in the tent door] Sarah was not visible, but the conversation
of the men under the tree was easily audible to her at the tent opening.

heard] Better, "was listening," which reproduces the Heb. participle.

which was behind him] Probably the LXX preserves the right
reading, "and she was behind it," i.e. the door.

11. *well stricken in age*] An Old English expression for well-
advanced in years: cf. "...his noble queen Well struck in years"
(Shakespeare, *Rich. III*, I. 1). Heb. "entered into days," LXX
προβεβηκότες, Lat. *provectae aetatis*. Cf. Luke i. 7; Heb. xi. 11, 12.

12. *Sarah laughed within herself*] This is the laughter, according
to J, which furnished a reason for the name "Isaac"; and on that
account it is here emphasized. See, for the reason in P, xvii. 17.

waxed old] The word in the original is forcible, and is used elsewhere for worn-out raiment, e.g. "shall wax old like a garment,"
Ps. cii. 26.

13. *Wherefore did Sarah laugh?*] The Divine nature of Abraham's
guest is shewn in His knowledge of Sarah's thought, cf. xvii. 19. Here,
for the first time, Abraham's Visitant is identified with Jehovah.

14. *too hard for the LORD*] Lit., as marg., *wonderful*. The LXX
rendering μὴ ἀδυνατεῖ παρὰ τῷ θεῷ ῥῆμα finds an echo in St Luke i.

J 15 season ¹cometh round, and Sarah shall have a son. Then Sarah denied, saying, I laughed not; for she was afraid. And he said, Nay; but thou didst laugh.

16 And the men rose up from thence, and looked toward Sodom: and Abraham went with them to bring them on
17 the way. And the LORD said, Shall I hide from Abraham
18 that which I do; seeing that Abraham shall surely become a great and mighty nation, and all the nations of the earth
19 shall be blessed in him? For I have known him, to the end that he may command his children and his household after him, that they may keep the way of the LORD, to do justice and judgement; to the end that the LORD may bring upon Abraham that which he hath spoken of him.

¹ Heb. *liveth*, or, *reviveth*.

37. Compare Jer. xxxii. 17, "Ah! Lord GOD! behold, thou hast made the heaven and the earth by thy great power...: there is nothing too hard for thee."

He who thus speaks of Jehovah, is Himself Jehovah. Cf. xvi. 11, xix. 13.

15. *I laughed not*] Sarah apparently emerges, in confusion and fear, to deny the guest's statement. This occasions the fourth repetition of the word "laugh" in these four verses, by the short reply, "Nay, but thou didst laugh."

16—33. COLLOQUY OF JEHOVAH WITH ABRAHAM, &c. (J.)

16. *looked toward Sodom*] The idea is that of directing the gaze from an eminence. A view of the Dead Sea is to be obtained from the hills in the neighbourhood of Hebron: cf. xix. 28. The LXX and Lat. add "and Gomorrah" after "Sodom."

to bring them on the way] See note on xii. 20.

17. *And the LORD said*] i.e. within Himself: cf. xx. 11, "I thought," lit. "I said."

Shall I hide from Abraham] With the thought of this verse, cf. Amos iii. 6, 7, "shall evil befall a city, and the LORD hath not done it? Surely the Lord God will do nothing, but he revealeth his secret unto his servants the prophets." Here Jehovah purposes to reveal His intention to Abraham on account of his position as one who was in covenant relation, and the recipient of the promise (*v.* 18).

18. *blessed in him*] See note on xii. 3.

19. *I have known him*] See Amos iii. 2. Personal knowledge is the basis of confidence and love; the choice of Abraham is no arbitrary election, but the result of knowledge.

to the end that, &c.] The purpose for which God has known and sought out Abraham is here epitomized; (1) that, through the obedience

And the LORD said, ¹Because the cry of Sodom and Go- 20
morrah is great, and ¹because their sin is very grievous; I 21
will go down now, and see whether they have done altogether according to the cry of it, which is come unto me;
and if not, I will know. And the men turned from thence, 22
and went toward Sodom: but Abraham stood yet before
the LORD. And Abraham drew near, and said, Wilt thou 23

¹ Or, *Verily*

of him and his folk, a true righteousness, according to "the way of the
LORD," may be propagated; (2) that the Divine fulfilment of the promise may be carried out unhindered. Family life is the sphere of
chosen service.

For the picture here given of a righteous and godly life, cf. xvii. 1.

20. *Because...because*] Better, as marg., *Verily...verily*.

the cry of Sodom and Gomorrah] See xix. 13. (1) Either, this is the
complaint concerning Sodom and Gomorrah going up to Heaven. The
genitive "of" is then objective, like "the report of Tyre" (Is. xxiii. 5),
"the spoil of thine enemies" (Deut. xx. 14). (2) Or, it is the cry by
the cities, which are personified, and which make their loud complaint
against the inhabitants. The genitive then is subjective. See iv. 10.

their sin is very grievous] Cf. xiii. 13; Ezek. xvi. 49, 50.

21. *I will go down*] Cf. xi. 5, 7. The Dead Sea lies in a deep
depression to which there would be a continuous descent from Hebron;
so that the words may be also understood quite literally. The strong
anthropomorphism is in the character of J.

22. *And the men turned*] There is nothing definitely to shew that
all three Angels are not here intended. But, as the passage stands,
Jehovah here separates Himself from the two Angels mentioned in xix. 1.

Abraham stood yet] Standing is the posture of prayer and intercession. The dialogue (1) emphasizes Abraham's intimacy with Jehovah, (2) heightens expectation of the catastrophe.

The Massoretic note on this verse suggests that the original reading
ran "and Jehovah stood yet before Abraham," and that this was altered
for reverential reasons. The alteration was included in the list of the
so-called *Tikkun Sopherim*, or "Corrections of the Scribes." The
versions, however, shew no uncertainty as to the reading. Targum of
Onkelos has "And Abraham still ministered in prayer before the LORD."

23. *Abraham drew near*] Abraham's intercession comes as a reply
to Jehovah's statement in vv. 20, 21, from which the doom of the cities
might be inferred. It forms one of the most striking and pathetic
passages in the book. It expresses the generous instincts of the
patriarch's nature. Nothing can exceed the dignified simplicity and
deference in the utterance of his submissive expostulation. What
adds to the effect, is that the servant of Jehovah, the nomad sheikh,
pleads on behalf of the people of the Plain, dwellers in cities, sunk

J 24 consume the righteous with the wicked? Peradventure there be fifty righteous within the city: wilt thou consume and not spare the place for the fifty righteous that are 25 therein? That be far from thee to do after this manner, to slay the righteous with the wicked, that so the righteous should be as the wicked; that be far from thee: shall not 26 the Judge of all the earth do right? And the LORD said,

in iniquity. His concern for Lot, doubtless, forms the motive of the intercession, though Lot's name and relationship are not put forward in extenuation of the plea. The great principle on which it rests is that the action of God cannot be arbitrary; and that Jehovah will not act as the heathen gods, but only in accordance with the perfect standard of justice. The virtues of mercy and forgiveness, which operate in the human heart, are assumed to be proportionately more potent in the counsels of Jehovah. If this abstract reasoning holds good, the safety of Lot and his family may be left securely in the hands of perfect justice.

consume] A word for utter destruction, as in xix. 15, 17.

the righteous with the wicked] Cf. especially the similar passage in Jer. v. 1, "run ye to and fro through the streets of Jerusalem...if ye can find a man, if there be any that doeth justly, that seeketh truth; and I will pardon her."

24. *spare the place*] The word in the Heb. means literally "and take away for the place," i.e. its guilt, and so "forgive," as in Num. xiv. 19.

25. *That be far from thee*] An exclamation of deprecation, like "God forbid," or the Lat. *nefas tibi sit*. LXX μηδαμῶς, Lat. *absit a te*. Cf. chap. xx. 4, "Lord, wilt thou slay even a righteous nation?"

that so the righteous should be as the wicked] This was one of the great problems of religious thought in ancient Israel. The Book of Job is devoted to the consideration of this mystery of human life. Under a Divine Government of the Universe, should the innocent be consumed in the same overthrow as the evil-doer? If the Israelite's sense of justice rebelled against the notion that suffering always implied sin, conversely it cherished the hope that the suffering of the innocent might vicariously be for the good of the community.

the Judge of all the earth] A very remarkable declaration that Jehovah is supreme throughout the world. Whether or not the writer admitted the existence of other gods in other lands, he here asserts the complete sovereignty of Jehovah: cf. vi. 1 ff., viii. 21, 22, xi. 1—9. This is not monotheism, but it is the stage next before it. The "Judge" of a Semitic people was ruler, judge, and advocate. God does not judge after the sight of the eyes, or the hearing of the ears, but righteous judgement. Cf. Deut. xxxii. 4; Isa. xi. 3.

do right] Lit. "do judgement." The Judge (*shôphêt*) will do judgement (*mishpât*). This is the foundation of a moral belief.

If I find in Sodom fifty righteous within the city, then I will J spare all the place for their sake. And Abraham answered 27 and said, Behold now, I have taken upon me to speak unto the Lord, which am but dust and ashes: peradventure there 28 shall lack five of the fifty righteous: wilt thou destroy all the city for lack of five? And he said, I will not destroy it, if I find there forty and five. And he spake 29 unto him yet again, and said, Peradventure there shall be forty found there. And he said, I will not do it for the forty's sake. And he said, Oh let not the Lord be angry, 30 and I will speak: peradventure there shall thirty be found there. And he said, I will not do it, if I find thirty there. And he said, Behold now, I have taken upon me to speak 31 unto the Lord: peradventure there shall be twenty found there. And he said, I will not destroy it for the twenty's sake. And he said, Oh let not the Lord be angry, and I will 32 speak yet but this once: peradventure ten shall be found there. And he said, I will not destroy it for the ten's sake. And the LORD went his way, as soon as he had left 33 communing with Abraham: and Abraham returned unto his place.

"Righteousness is one, whether in God or in man. It would be wrong in a human judge or ruler to condemn the righteous with the wicked, or destroy them indiscriminately...The fact that God is God does not withdraw Him and His actions from the sphere of moral judgement. Nothing would be right in God because He is God, which would not be right in Him were He man" (Davidson, *Theology of O.T.* p. 130). This is one great contrast between the Christian and the Mahommedan view of God.

27. *dust and ashes*] Two alliterative words in the Heb. (*âphar va-êpher*) which defy reproduction in English: cf. i. 2, iv. 14. For the dust of man's frame, cf. ii. 7, iii. 19. See a similar use of the phrase in Job xxx. 19, xlii. 6.

33. *communing with*] i.e. "speaking to," as in *vv.* 27, 29, 31.

unto his place] i.e. "the terebinths of Mamre" (*v.* 1), from which Abraham had gone forth to escort the Angels (*v.* 16). In the expression "the LORD went his way" (Heb. "went") the writer leaves us uninformed as to the manner of Jehovah's separation from Abraham. There is no mention of "Sodom," as the place to which he "went," as in *v.* 22.

For other instances in which human intercession is raised to avert Divine anger, and is the means of forgiveness, cf. Ex. xxxii. 9—14;

J 19 And the two angels came to Sodom at even; and Lot sat in the gate of Sodom: and Lot saw them, and rose up to meet them; and he bowed himself with his face to the 2 earth; and he said, Behold now, my lords, turn aside, I pray you, into your servant's house, and tarry all night, and wash your feet, and ye shall rise up early, and go on your way. And they said, Nay; but we will abide in the street 3 all night. And he urged them greatly; and they turned in unto him, and entered into his house; and he made them

Num. xiv. 15—20; Amos vii. 4—6. In all these cases, he that intercedes seeks, on the one hand, to enter into the mind of God in His holiness and in His mercy; and then, on the other, to be the spokesman and representative of the community whose sin he confesses, and in whose behalf he entreats forgiveness and deliverance.

CH. XIX. 1—23. VISIT OF THE TWO ANGELS TO LOT IN SODOM; LOT'S DELIVERANCE AND ESCAPE TO ZOAR (J).

1. *the two angels*] See xviii. 22. It has been conjectured that the original text had here, as in *vv.* 5, 8, 10, 12, "the men" (i.e. the "three men" of xviii. 2); and that the substitution of the words "the two angels" has been made from motives of reverence, in order (1) to harmonize the action of this chapter with the scene of Abraham's pleading with Jehovah in chap. xviii., and (2) to separate Jehovah from contact with the evil of Sodom.

at even] They had visited Abraham at noon: see xviii. 1.

in the gate of Sodom] The wide arches of ancient Oriental city gates contained recesses which were the resort of leading citizens; and in which business was transacted, bargains made, and justice administered, cf. xxiii. 10, 18, xxxiv. 20; Deut. xxi. 19; Ruth iv. 1.

bowed himself] See xviii. 2.

2. *my lords*] *adonai*. The Massoretic note upon this word is "profane," i.e. not the Divine name: see note on xviii. 3.

turn aside] Lot's words are a good example of Eastern hospitality. Possibly to this passage and xviii. 3 reference is made in Heb. xiii. 2.

in the street] We must be careful not to connect the modern idea of a "street" with this word, which means rather a wide open space. Cf. Judg. xix. 15; Ezra x. 9; Neh. viii. 1, "the broad place."

The refusal of "the men" is partly to be explained as a piece of Oriental courtesy, but partly, also, to elicit the avowal that what would be safe in other towns could not be risked in Sodom.

3. *he urged them greatly*] The gentle compulsion of Oriental courtesy. To let a stranger sleep out at night would be contrary to all canons of civility, cf. Jud. xix. 16—22.

GENESIS XIX. 3—9

a feast, and did bake unleavened bread, and they did eat. J
But before they lay down, the men of the city, *even* the 4
men of Sodom, compassed the house round, both young
and old, all the people from every quarter; and they called 5
unto Lot, and said unto him, Where are the men which
came in to thee this night? bring them out unto us, that
we may know them. And Lot went out unto them to the 6
door, and shut the door after him. And he said, I pray 7
you, my brethren, do not so wickedly. Behold now, I have 8
two daughters which have not known man; let me, I pray
you, bring them out unto you, and do ye to them as is good
in your eyes: only unto these men do nothing; ¹forasmuch
as they are come under the shadow of my roof. And they 9

¹ Or, *for therefore*

a feast] Lit. "a drinking feast," and thence "a banquet." Perhaps we may assume that the Angels appeared as poor men needing food and shelter. The neglect of the poor and needy is part of the prophet's reproach against Sodom in Ezek. xvi. 49.

unleavened bread] Cakes baked hastily without leaven or yeast; the "unleavened cakes" of Jud. vi. 19.

4. *the men of the city*] The repulsive incident recorded in this passage (*vv.* 4—11) contrasts the hospitable conduct of Lot with the gross behaviour of the people of Sodom towards strangers, and has for all time associated the name of the city with shameless vice (cf. Isa. iii. 9).

from every quarter] Lit. "from the end." As in 1 Kings xii. 31, the phrase means "from all classes of the people." The writer insists upon the fact that "all" of every age and class were involved in the same guilt. Compare the scene in Jud. xix. 23.

8. *forasmuch as*] R.V. marg. *for therefore*: cf. xviii. 5. Lot's proposal, so atrocious in our ears, may have been deemed meritorious in an Eastern country, where no sacrifice was considered too great to maintain inviolate the safety of a stranger who had been received in hospitality. That Lot should have thought of imperilling the honour of his family, and not have rather hazarded his own life, is due not so much to the weakness of the man as to the terribly low estimate of womanhood which prevailed at that time. A parallel is afforded by the story in Jud. xix. The three regulations of modern Arab law as to the protection of the stranger are recorded by Robertson Smith in his *Kinship*, p. 259, "(1) the man whose tent rope has touched thine is thy stranger; (2) so also is he who journeys with thee by day and sleeps by thy side at night; (3) the guest who eats with thee is under thy protection, until he has eaten with another."

GENESIS XIX. 9—14

said, Stand back. And they said, This one fellow came in to sojourn, and he will needs be a judge: now will we deal worse with thee, than with them. And they pressed sore upon the man, even Lot, and drew near to break the door. 10 But the men put forth their hand, and brought Lot into the 11 house to them, and shut to the door. And they smote the men that were at the door of the house with blindness, both small and great: so that they wearied themselves to find the door. 12 And the men said unto Lot, Hast thou here any besides? son in law, and thy sons, and thy daughters, and whomso- 13 ever thou hast in the city; bring them out of the place: for we will destroy this place, because the cry of them is waxen great before the LORD; and the LORD hath sent us to 14 destroy it. And Lot went out, and spake unto his sons in law, which ¹married his daughters, and said, Up, get you

¹ Or, *were to marry*

9. *Stand back*] LXX ἀπόστα ἐκεῖ, Lat. *recede illuc*; cf. "give place," Isai. xlix. 20.

This one fellow] Lot is reminded of his solitariness and of his foreign extraction.

came in to sojourn] The people contrast Lot's position as a sojourner (*gêr*) in the city with his claim to decide and play the judge.

11. *blindness*] An unusual word for "blindness," inflicted as a sudden temporary visitation, used here and 2 Kings vi. 18. LXX ἀορασία.

12. *And the men said*] The incident just described had revealed the corrupt condition of the city. It had been tried by a simple test, and found wanting. Sodom is doomed; but Lot is to be saved.

any besides] The deliverance of the man carries with it the deliverance of the household.

son in law, and thy sons, &c.] A strange collocation. We should expect the sons and daughters first. Then again, why "son in law" in the singular? LXX has γαμβροί, which is probably a correction; Lat. *generum*. The proposal of Holzinger to put "son in law" in the previous clause is no improvement. Its prominence would be an additional difficulty.

13. *we will destroy*] See *v*. 24.

the cry of them] i.e. the cry against the people of Sodom; see note on xviii. 20.

the LORD hath sent us] Defining the position of the men in this and the previous chapter, as distinct from, and messengers of, Jehovah.

14. *married his daughters*] Better, as R.V. marg., *were to marry*, as Lat. *qui accepturi erant*. This seems more probable than the rendering of the R.V., and LXX τοὺς εἰληφότας. The verb used here means

GENESIS XIX. 14—17

out of this place; for the LORD will destroy the city. But he seemed unto his sons in law as one that mocked. And ¹⁵ when the morning arose, then the angels hastened Lot, saying, Arise, take thy wife, and thy two daughters which are here; lest thou be consumed in the ¹iniquity of the city. But he lingered; and the men laid hold upon his ¹⁶ hand, and upon the hand of his wife, and upon the hand of his two daughters; the LORD being merciful unto him: and they brought him forth, and set him without the city. And ¹⁷ it came to pass, when they had brought them forth abroad, that he said, Escape for thy life; look not behind thee, neither stay thou in all the Plain; escape to the mountain,

¹ Or, *punishment*

literally "the takers of." For Lot's daughters were in the house with him: Lot went out to find his "sons in law": the word "sons in law" may mean "the betrothed." If the daughters had been married, they would not have been living with Lot.

as one that mocked] The same word in the Hebrew as that rendered "laughed" in xviii. 12, and "sporting" in xxvi. 8. The Lat. has *quasi ludens*="as one who was playing."

15. *when the morning arose*] At day-break. The doom was to be inflicted before sun-rise (cf. *v.* 23). If Lot was still in the city, he too would perish: hence the men's haste.

consumed] See xviii. 23.

iniquity] Better, as R.V. marg., *punishment*. See note, on the ambiguous meaning of the Hebrew word, in iv. 13; cf. 1 Sam. xxv. 24; 2 Sam. xiv. 9.

16. *But he lingered*] It was difficult for Lot to realize the immediate and overwhelming nature of the doom announced by his visitants. His feelings for home and its associations made him hesitate. The versions misunderstood the Heb.; LXX καὶ ἐταράχθησαν, Lat. *dissimulante illo*.

the LORD being merciful unto him] An interesting clause, shewing that the men were agents of Jehovah's tenderness, as well as of His severity, cf. Ps. xxxiv. 22: does it not also imply that, in the original version of the narrative, Jehovah is here one of "the men"?

17. *he said*] One of the men is spokesman, as in *v.* 21; but the plural "they said" is found in the LXX and Lat.

look not behind thee] The meaning of this direction, which recalls the story of Orpheus and Eurydice, is not quite obvious. It may be a prohibition either of irresolute lingering, or of regretful curiosity. It is, probably, also, a test of obedience, combined with the thought that man could not look upon Jehovah and live. Cf. xvi. 13; Ex. xix. 21.

the Plain] i.e. the *kikkar*: see xiii. 10.

J 18 lest thou be consumed. And Lot said unto them, Oh, not
19 so, ¹my lord: behold now, thy servant hath found grace in thy sight, and thou hast magnified thy mercy, which thou hast shewed unto me in saving my life; and I cannot escape to the mountain, lest ²evil overtake me, and I die:
20 behold now, this city is near to flee unto, and it is a little one: Oh, let me escape thither, (is it not a little one?) and
21 my soul shall live. And he said unto him, See, I have accepted thee concerning this thing also, that I will not
22 overthrow the city of which thou hast spoken. Haste thee,

¹ Or, *O Lord*   ² Or, *the evil*

the mountain] i.e. the mountainous region on the east of the Dead Sea, "the mountains of Moab."

18. *my lord*] R.V. marg. *O Lord*. The Massoretic note here, as in xviii. 3, is "holy," regarding the word as the Divine name. Certainly in this chapter Jehovah is not so directly identified with one of "the men" as in chap. xviii. The rendering "my lord" is, perhaps, to be preferred, as in xviii. 3. On the other hand, the mention of "Jehovah" in *v.* 16, and the words in *vv.* 22 and 24, "I cannot do anything till thou be come thither," and "Then the LORD rained upon Sodom," would sufficiently justify the other rendering. Jehovah and His Angel are one, cf. xvi. 7 ff. His Presence is in "the two" as in "the three men."

19. *found grace*] Cf. vi. 8 (J).

thy mercy] Lat. *misericordiam tuam*. The LXX rendering, τὴν δικαιοσύνην, is a good illustration of the latitude given to "righteousness" as embodying compassion. Cf. Matt. vi. 1.

I cannot escape to the mountain] Lot speaks as if he were too old (cf. *v.* 31) and weak for flight over rough ground. He fears he could not find refuge in the mountains in time.

evil] Better, as R.V. marg., *the evil*. The evil means the doom of impending catastrophe.

20. *is it not a little one*] i.e. "is it not a trifle (*miz'ar*)?" It is a "small" concession to grant; or a "small" distance to go. Evidently a play on the pronunciation of the word Zoar. Lot's entreaty that he may take refuge in Zoar causes the exemption of that city from the catastrophe. For Bela, as an old name of Zoar, see xiv. 2.

and my soul shall live] = "that my soul (=I) may live." For "my soul" as a vivid way of expressing the personal pronoun, see xii. 13.

21. *I have accepted thee*] Heb. "I have received," or "lifted up thy countenance," see note on iv. 7. Compare the expression "respecter of persons," e.g. Acts x. 34. Here Jehovah is a "receiver," or "favourer," of the person of Lot: cf. xxxii. 20; Mal. i. 8.

22. *I cannot do any thing*] Mercy limits the exercise of Divine Justice. "The righteous" is not to be consumed "with the wicked" (xviii. 23).

escape thither; for I cannot do any thing till thou be come thither. Therefore the name of the city was called ¹Zoar. The sun was risen upon the earth when Lot came unto Zoar. Then the LORD rained upon Sodom and upon Gomorrah brimstone and fire from the LORD out of heaven;

¹ That is, *Little*, ver. 20.

Zoar] See note on xiv. 2. Zoar is identified by tradition with a spot on the S.E. of the Dead Sea, where a peninsula projects from the coast. Cf. xiii. 10; Deut. xxxiv. 3; Isa. xv. 5; Jer. xlviii. 34. The name in the LXX Σηγώρ, Lat. *Segor*, gave the Dead Sea the name of the Sea of Zugar in the Middle Ages.

24—29. THE DESTRUCTION OF SODOM AND GOMORRAH, &C.

24. *Then the LORD*, &c.] The destruction of the cities of the Plain is an event to which frequent allusion is made in Holy Scripture. The impressive features of the Dead Sea must have continually lent force to the terrible tradition of an overthrow in times of remote antiquity. The barrenness of the soil, the absence of life in the water, the deposits of salt, of bitumen, and of sulphur, helped to connect a region, which was within sight of Jerusalem, with the thought of a judicial visitation by Jehovah, more terrible in character, if less in magnitude, than the Deluge itself. For the prophetic use of this catastrophe, see especially Deut. xxix. 23. Cf. Jer. xx. 16, xxiii. 14, xlix. 18, l. 40; Lam. iv. 6; Amos iv. 11; Zeph. ii. 9. In the N.T. see Luke xvii. 29; 2 Pet. ii. 6; Jude 7.

brimstone and fire] It is unreasonable to subject the description of this overthrow to the close scrutiny of modern science. Geologists now tell us that, within recent geological periods, there is no sign of volcanic activity in the Dead Sea region. If, therefore, as is assumed, the cities of the Plain lay in the Dead Sea valley, their overthrow was not occasioned by lava or burning ashes, like Pompeii, or Herculaneum, or St Pierre. It has been contended, and is not beyond the bounds of probability, that an earthquake, causing a sudden subsidence of the crust and accompanied by great fissures in the earth, caused the overthrow of buildings, and released great masses of bitumen, sulphur, &c., which are to be found in large quantities in that locality. The spontaneous combustion of escaping gas, the ignition of great masses of bituminous material, combined with the outflow of steam and hot water, would then have enveloped the whole country in dense smoke, and would have seemed to drop brimstone and fire from the sky. This line of explanation would also assume that the depression of the earth's surface led to the subsequent submergence of the four ruined cities beneath the waters of the Dead Sea; the lower end of which is exceedingly shallow. A careful scientific investigation of the whole

GENESIS XIX. 25—27

J 25 and he overthrew those cities, and all the Plain, and all the inhabitants of the cities, and that which grew upon the
26 ground. But his wife looked back from behind him, and
27 she became a pillar of salt. And Abraham gat up early in

question was undertaken by Blanckenhorn, the results of which are contained in the *Z.D.P.V.* 1896, p. 58, 1898, p. 78.

There is, however, in the Biblical story, no mention of an earthquake. The events recorded evidently refer to a catastrophe, the tradition of which was handed down by the early Hebrews, and popularly localized in the bare and terrible features of the Dead Sea scenery.

from the LORD *out of heaven*] The words "from the LORD" come in very strangely after "the LORD rained." Cf. Micah v. 7, "as dew from the LORD." For "out of heaven," cf. 2 Kings i. 12; Job i. 16.

25. *and he overthrew*] The word used is the one regularly employed elsewhere in the O.T. where the overthrow of the cities is mentioned. Like the word *mabbul* for the Flood, so this word, "overthrow" (*mahpêkah*, "overturning"), used here and in *v*. 29, became the technical term for this catastrophe. It suggests an earthquake.

"The Korán frequently refers to Sodom and Gomorrah by the title of *al mutafikât* 'the overturned' (Sur. ix. 71, liii. 54, lxix. 9)" (Cheyne).

26. *a pillar of salt*] Lot's wife for disobeying the command, recorded in *v*. 17, was, according to the tradition, changed into a pillar of salt. Our Lord's words, "Remember Lot's wife" (Luke xvii. 32), refer to the narrative in this passage. Her looking back indicated the place of her real treasure. She failed to trust whole-heartedly, or to obey. Compare the story of Orpheus and Eurydice (Ovid, *Met.* x. 51). Our Lord's warning is directed against the absorption of mind in temporal pleasures and interests. His allusion to this passage was one that all Jewish hearers understood. He does not raise the question of its historicity. He appeals to the teaching of the parable contained in the Scripture story.

Travellers speak of the remarkable ridge called *Jebel Uzdum* ("mountain of Sodom") at the S.W. extremity of the Dead Sea. Its fantastic pillars and ragged fragments attract attention. It consists of rock salt. One of these needles or pinnacles has been called by the people "Lot's wife." Such pinnacles would in process of time change their appearance owing to the effects of wind and rain. One known as "Lot's wife" existed in the days of our Lord. See Wisd. x. 7; Josephus, *Ant.* I. 11, 4.

"Suddenly we saw before us among the pinnacles of salt a gigantic 'Lot,' with a daughter on each arm hurrying off in a south-westerly direction, with their bodies bent forward as though they were in great haste, and their flowing garments trailing behind" (*Pal. Q.S.* 1870, p. 150).

27. *gat up early*] No emphasis is here laid in the Hebrew upon the

the morning to the place where he had stood before the J
LORD: and he looked toward Sodom and Gomorrah, and 28
toward all the land of the Plain, and beheld, and, lo, the
smoke of the land went up as the smoke of a furnace.

And it came to pass, when God destroyed the cities of 29 P
the Plain, that God remembered Abraham, and sent Lot
out of the midst of the overthrow, when he overthrew the
cities in the which Lot dwelt.

And Lot went up out of Zoar, and dwelt in the mountain, 30 J
and his two daughters with him; for he feared to dwell in
Zoar: and he dwelt in a cave, he and his two daughters.

earliness of the rise. The idiom amounts to saying "in the morning
Abraham arose and went to the place."

stood before the LORD] See xviii. 22.

28. *the smoke of the land*] The word is one used especially in
connexion with incense and sacrifice. It is not the usual word for
smoke, but rather corresponds to our "reek" or, as Driver, "steam."
Travellers relate that, owing to rapid evaporation, there always appears
a steamy mist rising up from the Dead Sea. Wisdom x. 6, 7, "While
the ungodly were perishing, wisdom delivered a righteous man, when
he fled from the fire that descended out of heaven on Pentapolis. To
whose wickedness a smoking waste still witnesseth...Yea and a disbelieving
soul hath a memorial there, a pillar of salt still standing."

a furnace] The word used in Ex. ix. 8, 10, xix. 18, "a furnace," or
"kiln," for burning lime, or making bricks.

29 (P). *when God destroyed*, &c.] This verse contains P's brief
summary of the whole event. This will explain the repetition of the
narrative, and the sudden substitution of "God" (*Elohim*) for "the
LORD" (Jehovah). The expression "God remembered Abraham" would
otherwise seem strange after the narrative in xviii.; but, as a matter
of fact, the sentence probably followed after xiii. 12, with P's account
of the separation of Abram and Lot. For "destroyed" (*shâhath*), cf.
vi. 13, 17, ix. 11, 15 (P).

30—38 (J). THE ORIGIN OF THE MOABITES AND AMMONITES.

30. *And Lot went up*] He left the Plain, and withdrew "to the
mountain," viz. "the mountains of Moab"; see *v.* 17.

he feared] Why did he fear to dwell in Zoar? Not, as has been
suggested, lest the people of Zoar should put him to death, as one who
either had escaped just punishment, or, like Jonah, had been the cause
of catastrophe; but lest Zoar, one of the cities of the Plain, should still
be overtaken by catastrophe.

in a cave] The definite article in the Hebrew has been thought to
mean either a well-known cavern, or a locality in which caves were
numerous. But compare the idiomatic use of the def. art. in viii. 7.

J 31 And the firstborn said unto the younger, Our father is old, and there is not a man in the earth to come in unto us
32 after the manner of all the earth: come, let us make our father drink wine, and we will lie with him, that we may
33 preserve seed of our father. And they made their father drink wine that night: and the firstborn went in, and lay with her father; and he knew not when she lay down, nor
34 when she arose. And it came to pass on the morrow, that the firstborn said unto the younger, Behold, I lay yesternight with my father: let us make him drink wine this night also; and go thou in, and lie with him, that we may preserve seed
35 of our father. And they made their father drink wine that night also: and the younger arose, and lay with him; and he knew not when she lay down, nor when she arose.
36 Thus were both the daughters of Lot with child by their
37 father. And the firstborn bare a son, and called his name Moab: the same is the father of the Moabites unto this
38 day. And the younger, she also bare a son, and called his name Ben-ammi: the same is the father of the children of Ammon unto this day.

37. *Moab*] A play on the word "Moab," on account of its general assonance with the Heb. *mê-âb* = "from a father"; an instance of derivation by folk-etymology.

38. *Ben-ammi*] "The son of my people"; or "the son of my father's kin"; see xvii. 14. "Unto this day," cf. xxvi. 33, xxxii. 32, xxxv. 20, xlvii. 26 (J).

There is no need for us to regard this repulsive story as literal history. It should be included among the popular narratives which grew up round the traditional origin of proper names. It has been held that the tradition may have had a local Moabite origin connected with some famous cavern, and that the people of Moab and Ammon may have had an old belief that their races arose in prehistoric times from the same ancestor, in accordance with this tale. Undoubtedly, there were ancient Eastern peoples to whom the incest here described would have seemed in no way atrocious.

It is, of course, also possible, that the story, as we have it in Gen., reflects the feelings of bitterness and hatred which were felt among the Israelites towards their neighbours on the east side of the Jordan. The antipathy expressed in Deut. xxiii. 3 and Neh. xiii. 1, 2 may well account for the circulation of traditions concerning the parentage of these two peoples, combining a popular explanation of their names with contumely and reproach as to their origin.

Again, it is conceivable that this story may contain a fragment of a

And Abraham journeyed from thence toward the land of 20 E

tradition, Moabite and Ammonite in its derivation, which recorded some stupendous catastrophe, from which, through the favour of the Deity, only Lot and his daughters, out of all the inhabitants of the world, were saved. The story may then have been regarded as reflecting not ignominy, but honour, upon those who were the means of preserving the whole human race from the peril of extinction. There is plausibility in this theory of Gunkel's. The words of the elder daughter, "there is not a man," seem to imply that all the inhabitants of the earth had been annihilated. Our ignorance of Moabite early traditions forbids us to go further than to admit the possibility of some such explanation.

Ch. XX. Abraham and Sarah at the Court of Abimelech at Gerar (E).

The incident recorded in this chap. resembles in its general features that recorded of Abraham in Egypt, xii. 10—20, and that recorded of Isaac at Gerar, xxvi. 6—11. In each case the patriarch, fearing for his own life, represents his wife to be his sister. The foreign prince desires to make the patriarch's wife one of his own harem. He is prevented from so doing. The truth is divulged. The patriarch's wife is restored, and the patriarch himself is enriched by gifts or by compensation. In each case the heathen prince acts honourably. As compared with J's story in xii. 10—20, it has been claimed by Stanley Cook that "E's story of Abraham at Gerar in Gen. xx. 1—17 displays a great advance in morality; the sin of adultery is condemned in the most emphatic terms, and it is regarded as a capital offence. The stress here laid upon the iniquity marks a stage in ethics comparable only with the Decalogue, where adultery is prohibited, and with the Deuteronomic code (xxii. 22), where also the penalty is death (stoning; cf. Ezek. xvi. 40, xxiii. 47; John viii. 5)[1]." But it is very doubtful whether E and J can be so widely separated. Admission to the harem was not marriage.

This chapter is the first continuous narrative taken from E, the Elohist or Ephraimitic source of the prophetic narrative. In its vivid narrative E resembles J. But it possesses its own distinctive features of language and style. See Introduction.

The fulfilment of the promise is again postponed, while the narrative records a last peril to faith and honour.

1. *from thence*] This passage is evidently derived from some distinct source. As it ignores the previous section dealing with Lot, and the last reference to Abraham is in xviii. 33, when he is at Mamre, the precise meaning of "from thence" must remain obscure.

---

[1] *Laws of Moses and Code of Hammurabi*, p. 106.

E the South, and dwelt between Kadesh and Shur; and he
2 sojourned in Gerar. And Abraham said of Sarah his wife,
She is my sister: and Abimelech king of Gerar sent, and
3 took Sarah. But God came to Abimelech in a dream of
the night, and said to him, Behold, thou art but a dead
man, because of the woman which thou hast taken; for she
4 is a man's wife. Now Abimelech had not come near her:
and he said, Lord, wilt thou slay even a righteous nation?
5 Said he not himself unto me, She is my sister? and she,
even she herself said, He is my brother: in the integrity of
my heart and the innocency of my hands have I done this.

the South] See note on xii. 9.

between Kadesh and Shur] For these places, see xiv. 7, xvi. 7.

he sojourned in Gerar] This causes a difficulty. Gerar is the court of the king Abimelech. In xxvi. 1, Abimelech is king of the Philistines. Gerar has, therefore, been identified with a spot a few miles south of Gaza (*Umm Gerar*). This, however, is hardly a place of sojourn "between Kadesh and Shur." Either, therefore, there is a lacuna between the two clauses of this verse, representing a journey from the Negeb into the Philistine region; or Gerar *may* be a place S.W. of Kadesh (*Wady Gerur*), whose king happened to have the same name as the Philistine king of Gerar in chap. xxvi. Of these alternatives the former is the more probable.

2. *She is my sister*] See notes on xii. 13. It seems almost incredible that, after the event recorded in xii. 13—20, Abraham should once again have displayed the same faults of cowardice and dissimulation. Sarah also is advanced in years; and, in xviii. 10—14, had received the promise of a son. The narrative most probably is a duplicate of the tradition of xii. 13—20. Its present position, between the promise of a son in xviii. 10—14, and its fulfilment in chap. xxi., becomes intelligible on the supposition of its derivation from an independent source, not connected with chap. xviii.

Abimelech] i.e. "my father is Melech." This is probably a name compounded with that of a Canaanite deity, Milk (=Molech in the English Bible).

3. *God came...in a dream*] Scholars have noticed that E frequently describes Divine interposition by means of a dream. Cf. *v.* 6, xxxi. 11, 24, xxxvii. 5, 9, xl. 5 ff., xli. 1 ff., xlvi. 2.

art but a dead man] i.e. "shalt die." This sentence is not literally fulfilled. Cf. ii. 17.

4. *a righteous nation*] Abimelech appeals to the instinct of justice, that God will not punish the innocent, as if they were guilty. Cf. xviii. 23.

5. *integrity*] Heb. "perfectness." Cf. vi. 9.

innocency of my hands] Cf. Ps. xxvi. 6.

GENESIS XX. 6—10

And God said unto him in the dream, Yea, I know that in 6 E
the integrity of thy heart thou hast done this, and I also
withheld thee from sinning against me: therefore suffered I
thee not to touch her. Now therefore restore the man's 7
wife; for he is a prophet, and he shall pray for thee, and
thou shalt live: and if thou restore her not, know thou that
thou shalt surely die, thou, and all that are thine. And 8
Abimelech rose early in the morning, and called all his
servants, and told all these things in their ears: and the
men were sore afraid. Then Abimelech called Abraham, 9
and said unto him, What hast thou done unto us? and
wherein have I sinned against thee, that thou hast brought
on me and on my kingdom a great sin? thou hast
done deeds unto me that ought not to be done. And 10

6. *from sinning against me*] The violation of moral law is sin against God.

suffered I thee not] The explanation of this sentence is supplied in v. 17.

7. *for he is a prophet*] Abraham is here given the title of "prophet," or "nâbî" (the first occurrence of it in Scripture). The prophet—the one who utters or pours forth—is one who is in intimate relations with God, moved by His Spirit, protected by His Power. From 1 Sam. ix. 9 we learn the *nabi* was in old times called *roeh*, or Seer. To call Abraham a "prophet" (*nâbî*) is, therefore, an anachronism, indicating the atmosphere of the monarchical period. The prophet was one who was privileged to have intercourse with God, and was bound to communicate "the word" to his own kith and kin (xviii. 19). He was their representative, their intercessor, their spokesman. He who has the vision, *rô'eh*, must declare the message, *nâbî*.

A comment on this passage is supplied by Ps. cv. 14, 15, "he suffered no man to do them wrong...and do my prophets no harm." Perhaps the prophets of Israel traced their "guild" back to Abraham as their founder, as well as to Moses, their greatest leader (Deut. xxxiv. 10).

pray] i.e. intercede. For the efficacy of a "prophet's" intercession, cf. Deut. ix. 20; 1 Sam. vii. 5, xii. 19, 23; Jer. vii. 16.

9. *What hast thou done unto us*] Syriac Peshitto "what have I done unto thee," which suits the second clause rather better.

deeds...that ought not to be done] Cf. xxxiv. 7; 2 Sam. xiii. 12. The moral standard of the heathen king here stands higher than that of Abraham the prophet. There were at Gerar, presumably, no written laws; but the custom of the people, with which was bound up its religion, was more powerful than law. The Code of Hammurabi reflects the moral standard of the most civilized community of the time.

E Abimelech said unto Abraham, What sawest thou, that
11 thou hast done this thing? And Abraham said, Because
I thought, Surely the fear of God is not in this place; and
12 they will slay me for my wife's sake. And moreover she is
indeed my sister, the daughter of my father, but not the
13 daughter of my mother; and she became my wife: and it
came to pass, when God caused me to wander from my

10. *What sawest thou*] i.e. "what hadst thou in view?" An unusual use of the verb "to see." Cf. Ps. lxvi. 18, "if I regard (lit. 'see') iniquity in my heart." Some scholars prefer, by a slight alteration of the text, the reading, "what didst thou fear?" *yarêtha* for *ra'îtha* (Bacher).

11. *Because I thought*] Lit. "I said": see note on xviii. 17.

Surely the fear of God] Abraham's defence is that he assumed a heathen people did not fear God; and, therefore, would not be afraid of any Divine retribution, if they took the life of a stranger (*gêr*). The stranger had no rights; his God would not be known. He would have no "avenger of blood." See note on iv. 15.

See the same idea underlying Joseph's words, "for I fear God" (xlii. 18).

they will slay me] He does not explain, why he feared that he would be slain for his wife's sake. Obviously it is for the reason mentioned in xii. 12. Sarah's youth and beauty are assumed: the murder of the stranger would enable the inhabitants of Gerar to seize her. For this murder there would be no redress; and, therefore, there would be little compunction.

12. *she is indeed my sister*] See xi. 29, xii. 19. The marriage with a half-sister was evidently permitted in David's time (cf. 2 Sam. xiii. 13); and it was practised in the days of Ezekiel (Ezek. xxii. 11); though forbidden by the laws of Lev. xviii. 9, 11, xx. 17; Deut. xxvii. 22. It is said to have been permitted in Phoenicia and Egypt.

Abraham's excuse is based upon a half truth. Sarah may have been truly his sister; but this statement was no moral justification for his suppression of the fact that she was his wife. The further excuse in *v.* 13, that as he travelled about he always practised this mental reservation concerning Sarah, scarcely adds dignity to his line of defence.

13. *God caused me to wander*] Referring to xii. 1. The Hebrew student will notice that the verb "caused me to wander" is in the plural, although, as a rule in the O.T., the word "God" (*Elohim*) is treated as sing. But it is sometimes the case that the plural is used, as here and in xxxi. 53, Jos. xxiv. 19, when an Israelite speaks to heathen, or else heathen are speaking of God, e.g. 1 Sam. iv. 8; 1 Kings xix. 2, xx. 10. For an exception, see xxxv. 7. Here the Massoretic note adds "holy," in order to call attention to the unusual construction.

father's house, that I said unto her, This is thy kindness which thou shalt shew unto me; at every place whither we shall come, say of me, He is my brother. And Abimelech 14 took sheep and oxen, and menservants and womenservants, and gave them unto Abraham, and restored him Sarah his wife. And Abimelech said, Behold, my land is before 15 thee: dwell where it pleaseth thee. And unto Sarah he 16 said, Behold, I have given thy brother a thousand pieces of silver: behold, ¹it is for thee a covering of the eyes to all that are with thee; and ²in respect of all thou art righted.

¹ Or, *he* ² Or, *before all* men

14. *And Abimelech took*] Abimelech's gift is intended to compensate Abraham for injury to his honour. The head of the household is regarded as embodying the rights of all who belong to him. The LXX and Heb. Sam. insert "a thousand pieces of silver and" before "sheep and oxen." This is due to a misunderstanding of *v.* 16.

15. *my land is before thee*] Cf. xiii. 9, xxxiv. 10.

16. *I have given thy brother*] Abimelech emphasizes the word which Sarah had used (*v.* 5), and which freed his conscience from any blame. By the sarcastic use of the word "brother," Abimelech implies that compensation for wrong done to her is due to Abraham as one of her family, not as her husband.

a thousand pieces of silver] Lit. "1000 silver." The word *shekel*, meaning "a weight," is omitted. Money in the patriarchal times was reckoned by weight: there were no stamped coins. The standard weight was supplied, as a rule, by metal, generally silver. Hence the word "silver" is in Hebrew often used for "money"; and the word *shekel*, or weight, is equivalent to "a piece of money." See note on xxiii. 16. 1000 shekels of silver would be worth about £137. 10*s*., reckoning a shekel = 2*s*. 9*d*. But the purchasing value of silver varies. A slave in Ex. xxi. 32 is worth 30 *shekels*.

it is for thee a covering of the eyes] R.V. marg. *he* (= A.V.) is unsuitable and improbable. "A covering of the eyes" is a metaphor for a gift, which will have the effect of appeasing indignation and of causing the offended person to forget, or be blind to, the offence. Cf. xxxii. 20, "I will appease him," lit. "cover his face"; 1 Sam. xii. 3, "of whose hand have I taken a ransom to blind mine eyes therewith"; Job ix. 24, "he covereth the faces of the judges." There is no need to suppose that there is any reference to a woman's veil (xxiv. 65), as if the money paid was to be in lieu of lost modesty, symbolized by the veil.

to all that are with thee] i.e. those of her family will recognize that full amends have been made. LXX καὶ πάσαις ταῖς μετὰ σοῦ introducing a special reference to Sarah's personal attendants.

in respect of all] R.V. marg. *before all* men. The text in the

E 17 And Abraham prayed unto God: and God healed Abimelech, and his wife, and his maidservants; and they bare 18 children. For the LORD had fast closed up all the wombs of the house of Abimelech, because of Sarah Abraham's wife.

J P 21 And the LORD visited Sarah as he had said, | and the
J 2 LORD did unto Sarah as he had spoken. | And Sarah
P conceived, and bare Abraham a son in his old age, | at the
3 set time of which God had spoken to him. And Abraham

original is very doubtful. The meaning is fairly clear. Sarah is righted, and her honour saved; but whether the translation should be "and in respect of all that has happened," or "and in regard to all men, thou art put right," remains uncertain.

LXX καὶ πάντα ἀλήθευσον = "and in all things observe truth," furnishes a good moral, but a fantastic rendering. Lat. *quocunque perrexeris: mementoque te deprehensam* is no translation of our text.

17. *Abraham prayed*] See note on *v.* 7. This verse explains *v.* 4. Barrenness was regarded as the sign of Divine displeasure, which might be averted by prayer and intercession: cf. xxv. 21, xxx. 2, 22; 1 Sam. i. 10. See note on xii. 17.

18. *For the LORD*] An editorial addition, explanatory of *v.* 17. "Jehovah" is here used for the only time in this narrative.

CH. XXI.

1—7. THE BIRTH OF ISAAC. (J and P.)
8—21. THE EXPULSION OF HAGAR AND ISHMAEL. (E.)
22—34. THE COVENANT BETWEEN ABRAHAM AND ABIMELECH AT BEER-SHEBA. (E and J.)

The greater part of this chapter is from E. But *vv.* 1ᵃ, 2ᵃ, and 7 are probably from J; and *vv.* 1ᵇ, 2ᵇ—5 from P; *v.* 6 is E.

1. *visited*] Cf. 1 Sam. ii. 21; Luke i. 68. The word is used for the dealings of God, sometimes, as here, in blessing, and sometimes in punishment.

The two clauses of this verse are identical in meaning: the first probably refers to xviii. 10—14 (J): the second to xvii. 16, 21 (P). If the second clause is from P, the substitution of "Jehovah" for "God" is probably either editorial, or a transcriptional error.

2. *in his old age*] Cf. *v.* 7, xviii. 11, xxiv. 36, xxxvii. 3, xliv. 20 (all from J); meaning literally "to his old age."

at the set time] Cf. xvii. 21 (P).

It is to this verse that allusion is made in Heb. xi. 11, "by faith even Sarah herself received power to conceive seed, when she was past age, since she counted him faithful who had promised."

called the name of his son that was born unto him, whom Sarah bare to him, Isaac. And Abraham circumcised his son Isaac when he was eight days old, as God had commanded him. And Abraham was an hundred years old, when his son Isaac was born unto him. | And Sarah said, God hath ¹made me to laugh; every one that heareth will laugh with me. And she said, Who would have said unto Abraham, that Sarah should give children suck? for I have borne him a son in his old age.

And the child grew, and was weaned: and Abraham made a great feast on the day that Isaac was weaned.

P 4 5

E 6 7

8

¹ Or, *prepared laughter for me*

3. *And Abraham called*, &c.] For the name Isaac, see note on xvii. 19. The father, in the P narrative, gives the name: see xvi. 15.

4. *circumcised*] Abraham fulfilled the command of xvii. 10 (P). That Isaac, the son of the promise, was circumcised on the 8th day is particularly mentioned by St Stephen, Acts vii. 8.

The mention of circumcision in this verse, the naming in *v.* 3, and Abraham's age in *v.* 5, are characteristic of P's style.

6. *God hath made me to laugh*] R.V. marg. *prepared laughter for me*. Once more in connexion with the birth of Isaac the thought of laughter recurs: see xvii. 17 (P), xviii. 12—15 (J). This time we have the tradition preserved by E. It is not clear that the two clauses of this verse mean the same thing. According to R.V. text, the first clause refers the laughter to Sarah's own happiness and exultation: the second clause refers it to the merry reception of the unexpected news by those who would laugh incredulously. According to R.V. marg., the latter meaning attaches also to the first clause; and both clauses, meaning the same thing, are explained by *v.* 7. The R.V. text is perhaps to be preferred. It preserves two traditional explanations of the laughter associated with Isaac's birth. Certainly the laughter of Sarah's personal happiness seems to be the point of St Paul's quotation from Isa. liv. 1, "rejoice thou barren that bearest not," in a passage where the Apostle is allegorizing this chapter (Gal. iv. 22—31).

with me] Better, *at me*. The preposition "with" is hardly correct, though it is supported by the LXX συγχαρεῖται, Lat. *corridebit mihi*. The original represents Sarah as the object of the laughter; and amusement, not derision, as its cause.

8—21 (E). THE EXPULSION OF HAGAR AND ISHMAEL.

A narrative from E which forms a parallel to that in chap. xvi. (J).

8. *was weaned*] Weaning was often, in the East, deferred until as late as the child's third or fourth year; see 1 Sam. i. 24. It is still regarded as the occasion for a family rejoicing.

GENESIS XXI. 9—12

E 9 And Sarah saw the son of Hagar the Egyptian, which she
10 had borne unto Abraham, ¹mocking. Wherefore she said
unto Abraham, Cast out this bondwoman and her son: for
the son of this bondwoman shall not be heir with my son,
11 even with Isaac. And the thing was very grievous in
12 Abraham's sight on account of his son. And God said
unto Abraham, Let it not be grievous in thy sight because
of the lad, and because of thy bondwoman; in all that
Sarah saith unto thee, hearken unto her voice; for in Isaac

¹ Or, *playing*

9. *mocking*] Better, as R.V. marg., *playing*. The original is the same verb, in the intensive mood, which is rendered "laugh," e.g. in *v.* 6. There is no need to introduce the meaning of "mockery," which would require an object. The verb used absolutely, and rendered, as in the marg., gives a suitable sense. The LXX and Latin so render it, adding words of explanation: παίζοντα μετὰ 'Ισαὰκ τοῦ υἱοῦ αὐτῆς, *ludentem cum Isaac filio suo*, as if Sarah, watching Ishmael playing with her own child, had been seized with a sudden fit of passionate jealousy. Ishmael was the elder, but he was the son of her handmaid; and in Sarah's eyes it was unfitting that Ishmael should even play with or near her own child.

The Rabbinic interpretations of this word were productive of strange speculations. St Paul refers to one of them, which understood the word to denote "teasing" and "persecution"; hence Gal. iv. 29. Other more fantastic attempts at exegesis connected this verse with Ishmael's sins of idolatry, of impurity, and even of attempts to take his brother's life.

10. "Hebrew custom provided for the recognition of the children of the maid-servant (Gen. xxx. 3), and Ishmael according to the Elohist (Gen. xxi. 10) was coheir with Isaac" (Stanley Cook, p. 140).

11. *And the thing was very grievous*] Lit. "was very evil," or "ill." Abraham was displeased, because he loved his son. Sarah's suggestion, however, was in accord with the prevalent harsh treatment of slaves. Abraham raises no objection on the grounds of common humanity, honour, or reason, to the proposal to expel Ishmael and Hagar.

12. *And God said*] It is revealed to Abraham by night (*v.* 14), that compliance with Sarah's demand will be overruled to fulfil the destiny of Hagar's child. The Israelite tradition, according to the comparatively low moral standard of its time, especially in connexion with the conditions of slave concubinage and its domestic results, attributed to the voice of God a command that in our ears sounds unfeeling and cruel.

in Isaac shall thy seed be called] Lit. "in Isaac shall seed be called

shall thy seed be called.   And also of the son of the bond- 13
woman will I make a nation, because he is thy seed.   And 14
Abraham rose up early in the morning, and took bread and
a ¹bottle of water, and gave it unto Hagar, putting it on
her shoulder, and the child, and sent her away: and she
departed, and wandered in the wilderness of Beer-sheba.
And the water in the bottle was spent, and she cast the 15
child under one of the shrubs.   And she went, and sat her 16
down over against him a good way off, as it were a bowshot:

¹ Or, *skin*

---

to thee." LXX ἐν Ἰσαὰκ κληθήσεταί σοι σπέρμα, which is quoted in Rom. ix. 7 and Heb. xi. 18. The meaning is that in Isaac and in his descendants Abraham will have those who will be called by his name.

Isaac is to be the father of the "children of promise." He stands, therefore, in the allegory (Gal. iv. 27, 28), in contrast with him "that was born after the flesh" (i.e. Ishmael). Isaac stands for those "born after the spirit."

13. *a nation*] Cf. xvi. 10, xvii. 20. The LXX and the Sam. read "a great nation."

14. *a bottle of water*] or, better, "a skin of water." LXX ἀσκός. The vessel for carrying water in the East is generally the skin of a goat. The recollection of this will explain passages like Matt. ix. 17. Its shape might be easy to carry or to hang up. Cf. Ps. cxix. 83.

and the child] These words imply that Hagar carried the child, as well as the skin of water, upon her shoulder. So the LXX καὶ ἐπέθηκεν ἐπὶ τὸν ὦμον αὐτῆς καὶ τὸ παιδίον. Lat., avoiding the difficulty, "tradiditque puerum."

According to P (cf. xvi. 16, xxi. 5), Ishmael would be a boy of over fourteen years of age. According to E, Ishmael is still a child (cf. *vv.* 15—17).

the wilderness of Beer-sheba] i.e. the high plateau at the extreme south of Palestine. The country is hilly and bare.

Beer-sheba the sanctuary of the south—the modern *Bir-es-Seba*. See, for the meaning of its name, *vv.* 29—34, xxvi. 33.

15. *cast the child*] This expression taken with the mention of the child in *vv.* 14, 18 ("hold him in thine hand"), 20 ("and he grew") implies that Ishmael is regarded in this story as a little boy, who could be carried by his mother.

under one of the shrubs] We should probably understand by this word the low scrub such as grows in the desert, like the broom, under which Elijah rested, 1 Kings xix. 4. The word used also occurs in ii. 5 in a general sense; see note.

16. *as it were a bowshot*] LXX ὡσεὶ τόξου βολήν, Lat. *quantum potest arcus jacere*.

The child's strength had given out before the mother's. She could

E for she said, Let me not look upon the death of the child. And she sat over against him, and lift up her voice and 17 wept. And God heard the voice of the lad; and the angel of God called to Hagar out of heaven, and said unto her, What aileth thee, Hagar? fear not; for God hath heard the 18 voice of the lad where he is. Arise, lift up the lad, and hold him in thine hand; for I will make him a great nation. 19 And God opened her eyes, and she saw a well of water; and she went, and filled the bottle with water, and gave the 20 lad drink. And God was with the lad, and he grew; and 21 he dwelt in the wilderness, and ¹became an archer. And he dwelt in the wilderness of Paran: and his mother took him a wife out of the land of Egypt.

¹ Or, *became, as he grew up, an archer*

not bring herself to watch her child die of thirst, and she could not leave him. She remained within hearing.

and lift up her voice and wept] The LXX probably preserves the right rendering "And the child lifted up its voice and wept," ἀναβοῆσαν δὲ τὸ παιδίον ἔκλαυσεν.

17. *God heard the voice of the lad*] The voice God heard was that of the lad. He had pity on the anguish, and gave ear to the cry, of the child. Once more we have a play upon the name of Ishmael with its meaning of "God heareth." Cf. xvi. 11.

the angel of God] A different manifestation to Hagar from that in chap. xvi. 7. "The angel" (cf. xxviii. 12, xxxi. 11, xxxii. 2) speaks "from heaven" (xxii. 11 E). God protects the handmaid and her child no less than the Chosen Family.

18. *a great nation*] Cf. *v.* 13 and xvi. 10.

19. *opened her eyes*] What she had not seen before, Hagar suddenly received power to see. Cf. Num. xxii. 31; 2 Kings vi. 17; Luke xxiv. 16, 31. LXX φρέαρ ὕδατος ζῶντος, "a spring of living water," in the desert.

20. *God was with the lad*] Cf. 22, xxvi. 3, xxxix. 2.

became an archer] R.V. marg. rightly, *became, as he grew up, an archer*. Lat. *factusque est juvenis sagittarius*. His descendants were famous in later times for their skill in the use of the bow (cf. Isa. xxi. 17). Cf. Jetur the son of Ishmael (xxv. 15), the reputed ancestor of the Ituraeans.

21. *the wilderness of Paran*] Mentioned in Num. x. 12, xii. 16, xiii. 3. It seems to have been the wild mountainous country south and east of Kadesh, and west of Edom, the modern *et-Tih*.

out of the land of Egypt] Hagar herself was an Egyptian, cf. xvi. 1. For the parent taking a wife for the son, cf. xxiv. 3, xxxiv. 4, xxxviii. 6;

And it came to pass at that time, that Abimelech and Phicol the captain of his host spake unto Abraham, saying, God is with thee in all that thou doest: now therefore swear unto me here by God that thou wilt not deal falsely with me, nor with ¹my son, nor with my son's son: but according to the kindness that I have done unto thee, thou shalt do unto me, and to the land wherein thou hast sojourned. And Abraham said, I will swear. And Abraham reproved Abimelech because of the well of water,

¹ Or, *my offspring, nor with my posterity*

Judg. xiv. 2. The preliminary steps for a marriage are taken by the parents of the parties; here, in the absence of the father, the mother selects the bride.

22—34 (E, J). THE COVENANT BETWEEN ABRAHAM AND ABIMELECH AT BEER-SHEBA.

22. *Abimelech*] This passage seems to be a continuation of chap. xx.

Phicol the captain of his host] For this title, cf. 1 Sam. xiv. 50; 2 Sam. ii. 8 (where it is applied to Abner); xxiv. 2 (to Joab). It shews that Abimelech was a petty king of some importance.

Here and in *v.* 32, the LXX inserts another name and title between Abimelech and Phicol, Ὀχοζὰθ ὁ νυμφαγωγὸς αὐτοῦ, "Ahuzzath his friend." This name occurs with that of Phicol again in xxvi. 26.

God is with thee] Cf. 20, xxvi. 28. Abimelech has had reason to discern the meaning of the description of Abraham, in xx. 7, as "a prophet."

23. *here*] The reference is to the name of Beer-sheba and its popular etymology from the Hebrew word "to swear." Abraham's departure from Gerar is not recorded, but was doubtless included in the E narative which is only fragmentarily preserved.

my son, &c.] R.V. marg. *my offspring, nor with my posterity*. The words which are not usual are found together in Job xviii. 19; Isa. xiv. 22; LXX μηδὲ τὸ σπέρμα μου μηδὲ τὸ ὄνομά μου, Lat. *posteris stirpique meae*. The original phrase is alliterative, like our "neither kith nor kin."

the kindness] Referring to the gifts to Abraham in xx. 14, and the free welcome extended to Abraham in xx. 15. Abimelech is desirous to seal these friendly relations by a definite compact. There is an abrupt transition, in *vv.* 25, 26, to occasions of friction.

25. *Abraham reproved*] Disputes about wells are some of the most common causes of strife among the Bedouin tribes. Abraham's complaint is that his servants had dug wells; that Abimelech's servants had

E 26 which Abimelech's servants had violently taken away. And Abimelech said, I know not who hath done this thing: neither didst thou tell me, neither yet heard I of it, but 27 to-day. And Abraham took sheep and oxen, and gave them unto Abimelech; and they two made a covenant. 28 And Abraham set seven ewe lambs of the flock by them- 29 selves. And Abimelech said unto Abraham, What mean these seven ewe lambs which thou hast set by themselves? 30 And he said, These seven ewe lambs shalt thou take of my hand, that it may be a witness unto me, that I have digged 31 this well. Wherefore he called that place Beer-sheba;

taken violent possession of them; that there had been no redress. The occasion of the treaty favoured a settlement of the dispute.

The verbs in *vv.* 25 and 26 are best rendered as frequentatives = "as often as Abraham complained to Abimelech, Abimelech used to reply he was entirely ignorant." Gesen. *Hebr. Gr.* § 112 *rr*.

27. *And Abraham took sheep*, &c.] Abraham makes a gift, according to the custom, at the conclusion of a treaty (cf. 1 Kings xv. 19) and is a pledge of his good faith. He also acknowledges his need of protection from the king.

made a covenant] Cf. xv. 18, xxvi. 31.

28. *seven ewe lambs*] The seven lambs which Abraham here sets apart are to be handed over to Abimelech, if he acknowledges Abraham as the possessor of the well, and ratifies the compact with an oath. The number "seven" (*sheba‘*) is one of the explanations of the name "Beer-sheba."

30. *that it may be a witness*] Abimelech's question and Abraham's answer are probably the technical terms of the usual transaction. The transfer of the seven lambs having taken place, it was a "witness" to the fact that Abraham was acknowledged by Abimelech to have digged the well. There is no mention of document or writing in the compact.

31. *Beer-sheba*] LXX φρέαρ ὁρκισμοῦ: the derivation here given is "because there they sware both of them." The word in Heb. 'they sware" (*nishb‘u*) is the reflexive form of the verb *shaba‘*. This derivation of Beer-sheba, as "the well of swearing," is clearly not a complete explanation of the word. The correct derivation—"th well of seven"—is probably hinted at in Abraham's pledge of the *seven* lambs. At Beer-sheba, there were also "seven" wells, which can even now be identified. But there is a close connexion between the Heb. word "seven," and the Heb. word "to swear"; and if, as seems probable, the Heb. *nishba‘* "to swear" meant originally "to bind oneself by staking, or pledging, seven things," we can see that th well of "seven" and the well of "swearing" were practically identical in significance.

because there they sware both of them. So they made a 32 E
covenant at Beer-sheba: and Abimelech rose up, and
Phicol the captain of his host, and they returned into the
land of the Philistines. | And *Abraham* planted a tamarisk 33 J
tree in Beer-sheba, and called there on the name of the
LORD, the Everlasting God. And Abraham sojourned in 34
the land of the Philistines many days.

And it came to pass after these things, that God did 22 E
prove Abraham, and said unto him, Abraham; and he

Beer-sheba stood on the southernmost boundary of Palestine, at the edge of the desert, about 50 miles S.W. of Jerusalem. In later days it was famous as a sacred place of pilgrimage, Amos v. 5, viii. 14.

32. *returned into the land of the Philistines*] The reference to the Philistines is an anachronism. It is doubtful whether the Philistines occupied S.E. Palestine before the reign of Raamses III (1202—1172 B.C.). See xxvi. 1.

33. *a tamarisk tree*] The *tamarix syriaca*. The Heb. word *êshel* puzzled the versions; LXX ἄρουραν, Lat. *nemus*. Tradition probably connected a famous tamarisk, close to the seven sacred springs, with the site of the sanctuary of Beer-sheba; cf. xxvi. 23—25. See, also, for "tamarisk tree," 1 Sam. xxii. 6, xxxi. 13.

the Everlasting God] Heb. *El-Ôlâm*. See notes on xiv. 18, xvii. 1. "The God of Ages," the name which Abraham here identifies in thought and worship with Jehovah. God does not change, though the defective knowledge of Him in early ages makes way in later time for the fuller Revelation to the Chosen Family.

CH. XXII. (E, J.)

1—19. THE SACRIFICE OF ISAAC. (E.)
20—24. THE GENEALOGY OF NAHOR. (J.)

1—19. From E; but *vv.* 15—18 are, probably, from another source, possibly R. As a piece of simple and vivid narrative, this passage from E's narrative is unsurpassed.

1. *after these things*] An indefinite note of time referring to Isaac's birth and the expulsion of Ishmael: cf. *v.* 20. See note on xv. 1.

God did prove Abraham] "Prove" in the sense of "make trial of," cf. Ex. xv. 25, xvi. 4; Deut. viii. 2, 16; Ps. lxvi. 10. The A.V. had "tempt," in the old English sense of "put to the test"=Lat. *tentare*. On the test of faith and obedience, to which human nature is continually subjected, see the N.T. passages: 1 Cor. x. 13; Heb. xi. 17; James i. 12, 13; 1 Peter i. 6, 7. "Deus tentat, ut doceat: diabolus tentat, ut decipiat" (Augustine *in Joan. Tract.* 30, Serm. 2). It is instructive to compare the "proving" of Abraham, which is here referred directly

GENESIS XXII. 1, 2

E **2** said, Here am I. And he said, Take now thy son, thine only son, whom thou lovest, even Isaac, and get thee into the land of Moriah; and offer him there for a burnt offering

to God Himself, with the "proving" of Job, which, in chaps. i. ii., is brought about by "the Satan."

and said unto him] Presumably in a dream during the night; cf. *v.* 3, "Abraham rose early"; compare xix. 27, xx. 8, xxi. 14.

Here am I] The first instance of this response. Cf. 11, xxvii. 1.

2. *thy son*] Observe the cumulative force of the successive words, "thy son," "only son," "whom thou lovest," "Isaac," indicating the severity of the test about to be applied to Abraham's faith.

only son] Ishmael is here disregarded, as in *vv.* 12 and 16. He is no longer considered one of the true family. The LXX τὸν ἀγαπητόν (Lat. *unigenitum*) is, however, perhaps due to the thought of Ishmael.

into the land of Moriah] Moriah is here the name of a country, containing mountains on one of which Abraham is to offer Isaac. The proper name "Moriah" is found elsewhere only in 2 Chron. iii. 1, "in Mount Moriah," i.e. the hill in Jerusalem, on which was the threshing-floor of Ornan, the Jebusite, where the Angel appeared to David. This was the site of the Temple of Solomon. Obviously the expression, "the land of Moriah," and the reference to the mountains in it, cannot here denote Jerusalem. Jerusalem was a town in the days of the patriarchs (see xiv. 18). More probably the Chronicler, in 2 Chron. iii. 1, has recorded the popular tradition of his own time, according to which the scene of the appearance to David and the site of the temple at Jerusalem were identified with the place of Isaac's sacrifice; and the name "Moriah," occurring in this passage of Genesis was therefore popularly, although inaccurately, assigned to the Temple hill.

What "the land of Moriah" was, we can no longer determine. Possibly the word "Moriah" is the Heb. adaptation of some earlier name, which was lost in the transmission of the story. The name Moriah probably contains a play upon the words meaning "to see" and "Jehovah," cf. *v.* 14. It provided a puzzle to the versions. Lat. *terra visionis*, Sym. γῇ ὀπτασίας, Aq. τὴν γῆν τὴν καταφανῆ, LXX τὴν γῆν τὴν ὑψηλήν.

The Syriac Peshitto renders, "the land of the Amorites," with which agrees the conjecture of Dillmann and Ball. Tuch and Bleek conjectured "the land of Moreh," cf. Gen. xii. 6; but the Hebron district of "the land of Moreh" would be much too close to Beer-sheba to suit the description in *v.* 4. Hence Wellhausen's conjecture "the land of the Hamorites" (i.e. Shechem: cf. Gen. xxxiv. and Judges ix. 28). Probably the name is irrecoverable by conjecture. Rabbinic interpretations called it "the place of fear," or "of worship." Joseph. *Ant.* I. § 13, τὸ Μόριον ὄρος.

for a burnt offering] A whole burnt-offering, viz. an offering of complete dedication to God. It was wholly consumed in the fire, as

GENESIS XXII. 2—7

upon one of the mountains which I will tell thee of. And 3 E
Abraham rose early in the morning, and saddled his ass,
and took two of his young men with him, and Isaac his
son; and he clave the wood for the burnt offering, and
rose up, and went unto the place of which God had told
him. On the third day Abraham lifted up his eyes, and 4
saw the place afar off. And Abraham said unto his young 5
men, Abide ye here with the ass, and I and the lad will
go yonder; and we will worship, and come again to you.
And Abraham took the wood of the burnt offering, and laid 6
it upon Isaac his son; and he took in his hand the fire and
the knife; and they went both of them together. And 7
Isaac spake unto Abraham his father, and said, My father:
and he said, Here am I, my son. And he said, Behold,
the fire and the wood: but where is the lamb for a burnt

distinct from an offering in which the offerers themselves participated:
see note on viii. 20. It was a propitiatory offering: cf. Lev. i. 4.

3. *And Abraham rose early*, &c.] Abraham's prompt unquestioning
obedience is here depicted in the description of his successive acts.
The mental struggle is passed over in silence. Calvin notes: "quasi
oculis clausis pergit quo jubetur." Cf. Wisdom x. 5, "wisdom knew
the righteous man and preserved him blameless unto God, and kept
him strong when his heart yearned towards his child."

the wood] Implying that the place of the sacrifice would be treeless.

the place] See note on xii. 6. Was it a local sanctuary?

of which God had told him] Cf. *v.* 2, the narrative is condensed.
The names of the "place" and the mountain spoken of by God are not
recorded.

4. *On the third day...afar off*] The "place" was on a lofty
eminence visible at a distance. Presumably "the third day" indicates
a journey of 30 or 40 miles. The journey from Beer-sheba to Jerusalem
is computed to take less than 24 hours.

5. *I and the lad*] Abraham's words are either intended to conceal
his intention; or they imply hope, against all hope. "Come again,"
i.e. come back to the young men. He will not let the servants know
the nature of the expedition.

6. *laid it upon Isaac*] Isaac carries the heavy weight of the wood;
Abraham, the more dangerous burden of the fire (i.e. a brazier) and the
knife.

7. *And Isaac spake*] The pathos of the narrative reaches its climax
in the simple expression of boyish curiosity, indicating a knowledge of
his father's regular usages of sacrifice.

"Here am I, my son?" is a little formal as a rendering. It is
equivalent to a father's reply: "Well, boy, what is it?"

E 8 offering? And Abraham said, God will ¹provide himself the lamb for a burnt offering, my son: so they went 9 both of them together. And they came to the place which God had told him of; and Abraham built the altar there, and laid the wood in order, and bound Isaac his son, and 10 laid him on the altar, upon the wood. And Abraham stretched forth his hand, and took the knife to slay his son. 11 And the angel of the LORD called unto him out of heaven, and said, Abraham, Abraham: and he said, Here am I.

¹ Heb. *see for himself.*

8. *provide himself*] Heb. *see for himself*, cf. xli. 33. Abraham's words express his self-control and his faith, and have a reference to *v.* 14. The provision by God of a lamb for a burnt-offering lies at the root of the interpretation of the present passage in its typical application to the Sacrifice of Christ. Cf. the mention of the Lamb in John i. 29, 36; 1 Peter i. 19; Rev. v. 12. The present passage is the first Lesson for the morning of Good Friday.

so they went...together] In the brief words of this simple and moving description is compressed a world of intense feeling. Cf. a similar phrase in 2 Kings ii. 6, 8.

9. *which God had told him of*] See *vv.* 1, 2.

built the altar there] Possibly referring to the altar of some well-known spot. Cf. note on the word "place," *v.* 3, xii. 6. For the definite article, see viii. 7. The altar needed rebuilding.

laid the wood in order] The technical phrase for arranging the wood on an altar of sacrifice. See Num. xxiii. 4; 1 Kings xviii. 33.

bound] LXX συμποδίσας. Another technical word, for binding the limbs of the sacrificial animal, only found here in O.T. Amongst the Jews the sacrifice of Isaac was known as "the binding (*'akêdah*) of Isaac." See Special Note at the end of the chapter. The submission of Isaac is not expressed, but implied. Isaac's age, according to the narrative of E in this chapter, appears to be that of a mere lad. Without the necessary recognition of the different sources from which the patriarchal narrative is derived, it has been supposed, on the strength of xxi. 34 and xxii. 1, that Isaac was now a young man. The note of Calvin, to whom the analysis of Genesis was unknown, is therefore justified: "atqui scimus tunc fuisse mediae aetatis, ut vel patre esset robustior, vel saltem par ad resistendum si viribus certandum esset.... Mira quidem est Mosis in narrando simplicitas, sed quae plus vehementiae continet quam si tragice omnia exaggeret."

10. *slay*] The technical sacrificial word for killing the victim by cutting its throat.

11. *the angel of the Lord*] See note on xvi. 11.

Abraham, Abraham] For the reiteration of the name, denoting

GENESIS XXII. 12—14

And he said, Lay not thine hand upon the lad, neither do 12 E thou any thing unto him: for now I know that thou fearest God, seeing thou hast not withheld thy son, thine only son, from me. And Abraham lifted up his eyes, and looked, 13 and ¹behold, behind *him* a ram caught in the thicket by his horns: and Abraham went and took the ram, and offered him up for a burnt offering in the stead of his son. And Abraham called the name of that place ²Jehovah- 14 jireh: as it is said to this day, In the mount of the LORD

---

¹ Or, according to many ancient authorities, *behold a* (Heb. *one*) *ram caught* ² That is, *The LORD will see*, or, *provide*.

---

special earnestness, compare xlvi. 2; Ex. iii. 4; 1 Sam. iii. 10; Acts ix. 4. Abraham's act is arrested at the last possible moment. The sacrifice of Isaac was practically completed, when the hand of Abraham raised the knife over his son. The moral surrender had been complete.

12. *for now I know*] Abraham has stood the test. Actual experience has justified Divine foreknowledge. The Angel of the LORD is here identified with the Almighty. By the words "lay not thine hand, &c.," Jehovah proclaims to Abraham and to his descendants His abhorrence of the cruelty of child sacrifice.

hast not withheld] The recollection of these words possibly underlies the phrase of St Paul in Rom. viii. 32, "He that spared not his own Son, but delivered him up for us all."

13. *and behold, behind* him] The R.V. marginal note refers to a difference of reading, arising from the similarity of the two Heb. letters for *r* (ר) and (ד) *d*. The word, rendered "behind," would, by the alteration of *r* into *d*, appear with the same consonants as the word meaning "one": and this reading is found in the LXX, Sam., Peshitto, Targums, and many Heb. MSS. But the text, "behind *him*," is to be preferred.

For the sudden appearance of a ram, cf. the similar suddenness of appearance in xviii. 2, xxi. 19. God's gifts may be near at hand, and not yet discerned; the recognition of God's voice brings a sudden realization of His gifts.

a ram] The conjecture that the word rendered "ram" (*ayil*) should, with different vowel points, be rendered a "hart" (*ayyâl*) is not to be approved. For (1) wild animals were not usually sacrificed by Hebrews; (2) *vv.* 7 and 8, by the mention of "lamb," prepare us for "a ram"; (3) the word "thicket" seems to imply the twisted horns of a ram being entangled in brushwood.

14. *Jehovah-jireh*] i.e. *the LORD will see*, or, *provide*. The name which Abraham here gives to the place combines the thought of

ER 15 ¹it shall be provided. | And the angel of the LORD called
16 unto Abraham a second time out of heaven, and said, By
myself have I sworn, saith the LORD, because thou hast
done this thing, and hast not withheld thy son, thine only

¹ Or, *he shall be seen*

Jehovah's continual and constant watchfulness with that of His special response to Abraham's utterance of faith, *v.* 8, "God will provide himself the lamb," in answer to Isaac's question, "where is the lamb?"

as it is said to this day] That is, it became a proverbial expression, cf. x. 9. What is meant by "to this day," is uncertain: but very possibly it refers to a proverb current among the Israelites, in connexion with the hill on which the Temple stood.

In the mount of the LORD] This phrase is used of the Temple hill in Ps. xxiv. 3; Isaiah ii. 3, xxx. 29.

it shall be provided] R.V. marg. *he shall be seen*. Presumably the proverb here mentioned combined two ideas: (1) that Jehovah was seen, or revealed Himself, in the mount; (2) that the lesson of Jehovah's provision for those that love and trust Him was taught to Abraham, the father of the faithful, in this mount.

The text is not free from doubt. According to other punctuations, we have two possible alternative renderings: (1) "in the mountain Jehovah is seen, or is revealed," so LXX (ἐν τῷ ὄρει Κύριος ὤφθη); (2) "in the mountain Jehovah seeth, or provideth." With a slight alteration of text, Gunkel renders: "for he said, To-day, in this mountain, God provideth." According to the same scholar the name of the mountain was *Jeruel*, or *Jeriel* (2 Chron. xx. 16). This he compares with Ariel, an old name of Jerusalem mentioned in Isa. xxix. 1, 7.

15. Verses 15—18 are probably taken from another version of the same story. They are inferior in literary excellence, and probably represent a later amplification.

a second time] The renewal and ratification of the blessing to Abraham expresses the Divine recognition of the patriarch's faith. The blessing, previously granted, is here renewed as a reward for obedience (*v.* 18).

16. *By myself have I sworn*] Cf. Ex. xxxii. 13; Isai. xlv. 23; Heb. vi. 13—17.

The remembrance of this oath is frequently invoked, cf. xxiv. 7, xxvi. 3, l. 24; Ps. cv. 9, "the covenant which he made with Abraham, and his oath unto Isaac"; Luke i. 73, "the oath which he sware unto Abraham our father."

saith the LORD] Lit. "the Oracle" or "revelation of Jehovah"; a rare expression in narrative, cf. Numb. xiv. 28, 1 Sam. ii. 30; but common in the Prophets, e.g. Jer. xviii. 5. The Angel, speaking in the first person, identifies Himself with Jehovah (cf. xvi. 10, xxi. 18, xxxi. 13). The introduction of the prophetic formula, "Oracle of Jehovah," into the words spoken by the Angel impersonating Jehovah, is peculiar.

son: that in blessing I will bless thee, and in multiplying 17 R
I will multiply thy seed as the stars of the heaven, and
as the sand which is upon the sea shore; and thy seed
shall possess the gate of his enemies; and in thy seed 18
shall all the nations of the earth ¹be blessed; because thou
hast obeyed my voice. | So Abraham returned unto his 19 E
young men, and they rose up and went together to Beer-
sheba; and Abraham dwelt at Beer-sheba.

¹ Or, *bless themselves*

17. *that in blessing,* &c.] The language of this benediction combines the substance of previous blessings pronounced upon the patriarch,
under three heads: (1) multiplication of seed; (2) victory over enemies;
(3) universal happiness.

bless] Cf. xii. 2.

as the stars of the heaven] Cf. xv. 5.

as the sand] Cf. xiii. 16.

the gate of his enemies] See note on xxiv. 60. The phrase denotes
conquest. LXX reads πόλεις, both here and in xxiv. 60.

18. *in thy seed*] See note on xii. 3. The words might be also
rendered "by thy seed."

be blessed] Better, as R.V. marg., *bless themselves*. See notes on
xii. 3, xviii. 18, xxvi. 4.

because thou hast obeyed] Lit. "because thou hast heard," or "listened
to." God's word may be a sound which is not heard; or it may be
a sound which is heard, but not listened to; or it may be a sound which
is heard, listened to, and obeyed.

19. *returned unto his young men*] See *v.* 5. It is characteristic of
the reserve of the writer, that no mention is made of joy or congratula-
tion or relief.

Beer-sheba] See xxi. 31. Abraham was dwelling at Beer-sheba at the
time when these things happened.

20—24. THE GENEALOGY OF NAHOR (J).

In this genealogy it is to be noted, (1) that the home of Nahor and
his sons is not Ur, but *Aram Naharaim*, as in xxiv. 10; (2) that the
sons of Nahor, like those of Ishmael (xxv. 13—16), Esau (xxxvi. 15—
19), and Jacob, are twelve in number, of whom eight are born to his
legitimate wife Milcah, and four to his concubine Reumah; (3) that the
names of the sons represent tribes, or tribal dwelling-places, in the
Aramaean, or Syrian, region on the N.E. of Palestine. The genealogy
seems to represent a recollection of the traditional names of the prehistoric ancestors of the Hebrew immigrants. Probably the introduction
of the genealogy at this point is due to the mention of Rebekah in *v.* 23,
which prepares the way for the story in xxiv. (J).

J 20   And it came to pass after these things, that it was told
Abraham, saying, Behold, Milcah, she also hath borne
21 children unto thy brother Nahor; Uz his firstborn, and
22 Buz his brother, and Kemuel the father of Aram; and
Chesed, and Hazo, and Pildash, and Jidlaph, and Bethuel.
23 And Bethuel begat Rebekah: these eight did Milcah bear
24 to Nahor, Abraham's brother. And his concubine, whose
name was Reumah, she also bare Tebah, and Gaham, and
Tahash, and Maacah.

20. *after these things*] Cf. *v.* 1.

Milcah] See xi. 27, 29. Nahor's marriage with his niece probably represents the fusion of two tribes.

21. *Uz his firstborn*] In x. 23 (P) Uz is the firstborn of Aram. Uz, as a locality in the Syrian region, is mentioned in Assyrian inscriptions. It may denote a branch of an Aramaean tribe, the *Uṣṣâ* of Shalmaneser II. It appears as the birthplace of Job (i. 1). Whether it is the same Uz as is mentioned in Jeremiah xxv. 20, Lam. iv. 21, is doubtful. Another, Edomite, Uz is mentioned in Gen. xxxvi. 28.

Buz] See Jer. xxv. 23, where the mention of Buz with Dedan and Tema seems to point to the borders of the Arabian desert. Elihu, the friend of Job, is a native of Buz (Job xxxii. 2).

Aram] Here the son of Kemuel and nephew of Uz: in x. 23 (P), Aram, the son of Shem, is the father of Uz. Evidently the traditions embodying the relationship of the tribes of the desert were current in very various forms.

22. *Chesed*] Presumably, not to be confounded with the ancestor of the S. Babylonian people, the *Chasdim*, or "Chaldees," mentioned in xi. 31 (P). More probably, the Bedouin tribe, mentioned in 2 Kings xxiv. 2, Job i. 17, as "the Chaldeans," quite distinct from the Chesed of Arpachshad (x. 22).

23. *Bethuel*] See xxiv. 15.

Rebekah] See chap. xxiv. No place, or clan, of this name is mentioned in the O.T.

24. *Reumah*] The children of the concubine denote a less intimate tribal relationship than the children of the legal wife.

Maacah] See 2 Sam. x. 6. A region to the north of Mount Hermon; cf. the mention of the Maacathites in Josh. xiii. 11, 13.

SPECIAL NOTE ON THE SACRIFICE OF ISAAC

This episode occupies an important place in the religious teaching of Genesis. It is (1) the crowning test applied to the faith of the patriarch Abraham, and (2) the supreme example of the difference between the God who revealed Himself to the patriarchs, and the gods of the nature-religions of the Semitic peoples.

It has, however, raised difficulties in the minds of many readers, who have been unable to reconcile the command to offer Isaac for a burnt-offering with their conception of a good God. The following points deserve, in this connexion, a careful consideration.

1. *Human Sacrifice.* This was a religious custom widely prevalent among the ancient Semites.

(a) *The Israelites.* Besides the present passage, there are to be found in the Pentateuch several passages strongly condemnatory of the usage (Levit. xviii. 21, xx. 2, 5; Deut. xii. 31, xviii. 10). But it is evident from the instances of Jephthah's daughter (Judg. xi. 29 ff.), and of Hiel's sons (1 Kings xvi. 34) that the practice was not easily eradicated. The prophets denounced it: "Shall I give my firstborn for my transgression, the fruit of my body for the sin of my soul?" (Micah vi. 7). In the dark days of the later kings, and subsequently, we gather that the people shewed an evil tendency to revert to this barbarity (see 2 Kings xvi. 3, xxi. 6, xxiii. 10; Isai. lvii. 5; Jer. vii. 31, xix. 5; Ezek. xvi. 20, 21, xx. 26, xxiii. 37: cf. Ps. cvi. 37, 38).

It hardly admits of doubt that the ancient laws of Israel, by which the firstborn were dedicated to God (Ex. xxii. 29), and by which an animal was to be sacrificed in order to redeem the firstborn son (Ex. xxxiv. 20), point back to the custom of an earlier age, in which the primitive Hebrews had practised the sacrifice of the firstborn. The redemption of the firstborn with a lamb at the Feast of the Passover (Ex. xiii. 12—15) has been considered by some to be traceable to a similar origin.

(b) *Other Nations.* Instances of the practice in connexion with Moloch worship are mentioned in passages quoted above from the O.T. Mesha, the king of Moab, in order to propitiate his god, Chemosh, and obtain the defeat of the Israelite invaders, sacrificed his eldest son (2 Kings iii. 27). In 2 Kings xvii. 31 "the Sepharvites" are said to "have burnt their children in the fire to Adrammelech and Anammelech, the gods of Sepharvaim."

The excavations, carried out in recent years at Gezer, Megiddo, and Taanach, have shewn that the practice was followed by "the primitive Semitic inhabitants of Palestine, and even, at least at Megiddo, in the Israelite period" (Driver's *Schweich Lectures*, pp. 68, 69).

There is evidence to shew that human sacrifice prevailed from the earliest times in Egypt, though the victims may generally have been taken from the ranks of the enemy (cf. Handcock, p. 75, quoting Budge's *Osiris*, pp. 197 ff.).

2. *The Command to sacrifice Isaac.* We may assume, then, that in Abraham's time the religious custom of human sacrifice prevailed among the peoples of the land. We have to think of the patriarch as he was, as a man of his own time and race. God spoke to him in language that he could understand. God proved his faith by a test, which, horrible as it sounds to our ears, was consonant with the feelings and traditions he had inherited from his forefathers. The command to sacrifice Isaac, in the year 2100 B.C., would not have suggested anything outrageous or abominable, as it does to our minds. We must remember that,

startling as it may appear, it would have seemed to the ancient inhabitants of Palestine far more wonderful that Abraham's God should have interposed to prevent the sacrifice, than that He should have given the order for its being offered. The command to sacrifice his son corresponded to the true religious instinct to offer up his best and highest.

3. *The Triumph of Abraham's Faith.* We are told that "God did prove Abraham." In the presence of the people of the land who practised this custom, would not conscience, the voice of God, again and again have whispered: "thou art not equal to the supremest surrender; thou art not prepared to give up 'thy son, thine only son, whom thou lovest, even Isaac'"? The command, then, to offer up Isaac came as a threefold test of faith: (i) did Abraham love and obey his God as sincerely as the heathen around him loved and obeyed their gods? (ii) did he, in the conflict of emotions, put his affection for his son before his love for his God? (iii) could he himself undertake to obey a command of his God, which was in direct conflict with that same God's repeated promises that in Isaac should his name be called[1]? It was this last which constituted the most acute trial of Abraham's faith. But he stood the test; and in the surrender of everything, will, affections, hope, and reason, he simply obeyed, trusting, that, as a son had been granted to him in his old age, when he was as good as one dead, so, in God's good providence, His promises would yet somehow be fulfilled, and Isaac would live.

The completeness of this faith was tested up to the moment when his hand was outstretched to commit the fatal act.

4. *The Nature of God.* The prohibition of the sacrifice of Isaac proclaimed a fundamental contrast between the God of Abraham and the gods of the nations round about. The knowledge of the God of Abraham was progressive: there was continually more to be learned of His Will and Nature. It was now shewn that human sacrifice could not any longer be thought to be acceptable to Him.

There was a true element in sacrifice which in Abraham's case had been tested to the uttermost. This was the surrender of the will and of the heart to God. The spirit of the offerer, not the material of the offering is the essence of sacrifice. This is the anticipation of Israelite prophecy (1 Sam. xv. 22; Isai. i. 11 ff.; Jer. vi. 20; Amos v. 21).

There was a false element in the current conceptions of sacrifice, which tended to make its efficacy depend upon material quantity and cost. In the case of a human offering, the suffering, bereavement, and agony, mental and physical, seemed only to augment its value. The Deity that required to be propitiated with human life, was capricious, insatiable and savage. This hideous delusion about God's Nature was finally to be dissipated. God had no pleasure in suffering or in death, in themselves. God was a God of love. Life should be dedicated unto Him, not in cruelty, but in service.

---

[1] Cf. "Nam quasi Deus secum ipse pugnet, puerum ad mortem postulat, in quo spem aeternae salutis proposuit. Itaque hoc posterius mandatum quidam erat fidei interitus" (Calvin).

Sacrifice in the Chosen Family was to be free from the taint of this practice. The substitution of an animal for a human victim was to be the reminder of a transition to a higher phase of morality. The Revelation of the Law of Love was to be traced back by the devout Israelite to the Patriarchal Era, and to the religious experience of Abraham, the founder of the race. The Episode is a spiritual Parable.

5. *The Rights of the Individual.* Among ancient Semitic peoples the rights of the individual were merged in those of the family or the tribe. Life and death were in the hands of the father. Isaac possessed no rights of his own. The same Revelation, that prohibited his sacrifice, proclaimed that every one born in the image of God had individual and inalienable rights and duties. Human personality had a sanctity and a freedom of its own. True sacrifice implied the surrender of self, not of another. The substitution of the ram was the memorial of the abrogation of an inhuman system, which disregarded mercy and outraged humanity.

6. *References in O.T., Apocrypha, and N.T.* There appears to be no other mention in the O.T. of the sacrifice of Isaac. Some have needlessly supposed it is alluded to in Is. xli. 8, "Abraham my friend"; cf. 2 Chron. xx. 7. There is probably a reference to it in Ecclus. xliv. 20, "And when he was proved he was found faithful." Cf. Wisdom x. 5, "Wisdom knew the righteous man...and kept him strong when his heart yearned toward his child." 1 Macc. ii. 52, "Was not Abraham found faithful in temptation?" 4 Macc. xvi. 18—20, "Remember that for the sake of God ye have come into the world...; for whom also our father Abraham made haste to sacrifice his son Isaac, the ancestor of our nation; and Isaac, seeing his father's hand lifting the knife against him, did not shrink." In the N.T. it is twice mentioned: Heb. xi. 17 ff., "By faith Abraham, being tried, offered up Isaac: yea, he that had gladly received the promises was offering up his only begotten son; even he to whom it was said, In Isaac shall thy seed be called: accounting that God is able to raise up even from the dead; from whence he did also in a parable receive him back." James ii. 21, "Was not Abraham our father justified by works, in that he offered up Isaac his son upon the altar?"

7. *Jewish Tradition* found a fertile subject in the 'akêdah, or binding, of Isaac. The following passage from the Targum of Palestine is a good example of Haggadah (i.e. legend, or explanatory tradition): "And they came to the place of which the Lord had told him. And Abraham builded there the altar which Adam had built, which had been destroyed by the waters of the deluge, which Noah had again builded, and which had been destroyed in the age of divisions [i.e. the dispersion of the peoples]. And he set the wood in order upon it, and bound Isaac his son, and laid him on the altar upon the wood. And Abraham stretched out his hand, and took the knife to slay his son. And Isaac answered and said to his father, Bind me properly, lest I tremble from the affliction of my soul, and be cast into the pit of destruction, and there be found profaneness in thy offering. Now the eyes of Abraham looked on the eyes of Isaac; but the eyes of Isaac looked towards the

angels on high, and Isaac beheld them, but Abraham saw them not. And the angels answered on high, Come, behold how these solitary ones who are in the world kill the one the other; he who slays delays not; he who is to be slain reacheth forth his neck. And the Angel of the Lord called to him, &c."

"According to Jose ben Zimra, the idea of tempting Abraham was suggested by Satan who said, 'Lord of the Universe! Here is a man whom thou hast blessed with a son at the age of one hundred years, and yet, amidst all his feasts, he did not offer thee a single dove or young pigeon for a sacrifice' (*Sanh.* 87 *b*; *Gen. R.* LV.). In Jose ben Zimra's opinion, the *'akedah* took place immediately after Isaac's weaning. This however is not the general opinion. According to the Rabbis, the *'akedah* not only coincided with, but was the cause of the death of Sarah, who was informed of Abraham's intention while he and Isaac were on the way to Mount Moriah. Therefore Isaac must then have been thirty-seven years old (*Seder 'Olam Rabbah*, ed. Ratner, p. 6; *Pirke R. El.* XXXI.; *Tanna debe Eliyahu R.* XXVII.)." *Jewish Encycl.* s.v. Isaac.

"The Jews implore the mercy of God by the sacrifice of Isaac, as Christians by the sacrifice of Christ" (Mayor, *Ep. James*, p. 97). The merits of Isaac's submission were regarded as abounding to the credit of the whole race; e.g. "For the merit of Isaac who offered himself upon the altar, the Holy One, blessed be He, will hereafter raise the dead" (*Pesikta Rab. Kahana*, p. 200, ed. Buber).

8. *Patristic References.* In the Fathers, the story was seized upon for purposes of Christian allegory. Isaac is the type of Christ who offers Himself a willing sacrifice. The ram caught in the thicket is the type of Christ fastened to the wood of the cross. Thus according to Procopius of Gaza, the words of the Angel, "seeing thou hast not withheld thy son, thine only son," imply, "neither will I spare my beloved Son for thy sake. For God so loved the world that he gave his only begotten Son... (John iii. 16). Wherefore also Paul did greatly marvel at His goodness, saying, 'Who spared not His own Son, but gave Him up for us all'" (Rom. viii. 32). His note on "the ram" is: "Aries mactatus ab interitu redemit Isaacum; sic Dominus occisus salvavit nos ab impendente aeterna morte" (ed. Migne, *P. G.* 87, Pars 1. p. 391).

Primasius: "Occisus est Isaac quantum ad voluntatem patris pertinet. Deinde redonavit illum Deus patriarchae in parabola, id est, in figura et similitudine passionis Christi...Aries significabat carnem Christi. Isaac oblatus est et non est interfectus sed aries tantum; quia Christus in passione oblatus est, sed divinitas illius impassibilis mansit" (quoted by Westcott, *Ep. Heb.* xi. 19).

The earliest reference occurs in the *Epistle of Barnabas*: "Seeing that there is a commandment in scripture, Whosoever shall not observe the fast shall surely die, the Lord commanded, because He was in His own person about to offer the vessel of His Spirit a sacrifice for our sins, that the type also which was given in Isaac who was offered upon the altar should be fulfilled" (chap. vii.). Lightfoot's *Apostolic Fathers*, p. 251.

And the life of Sarah was an hundred and seven and 23 P
twenty years: these were the years of the life of Sarah.
And Sarah died in Kiriath-arba (the same is Hebron), in 2

Irenaeus speaks of Abraham as "having with a willing mind yielded
up his own only-begotten and beloved son as a sacrifice to God,
in order that God also might be well pleased, on behalf of his seed,
to grant His own only-begotten and beloved Son as a sacrifice with a
view to our redemption" (ed. Stieren, i. p. 572).

St Augustine compares Isaac bearing the wood for the sacrifice with
Christ bearing His cross; while the ram, caught in the thicket, typifies
Jesus crowned with thorns: "Propterea et Isaac, sicut Dominus crucem
suam, ita sibi ligna ad victimae locum quibus fuerat imponendus ipse
portavit...Postremo quia Isaac occidi non oportebat, posteaquam est
pater ferire prohibitus, quis erat ille aries, quo immolato impletum est
significativo sanguine sacrificium? Nempe quando eum vidit Abraham,
cornibus in frutice tenebatur. Quis ergo illo figurabatur, nisi Jesus,
antequam immolaretur, spinis Judaicis coronatus?" (Aug. *De Civ. Dei*,
xvi. c. 32).

CH. XXIII. (P). **1, 2**, THE DEATH OF SARAH; **3—18**, ABRAHAM
PURCHASES FROM EPHRON THE HITTITE THE CAVE AND FIELD
OF MACHPELAH; **19**, HE BURIES SARAH THERE; **20**, ABRAHAM'S
PROPERTY.

THE BURIAL OF SARAH IN THE CAVE OF MACHPELAH.

This chapter is entirely from P, as is shewn by the characteristics of
language, by the frequent repetitions, by the legal and statistical minuteness (e.g. in *vv.* 17, 18), and the mention of Sarah's age. The narrative
preserved the tradition respecting the first possession of Canaanite soil
by the Israelite patriarchs. The veneration of the cave of Machpelah
as the traditional burying-place of the patriarchs will account for the
minuteness with which Abraham's purchase of the famous cave is here
described. It seems to set an anticipatory seal of possession upon the
land of promise. See xxv. 9, 10, xlix. 29—32, l. 13 (P).

The details given in this chapter are a faithful picture of the usages of
the East; but there is nothing to warrant the assertion that they are
peculiarly Babylonian.

1. *the life of Sarah*] Sarah died at the age of 127, 37 years after the
birth of Isaac. Cf. xvii. 1, 17, xxi. 5 (P).

2. *Kiriath-arba (the same is Hebron)*] Cf. xxxv. 27 (P). *Kiriath-
arba* means "the city of four," probably four confederate tribes. It was
the earlier name of Hebron, which itself may mean "Confederation."
The two names are mentioned in Judg. i. 10. In Josh. xiv. 15 and
xv. 13, where the early name is also mentioned, Arba is regarded as
a proper name. For Hebron as one of the dwelling-places of Abraham,
see xiii. 18.

P the land of Canaan: and Abraham came to mourn for
3 Sarah, and to weep for her. And Abraham rose up from
before his dead, and spake unto the children of Heth,
4 saying, I am a stranger and a sojourner with you: give
me a possession of a buryingplace with you, that I may
5 bury my dead out of my sight. And the children of Heth
answered Abraham, saying unto him, Hear us, my lord:
6 thou art [1]a mighty prince among us: in the choice of
our sepulchres bury thy dead; none of us shall withhold
from thee his sepulchre, but that thou mayest bury thy

[1] Heb. *a prince of God*.

Abraham came to mourn for Sarah] As if, at the time of Sarah's death, Abraham had been residing in some different place. He came to "mourn"; and this word refers to the Oriental solemnity of wailing for the departed.

3. *rose up*] The use of this word is explained by the habitual attitude of prostration in mourning. Cf. 2 Sam. xii. 16, 17, 20.

the children of Heth] See note on x. 15. Cf. xxvi. 34, xxvii. 46, xlix. 32 (P). Hittites seem to have amalgamated with native Canaanites. In P, here, and in xxviii. 1, 8, they seem to be identified with Canaanites. The settlements of Hittites in the N. of Palestine may have extended in groups and families southwards. But "the children of Heth" are here spoken of as the native inhabitants of Hebron. Ezekiel regards "Amorites" and "Hittites" as original dwellers in Palestine (xvi. 3, 45).

4. *a stranger and a sojourner*] Abraham describes himself, in a proverbial phrase, as one whose origin is foreign, and whose period of residence is uncertain. LXX πάροικος καὶ παρεπίδημος, Lat. *advena et peregrinus*; cf. Lev. xxv. 23; 1 Chron. xxix. 15; Ps. cv. 12; Heb. xi. 9. The same phrase is employed by St Peter in 1 Pet. ii. 11 to describe the shortness and uncertainty of life on earth, and to indicate that the true citizenship is in heaven. The "stranger," in the Heb., belongs to the phraseology of nomad life; "the sojourner," of settled life.

6. *my lord*] A title of respect, *Adoni* (see note on xviii. 3). LXX Κύριε, Lat. *domine*.

a mighty prince] Heb. *a prince of God*. The Hebrew idiom for the superlative, "a prince worthy to rank with the sons of God"; cf. Deut. xxxiii. 1. For other instances, cf. Ps. xxxvi. 6, "the mountains of God"=A.V. "the great mountains," Ps. lxxx. 10, "cedars of God"=A.V. "the goodly cedars." See note on x. 9, "Like Nimrod, a mighty hunter before the LORD." For "prince," *nâsî*, cf. Ezek. xii. 10, xvii. 21, xxx. 13, xxxii. 29, xxxviii. 2.

in the choice of, &c.] In the complimentary style of Orientals the preliminaries to a business transaction are characterized by the greatest deliberateness and the greatest generosity. The opening proposal is

dead. And Abraham rose up, and bowed himself to the 7 P
people of the land, even to the children of Heth. And 8
he communed with them, saying, If it be your mind that
I should bury my dead out of my sight, hear me, and intreat
for me to Ephron the son of Zohar, that he may give me 9
the cave of Machpelah, which he hath, which is in the end
of his field; for the full price let him give it to me in the
midst of you for the possession of a buryingplace. Now 10
Ephron was sitting in the midst of the children of Heth:
and Ephron the Hittite answered Abraham in the audience

that Abraham should make use of one of the "choicest" Hittite
sepulchres, for the burial of Sarah. Even if the offer was meant
seriously, Abraham will not accept it; he wishes to possess a burial-
place of his own. For the phrase "the choice," cf. Isa. xxii. 7, xxxvii.
24. It means what we should express familiarly as "the pick of."

Probably their complimentary phrase is intended to conceal their
dislike of selling a grave.

7. *bowed himself*] Abraham's humble demeanour towards the
people of the land doubtless conforms to the elaborate usages of
Oriental bargaining. But it is also probably here emphatically recorded as indicating Abraham's loneliness among the people of the
land, and, therefore, in ironical contrast with the time when his
descendants would conquer the Canaanites and possess their country.

the people of the land] Cf. xlii. 6 (P). This is the phrase, *'am
ha-âreṣ*, so common in post-exilic literature for "the heathen": compare "peoples of the land," Ezra x. 2, 11; Neh. x. 28, 30.

8. *communed with*] Heb. "spake with." The word "communed"
is unnecessarily formal as a translation, cf. xviii. 33.

9. *the cave of Machpelah*] Machpelah is not the name of the cave,
but of the locality; cf. 17, xlix. 30, l. 12. The old explanation that the
cave was so called, because it was "a double cave," has therefore been
questioned; but the LXX and the Lat. both render Machpelah as if it
were the equivalent of "double," LXX τὸ σπήλαιον τὸ διπλοῦν, Vulg.
speluncam duplicem. The name in the Hebrew always has the article,
as an appellative or descriptive noun. The tradition of the cave
being a double one is continuously maintained. Its correctness is
indisputable.

in the end of his field] Abraham here only asks for the cave at one
end of the field of Machpelah.

for the full price] Lit. "for full silver"; cf. 1 Chron. xxi. 22. The
payment was to be full value and in good money. See note on *v.* 16.
The expression is one which was also current in the Assyrian language.

10. *audience*] Lit. "ears," as in *vv.* 13, 16. The presence of
witnesses is evidently requisite for the validity of the transaction: cf.
Ruth iv. 9—11.

P of the children of Heth, even of all that went in at the gate
11 of his city, saying, Nay, my lord, hear me: the field give I thee, and the cave that is therein, I give it thee; in the presence of the sons of my people give I it thee: bury thy
12 dead. And Abraham bowed himself down before the
13 people of the land. And he spake unto Ephron in the audience of the people of the land, saying, But if thou wilt, I pray thee, hear me: I will give the price of the
14 field; take it of me, and I will bury my dead there. And
15 Ephron answered Abraham, saying unto him, My lord, hearken unto me: a piece of land worth four hundred shekels of silver, what is that betwixt me and thee? bury
16 therefore thy dead. And Abraham hearkened unto Ephron;

all that went in at the gate of his city] Cf. *v.* 18. A technical phrase to denote full citizens. The gate was the place of popular assembly for the elders of a city; cf. xix. 1.

A similar phrase occurs in xxxiv. 24, "all that went out at the gate." The classical illustration of business transactions conducted at "the gate" of a city is to be found in the Book of Ruth, chap. iv. 1 ff.

11. *the field give I thee*, &c.] As in *v.* 6, we have here the complimentary style of bargaining. Observe the successive stages: Abraham in *v.* 9 asks to buy the cave only; Ephron in *v.* 11 offers to give the whole field and the cave in it for nothing; Abraham in *v.* 13 offers to pay for the field; Ephron in *v.* 15 mentions the price for the land; Abraham in *v.* 16 duly pays for the field and the cave (*v.* 17).

12. *bowed himself*] See note on *v.* 7. He had been sitting, while Ephron was speaking.

13. *But if thou wilt*] Abraham answers in short, broken sentences, acknowledging the generous offer, but insisting on the payment of the price. Here, however, he makes an offer for "the field," not merely for "the cave in the end of the field"; cf. *v.* 9. He politely declines to notice the suggestion of a gift, but offers to buy.

15. *worth four hundred shekels of silver*] About £55. See note on xx. 16. On the Hebrew value of a *shekel*, cf. Ex. xxx. 13, Ezek. xlv. 12. In 2 Sam. xxiv. 24 David buys the threshing-floor and the oxen of Araunah for 50 shekels of silver. In the Code of Hammurabi a hireling would not receive more than 1 shekel a month as wages (S. A. Cook, p. 172).

what is that betwixt me and thee?] Ephron has mentioned a full price; he is poor, Abraham rich: the figure could not possibly be a hindrance to the bargain. The important thing is that he, the owner, is willing to sell. Abraham will, therefore, of course purchase.

GENESIS XXIII. 16—20

and Abraham weighed to Ephron the silver, which he had P
named in the audience of the children of Heth, four hundred shekels of silver, current *money* with the merchant.
So the field of Ephron, which was in Machpelah, which 17
was before Mamre, the field, and the cave which was
therein, and all the trees that were in the field, that were
in all the border thereof round about, were made sure unto 18
Abraham for a possession in the presence of the children
of Heth, before all that went in at the gate of his city.
And after this, Abraham buried Sarah his wife in the cave 19
of the field of Machpelah before Mamre (the same is
Hebron), in the land of Canaan. And the field, and the 20
cave that is therein, were made sure unto Abraham for
a possession of a buryingplace by the children of Heth.

16. *weighed*] The scales were ready. "Weighed" is the appropriate word for the payment of money in days when money was not coined. Coined money seems not to have been in use among the Israelites before the Exile. The price of an article was reckoned by the weight of metal —silver or bronze—given in exchange for it. The metal might consist of bars or rings. Possibly in Josh. vii. 21, "a wedge of gold" was a bar, or ingot. For other instances in which the word for "to pay" is in the Hebrew "to weigh," cf. 1 Kings xx. 39; Isa. lv. 2 ("spend"); Jer. xxxii. 9, 10; Zech. xi. 12. Sayce (quoted by Skinner, p. 338, n.) mentions evidence for "shekels stamped with a seal" in the period of Hammurabi (*Cont. Rev.* Aug. 1907).

silver, current money with the merchant] Lit. "silver passing over to the merchant," i.e. pieces of good metal used in commercial exchange. LXX τετρακόσια δίδραχμα ἀργυρίου δοκίμου ἐμπόροις, Lat. *quadringentos siclos argenti probatae monetae publicae*.

17. *So the field of Ephron*] This and the following verses contain, in language of legal minuteness, the description of the purchase. The sentence probably represents the form of a deed of sale, such as was included in Hebrew contracts. Similar minute details are found in Babylonian legal deeds of sale. Notice the particular mention of "the field," "the cave," "all the trees," "all the border," "made sure," "in the presence of," "all that went in at the gate of his city."

before Mamre] i.e. "in front of" = "to the east of," as in *v*. 19, cf. xvi. 12, xxv. 18; Num. xxi. 11; Deut. xxxii. 49 ("over against"). For Mamre, a locality either identified with, or contiguous to, Hebron, cf. xiii. 18, xxxv. 27.

18. *all that went in at*] See note on *v*. 10. The necessary witnesses of the transaction. There is no document to be attested.

20. *were made sure*] This verse repeats and summarizes the transaction which for all subsequent ages symbolized to the Israelites

J 24 And Abraham was old, *and* well stricken in age: and
2 the Lord had blessed Abraham in all things. And Abraham said unto his servant, the elder of his house, that ruled over all that he had, Put, I pray thee, thy hand under

their ancestral connexion with, and sacred rights in, the land of Canaan.

a buryingplace] Besides Sarah there were buried in the cave of Machpelah, Abraham (xxv. 9), Isaac (xxxv. 27, 29), Rebekah and Leah (xlix. 31), Jacob (l. 13).

The cave, which is traditionally identified with the burying-place of Abraham, is still regarded with immense veneration by the Mahommedans. A large mosque has been erected over it. In 1869 the Prussian Crown Prince Frederick, and in 1881 the late King Edward VII, who was then Prince of Wales, received permission to visit the cave. But, as a rule, Christians are not allowed to view it.

Ch. XXIV. The Story of Rebekah (J).

This chapter, which gives one of the most vivid descriptions of the unchanging features of Oriental life to be found in the O.T., is from J. The narrative falls into four divisions:

(1) **1—9.** Abraham's commission to his servant.
(2) **10—28.** The servant and Rebekah at the well.
(3) **29—53.** The betrothal of Rebekah.
(4) **54—67.** Abraham's servant brings Rebekah to Isaac.

That the story may figuratively preserve a tradition of the amalgamation of Aramaean clans with the main Hebrew body is quite probable. But the picturesque details of the narrative are drawn from the life, and are evidently based on personal experience.

1—9. Abraham's Commission to his Servant.

1. *well stricken in age*] Cf. xviii. 11. The Hebrew phrase means "going in days," just as we should say "advanced in years." Cf. Luke i. 7.

had blessed] Cf. v. 35.

2. *his servant, the elder of his house*] This servant has very generally been identified with the Eliezer mentioned in xv. 2. The identity is nowhere explicitly stated; but it should be noted that chap. xv. is derived from E, while this chapter comes from J, and the absence of any reference to Eliezer by name need not surprise us.

"The elder of his house," not necessarily the "eldest" of his house servants, but the one of chief authority and dignity (cf. l. 7), who, if there was no heir, would succeed to the property.

that ruled over all that he had] i.e. a trusted slave who acted as the steward of Abraham's property: see note on xv. 4. Cf. the

my thigh: and I will make thee swear by the LORD, the 3
God of heaven and the God of the earth, that thou shalt
not take a wife for my son of the daughters of the
Canaanites, among whom I dwell: but thou shalt go unto 4
my country, and to my kindred, and take a wife for my
son Isaac. And the servant said unto him, Peradventure 5

description of Joseph in xxxix. 4, 22; Ps. cv. 21; and of Ziba in
2 Sam. ix. 2—13 and xvi. 1—4.

Put...under my thigh] For this symbolical act, compare the request made by Jacob in xlvii. 29, where, in the expectation of death, he binds Joseph by the solemn pledge of this sign. Presumably Abraham is expecting his death; and he causes his servant to swear in the most solemn way that he will carry out his master's wish.

The words "under my thigh" probably contain a survival of a very ancient piece of symbolism. The word "thigh" is rendered "loins" in xlvi. 26, Ex. i. 5. The phrase here seems to refer to the organs of generation, and also, possibly, to the covenant rite of circumcision. The appeal is made to those who hereafter should be born, on the one hand, to attest the oath, and, on the other, to avenge its violation. Similar symbolic acts have been found to exist among other primitive races. A custom like this long outlives the recollection of its original significance. The ritual remains binding; its purpose may be forgotten.

3. *the God of heaven...earth*] This solemn title of Jehovah as God of the whole universe is more common in later Hebrew writings; cf. Ezra v. 11. This form of adjuration indicates the conviction of the writer that the God of the Hebrews was the God of the whole world, not merely of a particular locality or nation: compare xviii. 25. No change of country, no lapse of time, would constitute an exemption from the binding character of the oath.

of the daughters of the Canaanites] The dread of the marriage of an Israelite with a Canaanite which is found here, is also expressed in xxvi. 34, 35, xxvii. 46; Ex. xxxiv. 16; Deut. vii. 3; Ezra ix. 2. For "Canaanite," cf. x. 18, 19, xii. 6, xiii. 7 (J).

Religious feeling underlies this prohibition. The purity of the Hebrew race is to be maintained. Intermarriage would involve participation in religious rites. Separateness would give a corresponding freedom from moral contamination.

4. *my country...kindred*] Here, as in xxviii. 2 (P), the country and kindred of Abraham are to be sought, not in Ur of the Chaldees, but in the land of Haran, or Paddan-aram; cf. *v.* 7.

take a wife for my son Isaac] It was customary for the father to select a bride for his son; cf. xxxiv. 4; Judg. xiv. 2. The same custom prevailed in Babylon, as appears from the Code of Hammurabi, § 155, "if a man betroth a maiden to his son," &c.

" Marriage between cousins has been and still is particularly common

J the woman will not be willing to follow me unto this land: must I needs bring thy son again unto the land from 6 whence thou camest? And Abraham said unto him, Beware thou that thou bring not my son thither again. 7 The LORD, the God of heaven, that took me from my father's house, and from the land of my nativity, and that spake unto me, and that sware unto me, saying, Unto thy seed will I give this land; he shall send his angel before thee, and thou shalt take a wife for my son from 8 thence. And if the woman be not willing to follow thee, then thou shalt be clear from this my oath; only thou 9 shalt not bring my son thither again. And the servant put his hand under the thigh of Abraham his master, and 10 sware to him concerning this matter. And the servant

in the East (cp. Gen. xxiv. 4, xxix. 19; 1 Kings xiv. 31 and xv. 2), and the tie between them is closer and more sacred than that between an ordinary couple" (Burckhardt, *Ar. Prov.*, quoted in Stanley Cook, p. 99).

5. *bring...again*] Here and in *vv.* 6 and 8 and xxii. 5 the word "again" is used for "back." Abraham's tone is that of a man who is on his death-bed.

7. *the God of heaven*] The LXX adds "and the God of the earth," from *v.* 3. The phrase "the God of heaven" occurs in Ezra v. 12; Neh. i. 4, 5, ii. 4; Jonah i. 9; Tobit v. 16.

the land of my nativity] See xii. 1 (J). The land of Haran is clearly intended.

that sware unto me, &c.] The reference is to xii. 7; cf. also xiii. 15, xv. 18, xxii. 16.

he shall send his angel] It is noteworthy that Abraham does not here speak of Jehovah being present with the servant on his mission. The servant of Abraham will be guided by "the messenger, or angel," of Abraham's God. For "the angel of Jehovah" going before His people, cf. Ex. xiv. 19, xxiii. 20, xxxii. 34; Ps. xci. 11.

8. *thou shalt be clear from this my oath*] Cf. *v.* 41. The word "clear" is used in the sense of "innocent," or "guiltless," as in Josh. ii. 17, "we will be guiltless of this thine oath." "Clear" in this sense is old English. Cf. Shakespeare, *Macb.* I. 7, "...this Duncan...hath been so *clear* in his great office, that his virtues will plead like angels."

9. *concerning this matter*] Lit. "according to this word."

It has been supposed that the account of Abraham's death, according to J, followed at this point, and, if so, it was omitted by the compiler, who inserted by preference the account from P, in xxv. 7—11. It is pointed out that (1) the oath is administered to the servant, instead

took ten camels, of the camels of his master, and departed; [1]having all goodly things of his master's in his hand: and he arose, and went to [2]Mesopotamia, unto the city of Nahor. And he made the camels to kneel down without the city 11

> [1] Or, *for all the goods of his master were in his hand*
> [2] Heb. *Aram-naharaim*, that is, *Aram of the two rivers*.

of a simple order, in expectation of immediate death, cf. xlvii. 31; (2) the difficulties in *v.* 67 suggest that some alteration of the text has there been made, in order to harmonize the narrative with the subsequent mention of Abraham's death in chap. xxv.

10—28. REBEKAH AT THE WELL.

10. *ten camels*] The largeness of this retinue is intended (1) to impress strangers with the reality and value of the proposed connexion by marriage: (2) to provide for the adequate means of conveying the bride and her attendant hand-maidens, cf. *v.* 61.

having all...hand] R.V. marg. *for all the goods of his master were in his hand*. See xxv. 5. A slightly different turn is given to the sentence by the versions, LXX καὶ ἀπὸ πάντων τῶν ἀγαθῶν τοῦ κυρίου αὑτοῦ, Lat. *ex omnibus bonis ejus portans secum*.

The servant carried with him gifts for the bride and for her family on behalf of the bridegroom: see *vv.* 22 and 53.

Mesopotamia] *Aram-naharaim*, that is, *Aram of the two rivers*. This is the region watered by the Upper Euphrates which appears in the Tel-el-Amarna tablets with the name *Naharina*, or "the river land." The termination *-aim* denotes the dual number; and hence the proposed rendering "Aram of the two rivers." If so, the two rivers are the Euphrates and its confluent the Habor; not the Tigris and the Euphrates. Another explanation supposes that the two sides of the river Euphrates are implied by the dual. But it is doubtful whether the sound of the dual termination is anything more than an accident: compare other proper names with the same termination, e.g. Ephraim, Mahanaim, Jerusalaim; and see note on Mizraim (= Egypt) in x. 6.

The name "Mesopotamia" is derived from a later time, and is really applicable to a somewhat different region. For other mention of Mesopotamia, cf. Deut. xxiii. 4; Judg. iii. 8; 1 Chron. xix. 6. Instead of *Aram-naharaim*, P writes *Paddan-aram*. Cf. Gen. xxv. 20, xxviii. 2.

the city of Nahor] The city where Nahor dwelt after Abraham's departure. The name, not mentioned here, appears as Haran in xxvii. 43, xxviii. 10, xxix. 4: cf. xi. 31, Acts vii. 2.

11. *he made the camels to kneel down*] Throughout this chapter the camels are made to play a very prominent part. The camels being made to kneel, in order to wait and rest until they are given water, is a common scene in the East.

J by the well of water at the time of evening, the time that
12 women go out to draw water. And he said, O Lord, the
God of my master Abraham, send me, I pray thee, good
speed this day, and shew kindness unto my master Abra-
13 ham. Behold, I stand by the fountain of water; and the
daughters of the men of the city come out to draw water:
14 and let it come to pass, that the damsel to whom I shall
say, Let down thy pitcher, I pray thee, that I may drink;
and she shall say, Drink, and I will give thy camels drink
also: let the same be she that thou hast appointed for
thy servant Isaac: and thereby shall I know that thou hast
15 shewed kindness unto my master. And it came to pass,
before he had done speaking, that, behold, Rebekah came
out, who was born to Bethuel the son of Milcah, the wife
of Nahor, Abraham's brother, with her pitcher upon her

the time that...to draw water] We have here a familiar scene from Oriental life. The well is outside the gate of the town. It is the women's duty to draw water: cf. 1 Sam. ix. 11; John iv. 7. They come when the heat of the day is past.

12. *O Lord, the God of my master*] Referring to *v.* 7. The servant, though possibly (xv. 2) a native of Damascus, worships the God of Abraham; cf. *v.* 26.

13. *the fountain of water*] Two words are used in this passage which require to be distinguished: (1) "the fountain," or "spring" (*'ayin*), the water of which rises from the ground, or out of the rock; and (2) "the well" (*be'êr*), as in *vv.* 11, 20, the tank or cistern, protected with stones, and provided with steps leading down to the actual "fountain" or "spring"; cf. 16. The "well" is the LXX φρέαρ, Lat. *puteus*: the "fountain" is the LXX πηγή, Lat. *fons*, cf. xvi. 7.

14. *and let it come to pass*] The servant contemplates the possibility of repeated application and failure. The sign for which he makes petition is the voluntary offer on the part of a girl to give water, not only to himself, but also to his camels. This would be no mere formality, but a practical and laborious act of kindness towards a stranger, done probably in the presence of many bystanders and idlers; and therefore making a demand upon energy and moral courage as well as physical strength.

15. *Rebekah*] Here described as the daughter of Bethuel, as in *vv.* 24, 47; cf. xxii. 20—24, xxv. 20, xxviii. 2. The absence, however, of any mention of Bethuel except in *v.* 50, and the mention of Rebekah's mother and her brother Laban as the representatives of the house (*vv.* 28, 55), have led to the conjecture, that Bethuel was dead, and that his name in *v.* 50 is due to a gloss or a textual error.

her pitcher upon her shoulder] Cf. xxi. 14; Ex. xii. 34; Josh. iv. 5.

shoulder. And the damsel was very fair to look upon, a 16 J
virgin, neither had any man known her: and she went
down to the fountain, and filled her pitcher, and came up.
And the servant ran to meet her, and said, Give me to 17
drink, I pray thee, a little water of thy pitcher. And she 18
said, Drink, my lord: and she hasted, and let down her
pitcher upon her hand, and gave him drink. And when 19
she had done giving him drink, she said, I will draw for
thy camels also, until they have done drinking. And she 20
hasted, and emptied her pitcher into the trough, and ran
again unto the well to draw, and drew for all his camels.
And the man looked stedfastly on her; holding his peace, 21
to know whether the LORD had made his journey prosperous or not. And it came to pass, as the camels had 22
done drinking, that the man took a golden ring of ¹half
a shekel weight, and two bracelets for her hands of ten

¹ Heb. *a beka*. See Ex. xxxviii. 26.

Everything turned upon the girl having a pitcher: hence the mention
of this detail.

20. *trough*] There was a separate receptacle, probably of stone, for
watering the animals; Rebekah empties the rest of her pitcher into
this trough, and probably has to fill it several times in order to give
water enough for the 10 camels[1].

21. *looked stedfastly...his peace*] Lat. *contemplabatur eam tacitus*.
The servant was astonished to find that the sign for which he had
prayed had been given in the case of the first girl that had come
to draw water; hence his look of eagerness, questioning, and silent
thought.

22. *a golden ring*] The ring (*nezem*) was probably a nose-ring, cf.
v. 47. So the Samaritan version here reads "and put it on her nose."
LXX ἐνώτια, Lat. *inaures* = "earrings."

See for the *nezem* Prov. xi. 22, Isai. iii. 21, Ezek. xvi. 12, where in
each case a nose-jewel is indicated.

half a shekel weight] Heb. *beḳa*. See Ex. xxxviii. 26. Half a

---

[1] *Times*, p. 4, Aug. 18, 1913, "Studies in the Zoological Gardens, IV." "However
'patient of thirst,' in Thomson's phrase, the camel may be...it is also true that it
drinks inordinate quantities when it gets the chance....It is recorded that an individual
[camel] has drunk as much as 20 gallons at a sitting, a fact which throws new light on
the incident of Rebekah at the well. Abraham's servant...had ten camels, and after
he had refreshed himself from Rebekah's pitcher, 'she said, I will draw water for thy
camels also, until they have done drinking....And the man, wondering at her, held
his peace....' As well he might. 'Until they have done drinking'—the words were
written by one who knew camels; and Rebekah's acts of kindness to the stranger and
his beasts were of larger proportions than the casual reader of these days might infer."

J 23 shekels weight of gold; and said, Whose daughter art thou? tell me, I pray thee. Is there room in thy father's
24 house for us to lodge in? And she said unto him, I am the daughter of Bethuel the son of Milcah, which she bare
25 unto Nahor. She said moreover unto him, We have both
26 straw and provender enough, and room to lodge in. And
27 the man bowed his head, and worshipped the LORD. And he said, Blessed be the LORD, the God of my master Abraham, who hath not forsaken his mercy and his truth toward my master: as for me, the LORD hath led me in the way to
28 the house of my master's brethren. And the damsel ran, and told her mother's house according to these words.
29 And Rebekah had a brother, and his name was Laban:

shekel weighed one quarter of an ounce. There is only mention of one ring, and this is of light weight. The two bracelets weighed 10 shekels, or 5 ounces. These gifts reward her kindness in a lavish manner, and lead up to the request for a lodging at her home. On the shekel, see xx. 16, xxiii. 15.

23. *room*] Lit. "place" as in *v.* 25. Cf. Ps. xxxi. 8, "in a large room" (A.V.) = "in a large place" (R.V.).

25. *straw and provender*] The character of Rebekah comes out in her practical answer. Food and stabling for the 10 camels would be more difficult to find than a lodging for the man. The Latin renders "room to lodge in" somewhat freely by *locus spatiosus ad manendum*.

26. *the man bowed his head*] Cf. *v.* 48, xliii. 28 (J). Rebekah's mention of her family had dispelled the servant's last doubt; bowing his head he gives praise to Jehovah, the God of Abraham; cf. *v.* 12.

27. *who hath not forsaken his mercy and his truth*] For a very similar sentence, cf. Ruth ii. 20, "Blessed be he of the LORD who hath not left off his kindness." The word used here for "mercy" is the same as that rendered "kindness," *vv.* 12 and 14, and "kindly" in *v.* 49. The combination of the Heb. words for "mercy" and "truth" was almost proverbial; cf. xxxii. 10, xlvii. 29, "kindly and truly" (J), Ps. xcviii. 3. "Mercy" denotes the goodness, "truth" the fidelity of God, in the fulfilment of His promises.

brethren] i.e. "kindred," as in *v.* 48. See note on xiii. 8.

28. *her mother's house*] Her father probably was dead. The "house" is not the building, but the "household," cf. xviii. 19.

29—53. THE BETROTHAL OF REBEKAH.

29. *Laban*] Rebekah's brother Laban (cf. xxv. 20, xxviii. 2, xxix. 5) takes the part of the chief representative of Rebekah's family.

GENESIS XXIV. 29—36

and Laban ran out unto the man, unto the fountain. And it came to pass, when he saw the ring, and the bracelets upon his sister's hands, and when he heard the words of Rebekah his sister, saying, Thus spake the man unto me; that he came unto the man; and, behold, he stood by the camels at the fountain. And he said, Come in, thou blessed of the LORD; wherefore standest thou without? for I have prepared the house, and room for the camels. And the man came into the house, and he ungirded the camels; and he gave straw and provender for the camels, and water to wash his feet and the men's feet that were with him. And there was set meat before him to eat: but he said, I will not eat, until I have told mine errand. And he said, Speak on. And he said, I am Abraham's servant. And the LORD hath blessed my master greatly; and he is become great: and he hath given him flocks and herds, and silver and gold, and menservants and maidservants, and camels and asses. And Sarah, my master's wife bare a son to my master when she was old: and unto

Bethuel, their father, is mentioned along with him only in *v*. 50; and their mother in *vv*. 53, 55.

30. *when he saw the ring*] With a slight touch of ironical humour, the first hint is thus given of Laban's avaricious character. The sight of the gold seems to stimulate his courtesy to the servant.

31. *thou blessed of the LORD*] Cf. xxvi. 29. Laban's reference to Jehovah probably implies that he too, as a member of Abraham's kindred, was a worshipper of Jehovah the God of Abraham.

32. *the man*] i.e. Abraham's servant; he ungirded his own camels, and Laban gave them straw and fodder. The camel is a most valuable possession, but a delicate animal, needing care and attention.

he gave straw] i.e. Laban.

water] Cf. xviii. 4.

33. *meat*] i.e. "food." See note on i. 29.

I will not eat] The courtesies of the East would prohibit an enquiry into the stranger's name before he had partaken of food. The name might possibly reveal relations, e.g. those of blood-feud, which would exclude hospitality.

35. *hath blessed*] Cf. *v*. 1. The servant recounts the wealth of Abraham of which we have heard in xii. 16, xiii. 2. The servant's first object is to represent that, from a worldly point of view, a marriage with Abraham's son would be not only prudent, but desirable.

36. *unto him hath he given*] The servant here states that Abraham

J 37 him hath he given all that he hath. And my master made me swear, saying, Thou shalt not take a wife for my son of the daughters of the Canaanites, in whose land I dwell: 38 but thou shalt go unto my father's house, and to my 39 kindred, and take a wife for my son. And I said unto my master, Peradventure the woman will not follow me. 40 And he said unto me, The LORD, before whom I walk, will send his angel with thee, and prosper thy way; and thou shalt take a wife for my son of my kindred, and of my 41 father's house: then shalt thou be clear from my oath, when thou comest to my kindred; and if they give her 42 not to thee, thou shalt be clear from my oath. And I came this day unto the fountain, and said, O LORD, the God of my master Abraham, if now thou do prosper my way 43 which I go: behold, I stand by the fountain of water; and let it come to pass, that the maiden which cometh forth to draw, to whom I shall say, Give me, I pray thee, 44 a little water of thy pitcher to drink; and she shall say to me, Both drink thou, and I will also draw for thy camels: let the same be the woman whom the LORD 45 hath appointed for my master's son. And before I had done speaking in mine heart, behold, Rebekah came forth with her pitcher on her shoulder; and she went down unto the fountain, and drew: and I said unto her, 46 Let me drink, I pray thee. And she made haste, and let down her pitcher from her shoulder, and said, Drink, and I will give thy camels drink also: so I drank, and she 47 made the camels drink also. And I asked her, and said, Whose daughter art thou? And she said, The daughter of Bethuel, Nahor's son, whom Milcah bare unto him: and I

has already made over to Isaac the great bulk of his wealth, as is stated in xxv. 5. Those who suppose that the mention of Abraham's death originally occurred after *v.* 9, regard this sentence as indicating Abraham's final disposition of his property.

37. *And my master made me swear*] This and the four following verses recapitulate the substance of *vv.* 3—8. The *dénouement* of the story is thus retarded. Similarly in the following *vv.* (42—48) the suspense caused by the repetition tends to heighten the interest.

42. *And I came this day*] *Vv.* 42—48 recapitulate the substance of 12—27.

put the ring upon her nose, and the bracelets upon her
hands. And I bowed my head, and worshipped the LORD, 48
and blessed the LORD, the God of my master Abraham,
which had led me in the right way to take my master's
brother's daughter for his son. And now if ye will deal 49
kindly and truly with my master, tell me: and if not, tell
me; that I may turn to the right hand, or to the left.
Then Laban and Bethuel answered and said, The thing 50
proceedeth from the LORD: we cannot speak unto thee
bad or good. Behold, Rebekah is before thee, take her, 51
and go, and let her be thy master's son's wife, as the LORD
hath spoken. And it came to pass, that, when Abraham's 52

48. *my master's brother's daughter*] The servant definitely states the relationship of Rebekah; cf. xxii. 23. "Brother" may mean "relative" (xiii. 8, xiv. 14). Those who think Bethuel's name in this chapter (*vv.* 15, 24, 47 [50]) is inserted as a gloss, regard Rebekah as Abraham's niece, the daughter of Nahor, and refer to xxix. 5.

49. *deal kindly and truly*] Lit. "do kindness and truth"; cf. xlvii. 29. See note on *v.* 27.

to the right hand, or to the left] The servant asks for a prompt reply, so that, if his request is refused, he may consider what course next to pursue. For fanciful Rabbinic interpretations of "the right hand and the left," cf. Calvin's note, *futilis autem argutia quam adducunt quidam Hebraei quod iturus sit ad Lot vel ad Ismael.*

50. *Laban and Bethuel*] The only passage in which, if the text is correct, Bethuel takes a prominent part in the transaction. Even here Laban is mentioned before him. For some reason, Bethuel is in the background: cf. xxix. 5. Hence Kittel reads "and his house," *ûbêthô*; Holzinger, "and Milcah": see *v.* 53.

from the LORD] It is recognized that Jehovah, the God of the family, has brought this thing to pass.

speak...bad or good] They have no voice. God has settled the matter. To accept will mean a good marriage for Rebekah, but her separation, at a great distance, from her family. To refuse is to reject a chance for her wealth and happiness, as well as to act in apparent opposition to the signs of Jehovah's will. "Bad and good," "yes and no," are evenly balanced. It is a proverbial phrase, cf. xxxi. 24; Num. xxiv. 13; 2 Sam. xiii. 22.

51. *take...and go*] The betrothal is thus summarily settled. The bride is not consulted!

as the LORD hath spoken] Referring to the manner in which the will of Jehovah had evidently been made known. Events, not words, had been the means of revelation.

J servant heard their words, he bowed himself down to the
53 earth unto the Lord. And the servant brought forth
jewels of silver, and jewels of gold, and raiment, and gave
them to Rebekah: he gave also to her brother and to
54 her mother precious things. And they did eat and drink,
he and the men that were with him, and tarried all night;
and they rose up in the morning, and he said, Send me
55 away unto my master. And her brother and her mother
said, Let the damsel abide with us *a few* days, at the
56 least ten; after that she shall go. And he said unto
them, Hinder me not, seeing the Lord hath prospered
my way; send me away that I may go to my master.

52. *bowed himself down*] Cf. *vv.* 26, 48. The servant renders thanks to Jehovah before proceeding to ratify the betrothal.

53. *jewels...silver...gold...raiment*] The word "jewels" in the original is indefinite, and might be rendered "vessels," as LXX σκεύη and Lat. *vasa*. The servant's first act is to ratify the betrothal by making the betrothal gifts to the bride. Oriental custom required that, at the betrothal, gifts should be made to the parents or nearest representative relations of the bride. Mention of marriage gifts (*mohar*) to the bride's family is found also in xxxiv. 12; Ex. xxii. 16, 17; Deut. xxii. 19; 1 Sam. xviii. 25. The custom must be regarded as a remnant of still earlier times, when the bride was purchased, and the marriage ceremony consisted chiefly of a financial transaction. In this verse, the "precious things," given by the servant to Rebekah's brother and mother, constitute the customary *mohar* to the bride's family. This custom is also mentioned in the Code of Hammurabi, §§ 159—161.

It is noticeable that the "precious things" are given, not to Rebekah's father, Bethuel, but to her brother and mother. This is an important point in favour of the view, mentioned above, that Bethuel's name in *v.* 50 is an interpolation (see note on *v.* 15).

54—67. Abraham's Servant brings Rebekah to Isaac.

55. *her brother and her mother*] LXX and Lat. read "her brothers and her mother."

a few *days, at the least ten*] Heb. "days or ten," or, as we should say, "a week or ten days"; the word "or" meaning "or rather." LXX ἡμέρας ὡσεὶ δέκα, Lat. *saltem decem dies*. The Syriac Peshitto, "a month in days." A possible conjecture based on these variations is that of Olshausen, "a month of days, or ten."

56. *to my master*] The servant entreats that there should be no delay. He wishes to return with the bride to his master. Whether

And they said, We will call the damsel, and inquire at 57 J
her mouth. And they called Rebekah, and said unto her, 58
Wilt thou go with this man? And she said, I will go.
And they sent away Rebekah their sister, and her nurse, 59
and Abraham's servant, and his men. And they blessed 60
Rebekah, and said unto her, Our sister, be thou *the mother*
of thousands of ten thousands, and let thy seed possess the gate of those which hate them. And Rebekah 61
arose, and her damsels, and they rode upon the camels,
and followed the man: and the servant took Rebekah,
and went his way. And Isaac came [1]*from the way of* 62

[1] The Sept. has *through the wilderness*.

this is Abraham or Isaac, is not stated. But, judging from *v.* 65, there is ground for the supposition that Isaac is intended.

Otherwise, the servant's haste may be supposed to have been dictated by a knowledge of Abraham's failing condition. If so, it is strange that there is no mention of Abraham on the return.

59. *their sister*] Laban is thus referred to as the head of the family; cf. "your daughter" in xxxiv. 8.

her nurse] i.e. her special personal attendant; cf. xxix. 24, 29. The name of the nurse appears in xxxv. 8 as Deborah.

and his men] The servant's retinue, mentioned in *v.* 32; see note on *v.* 10.

60. *And they blessed Rebekah*] The farewell blessing and good wishes of the family referred in Oriental fashion to the two objects of desire, (1) that she should be the mother of many descendants; and (2) that they should be victorious over their enemies.

possess the gate of] Cf. xxii. 17. "The possessors of the gate" were the controllers of the affairs of the city.

61. *her damsels*] Rebekah took attendants with her besides the nurse mentioned in *v.* 59. See note on *v.* 10.

62. *from the way*] The reading of LXX, *through the wilderness*, is supported by the Samaritan, and gives a good meaning. Isaac had been dwelling in the Negeb, and had now come, "through the wilderness," to Beer-lahai-roi, to meet the returning messengers. The Hebrew text is probably corrupt. Literally rendered, it runs, "And Isaac came from the coming of the well"; this has been understood to mean "from the direction of the well," Lat. *per viam quae ducit ad puteum*. The clause evidently intends to state that the vicinity of Beer-lahai-roi (xvi. 14, xxv. 11) is the scene of the meeting between Isaac and Rebekah. Conjectural emendations, e.g. "from Beer-sheba to Beer-lahai-roi," or "from Beer-lahai-roi," are very doubtful.

J 63 Beer-lahai-roi; for he dwelt in the land of the South. And Isaac went out to meditate in the field at the eventide: and he lifted up his eyes, and saw, and, behold, there 64 were camels coming. And Rebekah lifted up her eyes, 65 and when she saw Isaac, she lighted off the camel. And she said unto the servant, What man is this that walketh in the field to meet us? And the servant said, It is my 66 master: and she took her veil, and covered herself. And the servant told Isaac all the things that he had done. 67 And Isaac brought her into his mother Sarah's tent, and took Rebekah, and she became his wife; and he loved her: and Isaac was comforted after his mother's death.

in the land of the South] Lit. in the land of the Negeb. See note on xii. 9.

63. *to meditate*] A strange and poetical word to be used in this context. It has given rise to very various renderings: LXX ἀδολεσχῆσαι, Lat. *ad meditandum*, Aq. ὁμιλῆσαι, Sym. λαλῆσαι, Syr. Pesh. "to walk about" (so Gesenius), with a slight variation of the reading. Rashi says the word means "prayer"; Ibn Ezra, "to walk between the shrubs"; Bötticher, "to fetch brushwood." Many modern scholars, e.g. Knobel, Ewald, Strack, and Gunkel, render "to wail," or "lament," comparing the use of the same word in Ps. lv. 2, 17 ("moan"), cxlii. 2 ("complaint"); and doubtless this rendering has the merit of agreeing with the mention of Isaac's need of being comforted (*v.* 67).

As the servant does not bring Rebekah to Abraham, there is good reason for the conjecture that Abraham's death had occurred.

64. *lighted off the camel*] i.e. she "alighted," or "leapt down from." Her action is that of Oriental courtesy: cf. Josh. xv. 18; Judg. i. 14; 1 Sam. xxv. 23; 2 Kings v. 21. See Thomson's *Land and Book*, p. 593, "Women frequently refuse to ride in the presence of men; and when a company of them are to pass through a town, they often dismount and walk."

65. *It is my master*] Referring to Isaac. The expression favours the suggestion that, according to the original version of the story, Abraham's death had been mentioned after *v.* 9 (see note); the servant's master was no longer Abraham.

took her veil] According to Oriental custom the bride was brought veiled into the presence of the bridegroom: cf. xxix. 23, 25.

67. *into his mother Sarah's tent*] The language of the Heb. text is here very obscure; and the original structure of it has probably been altered. Literally it means "into the tent Sarah his mother," a grammatical impossibility. It can hardly be questioned that the words "Sarah his mother" are a gloss upon the word "tent," which has found its way into the text.

The tent would be either Isaac's, or the chief tent in the women's quarters. Cf. xxxi. 33. This would explain the gloss.

And Abraham took another wife, and her name was **25** J
Keturah. And she bare him Zimran, and Jokshan, and **2**
Medan, and Midian, and Ishbak, and Shuah. And Jokshan **3**

after his mother's death] Once more the text seems to be doubtful. The literal translation of the Heb. is "after his mother": and the phrase is intolerably harsh. The versions have paraphrased the sentence. LXX καὶ παρεκλήθη Ἰσαὰκ περὶ Σάρρας τῆς μητρὸς αὐτοῦ, Lat. *ut dolorem qui ex morte matris ejus accidat temperaret*.

The probability is that the text of J ran, "after his father's death" (*'aḥarey môth 'âbîv*); but that, as the compiler decided to accept P's account of Abraham's death and burial (xxv. 7—11), it was necessary to harmonize this passage; and this was done by the substitution of "his mother" (*'immô*) for "his father's death" (*môth 'âbîv*).

CH. XXV.

ABRAHAM'S DESCENDANTS BY KETURAH, 1—6 (J).
ABRAHAM'S DEATH AND BURIAL, 7—11 (P).
THE DESCENDANTS OF ISHMAEL, 12—18 (P).

1—6. ABRAHAM'S DESCENDANTS BY KETURAH.

This section is from J.

The children by a concubine represent tribal relationship of a secondary and less intimate character. The domestic tradition in these verses preserves the recollection of an early connexion between the ancestors of Israel and the clans or tribes on the borders of the North Arabian desert.

1. *Abraham...another wife...Keturah*] We are not told the period in Abraham's history at which his marriage with Keturah took place. The mention of it here is introduced, in order to complete the account of his descendants, before the narrative passes on to the story of Isaac and Jacob.

Keturah] This name means "incense." It is conceivable that the name stands in some sort of relation to the "frankincense" trade, which was carried on, by regular routes, between Arabia and Syria and Egypt. In 1 Chron. i. 32 she is called "a concubine."

2. *And she bare him*] The genealogy of Keturah is found again in a shortened form in 1 Chron. i. 32. That we have to do with a tradition relating to tribes and places rather than to individuals, is clearly shewn by such names as Midian, Shuah, Sheba, and Dedan. In this verse six names are given. In view of other groups of *twelve* (cf. notes on xvii. 20, xxii. 21), this number is hardly accidental; see *v.* 12.

Zimran] Probably from a word meaning "wild goat": cf. Zimri, Num. xxv. 14.

Midian] The territory with which the Midianites are usually found associated is N.W. Arabia, the east side of the Gulf of Akaba. Groups of Midianites appear in the Sinaitic Peninsula (Ex. ii. 15, iii. 1

J   begat Sheba, and Dedan. And the sons of Dedan were
  4 Asshurim, and Letushim, and Leummim. And the sons
     of Midian; Ephah, and Epher, and Hanoch, and Abida,
  5 and Eldaah. All these were the children of Keturah. And
  6 Abraham gave all that he had unto Isaac. But unto the sons
     of the concubines, which Abraham had, Abraham gave gifts;
     and he sent them away from Isaac his son, while he yet
P 7 lived, eastward, unto the east country. | And these are

Extending their influence along the eastern side of the Dead Sea, Midianites appear as the enemies of Israel on the eastern side of the Jordan (Num. xxii. 4, xxv. 6, 17, xxxi. 1—12); and in Judg. vi. bands of Midianites overrun Palestine. On Midianite trade with Egypt, cf. xxxvii. 28, 36.

Shuah]=1 Chr. i. 32. Cf. Job ii. 11, "Bildad, the Shuhite." It has been identified somewhat precariously with the Assyrian *Suhu*, on the Euphrates, S. of Carchemish.

3. *Sheba...Dedan*] These places have already been mentioned by P in a different connexion (x. 7). The identity of the names illustrates the fact, that there were different Israelite traditions explaining the relation of the different members of the Hebrew-speaking families.

Asshurim, and Letushim, and Leummim] These plural names are noticeable as obviously denoting, not individuals, but peoples. The Asshurim are probably to be connected with the "Asshur" (R.V. "Assyria") of Ps. lxxxiii. 8, and possibly with the mention of Asshur in the present chapter (*v.* 18) and in Num. xxiv. 22. In both instances, an allusion to obscure tribes on the Arabian borders of Palestine is more suitable than to the Assyrian empire.

Ephah] Cf. Isa. lx. 6, "the dromedaries of Midian and Ephah," a passage confirming the probability that the present group of names is Arabian.

5. *And Abraham...Isaac*] See xxiv. 36. This disposition of his property seems to have been made some time before his death; and was intended to prevent disputes amongst the members of his family.

6. *the concubines*] i.e. Hagar and Keturah; although in xvi. 3 Hagar is called Abraham's wife, as also is Keturah in *v.* 1 of this chapter.

sent them away] The present passage belongs to J, a different source of tradition from chap. xxi. (E). It ignores the account of the expulsion of Hagar and Ishmael related in that chapter, and of the dwelling of Ishmael in the wilderness of Paran (xxi. 21).

unto the east country] i.e. the Syro-Arabian desert, on the east of Palestine. Gen. xxix. 1; Judg. vi. 3, 33, vii. 12, viii. 10; Isa. xi. 14; Jer. xlix. 28; Ezek. xxv. 4, 10 are passages in which "the children of the east" (*b'nê ḳedem*) are mentioned as the nomad occupants of this region.

the days of the years of Abraham's life which he lived, P
an hundred threescore and fifteen years. And Abraham 8
gave up the ghost, and died in a good old age, an old man,
and full *of years*; and was gathered to his people. And 9
Isaac and Ishmael his sons buried him in the cave of
Machpelah, in the field of Ephron the son of Zohar the
Hittite, which is before Mamre; the field which Abraham 10
purchased of the children of Heth: there was Abraham
buried, and Sarah his wife. And it came to pass after 11
the death of Abraham, that God blessed Isaac his son; |
and Isaac dwelt by Beer-lahai-roi.   J

7—11 (P). THE DEATH OF ABRAHAM.

This passage is from P, recording the age of Abraham and the place of his burial, and following directly upon the death and burial of Sarah (chap. xxiii.).

7. *And these are the days*] Cf. the age of Terah, xi. 32 (P). Abraham is 30 years younger than Terah at his death.

8. *gave up the ghost*] Cf. *v.* 7, xxxv. 29, xlix. 33 (P): the same word as "die" in vi. 17, vii. 21 (P).

in a good old age] This was part of the promised blessing: cf. xv. 15.

was gathered to his people] See note on xvii. 14. "His people" evidently has no local significance; but means those of his own family already dead, and now in *Sheôl*, "the under-world" of departed spirits. Cf. xxxv. 29, xlix. 29, 33 (P). There is no difference, then, between being "gathered to his people," and "to go to thy fathers" (xv. 15), and "to sleep with my fathers" (xlvii. 30; cf. Deut. xxxi. 16).

9. *Isaac and Ishmael*] The two sons are mentioned once more together, as paying the last tribute of honour to their father. The banishment of Ishmael, recorded by E in xxi., was not apparently included in the narrative of P, which avoids the notice of anything derogatory to the patriarchs.

in the cave of Machpelah, &c.] Isaac and Ishmael bury their father in the burial-place where he had laid Sarah his wife to rest. Cf. xxiii. 17—20.

11. *God blessed Isaac*] The fulfilment of xvii. 21. The traditions of Isaac are very meagre. Here, as in xxiv. 62, his dwelling-place is at Beer-lahai-roi, which was also connected with Ishmael (xvi. 14). In xxxv. 27, Hebron is spoken of as the dwelling-place of Isaac at a later period of his life.

12—18 (P). THE DESCENDANTS OF ISHMAEL.

The genealogy of Ishmael is thus disposed of, before the narrative resumes the history of the Chosen Family in the generations of Isaac

GENESIS XXV. 12—16

P 12 Now these are the generations of Ishmael, Abraham's son, whom Hagar the Egyptian, Sarah's handmaid, bare
13 unto Abraham: and these are the names of the sons of Ishmael, by their names, according to their generations: the firstborn of Ishmael, Nebaioth; and Kedar, and Adbeel,
14,15 and Mibsam, and Mishma, and Dumah, and Massa; Hadad,
16 and Tema, Jetur, Naphish, and Kedemah: these are the sons of Ishmael, and these are their names, by their villages, and by their encampments; twelve princes according

(v. 19). It is to be noticed that the sons of Ishmael are twelve in number, like the sons of Nahor (xxii. 21—24) and of Jacob.

12. *Now these are the generations*] Cf. v. 1, vi. 9, x. 1, xi. 10, 27 (P).

13. *and these are the names*] Cf. the genealogy in 1 Chron. i. 29—31.

Nebaioth] Mentioned also in xxviii. 9, xxxvi. 3, and in Isa. lx. 7, where the name is associated also with Kedar. Probably Nebaioth is to be identified with the *Nabajâti* of the inscriptions of Assurbanipal. The identification with the Nabataeans, of the Christian era, is now generally abandoned.

Kedar] Cf. Isa. lx. 7. Probably the Assyrian *Ḳidri*, a region on the Syro-Arabian frontier, mentioned as a hostile people in Ps. cxx. 5, dwelling in black tents (Cant. i. 5) and in open villages (Isa. xlii. 11; Jer. xlix. 28—31).

Possibly the *Cedraei* mentioned together with *Nabataei* by Pliny are to be identified with these tribes.

Dumah] Possibly the same as in Isa. xxi. 11.

15. *Hadad*] The name of a Syrian god; cf. Hadad (1 Kings xi. 14) and Ben-hadad (1 Kings xx. 1 ff.). It occurs again xxxvi. 35, 39.

Tema] A famous locality—modern *Teima*—on the trade-route between Syria and *Yemen*=S. Arabia, mentioned in Isa. xxi. 14; Job vi. 19.

Jetur] Mentioned along with Naphish in 1 Chron. v. 19. Jetur has usually been identified with the people known as the Ituraeans, who dwelt in the anti-Lebanon district. In the Roman period they were particularly famous as archers.

16. *by their villages, and...encampments*] The distinction is, probably, between settled habitations in open unwalled villages, and circles of black tents in which the Bedouins dwell. This distinction between the permanent and the movable dwellings of the Ishmaelites is not reproduced in the versions. LXX ἐν ταῖς σκηναῖς...ἐν ταῖς ἐπαύλεσιν, Lat. *per castella et oppida*.

See, also, for "encampments," the *tîrôth* of the Midianites (Num. xxxi. 10) and of "the children of the east" (Ezek. xxv. 4).

twelve princes] See note on v. 2. The fulfilment of xvii. 20 (P). The "princes" are "leaders," or *Sheikhs*, of clans.

to their nations. And these are the years of the life of 17 P
Ishmael, an hundred and thirty and seven years: and he
gave up the ghost and died; and was gathered unto his
people. And they dwelt from Havilah unto Shur that is 18
before Egypt, as thou goest toward Assyria: he ¹abode ²in
the presence of all his brethren.

And these are the generations of Isaac, Abraham's son: 19

¹ Or, settled Heb. fell.   ² Or, over against

nations] A technical term for "clan" ('*ummah*='*ummat* in Arabic); cf. Ps. cxvii. 1: elsewhere only Num. xxv. 15="a father's house."

17. *And these are*, &c.] The same phrases occur in this verse as in *vv*. 7 and 8.

gathered unto his people] See note on *v*. 8.

18 (J). *from Havilah unto Shur*] Cf. 1 Sam. xv. 7. See note on "Havilah," x. 29. It was apparently a locality in the N.E. of Arabia. On "Shur," see note on xvi. 7. It was on the eastern border of Egypt. It has been conjectured that this summary description of Ishmael's territory concluded J's narrative of Hagar and Ishmael (xvi. 1—14). It seems to indicate the whole extent of country between N.E. Arabia and the E. Egyptian frontier.

before Egypt] The preposition "before," i.e. "in front of," denotes "the eastern side." See note on xvi. 12.

as thou goest...Assyria] The mention of "Assyria" is here evidently quite out of place, and the explanation of Delitzsch that it means "up to, or as far as, the country under the rule of Assyria," is very forced and improbable. Either, therefore, the Asshur here mentioned is to be connected with the country of the "Asshurim" (*v*. 3), or we must suppose that the text has suffered some corruption. Hence Hupfeld conjectured "unto Shur."

abode] R.V. marg. *settled*; Heb. *fell*.

in the presence of] R.V. marg. *over against*. The same preposition as is rendered "before" in the previous clause. The words are the fulfilment of the angel's promise to Hagar in xvi. 12, where see note.

NARRATIVE OF JACOB (XXV.—XXXVI.).

19—34 (P and J). ESAU AND JACOB. ESAU SELLS HIS BIRTHRIGHT.

Vv. 19 and 20 are from P, 21—34 from J.

19. *And these are the generations*] See *v*. 12. With this familiar formula (cf. ii. 4) commences the next section from P, which deals with the story of Isaac and his two sons, Esau and Jacob.

P 20 Abraham begat Isaac: and Isaac was forty years old when he took Rebekah, the daughter of Bethuel the ¹Syrian of Paddan-aram, the sister of Laban the ¹Syrian, to be his
J 21 wife. | And Isaac intreated the LORD for his wife, because she was barren: and the LORD was intreated of him, and
22 Rebekah his wife conceived. And the children struggled together within her; and she said, If it be so, ²wherefore
23 do I live? And she went to inquire of the LORD. And the LORD said unto her,

¹ Heb. *Aramean*.   ² Or, *wherefore am I thus?*

20. *forty years old*] P gives the age of Isaac at the time of his marriage with Rebekah, thirty-five years before Abraham's death (*v.* 8).

Bethuel] P makes no mention here of Bethuel's being son of Nahor, the brother of Terah. The genealogy of J in xxii. 22 is ignored.

the Syrian] Heb. *Aramean*, as in xxviii. 5. Aram is mentioned in x. 22, 23 (P), as the fifth of the sons of Shem.

Paddan-aram] This is the name given in the P narrative for the country described as *Aram-naharaim* by J. See note on xxiv. 10. Cf. xxviii. 2, 5, 6, 7, xxxi. 18, xxxv. 9, 26, xlvi. 15, xlviii. 7 (*Paddan*), all from P. The word *Paddan* is Aramaic, and means probably "the field," modern Arabic *feddân* (= "acre"). In Assyrian *padanu* = "way" or "field," like Haran (xi. 32). According to Hosea xii. 12, "Jacob fled into the *field* of Aram," where "field" is the Heb. *sâdeh*, and denotes Haran, the country E. of Euphrates.

21—34 (J, E). This passage contains two short narratives, (1) the birth of Jacob and Esau (*vv.* 21—26), (2) the sale of Esau's birthright (27—34).

21. *barren*] As in the case of Sarah (xi. 30) and of Rachel (xxix. 31). Rebekah has at first no children. The Chosen People are the children of God's gift. In each generation patience is made the test of faith. Cf. the birth of Samson (Judg. xiii. 2) and Samuel (1 Sam. i.).

was intreated] Allowed Himself to be interceded with, i.e. listened to the prayer, as in 2 Sam. xxi. 14, xxiv. 25.

22. *struggled together*] LXX ἐσκίρτων. Cf. Luke i. 41. The future hostility between Israel and Edom was thus prefigured before their birth. Rebekah, afraid of some betokening of evil, becomes fearful and despondent.

Aquila συνεθλάσθησαν, Symmachus διεπάλαιον.

wherefore do I live] R.V. marg. *wherefore am I thus?* So LXX ἵνα τί μοι τοῦτο, Lat. *quid necesse fuit concipere?*

to inquire of the LORD] A technical phrase for seeking an answer from a Divine source. Cf. 1 Sam. ix. 9; Amos v. 4—6. We may suppose that Rebekah sought an oracle from Jehovah at some sacred place

> Two nations are in thy womb,
> And two peoples shall be separated even from thy
>   bowels:
> And the one people shall be stronger than the other
>   people;
> And the elder shall serve the younger.

And when her days to be delivered were fulfilled, behold, 24
there were twins in her womb. And the first came forth 25
¹red, all over like an hairy garment; and they called his

¹ Or, *ruddy*

at which a Divine revelation was granted, e.g. at Beer-sheba, xxi. 33, xxvi. 25.

23. *And the* LORD *said*] How the Divine answer was granted, whether by priest or soothsayer, by dream or by vision, we are not told. It is in the form of a rhythmic oracle, in four *stichoi*, or lines. The oracle proclaims, that (1) there are two children who shall be two nations; (2) from the first there shall be separation and discord between the two; (3) one shall overmaster the other; (4) the younger shall be the lord of the elder. The historic rivalry between Israel and Edom is thus prefigured.

separated...bowels] The English is ambiguous, as in Gal. i. 15, "the good pleasure of God who separated me even from my mother's womb." The meaning is, "even from birth" the destinies of the two men and of their descendants will be divergent: cf. xiii. 11, "and they separated themselves the one from the other."

the elder shall serve the younger] The subjugation of the Edomites by the Israelites took place in the days of David, 2 Sam. viii. 14. The same event is predicted by Jacob in xxvii. 40, where the additional prediction is made, that the subjugation will be only temporary. Israel, whose settlement in Palestine was later than that of the Edomites in the country of Seir, was regarded as the younger of the brother peoples. Edom was already a monarchy before Israel had settled down. But, occupying a richer country, Israel attained a higher civilization, and became a more powerful nation. For the hostility of Israel and Edom, see the prophet Obadiah. For St Paul's use of the present passage, see Rom. ix. 10—12.

25. *red*] R.V. marg. *ruddy*. The adjective refers to the skin rather than to the hair, as in the case of David (1 Sam. xvi. 12). The Heb. for "red," *admoni*, is intended as a play on the word "Edom," as if the Edomites were known as "the Reds," or "Redskins," on account of their warm complexion.

like an hairy garment] Cf. the description in xxvii. 11, 12, 16, 23. The word for "hairy" (*sē'ar*) contains a play on the word "Seir," the country of the Edomites.

J 26 name Esau. And after that came forth his brother, and his hand had hold on Esau's heel; and his name was called
P ¹Jacob: | and Isaac was threescore years old when she bare
J 27 them. | And the boys grew: and Esau was a cunning hunter, a man of the field; and Jacob was a ²plain man,
28 dwelling in tents. Now Isaac loved Esau, because he did

> ¹ That is, *One that takes by the heel* or *supplants*.
> ² Or, *quiet* Or, *harmless* Heb. *perfect*.

Esau] The origin of the name is uncertain, but it may possibly be connected with an Arabic word meaning "thick-haired." More doubtful is the suggested identification with Ὀυσῶος, a hunter in Phoenician mythology. Esau appears as the poetical name for Edom. See Jer. xlix. 8—10; Obad. 6, 8 ff.; Mal. i. 2, 3.

26. *had hold...heel*] As if, from the first, desirous to pull his brother back, and get in front of him. See the reference to this passage in Hos. xii. 3. The character of the man was thus prefigured at birth. The idea of overreaching, or outwitting, by cunning and strategy, inspired the early Israelite with admiration and amusement rather than with repulsion.

Jacob] That is, *One that takes by the heel* or *supplants*. The Heb. for "heel" is *'âḳêb*, and the name "Jacob" was popularly regarded as having been derived from the same root, with the meaning of "one who seeks to trip up or supplant"; compare the use of the word "supplant" in Jer. ix. 4. It appears as a place name = $Y'kb'r$, in Palestine, on the list of Thothmes III (c. 1450 B.C.), and as a personal name, *Ya'ḳub-ilu*, in a Babylonian tablet of Hammurabi's period (c. 2100 B.C.).

threescore years old] See note on *v.* 20 (P).

27. *a cunning hunter*] That is a skilful, expert hunter. The word "cunning" is used in its old English sense, with no idea of craft or deceit; see 1 Sam. xvi. 16. The Heb. means having a knowledge of the chase. LXX εἰδὼς κυνηγεῖν, Lat. *gnarus venandi*.

a man of the field] i.e. a man who spends his days in the open country. But this meaning is missed by the versions, LXX ἄγροικος, Lat. *agricola*.

a plain man] i.e., as R.V. marg., *quiet* or *harmless*, Lat. *integer*. "Plain," in Old English, is used for "simple," "honest": cf. "For he [Antonius] was a *plaine* man, without subletie" (North's Plutarch, *Antonius*, p. 979); "*Plaine*, faithful, true, and enimy of shame" (Spenser, *F. Q.*, I. 6, § 20).

The meaning seems to be that of a solid, simple, home-abiding man. LXX ἄπλαστος, Lat. *simplex*. Cf. the German *fromm*.

dwelling in tents] Cf. iv. 20. The life of Jacob, the herdsman and the shepherd, is contrasted with that of the fierce and roving huntsman. The ideal patriarchal habit of life seems to be pastoral.

28. *because...venison*] Cf. xxvii. 3, 4.

eat of his venison: and Rebekah loved Jacob. And Jacob 29
sod pottage: and Esau came in from the field, and he was
faint: and Esau said to Jacob, Feed me, I pray thee, 30
with ¹that same red *pottage*; for I am faint: therefore was
his name called ²Edom. And Jacob said, Sell me ³this 31
day thy birthright. And Esau said, Behold, I am at the 32

¹ Heb. *the red* pottage, *this red* pottage.   ² That is, *Red*.
³ Or, *first of all*

Rebekah loved Jacob] i.e. more than Esau. We have in this verse the division of the two pairs, Isaac and Esau, Rebekah and Jacob, on which turns the narrative in chap. xxvii.

The contrast between the hunter and the shepherd is drawn with a settled preference for the shepherd.

30. *Feed me...with*] i.e. "let me, I pray thee, swallow a little of."

that same red pottage] Heb. *the red* pottage, *this red* pottage. Esau's words repeat the adjective "red": either this was the name by which the pottage was known, or else Esau in his faintness and weariness is represented as simply pointing and gasping out "that red, red mess¹."

therefore was his name called] A separate tradition accounting for the origin of the name "Edom": see note on *v.* 25.

Edom] That is, *Red*.

31. *this day*] Rather, as R.V. marg., *first of all*. So also in *v.* 33. See 1 Sam. ii. 16, "they will surely burn the fat *presently*," where "presently"=Heb. "this day," i.e. "first of all." The same idiom explains 1 Kings xxii. 5, where "to-day" should be rendered "first of all."

Jacob seizes his opportunity: Esau is too faint to question or oppose: the coveted privilege may be won at once by a bold bid.

thy birthright] i.e. the rights and privileges of the firstborn. What these were is not defined. In xxvii. the blessing of the firstborn is chiefly regarded as a religious privilege rather than as a transfer of property. But it is clear from xliii. 33, xlviii. 13—19, that the firstborn was regarded as entitled to a more honourable position and to a larger share of the inheritance than his brethren (cf. Deut. xxi. 17). Jacob's action on this occasion is recorded without disapproval. There is probably a touch of humour in the tradition, that by a stroke of cleverness Jacob, the younger, deprived his elder brother Esau of the advantage of the birthright; and, hence, Israel obtained a richer and more fertile land than Edom. The carelessness of Esau rather than the meanness of Jacob seems to meet with the contempt of the narrator.

¹ "The phrase 'mess of pottage' does not occur in the A.V. of 1611, but is used proverbially of the means whereby Esau sold his birthright (Gen. xxv.). The actual phrase was used in the heading to this chapter of Genesis in the Bibles of 1537 and 1539, and in the Geneva Bible of 1560. Coverdale, in his Bible of 1535, used the phrase in other passages, viz. in 1 Chron. xvi. 3 and Prov. xx. 7, but not in Gen. xxv. See *A New English Dictionary* (Oxford University Press)," *Spectator*, Nov. 29, 1913.

J point to die: and what profit shall the birthright do to me? 33 And Jacob said, Swear to me ¹this day; and he sware 34 unto him: and he sold his birthright unto Jacob. And Jacob gave Esau bread and pottage of lentils; and he did eat and drink, and rose up, and went his way: so Esau despised his birthright.

¹ Or, *first of all*

32. *I am at the point to die*] Esau's words mean that he is dying of hunger, and has no thought of anything but the prospect of food. So LXX ἰδοὺ ἐγὼ πορεύομαι τελευτᾶν, Lat. *en morior*. A more improbable and very insipid interpretation makes Esau say, "I live as a hunter in continual danger of death."

33. *Swear to me*] Jacob is acute enough to secure the solemn ratification of his brother's act, done in the thoughtless moment of exhaustion. When Esau recovers his self-control, he will not be able to repudiate his action.

this day] R.V. marg. rightly, *first of all*. Cf. *v*. 31.

34. *lentils*] The pottage here described is made of a small reddish kind of bean much in use for food in Palestine, Arab. *'adas*. Cf. 2 Sam. xvii. 28, xxiii. 11 ; Ezek. iv. 9. It makes the reddish pottage now called in Palestine *mujedderah*, a very popular dish.

so Esau despised his birthright] These words summarize the narrative. Esau's character is portrayed as that of a careless, shallow man, living from hand to mouth, and paying no regard to things of higher or spiritual significance. It is this trait which is referred to in Heb. xii. 16, "or profane person as Esau, who for one mess of meat sold his own birthright." The advantage of the birthright may have been indefinite. But, as we may judge not only from the story in ch. xxvii., but also from that of xxxviii. 28—30 and xlviii. 13—19 (cf. Deut. xxi. 15—17), the privilege of the birthright was accounted sacred in the social life of the early Israelite. The Lat. paraphrases the sense of the last clause, *parvi pendens quod primogenita vendidisset*.

The birthright was Esau's by God's gift, not by his own merit. Hence it symbolized eternal blessing. Esau's repudiation of the unseen and intangible, for the sake of immediate self-gratification, is the symbol of a large proportion of human sin and thoughtlessness.

SPECIAL NOTE ON XXV. 26.

On the name "*Jacob*."

The popular Israelite derivation of the name "Jacob" from the Heb. word *'âḳêb*, "a heel," like so many other popular derivations, is simply based upon the resemblance in the sound of the proper name to a word in common use.

"It is another question," says Driver, "whether this explanation

And there was a famine in the land, | beside the first 6 J(R)
famine that was in the days of Abraham. | And Isaac J
went unto Abimelech king of the Philistines unto Gerar.

expresses the actual meaning of the name. It has been supposed, for instance, that *Jacob* is really an elliptical form of *Jaḳob'ēl*: in this case El, 'God,' would be the subject of the verb (like *Ishmā'ēl*, 'God heareth,' *Isrā'el*, 'God persisteth,' *Yeraḥme'ēl*, 'God is compassionate'), and the word might be explained from the Arab., 'God follows,' or... 'God rewards.' In fact there is now evidence that the name is much older than the date at which, according to the Biblical narrative, Jacob must have lived. Mr Pinches has found on contract tables of the age of Khammurabi (c. 2300 B.C.) the personal name *Ya'ḳub-ilu* (analogous to *Yashup-ilu*, *Yarbi-ilu*, *Yamlik-ilu*, *Yakbar-ilu*, etc., of the same age); and, according to Hommel (*AHT*. 203), the contracted form *Yakubu* occurs likewise. Further, in the lists of 118 places in Palestine conquered by Thothmes III (B.C. 1503—1449, Sayce and Petrie), which are inscribed on the pylons of the temple at Karnak, there occur (Nos. 78 and 102) the names *Y-ša-p-'a-ra* and *Y-'-ḳ-b-'â-ra*. These names (the Egyp. *r* standing, as is well known, also for *l*) can be only יספאל *Joseph-'ēl* and יעקבאל *Jaḳob-'ēl*; and we learn consequently that places bearing these names (cf. for the form the place-names *Jezre'ēl*, *Jabne'ēl*, Jos. xv. 11 [=*Jabneh*, 2 Chron. xxvi. 6]; *Yiphtaḥ'ēl*, Jos. xix. 14, 27; *Yeḳabze'ēl*, Neh. xi. 25; *Yirpe'ēl*, Jos. xviii. 27) existed in Palestine, apparently in the central part, in the 15th cent. B.C. What connexion, if any, exists between these names and those of the patriarchs, may never perhaps be ascertained; but their existence at such a date in Palestine is remarkable. These facts, however, make it not improbable that (as had indeed been supposed even before their discovery) names of the type of *Jacob*, *Joseph*, *Jephthah*, etc., are elliptical forms of a more original *Jaḳob'ēl*, *Joseph'ēl*, etc. But, however that may be, to the Hebrews, as we know them, the idea which *Jacob* suggested, and in which it was supposed to have originated, was that of *supplanter*." Driver in Art. *Jacob* in Hastings' *Dict. of the Bible*, ii. 526[b].

CH. XXVI. 1—33 (J). ISAAC IN THE LAND OF THE PHILISTINES.

1—6 (J and R). The covenant with Abraham renewed to Isaac.
7—11. Isaac and Rebekah at the court of Abimelech.
12—17. Isaac's prosperity.
18—22. Isaac's wells.
23—25. Isaac at Beer-sheba.
26—33. Abimelech's covenant with Isaac.
34, 35 (P). Esau's Hittite wives.

1. *beside the first famine*] Referring to the famine mentioned in xii. 10. This clause is probably added by the Compiler (R).

Abimelech king of the Philistines] This can hardly be the Abimelech

J   2 And the LORD appeared unto him, and said, Go not down
(R)   into Egypt; | dwell in the land which I shall tell thee of : |
J   3 sojourn in this land, and I will be with thee, and will bless
(R)   thee; | for unto thee, and unto thy seed, I will give all these
lands, and I will establish the oath which I sware unto
4 Abraham thy father; and I will multiply thy seed as the
stars of heaven, and will give unto thy seed all these lands;
and in thy seed shall all the nations of the earth [1]be
5 blessed; because that Abraham obeyed my voice, and kept
my charge, my commandments, my statutes, and my laws. |

[1] Or, *bless themselves*

mentioned in xx. 2. Possibly we ought to regard Abimelech as the dynastic name of the Philistine rulers. Strictly speaking, this portion of Palestine having not yet been occupied by the Philistines, their name is here used by a not unnatural anachronism on the part of the Hebrew writer, to whom the Philistines were well known on the S.W. of the Israelite territory[1]. See notes on x. 14, xxi. 32.

Gerar] On the road from Palestine into Egypt: evidently a town of some importance; see x. 19, xx. 1.

2. *appeared*] The promises here made to Isaac are, for the most part, reiterated from xii. 2, 3, xv. 5, xvii. 6—8, xxii. 15—18.

which I shall tell thee of] Cf. the similar phrase in xii. 1, xxii. 2.

3. *sojourn...land*] The temporary dwelling of one who as a stranger had none of the rights of a native inhabitant; so LXX παροικει; Lat. *peregrinare*. See note on xxiii. 4, and cf. Heb. xi. 9.

I will be with thee] See *v.* 24, xxi. 20, xxviii. 15. God's Presence is the pledge of man's blessing.

unto thee, &c.] The promises made to Abraham are here renewed to Isaac; see note on xiii. 14—17.

these lands] The plural is uncommon. Lat. *universas regiones has*.

the oath...sware] See xxii. 16—18.

4. *as the stars of heaven*] See note on xiii. 1—6; cf. xv. 5, xxii. 17.

be blessed] R.V. marg. rightly, *bless themselves*. See xii. 3, xxii. 18.

5. *because that*, &c.] The blessing of Isaac is here treated as the reward of the obedience of Abraham; the emphasis is laid on the unity and continuity of the Chosen Family.

my charge...my laws] A strange redundancy of expression, reminding us of the style of Deut. The four words "charge," "commandments," "statutes," "laws," correspond to the more simple phrase "the way of the LORD" in xviii. 19. The observance of legal enactments, ascribed to Abraham, is, strictly speaking, an anachronism. Cf. Deut. xi. 1, "Therefore thou shalt love the LORD thy God, and keep his charge, and his statutes, and his judgements, and his commandments, alway"; 1 Kings ii. 3.

---

[1] See *The Philistines, Their History and Civilization*, The Schweich Lectures, 1911, p. 39, by Professor R. A. S. Macalister. (1913.)

GENESIS XXVI. 6—12

And Isaac dwelt in Gerar: and the men of the place asked 6
him of his wife; and he said, She is my sister: for he 7 J
feared to say, My wife; lest, *said he*, the men of the
place should kill me for Rebekah: because she was fair to
look upon. And it came to pass, when he had been there 8
a long time, that Abimelech king of the Philistines looked
out at a window, and saw, and, behold, Isaac was sporting
with Rebekah his wife. And Abimelech called Isaac, and 9
said, Behold, of a surety she is thy wife: and how saidst
thou, She is my sister? And Isaac said unto him, Because
I said, Lest I die for her. And Abimelech said, What is 10
this thou hast done unto us? one of the people might
lightly have lien with thy wife, and thou shouldest have
brought guiltiness upon us. And Abimelech charged all 11
the people, saying, He that toucheth this man or his wife
shall surely be put to death. And Isaac sowed in that land, 12

7—11 (J). ISAAC AND REBEKAH AT THE COURT OF ABIMELECH.

In this narrative Isaac from motives of fear tells the inhabitants of Gerar that Rebekah is his sister. The resemblance to the similar narratives in the story of Abraham (1) in Egypt, xii. 13, (2) at Gerar, chap. xx., is obvious.

The plea of the relationship of a half-sister could be made for Sarah, but not for Rebekah. The same story was repeated in slightly different versions. It commemorated (*a*) the moral weakness of the patriarch, and (*b*) the protection which was accorded by Jehovah to the ancestors of the Israelite people. Contact with civilization brought perils no less real than the solitary life of the nomad.

7. *my sister*] See xii. 12, 13, xx. 5.

8. *at a window*] The account suggests that Isaac and Rebekah were in the courtyard overlooked by the king's residence. Cf. 2 Sam. xi. 2.

sporting] See xxi. 9 marg., "playing." The word in the original is the same as that from which the name "Isaac" was popularly derived; cf. xvii. 17, 19, xxi. 6. Here the meaning seems to be that of "fondling," the caress of husband and wife, rather than of brother and sister. LXX παίζοντα, Lat. *jocantem*.

10. *lightly*] Lit. "as a little": i.e. "it might easily have happened." See xii. 18, xx. 10. For "lien"="lain," cf. Ps. lxviii. 13 (A.V. and P.B.V.).

guiltiness] Heb. *âshâm*; LXX ἄγνοιαν; Lat. *grande peccatum*. In spite of ignorance, national guilt would be involved in such an outrage as marriage with the wife of another man. For "guiltiness," "guilt," cf. Ps. lxviii. 22; Prov. xiv. 9.

J and found in the same year an hundredfold: and the LORD
13 blessed him. And the man waxed great, and grew more
14 and more until he became very great: and he had possessions of flocks, and possessions of herds, and a great household:
15 and the Philistines envied him. Now all the wells which his father's servants had digged in the days of Abraham his father, the Philistines had stopped them, and filled them
16 with earth. And Abimelech said unto Isaac, Go from us;
17 for thou art much mightier than we. And Isaac departed thence, and encamped in the valley of Gerar, and dwelt
18 there. And Isaac digged again the wells of water, which they had digged in the days of Abraham his father; for the Philistines had stopped them after the death of Abraham: and he called their names after the names by which

12—17 (J). ISAAC'S PROSPERITY.

12. *an hundredfold*] Lit. "a hundred measures." LXX ἑκατοστεύουσαν κριθήν = "barley bearing a hundredfold," mistaking the Hebrew word for "measure," and confusing it with that for "barley." So also the Syriac Pesh. "An hundredfold," i.e. one hundred for one.

Isaac's agricultural pursuits offer a contrast to the roaming life of a nomad. But see, in Jacob's career, xxx. 14, xxxvii. 7.

blessed him] See *v*. 3, xxiv. 1, 35.

14. *and a great household*] i.e. a large number of slaves and attendants.

15. *his father's servants*] Cf. xxi. 25.

had stopped them] Wells were of priceless value to large owners of cattle and sheep. The "Philistines" adopted the most malignant method of spiting the Hebrews, and of rendering their continued sojourn in the land impossible. See 2 Kings iii. 25.

16. *Go from us*] Abimelech recognized that, after such conduct on the part of his people, it would be best in the interests of peace that Isaac should withdraw. Isaac's attitude is one of concession and compliance towards the people among whom he sojourns. He is the type of the race that grows rich, but excites envy and hatred in the land of its sojourn.

17. *the valley of Gerar*] The word "valley" (*nahal*) represents the bed of a stream, often dry during summer. Here, possibly, it is the *Wady Jerâr*, into which several other *wadies* open.

18—22 (J). ISAAC'S WELLS.

18. *in the days of Abraham*] Instead of "in the days," Sam., LXX, and Lat. read "the servants," i.e. "which the servants of Abraham his father had digged."

GENESIS XXVI. 18—24

his father had called them. And Isaac's servants digged 19 J in the valley, and found there a well of ¹springing water. And the herdmen of Gerar strove with Isaac's herdmen, 20 saying, The water is ours: and he called the name of the well ²Esek; because they contended with him. And they 21 digged another well, and they strove for that also: and he called the name of it ³Sitnah. And he removed from thence, 22 and digged another well; and for that they strove not: and he called the name of it ⁴Rehoboth; and he said, For now the LORD hath made room for us, and we shall be fruitful in the land. And he went up from thence to Beer-sheba. 23 And the LORD appeared unto him the same night, and said, 24 I am the God of Abraham thy father: fear not, for I am with thee, and will bless thee, and multiply thy seed for my

---

¹ Heb. *living*.
² That is, *Contention*.
³ That is, *Enmity*.
⁴ That is, *Broad places*, or, *Room*.

19. *springing*] Heb. *living*. A well (*be'êr*) might contain either the water that came from a spring, as here; or water that was stored from rainfall. The word rendered "springing" appears as "running" in Lev. xiv. 5 and as "living" in Jer. ii. 13; cf. Zech. xiv. 8; Joh. iv. 10.

20. *Esek*] That is, *Contention*. LXX Ἀδικία; Lat. *Calumnia*. In this and the two following verses we have popular tradition as to the origin of the names of wells in the region associated with the sojournings of the patriarch.

21. *Sitnah*] That is, *Enmity*. This name is connected with the same root as the word *satan*, "adversary"; cf. Num. xx. 22; 1 Sam. xxix. 4. It has been doubtfully identified with a modern name, *Wady-Sutem*.

22. *Rehoboth*] That is, *Broad places*, or, *Room*. LXX Εὐρυχωρία; Lat. *Latitudo*. This has been identified by modern travellers with a place called *er-Ruhaibeh*, 20 miles S.W. of Beer-sheba, where there is a well.

we shall be fruitful] i.e. prosperous. Prosperity depended upon unhindered access to a supply of water. The same word is used as in i. 22, xli. 52, xlix. 22.

23—25 (J). ISAAC AT BEER-SHEBA.

24. *the same night*] The manner of the appearance of Jehovah is not defined. Was it "in a vision" (xv. 1), or "in a dream" (xx. 3)?

fear not] The words of encouragement are probably spoken in reference to the hostility Isaac had recently experienced, and to his loneliness in the land of his sojournings; cf. xv. 1 (J).

I am with thee] Cf. v. 3, xxviii. 15, xxxi. 3. Isaac might feel lonely

J 25 servant Abraham's sake. And he builded an altar there, and called upon the name of the LORD, and pitched his
26 tent there: and there Isaac's servants digged a well. Then Abimelech went to him from Gerar, and Ahuzzath his
27 friend, and Phicol the captain of his host. And Isaac said unto them, Wherefore are ye come unto me, seeing ye
28 hate me, and have sent me away from you? And they said, We saw plainly that the LORD was with thee: and we said, Let there now be an oath betwixt us, even betwixt us and
29 thee, and let us make a covenant with thee; that thou wilt do us no hurt, as we have not touched thee, and as we have done unto thee nothing but good, and have sent thee away

as a stranger (*gêr*) in the land, but he was assured of the presence of Jehovah wherever he went.

for my servant...sake]. See note on *v*. 5. The title "my servant" here given to Abraham is only found in this place in Genesis. LXX reads "thy father." But it was the obedience of Abraham that won for him this great title: cf. Isai. xli. 8, "Israel my servant...Abraham my friend."

25. *builded...there*] As Abraham had done, xii. 7, xiii. 18.

called...LORD] See notes on iv. 26, xxi. 33.

digged a well] According to xxi. 30 a well had already been digged by Abraham. The word in the Hebrew is not the same as that used in *v*. 22; see l. 5.

26—33 (J). ABIMELECH'S COVENANT WITH ISAAC.

26. *Then Abimelech*] The king of Gerar discerns that Isaac's prosperity can only be explained by the special blessing of Jehovah his God (*v*. 29). He deems it wise policy to make terms with so powerful a person. Abimelech is accompanied by his two officers of state.

Ahuzzath his friend] This proper name has a termination like that of the Philistine name "Goliath" (1 Sam. xvii. 4). The king's "friend" was probably his chief favourite and councillor; cf. 2 Sam. xv. 37; 1 Kings iv. 5; 1 Chron. xxvii. 33. The LXX strangely renders by νυμφαγωγός, "the friend of the bridegroom" (cf. Judg. xiv. 11, 20, xv. 2, 6), i.e. "the intimate friend."

Phicol] See xxi. 22. Possibly also a Philistine name. Phicol represented the army, Ahuzzath the court.

28. *an oath*] A compact sealed by an oath. Cf. Deut. xxix. 12; Neh. x. 29.

covenant] See on this word (*b'rîth*) the note on xv. 18.

29. *as we have...but good*] This statement, scarcely veracious in view of *vv*. 15, 20, 21, is evidently made in the interests of policy.

in peace: thou art now the blessed of the LORD. And he 30 J made them a feast, and they did eat and drink. And 31 they rose up betimes in the morning, and sware one to another: and Isaac sent them away, and they departed from him in peace. And it came to pass the same day, that 32 Isaac's servants came, and told him concerning the well which they had digged, and said unto him, We have found water. And he called it Shibah: therefore the name of the 33 city is Beer-sheba unto this day.

And when Esau was forty years old he took to wife 34 P Judith the daughter of Beeri the Hittite, and Basemath the daughter of Elon the Hittite: and they were ¹a grief of 35 mind unto Isaac and to Rebekah.

¹ Heb. *bitterness of spirit*.

the blessed of the LORD] Cf. *v.* 12 and xxiv. 31.

30. *a feast*] A "feast" was partaken of by the two parties in a covenant. Cf. xxxi. 54. Here it is an evening "drinking banquet"; cf. xix. 3.

31. *betimes*] More often rendered "early"; cf. 2 Chron. xxxvi. 15. The etymology of the Old English word is "by time," i.e. "in good time." See Ps. v. 3 (P.B.V.).

sware] Cf. on xxi. 31.

33. *Shibah*] This word, denoting "oath-taking" or "swearing," is here given as the explanation of the name "Beer-sheba." For another tradition as to the origin of the name, see xxi. 31. The narrative there is from E; the narrative here from J. *Shebûah*, of which *shib'ah* is a rare variety, is an "oath"; *sheba'* is "seven." Aquila and Symmachus πλησμονή; Lat. *abundantiam*; reading *sib'ah*.

unto this day] See note on xxii. 14.

34, 35 (P). ESAU'S HITTITE WIVES.

34. *forty years old*] The same age as Isaac, when he married Rebekah, xxv. 20.

Judith...Basemath...Hittite] See xxxvi. 2, 3. Judith and Basemath are here described as "Hittites," by which name were known, according to P, some of the principal inhabitants of the land; cf. note on xxiii. 3. Groups of Hittites doubtless had come from the north and settled in Canaan. But in P there is little difference between Canaanites and Hittites.

35. *a grief of mind*] Heb. *bitterness of spirit*. Cf. xxvii. 46, xxviii. 8. Isaac and Rebekah regarded a mixed marriage with the people of the land as a source of dishonour to the race; cf. xxiv. 3.

GENESIS XXVII. 1—6

J 27 And it came to pass, that when Isaac was old, and his eyes were dim, so that he could not see, he called Esau his elder son, and said unto him, My son: and he said unto
2 him, Here am I. And he said, Behold now, I am old,
3 I know not the day of my death. Now therefore take, I pray thee, thy weapons, thy quiver and thy bow, and go
4 out to the field, and take me venison; and make me savoury meat, such as I love, and bring it to me, that I may
5 eat; that my soul may bless thee before I die. And Rebekah heard when Isaac spake to Esau his son. And Esau went to the field to hunt for venison, and to bring it.
6 And Rebekah spake unto Jacob her son, saying, Behold, I heard thy father speak unto Esau thy brother, saying,

By "a grief of mind" we should understand soreness and disappointment; cf. Prov. xiv. 10. The LXX ἐρίζουσαι, Lat. *offenderant animam*, took the meaning to be that Judith and Basemath were quarrelsome, and had given offence to Esau's parents.

CH. XXVII. 1—45 (J, E). THE BLESSING OF ISAAC AND JACOB'S DECEIT.

This narrative is taken from J, though possibly it includes extracts from E. It is a famous and graphically written piece of literature. The lifelike personal touches are not allowed to obscure the element of racial or national motive, which describes the outwitting of the older and more stupid Edomite by the younger and cleverer Israelite.

1. *Isaac was old*] According to P, Isaac was forty years old when he married Rebekah (xxv. 20); sixty years old when Esau and Jacob were born (xxv. 26); and a hundred years old when Esau married Judith and Basemath (xxvi. 34).

his eyes were dim] The narrative assumes that Isaac is in extreme old age, and feeling the nearness of death (cf. xlviii. 10). Cf. 1 Kings xiv. 4.

he called Esau] His favourite son (cf. xxv. 28).

2. *I know not the day of my death*] Isaac expects that death is at hand, and fears lest he should die without having pronounced the blessing on his son. The dying utterance was deemed prophetic, xlviii. 21, l. 24; 2 Sam. xxiii. 1—5.

3. *thy weapons*] The quiver and bow are the huntsman's weapons. Esau as "a man of the field" (xxv. 27) is to go out "to the field," i.e. the open country. Targum of Onkelos, "thy sword and thy bow"; cf. xlviii. 22.

4. *that my soul may bless thee*] Cf. 19, 25, 31. See note on xii. 13. A sacrificial meal is not intended. The strengthening food is from the chase, not the flesh of domestic animals.

Bring me venison, and make me savoury meat, that I 7 J
may eat, and bless thee before the LORD before my death.
Now therefore, my son, obey my voice according to that 8
which I command thee. Go now to the flock, and fetch 9
me from thence two good kids of the goats; and I will
make them savoury meat for thy father, such as he loveth:
and thou shalt bring it to thy father, that he may eat, so 10
that he may bless thee before his death. And Jacob said to 11
Rebekah his mother, Behold, Esau my brother is a hairy
man, and I am a smooth man. My father peradventure 12
will feel me, and I shall seem to him as a ¹deceiver; and I
shall bring a curse upon me, and not a blessing. And his 13
mother said unto him, Upon me be thy curse, my son:

¹ Or, *mocker*

7. *before the* LORD] i.e. in the presence of Jehovah, and in acknowledgment of His power, the human blessing will be pronounced, and will be effectual. The supposition that "before the LORD" means before an image of Jehovah in the house, is an arbitrary one. A local sanctuary, such as we may suppose was sought by Rebekah (xxv. 22), is not here implied. Isaac contemplates a religious act of blessing performed under the inspiring consciousness of the Divine Presence.

8. *obey my voice*] Jacob is Rebekah's favourite; cf. xxv. 28. Rebekah is prepared to deceive Isaac, in order that Jacob may obtain the coveted blessing. As in chap. xxiv., she shews energy and decision. She believes that Isaac's blessing of Esau would have the effect of reversing the oracle she herself had received (xxv. 23) and nullifying the privilege Jacob had purchased (xxv. 33). She is jealous for his sake.

11. *And Jacob said*, &c.] Jacob objects to the proposal, not because of its deceitfulness, but because of the risk of detection.

a hairy man] See xxv. 25 (E).

12. *will feel me*] Isaac's sight was no longer good enough to distinguish between his sons; but the sense of touch would remove all doubt.

a deceiver] Better, as R.V. marg., *a mocker*. LXX ὡς καταφρονῶν, "a profane trifler," one who treats in a contemptuous way the solemn religious blessing of his father. A rare Heb. word, rendered "scoff," 2 Chron. xxxvi. 16.

a curse] Jacob apprehends that his profanity will be visited by a solemn religious denunciation. If so, he will be a loser, not a gainer, by the trick. The thought of risk, not the deception, troubles him.

13. *thy curse*] i.e. "the penalty pronounced upon thee." Rebekah is prepared to take upon herself the evil consequences. Absorbed

GENESIS XXVII. 13—20

14 only obey my voice, and go fetch me them. And he went, and fetched, and brought them to his mother: and his
15 mother made savoury meat, such as his father loved. And Rebekah took the goodly raiment of Esau her elder son, which were with her in the house, and put them upon Jacob
16 her younger son: and she put the skins of the kids of the goats upon his hands, and upon the smooth of his neck:
17 and she gave the savoury meat and the bread, which she
18 had prepared, into the hand of her son Jacob. And he came unto his father, and said, My father: and he said,
19 Here am I; who art thou, my son? And Jacob said unto his father, I am Esau thy firstborn; I have done according as thou badest me: arise, I pray thee, sit and eat of my
20 venison, that thy soul may bless me. And Isaac said unto his son, How is it that thou hast found it so quickly, my son? And he said, Because the LORD thy God sent me

in her plan, she will not waste time upon the consideration of ill results. The character of Lady Macbeth in Shakespeare admits of comparison with that of Rebekah in this scene.

15. *the goodly raiment*] "Goodly," lit. "choice," "desirable." By this is meant the clothes worn by Esau on festivals and solemn occasions. Their odour was familiar, *v.* 27. It was the ancient Jewish idea that *priestly* garments were meant.

with her in the house] We are to infer from this expression that in this narrative of J (E) there is no knowledge of Esau's marriage with the Hittite women as recorded by P in xxvi. 34. Esau as a married man would have had a separate establishment. His festal attire would not have been in his mother's keeping.

16. *the skins of the kids*] An extraordinary comment upon the description of Esau as "a hairy man" (xxv. 25).

18. *who art thou, my son*] These words indicate the state of blindness of Isaac. The element of doubt arises from an imperfect recognition of the voice.

19. *And Jacob said*] Jacob's reply combines (*a*) a statement of direct falsehood and (*b*) a specious assumption of virtue in the prompt obedience to his father's command.

20. *How is it...quickly*] Isaac's question implies a second shadow of doubt. This time it arises not from the voice, but from the disquieting thought of the extraordinary rapidity of the huntsman's good fortune.

Because the LORD thy God] Jacob takes a third step in deceitfulness. To the lie and the vaunt of *v.* 19 he now adds the profanity of claiming the Divine assistance. But, at least, he says "the LORD thy God": his conscience does not quite permit him to say "the LORD my God."

GENESIS XXVII. 20—27

good speed. And Isaac said unto Jacob, Come near, I 21
pray thee, that I may feel thee, my son, whether thou be my
very son Esau or not. And Jacob went near unto Isaac 22
his father; and he felt him, and said, The voice is Jacob's
voice, but the hands are the hands of Esau. And he dis- 23
cerned him not, because his hands were hairy, as his brother
Esau's hands: so he blessed him. And he said, Art thou 24
my very son Esau? And he said, I am. And he said, 25
Bring it near to me, and I will eat of my son's venison, that
my soul may bless thee. And he brought it near to him,
and he did eat: and he brought him wine, and he drank.
And his father Isaac said unto him, Come near now, and 26
kiss me, my son. And he came near, and kissed him: 27
and he smelled the smell of his raiment, and blessed him,
and said,

See, the smell of my son
Is as the smell of a field which the LORD hath blessed:

sent me good speed] Lit. "caused it opportunely to come into my presence," the same word as in xxiv. 12. Lat. *voluntas Dei fuit ut cito occurreret mihi quod volebam.* The reference to the Divine Name adds to the deceit a taint of pious hypocrisy.

21. *Come near*] Isaac's shadow of suspicion has not yet been dispelled, even by the invocation of the Divine Name. He requires to be assured by the very test that Jacob, in *v.* 12, had dreaded would defeat his mother's stratagem. This point raises the excitement of the story.

22. *And Jacob went near*] Luther says, "Had I been Jacob, I should have dropped the dish."

The voice is Jacob's voice] Here is expressed the original source of Isaac's hesitation. The touch of his arms dispels all doubt; cf. *vv.* 14, 16.

23. *blessed*] Anticipating *vv.* 26—29.

25. *did eat...drank*] The feast, consisting of food and drink, is the preliminary to the solemn ceremony of blessing, just as it precedes the rites of a covenant; cf. xxvi. 30; xxxi. 54.

27. *he smelled*] The scent of the "field" forms the starting-point of the Oracle, or Song, of Blessing. The blessing is concerned not with the personal destiny of Jacob, but with the national history of the Israelite people. Cf. the blessing of Jacob on Joseph (xlix. 22 ff.). What "the smell of his raiment" had to do with "the goodly raiment" of *v.* 15, is not explained.

as the smell of a field] Cf. Hos. xiv. 6, "and his smell as Lebanon." Isaac's words refer to the "field" of xxv. 27, xxvii. 5, the country

> J 28   And God give thee of the dew of heaven,
>   And of the fatness of the earth,
>   And plenty of corn and wine:
>   29   Let peoples serve thee,
>   And nations bow down to thee:
>   Be lord over thy brethren,

of the huntsman. Before Isaac's mind rises up the picture of a rich and fruitful land.

which the LORD hath blessed] i.e. by fertility. The versions prefix an adjective denoting "plenty" before the word "field." LXX ἀγροῦ πλήρους; Lat. *agri pleni*.

Isaac's utterance is in poetical form. The two clauses in this verse serve as a prelude to the blessing of *vv.* 28 and 29.

28. *And God give thee*] The blessing of the firstborn in this and the following verse is solemnly pronounced by Isaac. It is irrevocable; see *v.* 33. It invokes (*a*) blessings of fertility upon the soil, (*b*) blessings of victory over other nations, (*c*) blessings of predominance over kindred tribes and clans.

This invocation is closed by the short and solemn utterance of a curse against the foe, and of a benediction upon the friend.

the dew of heaven] The blessing from above, cf. xlix. 25, "with blessings of heaven above." In a hot country the dew falling heavily by night is a source of fruitfulness to the land; and gives refreshing coolness to the atmosphere. Cf. Deut. xxxiii. 13, 28; Zech. viii. 12.

the fatness of the earth] The other side of the blessing of prosperity is supplied by the fertility of the soil, for which the Heb. expression is "the fat things." By "the earth" is clearly indicated a parallel to "the heaven" in the previous clause. There is no need for supposing, as some scholars have done, that Isaac here identifies Canaan with "the earth." See Num. xiii. 20; Neh. ix. 25, 35, "fat land"; Is. xxviii. 1, "fat valley"; Ezek. xxxiv. 14, "fat pasture."

plenty of corn and wine] The two most typical illustrations of agricultural wealth; cf. Ex. xxii. 5; Num. xx. 17. We find "corn," "wine," and "oil," represented as the three blessings of the soil in Deut. vii. 13; and "corn" and "wine" in Deut. xxxiii. 28; Ps. iv. 7.

29. *Let peoples*, &c.] The first half of this verse seems to refer to conquest over foreign foes; the second half to pre-eminence among the kindred races. The complete fulfilment of this prediction cannot have taken place before the times of David (cf. 2 Sam. viii.) and Solomon. The "peoples" and "nations," who "served" and "bowed down," were the Canaanites; the "brethren" and the "mother's sons" were the Edomites, Ammonites, Moabites, and Amalekites.

lord...brethren] These words recall the oracle given to Rebekah in xxv. 23. The irony of the situation is that Isaac, predicting, as he supposes, Esau's predominance over Jacob, seems to be reversing the

And let thy mother's sons bow down to thee:
Cursed be every one that curseth thee,
And blessed be every one that blesseth thee.

30 And it came to pass, as soon as Isaac had made an end of blessing Jacob, and Jacob was yet scarce gone out from the presence of Isaac his father, that Esau his brother came in from his hunting. 31 And he also made savoury meat, and brought it unto his father; and he said unto his father, Let my father arise, and eat of his son's venison, that thy soul may bless me. 32 And Isaac his father said unto him, Who art thou? And he said, I am thy son, thy firstborn, Esau. 33 And Isaac trembled very exceedingly, and said, Who then is he that hath taken venison, and brought it me, and I have eaten of all before thou camest, and have blessed him? yea, *and* he shall be blessed. 34 When Esau heard the words

decree, "the elder shall serve the younger." In reality he ratifies and endorses it.

thy brethren] The word is here poetically used in the sense of "kindred." The blessing impersonates the nation in the individual. It prefigures kindred races in the individual's brethren: see note on *v.* 40. This blessing, as applied to Jacob, was fulfilled in the subjugation of Edom, Moab, and Ammon in the reign of David.

Cursed be every one] For this formula concluding a blessing, cf. xii. 3, and Num. xxiv. 9. Words of good omen end the utterance.

30. *Jacob was yet...out*] These words dramatically represent to us the rapid succession of the two scenes, and remind us that, had Esau arrived a few minutes earlier, the *dénouement* would have been entirely different. Rebekah's trick has been wholly successful. Jacob has won the blessing of the firstborn; he has won it with scarcely a minute to spare. A moment earlier; and he would have been detected "flagrante delicto." The detection was bound to be made. But the risk was run for the sake of the irreversible and sacred "blessing of primogeniture," conferred by a dying father.

31. *Let my father arise*] Cf. 19. The effect of this scene is heightened by the use of almost identical language.

32. *thy son, thy firstborn, Esau*] For this triple emphasis, cf. xxii. 2. Esau answers, as if he were surprised that Isaac should have asked who he was, or possibly at the agitated manner of the questioner.

33. *trembled very exceedingly*] Isaac's agitation is expressed in the original with an emphasis which our version can hardly reproduce. Lat. "*expavit Isaac stupore vehementi et ultra quam credi potest admirans*," where two renderings seem to be combined. LXX ἐξέστη ἔκστασιν μεγάλην σφόδρα.

and he shall be blessed] Isaac, even in this moment of agitation,

J of his father, he cried with an exceeding great and bitter cry, and said unto his father, Bless me, even me also, O my 35 father. And he said, Thy brother came with guile, and 36 hath taken away thy blessing. And he said, Is not he rightly named Jacob? for he hath supplanted me these two times: he took away my birthright; and, behold, now he hath taken away my blessing. And he said, Hast thou 37 not reserved a blessing for me? And Isaac answered and said unto Esau, Behold, I have made him thy lord, and all his brethren have I given to him for servants; and with corn and wine have I sustained him: and what then shall I 38 do for thee, my son? And Esau said unto his father, Hast thou but one blessing, my father? bless me, even me also,

admits that the blessing of the firstborn has been pronounced with all due regularity, and is irrevocable. The Divine purpose has been affirmed. Esau, the firstborn, has not received the blessing. It could, therefore, only have been Jacob, the supplanter, whose voice at the first Isaac had thought he recognized.

34. *an exceeding...cry*] These are the words to which reference is made in Heb. xii. 17. Esau had hoped to win back through his father's fondness the privileges which he himself had bartered away through his own thoughtless folly. His disappointment is all the greater, because he believed that he was about to recover that which his conscience told him he had already forfeited in an unworthy and trifling spirit.

35. *Thy brother...guile*] Isaac at once concludes that the deceiver was Jacob, and acknowledges that Jacob's trick has succeeded.

36. *rightly named Jacob*] See note on xxv. 26.

supplanted] i.e. "outwitted," "overreached by guile." The word in the original is of the same root as the word "Jacob." It is as if Esau had said "he hath 'Jacob-ed' me these two times"; "he hath twice overreached me." See Jer. ix. 4. LXX ἐπτέρνικε, Lat. *supplantavit*. Our word "supplant" is probably derived from this context.

he took away my birthright] See xxv. 29—34. Esau now applies the words "took away" to the transaction in which he was foolish enough, not only to sell his birthright for a "mess of pottage," but also to ratify his action with an oath. He tries to hide his own folly by denouncing his brother's part in the affair.

my blessing] The word "my blessing" is spelt in the Heb. with the same consonants as "my birthright," but with two letters transposed. The difference between the birthright or *primogenita*, and the blessing or *benedictio*, is that between a title of privilege and the patent which confers it.

38. *but one blessing*] Esau's words shew the importance attached to the blessing invoked by the dying head of the family. Isaac's words

O my father. And Esau lifted up his voice, and wept. J
And Isaac his father answered and said unto him, 39
  Behold, ¹of the fatness of the earth shall be thy dwelling,

¹ Or, *away from*

in the preceding verse, coupled with Esau's exclamation, imply that there was only one blessing. Esau knows that the blessing once given cannot be recalled.

wept] Cf. xxi. 16. "Those tears of Esau, the sensuous, wild, impulsive man,—almost like the cry of some 'trapped creature,' are among the most pathetic in the Bible" (Davidson, *Hebrews*, 242).

39. *Behold*, &c.] Isaac's utterance again takes the form of poetry. His prediction as to Esau's future is contained in 6 strophes; 1 and 2 refer to the physical conditions of the nation's existence; 3 to its manner of life; 4 to its temporary subjection to Israel; 5 to its revolt; 6 to its ultimate independence.

of] Better, as R.V. marg., *away from*. The Heb. preposition *min*, "from," admits of both renderings. The oracle is intentionally ambiguous. In *v*. 28 ("*of* the dew...*of* the fatness") there can be no doubt the preposition is used in its partitive sense. (*a*) The English versions in this verse translate *min* by "of," as in *v*. 28. It might be expected that a preposition used by the same person, with the same nouns, and in a similar context in the same passage, would be identical in meaning. According to this rendering, Isaac promises to Esau a country blessed with rich soil and favourable physical conditions: but he cannot promise a settled or happy government; only a struggle for existence, a temporary servitude, and final freedom. This interpretation, however, seems to miss the point of Isaac's prediction as to the future material conditions of Esau's lot. The land of Edom was rugged and mountainous; Esau will live by the sword, not by the fertility of the soil.

(*b*) It is better to follow the margin, "away from"; cf. 2 Sam. i. 22. Isaac has really only one blessing; cf. *v*. 33. Esau's future will not be as Jacob's. His country in Mount Seir will not be rich and fertile, like the land of Canaan. His people will not be peaceful cultivators of the soil; they will dwell in the mountains, and get their livelihood as robbers. Edom will serve Israel; but only for a time. This is the climax of the prediction. In spite of hardships, in spite of social inferiority, and in spite of subjugation, Edom shall at last win freedom. According to this interpretation, Isaac's words contain no soft blessing; but a stern, truthful, continuous prediction, describing (1) the barrenness and aridity of the soil of Edom, (2) the warlike temper of the people, (3) their subjugation to Israel, (4) their ultimate revolt and freedom.

The blessing of Jacob excludes the blessing of Esau; but does not shut out the hope of successful rebellion against the favoured brother. The play of words, produced by the different use of the same preposition, is what might be expected in the language of an ancient oracle; and is

J

And ¹of the dew of heaven from above;
40 And by thy sword shalt thou live, and thou shalt serve thy brother;
And it shall come to pass when thou shalt break loose,
That thou shalt shake his yoke from off thy neck.

41 And Esau hated Jacob because of the blessing wherewith his father blessed him: and Esau said in his heart, The days of mourning for my father are at hand; then will I slay my

¹ Or, *away from*

quite congenial to the genius of Heb. literature. For the oracular and different use of the same words, cf. xl. 13, 19.

fatness...dew of heaven] See note on *v.* 28.

40. *by thy sword*] The soil will not furnish means of subsistence. The life of marauders dwelling in mountain fastnesses is here depicted. They will raid their brother's borders. They will cut off the merchants travelling with caravans and camels between the Red Sea and Syria.

thou shalt serve thy brother] Cf. xxv. 23. The people of Edom were first subjugated by Israel in the reign of David. Cf. 2 Sam. viii. 14.

break loose] Better, as Driver, "become restless." The word in the original is obscure, being found elsewhere only in Ps. lv. 2, "restless"; Jer. ii. 31, "broken loose"; Hos. xi. 12 (R.V. marg. *is yet unstedfast with*). Probably the metaphor is that of an animal shaking itself free from restraint. The A.V. "shalt have dominion" is quite impossible. Dillmann, "when thou shalt make efforts, or strive," as the Arabian and Ethiopian versions.

Lat. *tempusque veniet, cum excutias et solvas jugum ejus.*

shake...neck] The metaphor is that of the bull refusing the yoke. Edom successfully threw off the yoke of the kingdom of Judah in the reigns of Jehoram, 2 Kings viii. 20—22, and Ahaz, 2 Kings xvi. 6. But freedom from the dominion of Israel was followed by submission to Assyria. Edom appears among those who paid tribute to the Assyrian king Tiglath-Pileser III (731 B.C.), the Pul of 2 Kings xv. 19, 20.

41. *The days of mourning*, &c.] Cf. l. 3, 4, 10. The meaning is obvious. Esau says in his heart, "Isaac my father is on the point of death: no sooner shall he die, than I will take revenge. Even while the customary mourning is going on, I will slay Jacob." Before seven days have elapsed (cf. l. 3) he will have had his revenge. For "say in one's heart," cf. viii. 21, xxiv. 45 (J).

Very improbable is the interpretation which makes "the days of mourning, &c." mean "the days of mourning by my father," i.e. "for the death of Jacob."

then will I slay] The word "then" is simply "and" in the original. The clause is consecutive. There is no adverb defining the point of time. But the idiom emphasizes the dependence of the second clause upon the first.

brother Jacob. And the words of Esau her elder son were 42
told to Rebekah; and she sent and called Jacob her younger
son, and said unto him, Behold, thy brother Esau, as touching thee, doth comfort himself, *purposing* to kill thee. Now 43
therefore, my son, obey my voice; and arise, flee thou to
Laban my brother to Haran; and tarry with him a few days, 44
until thy brother's fury turn away; until thy brother's anger 45
turn away from thee, and he forget that which thou hast
done to him: then I will send, and fetch thee from thence:
why should I be bereaved of you both in one day?

42. *the words of Esau*] Esau's threat in the previous verse was "said in his heart"; but his was not a nature to keep a secret. His intention was soon the subject of talk.

doth comfort himself] A strange, but expressive phrase, lit. "is comforting himself with regard to thee, in order to kill thee": as we should say, "hugs himself," or "takes satisfaction," in the thought that he will shortly kill thee. The versions LXX ἀπειλεῖ "threatens," Lat. *minatur* translate erroneously.

43. *obey my voice*] Rebekah takes full responsibility upon herself, in fulfilment of her promise in *v.* 13, "upon me be thy curse, my son, only obey my voice."

44. *a few days*] Cf. xxix. 20, "but a few days," in the sense of "a short time." Rebekah's plan was, in this respect, destined to be signally frustrated, cf. xxix. 30, xxxi. 41. She was separated from her favourite son for over 20 years.

45. *I will send, and fetch thee*] There is no mention of this part of Rebekah's promise being fulfilled.

be bereaved of you both] The expression seems to be a reference to the custom of blood-revenge, as in 2 Sam. xiv. 7. The life of the murderer would be required by the family. He must either be banished from the family, or judicially put to death. In either case the parents would be "bereaved of both."

Or, possibly, "you both" refers to Isaac, her husband, and Jacob, her favourite son. On the day of Isaac's death, Esau intended to slay Jacob.

46 and ch. xxviii. 1—9. This passage is from P, as is shewn by the characteristic language and phraseology. It supplies a different motive for Jacob's journey. He is to go to Paddan-aram, xxviii. 2, not to Haran as in xxvii. 43. Jacob's deception is ignored; his departure is on a journey for a visit, and on a mission for a wife, not in flight from fear of assassination. Esau, in xxviii. 6, makes no reference to the events recorded in chap. xxvii. The passage interrupts the story of Jacob in J, which is resumed in xxviii. 10; it gives a parallel and distinct treatment of Jacob's journey into the Aramaean region: it refers back to a previous passage from P, which records how Esau had married two

P **46** And Rebekah said to Isaac, I am weary of my life because of the daughters of Heth: if Jacob take a wife of the daughters of Heth, such as these, of the daughters of **28** the land, what good shall my life do me? And Isaac called Jacob, and blessed him, and charged him, and said unto him, Thou shalt not take a wife of the daughters of **2** Canaan. Arise, go to Paddan-aram, to the house of Bethuel thy mother's father; and take thee a wife from thence of the **3** daughters of Laban thy mother's brother. And ¹God Almighty bless thee, and make thee fruitful, and multiply **4** thee, that thou mayest be a company of peoples; and give thee the blessing of Abraham, to thee, and to thy seed with

¹ Heb. *El Shaddai*.

"Hittite" wives (xxvi. 34, 35). Rebekah fears Jacob may do the same; Jacob is sent away with Isaac's blessing (xxviii. 3, 4), and without reference to the great deception.

46. *I am weary of my life*] See note on xxvi. 34, 35. The "daughters of Heth" clearly mean Esau's two wives. This passage resumes the P narrative of xxvi. 35.

what good, &c.] Cf. Rebekah's words, xxv. 22, "if it be so, wherefore do I live?"

xxviii. **1.** *and blessed him*] This mention of Isaac's blessing of Jacob, without reference to the deception in chap. xxvii., is a clear indication of the distinctness of origin of this passage from that which precedes it.

Thou shalt not...Canaan] Cf. xxiv. 3. "The daughters of Canaan" cannot be distinguished from "the daughters of Heth" (xxvii. 46).

2. *Paddan-aram*] See note on xxv. 20. This is the name given by P (cf. xxxi. 18, xxxiii. 18, xxxv. 9, 26, xlvi. 15) to the region which in the J narrative is called "Haran": another indication of the literary distinctness of this passage from that which immediately precedes it: see xxvii. 43.

3. *God Almighty*] Heb. *El Shaddai*. This Divine Name is here communicated by Isaac to Jacob: see note on xvii. 1 (P).

make...multiply] See note on i. 22: a phrase characteristic of P, cf. viii. 17, ix. 1, 7, xvii. 20, xxxv. 11, xlviii. 4.

a company of peoples] A phrase used in the blessings, in P's narrative, xxxv. 11, xlviii. 4. The Heb. *k'hal 'ammîm* combines the two terms used for "assembly" (*kâhâl*) and "people" (*'am*), as in Ezek. xxiii. 24, xxxii. 3. LXX renders εἰς συναγωγὰς ἐθνῶν. Compare "a multitude of nations" in xvii. 5 (P).

4. *the blessing of Abraham*] Probably a reference to xvii. 8. The same blessing as Abraham received is now pronounced by Isaac upon Jacob, recognizing him as the religious representative of the family, and ignoring Esau. This verse would be almost unintelligible, if we were

thee; that thou mayest inherit the land of thy sojournings, P
which God gave unto Abraham. And Isaac sent away 5
Jacob: and he went to Paddan-aram unto Laban, son of
Bethuel the ¹Syrian, the brother of Rebekah, Jacob's and
Esau's mother. Now Esau saw that Isaac had blessed 6
Jacob and sent him away to Paddan-aram, to take him a
wife from thence; and that as he blessed him he gave him
a charge, saying, Thou shalt not take a wife of the daughters
of Canaan; and that Jacob obeyed his father and his 7
mother, and was gone to Paddan-aram: and Esau saw that 8
the daughters of Canaan pleased not Isaac his father; and 9
Esau went unto Ishmael, and took unto the wives which he
had Mahalath the daughter of Ishmael Abraham's son, the
sister of Nebaioth, to be his wife.

¹ Heb. *Aramean*.

not on literary grounds sure that this section is from the P tradition, and
is independent of the J narrative (chap. xxvii.), which describes Isaac's
age and Jacob's deceit towards his father in obtaining the blessing of
the firstborn. This is not the blessing of a dying man, but of a father
parting with a son. It repeats, in a summary form, the national aspect
of Abraham's blessing. It lacks the poetical vigour and spiritual
interest of the blessing in J (xxvii. 27—29).

the land of thy sojournings] A P phrase: see note on xvii. 8, and
cf. xxxvi. 7, xxxvii. 1. It is here applied by Isaac to Jacob's residence
in Canaan after his return from Paddan-aram.

5. *and he went to Paddan-aram unto Laban*] In this short sentence
the narrative of P disposes of the journey of Jacob, which is described
in much greater detail in the parallel narratives from J and E, preserved in *vv.* 10—22 and chap. xxix.

the Syrian] Heb. *Aramean*. Cf. xxv. 20; Deut. xxvi. 5.

6. *Now Esau saw*] The conduct of Esau in this passage is prompted
by the desire to obtain a blessing such as Isaac had given Jacob in
vv. 3, 4. In order to propitiate his father, he contracts a marriage with
his first cousin, the daughter of Ishmael. Neither in this, nor in the
following verse, is there implied any resentment on the part of Esau
towards Jacob, or any other reason for Jacob's journey to Paddan-aram
beyond that of marriage with one of his own kindred.

9. *unto the wives*] i.e. in addition to Judith and Basemath (xxvi. 34).

Mahalath...the sister of Nebaioth] Nebaioth was the firstborn son
of Ishmael (xxv. 13). In xxxvi. 3, the name of Ishmael's daughter,
sister of Nebaioth, appears as Basemath. Here she is called Mahalath;
while Basemath, in xxvi. 34, is the name of one of Esau's Hittite wives.

Ishmael is mentioned in this verse as the uncle of Esau. The reference is personal, though it may also denote tribal kinship. According

J 10   And Jacob went out from Beer-sheba, and went toward
E 11 Haran. | And he lighted upon ¹a certain place, and tarried
there all night, because the sun was set; and he took one
of the stones of the place, and put it under his head,
12 and lay down in that place to sleep. And he dreamed,
and behold a ladder set up on the earth, and the top of it

¹ Heb. *the place*.

to P's chronology, it would appear that Ishmael was at this time
114 years old, and lived for 23 years more. Cf. xvii. 24, 25, xxv. 17, 26,
xxvi. 34.

10—22. This section taken from J and E follows upon xxvii. 45.
Observe the mention of Haran in *v.* 10 (cf. xxvii. 43), and the mention
of Beer-sheba as the dwelling-place of Isaac in *v.* 10 (cf. xxvi. 23).
Vv. 10, 13—16, 19 are probably from J; *vv.* 11, 12, 17, 18, 20—22
from E.

This passage, recording Jacob's dream at Bethel, and the passage
in xxxii. 22—32, recording Jacob's wrestling with the Angel, relate the
most famous and significant events in the narrative of the patriarch
Jacob. The present passage is in some respects one of the most
suggestive and impressive in religious literature. The distinctive
features of the narrative have been an inspiration in the poetry and
prose of religious literature, e.g. the hymn "Nearer, my God, to Thee."

11.   *And he lighted*] i.e. he by chance reached, like our colloquial
"hit upon." The Divine purpose of the revelation made to Jacob is
contrasted in this word with the fortuitousness of Jacob's action.

a certain place] Heb. *the place*. For the special significance of
"place," with the possible meaning of "sacred spot," see note on
xii. 6. The scene of this story is afterwards (*v.* 19) identified as Bethel:
and it is natural to assume that the famous story of the Theophany to
Jacob was preserved and honoured at the shrine of Bethel.

put it under his head] Jacob makes a pillow of the stone: his action
in so doing, though it may sound strange to English readers, can be
illustrated by the ordinary experience of those who are acquainted with
Arab life and Oriental travel.

12.   *And he dreamed*] The vision, about to be described, is conveyed
through the medium of a dream; cf. xx. 3.

a ladder] It has been suggested, e.g. by Stanley (*Sinai and Palestine*,
p. 219) that the ledges of rock, one above the other, on the Bethel hill
produced an impression on the faculties of Jacob, which took the shape,
in his dream, of a flight of steps. By "a ladder," LXX κλίμαξ, Lat.
scala, we must not understand a house ladder, with uprights and rungs
of wood; but, rather, a stairway, or ascent by successive terraces.
Possibly, the "ladder" here mentioned resembled the ascent to
Babylonian and Assyrian temples, in which the shrine or sanctuary,
on the summit, was reached by steps leading through seven terraces,
corresponding to the seven planets: see note on xi. 4.

reached to heaven: and behold the angels of God ascending E
and descending on it. | And, behold, the LORD stood ¹above 13 J

¹ Or, *beside him*

on the earth...to heaven] The distinctive feature of the vision is the communication between earth and heaven.

For the impression produced upon the mind of a modern traveller by the scenery of this spot, see footnote[1].

the angels of God] For this unusual expression, cf. xxxii. 1, 2. The expression "the angel of God" is common, but that of "the angels of God" is most rare. We are to suppose that to the sleeper's eyes were revealed the heavenly hosts, the members and attendants of the heavenly court (see notes on i. 26 and vi. 2).

ascending and descending] See the use made of this vision in our Lord's words to Nathanael, John i. 51. "Ascending" comes before "descending," which reminds us that the process of Divine ministration to the sons of men has been going on before it is finally revealed to their spiritual faculties. "Ascending," with tasks completed: "descending," with fresh commissions from above.

13. *the LORD stood*] Lit. "was set, established, stationed," LXX ἐπεστήρικτο, Vulg. "innixum." The appearance of Jehovah is mentioned, but not described.

above it] Better, probably, as R.V. marg., *beside him*. Both renderings are possible. We should perhaps prefer that of the margin. The preposition is the same as in the account of the appearance of the three men to Abraham, xviii. 2 ("Lo, three men stood over against him"). On the other hand, the versions LXX ἐπ' αὐτῆς, Lat. and Syr. Pesh., render as R.V. text. But the substance of *vv.* 13, 14, 15 is a *personal* revelation to Jacob. It is distinct from the vision of *v.* 12, which, on a great and impressive scale, taught the general lesson of the union between earth and heaven. There is, therefore, reason for preferring the personal allusion, either "beside him," or "over (i.e. bending over) him." Jacob is lying down: Jehovah is standing by him. Jacob is made to realize the ever-protecting Presence, at his side, or watching over him.

[1] "One of the most singular stone formations west of the Jordan in Palestine is to be seen in the great stonefield a little to the north of the modern town of Beitin, the ancient Bethel....Huge stones seem to be piled one upon another to make columns nine or ten feet or more in height. In reality these columns are produced by erosion, and the different density of the strata has led to greater erosion in one part than in another, so that they taper and bulge in manifold and various shapes. So strong is the resemblance to construction made by men's hands that I myself have gone to this spot, not once but several times, and examined every stone, to make sure that there could be no mistake in my impression, and I have found that others have done the same thing. It is only after such a careful examination of the site that one convinces one's self that in reality these stone pillars are the work of nature, not of man....Surely it is a point at which heaven and earth meet. And there stand the pillars which the mighty heroes of antiquity erected....It was only the giant men of olden times who could set up as memorials of communion with God these mighty stones at this point where heaven and earth are so clearly united" (Peters, *Early Hebrew Story*, pp. 111, 112).

J it, and said, I am the LORD, the God of Abraham thy father, and the God of Isaac: the land whereon thou liest, to thee 14 will I give it, and to thy seed; and thy seed shall be as the dust of the earth, and thou shalt ¹spread abroad to the west, and to the east, and to the north, and to the south: and in thee and in thy seed shall all the families of the 15 earth be blessed. And, behold, I am with thee, and will keep thee whithersoever thou goest, and will bring thee again into this land; for I will not leave thee, until I have 16 done that which I have spoken to thee of. And Jacob awaked out of his sleep, and he said, Surely the LORD is E 17 in this place; and I knew it not. | And he was afraid, and said, How dreadful is this place! this is none other but 18 the house of God, and this is the gate of heaven. And

¹ Heb. *break forth*.

and said] The blessing of Jacob consists of (1) the Divine personal revelation; (2) the promise of the land (*v*. 13); (3) the multiplication of his descendants (*v*. 14); (4) the world's blessing through his seed (*v*. 14); (5) the personal promise of Presence and Protection (*v*. 15).

thy father] i.e. thy ancestor. Abraham's name is mentioned as that of the first recipient of the Divine promise.

the land] The renewal of the promise to Abraham, xiii. 14—16.

14. *as the dust of the earth*] Cf. xiii. 16.

spread abroad] Heb. *break forth*. Cf. xxx. 30, "increased," 43, Ex. i. 12.

to the west] Cf. xiii. 14.

in thee...be blessed] See note on xii. 3.

15. *I am with thee*] Cf. xxvi. 24, xxxi. 3. The personal promise to Jacob consists of (1) Divine Presence (*with thee*): (2) Divine preservation (*keep thee*): (3) Divine restoration (*bring again*): (4) Divine fulfilment of promise (*until I have done*).

16. *in this place*] Jacob's words express astonishment that Jehovah should have manifested Himself (*a*) in a place remote from his father's home; (*b*) to himself a solitary wanderer.

this place] Compare Ex. iii. 5, "the place whereon thou standest is holy ground"; Jos. v. 15, "the place whereon thou standest is holy."

17. *How dreadful*] This adjective is rendered unsuitable by colloquial usage. The sense would be better given by "awesome" or "terrible." Jacob believes that he has been in the presence of Jehovah and of the heavenly host. The belief that those who saw "the angel of the LORD" face to face would die is expressed in the terror of Jacob. Cf. Jud. vi. 22, 23, xiii. 21, 22.

the house of God] Heb. *bêth Elohim*, i.e. "a dwelling-place of the

Jacob rose up early in the morning, and took the stone E
that he had put under his head, and set it up for a pillar,
and poured oil upon the top of it. | And he called the 19 J
name of that place ¹Beth-el: but the name of the city was
Luz at the first. | And Jacob vowed a vow, saying, If God 20 E
will be with me, and will keep me in this way that I go, and

1 That is, *The house of God*.

Divine Being." This clause contains the popular etymology of the name *Bethel*.

18. *for a pillar*] Heb. *maṣṣēbah*. This word is used in the O.T. for the sacred upright stone which stood by the altar, and was one of the usual features of worship and sacrifice at a "high place" (*bâmah*). Its use is condemned in Deut. xvi. 22. But in Hos. iii. 4 it is associated with other forms of Israelite worship.

Here the erection and consecration of a stone as the memorial of the Divine manifestation, correspond with the religious use of such upright stones for purposes of ceremonial and symbolical offerings. Cf. xxxi. 45; Ex. xxiv. 4; Josh. iv. 3, xxiv. 26, 27; 1 Sam. vii. 12.

At the excavations in Gezer, eleven *maṣṣēbahs* were found standing close to the altar of the Canaanite "high place," cf. Driver's *Schweich Lectures*.

poured oil] Oil was used as the symbol of an offering made to the Divine Being, whose presence or abode is connected with the consecrated stone. For the use of oil in consecration, cf. Ex. xxx. 25—30; Lev. viii. 10; Num. vii. 1. There are many instances in ancient literature of sacred stones which were anointed with oil (λίθοι λιπαροί). Compare Tylor's *Primitive Culture*³, ii. 160—167.

19. *Beth-el*] That is, *The house of God*: see xxxv. 1, 6. This place was one of the most famous sanctuaries in Canaan. It was selected by Jeroboam as one of the High Places at which he set up the calves of gold (1 Kings xii. 29—33). For its repute and popularity as a sanctuary and place of pilgrimage, see Amos vii. 13: close by the altar of Bethel would stand the pillar connected with its worship, and associated with this story of Jacob. The site has been identified with the modern *Beitin*.

Luz] The old city's name mentioned also in xxxv. 6, xlviii. 3, Judg. i. 23, not identical with, but close to Bethel, Jos. xvi. 2. The narrative does not suggest that Jacob's dream was in the vicinity of a town.

20. *vowed a vow*] See xxxi. 13. This is the first mention in the O.T. of a religious vow, i.e. a solemn promise, enforced by an adjuration of the Deity, to dedicate, or wholly set apart, some offering or gift.

If God will be with me] Jacob's vow is made with special reference to the personal promise in *v*. 15. Its three conditions are: (1) Divine presence (*with me*), (2) Divine preservation (*keep me*), (3) Divine restoration (*so that I come again*).

E 21 will give me bread to eat, and raiment to put on, so that I come again to my father's house in peace, ¹then shall the
22 LORD be my God, and this stone, which I have set up for a pillar, shall be God's house: and of all that thou shalt give me I will surely give the tenth unto thee.

29 Then Jacob ²went on his journey, and came to the land
J 2 of the children of the east. | And he looked, and behold a

¹ Or, *and the* LORD *will be my God, then this stone &c.*
² Heb. *lifted up his feet.*

21. *to my father's house in peace*] It does not appear that this was literally fulfilled. Jacob, on his return, did not dwell at his father's house. But, perhaps, "father's house" means "the land of his fathers." "In peace," a common Heb. phrase, noticeable here for the rendering of LXX μετὰ σωτηρίας, "with safety."

then shall the LORD *be my God*] The rendering of the margin, *and the* LORD *will be my God, then this stone,* &c., is that of the ancient versions, LXX, Lat. and Syr.: that of the text is on the whole preferable. The crowning thought is that in days to come, Jehovah, who has been the God of Abraham and Isaac, shall also be the God of Jacob. This forms the substance of Jacob's vow; to which is added, that Bethel, as well as Beer-sheba and Hebron, shall be a place of Jehovah's worship. Jacob's vow, with the conditions attached to it, reflects his calculating character. But it acknowledges that Jehovah is the God who has revealed Himself to his fathers, and is distinct from mere nature-gods.

22. *God's house*] See note on *v.* 17. Here the title "God's house" is applied to the stone itself.

of all...give the tenth] Very strange is this concluding promise to pay a tithe to Jehovah. In xiv. 20, Abraham pays a tithe to Melchizedek of Jerusalem (?). The payment of tithe was maintained at Bethel in the times of the Israelite monarchy, cf. Amos iv. 4. The mention of Jacob's promise at Bethel to pay a tenth to Jehovah, shews that this Israelite religious usage was believed to go back to pre-Mosaic times. For the Levitical tenth or tithe, cf. Lev. xxvii. 30—33.

CHS. XXIX., XXX. JACOB IN HARAN, FROM J AND E.

xxix. 1—14.   Jacob at the well.
    15—30.   Jacob's marriage with Leah and Rachel.
  31—xxx. 24.   Birth of Jacob's children.
    25—43.   Jacob serves Laban for a wage in flocks and herds.

1. *went on his journey*] Heb. *lifted up his feet.*

the children of the east] A phrase generally used of the nomad Arab tribes to the east of Palestine: see note on xxv. 6. Cf. Num. xxiii. 7; Jud. vi. 3. Here it is used for the Aramaeans of Haran, N.E. of Palestine.

GENESIS XXIX. 2—7

well in the field, and, lo, three flocks of sheep lying there **J**
by it; for out of that well they watered the flocks: and the
stone upon the well's mouth was great. And thither were 3
all the flocks gathered: and they rolled the stone from the
well's mouth, and watered the sheep, and put the stone
again upon the well's mouth in its place. And Jacob said 4
unto them, My brethren, whence be ye? And they said,
Of Haran are we. And he said unto them, Know ye 5
Laban the son of Nahor? And they said, We know him.
And he said unto them, Is it well with him? And they 6
said, It is well: and, behold, Rachel his daughter cometh
with the sheep. And he said, Lo, it is yet high day, neither 7

In Hos. xii. 12 Jacob is said to have "fled into the field of Aram."

2. *in the field*] There is no exact description of the place where this well was. It was not, apparently, the same as "the well of water," "without the city," in xxiv. 11.

for out of that well] This clause and *v*. 3 are parenthetical, describing the custom of the country, i.e. "they were *wont to* water": "were *wont to* roll and put the stone again."

the stone upon the well's mouth] A well was a cistern or tank, often covered with a large stone requiring two or three men to remove it. This stone protected the water from the rays of the sun and from mischief or pollution. In the present instance the well seems to have belonged to the community, and was not opened for use, until all the herdsmen and shepherds had come.

4. *unto them*] i.e. the shepherds of the three flocks mentioned in *v*. 2.

Of Haran] See xxvii. 43. There is nothing to shew whether Haran, the town, was near or far off.

5. *Laban...of Nahor*] See note on xxiv. 15. In xxiv. 24 Rebekah is daughter of Bethuel, the son of Nahor. In xxiv. 29 ff. Laban is Rebekah's brother. Here he is son of Nahor. It is possible that the tradition, followed here and in chap. xxiv., differs from that of the genealogy in xxii. 20—23; or that Nahor is mentioned as more famous than Bethuel his son. Cf. Jehu who is called "son of Nimshi" (2 Kings ix. 20), though, in reality, his grandson (2 Kings ix. 2, 14).

6. *Rachel*] The name means "Ewe," a personal name, though, possibly, also tribal. In very early times, the designation of an animal seems often to have been transferred to a family or clan in connexion with the "totem," or animal associated in worship with the spirit-god of the community.

7. *it is yet high day*] Lit. "the day is great"; like the Fr. "*il fait grand jour*." Lat. *adhuc multum diei super est*. Jacob is a practical shepherd; he says "there is still the whole afternoon: what is the

J is it time that the cattle should be gathered together: water
8 ye the sheep, and go and feed them. And they said, We
cannot, until all the flocks be gathered together, and they
roll the stone from the well's mouth; then we water the
9 sheep. While he yet spake with them, Rachel came with
10 her father's sheep; for she kept them. And it came to
pass, when Jacob saw Rachel the daughter of Laban his
mother's brother, and the sheep of Laban his mother's
brother, that Jacob went near, and rolled the stone from the
well's mouth, and watered the flock of Laban his mother's
11 brother. And Jacob kissed Rachel, and lifted up his voice,
12 and wept. And Jacob told Rachel that he was her father's
brother, and that he was Rebekah's son: and she ran and
13 told her father. And it came to pass, when Laban heard
the tidings of Jacob his sister's son, that he ran to meet

good of wasting time, and delaying to water the sheep?" It was not yet time to gather together the animals to bring them back for the night.

8. *We cannot*] The local custom was not to be broken. All the flocks were to be collected, before any were to be watered; and then those who had come first had the privilege of watering their flocks first.

10. *went near, and rolled*] Jacob disregards the rule of the well; and at the risk of incurring the wrath of the local herdsmen and shepherds, by a feat of great personal strength, removes unaided the stone covering, and renders Rachel the service of watering Laban's flock. The shepherds were apparently kept quiet by the appearance of the stranger's energy and strength. For the whole scene, cf. the story of Moses, Ex. ii. 16—21.

11. *Jacob kissed...wept*] This demonstrative display of feeling is Homeric in its simplicity. The suddenness of Jacob's opportune meeting with his relatives, the removal of doubt and anxiety from his mind on entering a strange country, and the apparition of his young and fair cousin, had all deeply stirred his emotional nature. Cf. the tears of Joseph, xlv. 2, 14.

12. *her father's brother*] In the sense of "relative"; strictly speaking, her father's sister's son. Cf. *v.* 15 and xiii. 8.

ran and told] We are reminded of Rebekah's action in xxiv. 28, 29.

13. *Laban*] According to the P narrative, xxvi. 34, it was over forty years since Laban had said farewell to his sister Rebekah. He now effusively greets and welcomes her son. Perhaps he recollects the gifts of Rebekah's dowry (xxiv. 30), and also perceives in Jacob a strong and capable worker.

the tidings] LXX τὸ ὄνομα = "the name," with the omission of one letter in the original (*shêm* for *shêmaʻ*).

him, and embraced him, and kissed him, and brought him
to his house. And he told Laban all these things. And
Laban said to him, Surely thou art my bone and my flesh.
And he abode with him the space of a month. | And Laban
said unto Jacob, Because thou art my brother, shouldest
thou therefore serve me for nought? tell me, what shall thy
wages be? And Laban had two daughters: the name of
the elder was Leah, and the name of the younger was
Rachel. And Leah's eyes were tender; but Rachel was
beautiful and well favoured. And Jacob loved Rachel;
and he said, I will serve thee seven years for Rachel thy
younger daughter. And Laban said, It is better that I give
her to thee, than that I should give her to another man:
abide with me. And Jacob served seven years for Rachel;

kissed] The Hebrew verb expresses the warmth of the salutation.

14. *my bone and my flesh*] See note on ii. 23, and cf. xxxvii. 27.
Laban readily acknowledges the relationship which Jacob claims.

the space of a month] Lit. "a month of days." See on xxiv. 55, "*a few days*."

15—30. JACOB'S MARRIAGE WITH LEAH AND RACHEL.

15. *Because...brother*] Lit. "art thou a brother, and shouldest thou serve me for nothing?" For "brother," see note on *v.* 12. Laban asks Jacob to state on what terms he would serve.

16. *Leah*] The meaning of "Leah" is uncertain. According to some scholars, who see in it a *totem* name, it should be compared with an Arabic word meaning "a wild cow"; according to others, with an Assyrian word meaning "a lady."

17. *Leah's eyes were tender*] i.e. weak or soft, wanting in clearness and brilliancy. The eye was the chief feature of Oriental beauty. The versions rather exaggerate the sense. LXX ἀσθενεῖς="weak," Lat. *lippis oculis*, Aq. Sym. ἀπαλοί="tender."

beautiful and well favoured] Lit. "fair of form and fair of looks."
The Old English "favoured" has reference to personal appearance; cf. xli. 2, 4.

18. *I will serve...Rachel*] He has no money to offer; he is ready to give seven years' service without wages, in order to win Rachel as his bride. He cannot as bridegroom, or suitor, offer the usual gifts, or *mohar* (see note on xxiv. 53). So he offers the equivalent in work. See the reference to this incident in Hos. xii. 12.

19. *It is better*] Laban means that it is in the interests of the family his daughter should be married to one of their own kindred. The marriage of first cousins is considered especially desirable among the Bedouin.

E	and they seemed unto him but a few days, for the love he
	21 had to her. And Jacob said unto Laban, Give me my wife, for my days are fulfilled, that I may go in unto her.
	22 And Laban gathered together all the men of the place, and
	23 made a feast. And it came to pass in the evening, that he took Leah his daughter, and brought her to him; and he
P	24 went in unto her. | And Laban gave Zilpah his handmaid
E	25 unto his daughter Leah for an handmaid. | And it came to pass in the morning that, behold, it was Leah: and he said to Laban, What is this thou hast done unto me? did not I serve with thee for Rachel? wherefore then hast thou
	26 beguiled me? And Laban said, It is not so done in our
	27 place, to give the younger before the firstborn. Fulfil the week of this one, and we will give thee the other also for

20. *for the love*] These simple and touching words are noticeable for their beauty in a narrative which in many of its details is repulsive to our notions of delicacy.

22. *made a feast*] The marriage feast was a great affair. The ceremonial lasted for seven days. Cf. Judg. xiv. 10, 12; Tobit xi. 19. "All the men of the place," not only "brethren," i.e. "relations," are invited. "The place" is the residence of a large community, cf. v. 26.

23. *he took Leah*] The bride was brought to the bridegroom enveloped in a veil; cf. xxiv. 65. "The bridegroom can scarcely ever obtain even a surreptitious glance at the features of his bride until he finds her in his absolute possession." Lane, *Manners and Customs of the Modern Egyptians*.

24 (P). *Zilpah his handmaid*] For the custom of the bride being attended by her own servant to her new home, cf. xxiv. 59.

25. *beguiled*] i.e. "deceived," as Jos. ix. 22; but a different word in the Hebrew from that in iii. 13. Laban had succeeded in astutely bestowing his less attractive daughter in marriage.

26. *It is not so done*] Cf. xx. 9, xxxiv. 7; 2 Sam. xiii. 12. Laban's excuse was specious, that it was necessary to conform to local customs, and that Jacob, as a stranger, did not know them. But, if so, he should in decency and honour have explained the custom to Jacob before consenting to the marriage with the younger sister. In this disgraceful deception Laban's character is revealed; while Jacob, who deceived his father and his brother, is made to suffer himself from deception.

27. *Fulfil the week*] Laban's proposal is that when the week's marriage festivities for Leah are over, Jacob shall take Rachel as his second wife, on condition that he gives his services for another period of seven years. Nothing would justify the interruption of the seven days' marriage ceremonial.

the service which thou shalt serve with me yet seven other
years. And Jacob did so, and fulfilled her week: | and he 28
gave him Rachel his daughter to wife. And Laban gave to 29
Rachel his daughter Bilhah his handmaid to be her hand-
maid. | And he went in also unto Rachel, and he loved 30
also Rachel more than Leah, and served with him yet seven
other years.

E
P

E

And the LORD saw that Leah was hated, and he opened 31 J
her womb: but Rachel was barren. And Leah conceived, 32
and bare a son, and she called his name Reuben: for she
said, Because the LORD ¹hath looked upon my affliction;

¹ Heb. *raah beonyi.*

Marriage with two sisters was evidently free from objection in the primitive days of the Israelites; and, perhaps for that reason, it is introduced into the prophetical symbolism of Jer. iii. 6 ff. and Ezek. xxiii. But, in the Levitical law, marriage with two sisters simultaneously is forbidden; Lev. xviii. 18.

XXIX. 31—XXX. 24. BIRTH OF JACOB'S CHILDREN.

31—35 (J); xxx. 1—24 (J, E and P).

In this section is narrated the account of the birth of eleven sons and one daughter. Six of the sons, viz. Reuben, Simeon, Levi, Judah, Issachar and Zebulun, and the daughter Dinah, are the children of Leah; Gad and Asher are the sons of Zilpah, Leah's handmaid; Dan and Naphtali are the sons of Bilhah, Rachel's handmaid; and Joseph is the son of Rachel. These are all born to Jacob in Haran. The only son born in Canaan is Benjamin (see xxxv. 16—19).

It has been conjectured that this account not only furnishes the popular etymology of the names of the tribes of Israel, but may also symbolize, under the terms of family life, the growth of Israelite clans into a united, though composite, people in the land of Mesopotamia, before the migration into Canaan.

The explanation of the meaning of the names is of the usual popular kind, based upon resemblances of sound. The fact that in some cases more than one etymology is given reflects the composite nature of the narrative (cf. xxx. 16 and 18, 20, 23 and 24).

31. *hated*] By this is meant that Jacob had less affection for Leah than for Rachel. Cf. Deut. xxi. 15, "if a man have two wives, the one beloved and the other hated." In order to prevent the evil effects of jealousy, the marriage by one man of two sisters is forbidden in Lev. xviii. 18. See, also, Mal. i. 2, 3, "I loved Jacob, but Esau I hated."

32. *Reuben*] The name is evidently here assumed to consist of two words, *re'û* = "behold ye," *ben* = "a son."

hath...affliction] Heb. *râ'ah be'onyi*. The sound of these two words

J 33 for now my husband will love me. And she conceived again, and bare a son; and said, Because the LORD [1]hath heard that I am hated, he hath therefore given me this *son*
34 also: and she called his name [2]Simeon. And she conceived again, and bare a son; and said, Now this time will my husband be [3]joined unto me, because I have borne him
35 three sons: therefore was his name called Levi. And she conceived again, and bare a son: and she said, This time will I [4]praise the LORD: therefore she called his name [5]Judah; and she left bearing.

E 30 And when Rachel saw that she bare Jacob no children, Rachel envied her sister; and she said unto Jacob, Give me

[1] Heb. *shama*.   [2] Heb. *Shimeon*.   [3] From the root *lavah*.
[4] From the Heb. *hodah*.   [5] Heb. *Jehudah*.

forms some kind of a play on the name Reuben, and represents a popular and unscientific etymology. In some MSS. of LXX and the Syriac, and in Josephus, the name appears as "Reubel," which has been compared with the Arabic *Ri'bal*, meaning "a lion"; or it may be compounded with the name of the god *Bel* or *Baal*. The tribe Reuben settled between the Jabbok and the Arnon. See Judg. v. 15, 16.

"My affliction." LXX τὴν ταπείνωσιν = "low estate"; cf. 1 Sam. i. 11; Luke i. 48.

33. *heard*] Heb. *shama*; cf. xvi. 11.

Simeon] Heb. *Shimeon*. The meaning of this name is very likely that of an animal, "the hyaena"; cf. the Arabic *sim'*, the hybrid offspring of the hyaena and the female wolf.

34. *joined*] From the root *lavah*, "to join." In Numb. xviii. 2, 4, this word *lavah* is especially used of the *attachment* of the sons of Levi to the service of Jehovah, as the priestly tribe. According to many scholars, the name denotes *the* tribe *par excellence* of the Leah group; which, owing to some great disaster, was broken up, and the name survived only in the guild of Priests and their assistants. See on chap. xxxiv. and xlix. 5—7. On the meaning of Leah, see note on xxix. 16.

35. *praise*] From the Heb. *hôdah*.

Judah] Heb. *Jehudah*. This is the regular form of the name in the O.T. The origin of the name is uncertain; but its sound resembles that of the word for "praise." On Judah, see notes on chap. xxxviii. and xlix. 8—12.

CH. XXX. 1—24.

1. *envied*] The desire for children and the dread of the reproach of childlessness are frequently referred to in Scripture, e.g. 1 Sam. i. In this chapter the childlessness of Rachel should be compared with

children, or else I die. And Jacob's anger was kindled 2 E
against Rachel: and he said, Am I in God's stead, who
hath withheld from thee the fruit of the womb? And she 3
said, Behold my maid Bilhah, go in unto her; that she may
bear upon my knees, and I also may ¹obtain children by
her. | And she gave him Bilhah her handmaid to wife: and 4 J
Jacob went in unto her. And Bilhah conceived, and bare 5
Jacob a son. | And Rachel said, God hath ²judged me, and 6 E
hath also heard my voice, and hath given me a son: there-
fore called she his name Dan. | And Bilhah Rachel's 7 J
handmaid conceived again, and bare Jacob a second son.
And Rachel said, With ³mighty wrestlings have I ⁴wrestled 8
with my sister, and have prevailed: and she called his name
Naphtali. When Leah saw that she had left bearing, she 9

¹ Heb. *be builded by her*.   ² Heb. *dan*, he judged.
³ Heb. *wrestlings of God*.   ⁴ Heb. *niphtal*, he wrestled.

that of Sarah and Rebekah (xvi. 5, xxv. 21). It is part of the discipline
of the covenant.

2. *Am I in God's stead*] See l. 19. For God as the author and giver
of human life, cf. xvi. 2, xxix. 31; 1 Sam. i. 5. A similar exclamation
occurs in 2 Kings v. 7.

3. *bear upon my knees*] By this phrase Rachel means that she will
recognize and adopt as her own the children by her handmaid, Bilhah.
For the phrase, cf. l. 23; Job iii. 12. The child being received on the
knees of the parent was regarded as being accepted into the family.
The words retain the trace of a primitive ceremony of legitimatization
and adoption.

obtain children] Heb. *be builded by her*. The same figure of a house
is used by Sarah, referring to Hagar in xvi. 2, where see note.

6. *judged*] Heb. *dan*, "he judged." When Rachel says "he has
judged me," she means "God has decided in my favour." For this
use of "judge" in the sense of "vindicate," cf. Ps. xliii. 1, "Judge
me, O God, and plead my cause"; liv. 1, "Save me, O God,...and
judge me." The name "Dan" is possibly an abbreviation of a longer
form, such as Daniel, and Abidan (Numb. i. 11).

Dan and Naphtali, as Bilhah's children, are associated with the
Rachel children in tribal history; cf. Judg. v.

8. *mighty wrestlings*] Heb. *wrestlings of God*. The "wrestlings
of God" may mean either "mighty wrestlings," "of God" being added
as an intensive or superlative (cf. xxiii. 6, "a mighty prince"); or
"wrestlings," i.e. "strugglings in prayer for God's blessing" of children. The original meaning has probably been lost.

wrestled] Lit. "twisted myself." The participle *niphtâl* means
"crooked" (Prov. viii. 8).

J took Zilpah her handmaid, and gave her to Jacob to wife.
10 And Zilpah Leah's handmaid bare Jacob a son. And Leah
11
12 said, ¹Fortunate! and she called his name ²Gad. And
13 Zilpah Leah's handmaid bare Jacob a second son. And
Leah said, ³Happy am I! for the daughters will ⁴call me
14 happy: and she called his name Asher. And Reuben went
in the days of wheat harvest, and found ⁵mandrakes in the
field, and brought them unto his mother Leah. Then
Rachel said to Leah, Give me, I pray thee, of thy son's
15 mandrakes. And she said unto her, Is it a small matter
that thou hast taken away my husband? and wouldest
thou take away my son's mandrakes also? And Rachel

---

¹ Heb. *With Fortune!* Another reading is, *Fortune is come.*
² That is, *Fortune.* ³ Heb. *With my happiness!* ⁴ Heb. *asher*, to call happy. ⁵ Or, *love-apples*

11. *Fortunate*] Heb. *with fortune!* Another reading is, *Fortune is come.* The versions (LXX ἐν τύχῃ = "with fortune," Lat. *feliciter*) follow the reading of the Hebrew text (*Ke'thîb*). The other reading, followed by the Massoretic tradition (*Ḳerî*), is found in the Targum of Onkelos. Gad seems to have been the name of an ancient Aramaean god of fortune, whose worship existed among the Canaanites. Cf. the names Baal-gad (Josh. xi. 17), and Migdal-gad (Josh. xv. 37). The Jews in Babylon made offerings to this god of good fortune; cf. Isa. lxv. 11. In Judg. v. 17, Gilead takes the place of Gad.

13. *call me happy*] Heb. *asher*, to call happy. The "daughters" are probably the daughters of the land. Cf. Song of Songs vi. 9, "the daughters saw her and called her blessed"; cf. Luke i. 48. These two Hebrew traditional etymologies do not exclude the possibility that the names of Asher and Gad may have been drawn from the names of primitive gods of prosperity. Asher, or *Aseru*, appears in Egyptian inscriptions of the time of Rameses II (14th cent. B.C.) as the name of a district in N.W. Palestine.

14. *mandrakes*] R.V. marg. *love-apples*. The mandrake (*mandragora vernalis*) is a tuberous plant, with yellow plumlike fruit. It was supposed to act as a love-charm. It ripens in May, which suits the mention (*v.* 14) of wheat harvest. It has an odour of musk; cf. Song of Songs vii. 13, "the mandrakes give forth fragrance." It has been conjectured that the word *duda'im* is connected with the name of Dudah, the love-god mentioned on the inscription of Mesha (line 12); that Reubenites, adjoining the Moabites, were worshippers of Dudah; and that, on this account, Reuben is spoken of as the finder of the love-apples. The mandrake is called by the native inhabitants of Palestine *baid el-jinn*, "the eggs of the *jinn*."

said, Therefore he shall lie with thee to-night for thy 　J
son's mandrakes. And Jacob came from the field in the 16
evening, and Leah went out to meet him, and said, Thou
must come in unto me; for I have surely hired thee with my
son's mandrakes. And he lay with her that night. | And 17　E
God hearkened unto Leah, and she conceived, and bare
Jacob a fifth son. And Leah said, God hath given me my 18
¹hire, because I gave my handmaid to my husband: and
she called his name Issachar. And Leah conceived again, 19
and bare a sixth son to Jacob. And Leah said, God hath 20
endowed me with a good dowry; | now will my husband 　J
²dwell with me, because I have borne him six sons: | and 　E
she called his name Zebulun. And afterwards she bare a 21
daughter, and called her name Dinah. And God remem- 22
bered Rachel, and God hearkened to her, and opened her
womb. And she conceived, and bare a son: and said, God 23

---

¹ Heb. *sachar*. 　　　² Heb. *zabal*, he dwelt.

18. *hire*] Heb. *sâchâr* = "wages," "reward."

Issachar] The name receives a twofold explanation, in its derivation from *sâchâr*: (1) as the passive of the verb, in the sense of "he shall be hired or rewarded"; (2) as the combination of *îsh*, "man," and *sâchâr*, "hire," i.e. "a man of hire." In *v*. 16 Leah "hires" Jacob with the mandrakes given to Rachel; in *v*. 18 she calls Issachar the "hire" or wage, which she receives for giving Zilpah to Jacob.

20. *dwell*] Heb. *zabal*, "he dwelt." In this verse we have two explanations of the name "Zebulun." In the first clause Leah says "God has endowed (*zabad*) me with a good dowry (*zebed*)"; cf. the names Zabdi (Jos. vii. 1) and Zebedee (Mark i. 19). In the second clause the derivation is taken from the word *zabal*, "he dwelt." Presumably both popular etymologies were current. The interchange of *d* and *l* sounds is well known; cf. δάκρυον = Lat. *lachryma*. Assyriologists suggest a derivation from the Assyrian *zabalu*, "lift up," "exalt," "honour."

The two tribes of Issachar and Zebulun occupied adjoining territories.

21. *Dinah*] This name must have been similar in meaning to that of Dan; cf. *v*. 6. This is the only daughter of Jacob whose name is mentioned. The "daughters" in xxxvii. 35, xlvi. 7, may have been daughters-in-law.

It is noticeable that no mention of Dinah is made in xxxii. 22, where Jacob's "eleven children" are spoken of; and it has been suggested that her name here is a later editorial insertion to harmonize the list of children with the story of ch. xxxiv.

GENESIS

EJ 24 hath taken away my reproach: | and she called his name Joseph, saying, The LORD ¹add to me another son.

25 And it came to pass, when Rachel had borne Joseph, that Jacob said unto Laban, Send me away, that I may go
26 unto mine own place, and to my country. Give me my wives and my children for whom I have served thee, and let me go: for thou knowest my service wherewith I have
27 served thee. And Laban said unto him, If now I have found favour in thine eyes, *tarry: for* I have divined that

¹ Heb. *joseph*.

23. *God hath taken away*] The Hebrew for "hath taken away" (*âsaph*) is clearly regarded as one etymology of the name Joseph.

my reproach] See note on *v*. 1. Cf. Isa. iv. 1, "Take thou away our reproach"; Luke i. 25, "to take away my reproach among men."

24. *add*] Heb. *jôsêph*. This clause gives another etymology of the name Joseph from *yâsaph*, "he hath added." These two traditional interpretations of the name are taken, the one from E, the other from J narrative. According to E, the name means *âsaph Elohim*, "God hath taken away"; according to J, it means *yôsêph Jehovah*, "may Jehovah add." This name is very possibly to be read in the list of Thothmes III (No. 78) as *Joseph-el* (*Ysp'r*); see p. 273. Similarly *Yašu-pili* appears in documents of Hammurabi's time as a proper name.

25—43 (J, E). JACOB'S WAGES.

In this passage and in the following chapter Laban is depicted in the Israelite narrative as the typical Aramaean, a crafty, selfish, grasping man of business. Jacob, however, in spite of Laban's duplicity, prospers exceedingly. By greater cunning he outwits Laban himself, and God gives him protection and prosperity.

26. *my wives and my children*] Jacob's request implies that Laban as the head of the family possessed control over his married daughters and their children, who were included in Jacob's wages.

27. *If now I have found*, &c.] Cf. xviii. 3, xxxiii. 10 (J). Laban's sentence is unfinished. The words "tarry: for" are inserted to complete the aposeiopesis. Laban wishes to retain Jacob, and to propitiate him with flattering words. The bargain so far has been all in his favour.

I have divined] Lit. "I have observed signs." The word occurs in xliv. 5, 15, where it is used of obtaining an answer by means of magic. Here Laban means he has "discerned" by clear indications. Perhaps there may be a reference to the custom of consulting the household gods or *teraphim*. Cf. xxxi. 19. LXX οἰωνισάμην, Lat. *experimento didici*. See also 1 Kings xx. 33 marg.

the LORD hath blessed me for thy sake. And he said, 28 J
Appoint me thy wages, and I will give it. And he said 29
unto him, Thou knowest how I have served thee, and how
thy cattle hath fared with me. For it was little which thou 30
hadst before I came, and it hath ¹increased unto a multitude; and the LORD hath blessed thee ²whithersoever I
turned: and now when shall I provide for mine own house
also? And he said, What shall I give thee? And Jacob 31
said, Thou shalt not give me aught: if thou wilt do this
thing for me, I will again feed thy flock and keep it. I will 32
pass through all thy flock to-day, removing from thence
every speckled and spotted one, and every black one among
the sheep, and the spotted and speckled among the goats:
and *of such* shall be my hire. So shall my righteousness 33
answer for me hereafter, when thou shalt come concerning
my hire that is before thee: every one that is not speckled

¹ Heb. *broken forth.* ² Heb. *at my foot.*

hath blessed me] This is a new feature in the story, and prepares the way for the following section.

for thy sake] LXX τῇ σῇ εἰσόδῳ = "at thy arrival," reading *b'ragl'ka* for *biglal ka*.

30. *increased*] Heb. *broken forth.* See xxviii. 14.

whithersoever I turned] Heb. *at my foot.* For the same idiom, cf. Isa. xli. 2 (text and marg.).

32. *I will pass*, &c.] Jacob's proposal to Laban is that he should serve for a wage, to be given, not in money, but in animals. The sheep in Syria are nearly always white, and the goats black; cf. Cant. iv. 1. Jacob asks that his wage should consist of the sheep that were not white and the goats that were not black. Laban's flocks would be, according to this arrangement, the great mass of the animals. To Jacob's share would fall the exceptions, the spotted and black among the sheep, the spotted and speckled among the goats.

33. *my righteousness*] i.e. my uprightness, honesty, and straightness of dealing.

answer for me] i.e. "testify with regard to me"; or, better, as in 1 Sam. xii. 3, 2 Sam. i. 16, "witness against me."

every one that is not] Jacob promises that, when Laban visits his flocks, if he shall find among them any quite black goats or white sheep, he is at liberty to regard them as having been stolen by Jacob. He might at once seize them.

The compact was all in Laban's favour; but neither of the men trusts the other.

and spotted among the goats, and black among the sheep,
34 that *if found* with me shall be counted stolen. And Laban
said, Behold, I would it might be according to thy word.
35 And he removed that day the he-goats that were ringstraked
and spotted, and all the she-goats that were speckled and
spotted, every one that had white in it, and all the black
ones among the sheep, and gave them into the hand of his
36 sons; and he set three days' journey betwixt himself and
37 Jacob: and Jacob fed the rest of Laban's flocks. And
Jacob took him rods of fresh ¹poplar, and of the almond
and of the plane tree; and peeled white strakes in them,
38 and made the white appear which was in the rods. And he
set the rods which he had peeled over against the flocks in
the gutters in the watering troughs where the flocks came to
39 drink; and they conceived when they came to drink. And
the flocks conceived before the rods, and the flocks brought

¹ Or, *storax tree*

35. *into the hand of his sons*] Laban in accepting Jacob's offer determines to make the very best of the new arrangement. Any particoloured goats, and any black sheep in his flock, "he removed that day," and put into the keeping of his own sons, so that they might not afterwards be claimed by Jacob. Jacob will begin the new term of service with nothing in his favour. All the sheep that he will tend will be white, and all the goats black.

36. *three days' journey*] In order to prevent the least possibility of confusion or of intermingling, Laban separates his sons' flocks by a great distance from those which Jacob is to tend.

37. *poplar*] R.V. marg. *storax tree*. The Hebrew name is *libneh*, and is probably connected with the word *laban*, meaning "white." By some it is identified with the *styrax officinalis*.

plane tree] In the Hebrew *'armon*, i.e. "naked," a name derived from the annual scaling of the bark of the tree. The *platanus orientalis* was held in high veneration in the East. Cf. Ezek. xxxi. 8.

white strakes] Jacob's trick turns upon the *whiteness* of the rods; and this supplies a play upon the name "Laban" (="white"), who is outwitted by Jacob. The device is said to be well known to shepherds. "Strake" is Old English for "streak"; cf. Lev. xiv. 37.

38. *over against*] Jacob places the white peeled rods in front of the flocks, when they come to drink at the breeding season. It was the popular belief that such objects, being presented to the eye at such a season, would be likely to affect the colouring of the progeny.

gutters] This word is explained by the phrase following, "watering troughs"; cf. Ex. ii. 16.

GENESIS XXX. 39—43

forth ringstraked, speckled, and spotted. And Jacob 40 J separated the lambs, | and set the faces of the flocks toward the ringstraked and all the black in the flock of Laban; | and he put his own droves apart, and put them not J unto Laban's flock. And it came to pass, whensoever the 41 stronger of the flock did conceive, that Jacob laid the rods before the eyes of the flock in the gutters, that they might conceive among the rods; but when the flock were feeble, 42 he put them not in: so the feebler were Laban's, and the stronger Jacob's. And the man increased exceedingly, and 43 had large flocks, and maidservants and menservants, and camels and asses.

40. *set the faces...Laban*] This is a very obscure sentence in the original. It probably describes a second device practised by Jacob. At the breeding time he caused the ewes which belonged to Laban to pasture within view of his own parti-coloured and black animals, in order to increase the tendency of Laban's flock to produce spotted and parti-coloured lambs. The difficulty, however, of the language has made some scholars suppose that the words "and set...of Laban" are a gloss. As they stand, they seem to contradict *vv.* 33, 36, according to which Laban had already removed to a distance the parti-coloured animals.

41. *the stronger*] A third device on Jacob's part. He is careful, at the breeding season, to pick out only the finer animals before which to place the peeled rods. Hence he obtained for his own share the young of the better animals.

42. *the feebler...the stronger*] These words were a difficulty to the versions. LXX τὰ ἄσημα...τὰ ἐπίσημα, Lat. *quae erant serotina...quae primi temporis*. So Aq. Sym. πρώϊμα ὄψιμα, and Targum of Onkelos "early" and "late," referring to the time of breeding. The earlier breeding sheep were the stronger. Pliny, *H.N.*, viii. 187, *postea concepti invalidi* (quoted by Skinner).

43. *increased exceedingly*] Cf. the description of the wealth of Abraham and Isaac, xiii. 2, xxiv. 35, xxvi. 13, 14.

Cf. Shakespeare, *Merchant of Venice*, Act I. Scene iii.:

> "*Shy.*   mark what Jacob did.
> When Laban and himself were compromised
> That all the eanlings which were streak'd and pied
> Should fall as Jacob's hire....
> The skilful shepherd peel'd me certain wands,...
> He stuck them up before the fulsome ewes,
> Who, then conceiving, did in eaning time
> Fall parti-colour'd lambs, and those were Jacob's.
> This was a way to thrive, and he was blest."

J 31 And he heard the words of Laban's sons, saying, Jacob hath taken away all that was our father's; and of that
E 2 which was our father's hath he gotten all this ¹glory. | And Jacob beheld the countenance of Laban, and, behold, it
J 3 was not toward him as beforetime. | And the LORD said unto Jacob, Return unto the land of thy fathers, and to thy
E 4 kindred; and I will be with thee. | And Jacob sent and
5 called Rachel and Leah to the field unto his flock, and said unto them, I see your father's countenance, that it is not toward me as beforetime; but the God of my father hath
6 been with me. And ye know that with all my power I have
7 served your father. And your father hath deceived me, and changed my wages ten times; but God suffered him not

¹ Or, *wealth*

CH. XXXI. (J, E.)

1—21. THE FLIGHT OF JACOB.
22—55. THE PURSUIT OF LABAN, AND THE COVENANT BETWEEN LABAN AND JACOB AT GILEAD.

The greater part of this chapter is taken from E. The discrepancies between it and the previous chapter are to be explained by the compiler's prevalent use in that chapter of J and in this of E.

1. *Laban's sons*] See xxx. 35. It has hitherto been a contest of wits between Laban and Jacob. Jacob has had the best of it. Laban's sons are jealous and thoroughly alienated.

glory] R.V. marg. *wealth*. The Hebrew word *kâbôd*, usually rendered "honour" or "glory," has sometimes the meaning of "wealth," as here and Ps. xlix. 17, "for when he dieth he shall carry nothing away, his glory shall not descend after him." Cf. Isa. x. 3.

2. *the countenance of Laban*] Here, and in *v.* 5, Laban's countenance toward Jacob is said to be altered. For this idiomatic use of "the countenance" as expressing feeling, cf. iv. 5.

3. *And the LORD said*] In a dream; cf. *v.* 11.

the land of thy fathers] i.e. Canaan, as the country of Abraham and Isaac.

I will be with thee] The renewal of the promise of the Divine Presence made to Jacob in xxviii. 15; cf. xxi. 22, xxvi. 24.

7. *changed my wages*] The account given in the following passage differs from that in the preceding chapter, xxx. 25—31. There Jacob specified the conditions, to which Laban acceded; and then Jacob resorted to artifice, in order to improve his position. Here it is Laban that has specified the wages, and arbitrarily changed them (cf. *v.* 41)

to hurt me. If he said thus, The speckled shall be thy 8 E
wages; then all the flock bare speckled: and if he said
thus, The ringstraked shall be thy wages; then bare all the
flock ringstraked. Thus God hath taken away the cattle of 9
your father, and given them to me. And it came to pass 10
at the time that the flock conceived, that I lifted up mine
eyes, and saw in a dream, and, behold, the he-goats which
leaped upon the flock were ringstraked, speckled, and
grisled. And the angel of God said unto me in the dream, 11
Jacob: and I said, Here am I. And he said, Lift up now 12
thine eyes, and see, all the he-goats which leap upon the
flock are ringstraked, speckled, and grisled: for I have seen
all that Laban doeth unto thee. I am the God of Beth-el, 13

from time to time. But in every case, by the providence of God, not by Jacob's cleverness, the result has worked out advantageously to Jacob. In ch. xxx. we had principally, probably, the narrative of J; in this chapter, that of E is predominantly employed.

ten times] A phrase used to denote frequency, as in *v.* 41, Numb. xiv. 22, Neh. iv. 12, Job xix. 3, by a round number; Lat. *decem vicibus*. But LXX, not understanding the Hebrew word rendered "times" (*mônîm*), seems to have transliterated it with the rendering ἀμνῶν, "lambs" (or is this for μνῶν?), i.e. "ten lambing seasons."

8. *If he said thus*] Applying to Laban the proposal made by Jacob in xxx. 32.

10. *in a dream*] Cf. xx. 3. It is thus revealed to Jacob (*vv.* 10—12) that the birth, in such numbers, of spotted and parti-coloured young is due to God's goodness towards him, and in order to requite Laban (*v.* 12).

grisled] i.e. "gray" (Fr. *gris*). This Old English word, now generally spelt "grizzled," occurs also in Zech. vi. 3, 6. Compare, in Bacon's *Essays*, "pusled" for "puzzled."

11. *And the angel of God*] The vision combines the account of the events connected with the wages in xxx. 31—42 with the mention of the Divine word to Jacob in *v.* 3.

Notice the frequent use of "God" (Elohim), not LORD (Jehovah), in this chapter, *vv.* 9, 11, 16, 24, 42.

13. *the God of Beth-el*] i.e. the God who appeared unto thee at Beth-el; see xxxv. 7. For the mention of the pillar and the vow, see xxviii. 18—22. By the words "I am the God of Beth-el," the Angel is shewn to be not a created angel, but Jehovah Himself in a manifested form; cf. Ex. xxiii. 20, 21, "Behold, I send an angel before thee... my name is in him." See notes on xvi. 10, xxi. 17, 18, xxii. 11, 12. The Hebrew text is ungrammatical: LXX ὁ Θεὸς ὁ ὀφθείς σοι ἐν τόπῳ Θεοῦ.

GENESIS XXXI. 13—19

E where thou anointedst a pillar, where thou vowedst a vow unto me: now arise, get thee out from this land, and return 14 unto the land of thy nativity. And Rachel and Leah answered and said unto him, Is there yet any portion or 15 inheritance for us in our father's house? Are we not counted of him strangers? for he hath sold us, and hath 16 also quite devoured [1]our money. For all the riches which God hath taken away from our father, that is ours and our children's: now then, whatsoever God hath said unto thee, 17 do. Then Jacob rose up, and set his sons and his wives
P 18 upon the camels; and he carried away all his cattle, | and all his substance which he had gathered, the cattle of his getting, which he had gathered in Paddan-aram, for to go to
E 19 Isaac his father unto the land of Canaan. | Now Laban was gone to shear his sheep: and Rachel stole the teraphim

[1] Or, *the price paid for us*

14. *Is there yet*] i.e. "we have no reason any longer to expect." Leah and Rachel had both been alienated from their father by his disregard of their feelings and by his mean grasping policy.

portion or inheritance] A proverbial phrase: see 2 Sam. xx. 1; 1 Kings xii. 16.

15. *strangers*] i.e. foreigners, people of another kindred or country.

sold us] Referring to the bargain by which Jacob had obtained his two wives at the price of fourteen years' service (xxix. 15—20, 27).

our money] Better, as marg., *the price paid for us*. Laban had taken to himself the full profits of Jacob's fourteen years' service as the gift, or *mohar*, to the bride's family; but had assigned nothing of it as the dowry or gift to the two brides. Cf. xxiv. 53. This conduct they imply was contrary to usual custom, and was part of his stinginess. It was too late now to expect him to give anything back.

18 (P). *all his substance*] It would appear that this verse, taken from P, is the brief summary of Jacob's departure given in that narrative. The words for "substance" and "his getting," the mention of "Paddan-aram," and the redundancy of the language, are characteristic of P.

to Isaac his father] The narrative of JE (xxvii. 1, xxviii. 21) would suggest that Isaac had died long previously.

19. *gone to shear his sheep*] Jacob selected, as an opportune moment for flight, Laban's absence from home and attendance at the important festival of sheep-shearing. Among shepherds this was an occasion of feasting, which lasted several days. Cf. 1 Sam. xxv. 2, 7, 11; 2 Sam.

GENESIS XXXI. 19—23

that were her father's. And Jacob [1]stole away unawares to Laban the Syrian, in that he told him not that he fled. So he fled with all that he had; and he rose up, and passed over [2]the River, and set his face toward the mountain of Gilead.

And it was told Laban on the third day that Jacob was fled. And he took his brethren with him, and pursued after him seven days' journey; and he overtook him in the

[1] Heb. *stole the heart of Laban the Aramean.*
[2] That is, the Euphrates.

xiii. 23. Jacob, by seizing this opportunity, is able to get clear away, cross the Euphrates, and start homewards.

the teraphim] The *teraphim* were the household gods, like the Latin *Penates*, sometimes small in size, as would appear from this verse and *vv.* 30, 34; but sometimes, as is to be inferred from 1 Sam. xix. 13, large enough to be shaped like human figures. Their presence in the houses of Israelites was common; cf. Judg. xvii. 4, 5; Hos. iii. 4. But they seem to have been a source of superstition. The narrative in xxxv. 2, 1 Sam. xv. 23, 2 Kings xxiii. 24, shews that their use was opposed to the best spirit of Israelite religion. The versions here render "teraphim" by "idols," LXX τὰ εἴδωλα, Lat. *idola*.

The mention of them here and in xxxv. 2—4 seems to connect their use with Aramaean influences. There is no reference to them in the story of Abraham and Isaac. Rachel hopes to bring with her the good genius of her own home.

20. *stole away*, &c.] Heb. *stole the heart of Laban the Aramean.* Cf. *v.* 26. Jacob outwitted Laban; fled secretly, and got three days' start. For the phrase, cf. the Greek κλέπτειν νοῦν, "to steal the mind," i.e. to deceive; see 2 Sam. xv. 6.

21. *the River*] i.e. *the Euphrates.* See note on xv. 18. Cf. Ps. lxxii. 8, "from the River unto the ends of the earth." "Haran" (xxiv. 4) was Laban's home.

toward the mountain of Gilead] i.e. towards the hill-country on the east side of Jordan. The name "Gilead" is here used in its widest application.

22—55. THE PURSUIT OF LABAN, &c.

23. *his brethren*] i.e. the men of his kindred and clan, as in *vv.* 25, 32. Jacob is similarly attended; cf. *vv.* 37, 46, 54, xxiv. 60.

seven days' journey] The distance from Haran to the land of Gilead for a company with flocks and herds would require a longer time. It is computed to be over 300 miles in a straight line. But we do not

E 24 mountain of Gilead. And God came to Laban the Syrian in a dream of the night, and said unto him, Take heed to thyself that thou speak not to Jacob either good or bad.
25 And Laban came up with Jacob. Now Jacob had pitched his tent in the mountain: and Laban with his brethren
26 pitched in the mountain of Gilead. And Laban said to Jacob, What hast thou done, that thou hast stolen away unawares to me, and carried away my daughters as captives
27 of the sword? Wherefore didst thou flee secretly, and ¹steal away from me; and didst not tell me, that I might have sent thee away with mirth and with songs, with tabret
28 and with harp; and hast not suffered me to kiss my sons
29 and my daughters? now hast thou done foolishly. It is in the power of my hand to do you hurt: but the God of

---

¹ Heb. *didst steal me*.

---

need to be very exacting about geographical accuracy in old-world popular stories.

The point to notice is that Jacob was encumbered with his flocks and herds and household, and that Laban, travelling without encumbrance in pursuit, overtook him in ten days from his flight.

24. *And God came*] Cf. *v.* 11. For this revelation to Laban the Syrian, compare the revelation to Abimelech, king of Gerar, in xx. 3. It is God, not the "angel of God" (*v.* 11), who appears to Laban.

either good or bad] A phrase used by Laban himself in xxiv. 50.

25. *in the mountain*] Very probably the name has dropped out of the text. We should expect a proper name to balance "the mountain of Gilead" in the second clause. The opposing camps were lodged on hill-tops over against each other. Perhaps Mizpah, mentioned in *v.* 49, was the name that is here missing.

26. *What hast thou done?*] Cf. iv. 10. Laban's reproach in *vv.* 26—30 is expressed in terms of forbearance and injured innocence: why had Jacob fled secretly? why not suffer himself to be dismissed with dignity? For the sake of the God of Isaac Laban will say no more, but he must protest against the theft of his household gods.

27. *steal away from me*] Heb. *didst steal me*; cf. *v.* 20.

sent thee away] The same word as in xii. 20, "And they brought him on the way." The suggestion of a musical accompaniment is rhetorical. The "tabret" (*tôph*) is the "timbrel" or "tambourine."

28. *sons...daughters*] Laban's grandchildren; cf. *vv.* 43, 55.

29. *in the power of my hand*] A Hebrew idiom occurring in Deut. xxviii. 32, Neh. v. 5, Prov. iii. 27, Micah ii. 1. The word "power" is "*Êl*," usually rendered "God"; in this idiom it denotes "power" or "might" in the abstract.

your father spake unto me yesternight, saying, Take heed to E
thyself that thou speak not to Jacob either good or bad.
And now, *though* thou wouldest needs be gone, because 30
thou sore longedst after thy father's house, *yet* wherefore
hast thou stolen my gods? And Jacob answered and said to 31
Laban, Because I was afraid: for I said, Lest thou shouldest
take thy daughters from me by force. With whomsoever 32
thou findest thy gods, he shall not live: before our brethren
discern thou what is thine with me, and take it to thee.
For Jacob knew not that Rachel had stolen them. And 33
Laban went into Jacob's tent, and into Leah's tent, and
into the tent of the two maidservants; but he found them
not. And he went out of Leah's tent, and entered into
Rachel's tent. Now Rachel had taken the teraphim, and 34
put them in the camel's furniture, and sat upon them. And
Laban felt about all the tent, but found them not. And she 35
said to her father, Let not my lord be angry that I cannot
rise up before thee; for the manner of women is upon me.
And he searched, but found not the teraphim. And Jacob 36
was wroth, and chode with Laban: and Jacob answered and
said to Laban, What is my trespass? what is my sin, that

the God of your father] Laban's conscience smites him, as is implied by the vision recorded in *v.* 24.

30. though *thou wouldest needs be gone*] Lit. "thou art actually gone."

my gods] "My *Elohim*, or god," here in the sense of the figures of the household gods, as in Judg. xviii. 24, and possibly in Exod. xxi. 6, xxii. 7, 8, xxxii. 1.

31. *I was afraid*] Jacob's defence is brief: (1) he fled because he could not trust Laban, who, he thought, would keep his daughters by force; (2) as to the *teraphim*, he was innocent; if any of his party had stolen them, they should be punished by death.

32. *our brethren*] Cf. *v.* 23.

33. *tent*] Four tents are mentioned, one occupied by Jacob, one each by Leah and Rachel, and one by handmaidens. LXX renders by οἶκον = "house."

34. *the camel's furniture*] By this is probably meant the wicker framework of the camel's saddle, with its trappings and hangings, LXX τὰ σάγματα, Lat. *stramenta*.

35. *rise*] i.e. in honour to her father. For the custom of rising to do honour to age, see Lev. xix. 32.

36. *trespass...sin*] i.e. (*a*) the particular outrage against the rights of

E 37 thou hast hotly pursued after me? Whereas thou hast felt about all my stuff, what hast thou found of all thy household stuff? Set it here before my brethren and thy brethren, 38 that they may judge betwixt us two. This twenty years have I been with thee; thy ewes and thy she-goats have not cast their young, and the rams of thy flocks have I not 39 eaten. That which was torn of beasts I brought not unto thee; I bare the loss of it; of my hand didst thou require 40 it, whether stolen by day or stolen by night. Thus I was; in the day the drought consumed me, and the frost by 41 night; and my sleep fled from mine eyes. These twenty years have I been in thy house; I served thee fourteen years for thy two daughters, and six years for thy flock: and 42 thou hast changed my wages ten times. Except the God of my father, the God of Abraham, and the Fear of Isaac, had been with me, surely now hadst thou sent me away empty. God hath seen mine affliction and the labour of my hands,

kinship, and (*b*) moral offence generally. Jacob regards the charge of the theft of the *teraphim* as a mere pretext, devised by Laban in order to ransack his goods. For the word rendered "trespass," "transgression," "rebellion," cf. l. 17; 1 Sam. xxiv. 12; 1 Kings xii. 19; 2 Kings viii. 20.

38. *This twenty years*] Jacob's indignant protest proclaims (1) his length of service, (2) his perfect honesty, (3) his uncomplaining endurance of hardship, in spite of capricious changes in his wage. And now that he has left Haran, it was only because of God's mercy, and not through Laban's kindness, that he did not go empty-handed.

39. *I brought not unto thee*] Jacob allowed himself to be the loser by the animals that were killed by wild beasts. Instead of bringing the mangled remains so that their value might not be deducted, he cheerfully bore the full loss: see Ex. xxii. 12, 13; Amos iii. 12. Jacob had exceeded the standard of fairness which was required by custom: "I bare the loss of it," i.e. "I used to make myself responsible for the loss."

40. *drought...frost*] The extremes of midday heat and midnight frost. For the variations of temperature, cf. Jer. xxxvi. 30.

41. *ten times*] Cf. *v*. 7.

42. *the God of my father*] Cf. *v*. 5.

the Fear of Isaac] Cf. *v*. 53. A remarkable phrase, denoting the personal God who was the object of Isaac's worship. Cf. Isa. viii. 13, "Neither fear ye their fear. The LORD of Hosts...let him be your fear." It clearly shews not that Isaac was regarded as a deity; but that He whom Isaac feared was the true God of Jacob.

sent me away empty] A regular phrase for destitution; cf. Job xxii. 9; Luke i. 53.

and rebuked thee yesternight. And Laban answered and 43 E
said unto Jacob, The daughters are my daughters, and the
children are my children, and the flocks are my flocks, and
all that thou seest is mine: and what can I do this day unto
these my daughters, or unto their children which they have
borne? And now come, let us make a covenant, I and 44
thou; and let it be for a witness between me and thee.
And Jacob took a stone, and set it up for a pillar. | And 45 46 J
Jacob said unto his brethren, Gather stones; and they took
stones, and made an heap: and they did eat there by the
heap. | And Laban called it ¹Jegar-sahadutha: but Jacob 47 (R)
called it ²Galeed. | And Laban said, This heap is witness 48 J

1 That is, *The heap of witness*, in Aramaic.
2 That is, *The heap of witness*, in Hebrew.

rebuked thee] Cf. *v*. 29.

43. *my daughters*] Laban's reply, consisting of the claim of complete parental control over Leah and Rachel and their children and their husband's flocks, is no sort of reply to Jacob's complaint.

44. *a covenant*] Cf. xxvi. 28.

a witness] Heb. '*ed*. This word gives the keynote to the transaction, and introduces the play on the word Gilead in *v*. 47. But "a covenant" is not "a witness." Surely some words have dropped out. Several commentators suggest: "And let us make a heap, and let it be for a witness."

45. *Jacob*] The name "Jacob" is here almost certainly a gloss. We should read either "and he took a stone," or "and Laban took a stone." In *v*. 51 Laban says that he set up the pillar or *maṣṣēbah*. Laban erects the pillar; Jacob makes the heap of stones.

a pillar] Heb. *maṣṣēbah*. As Jacob had done at Bethel, xxviii. 18.

46. *his brethren*] i.e. his followers and companions; see *vv.* 23, 32.

an heap] Heb. *gal*. What we should now call a "cairn," on the top of a mountain. Lat. *tumulus*.

47. *And Laban called it*] This verse, which anticipates and does not agree with *vv*. 48 and 49, must be a learned gloss.

Laban the Syrian (cf. *v*. 20, xxviii. 5) gives an Aramaic name, Jacob the Hebrew gives a Hebrew name. In the region of Gilead, in later times, both languages were probably spoken[1].

---

[1] "Pillars of testimony" occur to-day in groups at many places, especially where the traveller first catches sight of some sacred spot. Thereupon he sets stones one upon the other in the shape of a column, and says, "Oh, so and so (mentioning the name of the saint whose *weli* he sees), as I by this bear testimony to thee, so do thou bear testimony to me in the day of judgment" (Peters, *Early Hebrew Story*, p. 111 f.).

GENESIS XXXI. 48—52

J between me and thee this day. Therefore was the name
49 of it called Galeed: and [1]Mizpah, for he said, The LORD
watch between me and thee, when we are [2]absent one from
50 another. If thou shalt afflict my daughters, and if thou
shalt take wives beside my daughters, no man is with us;
E 51 see, God is witness betwixt me and thee. | And Laban said
to Jacob, Behold this heap, and behold the pillar, which I
52 have set betwixt me and thee. This heap be witness, and

[1] That is, *The watch-tower*.   [2] Heb. *hidden*.

48. *Therefore was the name*, &c.] A popular etymology thus accounted for the name "Gilead" by derivation from "Galeed." Probably, some well-known "cairn" on the hill-frontier of Gilead was the reputed scene of the compact between Laban and Jacob. That border feuds were waged between Aramaeans and Israelites, and that the boundaries between the two nations were marked by cairns, is indicated in this story.

49. *Mizpah*] That is, *The watch-tower*. Cf. Judg. xi. 29, "Mizpeh of Gilead," and *v.* 34, "Mizpah." Probably a common name for a height. The mention of this name comes in very abruptly at this point, and may be a gloss. The Sam. reads *maṣṣēbah*, LXX καὶ ἡ ὅρασις = "the vision." It has been suggested that the high point here indicated might be the Rammath-mizpeh of Josh. xiii. 25, or the Mizpah in Gilead of Judg. xi. 11. A third name for "the heap of stones" is very awkward, and the grammar barely tolerable. The text has undergone some dislocation.

The LORD] LXX ὁ Θεός. Jehovah is the third party in the solemn contract: He is witness; He will uphold the right, and punish the violator of the bond; cf. xvi. 5.

between me and thee] The cairn on the hill is to be the witness of the covenant between two sets of people separated at a distance from one another, and tempted to take advantage of one another. The popular use of the word Mizpah, based on this verse, ignores the context, and, in particular, *v.* 50. God is here invoked, because of the mutual distrust of the two parties, to watch lest one or the other should violate the compact.

absent] Heb. *hidden*, i.e. "separated and out of sight."

50. *wives beside my daughters*] So that Leah and Rachel may not be exposed to the risk of any indignity. "Afflict," cf. "dealt hardly" (xvi. 6).

51. *heap...set*] Jacob had caused the heap to be collected; Laban had erected the pillar: see note on *v.* 45. Two compacts are made: (1) Jacob will not ill-treat Laban's daughters, *v.* 50; (2) neither Laban nor Jacob will pass the boundary heap of stones to do the other harm, *v.* 52. The heap of stones and the pillar are the witness of the agreement.

GENESIS XXXI. 52—55   319

the pillar be witness, that I will not pass over this heap to   E
thee, and that thou shalt not pass over this heap and this
pillar unto me, for harm. The God of Abraham, and the 53
God of Nahor, the ¹God of their father, judge betwixt us.
And Jacob sware by the Fear of his father Isaac. And 54
Jacob offered a sacrifice in the mountain, and called his
brethren to eat bread: and they did eat bread, and tarried
all night in the mountain. And early in the morning Laban 55
rose up, and kissed his sons and his daughters, and blessed
them: and Laban departed, and returned unto his place.

¹ Or, *gods*

53. *The God of Abraham...Nahor*] The verb "judge" is in the plural. See note on xx. 13 for the rare use of the plural verb with "Elohim." Laban speaks of the God of Abraham, i.e. of the Hebrews in Canaan, and of the God of Nahor, i.e. of the Hebrews in Haran, and as a Syrian may possibly have regarded them as distinct deities. The plural with *Elohim* is found in xx. 13, xxxv. 7.

the God of their father] R.V. marg. *gods*. These words are not found in the LXX and some Hebrew MSS., and are probably a gloss. If they are omitted, the God of Abraham and the God of Nahor were treated in the original form of the narrative as separate, not identical, deities.

the Fear of his father Isaac] See note on *v.* 42.

54. *offered a sacrifice*] Lit. "killed a sacrifice." The killing of an animal for sacrifice was the occasion of a feast. The sacrifice consisted not only in an offering to the Deity, but also in the eating of portions of the sacrificial victim by both the contracting parties of the covenant; cf. xxvi. 30.

eat bread] i.e. to take a meal. To partake of food together was the sign of restored friendship and trust between disputing parties.

55. *sons and...daughters*] Cf. *vv.* 28, 43. His grandchildren as well as his two daughters.

unto his place] i.e. his home in Haran; cf. xviii. 33; Num. xxiv. 25.

CH. XXXII. (J, E.) JACOB AT MAHANAIM AND PENUEL.

1—2.   JACOB AT MAHANAIM.
3—12. THE APPROACH OF ESAU, AND JACOB'S PRAYER.
13—21. JACOB'S PRESENT TO ESAU.
22—32. JACOB'S WRESTLING WITH THE ANGEL.

In this section *vv.* 1 and 2 are from E; 3—13ᵃ from J (notice the different explanations given of the origin of the name "Mahanaim" in

E 32 And Jacob went on his way, and the angels of God met
2 him. And Jacob said when he saw them, This is God's
host: and he called the name of that place ¹Mahanaim.

J 3 And Jacob sent messengers before him to Esau his
4 brother unto the land of Seir, the field of Edom. And he

---

¹ That is, *Two hosts*, or, *companies*.

---

v. 2 and in *vv.* 7, 8); *vv.* 13ᵇ—21 are very probably from E, since 21ᵇ
seems to take up the thread of 13ᵃ.

1. *the angels of God*] See note on xxviii. 12. The appearance of
the angels to Jacob on his return home, as on his journey thither,
gives him the assurance of God's presence. In chap. xxviii. it was a
dream; here we are told the angels "met him."

2. *This is God's host*] The Heb. word for "host" (*maḥaneh*) is
usually, and ought here to be, rendered "camp." The angels are regarded as the warriors of Jehovah; cf. the narrative in Josh. v. 13—15,
and 1 Kings xxii. 19; Ps. ciii. 21, cxlviii. 2.

Mahanaim] That is, *Two hosts*, or, *companies*. The termination
-aim denotes the dual. Possibly Jacob here refers to the two "companies," or "encampments," one of the angels, and the other of his
own followers. The LXX renders παρεμβολαί = "camps"; Lat. *Mahanaim, id est, Castra*, without reference to the dual number. For
another derivation of the name, see on *vv.* 7, 10.

Mahanaim was in later times a place of considerable importance.
During Absalom's rebellion it was the residence and head-quarters of
David; see 2 Sam. xvii. 24, 27. Cf. 2 Sam. ii. 8, 12, 29; 1 Kings ii. 8.
The site is uncertain: from *v.* 11 it would appear to be not far from the
banks of the Jordan, and from *v.* 22 to lie north of the Jabbok (modern
Zerka). In Josh. xiii. 26—30, it appears to lie on the confines of Gad
and Manasseh.

3—12 (J). THE APPROACH OF ESAU, AND JACOB'S PRAYER.

3. *the land of Seir*] This name for the country occupied by the
Edomites (xiv. 6) seems to mean the "shaggy," or "rough," "forest-
covered" country; see xxxiii. 14, 16, xxxvi. 8. It is applied not only
to the mountains on the east of the *Arabah* desert, but also to the
mountain country of the *Arabah* and the southern borders of Palestine.

the field of Edom] The future home of Esau's descendants is here
so called by a not unnatural anachronism. Cf. xiv. 7, "the country of
the Amalekites"; xxi. 34, "the land of the Philistines."

The description of the country by the twofold name "land of Seir"
and "field of Edom" indicates the two sources of the narrative.

GENESIS XXXII. 4—10

commanded them, saying, Thus shall ye say unto my lord J
Esau; Thus saith thy servant Jacob, I have sojourned
with Laban, and stayed until now: and I have oxen, and 5
asses *and* flocks, and menservants and maidservants: and
I have sent to tell my lord, that I may find grace in thy
sight. And the messengers returned to Jacob, saying, 6
We came to thy brother Esau, and moreover he cometh to
meet thee, and four hundred men with him. Then Jacob 7
was greatly afraid and was distressed: and he divided the
people that was with him, and the flocks, and the herds,
and the camels, into two companies; and he said, If Esau 8
come to the one company, and smite it, then the company
which is left shall escape. And Jacob said, O God of my 9
father Abraham, and God of my father Isaac, O LORD,
which saidst unto me, Return unto thy country, and to thy
kindred, and I will do thee good: ¹I am not worthy of 10
the least of all the mercies, and of all the truth, which thou

¹ Heb. *I am less than all &c.*

4. *my lord Esau*] Jacob adopts the language of extreme courtesy and respect. Cf. xviii. 3, xliii. 20, xliv. 18.

5. *find grace*] Cf. xviii. 3, xxxiii. 8, 15, xxxiv. 11, xlvii. 25. Jacob hopes to be reconciled and desires to propitiate his brother. He has not forgotten his brother's threats (xxvii. 41).

6. *four hundred men*] Where Esau was, and how he had become the head of a force of four hundred men, is not related, but may have formed part of another narrative. His intentions, if not hostile, are suspicious (cf. xxxiii. 4).

7. *two companies*] The word for "companies" is the same as that rendered "host" in *v.* 2, except that it occurs in the plural (*mahanoth*). This is evidently another explanation of the origin of the name Mahanaim. It is a pity that the same word, "camp," has not been used here and in *vv.* 2, 8, 10, 21, in order to bring out the two etymologies that were current.

9. *O God, &c.*] Jacob's prayer consists of (1) an invocation; (2) a reminder of the promise; (3) a humble acknowledgment of mercies; (4) an entreaty (*a*) for protection, and (*b*) for the fulfilment of the covenant promise. Jacob's prayer, followed by the symbolic scene of the wrestling with the angel (*vv.* 24—32), is an indication that, through discipline, the patriarch's character has been made ready for the exercise of the faith of which it was capable, and for submission to the Will which it had begun to recognize. The absence of confession of sin has been remarked upon. The self-sufficiency still lingers; see *v.* 11.

which saidst] The reference is to xxxi. 3.

10. *I am not worthy*] Heb. *I am less than all*, &c. The meaning

J hast shewed unto thy servant; for with my staff I passed over this Jordan; and now I am become two companies. 11 Deliver me, I pray thee, from the hand of my brother, from the hand of Esau: for I fear him, lest he come and 12 smite me, the mother with the children. And thou saidst, I will surely do thee good, and make thy seed as the sand 13 of the sea, which cannot be numbered for multitude. And he lodged there that night; and took of that which he had 14 with him a present for Esau his brother; two hundred she-goats and twenty he-goats, two hundred ewes and twenty 15 rams, thirty milch camels and their colts, forty kine and 16 ten bulls, twenty she-asses and ten foals. And he delivered them into the hand of his servants, every drove by itself:

is, "I am too small and insignificant to deserve." For this idiom, cf. iv. 13, xviii. 14.

mercies...truth] See xxiv. 27, 49: i.e. "manifestations of graciousness and fidelity."

with my staff] i.e. with only my shepherd's stick (*makkêl*) in my hand, Exod. xii. 11; Num. xxii. 27.

I passed over this Jordan] Jacob is on the banks of the Jabbok; but evidently the distance from the river Jordan was not considerable.

two companies] Heb. *mahanoth*. Another evident allusion to the name Mahanaim; cf. vv. 2, 7.

11. *from the hand of Esau*] Jacob in his prayer makes no reference to the possible cause of Esau's anger, and expresses no consciousness of, nor sorrow for, his own wrong-doing towards either Esau or Isaac.

the mother with the children] A proverbial phrase for "the mother and family"; cf. Hos. x. 14.

12. *thou saidst*] See xxviii. 14.

as the sand of the sea] See xiii. 16, xxii. 17, and cf. xvi. 10.

13—21. Jacob's Present to Esau.

13. *a present*] Heb. *minhah*. Cf. xliii. 11, 15. See note on iv. 3. Jacob hopes that a substantial present will turn away the resentment of his brother. Prov. xviii. 16, "a man's gift maketh room for him"; xxi. 14, "a gift in secret pacifieth anger"; cf. Abigail's present to David, 1 Sam. xxv. 18, 27.

14. *two hundred, &c.*] The numbers here given enable us to form some idea of the great size of Jacob's caravan. The animals are apparently mentioned in the order of their value, beginning with the least valuable.

Jacob hopes by the arrival of a succession of gifts to break down Esau's bitter grudge against him. For "a brother offended," cf. Prov. xviii. 19.

GENESIS XXXII. 16—23

and said unto his servants, Pass over before me, and put **J**
a space betwixt drove and drove. And he commanded the 17
foremost, saying, When Esau my brother meeteth thee, and
asketh thee, saying, Whose art thou? and whither goest
thou? and whose are these before thee? then thou shalt 18
say, *They be* thy servant Jacob's; it is a present sent unto
my lord Esau: and, behold, he also is behind us. And he 19
commanded also the second, and the third, and all that
followed the droves, saying, On this manner shall ye speak
unto Esau, when ye find him; and ye shall say, Moreover, 20
behold, thy servant Jacob is behind us. For he said, I will
appease him with the present that goeth before me, and
afterward I will see his face; peradventure he will accept
me. So the present passed over before him: and he himself 21
lodged that night in the company.

And he rose up that night, and took his two wives, and 22
his two handmaids, and his eleven children, and passed
over the ford of Jabbok. And he took them, and sent 23

20. *I will appease him*] Lit. "I will cover his face," in the sense of "I will propitiate." The present will so "cover his face," that Esau cannot look upon Jacob's offence; cf. xx. 16. LXX renders ἐξιλάσομαι τὸ πρόσωπον αὐτοῦ. Cf. Prov. xvi. 14 (the pacifying of a king's wrath with a gift).

accept me] Lit. "lift up my face." Cf. iv. 7, xix. 21; Mal. i. 8.

21. *company*] Lit. "camp"; cf. *v.* 7.

22—32. JACOB'S WRESTLING WITH THE ANGEL.

This passage forms the climax of Jacob's history. It records the occasion on which his name is changed to Israel, and describes his personal meeting with the Divine Being, whose blessing he obtains. The religious significance of the story turns upon (1) the sudden mysterious wrestling by night; (2) Jacob's persistence in his demand for a blessing; (3) the blessing given, and symbolized by the new name, Israel; (4) the physical disability, a memorial of acceptance and spiritual victory, and a symbol of the frailty of earthly strength, in the crisis of life, when God meets man face to face. See the hymn "Come, O thou Traveller unknown" (Chas. Wesley).

22. *the ford of Jabbok*] This river, the modern *Zerka*, is a tributary of the Jordan on its eastern bank. The narrative does not state on which bank of the Jabbok the angel appeared to Jacob. According to *v.* 22 Jacob had crossed the stream; according to *v.* 23 he had not. If, as seems probable, *vv.* 24—32 follow *v.* 22 and belong to J (*v.* 23 belonging to the E narrative), Jacob met the angel on the S. bank of the Jabbok.

J 24 them over the stream, and sent over that he had. And Jacob was left alone; and there wrestled a man with him
25 until the breaking of the day. And when he saw that he prevailed not against him, he touched the hollow of his thigh; and the hollow of Jacob's thigh was strained, as he
26 wrestled with him. And he said, Let me go, for the day breaketh. And he said, I will not let thee go, except thou
27 bless me. And he said unto him, What is thy name? And
28 he said, Jacob. And he said, Thy name shall be called

23. *the stream*] The Jabbok is called a "stream" (*nahal*) in Deut. iii. 16; Josh. xii. 2. On the word rendered "stream," see note on xxvi. 17.

24. *And Jacob...alone*] It is natural to suppose that Jacob remained behind to think and to pray at this crisis of his life. He was given over to anxious fears; the darkness and loneliness intensified them. The thought that God had left him, or was opposed to him, overwhelmed him.

there wrestled a man] The brevity of the account leaves it unexplained, who the man is, how he appeared, and how the contest began. The word for "wrestled," *yēâbêk*, is very possibly intended to be a play on the name of the river Jabbok as if it meant "twisting." In *v.* 28, and in Hos. xii. 4, a different word, "to strive," is used for the "wrestling" of Jacob. It is this scene of "wrestling" which has become, in the language of spiritual experience, the classical symbol for "agonizing" in prayer.

25. *he saw*] In the narrative, as we have it, these words refer to the mysterious combatant with whom Jacob wrestled. But the omission of the subject both in this and the subsequent clause, in the Hebrew as well as in the English, leaves the meaning ambiguous. That it was Jacob, and not "the man," who by some trick of wrestling got the mastery, may have been the version of the story referred to in Hos. xii. 4, "he had power over the angel, and prevailed."

26. *the day breaketh*] A survival of the old belief that unearthly visitants of the night must be gone before daybreak. In Plautus, *Amphitr.* 532 f., Jupiter says, "Cur me tenes? Tempus est: exire ex urbe, priusquam lucescat, volo." Shakespeare, *Hamlet*, Act I. Scene i.:

"*Ber.* It was about to speak, when the cock crew.
Hor. And then it started like a guilty thing."

See note on xix. 15, 23.

except thou bless me] Jacob had suddenly realized, through the touch of physical suffering, that he was in the grasp of more than mortal power. He neither shrinks, nor desists, but maintains his hold and asks for a blessing.

27. *What is thy name?*] This question, concerning the name which the Questioner knows, leads up to the solemn pronunciation of Jacob's new title.

no more Jacob, but ¹Israel: for ²thou hast ³striven with   J
God and with men, and hast prevailed. And Jacob asked 29
him, and said, Tell me, I pray thee, thy name. And he
said, Wherefore is it that thou dost ask after my name?
And he blessed him there. And Jacob called the name of 30
the place ⁴Peniel: for, *said he*, I have seen God face to

---

¹ That is, *He who striveth with God*, or, *God striveth*. ² The
Sept. and Vulgate have, *thou hast had power with God, and thou shalt
prevail against men.* ³ Or, *had power with* ⁴ That is,
The face of God.

---

28. *Israel*] That is, *He who striveth with God*, or, *God striveth*.
The name is clearly a title of victory, from a root meaning "to persevere." (*a*) The meaning seems here to be applied to Jacob as "the perseverer with God." It is commonly compared with Jerubbaal = "he that striveth with Baal" (Judg. vi. 32). The prophet Hosea gives this meaning in xii. 3, 4, "in his manhood [or 'strength'] he had power [or 'persevered,' 'strove'] with God; yea, he had power over the angel, and prevailed." (*b*) The meaning, on the analogy of similarly formed words, would be "El persevereth"; and would be exactly similar to Seraiah = "Jah perseveres"; Ishmael = "God hears." Another suggested derivation is from *sar* = "prince." See another account of the origin of the name "Israel" given by P in xxxv. 10.

The narrative of J, from this point onwards, shews a marked preference for the name "Israel" in its application to the patriarch.

The name of "Israel" has been found, as is generally believed, in the inscription of the Egyptian king, Merneptah (circ. 1230 B.C.), as *Ysir'r*; and in Assyrian inscriptions as *Sirlai*.

thou hast striven, &c.] R.V. marg. *thou hast had power with God, and thou shalt prevail against men.* LXX ἐνίσχυσας...δυνατὸς ἔσῃ; Lat. *fortis fuisti...praevalebis*. Jacob had prevailed in his contest with Laban; now, also, the promise of deliverance from Esau is contained in the *past* tense, "hast striven and hast prevailed." The rendering of the R.V. text gives the literal translation of the Hebrew. The past and the future are embraced in one thought.

29. *And he blessed him*] The name is refused, but the blessing previously asked for (*v.* 26) is granted. The same occurrence is recorded in Judg. xiii. 17—21. The prayer may not always be right or wise. But the blessing is not refused, because the literal answer is not given. The blessing is the sign of God's Presence and the pledge of man's salvation.

30. *Peniel*] R.V. marg. *The face of God*. In the Sam. version, Syr., and Lat., it is called "Penuel," as in *v.* 32. Popular tradition explained the etymology of the name of the place by the story of Jacob.

The face of God was to be seen in the Angel: he that looked on the Angel saw the Presence of Jehovah.

J 31 face, and my life is preserved. And the sun rose upon him as he passed over Penuel, and he halted upon his
(R) 32 thigh. | Therefore the children of Israel eat not the sinew of the hip which is upon the hollow of the thigh, unto this day: because he touched the hollow of Jacob's thigh in the sinew of the hip.

J 33 And Jacob lifted up his eyes, and looked, and, behold, Esau came, and with him four hundred men. And he divided the children unto Leah, and unto Rachel, and

I have seen God...preserved] The belief that to see God was to die prevailed amongst the Israelites; see xvi. 13; Exod. xix. 21, xxiv. 10, 11, xxxiii. 20; Deut. v. 24; Judg. vi. 22, xiii. 22. Jacob has seen the Divine Being, *Elohim*, and lives.

Jacob, on his deathbed, refers to this event (xlviii. 16): "The Angel which redeemed me from all evil, bless the lads."

face to face] See Exod. xxxiii. 11; Deut. xxxiv. 10

31. *And the sun rose*] See *v.* 24.

Penuel] The name of a town in Judg. viii. 8; 1 Kings xii. 25. The site is doubtful, but was evidently not far from the confluence of the Jabbok and the Jordan.

32. *Therefore the children of Israel*] The Compiler adds this note, which explains the Israelite custom of abstaining from eating the muscle in an animal, corresponding to the muscle, or sinew, in the thigh of Jacob that was touched by God: it was regarded as sacred.

This tendon is commonly supposed to be the sciatic muscle, *nervus ischiaticus*, running from the thigh to the ankle. No mention of this practice of ritual abstinence occurs in the Levitical law; but it is referred to in the Talmud *Tract Chullin*, cap. vii.

he touched] The subject to the verb is not expressed, out of motives of reverence.

"The nature of the lameness produced by injury to the sinew of the thigh socket is explained by the Arabic lexx., *s.v. ḥārifat*; the man can only walk on the tips of his toes" (!).—Robertson Smith, *Rel. Sem* (380, n. 1).

Ch. XXXIII.

1—17. Meeting of Jacob and Esau (J).

18—20. Jacob at Shechem (P and E).

1. *And Jacob lifted up his eyes, &c.*] For this phrase, cf. xviii. 2, xxiv. 63, xxxi. 10 (J).

four hundred men] See xxxii. 6.

he divided, &c.] Jacob disposes of his household, placing in the rear those who were most dear to him, so that in the event of an attack by Esau they might have the best chance of escape.

unto the two handmaids. And he put the handmaids 2 J
and their children foremost, and Leah and her children
after, and Rachel and Joseph hindermost. And he himself 3
passed over before them, and bowed himself to the ground
seven times, until he came near to his brother. And Esau 4
ran to meet him, and embraced him, and fell on his neck,
and kissed him: and they wept. And he lifted up his 5
eyes, and saw the women and the children; and said, Who
are these with thee? And he said, The children which
God hath graciously given thy servant. Then the hand- 6
maids came near, they and their children, and they bowed
themselves. And Leah also and her children came near, 7
and bowed themselves: and after came Joseph near and
Rachel, and they bowed themselves. And he said, What 8
meanest thou by all this company which I met? And he

3. *before them*] Jacob himself goes in front of his household to protect them.

seven times] Jacob prostrates himself before his brother, in token of complete subservience. Not content with one prostration, he bows seven times to the ground, with which has aptly been compared a letter from a Canaanite to the king of Egypt in the Tel-el-Amarna tablets: "At the feet of the king, my lord, seven times and seven times do I fall."

4. *And Esau*] Esau's conduct on this occasion is that of a good-natured and forgiving disposition. There is no statement of his having intended any mischief to Jacob. His appearance with four hundred men seems to have been accidental, and not with hostile intent against Jacob. He behaves throughout magnanimously and simply.

fell on his neck] In xlv. 14, xlvi. 29 (J), this demonstration of feeling is followed by "weeping."

kissed him] On the Hebrew word for "kissed him" the Massoretic, or traditional, Hebrew text has this note: "All of it punctuated," i.e. every letter dotted. Probably the text was at an early date uncertain. The Rabbinic explanation is strange, i.e. "because he did not come to kiss him, but to bite him," and the tradition goes on to say that Jacob's neck was turned into marble!

they wept] The strong emotion of orientals; cf. xlv. 2.

The Targum of pseudo-Jonathan, following up the absurd Rabbinic tradition arising from the Israelite hatred of Edom, explains that Jacob wept because his neck was painful, and Esau because he had pain in his teeth!

8. *all this company*] Lit. "all this camp." Esau refers to the

GENESIS XXXIII. 8—13

9 said, To find grace in the sight of my lord. And Esau said, I have enough; my brother, let that thou hast be thine.
10 And Jacob said, Nay, I pray thee, if now I have found grace in thy sight, then receive my present at my hand: [1]forasmuch as I have seen thy face, as one seeth the face of
11 God, and thou wast pleased with me. Take, I pray thee, my [2]gift that is brought to thee; because God hath dealt
12 graciously with me, and because I have [3]enough. And he urged him, and he took it. And he said, Let us take our
13 journey, and let us go, and I will go before thee. And he said unto him, My lord knoweth that the children are

---

[1] Or, *for therefore have I seen*   [2] Heb. *blessing.*   [3] Heb. *all.*

---

droves sent on ahead as a present by Jacob (xxxii. 13—22). The word "camp" (*mahaneh*) is an additional reference to Mahanaim.

9. *enough*] Heb. "abundance," or "plenty."

10. *forasmuch as I have seen*] R.V. marg. *for therefore have I seen.* See xviii. 5, xix. 8 (J).

as one seeth the face of God] Jacob desires to imply that to have seen the face of Esau, and to have found him friendly, was as if one had looked on the face of God, and found it favourable. The phrase is therefore an elaborate compliment, such as is found in 1 Sam. xxix. 9, 2 Sam. xiv. 17, where David is compared to an angel of God. We can hardly doubt that this turn of compliment contains a side allusion to the name of the locality, Peniel. Cf. xxxii. 30, 31.

The phrase "to see the face" is equivalent to being "admitted into the royal presence"; cf. xliii. 3, 5; 2 Kings xxv. 19.

11. *gift*] Heb. *blessing*; LXX τὰς εὐλογίας μου; Lat. *benedictionem.* The "gift" is the material side of the "blessing"; and the word "blessing" is thus used for a gift, in Josh. xv. 19; Judg. i. 15; 1 Sam. xxv. 27, xxx. 26; 2 Kings v. 15. The word *benedictio* was similarly used to denote a gift in the Middle Ages. The "liberal soul" of Prov. xi. 25 is a "soul, or person, of blessing."

enough] Heb. "all." Jacob means that in the kindness of Esau he has everything. Perhaps also there is an allusion to the Divine blessing in xxxii. 29.

urged] Until Esau had accepted the gift, Jacob's suspicious nature could not feel secure.

12. *And he said*] Esau speaks. He assumes that Jacob will be glad to receive the protection of his armed men. Jacob declines, not wishing to incur the risk of friction arising from a collision between two large companies; and will not accept a kindness which might compromise his independence. It was wiser to separate, while they were still amicable. The natures remain the same; Esau's thoughtless, Jacob's calculating.

tender, and that the flocks and herds with me give suck: J
and if they overdrive them one day, all the flocks will die.
Let my lord, I pray thee, pass over before his servant: 14
and I will lead on softly, according to the pace of the cattle
that is before me and according to the pace of the children,
until I come unto my lord unto Seir. And Esau said, 15
Let me now leave with thee some of the folk that are with
me. And he said, What needeth it? let me find grace in
the sight of my lord. So Esau returned that day on his 16
way unto Seir. And Jacob journeyed to Succoth, and built 17
him an house, and made booths for his cattle: therefore the
name of the place is called ¹Succoth.

And Jacob came ²in peace to the city of Shechem, which 18 P

¹ That is, *Booths*.   ² Or, *to Shalem, a city*

13. *tender*] i.e. young and unequal to the fatigues of travel.

14. *softly*] Lit. "according to my gentleness," i.e. at a quiet and leisurely rate.

according to the pace of the cattle] Lit. "of the property" in herds and flocks (*m'lă'cah*, as in Exod. xxii. 7, 10; 1 Sam. xv. 9).

unto Seir] Jacob here implies that he was intending to visit his brother in Seir. He has no intention of settling there, and at the most he expresses a courteous hope of a temporary sojourn.

15. *What needeth it?*] i.e. why should you do so? Jacob courteously declines his brother's offer.

Esau here is withdrawn from the scene. The part which he has played in this chapter is dignified and chivalrous. He forgives and forgets. He has the force at his command, but will not make an unworthy use of it.

17. *Succoth*] This verse preserves the traditional explanation of the origin of the name *Succoth*, "booths," "huts"; LXX σκηναί. The site of Succoth is not yet identified with any certainty. From this passage we may infer, that it lay on the east of the Jordan, and south of the Jabbok. For other references to Succoth, cf. Josh. xiii. 27; Judg. viii. 5, 8; Ps. lx. 6, cviii. 7.

an house] Jacob is here stated to have erected not a "tent" or a "booth," but a "house," as a sign of the more permanent character of his sojourn in the land.

18—20. JACOB AT SHECHEM.

18. *in peace*] R.V. marg. *to Shalem, a city of.* The rendering in the margin is possible. It is supported by LXX and Vulg. There is a village, *Salim*, still to be found near Shechem. On the other hand, the context speaks of Jacob "before the city" of Shechem; and

P is in the land of Canaan, when he came from Paddan-
E 19 aram; and encamped before the city. | And he bought the
parcel of ground, where he had spread his tent, at the hand
of the children of Hamor, Shechem's father, for an hundred
20 ¹pieces of money. And he erected there an altar, and called
it ²El-elohe-Israel.

> ¹ Heb. *kesitah*.   ² That is, *God, the God of Israel*.

the fact of his arrival there "in peace" is not without significance in view of the events narrated in ch. xxxiv.

Canaan...Paddan-aram] The transition in this verse is abrupt. Jacob is suddenly transferred from the east to the west side of the Jordan. The clause, "when he came from Paddan-aram," seems to ignore the previous chapters, and is clearly taken from a different source, viz. P.

before the city] "In front of it," lit. "in the presence of the city" of Shechem. It is the preposition rendered "before" in xix. 13.

19. *the parcel of ground*] or "the portion of the field." Lat. *partem agri*. For "parcel," Fr. "parcelle," from Lat. *particula*, see Josh. xxiv. 32; Ruth iv. 3. Cf. "Many a thousand, Which now mistrust no parcel of my fear" (Shakespeare, 3 *Hen. VI*, v. 6).

his tent] Jacob has resumed dwelling in tents, see *v.* 17.

the children of Hamor, Shechem's father] This apparently means the people of the tribe of Hamor; and Hamor was the founder, or chieftain, of the city of Shechem. The confusion between the "sons of Hamor, Shechem's father," and "Shechem the son of Hamor," in xxxiv. 2, caused LXX in this verse to omit "sons of."

LXX, by rendering Συχέμ for the name of the man, and Σίκιμα (cf. xii. 6) for the name of the city, draws a distinction which it is not always possible to observe in English.

pieces of money] Heb. *kesitah*. Apparently a *kesitah* was a piece of metal used for money; elsewhere it is mentioned only in Josh. xxiv. 32; Job xlii. 11. Whether it denotes a small coin, or an ingot, cannot be determined. The versions, LXX, Lat. and Targ. Onkelos, render "lambs¹": Targ. Jon. and Jerus., "pearls."

The purchase of this plot of ground was historically important. It was the burial-place of the bones of Joseph (cf. Josh. xxiv. 32; Acts vii. 16). The possession of such small pieces of territory (cf. the purchase of Machpelah ch. xxiii.) constituted no claim for the possession of the country: the patriarchs were "strangers and sojourners," xxiii. 4.

20. *erected*] Lit. "set up." A verb used elsewhere, not of an altar, but of a "pillar" or upright stone. Cf. xxxv. 14, 20 and Josh. xxiv. 26. Hence many prefer here to read "pillar" (*maṣṣēbah*) instead of "altar" (*mizbēah*).

El-elohe-Israel] R.V. marg. That is, *God, the God of Israel*. The

---

¹ LXX (ἑκατὸν ἀμνῶν="a hundred lambs") "vel *agnos ipsos* intellegere potuerunt, vel *nummos agnorum imagine signatos*." Schleusner, *Lex. Vet. Test.*, s.v. ἀμνός.

altar, or stone, is denoted by the name of Êl, the God of Israel. The origin of some sacred stone, well known to the Israelites, was thus accounted for. The stone and the Divine Being associated with it are identified: see xxviii. 22, xxxv. 7. "Israel's God is El" is a profession of faith in the one true God made at the moment when Jacob comes to dwell among the heathen Canaanites.

CH. XXXIV.

The story of Dinah and of the destruction of Shechem presents numerous difficulties which are hard to explain.

(1) The reader is surprised at finding that Jacob and his sons, who had fled from Laban and had been at the mercy of Esau, are now able, though dwelling in the midst of strangers, to seize and destroy one of the most important cities in central Canaan, and to carry off as captives the women and children of Shechem (*vv*. 27—29).

(2) This bloody deed is represented, in *vv*. 25, 30, as being done by Simeon and Levi. But, in the main portion of the chapter, all the sons of Jacob are described as implicated in the act of treachery and slaughter.

(3) Dinah appears in this chapter as a young woman; whereas we should be led to infer, both from the mention of her birth in xxx. 21 (cf. xxxi. 41), and from the age assigned to Joseph in xxxvii. 2 at a period evidently considerably later, that she was still of tender years at the time when Jacob left Haran. According to this narrative, a considerable interval of time must, therefore, be supposed to have occurred since the arrival of Jacob in Canaan.

The narrative, like that in ch. xiv., is an exception to the series of peaceful scenes from patriarchal life and character. Probably, it contains in its main outlines the reminiscence of early tribal history. If so, the repulsive details of the story may be regarded, not so much as incidents of personal history, as the symbolical description of early tribal relations. The main outline of the tradition may have been as follows: Dinah was the name of a small Israelite tribe, which, at the time of the occupation of Canaan, became attached to, and finally amalgamated with, and absorbed in, the native Shechemite clans. The Israelite tribes, Simeon and Levi, sought to rescue and avenge their sister tribe, and, after a pretended alliance, fell upon the Shechemites and treacherously massacred them. That they themselves were in turn almost overwhelmed by a Canaanite coalition, seems probable in view of the facts that (1) the Shechemites retained their independence (cf. Judg. ix.); (2) the tribes of Levi and Simeon are not referred to in the song of Deborah (Judg. v.), and practically drop out of Israelite history as effective for warlike purposes. The act of violence was disavowed by the nation of Israel, cf. *v*. 30.

In the present narrative two slightly different versions of the same tradition are combined. In one version, Shechem is the prominent speaker (*vv*. 11, 12); Shechem submits to the condition of circumcision

GENESIS XXXIV. 1—5

E* 34 And Dinah the daughter of Leah, which she bare unto
2 Jacob, went out to see the daughters of the land. And
Shechem the son of Hamor the Hivite, the prince of the
J* land, saw her; | and he took her, and lay with her, and
3 humbled her. And his soul clave unto Dinah the daughter
of Jacob, and he loved the damsel, and spake [1]kindly
E* 4 unto the damsel. | And Shechem spake unto his father
J* 5 Hamor, saying, Get me this damsel to wife. | Now Jacob
heard that he had defiled Dinah his daughter; and his sons

[1] Heb. *to the heart of the damsel.*

(*v.* 19); Simeon and Levi slaughter Shechem and his father Hamor, and carry away Dinah (*v.* 26). In the other version, Hamor the father of Shechem is the more prominent person (*vv.* 4, 6, 8—10, 13—17, 20—25), while the affair is made to concern the people, as much as the family: again, the attack on the city, the massacre, and the looting, are represented as the deed of all the brothers of Dinah (*vv.* 27—29). The second version, therefore, relates the story on a larger and more dreadful scale than the first.

It is very doubtful whether either of the two versions can be identified with J or E or P. Skinner remarks: "The first recension must have taken literary shape within the Yahwistic school, and the second may have been current in Elohistic circles; but neither found a place in the main document of the school to which it belonged, and its insertion here was an afterthought suggested by a supposed connection with xxxiii. 19 (E)." The two versions are amalgamated somewhat as follows:

J* (=Jahvistic school): 2^{b*}, 3, 5 (?), 7 (?), 11, 12, 19, (25), 26, 30, 31.
E* (=Elohistic school): 1, 2^a, 4, 6, 8—10, 13—18, 20—24, (25), 27—29.

1. *Dinah*] See xxx. 21, xxxi. 41, from which passages the age of Dinah at the time of Jacob's flight from Haran may be computed. She was nearly the last of Jacob's children born in Haran.

2. *Hivite*] See x. 17. The name of a Canaanite tribe. In Josh. ix. 7 the Hivites are found in Gibeon; but, from Judg. iii. 3 and Josh. xi. 3, their dwelling-place was traditionally connected with Lebanon.

LXX has "Horite," as in Josh. ix. 7.

"Hamor," as the name of an animal, means "he-ass."

the prince] This word, in Heb. *nasi*, is used frequently by P, xvii. 20, xxiii. 6, xxv. 16. Lat. *princeps*.

3. *his soul*] i.e. his affections. Heb. *nephesh*. Cf. xii. 13, xxvii. 4. *kindly*, &c.] Heb. *to the heart of the damsel*. The same phrase, sometimes rendered "comfortably," occurs in l. 21; 2 Sam. xix. 7; Isa. xl. 2; Hos. ii. 14.

4. *Get me*] The parents were accustomed to obtain a wife for their son: see xxi. 21, xxiv. 3, 4; Judg. xiv. 2.

were with his cattle in the field: and Jacob held his 6 J*
peace until they came. | And Hamor the father of Shechem 6 E*
went out unto Jacob to commune with him. | And the 7 J*
sons of Jacob came in from the field when they heard
it: and the men were grieved, and they were very wroth,
because he had wrought folly in Israel in lying with Jacob's
daughter; which thing ought not to be done. | And Hamor 8 E*
communed with them, saying, The soul of my son Shechem
longeth for your daughter: I pray you give her unto him
to wife. And make ye marriages with us; give your 9
daughters unto us, and take our daughters unto you. And 10
ye shall dwell with us: and the land shall be before you;
dwell and trade ye therein, and get you possessions therein. |
And Shechem said unto her father and unto her brethren, 11 J*
Let me find grace in your eyes, and what ye shall say unto
me I will give. Ask me never so much dowry and gift, 12
and I will give according as ye shall say unto me: but

6. *And Hamor*] This verse continues *v.* 4. The intervening *v.* 5 is continued in *v.* 7.

7. *wrought folly*] The word *nebâlah* denotes "senseless wickedness," an offence against honour and morality: cf. the use of the word in Deut. xxii. 21; Jos. vii. 15; Judg. xix. 23, 24; 2 Sam. xiii. 12.

in Israel] The addition of these words (as in Deut. xxii. 21; Judg. xx. 6, 10; Jer. xxix. 23) is of course an anachronism, when put into the mouth of Jacob; and indicates a time of authorship when this phrase had become proverbial.

ought not to be done] See notes on xx. 9, xxix. 26.

9. *make ye marriages with us*] Hamor's proposition is to the effect that the Israelites and the Shechemites should be amalgamated on the basis of (1) intermarriage, (2) trading rights, (3) rights of occupation of land. For the detestation of intermarriage with the Canaanites, see Deut. vii. 3; Josh. xxiii. 12; Ezra ix. 2.

11. *And Shechem*] Here, and in *v.* 12, Shechem makes his own overtures to Jacob and his sons. In *vv.* 6, 8—10, Hamor has been negotiating on behalf of Shechem.

12. *dowry and gift*] The "dowry," or *mohar*, is the present made to the parents or relations, cf. xxiv. 53; Ex. xxii. 16; 1 Sam. xviii. 25. The rendering "dowry" hardly, therefore, gives the correct idea to English readers. The "gift," on the other hand, was the present made by the bridegroom to the bride, as in xxiv. 53, xxix. 18. In Ex. xxii. 16, as in the present passage, the "dowry" is a payment to the parents as "compensation" for wrong, as well as "purchase-money" for the wife; cf. Deut. xxii. 28, 29.

E* 13 give me the damsel to wife. | And the sons of Jacob answered Shechem and Hamor his father with guile, and 14 spake, because he had defiled Dinah their sister, and said unto them, We cannot do this thing, to give our sister to one that is uncircumcised; for that were a reproach unto us: 15 only on this condition will we consent unto you: if ye will be as we be, that every male of you be circumcised; 16 then will we give our daughters unto you, and we will take your daughters to us, and we will dwell with you, and we 17 will become one people. But if ye will not hearken unto us, to be circumcised; then will we take our daughter, and 18 we will be gone. And their words pleased Hamor, and

J* 19 Shechem Hamor's son. | And the young man deferred not to do the thing, because he had delight in Jacob's daughter: and he was honoured above all the house of his father. |

E* 20 And Hamor and Shechem his son came unto the gate of their city, and communed with the men of their city, saying, 21 These men are peaceable with us; therefore let them dwell

13. *the sons of Jacob*] In vv. 13—18 we have the treacherous proposal, made by the sons of Jacob, by which they would be able to revenge themselves upon the Shechemites, and attack them, when they would be incapacitated for defence.

14. *uncircumcised*] The passage contains the interesting and early tradition, that circumcision was not practised by the Canaanite dwellers in Shechem. On the widespread prevalence of this rite, see note on ch. xv. In J and E, Israelite circumcision is specially connected with the names of Moses and Joshua (Ex. iv. 25; Josh. v. 2). The peculiar treachery of Jacob's sons is made to turn upon their insistence on the sacred national rite of circumcision. The condition which Shechem, in v. 19 (J*), undertakes to satisfy, is not explained, in view of E*'s account (vv. 13—18).

a reproach] Compare the similar expression in Josh. v. 9, where it appears that the Egyptians reproached the Israelites for their neglect of circumcision.

19. *to do the thing*] This verse describes Shechem's eagerness to fulfil some condition required by Jacob. We cannot say for certain, whether this personal requirement was the same as that contained above, i.e. the obligation of circumcision (vv. 15—17).

honoured above all] These words must have had some reference to the terms, presumably of a humiliating nature, to which he had consented. He was the most distinguished personage in the city. If he was willing, no one else in the community need object.

20. *the gate of their city*] The place for the transaction of public business: see note on xix. 1, xxiii. 10.

in the land, and trade therein; for, behold, the land is E*
large enough for them; let us take their daughters to us for
wives, and let us give them our daughters. Only on this 22
condition will the men consent unto us to dwell with us,
to become one people, if every male among us be circumcised,
as they are circumcised. Shall not their cattle and their sub- 23
stance and all their beasts be ours? only let us consent unto
them, and they will dwell with us. And unto Hamor and unto 24
Shechem his son hearkened all that went out of the gate
of his city; and every male was circumcised, all that went
out of the gate of his city. And it came to pass on 25
the third day, when they were sore, that | two of | the sons J*E*
of Jacob, | Simeon and Levi, Dinah's brethren, | took each J*E*
man his sword, and came upon the city ¹unawares, and
slew all the males. | And they slew Hamor and Shechem 26 J*
his son with the edge of the sword, and took Dinah out
of Shechem's house, and went forth. | The sons of Jacob 27 E*

¹ Or, *boldly*

23. *cattle...substance*] It would be a good business transaction.

24. *all that went out of the gate*] i.e. all the citizens: cf. "all that
went in at the gate," xxiii. 10, 18.

25. *And it came to pass*] In this verse the Compiler has combined
the two versions: (1) that which ascribes the treacherous deed to the
sons of Jacob generally; and (2) that in which Simeon and Levi alone
are the perpetrators of the massacre.

when they were sore] The effects of the operation rendered the
Shechemite males powerless to defend themselves. In this version
there is a vein of coarse and repulsive humour. The Canaanites were
not only put to the sword, but by their submission to the Israelite
rite they had been outwitted. At the time of the attack, they were
unable to offer any resistance.

unawares] Better than R.V. marg. *boldly*. LXX ἀσφαλῶς = "safely,"
Lat. *confidenter*. The meaning is that the people of Shechem were
secure and unsuspecting, when the attack was made. Not the courage
of the assailants, but the sense of security on the part of their victims,
is indicated. Cf. "the careless Ethiopians" (Ezek. xxx. 9).

26. *slew Hamor and Shechem...took Dinah...went forth*] In this
verse we have the narrative in which Simeon and Levi (cf. *vv.* 25, 30)
alone entered the city, slew Hamor and Shechem, took Dinah from
Shechem's house, and made off with her. Their act is one of family
vengeance for the honour of their sister.

with the edge of the sword] Lit. "according to the mouth of the
sword," i.e. according to the sword's power to devour, unmercifully.
Cf. 2 Sam. ii. 26, xi. 25.

E*　came upon the slain, and spoiled the city, because they
28　had defiled their sister. They took their flocks and their
　　herds and their asses, and that which was in the city,
29　and that which was in the field; and all their wealth, and
　　all their little ones and their wives, took they captive
J* 30　and spoiled, even all that was in the house. | And Jacob
　　said to Simeon and Levi, Ye have troubled me, to make
　　me to stink among the inhabitants of the land, among the
　　Canaanites and the Perizzites: and, I being few in number,
　　they will gather themselves together against me and smite
31　me; and I shall be destroyed, I and my house. And they
　　said, Should he deal with our sister as with an harlot?
E 35　And God said unto Jacob, Arise, go up to Beth-el, and

27. *The sons of Jacob*] This verse and *vv.* 28, 29 record the version in which all the sons of Jacob united to massacre the males of Shechem, carried away captive the wives and children, and took possession of the wealth and property of the inhabitants: cf. Num. xxxi. 9, 11.

30. *And Jacob*, &c.] This and the following verse continue the narrative of *v.* 26. Jacob reproaches his two sons for the murder, on account of which the people of the land will be infuriated with Jacob and his house. Cf. xlix. 5—7.

troubled] The same word used in the story of Achan (Josh. vi. 18, vii. 25; 1 Chron. ii. 7). Jacob's rebuke turns, not so much upon the dastardly treachery and cruelty of his sons, as upon the evil effects it will produce, and upon the insecurity it will bring upon himself and his house.

make me to stink] A common Heb. metaphor: cf. Ex. v. 21 ("make savour to be abhorred"); 1 Sam. xiii. 4 ("had in abomination"), xxvii. 12 ("made...abhor"); 1 Chron. xix. 6 ("made...odious").

the Canaanites and the Perizzites] See note on xiii. 7.

being few in number] Cf. 1 Chron. xvi. 19.

31. *Should he deal*] Simeon and Levi regard the incident as one in which the honour of the clan was involved, and as if they had only one course of action to follow with regard to Shechem and Hamor.

Ch. XXXV. (E, J, P.)

1—8 (E).　Jacob at Bethel.

9—15 (14 J) (P).　The appearance of God to Jacob. His name changed to Israel.

16—22ᵃ.　Birth of Benjamin, death of Rachel (J).

22ᵇ**—29.**　The names of Jacob's sons and the death of Isaac (P).

1. *go up to Beth-el*] From Shechem to Bethel is an ascent of 1000 feet. Bethel is 2890 feet above the sea.

dwell there: and make there an altar unto God, who E
appeared unto thee when thou fleddest from the face of
Esau thy brother. Then Jacob said unto his household, 2
and to all that were with him, Put away the strange gods
that are among you, and purify yourselves, and change your
garments: and let us arise, and go up to Beth-el; and I will 3
make there an altar unto God, who answered me in the
day of my distress, and was with me in the way which
I went. And they gave unto Jacob all the strange gods 4
which were in their hand, and the rings which were in their
ears; and Jacob hid them under the ¹oak which was by
Shechem. And they journeyed: and ²a great terror was 5

¹ Or, *terebinth*   ² Heb. *a terror of God*.

LXX εἰς τὸν τόπον Βαιθήλ = "unto the place Bethel," cf. xii. 6—8, xiii. 4, xxviii. 11.

an altar] Jacob is commanded to worship at Bethel in fulfilment of his vow, xxviii. 22.

2. *strange gods*] The images of the gods of foreigners, i.e. of another family, tribe, or nation. Rachel had carried away, from Haran, the household gods of her father's family. Cf. xxxi. 19, 30, 32—35. The presence of the gods of the foreigner was displeasing in the sight of the God of Israel. Cf. Josh. xxiv. 23, "Now therefore put away the strange gods which are among you, and incline your heart unto the LORD, the God of Israel"; words which were also spoken at Shechem.

purify yourselves] Cf. Ex. xix. 10; Lev. xv. 5. Purification was effected by ceremonial washings.

3. *who answered me*] Jacob here refers to his flight from Esau (chap. xxviii.), not, as some have supposed, to his flight from Laban (chap. xxxi.).

in the day of my distress] Cf. Ps. xx. 1, "The LORD answer thee in the day of trouble; the name of the God of Jacob set thee up on high."

was with me] Cf. xxviii. 20, xxxi. 3.

4. *in their hand*] i.e. in their possession.

the rings...ears] The rings mentioned were probably not simple earrings as in xxiv. 22, but rings worn as charms, and amulets, having symbols of heathen deities. Cf. Hos. ii. 13.

the oak] R.V. marg. *terebinth*. It is noteworthy that Joshua, under the same "oak" of Shechem (Josh. xxiv. 26), testified against the primitive worship of strange gods; cf. Josh. xxiv. 2, 14, 23. For the "terebinth," cf. xii. 6. The same sacred tree is possibly mentioned in Judg. ix. 6.

5. *a great terror*] Heb. *a terror of God*. The inhabitants were under the influence of a mysterious dread or panic, inspired by God. Cf. Ex. xv. 16, xxiii. 27; Deut. ii. 25; Josh. ii. 9; 2 Chron. xiv. 14.

E upon the cities that were round about them, and they did 6 not pursue after the sons of Jacob. So Jacob came to Luz, which is in the land of Canaan (the same is Beth-el), 7 he and all the people that were with him. And he built there an altar, and called the place ¹El-beth-el: because there God was revealed unto him, when he fled from the 8 face of his brother. And Deborah Rebekah's nurse died, and she was buried below Beth-el under the oak: and the name of it was called ²Allon-bacuth.

P 9 And God appeared unto Jacob again, when he came 10 from Paddan-aram, and blessed him. And God said unto him, Thy name is Jacob: thy name shall not be called

¹ That is, *The God of Beth-el.* ² That is, *The oak of weeping.*

did not pursue] These words which imply that "the sons of Jacob" had by their violence given just cause of provocation, presuppose ch. xxxiv.

6. *Luz*] See xxviii. 19, xlviii. 3.

7. *the place*] See notes on xii. 6, xxviii. 11.

El-beth-el] That is, *the god of Beth-el.* Here, as in xxxiii. 20, the altar receives the name of the deity.

was revealed] Referring to xxviii. 12, 13. In the Heb. "was revealed" is in the plural: see note on xx. 13, cf. Josh. xxiv. 19. Dillmann (*Theologie d. A.T.*, p. 211) explains this by saying that "Elohim" here is "God with the angels." The Divine Presence is regarded as hidden or covered, and needing to be "revealed"; cf. Num. xxiv. 4, 16.

8. *Deborah*] The mention of Deborah, Rebekah's nurse, is surprising. She is mentioned, though not by name, in xxiv. 59. Probably her name was well known in other Israelite traditions which have not survived. If we relied on the chronology of P, we should have to call attention to the fact that, according to its statements (xxv. 20, xxxv. 28), Deborah had left Haran with Rebekah 140 years before.

below Beth-el] On lower ground, probably to the south; cf. 1 Sam. vii. 11, "under Beth-car"; 1 Kings iv. 12, "beneath Jezreel."

Allon-bacuth] That is, *the oak of weeping.* It is a coincidence, but nothing more, that Deborah, the prophetess, dwelt between Ramah and Bethel, under a palm tree, Judg. iv. 5. Is this the "oak of Tabor" (1 Sam. x. 3)?

9—15 (P). This passage contains the account of (1) an appearance of God to Jacob, (2) the change of his name to Israel, and (3) the renewal of the Divine promises granted at Bethel. All this is parallel to the narrative in xxviii. 10—22; it presents P's explanation of the names Israel and Bethel, both of which have already been accounted for in J and E.

9. *when he came...Paddan-aram*] As in xxxiii. 18, P ignores the

any more Jacob, but Israel shall be thy name: and he   P
called his name Israel. And God said unto him, I am 11
¹God Almighty: be fruitful and multiply; a nation and
a company of nations shall be of thee, and kings shall come
out of thy loins; and the land which I gave unto Abraham 12
and Isaac, to thee I will give it, and to thy seed after thee
will I give the land. And God went up from him in the 13
place where he spake with him. | And Jacob set up a pillar in 14 J
the place where he spake with him, a pillar of stone: and he
poured out a drink offering thereon, and poured oil thereon. |
And Jacob called the name of the place where God spake with 15 P
him, Beth-el. | And they journeyed from Beth-el; and there 16 J

¹ Heb. *El Shaddai*.

whole J and E narrative since the departure from Haran; which country appears in P as Paddan-aram.

10. *Israel shall be thy name*] This change of name has been mentioned by J in xxxii. 28. For the change, cf. xvii. 5, 15, where Abraham and Sarah receive a change of name associated with a special promise.

11. *God Almighty*] Heb. *El Shaddai*. See note on xvii. 1. The phrases in this verse, "God Almighty," "be fruitful and multiply," "company of nations," are characteristic of P's style.

a nation, &c.] Cf. the promises in xvii. 5, 6, 16. Here the mention of "kings" renews the promise to Sarah in xvii. 16 (P).

13. *And God went up*] An expression descriptive of the manifestation in some external form, in which God appeared to Jacob. Cf. xviii. 33, "And the LORD went his way."

14. *And Jacob*, &c.] This verse, probably from J, contains a parallel account to that of E in xxviii. 18. Jacob erects a pillar, or upright stone (*maṣṣēbah*): and this he consecrates with a libation of oil and a drink offering. Whether this is the account of another pillar at Bethel, or is a parallel version of the account in ch. xxviii., is uncertain.

16—22ᵃ (J). BIRTH OF BENJAMIN AND DEATH OF RACHEL.

"The meaning of the statement that Rachel died when Benjamin was born is that the formation of the new tribe Benjamin broke up the old tribe Rachel" (Bennett). But it would be a mistake to attempt to distinguish too closely the personal and tribal elements in the narrative. Events in personal life may be recorded for their symbolical significance. The story of Jacob, as distinct from that of Joseph, closes with Rachel's death.

16. *some way*] The word in the Heb. denotes a measure of distance. What it was, however, cannot be determined. It is found in xlviii. 7 and 2 Kings v. 19. LXX renders as a proper name *Chabratha*.

J was still some way to come to Ephrath: and Rachel travailed,
17 and she had hard labour. And it came to pass, when she
was in hard labour, that the midwife said unto her, Fear not;
18 for now thou shalt have another son. And it came to pass,
as her soul was in departing (for she died), that she called
his name ¹Ben-oni: but his father called him ²Benjamin.
19 And Rachel died, and was buried in the way to Ephrath
20 (the same is Beth-lehem). And Jacob set up a pillar upon

> ¹ That is, *The son of my sorrow*.
> ² That is, *The son of the right hand*.

to Ephrath] The name of a place otherwise unknown, in Benjamite territory, south of Bethel: not Bethlehem (Micah v. 2); see *v.* 19.

17. *another son*] Lit. "for this also is a son for thee." Perhaps the reference is to Rachel's prayer (xxx. 24), "the LORD add to me another son," when Joseph was born.

18. *her soul*] The *nephesh*, or "soul," the vital principle: cf. 1 Kings xvii. 21, "let this child's soul come unto him again."

Ben-oni] i.e. *the son of my sorrow*. Rachel, as she dies, names her son; but the father cannot acquiesce in a name of such sad memories.

Benjamin] i.e. *the son of the right hand*. Jacob refuses to give his child an ill-omened name. The right hand was regarded as the auspicious side. Cf. xlviii. 13, 17—19; 1 Kings ii. 19; Ps. xlv. 9, lxxxix. 13. The tribe of Benjamin occupied the southernmost territory of the sons of Rachel, viz. on the right of Ephraim, facing eastwards. According to Sayce (*E.H.H.*, p. 79) this is the explanation of the name, which then might be rendered "southerner"; and the present story would imply the formation of the tribe after the occupation of Canaan.

The words of Rachel, as she dies, should be compared with the allusion in Jeremiah xxxi. 15. The condensed account in this passage makes no reference to the grief of Jacob; but this is expressed in xlviii. 7 by a pathetic sentence.

19. *Ephrath* (*the same is Beth-lehem*)] The words, "the same is Beth-lehem," create a difficulty; they occur also in xlviii. 7, and seem to be confirmed by Ruth iv. 11; Micah v. 2, "Bethlehem Ephrathah," where the reference is to Bethlehem, S. of Jerusalem. But (1) judging from the present passage we should suppose that Rachel's tomb was a little south of Bethel: (2) from Jer. xxxi. 15 it would appear that Rachel's death and burial were connected with Ramah, a place 5 miles north of Jerusalem: (3) from 1 Sam. x. 2 we learn that Rachel's sepulchre is in the border of Benjamin, i.e. north of Jerusalem. There is clearly, therefore, a discrepancy. Perhaps two traditions were current respecting the sepulchre; one placing it near Ramah, on the borders of Benjamin, south of Bethel; the other placing it near Bethlehem, south of Jerusalem. The words, "the same is Beth-lehem," look like a gloss,

her grave: the same is the Pillar of Rachel's grave unto this day. And Israel journeyed, and spread his tent beyond the tower of Eder. And it came to pass, while Israel dwelt in that land, that Reuben went and lay with Bilhah his father's concubine: and Israel heard of it. J 21 22

Now the sons of Jacob were twelve: the sons of Leah; Reuben, Jacob's firstborn, and Simeon, and Levi, and Judah, and Issachar, and Zebulun: the sons of Rachel; Joseph and Benjamin: and the sons of Bilhah, Rachel's handmaid; Dan and Naphtali: and the sons of Zilpah, Leah's handmaid: Gad and Asher: these are the sons of P 23 24 25 26

erroneously inserted into the text. "Ephrath," by itself, was not an uncommon name. In all probability, if the words are an erroneous gloss, they are responsible for the Biblical discrepancy, and are accountable for the Christian tradition of Rachel's tomb N. of Bethlehem.

21. *Israel*] Observe the employment of the new name as an alternative for Jacob, with especial frequency in the J narrative.

the tower of Eder] i.e. "the tower of the flock." It is uncertain whether "Eder" is a proper name or not. For a similar uncertainty, cf. xxxiii. 18. The place is evidently situated between Ephrath (*v.* 19) and Hebron (xxxvii. 14). The identification of Eder with Jerusalem on the strength of Micah iv. 8 ("O tower of the flock [or, "Eder"], the hill of the daughter of Sion") is improbable.

22ª. *Reuben*] The incest of Reuben is alluded to in xlix. 3, 4. The Compiler abbreviates what must have been a repulsive tradition. But, as in ch. xxxiv., the tradition may possibly contain, in figurative language, some reminiscence of early tribal relations. Very little is known of the tribe of Reuben; but in Num. xvi. the tribe of Reuben endeavours to displace Moses on the strength of its primogeniture: and in Josh. xv. 6, "the stone of Bohan son of Reuben," in the heart of Canaan, may contain the reminiscence of some early unrecorded tribal encroachment.

Israel heard of it] As in xxxiv. 30, 31, the tradition breaks off abruptly.

22ᵇ.—29 (P). JACOB'S SONS, AND THE DEATH OF ISAAC.

22ᵇ. *the sons of Jacob*] The names of Jacob's sons are enumerated after the mention of Benjamin's birth. But the enumeration is that of P, which assumes that all the sons of Jacob, including Benjamin, were born to him in Paddan-aram (*v.* 26), in direct contradiction to *vv.* 16—18 (J).

twelve] A sacred number, found also in the sons of Nahor and Ishmael (xvii. 20, xxii. 20—24, xxv. 16).

P 27 Jacob, which were born to him in Paddan-aram. And Jacob came unto Isaac his father to Mamre, to Kiriath-arba (the same is Hebron), where Abraham and Isaac sojourned. 28 And the days of Isaac were an hundred and fourscore 29 years. And Isaac gave up the ghost, and died, and was gathered unto his people, old and full of days; and Esau and Jacob his sons buried him.

27. *Isaac*] The mention of Isaac, after so long an interval, is surprising. But the P narrative carefully records the death and age of each patriarch. According to J, Isaac was living at Beer-sheba, when Jacob left his home (xxviii. 10). According to P, Isaac died 80 years later at Mamre in close proximity to the burial-place of his father. Isaac was 40 years old when he married Rebekah (xxv. 20); 60 years old at the birth of Esau and Jacob (xxv. 26); at least 100 years old when Jacob went to Haran (xxvii. 46, cf. xxvi. 34), and, therefore, over 120 when Jacob returned from Haran.

Mamre] Cf. xiii. 18, xxiii. 19.

Kiriath-arba] Cf. xxiii. 2.

28. *the days of Isaac*] Isaac is here credited with a longer life by 5 years than Abraham. Cf. xxv. 7. Comparing this verse with xxv. 20, xxvi. 34, Jacob, according to P, was 120 years old at his father's death; he had left his father at the age of 40; and had resided in Canaan for nearly 60 years. There is no mention of his having visited Isaac again.

29. *gave up the ghost*, &c.] Cf. the same phrase in xxv. 8, xlix. 33.

Esau and Jacob] According to P, Esau and Jacob meet at the burial of Isaac, just as Ishmael and Isaac met to bury Abraham, xxv. 9.

The Book of Jubilees (chs. xxxvii., xxxviii.) relates that, after Isaac's death, Esau was stirred up by his sons to attack Jacob with an army; and that Esau said: "If the boar can change its skin, and make its bristles as soft as wool...then will I observe the tie of brotherhood with thee, &c." Whereupon Jacob, listening to the advice of Judah his son, "bent his bow and sent forth the arrow and struck Esau his brother on the right breast and slew him."

CH. XXXVI. (P.) THE GENERATIONS OF ESAU.

In this chapter are preserved traditions of great antiquarian interest relating to Edom, one of the races most nearly allied to Israel. After the burial of Isaac, the P narrative disposes of the "generations of Esau," before dealing with "the generations of Jacob" (xxxvii. 2).

The Edomites were an invading people who occupied the mountainous country of Seir. They subjugated the natives who were called Horites (xiv. 6), and, while largely dispossessing them, also became fused with them by intermarriage and peaceful settlement; cf. Deut. ii. 12,

GENESIS XXXVI. 1—3

Now these are the generations of Esau (the same is Edom). **36** P
Esau took his wives of the daughters of Canaan; Adah the **2**
daughter of Elon the Hittite, and Oholibamah the daughter
of Anah, the ¹daughter of Zibeon the Hivite; and Basemath **3**

> ¹ Some ancient authorities have, *son*. See ver. 24.

22. The subjugation of the Horites by the Edomites presents a close parallel to that of the Canaanites by the Israelites.

The chapter falls into seven sections.

vv.		
1—5.	(1)	Esau's wives and children.
6—8.	(2)	Esau's immigration into Seir.
9—14.	(3)	The genealogy of the sons of Esau.
15—19.	(4)	The tribal chiefs of Esau.
20—30.	(5)	The genealogy of the Horites and their chiefs.
31—39.	(6)	Kings of Edom.
40—43.	(7)	A supplementary list of Edomite chiefs.

The contents of this chapter are probably chiefly derived from P: but it is clear from the discrepancies in some of the names that various materials have been employed. It is natural to suppose that the compiler of this section enjoyed the privilege of access to Edomite documents.

1 Chron. i. 35—54 repeats, with some variations, and in an abbreviated form, the lists of names in *vv.* 4, 5, 11—13, 20—28, 31—43.

1—5. ESAU'S WIVES AND CHILDREN.

1. *the same is Edom*] A gloss introduced here and in *vv.* 8, 19.

2. *Esau took his wives*] The list of Esau's wives in this chapter does not agree with that in xxvi. 34 and xxviii. 9.

(*a*) In this passage and in *vv.* 9—14 Esau's wives are (1) Adah, the daughter of Elon the Hittite; (2) Oholibamah, the daughter of Anah, the daughter of Zibeon the Hivite; (3) Basemath, the daughter of Ishmael, and sister of Nebaioth.

(*b*) In xxvi. 34 (P) and xxviii. 9 (P) Esau's wives are (1) Judith, the daughter of Beeri the Hittite; (2) Basemath, the daughter of Elon the Hittite; (3) Mahalath, the daughter of Ishmael, and sister of Nebaioth. Thus there are two widely differing versions of P tradition. For the differences are too considerable to have arisen from corruptions in the text.

Anah, the daughter of Zibeon the Hivite] "Daughter," as in *v.* 14. But the reading "son" is found in LXX, Sam. and Syr. Pesh., and is to be preferred; see *v.* 24. "Daughter" is probably a correction, on the assumption that "Anah" was a feminine name.

the Hivite] For "Hivite" should be read "Horite," if the Anah of *v.* 2 be the same as the Anah in *v.* 24. Probably, in *v.* 25, "the daughter of Anah" has been introduced as a gloss.

P 4 Ishmael's daughter, sister of Nebaioth. And Adah bare to
5 Esau Eliphaz; and Basemath bare Reuel; and Oholibamah
bare Jeush, and Jalam, and Korah: these are the sons of
6 Esau, which were born unto him in the land of Canaan. And
Esau took his wives, and his sons, and his daughters, and all
the souls of his house, and his cattle, and all his beasts, and
all his possessions, which he had gathered in the land of
Canaan; and went into a land away from his brother Jacob.
7 For their substance was too great for them to dwell together;
and the land of their sojournings could not bear them be-
8 cause of their cattle. And Esau dwelt in mount Seir: Esau is
9 Edom. And these are the generations of Esau the father of
10 [1]the Edomites in mount Seir: these are the names of
Esau's sons; Eliphaz the son of Adah the wife of Esau,
11 Reuel the son of Basemath the wife of Esau. And the
sons of Eliphaz were Teman, Omar, [2]Zepho, and Gatam, and

[1] Heb. *Edom*.   [2] In 1 Chr. i. 36, *Zephi*.

4. *Eliphaz*] Familiar as the name of one of Job's friends, Job ii. 11.
Reuel] The same name as that of Moses' father-in-law, a Midianite, Ex. ii. 18.

6—8. ESAU IN MOUNT SEIR.

6. *a land away from his brother Jacob*] The Syr. reads "the land of Seir," which is possibly the original reading. The Lat. *abiit in alteram regionem*. The present passage ignores the previous mention of Esau's residence in "the land of Seir, the field of Edom," xxxii. 3. Seir was the mountainous country between the Dead Sea and the Elamitic Gulf.

7. *For their substance was too great*] The departure of Esau into Seir is here explained as necessitated by the growing wealth of Esau and Jacob in Canaan: cf. the separation of Abraham and Lot in ch. xiii. Obviously the explanation given here does not agree with the representation in xxxii. 3 and xxxiii. 14—16. "Substance," cf. xii. 5, xv. 14.

8. *mount Seir*] The mountain country of Seir, a region, not a mountain, lying to the east of the Arabah.

9—14. The "sons" of Esau by Adah, Basemath, and Oholibamah must be regarded as the names of clans, and, like the sons of Ishmael and Israel, are 12 in number (Amalek, the son of Esau's concubine, Timna, is excluded from this list of twelve).

9. *the Edomites*] Heb. *Edom*, as in *v*. 43: cf. 1 Sam. xiv. 47.
10. *Eliphaz*] See *v*. 4.
Reuel] See *v*. 4.
11. *Teman*] A district in the north of Edom. Cf. Ezek. xxv. 13;

Kenaz. And Timna was concubine to Eliphaz Esau's 12 P
son; and she bare to Eliphaz Amalek: these are the sons
of Adah Esau's wife. And these are the sons of Reuel; 13
Nahath, and Zerah, Shammah, and Mizzah: these were the
sons of Basemath Esau's wife. And these were the sons 14
of Oholibamah the daughter of Anah, the daughter of
Zibeon, Esau's wife: and she bare to Esau Jeush, and
Jalam, and Korah. These are the ¹dukes of the sons of 15
Esau: the sons of Eliphaz the firstborn of Esau; duke
Teman, duke Omar, duke Zepho, duke Kenaz, duke Korah, 16
duke Gatam, duke Amalek: these are the dukes that came
of Eliphaz in the land of Edom; these are the sons
of Adah. And these are the sons of Reuel Esau's son; 17
duke Nahath, duke Zerah, duke Shammah, duke Mizzah:
these are the dukes that came of Reuel in the land of

¹ Or, *chiefs*

Amos i. 12; Obad. 9. Its reputation for "wise men" is alluded to in Jer. xlix. 7; Baruch iii. 22, 23. Job's friend Eliphaz is a Temanite, Job ii. 11. The Heb. word *têmân* means "south," i.e. what is on the right hand, facing east.

Kenaz] Probably connected with the Kenizzites (xv. 19), an Edomite family, which attached itself to the tribe of Judah in southern Palestine.

12. *Amalek*] Here a grandson of Esau; but, as the descendant from a concubine, he denotes a subordinate clan. Amalekites infested the Sinaitic Peninsula (Ex. xvii. 8—15; Deut. xxv. 17) and harried southern Palestine (1 Sam. xv. 2).

15—19. THE TRIBAL CHIEFS OF ESAU.

15. *the dukes*] Better, as marg., *chiefs*. The word "duke" has been introduced into the English version from the Lat. *dux* which translates the LXX ἡγεμών. The Heb. *allûph* is connected with *eleph* = 1000, or "a clan"; and hence is used for "the chieftain of a clan," or "a chiliarch," especially in Edom: cf. Ex. xv. 15; Zech. ix. 7, xii. 5, 6.

"Duke," in Old English, was not limited to the highest rank of nobility. It meant "leader" or "chief." Cf. Wiclif, *Matt.* ii. 6, "And thou Bethleem...for of thee a *duyk* shall go out"; Latimer, *Serm.*, p. 31, "Gideon a *duke* which God raised up."

duke Teman] A better idea would be conveyed to English readers, if the rendering were "the chieftain of Teman, of Omar, &c."

16. *duke Korah*] This name is out of place. It has come in from *v.* 18. The other names in *vv.* 15, 16 are drawn from *vv.* 11 and 12, while Korah, which occurs in *v.* 14, is mentioned again in *v.* 18.

GENESIS XXXVI. 17—24

P 18 Edom; these are the sons of Basemath Esau's wife. And these are the sons of Oholibamah Esau's wife; duke Jeush, duke Jalam, duke Korah: these are the dukes that came 19 of Oholibamah the daughter of Anah, Esau's wife. These are the sons of Esau, and these are their dukes: the same is Edom.

20 These are the sons of Seir the Horite, the inhabitants of the land; Lotan and Shobal and Zibeon and Anah, 21 and Dishon and Ezer and Dishan: these are the dukes that came of the Horites, the children of Seir in the 22 land of Edom. And the children of Lotan were Hori 23 and ¹Hemam; and Lotan's sister was Timna. And these are the children of Shobal; ²Alvan and Manahath and 24 Ebal, ³Shepho and Onam. And these are the children of Zibeon; Aiah and Anah: this is Anah who found the hot springs in the wilderness, as he fed the asses

---

¹ In 1 Chr. i. 39, *Homam*.   ² In 1 Chr. i. 40, *Alian*.
³ In 1 Chr. i. 40, *Shephi*.

20—30. The Horites—the aboriginal inhabitants of the country—"the sons of Seir, the Horite," were possibly so called from the word *hor*, "a hole"; cf. 1 Sam. xiii. 6, xiv. 11. This derivation has long been maintained, and is possibly correct, the Horites being regarded as troglodytes, or cave-dwellers. In Obad. 3 Edom is apostrophized, "O thou that dwellest in the clefts of the rock." On the other hand another derivation has recently commended itself, Hor being identified with the Egyptian *Haru* which is found in Egyptian inscriptions for "Syria." But there is good support from the rocks of Petra and the excavations at Gezer for the "cave-dweller" explanation of the word.

20. *the inhabitants of the land*] The aborigines: see xiv. 6; Deut. ii. 12.

24. *Zibeon*] means "an hyaena."

Anah] See note on *v.* 2. Whether son or brother (*v.* 20) of Zibeon, Anah stands for a clan.

the hot springs] There must have been some well-known story about Anah and his discovery of certain hot springs, while he was, like Saul in 1 Sam. ix., searching for strayed asses. Hot springs are found not far from the pilgrim road to Mecca. The tradition probably claimed their possession for the clan of Anah.

The word for "hot springs" presented a difficulty. The A.V. and Luther render "mules," and LXX makes it a proper name τὸν Ἰαμείν,

of Zibeon his father. And these are the children of 25 P
Anah; Dishon and Oholibamah the daughter of Anah.
And these are the children of ¹Dishon; ²Hemdan and 26
Eshban and Ithran and Cheran. These are the children 27
of Ezer; Bilhan and Zaavan and ³Akan. These are the 28
children of Dishan; Uz and Aran. These are the dukes 29
that came of the Horites; duke Lotan, duke Shobal, duke
Zibeon, duke Anah, duke Dishon, duke Ezer, duke Dishan: 30
these are the dukes that came of the Horites, according to
their dukes in the land of Seir.

And these are the kings that reigned in the land of 31
Edom, before there reigned any king over the children

---

¹ Heb. *Dishan*.   ² In 1 Chr. i. 41, *Hamran*.
³ In 1 Chr. i. 42, *Jaakan*.

---

while Targ. Onk. renders "the Emim"; but Lat. *aquas calidas* correctly.

25. *Anah*] This is the clan of Anah of *v.* 20, and probably also of *v.* 24.

Oholibamah] See *v.* 2. Probably the words "the daughter of Anah" have been carelessly inserted from *v.* 2 as a gloss.

26. *Dishon*] Heb. *Dishan*, "a mountain goat" (Deut. xiv. 5).

28. *Uz*] See x. 23, xxii. 21. Possibly a branch of the Aramaean race (cf. Job i. 1) had settled among the Horites, S.E. of Palestine.

30. *according to their dukes*] Rather, "according to their clans." So LXX, ἐν ταῖς ἡγεμονίαις.

31—39. KINGS OF EDOM.

31. *any king*] From this verse we infer that the writer lived at a time subsequent to the foundation of the Israelite monarchy. The definition, however, of the date is not quite clear in the opinion of some scholars. It is simplest to render, "before there reigned a king for Israel," i.e. before the time of Saul. But it is noteworthy that LXX Cod. A renders, "before there reigned any king in Jerusalem." Dillmann translates "before an Israelite king reigned," i.e. over Edom, referring to the subjugation of the Edomites by David. The tradition shews that Edom had a settled constitution before Israel. In Scriptural terms Esau was "the elder." It is to be observed that the Edomite kings, (1) had different places of residence, (2) were not hereditary kings. Perhaps they may be compared with the local judges of Israel. "The land of Edom" is the whole territory, more extensive than "mount Seir" (*v.* 8). There was a "king of Edom" in Moses' time (Num. xx. 14).

P 32 of Israel. And Bela the son of Beor reigned in Edom;
33 and the name of his city was Dinhabah. And Bela died, and Jobab the son of Zerah of Bozrah reigned in
34 his stead. And Jobab died, and Husham of the land of
35 the Temanites reigned in his stead. And Husham died, and Hadad the son of Bedad, who smote Midian in the
36 field of Moab, reigned in his stead: and the name of his city was Avith. And Hadad died, and Samlah of Masrekah
37 reigned in his stead. And Samlah died, and Shaul of
38 Rehoboth by the River reigned in his stead. And Shaul died, and Baal-hanan the son of Achbor reigned in his
39 stead. And Baal-hanan the son of Achbor died, and

32. *Bela the son of Beor*] In the Hebrew the addition of the letter *m* would give us the proper name "Balaam the son of Beor" (Num. xxii. 5). So Targum of Jonathan reads. Hence some have conjectured that we have here an alternative tradition respecting Balaam, as king of Edom.

Bela is also the name of a town, Zoar (xiv. 2).

33. *Bozrah*] A town lying 20 miles south-east of the Dead Sea, of great importance in old times—perhaps the chief Edomite city. Cf. Isa. xxxiv. 6, lxiii. 1; Jer. xlix. 13, 22; Amos i. 12. It has been identified with the modern *Busera*. The name means "fortification."

34. *the Temanites*] See v. 11.

35. *Hadad*] A name familiar as that of a Syrian deity, occurring in the royal names "Ben-Hadad" and "Hadad-Ezer." The defeat of "Midian in the field of Moab," the solitary note of history, illustrates the extent to which the power of Edom at one time was developed. See note on the same name, xxv. 2. Ewald conjectured that this king Hadad I was a contemporary of Gideon's, and joined in resistance to the Midianite invasion, circ. 1100 (Judg. vi. ff.).

Avith] LXX reads "Gittaim."

36. *Samlah*] LXX (in some MSS.) "Salmah," almost the same name as "Solomon."

37. *Shaul*] This is the same name in Hebrew as "Saul."

Rehoboth by the River] The R.V. by printing "River" with a capital adopts the interpretation that the Euphrates is here intended. If so, Rehoboth may be *Rahaba* a little south of the junction of the Habor with the Euphrates. But it may be asked, what connexion can there be between Edom and the Euphrates? Hence some prefer to explain by the "river of Egypt," the *Wady el Arish*, viz. the boundary between Palestine and Egypt, from which the Rehoboth of xxvi. 22 would not be very remote. But "the River" is *nahar*; "the river of Egypt" is *nahal mizraim*.

Achbor] Meaning "jerboa." The name occurs in 2 Kings xxii. 14; Jer. xxvi. 22, xxxvi. 12.

38. *Baal-hanan*] i.e. "Baal is favourable," suggesting the worship

¹Hadar reigned in his stead: and the name of his city was P
²Pau; and his wife's name was Mehetabel, the daughter
of Matred, the daughter of Me-zahab. And these are the 40
names of the dukes that came of Esau, according to their
families, after their places, by their names; duke Timna,
duke ³Alvah, duke Jetheth; duke Oholibamah, duke Elah, 41
duke Pinon; duke Kenaz, duke Teman, duke Mibzar; 42
duke Magdiel, duke Iram: these be the dukes of Edom, 43
according to their habitations in the land of their possession.
This is Esau the father of ⁴the Edomites.

¹ In 1 Chr. i. 50, and some ancient authorities, *Hadad*.
² In 1 Chr. i. 50, *Pai*.   ³ In 1 Chr. i. 51, *Aliah*.   ⁴ Heb. *Edom*.

of Baal; cf. Elhanan, Johanan. The name is the same in meaning as
Hannibal.

39. *Hadar*] Probably, as 1 Chr. i. 50 and some ancient authorities,
Hadad. Possibly this Hadad II (see *v*. 35) was the Hadadezer deposed
by David (2 Sam. viii. 3 ff.). Hadad III shook off the yoke of Israel
(1 Kings xi. 21 ff.; cf. Gen. xxvii. 40).

Pau] In 1 Chr. i. 50, *Pai*. LXX reads Φόγωρ = Peor, cf. Num. xxiii. 28.

Mehetabel] = "El does good," a proper name occurring in Neh. vi. 10.
These names shew how close was the similarity between the languages
of the Edomites and the Israelites.

40—43. EDOMITE CHIEFS.

40. *families...places...names*] This short supplementary list of chiefs
consists of names partly tribal, partly local, and partly personal.

duke Timna] i.e. the chieftain of Timna; cf. note on *v*. 15.

Alvah] In 1 Chr. i. 51, *Aliah*. In *v*. 23, *Alvan*.

41. *duke Elah*] Probably the chief of the tribe that resided on the
coast of Elath. The name appears in the kinship of Caleb (1 Chron.
iv. 15).

Pinon] Possibly the same as Punon (cf. Num. xxxiii. 42) between
Petra and Zoar.

43. *the Edomites*] Heb. *Edom*; cf. *v*. 9.

CHS. XXXVII.—L. (JE.) THE NARRATIVE OF JOSEPH AND HIS BRETHREN.

The remaining chapters of the book, with the exception of chap.
xxxviii., deal with the story of Joseph. In its way this story is probably
unsurpassed. Its vividness of narrative is extraordinary. It contains
scenes of great pathos. In the delineation of character, it exhibits
strength and simplicity of portraiture. Joseph's career is dramatic in
its vicissitudes. Throughout all the events of his chequered life, God's

P 37 And Jacob dwelt in the land of his father's sojournings,
2 in the land of Canaan. These are the generations of Jacob.
J Joseph, being seventeen years old, | was feeding the flock
with his brethren; and he was a lad with the sons of
Bilhah, and with the sons of Zilpah, his father's wives:

overruling Providence is seen to be guiding him. He is led by the
discipline of sorrow and misfortune to the position in which he is
ultimately to prepare a home for his father and his brethren. His
generous magnanimity recompenses with complete forgiveness the
men who had basely plotted his death.

The Joseph section, xxxvii.—l., is denoted by P "These are the
generations of Jacob" (xxxvii. 2), just as the story of Jacob had
been introduced by the summary description of P, "these are the
generations of Isaac" (xxv. 19).

The story of Joseph was deservedly a favourite among the Israelites.
It was current in slightly different versions. The two versions of
J and E have been combined by the Compiler. A superficial reader,
perhaps, will not recognize the slight discrepancies which have
survived in the composite narrative. A careful study, especially in
chap. xxxvii., enables us to distinguish the different treatment of the
story. The main difference appears in the crisis of the narrative.

According to E, Joseph's brethren, offended at his dreams,
resolved to slay him, and cast his body into a tank. Reuben, secretly
anxious to rescue him, prevails on his brethren to abstain from bloodshed, and to cast him alive into a tank and leave him there to his fate.
A passing caravan of Midianites pull Joseph out of the tank, kidnap
him (cf. xl. 15), and carry him away to Egypt. Reuben, on finding the
tank empty, is overwhelmed with distress: see xxxvii. 19, 20, 22, 23^b,
24, 28^{ac}, 29, 30, 31^b, 34.

According to J, Joseph's brethren, who hate him because of his
father's preference, on seeing a caravan of Ishmaelites, determine, at the
urgent advice of Judah, to sell Joseph. They draw him out of the
tank and sell him for 20 pieces of silver: see xxxvii. 18^b, 21, 23^a,
25—27, 28^b, 31^a, 32, 33, 35.

1, 2^a (P). From P, as is shewn by the word "sojournings," and
the phrase "these are the generations," and the mention of Joseph's
age.

1. *sojournings*] Cf. xvii. 8, xxviii. 4, xxxvi. 7 (P).

2. *These are the generations*, &c.] The formula of a new section
in P.

2^b—36 (JE). JOSEPH SOLD INTO EGYPT.

2^b (J). *and he was a lad with*, &c.] The English here gives an
awkward rendering. The meaning is, "he was keeping sheep, being
still a lad, with his brethren, the sons of Bilhah and Zilpah," i.e. Dan
and Naphtali, Gad and Asher. Joseph's home at this time seems to

and Joseph brought the evil report of them unto their father. Now Israel loved Joseph more than all his children, because he was the son of his old age: and he made him ¹a coat of many colours. And his brethren saw that their father loved him more than all his brethren; and they hated him, and could not speak peaceably unto him. | And Joseph dreamed a dream, and he told it to his brethren: and they hated him yet the more. And he said unto them, Hear, I pray you, this dream which I have dreamed: for, behold, we were binding sheaves in

¹ Or, *a long garment with sleeves*

have been at Hebron (cf. xxxv. 27). The life of Joseph, the elder son of the favourite wife, spent in the field with the sons of the concubines, was not likely to be happy.

the evil report] What this was, does not appear; cf. 1 Sam. ii. 23. But Joseph's action brought upon him the odium of tale-bearing. On the words for "evil report" cf. Num. xiii. 32, xiv. 36, 37 (P).

3, 4 (J). JOSEPH AND HIS BRETHREN.

3. *Israel*] In J this name is generally used. Contrast the use of Jacob by P in *v.* 2.

the son of his old age] This is hardly the description that we should expect from chap. xxx. 22—24, which records the birth of Joseph. The phrase is used in xliv. 20 of Benjamin with greater appropriateness.

a coat of many colours] Rather, as R.V. marg., *a long garment with sleeves*. The familiar rendering "a coat of many colours," derived from LXX χιτῶνα ποικίλον, Vulg. *tunicam polymitam*, is certainly incorrect. It is literally "a tunic of palms," i.e. reaching to the palms of the hands and the soles of the feet, differing from an ordinary tunic by having sleeves, and by reaching to the feet. The same word is used in 2 Sam. xiii. 18 of a dress worn by a princess, where LXX χιτὼν καρπωτός and Lat. *tunica talaris* are correct. The rendering of the margin, of Pesh., Symm. (χειριδωτόν) and Aquila (χιτὼν ἀστραγάλων), if less picturesque, is more accurate.

The unwise favouritism shewn by his father heightened the unpopularity of the boy.

5—11 (E). JOSEPH'S DREAMS.

5. *dreamed a dream*] The influence of dreams in the E narrative is conspicuous; cf. xx. 3. Dreams were regarded by the Oriental as intimations from another world, and were invested with the sanctity of a divine oracle. The dream and its significance entered deeply into the religious conceptions of the ancient races.

7. *sheaves*] Joseph's dream presupposes that the patriarch was

E the field, and, lo, my sheaf arose, and also stood upright; and, behold, your sheaves came round about, and made 8 obeisance to my sheaf. And his brethren said to him, Shalt thou indeed reign over us? or shalt thou indeed have dominion over us? And they hated him yet the 9 more for his dreams, and for his words. And he dreamed yet another dream, and told it to his brethren, and said, Behold, I have dreamed yet a dream; and, behold, the sun and the moon and eleven stars made obeisance to 10 me. And he told it to his father, and to his brethren; and his father rebuked him, and said unto him, What is this dream that thou hast dreamed? Shall I and thy mother and thy brethren indeed come to bow down our-11 selves to thee to the earth? And his brethren envied him;
J 12 but his father kept the saying in mind. | And his brethren

leading a settled and agricultural life (cf. xxvi. 12). In xlvi. 31—34 Jacob and his family are shepherds and herdsmen, but the fact that the failure of crops compels them to seek for corn in Egypt, xlii. 1, shews that they were partly dependent upon local crops. Cf. xii. 10, xxxvi. 1.

8. *reign over us*] Perhaps with a reference to the future kingdom of Ephraim, or to the leadership of "the house of Joseph" (Judg. i. 22).

9. *another dream*] The repetition (cf. xli. 5—32) seems to indicate stronger certainty and greater importance. The first dream had its symbolism on earth, the second in the heavens. The first included the brethren only. The second included the father and the mother in the same act of obeisance with the brethren. Israel, in its widest sense, as a father's house, is to recognize the predominance of Joseph.

eleven stars] Supposed by some scholars to refer to the signs of the Zodiac (cf. 2 Kings xxiii. 5 marg.), the twelfth being either Joseph or obscured by Joseph. But the theory is improbable: it is not "*the* eleven stars."

10. *thy mother*] Implying that Rachel was still alive. Her death was recorded in xxxv. 19 (J). Presumably this version (E) assumed that her death occurred later.

The sun represented his father, and the moon his mother; each of his brethren is represented by a star. There is nothing in this scene which really favours astronomical or astral theories of interpretation.

11. *envied*] This is the envy of malice rather than of jealousy: it denotes resentment against Joseph for being favoured, and a desire to see him deprived of his privileges.

kept the saying in mind] Lit. "kept the word." LXX διετήρησεν. Lat. *rem tacitus considerabat*. This phrase is the origin of the words in Luke ii. 51, "kept all these sayings in her heart." Jacob rebuked Joseph, but evidently was so deeply impressed with the remarkable

GENESIS XXXVII. 12—18

went to feed their father's flock in Shechem. And Israel 13 J
said unto Joseph, Do not thy brethren feed the flock in
Shechem? come, and I will send thee unto them. And
he said to him, Here am I. And he said to him, Go 14
now, see whether it be well with thy brethren, and well
with the flock; and bring me word again. So he sent him
out of the vale of Hebron, and he came to Shechem.
And a certain man found him, and, behold, he was 15
wandering in the field: and the man asked him, saying,
What seekest thou? And he said, I seek my brethren: 16
tell me, I pray thee, where they are feeding *the flock*.
And the man said, They are departed hence: for I heard 17
them say, Let us go to Dothan. And Joseph went after
his brethren, and found them in Dothan. And they saw 18

and seemingly improbable character of the twice repeated dream, that
he secretly cherished a presentiment of its fulfilment (xlii. 6).

12—17 (J). JOSEPH'S MISSION TO HIS BRETHREN IN SHECHEM.

12. *in Shechem*] The region of Shechem was famous for its
fertility and pasturage. The fact that Jacob's brethren selected it
for pasturing their flocks, indicates that the Dinah narrative, recorded
in chap. xxxiv., belongs to a separate group of Israelite tradition.
Clearly Dinah, if we may judge from xxx. 21 and 22—24, was of
the same age as Joseph. Joseph in the present chapter (cf. *v.* 2) is
17 years old, while Dinah, to judge from xxxiv. 1, must have been
not less than 15; accordingly the events of that chapter would have
been of quite recent occurrence. Evidently the present J narrative is
independent of them.

Seeing that Jacob, according to *v.* 14, was residing in Hebron,
Shechem and Dothan would be a very great distance away from the
patriarch's residence. Apparently the writer assumes that the whole
country was open grazing ground.

14. *the vale of Hebron*] The residence of Jacob; cf. xxxv. 27.

15. *a certain man*] Evidently Joseph and his brethren were well
known, and not unfavourably, in the region of Shechem. The lad's
wandering in uncertainty appeals to the reader's sympathy. The
Targum of Palestine says the "man" was the angel Gabriel.

17. *Dothan*] Familiar to us as the name of the city in which Elisha
was beset by foes and divinely protected (2 Kings vi. 13—15). The
modern *Tel Dothan* probably preserves the site, a hill on the S. side
of the plain of Jezreel, and some 15 miles N. of Shechem. It is
mentioned frequently in the book of Judith. Modern writers speak
of its rich pasturage.

J	him afar off, and before he came near unto them, they
E 19	conspired against him to slay him.	And they said one
20	to another, Behold, this ¹dreamer cometh. Come now therefore, and let us slay him, and cast him into one of the pits, and we will say, An evil beast hath devoured him:
J 21	and we shall see what will become of his dreams.	And [Reuben] heard it, and delivered him out of their hand; and
E 22	said, Let us not take his life.	And Reuben said unto them, Shed no blood; cast him into this pit that is in the

¹ Heb. *master of dreams.*

18—36 (JE). JOSEPH IS SOLD INTO EGYPT.

The composite character of the narrative becomes at this point very evident. J (*vv.* 21, 25—27, 28ᵇ, 31—35) relates that *Judah* restrains his brethren from murder, and persuades them to sell Joseph to passing Ishmaelites, who sell him as a slave to an Egyptian noble. E (*vv.* 22—25 (*bread*), 28ᵃ (*pit*), 28ᶜ—30, 36) relates that *Reuben* interposes, and saves Joseph from his brethren: by his advice Joseph is cast into a tank, where he is found by passing Midianite merchants, who draw him out, take him to Egypt, and sell him to Potiphar, "captain of the guard." Reuben returning to the tank, after the interval for food, finds it empty.

19. *this dreamer*] Heb. *master of dreams.* This and the following verse are from E. Joseph's brethren speak derisively of this "master (Heb. *baal*) of dreams" (cf. xlix. 23, "archers"="masters of arrows"; 2 Kings i. 8, "a hairy man"="a master of hair"). They will kill him, and so stop his dreams from coming true.

20. *one of the pits*] Cisterns, or tanks, are necessary in that country for the storage of water. Long droughts are frequent, and the heat very great. Water is needed for the flocks and herds. The tanks are frequently covered with a stone. The aperture is narrow, and the sides of the tank converging.

21. *Reuben*] Reuben's name is probably here substituted by the Compiler (R) for that of Judah. Reuben speaks in *v.* 22; and it is unlikely that two consecutive clauses would begin with Reuben speaking. Probably this verse comes from J, and is carried on in *vv.* 26, 27, with Judah's attempt to rescue Joseph.

22. *And Reuben said*] This and the next two verses are from E. Reuben, the eldest, interposes to save his brother's life; cf. xlii. 37.

Shed no blood] Reuben's warning is that there should be no bloodshed, as if murder without bloodshed would be a less evil. His proposal is that Joseph should be thrown into a cistern or tank, which they knew of hard by, and that he should be left there to perish, Reuben intending himself to deliver him. Reuben is not brave enough to oppose his brothers; but hopes to outwit them. He appeals to the horror of bloodshed. Blood cries out against the murderer: see note on iv. 11.

wilderness, but lay no hand upon him: that he might E
deliver him out of their hand, to restore him to his father.
And it came to pass, when Joseph was come unto his 23
brethren, that they stript Joseph of his coat, the coat of
many colours that was on him; and they took him, and 24
cast him into the pit: and the pit was empty, there was no
water in it. And they sat down to eat bread: | and they 25 J
lifted up their eyes and looked, and, behold, a travelling
company of Ishmaelites came from Gilead, with their
camels bearing ¹spicery and ²balm and ³myrrh, going to

¹ Or, *gum tragacanth* Or, *storax*   ² Or, *mastic*   ³ Or, *ladanum*

24. *the pit was empty*] Cf. the incident in the life of Jeremiah (Jer. xxxviii. 6). Presumably this was the reason why Reuben proposes to "cast him into this pit" (*v.* 22).

25. *to eat bread*] i.e. to take their meal; cf. xxxi. 54, xliii. 25. The E narrative is here interrupted, and is resumed at *v.* 28.

25ᵇ. *a travelling company*] "A caravan." Cf. Job vi. 19, "the caravans of Tema, the companies of Sheba"; Isa. xxi. 13, "travelling companies of Dedanites." Dothan lay on the trade route that led from Gilead through the valley of Jezreel towards Egypt.

Ishmaelites] This must be regarded as a descriptive title for bands of traders at the time of the composition of this narrative. Ishmael, according to the P genealogies in Genesis, was Jacob's uncle; and the sons of Ishmael were cousins of Joseph. Here the title is used almost in the sense of "Bedouin nomads."

from Gilead] The trade route followed by caravans passed (1) from Gilead on the east of the Jordan, (2) by a ford, across the Jordan, (3) by Beth-Shean or *Beisan*, down the plain of Jezreel, and so (4) by Lydda and the coast, to Egypt.

spicery] R.V. marg. *gum tragacanth*, or, *storax*. "Spicery" is too vague a word. LXX θυμιαμάτων. Lat. *aromata*. "Tragacanth" is "the resinous gum of the *Astragalus gummifer*." "*Spice*, Old Fr. *espice* (*épice*), is derived from *species*. The mediaeval merchants recognised four 'kinds'=*species* of aromatic trade; hence 'spice,' viz. saffron, cloves, cinnamon, nutmegs." Weekley's *Romance of Words*, p. 129 (1912).

balm] R.V. marg. *mastic*, for which Gilead was famous; cf. xliii. 11; Jer. viii. 22, xlvi. 11, li. 8; Ezek. xxvii. 17. It was used for incense, and medicinally for wounds. It is said to be the gum of the mastic tree, *pistacia lentiscus*.

myrrh] R.V. marg. *ladanum*, a gum obtained from the *cistus creticus*, or rock-rose. Myrrh, *lôt*=LXX στακτή (cf. xliii. 11), appears as *ladunu* in Assyrian inscriptions describing tribute from Syria to Tiglath-Pileser IV. The caravan trade with Egypt was evidently largely occupied with materials for the practice of physicians, embalmers, and priests.

J 26 carry it down to Egypt. And Judah said unto his brethren, What profit is it if we slay our brother and
27 conceal his blood? Come, and let us sell him to the Ishmaelites, and let not our hand be upon him; for he is our brother, our flesh. And his brethren hearkened
E 28 unto him. | And there passed by Midianites, merchantmen; and they drew and lifted up Joseph out of the pit, |
J and sold Joseph to the Ishmaelites for twenty pieces of
E 29 silver. | And they brought Joseph into Egypt. And Reuben returned unto the pit; and, behold, Joseph was
30 not in the pit; and he rent his clothes. And he returned unto his brethren, and said, The child is not; and I,

26. *conceal his blood*] Referring to the superstition that blood, which was not covered, would cry for vengeance: see note on iv. 10. Cf. Job xvi. 18; Isai. xxvi. 21; Ezek. xxiv. 7.

27. *let us sell him*] Judah proposes to sell Joseph, in order to save his life. Judah takes the lead in J's version, as Reuben in E's. See xliii. 3 ff., xliv. 18 ff.

28. *Midianites*] The first part of this verse resumes E's narrative from v. 25. According to E, "Midianites," merchantmen, pass by, traders from the desert on the east of Jordan. The term is descriptive, and not genealogical: for Midian, like Ishmael, was a son of Abraham (xxv. 2). The suggestion that "Midianites" is a name representing the North Arabian Minaeans seems to ignore the Heb. character of the story. The name is without the definite article; it cannot, therefore, refer to "the Ishmaelites" of v. 27, whose description, though similar, is quite distinct. LXX οἱ Μαδιηναῖοι ἔμποροι. Lat. *Madianitae negotiatores*.

they drew and lifted up] According to E, the Midianites did this, and carried off Joseph, while his brothers were engaged in their meal. According to this account, Joseph was kidnapped, or, as he himself says (xl. 15), "stolen away," not sold.

28^b. *and sold*] This is from J. Joseph's brethren, by Judah's advice, sell him to the Ishmaelites. This clause follows upon v. 27.

twenty pieces of silver] i.e. shekels, as xx. 16. In Lev. xxvii. 5, 20 shekels is the price for a slave between the ages of 5 and 20. 30 shekels is the price for a slave in Ex. xxi. 32. On the value of a shekel, see xxiii. 15.

29. *And Reuben*] Reuben returning to "the pit" finds it empty. The Midianites had carried off the lad. Reuben's distress reveals his purpose to his brethren. Clearly this is a different picture from that of the sale of Joseph to the Ishmaelites.

30. *The child is not*] Cf. xlii. 13, 32, 36, xliv. 31; Jer. xxxi. 15; Lam. v. 7. The word "child," *yeled*, is appropriate for a small boy: see xxi. 8, 14.

whither shall I go? | And they took Joseph's coat, and 31 EJ
killed a he-goat, and dipped the coat in the blood; and 32
they sent the coat of many colours, and they brought it
to their father; and said, This have we found: know now
whether it be thy son's coat or not. And he knew it, and 33
said, It is my son's coat; an evil beast hath devoured
him; Joseph is without doubt torn in pieces. And Jacob 34
rent his garments, and put sackcloth upon his loins, and
mourned for his son many days. And all his sons and all 35
his daughters rose up to comfort him; but he refused to
be comforted; and he said, For I will go down to ¹the
grave to my son mourning. And his father wept for him. |

¹ Heb. *Sheol*, the name of the abode of the dead, answering to the Greek Hades, Acts ii. 27.

31—35. The continuation of the J clause in *v.* 28. Having sold Joseph to the Ishmaelites, the brothers have to plan how to explain his disappearance to Jacob.

According to J, they sent the coat to Jacob: according to E, they dipped it in blood, and brought it to Jacob.

33. *an evil beast*] Jacob interprets the message, as they had intended. They never asserted his death, but asked him to draw the inference. The clause is repeated from *v.* 20.

34. *rent his garments*, &c.] Jacob mourned with the mourning rites of the Israelites. The rent clothes, the sackcloth, and the ashes, denote the exact opposite of festal array, new garments, soft raiment, and ointment.

For "sackcloth" in mourning, see 1 Kings xxi. 27; 2 Kings vi. 30.

35. *his daughters*] Either a different version from that in chap. xxx. where Dinah is his only daughter; or referring to his sons' wives.

the grave] Heb. *Sheol*, the name of the abode of the dead, answering to the Greek $ᾅδης$, e.g. Acts ii. 27. *Sheol*, as the region of the dead, is, according to Hebrew ideas, the locality beneath the ground, where the disembodied spirits led a shadowy existence. See Isai. xiv. 9—20. Jacob thinks that he will arrive in *Sheol*, as he had been on the earth, in mourning for his lost son. See xlii. 38. The shade of his son will there recognize the signs of his father's grief for his sake. "To bring a man's gray hairs with sorrow to the grave" (here and xlii. 38, xliv. 29, 31) does not, therefore, only mean "to bring a man prematurely aged to his grave," but also "to bring an old man to the place of departed spirits in a state of lamentation for bereavement."

E 36 And the ¹Midianites sold him into Egypt unto Potiphar, an officer of Pharaoh's, the ²captain of the guard.

¹ Heb. *Medanites*.   ² Heb. *chief of the executioners*.

36. *Midianites*] Heb. *Medanites*. This verse, from E, resumes the narrative from *vv*. 29, 30.

Potiphar] An Egyptian name, denoting "the gift of Ra," the sun-god. It appears as "Potiphera," xli. 45, xlvi. 20. LXX Πετεφρῆς, Lat. *Putiphar*, reproducing the Egyptian *Pedephrē*= "he whom the sun-god gives."

officer] Lit. "eunuch." Probably a word used to denote an official about the court. Heb. *saris*, LXX σπάδων, Lat. *eunuchus*. Some Assyriologists prefer the derivation from *ša rêši*= "he who is the head." But there seems to be no sufficient reason to call in question the meaning which the word has in Hebrew, Aramaic, and Arabic. The class to which the *saris* belonged has always infested Oriental courts, and the name was therefore likely to acquire a general significance as "a court official." Cf. 2 Kings xviii. 17 (Rab-saris); Jer. xxxix. 3, 13; Dan. i. 3.

Pharaoh] i.e. the king of Egypt. The title, but not the personal name, of the sovereign: see note on xii. 15.

captain of the guard] Heb. *chief of the executioners*, and, as such, having charge of the prisoners (xl. 3, 4, xli. 12). Cf. "captain of the guard," 2 Kings xxv. 8; Jer. xxxix. 9, xli. 10, xliii. 6, lii. 12; Dan. ii. 14. Another very possible rendering is "chief of the butchers" (cf. xl. 2, "chief of the bakers"), the officer over the men who killed the animals for the food of the king's house, and one of the principal officials in an ancient court. The Heb. word in the sing. is "cook" in 1 Sam. ix. 23, 24, i.e. the man who killed the animal for food and cooked it.

If so, the rendering of the LXX ἀρχιμάγειρος, "head cook," "head of the kitchen department," is nearer the truth than that of the Lat. *magister militum*.

Ch. XXXVIII.

The contents of this chapter are derived from J. The narrative forms an abrupt interruption of the Joseph story. The subject-matter is peculiarly unattractive; but the insertion of the section at this point is probably due to the desire to give prominence to the position of Judah among the sons of Jacob.

The story of Judah and Tamar conceivably resembles that of Simeon and Levi in chap. xxxiv., and that of Reuben in xxxv. 21 f., in that it may be regarded as symbolizing tribal relations rather than as recording personal history. The daughter of Shua, the wife of Judah, is of Canaanite origin (*vv*. 2, 3). She represents the assimilation of Canaanite clans into the clans of the tribe of Judah. If this view be correct, then the primary object of the narrative is to preserve the tradition which connected leading families from the border races, e.g. Perez and Zerah (*vv*. 29, 30), with the great tribe of Judah. We may also

GENESIS XXXVIII. 1—8

And it came to pass at that time, that Judah went down **38 J** from his brethren, and turned in to a certain Adullamite, whose name was Hirah. And Judah saw there a daughter 2 of a certain Canaanite whose name was Shua; and he took her, and went in unto her. And she conceived, and bare 3 a son; and he called his name Er. And she conceived 4 again, and bare a son; and she called his name Onan. And she yet again bare a son, and called his name Shelah: 5 and he was at Chezib, when she bare him. And Judah 6 took a wife for Er his firstborn, and her name was Tamar. And Er, Judah's firstborn, was wicked in the 7 sight of the LORD; and the LORD slew him. And Judah 8 said unto Onan, Go in unto thy brother's wife, and perform

possibly see a subordinate object in the record of the tradition of a pre-Mosaic origin for the institution of the levirate marriage.

    1—11. Judah's wife and three sons.
    12—26. Tamar and Judah.
    27—30. The birth of Perez and Zerah.

1. *at that time*] Cf. xxi. 22. The notes of time in this chapter are very indefinite. Cf. 12, "in process of time." The marriage of Judah with the daughter of Shua, the birth of his three sons, Er, Onan, and Shelah, and the marriage of the first two with Tamar, evidently represent a long interval.

Adullamite] Judah moved from the high ground near Hebron to the lower, i.e. southern, country. The town of Adullam (Josh. xii. 15, xv. 35) is now identified with the ruins ʽ*Aid-el-mâ*, 17 miles S.W. of Jerusalem and about 12 N.W. from Hebron. See 1 Sam. xxii. 1.

Judah and Simeon in Judges i. 1—20 are represented as acting by themselves, and their names do not appear in Deborah's Song commemorating the patriotism of the Israelite tribes.

2. *Shua*] Note that "Shua," like Hirah in *v*. 1, is the name of a man. See *v*. 12. Bath-Shua, i.e. "the daughter of Shua," is all the description given of Judah's wife.

3. *and he called*] Better, "And she called his name Er." The mother calls the name, as in *v*. 4. The reading "she called" is found in some Heb. MSS., Sam. and Targ. Jer. "Er" and "Onan," see xlvi. 12.

5. *Chezib*] The same name as Achzib in Josh. xv. 44.

6. *Tamar*] = "a date palm." A female name, occurring twice in the family of David (2 Sam. xiii. 1, xiv. 27).

Judah, as head of the family, selects a wife for his firstborn, as in xxiv. 3, xxxiv. 4.

8. *perform*] The first instance of the "levirate" (Lat. *lĕvir*, "brother-in-law") law which made it obligatory for a surviving brother to marry

J the duty of an husband's brother unto her, and raise
9 up seed to thy brother. And Onan knew that the seed should not be his; and it came to pass, when he went in unto his brother's wife, that he spilled it on the ground,
10 lest he should give seed to his brother. And the thing which he did was evil in the sight of the LORD: and he
11 slew him also. Then said Judah to Tamar his daughter in law, Remain a widow in thy father's house, till Shelah my son be grown up: for he said, Lest he also die, like his brethren. And Tamar went and dwelt in her father's
12 house. And in process of time Shua's daughter, the wife of Judah, died; and Judah was comforted, and went up unto his sheepshearers to Timnah, he and his friend
13 Hirah the Adullamite. And it was told Tamar, saying, Behold, thy father in law goeth up to Timnah to shear
14 his sheep. And she put off from her the garments of her widowhood, and covered herself with her veil, and

the widow of his brother, if the latter should die childless. See Deut. xxv. 5; Matt. xxii. 24. The eldest son of a levirate marriage succeeded to the deceased's name and inheritance.

11. *in thy father's house*] A widow without children went back to her father's family; cf. Lev. xxii. 13; Ruth i. 8. A widow with children remained in the family of her husband, and under its protection. Judah evidently believes that the deaths of Er and Onan are somehow due to Tamar. Rather, then, than subject his youngest son Shelah to the risk of a similar fate, he sends Tamar back to her own people, on the pretext that Shelah is too young at present to perform the levirate duty. Compare the story in Tobit iii., where Sarah's seven husbands are cut off in succession.

12—26. TAMAR AND JUDAH.

12. *Timnah*] Possibly the same as in Josh. xv. 10, 57; Judg. xiv. 1.
13. *shear his sheep*] Sheep-shearing was an occasion of festivity, and often of licentiousness. See note on xxxi. 19. Cf. 1 Sam. xxv. 2 ff.; 2 Sam. xiii. 23 f.
14. *And she put off,* &c.] The neglect on Judah's part to satisfy the requirements of the levirate rule provoked Tamar to have recourse to trickery. To our moral sense such conduct is bad and disgusting. But to Orientals, whose life depended so largely upon the sanctity of racial customs, her action may have seemed not only entertaining in its cleverness, but even honourable and justifiable in its devotion to a deceased husband's rights.

her veil] Tamar apparelled herself in the guise of a religious prostitute (*ḳedêshah, v.* 21), one who dedicated herself to the goddess

wrapped herself, and sat in the gate of Enaim, which is
by the way to Timnah; for she saw that Shelah was
grown up, and she was not given unto him to wife. When 15
Judah saw her, he thought her to be an harlot; for she
had covered her face. And he turned unto her by the 16
way, and said, Go to, I pray thee, let me come in unto
thee: for he knew not that she was his daughter in law.
And she said, What wilt thou give me, that thou mayest
come in unto me? And he said, I will send thee a kid 17
of the goats from the flock. And she said, Wilt thou give
me a pledge, till thou send it? And he said, What pledge 18
shall I give thee? And she said, Thy signet and thy cord,
and thy staff that is in thine hand. And he gave them
to her, and came in unto her, and she conceived by him.
And she arose, and went away, and put off her veil 19
from her, and put on the garments of her widowhood.
And Judah sent the kid of the goats by the hand of his 20
friend the Adullamite, to receive the pledge from the
woman's hand · but he found her not. Then he asked the 21
men of her place, saying, Where is the ¹harlot, that was at

¹ Heb. *kedeshah*, that is, a woman dedicated to impure heathen worship. See Deut. xxiii. 17, Hos. iv. 14.

Astarte, the Babylonian Istar. The veil was one of the symbols of Istar.

in the gate of Enaim] i.e. in the open space at the entrance into the town. The name of the town means "wells," possibly *Enam*, mentioned in Josh. xv. 34, in the same context with Adullam.

by the way] i.e. on "the way side" (*v.* 21): see Jer. iii. 2; Ezek. xvi. 15—25.

15. *covered her face*] Cf. Prov. vii. 10. The attire indicated the character she had assumed.

18. *signet...cord...staff*] The signet ring is frequently worn by Arabs on a cord fastened round the neck. Cf. Song of Songs viii. 6, "set me as a seal upon thine heart." The signet ring and the staff, which was often carved and highly ornamented, would be the most personal possessions of a *Sheikh*, and, as pledges, a most certain means of identification. This astute manoeuvre is the turning-point of the whole story.

21. *harlot*] Heb. *ḳedêshah*, that is, a woman dedicated to impure heathen worship: see Deut. xxiii. 17; Hos. iv. 14. The Heb. word denotes "a woman dedicated to the service of some god, or goddess." Her dedication consisted in the sacrifice of her chastity. This

J Enaim by the way side? And they said, There hath
22 been no ¹harlot here. And he returned to Judah, and
said, I have not found her; and also the men of the place
23 said, There hath been no ¹harlot here. And Judah said,
Let her take it to her, lest we be put to shame: behold,
24 I sent this kid, and thou hast not found her. And it
came to pass about three months after, that it was told
Judah, saying, Tamar thy daughter in law hath played
the harlot; and moreover, behold, she is with child by
whoredom. And Judah said, Bring her forth, and let her
25 be burnt. When she was brought forth, she sent to her
father in law, saying, By the man, whose these are, am
I with child: and she said, Discern, I pray thee, whose
26 are these, the signet, and the cords, and the staff. And
Judah acknowledged them, and said, She is more righteous
than I; forasmuch as I gave her not to Shelah my son.
27 And he knew her again no more. And it came to pass in
the time of her travail, that, behold, twins were in her

¹ Heb. *kedeshah*, that is, a woman dedicated to impure heathen worship. See Deut. xxiii. 17, Hos. iv. 14.

repulsive and strangely degrading custom prevailed generally among Semitic races, and was associated with the impure and immoral rites of the Phoenician, Syrian, and Babylonian worship.

23. *Let her take it to her*] i.e. let her retain the pledges, lest by making enquiries Judah should be exposed to shame.

24. *let her be burnt*] Judah, as the head of the family, acts as judge having power of life and death, cf. xxxi. 32. It is remarkable that the matter is not referred to Jacob; but, presumably, this story constitutes a separate tribal tradition, in which Judah stands as the chief authority.

Judah sentences her to death as an adulteress. He treats her as the betrothed of Shelah, and the childless widow of Er. The penalty for adultery in the Levitical law was death by stoning (cf. Lev. xx. 10 with Deut. xxii. 22; Ezek. xvi. 40; John viii. 5). Death by burning, the penalty of a priest's daughter, Lev. xxi. 9, was the more ancient usage. The penalty of burning is recorded in the Code of Hammurabi; and occurs in ancient Egyptian sentences for adultery.

26. *more righteous*] Judah acknowledges that Tamar had a claim upon the observance of marriage customs, and that he had done wrong in neglecting her, and in ignoring the sacred obligations of tribal "levirate" marriage, upon which depended the very existence of an Oriental community. The Heb. verb means "to be right, to have right on one's side"; and Judah's words might be rendered "she is in her rights as against me" (cf. Davidson's *Theology of the O.T.*, p. 267).

womb. And it came to pass, when she travailed, that one 28 J
put out a hand: and the midwife took and bound upon
his hand a scarlet thread, saying, This came out first.
And it came to pass, as he drew back his hand, that, 29
behold, his brother came out: and she said, ¹Wherefore
hast thou made a breach for thyself? therefore his name
was called ²Perez. And afterward came out his brother, 30
that had the scarlet thread upon his hand: and his name
was called Zerah.

And Joseph was brought down to Egypt; and | Potiphar, 39 J(R)

¹ Or, *How hast thou made a breach! a breach be upon thee!*
² That is, *A breach.*

27—30. BIRTH OF PEREZ AND ZERAH.

29. *Wherefore hast*, &c.] *How hast thou made a breach! a breach be upon thee!*

Perez] That is, *a breach*. For Perez, see Ruth iv. 12, 18.

30. *Zerah*] A word which probably meant "the rising of the sun"; but was apparently in popular etymology connected with a word meaning "scarlet." See, for Zerah, an Edomite, xxxvi. 13, 17, 33.

In this narrative we may discern a reminiscence of a time in which the clans of Er and Onan disappeared from the tribe of Judah; while those of Perez and Zerah, connected with native Canaanites, became incorporated with it, but were rivals with one another, Zerah, though the more ancient, being obliged to yield to the greater vigour of Perez.

CH. XXXIX. (J.) JOSEPH AND POTIPHAR'S WIFE.

The story of Joseph is in this chapter resumed, in the J version, from xxxvii. 35. In this version Joseph in Egypt is a slave who has been sold by his brethren to the Ishmaelites, and then by the Ishmaelites to an Egyptian of rank, whose name is not given. This Egyptian makes him the chief servant in his household. The Egyptian's wife brings an accusation against Joseph for which the Egyptian commits him to prison.

In the present chapter the two versions of the Joseph narrative are harmonized by the Compiler giving to the Egyptian, who bought Joseph from "the Ishmaelites," the name of Potiphar, to whom, according to E, "the Midianites" sold him in xxxvii. 36.

  1—6. Joseph's prosperity.
  7—20. The false accusation.
  21—23. Joseph in prison.

1. *was brought down*] This follows upon xxxvii. 28.

Potiphar, &c.] See note on xxxvii. 36. These words the Compiler seems to have added from E to harmonize the two accounts. J merely

(R)J an officer of Pharaoh's, the captain of the guard, | an Egyptian, bought him of the hand of the Ishmaelites, 2 which had brought him down thither. And the LORD was with Joseph, and he was a prosperous man; and he was in 3 the house of his master the Egyptian. And his master saw that the LORD was with him, and that the LORD made 4 all that he did to prosper in his hand. And Joseph found grace in his sight, and he ministered unto him: and he made him overseer over his house, and all that he had he 5 put into his hand. And it came to pass from the time that he made him overseer in his house, and over all that he had, that the LORD blessed the Egyptian's house for Joseph's sake; and the blessing of the LORD was upon all 6 that he had, in the house and in the field. And he left all that he had in Joseph's hand; and ¹he knew not aught *that was* with him, save the bread which he did eat. And 7 Joseph was comely, and well favoured. And it came to

¹ Or, *with him he knew not*

read "And an Egyptian bought him"; cf. *v*. 2, "in the house of his master the Egyptian." The words "an Egyptian," "the Egyptian" would have been needless in *vv*. 1, 2, after the full description of Potiphar as "an officer of Pharaoh's, the captain of the guard."

2. *the* LORD *was with Joseph*] This is the *motif* of the whole section. Jehovah stands by Joseph whether in trouble or in prosperity, in good report or in evil; cf. *vv*. 3, 5, 21, 23. Joseph was one of those rare characters in which great personal attractiveness in manner and appearance was combined with high principle and good intellectual powers.

in the house] i.e. not sent out to labour in the field.

4. *ministered unto him*] Joseph's character and capacities were first tested by personal service, and afterwards by the responsibility of general supervision.

overseer] Joseph was made steward of the whole household, a position of which we find mention in early Egyptian records. Cf. xliii. 16, xliv. 1.

5. *for Joseph's sake*] Cf. xxx. 27 (J).

6. *he knew not...him*] The R.V. marg., *with him he knew not*, gives the correct meaning. Joseph's master trusted everything to him. Everything went on smoothly; and with Joseph as manager he had no need to think of a thing, except as regards food. It is also just possible that "save the bread, &c.," implies that food, owing to the strictness of Egyptian scruples (cf. xliii. 32), could not be committed to the care of a foreigner. Joseph was controller, or steward, of the household.

GENESIS XXXIX. 7—13

pass after these things, that his master's wife cast her eyes
upon Joseph; and she said, Lie with me. But he re- 8
fused, and said unto his master's wife, Behold, my master
¹knoweth not what is with me in the house, and he hath
put all that he hath into my hand; ²there is none greater 9
in this house than I; neither hath he kept back any thing
from me but thee, because thou art his wife: how then
can I do this great wickedness, and sin against God? And 10
it came to pass, as she spake to Joseph day by day, that
he hearkened not unto her, to lie by her, *or* to be with her.
And it came to pass about this time, that he went into the 11
house to do his work; and there was none of the men
of the house there within. And she caught him by his 12
garment, saying, Lie with me: and he left his garment
in her hand, and fled, and got him out. And it came to 13
pass, when she saw that he had left his garment in her

J

¹ Or, *knoweth not with me what is &c.*   ² Or, *he is not*

7—20. THE FALSE ACCUSATION.

8. *knoweth not*, &c.] Here, as in *v*. 6, the marg., *knoweth not with me what is*, gives the meaning of the passage.

9. *there is none greater*] The margin, *he is not*, is correct. The rendering of the text is not only less accurate, but far less vigorous. The LXX and Vulg. have similarly missed the meaning.

how then...against God] Observe how, in J, Elohim, not Jehovah, is used of God in a passage where Joseph is speaking to a non-Israelite. Joseph repels the immoral overtures of his master's wife on the ground, (1) of honour towards the master who trusted him in everything; and (2) of goodness and virtue, the duty of a man living in the presence of God. "This great wickedness"; Joseph takes the simplest line of resisting temptation. The thing is wrong in God's sight; and that is enough for him. Egyptologists have illustrated this part of Joseph's story from the ancient Egyptian "Tale of the two brothers" (contained in the *d'Orbiney Papyrus*, 19th Dynasty), in which the wife of the elder seeks to seduce the honour of the younger. The tale belongs to the Egyptian literature of the 14th cent. B.C.¹ "Against God": the consciousness of the personal presence of Jehovah "made all sins to be actions directly done against Him" (Davidson). So the Psalmist, although confessing wrong against his fellow-men, says, "Against thee, thee only, have I sinned" (Ps. li. 4).

13. *his garment*] This accident provided the only circumstantial piece of evidence for the charge brought against him.

See Appendix E.

GENESIS XXXIX. 13—21

J 14 hand, and was fled forth, that she called unto the men of her house, and spake unto them, saying, See, he hath brought in an Hebrew unto us to mock us; he came in 15 unto me to lie with me, and I cried with a loud voice: and it came to pass, when he heard that I lifted up my voice and cried, that he left his garment by me, and fled, and 16 got him out. And she laid up his garment by her, until 17 his master came home. And she spake unto him according to these words, saying, The Hebrew servant, which thou hast brought unto us, came in unto me to 18 mock me: and it came to pass, as I lifted up my voice and cried, that he left his garment by me, and fled out. 19 And it came to pass, when his master heard the words of his wife, which she spake unto him, saying, After this manner did thy servant to me; that his wrath was kindled. 20 And Joseph's master took him, and put him into the prison, |
(R)J the place where the king's prisoners were bound: | and he was 21 there in the prison. But the LORD was with Joseph, and

14. *an Hebrew*] The designation used by foreigners for "an Israelite" (cf. xli. 12, xliii. 32), and probably for any one who belonged to the group of peoples, Israelite, Moabite, Ammonite, Edomite, who invaded and settled down in Palestine and the adjacent territories. The word is an appeal to the racial prejudice against Asiatic strangers.

to mock] Cf. Prov. i. 26. The idea is of wanton insult.

us] As if none of the women in the house would be secure from insult, when the master's wife had been subjected to such an affront from this young upstart foreigner. She implies that her husband's confidence in his Hebrew slave meant disregard for the family's honour.

16. *laid up*] i.e. laid on one side, and kept ready to be produced as evidence.

20. *into the prison*] Lit. "into the house of roundness," or "the round house." Possibly the Heb. expression, "the house of *sohar*," may be an attempt to transliterate an Egyptian word, with a similar sound, by means of a familiar Heb. word *sohar*. LXX ὀχύρωμα, Lat. *carcer*. It only occurs here, and *v.* 23, and xl. 3, 5. On the whole, if Joseph's master believed the tale that had been told him, the punishment inflicted was less violent than we should have expected in such an age.

the place...were bound] These words are considered by many scholars to be introduced by the Compiler, in order to lead up to the description of the prison scene in the E narrative of ch. xl.

21. *But the LORD*, &c.] See note on *v.* 2. The favour of Jehovah

shewed kindness unto him, and gave him favour in the sight of the keeper of the prison. And the keeper of the prison committed to Joseph's hand all the prisoners that were in the prison; and whatsoever they did there, he was the doer of it. The keeper of the prison looked not to any thing that was under his hand, because the LORD was with him; and that which he did, the LORD made it to prosper.

And it came to pass after these things, that the butler of the king of Egypt and his baker offended their lord the king of Egypt. And Pharaoh was wroth against his two officers, against the chief of the butlers, and

towards Joseph is the cause of Joseph's acceptability with the keeper of the prison. He receives the same degree of confidence in prison, as he had received from the master whom he had served as steward.

CH. XL. (E.) JOSEPH INTERPRETS THE DREAMS OF PHARAOH'S OFFICERS.

The contents of this chapter are from E. Joseph's master (cf. xxxvii. 36) is the officer in whose house is the prison; and he commits to the charge of Joseph, his slave, the two court-officials whose dreams Joseph correctly interprets.

The section leads up to the *dénouement* in ch. xli. The details are skilfully drawn. The scene is pronounced by Egyptologists to be faithful to the conditions of Egyptian life in the 14th century B.C.

Though the narrative is from E, the Compiler endeavours to harmonize the account with that of J by inserting words in *vv.* 3, 5, and 15.

   1—8. The two officers in prison.
   9—19. The interpretation of their dreams.
   20—23. Their fulfilment.

1—8. THE TWO OFFICERS IN PRISON.

1. *after these things*] A vague definition of time: see xv. 1, xxii. 1, xxxix. 7.

the butler] In *vv.* 2, 20 he is called "the chief butler." The word is rendered in Neh. i. 11, "cupbearer," an officer who looked after the king's cellar.

his baker] In *vv.* 2 and 22 he is called "the chief baker," an officer who looked after the king's bakehouse. These officials filled high positions at the Egyptian court. Cf. xxxvii. 36.

offended] Lit. "sinned"; so LXX ἥμαρτον, Lat. *peccarent*.

2. *his...officers*] Lit. "his eunuchs"; see note on xxxvii. 36.

E 3 against the chief of the bakers. And he put them in ward in the house of the captain of the guard, into the
4 prison, the place where Joseph was bound. And the captain of the guard charged Joseph with them, and he ministered
5 unto them: and they continued a season in ward. And they dreamed a dream both of them, each man his dream, in one night, each man according to the inter-
(R) pretation of his dream, | the butler and the baker of the
E 6 king of Egypt, which were bound in the prison. | And Joseph came in unto them in the morning, and saw them,
7 and, behold, they were sad. And he asked Pharaoh's officers that were with him in ward in his master's house,
8 saying, Wherefore look ye so sadly to-day? And they said

3. *in ward*] Cf. *vv.* 4 and 7. An old English expression; cf. Shakespeare, 2 *Hen. VI*, v. i.:

"I know, ere they will have me go to *ward*,
They'll pawn their swords for my enfranchisement."

He committed them for safe keeping, while the enquiry into the charges against them went on.

captain of the guard] See note on xxxvii. 36.

the prison] = "the round house," as in xxxix. 20. This clause seems to have been introduced, in order to harmonize the tradition of Joseph's position in the house of the "captain of the guard" with the account of his imprisonment in xxxix. 20—23.

According to E, Pharaoh placed his two officials in confinement, but not in the prison, in the keeping of the "captain of the guard."

4. *charged Joseph with them*] i.e. put them under the care of Joseph, who is to be in attendance on them, not as a fellow-prisoner, but as a servant in his master's house. Compare the words of "the chief butler" in xli. 12 (also from E), "there was with us there a young man, an Hebrew, *servant to the captain of the guard*." This is different from the idea given in xxxix. 22, where he is a prisoner, and appointed by the "keeper of the prison" to look after the other prisoners.

a season] Lit. "days."

6. *sad*] Gloomy and depressed, the word rendered "worse liking" in Dan. i. 10. There was a general belief in dreams, as a means of conveying supernatural information. In the case of these two officers, their anxiety as to their fate added to the desire to learn the meaning of the strange dreams which had so deeply impressed them. The coincidence in time and the general resemblance between the two dreams could not be accidental.

7. *look ye so sadly*] Lit. "are your faces bad," cf. Neh. ii. 2.

GENESIS XL. 8—13

unto him, We have dreamed a dream, and there is none
that can interpret it. And Joseph said unto them, Do not
interpretations belong to God? tell it me, I pray you.
And the chief butler told his dream to Joseph, and said 9
to him, In my dream, behold, a vine was before me;
and in the vine were three branches: and it was as though 10
it budded, *and* its blossoms shot forth; *and* the clusters
thereof brought forth ripe grapes: and Pharaoh's cup was 11
in my hand; and I took the grapes, and pressed them into
Pharaoh's cup, and I gave the cup into Pharaoh's hand.
And Joseph said unto him, This is the interpretation of it: 12
the three branches are three days; within yet three days 13
shall Pharaoh lift up thine head, and restore thee unto

8. *none that can interpret it*] The Egyptians regarded the interpretation of dreams as a science requiring special study; or as a department of magic needing special initiation. Had the two officials been at liberty, they would have each repaired to their special soothsayer or dream-interpreter for an explanation of the dream that had so greatly disturbed them.

belong to God] Joseph claims that the interpretation of dreams is neither science nor magic. The man, to whom God reveals His secrets, alone can interpret them. He himself does not pretend to interpret. But, possibly, God may make use of His servant to make known His mind, cf. xli. 16, 38, 39 and Dan. ii. 19, 28, 47.

9—19. THE INTERPRETATION OF THEIR DREAMS.

10. *it was as though it budded*] Another rendering is "and as it budded, its blossoms shot forth." But the rendering in the text is grammatically to be preferred. The dream combines, as it were, in a moment the successive stages, by which the vine first budded and blossomed, then brought forth grapes, the grapes ripened, and their juice was transformed into wine. Things will happen in a dream which do not admit of a scientific explanation.

11. *pressed them into Pharaoh's cup*] The cupbearer did not squeeze grapes into his master's cup in order to make wine. He squeezed, and at once the cup was full of wine. This is one of the fancies occurring in a dream. Dream-land is true to experience, and yet possesses, here and there, odd fantastic features. It is a feature in this dream that all the difficulties are successfully overcome; the chief butler, at the end of it, holds Pharaoh's cup.

13. *lift up thine head*] i.e. "will lift it up with favour," as in 2 Kings xxv. 27; Jer. lii. 31. The "countenance," which is sad, or in trouble, hangs down and needs to be lifted up: see note on iv. 6, 7. As the phrase is also used of "the chief baker" in an unfavourable

E thine office: and thou shalt give Pharaoh's cup into his hand, after the former manner when thou wast his butler. 14 But have me in thy remembrance when it shall be well with thee, and shew kindness, I pray thee, unto me, and make mention of me unto Pharaoh, and bring me 15 out of this house: for indeed I was stolen away out of (R) the land of the Hebrews: | and here also have I done **E** 16 nothing that they should put me into the dungeon. | When the chief baker saw that the interpretation was good, he said unto Joseph, I also was in my dream, and, behold, 17 three baskets of white bread were on my head: and in the uppermost basket there was of all manner of bakemeats for Pharaoh; and the birds did eat them out of the

sense (*vv*. 19, 20), it might conceivably be employed for the official notice of release to a prisoner, either for pardon or for punishment. But this is not probable; see note on *v*. 19.

14. *But have me*, &c.] Joseph claims no reward for his interpretation beyond that of an act of kindness.

15. *stolen away*] i.e. "kidnapped": see xxxvii. 28. According to E Joseph was not sold by his brethren, but stolen by the Midianites.

the land of the Hebrews] For the use of the word "Hebrew," cf. xiv. 13, xxxix. 14 and xli. 12. It was the designation in use by foreigners for "the dwellers in Palestine." In Joseph's mouth the phrase is an anachronism, even if it means the whole region in which the Hebrew races of Israel, Ishmael, Moab, Ammon, and Edom, were establishing themselves. Whether "the Hebrews" are to be identified with the Ḫabiri of the Tel-el-Amarna tablets, is a disputed question. But "the land of the Hebrews" is not a Hebrew phrase that would naturally be used of Canaan before it had been conquered and occupied by the tribes of Israel. See Appendix D, ii., iii. on the Ḫabiri and the ʽApuriu.

and here also...the dungeon] This clause is very probably introduced by the Compiler in order to harmonize the present chapter with the account of Joseph's position in xxxix. 20—23. LXX εἰς τὸν λάκκον τοῦτον, Lat. *in lacum*.

16. *I also*] The chief baker is encouraged to relate his dream. There are certain conspicuous similarities in the two dreams: (1) each man is discharging his own special office; (2) the number "3" is a feature in both.

of white bread] LXX τρία κανᾶ χονδριτῶν, Lat. *tria canistra farinae*. Instead of "white bread," some scholars prefer the rendering "baskets of open wicker-work," viz. "baskets shewing their contents" (so Rashi). Symmachus, βαϊνά = "baskets of palm-branches."

17. *bakemeats*] LXX ἔργον σιτοποιοῦ, Lat. *cibos qui fiunt arte pistoria*: as we say, "all kinds of confectionery." The bakemeats are

basket upon my head. And Joseph answered and said, This is the interpretation thereof: the three baskets are three days; within yet three days shall Pharaoh lift up thy head from off thee, and shall hang thee on a tree; and the birds shall eat thy flesh from off thee. And it came to pass the third day, which was Pharaoh's birthday, that he made a feast unto all his servants: and he lifted up the head of the chief butler and the head of the chief baker among his servants. And he restored the chief butler unto his butlership again; and he gave the cup into Pharaoh's hand: but he hanged the chief baker: as Joseph had interpreted to them. Yet did not the chief butler remember Joseph, but forgat him. 18 E 19 20 21 22 23

only in the top basket. If the birds took them, he had nothing in the other baskets to bring to Pharaoh's table.

the birds] The birds, darting down upon the food and carrying it off, doubtless seemed of evil augury; cf. the appearance of the birds in xv. 11. It was like a nightmare! The baker found himself powerless to frighten the birds away. The great kites in Egypt, the bird scavengers of the land, are always wheeling in the air, ready to pounce down upon choice morsels, if they see the slightest chance of carrying them off.

19. *lift up thy head from off thee*] Joseph, by a use of the same phrase as in *v.* 13, introduces the sudden unfavourable interpretation: "from off thee" shews that it means here "decapitation," not (see note on *v.* 13) "he will release thee from imprisonment, in order to be executed." For the word-play, which uses the same word in two senses, cf. xxvii. 39.

hang thee on a tree] The decapitated corpse of the malefactor would be impaled, and allowed to hang exposed to public view, and to become the prey of wild animals and obscene birds. This picture was terrible to the Egyptian mind, which attached great value to preservation of the body as the ultimate medium of the soul's (=*ka*) existence. For "hanging," see Josh. x. 26; 2 Sam. iv. 12, xxi. 9, 10.

20—23. The Fulfilment.

20. *Pharaoh's birthday*] Cf. Matt. xiv. 6; Mark vi. 21. Proclamations of amnesty on royal birthdays have been universal. They can be illustrated from the royal proclamations preserved in Egyptian inscriptions.

The title "Pharaoh" (=Egypt. *Pr‘ô*, "Great House") is constantly used without a personal surname before the 22nd Dynasty (945—745 B.C.).

23. *forgat him*] These words are an artistic conclusion to this interesting section. The chief butler's forgetfulness, in the enjoyment of his own good fortune, (1) is sadly natural; (2) increases our sympathy

E 41 And it came to pass at the end of two full years, that Pharaoh dreamed: and, behold, he stood by the [1]river. 2 And, behold, there came up out of the river seven kine,

[1] Heb. *Yeor*, that is, the Nile.

with Joseph; (3) heightens the expectation of the reader as to the manner of his deliverance.

CH. XLI. (E (JP).) JOSEPH AND PHARAOH'S DREAMS.

This is a continuation of ch. xl., and is mainly derived from E. In this section Joseph as the servant of God is not only rescued from the position of a slave, but exalted to be the first minister in Egypt. Pharaoh's dreams offer the occasion for Joseph's liberation. The incidents in the previous chapter, after a long disciplinary interval of waiting, are the cause of his being remembered by the chief butler. He is summoned into the presence of Pharaoh himself. His interpretation of Pharaoh's dreams is rewarded by a startling elevation into highest office[1].

The Compiler, in order to harmonize the accounts, introduces in v. 14 the mention of "the prison," which is taken from J.

            1—7.   Pharaoh's dreams.
            8—32.   Joseph as Interpreter.
            33—36. Joseph's counsel.
            37—46. Joseph as Grand Vizier.
            47—49. The seven good years.
            50—52. Joseph's sons.
            53—57. The years of famine.

—7. PHARAOH'S DREAMS.

1. *two full years*] i.e. from the execution of the chief baker.

river] Heb. *Yeor*, i.e. the Nile, as always in the O.T., except Job xxviii. 10; Isai. xxxiii. 21; Dan. xii. 5, 6. The Heb. word reproduces the Egyptian. According to Egyptologists it stands for the Egyptian *aur*, "stream," or *aur-aa*, "the great stream," Assyr. *ia'uru*, "stream."

2. *out of the river*] The Nile is the source of the fertility and wealth of Egypt. The cows issuing from the Nile would be a symbol of fertility. The Egyptian goddess Hathor is represented with the head of a cow.

seven kine] The number "seven" is commonly employed for the purposes of symbolism. The god Osiris is represented in Egyptian drawings as an ox accompanied by seven cows.

---

[1] "The points of resemblance between Dan. ii. and Gen. xl.—xli. are very striking. In both accounts we have a young Hebrew raised by the favour of a heathen king to great political prominence owing to his extraordinary God-given ability to interpret dreams. In both versions the heathen astrologers make the first attempt to solve the difficulty, which results in failure, whereupon the pious Israelite, being summoned to the royal presence, in both cases through the friendly intervention of a court official, triumphantly explains the mystery to the king's satisfaction." *Encycl. Brit.* edn. 11, art. "Daniel."

well favoured and fatfleshed; and they fed in the reed-
grass. And, behold, seven other kine came up after them 3
out of the river, ill favoured and leanfleshed; and stood
by the other kine upon the brink of the river. And the 4
ill favoured and leanfleshed kine did eat up the seven
well favoured and fat kine. So Pharaoh awoke. And 5
he slept and dreamed a second time: and, behold, seven
ears of corn came up upon one stalk, ¹rank and good. And, 6
behold, seven ears, thin and blasted with the east wind,
sprung up after them. And the thin ears swallowed up the 7
seven ¹rank and full ears. And Pharaoh awoke, and,
behold, it was a dream. And it came to pass in the morn- 8
ing that his spirit was troubled; and he sent and called for
all the ²magicians of Egypt, and all the wise men thereof:

¹ Heb. *fat*.   ² Or, *sacred scribes*

reed-grass] The Heb. word *ahu* transliterates the Egyptian *ahu*, or *iḥi*. It is found also in *v.* 18; Job viii. 11; Hos. xiii. 15. LXX ἄχει, which occurs also in Isa. xix. 7; Ecclus. xl. 16. Jerome, commenting on Isa. xix. 7, explains ἄχει as *quicquid in palude virens nascitur*. The word, derived from a root meaning "green," is applied to the Nile reed-grass whose vivid green, under that bright sky, strikes every traveller in Egypt[1].

4. *did eat up*] The fantastic side of the dream. Cf. xl. 11, 17.

5. *a second time*] Here, as in xxxvii. 9 and xl. 16, the duplication of the dream seems to place its significance beyond dispute. The resemblance of the dreams is found in (1) the number "seven"; (2) in the good products being consumed by the bad. The first dream was concerned with the sacred animal of Egypt; the second with Egypt's chief source of wealth.

rank] Heb. *fat*, i.e. rich and good.

6. *blasted with the east wind*] The east wind in the O.T. is always a synonym for dryness, parching heat, and violence. Cf. Ezek. xvii. 10, xix. 12; Hos. xiii. 15; Jonah iv. 8. In Egypt the S.E. wind is the dreaded *khamsin*, which brings the sandstorms in the spring, Ar. *sirocco*.

8—32. JOSEPH AS INTERPRETER.

8. *his spirit was troubled*] Compare the effect of the dreams in xl. 6; Dan. ii. 1—3.

all the magicians] or, as R.V. marg., *sacred scribes*. The Heb. *ḥartummim* used in this chapter and Ex. vii.—ix. probably designates

---

[1] "Pro junco papyrum transtulerunt LXX, de quo charta fit, addentes de suo *Achi, viride*, quod in Hebraeo non habetur. Cumque ab eruditis quaererem, quid hic sermo significaret, audivi ab Aegyptiis hoc nomine lingua eorum *quicquid in palude virens nascitur* appellari" (*Comm. in Esai*, § 291).

E and Pharaoh told them his dream; but there was none
9 that could interpret them unto Pharaoh. Then spake the
chief butler unto Pharaoh, saying, I [1]do remember my
10 faults this day: Pharaoh was wroth with his servants, and
put me in ward in the house of the captain of the guard,
11 me and the chief baker: and we dreamed a dream in
one night, I and he; we dreamed each man according
12 to the interpretation of his dream. And there was with
us there a young man, an Hebrew, servant to the captain
of the guard; and we told him, and he interpreted to us
our dreams; to each man according to his dream he did
13 interpret. And it came to pass, as he interpreted to
us, so it was; [2]me he restored unto mine office, and
14 him he hanged. Then Pharaoh sent and called Joseph, |
(R) and they brought him hastily out of the dungeon: |

[1] Or, *will make mention of*
[2] Or, *I was restored...and he was hanged*

the priestly class, which was credited with the knowledge of all sacred mysteries, cf. *v.* 24; Ex. vii. 11, &c. LXX renders by ἐξηγηταί ="interpreters," Lat. *conjectores*. The rendering "magicians" represents "possessors" of occult knowledge or magic." The same Heb. word is used in Dan. ii. 2, probably in imitation of this passage; but it does not occur elsewhere. Possibly the word is derived from a root meaning "to cut" or "engrave," from which came *heret*, "stylus" or "pen." Cf. Tacitus, *Hist.* iv. 83, *Ptolemaeus...sacerdotibus Aegyptiorum, quibus mos talia intellegere, nocturnos visus aperit.*

9. *I do remember*] R.V. marg., *will make mention of*, gives the right meaning of the Heb. LXX ἀναμιμνήσκω, Lat. *confiteor*.

my faults] Lit. "my sins" (cf. xl. 1). He is not referring to his forgetfulness (xl. 23), but to his offences against Pharaoh.

12. *servant to the captain of the guard*] It will be remembered that, in the E story, Joseph is the slave of the captain, and not a fellow-prisoner of the chief butler.

13. *me he restored...and him he hanged*] R.V. marg. *I was restored...and he was hanged*. Probably, the construction in the original is impersonal, i.e. "me they restored, and him they hanged." In addressing Pharaoh, and in alluding to Pharaoh's actions, this impersonal use of the 3rd pers. sing. is doubtless the language of etiquette.

14. *and they...dungeon*] A clause probably introduced, like that in xl. 15, in order to harmonize the E with the J version. In E, Joseph is a slave, not a prisoner: in J he is a prisoner, cf. xxxix. 21—23.

GENESIS XLI. 14—25

and he shaved himself, and changed his raiment, and came in unto Pharaoh. And Pharaoh said unto Joseph, I have dreamed a dream, and there is none that can interpret it: and I have heard say of thee, that when thou hearest a dream thou canst interpret it. And Joseph answered Pharaoh, saying, It is not in me: God shall give Pharaoh an answer of peace. And Pharaoh spake unto Joseph, In my dream, behold, I stood upon the brink of the river: and, behold, there came up out of the river seven kine, fatfleshed and well favoured; and they fed in the reedgrass: and, behold, seven other kine came up after them, poor and very ill favoured and leanfleshed, such as I never saw in all the land of Egypt for badness: and the lean and ill favoured kine did eat up the first seven fat kine: and when they had eaten them up, it could not be known that they had eaten them; but they were still ill favoured, as at the beginning. So I awoke. And I saw in my dream, and, behold, seven ears came up upon one stalk, full and good: and, behold, seven ears, withered, thin, *and* blasted with the east wind, sprung up after them: and the thin ears swallowed up the seven good ears: and I told it unto the magicians; but there was none that could declare it to me. And Joseph said unto Pharaoh, The dream of

shaved himself] The Egyptians paid extreme care to matters of cleanliness. They were very generally themselves clean shaven. LXX and Lat. render "they shaved him."

16. *It is not in me*] Rather, "nay, far from it," as in xiv. 24. Joseph, as in xl. 8, disclaims any power in himself. God's servant may be His *propheta*, or spokesman; but he is not as God, nor is he a magician.

an answer of peace] Joseph replies, with suitable courtesy, literally, "God will make answer with the peace of Pharaoh." The answer of God will be the well-being of Pharaoh. "Peace," i.e. "welfare," as in xxxvii. 14, "whether it be well," lit. "peace."

LXX ἄνευ τοῦ θεοῦ οὐκ ἀποκριθήσεται τὸ σωτήριον, the meaning of which is doubtful: "without God there will be no answer of peace." Lat. *absque me Deus respondebit prospera Pharaoni*. The Syriac makes a question of it, "Thinkest thou that apart from God one will answer?" on the lines of Balaam's answer in Num. xxii. 18, 38.

23. *withered*] The Hebrew word occurs here only in O.T., and is omitted by LXX and Lat.

E Pharaoh is one: what God is about to do he hath declared
26 unto Pharaoh. The seven good kine are seven years;
and the seven good ears are seven years: the dream is
27 one. And the seven lean and ill favoured kine that came
up after them are seven years, and also the seven empty
ears blasted with the east wind; they shall be seven years
28 of famine. That is the thing which I spake unto Pharaoh:
what God is about to do he hath shewed unto Pharaoh.
29 Behold, there come seven years of great plenty throughout
30 all the land of Egypt: and there shall arise after them
seven years of famine; and all the plenty shall be forgotten
in the land of Egypt; and the famine shall consume the
31 land; and the plenty shall not be known in the land by
reason of that famine which followeth; for it shall be
32 very grievous. And for that the dream was doubled unto
Pharaoh twice, it is because the thing is established by
33 God, and God will shortly bring it to pass. Now therefore let Pharaoh look out a man discreet and wise, and
34 set him over the land of Egypt. Let Pharaoh do *this*, and
let him appoint overseers over the land, and take up the

25. *is about to do*] Lit. "is doing." Lat. *facturus est*. Joseph's interpretation of the two dreams is the same.

32. *doubled...twice*] This is a literal rendering. The repetition of the dream shewed emphatically that the thing was "established," i.e. made fixed and sure, by the decree of God. Cf. Ps. xciii. 2, "Thy throne is established"; Hos. vi. 3, "sure as the morning."

will shortly bring it to pass] Lit. "hasteneth to do it." Hence there is urgent need to take measures in good time to meet the crisis which is bound to come.

33—36. Joseph's Counsel.

33. *let Pharaoh*, &c.] Joseph leaves the office of interpreter, and takes upon himself to give political counsel to the king of Egypt.

34. *Let Pharaoh do* this] Joseph's advice is (1) to appoint a "grain administrator," *praefectus rei frumentariae*; (2) to appoint local officers, "over-seers," LXX τοπάρχαι, for the various districts of Egypt; (3) to exact for the crown 20 per cent., "the fifth part," of the grain of the country.

Some think an inconsistency is involved in the recommendation of one supreme officer (*v*. 33) and the recommendation of local overseers (*v*. 34). The two, however, are practically inseparable elements in a sound administrative scheme.

take up the fifth part of the land] Lit. "let him fifth the land,"

GENESIS XLI. 34—39

fifth part of the land of Egypt in the seven plenteous
years. And let them gather all the food of these good 35
years that come, and lay up corn under the hand of
Pharaoh for food in the cities, and let them keep it.
And the food shall be for a store to the land against the 36
seven years of famine, which shall be in the land of Egypt;
that the land perish not through the famine. And the thing 37
was good in the eyes of Pharaoh, and in the eyes of all his
servants. And Pharaoh said unto his servants, Can we 38
find such a one as this, a man in whom the spirit of
God is? And Pharaoh said unto Joseph, Forasmuch as 39
God hath shewed thee all this, there is none so discreet

E

i.e. secure for the crown one-fifth of the annual grain produce of Egypt during the seven years of fertility. In this passage from E, the imposition of a 20 per cent. duty is a special regulation proposed by Joseph to meet the exigencies of the impending famine. In xlvii. 24, from J, it appears as a permanent Egyptian usage, owing its origin to the initiation of Joseph.

35. *let them gather all the food*] This is rhetorical, and need not be pressed as contradicting the exaction of the one-fifth in *v.* 34. But see *v.* 48.

lay up corn] i.e. store up the grain in the keeping of the king's officers. The establishment of state granaries appears here for the first time in history.

under the hand of Pharaoh] The king's authority is never to be relaxed. The measures proposed will enhance the monarchy.

36. *for a store*] i.e. a reserve. The Hebrew narrative is proud to attribute to Joseph the origination of the granaries, which formed part of the elaborate organization of the Egyptian kingdom, and must have profoundly impressed the simpler Israelite people.

37—46. JOSEPH AS GRAND VIZIER.

38. *such a one as this*] Pharaoh and his servants are represented as discerning in Joseph the supreme gifts of one who combined the supernatural power of interpreting dreams with the practical wisdom and sagacity of a statesman.

in whom the spirit of God is] The same phrase is employed by Belshazzar when he addresses Daniel: Dan. v. 14, "I have heard of thee, that the spirit of the gods is in thee, and that light and understanding and excellent wisdom is found in thee." The presence and operation of the Spirit of God, in the O.T., account for those special manifestations which surpass the limits of ordinary human capacity, in wisdom or prowess. Cf. Ex. xxxi. 3; Num. xxvii. 18; Judg. iii. 10, xiv. 6.

39. *Forasmuch as*] Lit. "after that."

E 40 and wise as thou: thou shalt be over my house, and according unto thy word shall all my people ¹be ruled: only in the
41 throne will I be greater than thou. And Pharaoh said unto Joseph, See, I have set thee over all the land of Egypt.
42 And Pharaoh took off his signet ring from his hand, and put it upon Joseph's hand, and arrayed him in vestures of ²fine
43 linen, and put a gold chain about his neck; and he made him to ride in the second chariot which he had; and they cried

¹ Or, *order themselves* Or, *do homage*
² Or, *cotton*

40. *over my house*] Pharaoh exalts the Hebrew slave at one step to become his Grand Vizier; cf. Ps. cv. 21; 1 Macc. ii. 53. Whether there was a vacancy in this office into which Joseph was promoted, or whether he displaced an existing official, the tradition does not record. "My house" seems to mean "my palace," or "my court." The elevation of a Syrian slave to such high rank is apparently not without example in the records of the Egyptian kings. See Appendix E on "Joseph as Vizier." For the title of "governor of the palace," cf. 1 Kings iv. 6; Isai. xxii. 15.

be ruled] The meaning is very doubtful; possibly, as R.V. marg., *order themselves*, or, *do homage*. Lit. (if the text be correct) "and upon thy mouth shall all my people kiss." In illustration of this expression some have quoted Hos. xiii. 2; Prov. xxiv. 26. It is objected that "the kiss of homage" was not a kiss upon the mouth. Hence scholars have preferred a different rendering, "according to thy mouth," i.e. "at thy command" (cf. xlv. 21), "shall my people order, or dispose, themselves." So, probably, LXX ἐπὶ τῷ στόματί σου ὑπακούσεται, Lat. *obediet*. Perhaps, however, the text is corrupt.

42. *signet ring*] i.e. the official ring with which state documents would be sealed. The king thus symbolically transferred to Joseph absolute authority. Cf. 1 Macc. vi. 15, "gave him his diadem and his robe and his signet ring." See also the use of the king's ring in Esth. iii. 10, 12, viii. 2, 8, 10.

fine linen] Possibly, as R.V. marg., *cotton*. The Hebrew *shêsh* has been identified with the Egyptian *schenti*, meaning something woven. LXX and Lat. render it by an adjective meaning "made of byssus," i.e. fine flax. This was probably the material worn by the royal and state officials. Possibly it was the same material as that in which the Egyptian mummies were wound.

a gold chain] Presumably Pharaoh invested Joseph with his own golden necklace, a sign of honour which the narrative delights to record.

The position to which Joseph is elevated is that of "Grand Vizier" or *T'ate*, as he was called in the Egyptian dialect.

43. *the second chariot*] It has been objected that horses and chariots

GENESIS XLI. 43—45

before him, [1]Bow the knee: and he set him over all the land of Egypt. And Pharaoh said unto Joseph, I am Pharaoh, and without thee shall no man lift up his hand or his foot in all the land of Egypt. And Pharaoh called Joseph's name Zaphenath-paneah; and he gave him to wife Asenath the daughter of Poti-phera priest of On.

[1] *Abrech*, probably an Egyptian word, similar in sound to the Hebrew word meaning *to kneel*.

first appear in Egyptian inscriptions in the 18th Dynasty (1580—1350 B.C.). But they were introduced into use in Egypt under the rule of the Hyksos (13th to 17th Dynasty). The Egyptian word for "chariot," *mrkbt*, is borrowed from the Semitic. The "second" would be the next best to Pharaoh's. Joseph might not ride in Pharaoh's chariot.

Bow the knee] Heb. *abrech*. The meaning of the word has been much disputed. It was omitted by the LXX; but the meaning "bow the knee" appears in the Lat. *ut genuflecterent*, and in Aquila. Jerome prefers the extraordinary rendering "tender father": '*âb* being the Hebrew for "father," *rēkh* for "tender" or "delicate," he explains that it is thus signified, how in wisdom Joseph was the father of all, but in age a tender youth.

There seems, at present, to be no solution of the puzzle offered by the word *Abrech*. Spiegelberg suggests that it is the transliteration of the Egyptian '*b r-k*, equivalent to "Attention!," or the "O yes, O yes," of the crier. The Egyptian *abu-rek*, "thy command is our desire," i.e. "at thy service," was conjectured by Lepage Renouf.

45. *Zaphenath-paneah*] An Egyptian name for which the meaning is given by some Egyptologists "God speaks, and He lives," i.e. *De-pnute-ef-ônch*. A proper name of this form does not as yet however appear to have been found in the Egyptian inscriptions before the 20th Dynasty, i.e. the 13th century B.C. The LXX endeavoured to transliterate the name by Ψονθομφανήχ. The Vulg. renders *salvator mundi*; and Jerome records *ab Egyptiis didicimus, quod in linguâ eorum resonet salvator mundi*.

Josephus (*Ant.* II. 91), Targum of Onkelos, and the Syriac rendered the name by "Revealer of Secrets"; and this was very generally accepted in Christian tradition, the derivation being assumed to be from the Hebrew root *zâphan*, "to conceal."

Asenath] A proper name, meaning "Belonging to the goddess Neith."

Poti-phera] As in v. 50 and xlvi. 20. This is the same name, spelled fuller, as in xxxvii. 36 (see note), xxxix. 1, meaning "the gift of the sun-god." We may compare the Greek name Heliodorus.

priest of On] "On," known in later times as Heliopolis, was situate about 7 miles N.E. of Cairo; and was the great centre of

EP 46 And Joseph went out over the land of Egypt. | And Joseph was thirty years old when he stood before Pharaoh king of Egypt. And Joseph went out from the presence of
E 47 Pharaoh, and went throughout all the land of Egypt. | And in the seven plenteous years the earth brought forth by
48 handfuls. And he gathered up all the food of the seven years which were in the land of Egypt, and laid up the food in the cities: the food of the field, which was round
49 about every city, laid he up in the same. And Joseph laid up corn as the sand of the sea, very much, until he left
50 numbering; for it was without number. And unto Joseph

Egyptian *Ra*, or Sun, worship. The obelisk still standing at Heliopolis was there in Joseph's time. By his marriage with Asenath, Joseph became connected with one of the principal Egyptian families. Potiphera, the priest of On, would have been a man of eminence; but should not be confounded with "the captain of the guard" (xxxvii. 36). Late Jewish tradition identified the two names; and asserted that Asenath had reported to her father her mother's shameless conduct, whereupon he gave Asenath to Joseph as wife, in order that Joseph might be cleared of any shadow of blame. But this is mere romance.

46. *thirty years old*] This verse probably contains the brief record of P; according to which Joseph had spent thirteen years in Egypt before his elevation, and was aged seventeen when he was brought into Egypt, xxxvii. 2. There elapsed seven years of plenty and two of the years of famine, before his brothers came down to Egypt (xlv. 11). Accordingly, Joseph must have been in Egypt over twenty years before they came. Benjamin had been born some time before Joseph disappeared (xxxv. 18). Hence, so far from Benjamin being "a little one" (xliv. 20), he must have been well over twenty, when Joseph saw his brethren. The computation illustrates the impossibility of harmonizing discrepancies, if the existence of independent narratives, or parallel versions of tradition, be rejected. When the separate character of the P record is recognized, the difficulties disappear.

47—49 (J, E). The seven Good Years.

48. *of the seven years*] Probably we should add here, with LXX and Sam., "of plenty," which seems to have dropped out of the Hebrew text.

laid up the food] On the state granaries of Egypt and the duties of the official who supervised them, the student is referred to Erman's *Life in Ancient Egypt* (E. T.), p. 108. The chief "cities" of the districts, or νομοί, into which Egypt was divided, seem here to be referred to.

49. *as the sand of the sea*] For this comparison cf. xxii. 17, xxxii. 12.

Egyptians measuring the wheat and depositing it in the granaries.

From Mr P. S. Handcock's *Latest Light on Bible Lands*, by kind permission of the S.P.C.K.

were born two sons before the year of famine came, which E
Asenath the daughter of Poti-phera priest of On bare
unto him. And Joseph called the name of the firstborn 51
¹Manasseh: For, *said he*, God hath made me forget all
my toil, and all my father's house. And the name of the 52
second called he ²Ephraim: For God hath made me
fruitful in the land of my affliction. And the seven years 53
of plenty, that was in the land of Egypt, came to an end.
And the seven years of famine began to come, according 54
as Joseph had said: and there was famine in all lands;
but in all the land of Egypt there was bread. And when 55
all the land of Egypt was famished, the people cried to
Pharaoh for bread: and Pharaoh said unto all the Egyptians,
Go unto Joseph; what he saith to you, do. And the famine 56
was over all the face of the earth: and Joseph opened
all the storehouses, and sold unto the Egyptians; and the

¹ That is, *Making to forget*.
² From a Hebrew word signifying *to be fruitful*.

50—52 (E). JOSEPH'S SONS.

51. *Manasseh*] That is, *Making to forget*. There is to be no thought of return to his father's house. The name makes us ask the question why Joseph, when supreme in Egypt, sent no message to his father, who was living in a region distant only a few days' journey. That there were continual communications between Egypt and Canaan is conclusively shewn by the Tel-el-Amarna tablets, and by the subsequent events in the present narrative.

52. *Ephraim*] For the Hebrew word *to be fruitful*, cf. xxviii. 3, xxxv. 11, xlviii. 4. There is a play on the resemblance in the sound of the name to the Hebrew root (*prh*) meaning "fruitfulness." The same play on the two words is found in Hos. xiii. 15, "fruitful among his brethren," referring to Ephraim.

made me fruitful] i.e. "hath given me sons." But, as a title for the tribe of Ephraim, it is natural to connect it with the fertility of the territory which it occupied.

53—57. THE YEARS OF FAMINE.

54. *all lands*] Cf. *v.* 57. The famine is represented as afflicting not only Egypt, but all the neighbouring lands which constituted the known world of the Israelites. Cf. xliii. 1. For a similar hyperbole, cf. "all the world" (Luke ii. 1; John xxi. 25); "a great famine over all the world" (Acts xi. 28).

56. *all the storehouses*] The Hebrew text is in error: lit. "all

GENESIS XLI. 56—XLII. 5

E 57 famine was sore in the land of Egypt. And all countries came into Egypt to Joseph for to buy corn; because the famine was sore in all the earth.

42 Now Jacob saw that there was corn in Egypt, and Jacob
2 said unto his sons, Why do ye look one upon another? And he said, Behold, I have heard that there is corn in Egypt: get you down thither, and buy for us from thence; that we
3 may live, and not die. And Joseph's ten brethren went
4 down to buy corn from Egypt. But Benjamin, Joseph's brother, Jacob sent not with his brethren; for he said, Lest
J 5 peradventure mischief befall him. | And the sons of Israel

that was in them." The versions have supplied the right meaning. LXX πάντας τοὺς σιτοβολῶνας, Lat. *universa horrea*, i.e. "all the granaries."

57. *all countries*] Cf. v. 52, as we should say, "the whole world." This verse prepares us for the crisis in the Joseph narrative recorded in the following chapter.

CH. XLII. (E (J).) JOSEPH'S BRETHREN IN EGYPT.

1—5. The descent into Egypt.
6—17. The first interview with Joseph.
18—26. The second interview.
27—38. The return to Canaan.

The whole of this chapter, except vv. 5, 6ᵃ, 27, 28, is probably from the E narrative. The dramatic interest of the story is admirably sustained. Joseph delays to disclose his identity, until by a succession of tests he has been convinced of his brethren's honesty.

1—5. THE DESCENT INTO EGYPT.

1. *look one upon another*] In silence, as if desperate. Jacob's words indicate the energy and resourcefulness of the old man, as compared with the helpless despondency of the sons.

2. *down thither*] Egypt being regarded as on the low ground, in comparison with Palestine; cf. xii. 10, xiii. 1, xliii. 4, 15, xlvi. 3, 4.

3. *ten brethren*] Jacob's sons are here mentioned, not as heads of families, or as separate householders, but as the capable male members of a single family. The whole ten are needed, in order to carry back corn enough corn.

4. *mischief*] See *v.* 38. Jacob dares not part with Benjamin, for whom, both as his youngest child and as the surviving son of Rachel, he has special affection. On this trait the whole narrative turns, cf. *v.* 38, xliv. 20, 30, 31.

5 (? J). *And the sons of Israel*, &c.] "Sons of Israel," cf. xlv. 21, xlvi. 5. The verse reads like the commencement of a new section;

came to buy among those that came: for the famine was in J
the land of Canaan. And Joseph was the governor over 6
the land; he it was that sold to all the people of the land: |
and Joseph's brethren came, and bowed down themselves E
to him with their faces to the earth. And Joseph saw his 7
brethren, and he knew them, but made himself strange unto
them, and spake roughly with them; and he said unto them,
Whence come ye? And they said, From the land of
Canaan to buy food. And Joseph knew his brethren, but 8

while the words "for the famine, &c." are not necessary after *vv*. 1—4. The change from the name of "Jacob" (*vv*. 1—4) to that of "Israel" is another indication that this verse is drawn from a different source of narrative from *vv*. 1—4.

6—17. THE FIRST INTERVIEW WITH JOSEPH.

6. *governor*] The late, and not very common, word here used in the Hebrew (*shâlît*) denotes the position of "Grand Vizier[1]," "the T"ate," or chief officer of state: see note on xli. 42. It is akin to our word "Sultan," and rendered "ruler" in Eccles. vii. 19, x. 5.

he it was that sold] We need not suppose that Joseph in person always conducted the business transactions; but a group of foreign purchasers would be brought into his presence to be interrogated.

bowed down themselves] Cf. *v*. 9. Joseph's dreams are fulfilled: see xxxvii. 7, 9, 10.

7. *knew them*] Joseph at once recognized his brethren. They did not recognize him. From a boy he had become a man; they were grown men when they sold him, and were comparatively unaltered. He in stature, dress, hair, and ornament must have been wholly changed from the rough shepherd lad of Canaan. According to E (xli. 1, 47) more than nine years, according to P (xxxvii. 2, xli. 46) more than twenty years had elapsed, since he had been separated from his home in Canaan.

made himself strange] In order to account for Joseph's treatment of his brethren, the two most common explanations have been that he sought (1) to prove them, and (2) to punish them. His motives were, doubtless, mixed. The welfare of his father and of his own brother is uppermost in his thoughts. As he does not see them, he doubts whether the brethren who had treated him so shamefully will have maintained any regard for the life of his aged father or his young brother. He assumes a tone of harshness which he does not feel; and suffers a vein of generous hospitality and munificence to mingle with severity in the treatment of his brethren, so as to add to their mystification and confusion.

---

[1] On the "Grand Vizier" of Egypt, see Appendix E. The name of one of the Hyksos kings, Salatis, presents a resemblance to *shâlît*, which has been remarked upon (Budge, *Hist. Eg.* III. 146, note 1).

9 they knew not him. And Joseph remembered the dreams which he dreamed of them, and said unto them, Ye are 10 spies; to see the nakedness of the land ye are come. And they said unto him, Nay, my lord, but to buy food are thy 11 servants come. We are all one man's sons; we are true 12 men, thy servants are no spies. And he said unto them, Nay, but to see the nakedness of the land ye are come. 13 And they said, We thy servants are twelve brethren, the sons of one man in the land of Canaan; and, behold, the 14 youngest is this day with our father, and one is not. And Joseph said unto them, That is it that I spake unto 15 you, saying, Ye are spies: hereby ye shall be proved: by the life of Pharaoh ye shall not go forth hence, except 16 your youngest brother come hither. Send one of you, and let him fetch your brother, and ye shall be bound, that your words may be proved, whether there be truth in you: 17 or else by the life of Pharaoh surely ye are spies. And he

9. *Ye are spies*] The pretext for this sudden accusation lies in the constant exposure of the Egyptians, on their eastern border, to raids and attacks from nomad hordes of Asiatics. Joseph's words are therefore quite natural. LXX κατάσκοποι, Lat. *exploratores*.

the nakedness of the land] Referring not to the desolation produced by the famine (as Targum of Onkelos), but to the weak and unprotected parts of the frontier : so the Lat. *infirmiora terrae*: the LXX τὰ ἴχνη τῆς χώρας = "the tracks (?) of the country," is perplexing. Symm. τὰ κρυπτά.

11. *true men*] Lit. "straight," i.e. genuine and above suspicion.

13. *We...twelve brethren*] In this verse, as in *v*. 32, it appears that Joseph's brethren proffer this information of their own accord, in order to convince the ruler that they were simple private persons. According to J (xliii. 7, xliv. 19), Joseph extracted the information by direct questioning.

one is not] See xxxvii. 30.

14. *That is it that I spake*] Joseph seems to say that their claim to be all the sons of one man is improbable and suspicious. If these suspicions are to be removed, their statements must be verified. Their statement was either the needless embroidery of a falsehood, or it was a detail of actual life that could easily be proved. Joseph's real object is to find out about Benjamin, whether he was alive, and well treated by his brothers. It is a delicate touch in the story, that he abstains from cross questioning them about the brother that "is not."

15. *by the life of Pharaoh*] An Egyptian form of oath, in the sense of "as sure as Pharaoh is alive to punish, or avenge." Dillmann

GENESIS XLII. 17—22

put them all together into ward three days. And Joseph 18
said unto them the third day, This do, and live; for I fear
God: if ye be true men, let one of your brethren be bound 19
in your prison house; but go ye, carry corn for the famine
of your houses: and bring your youngest brother unto me; 20
so shall your words be verified, and ye shall not die. And
they did so. And they said one to another, We are verily 21
guilty concerning our brother, in that we saw the distress of
his soul, when he besought us, and we would not hear;
therefore is this distress come upon us. And Reuben 22

says, "the oath is very suitable here, as the Egyptians honoured their
kings, ὡς πρὸς ἀλήθειαν ὄντας θεούς (Diod. i. 90)," i.e. as truly divine.
The oath by the life of the king is found in an Egyptian inscription
of the 20th century B.C.

17. *put them...into ward*] i.e. "in charge, or safe keeping"; as in xl. 3.
Not "in prison," as in xxxix. 20. Joseph's treatment sounds to us
harsh and cruel. Arbitrary confinement, however, was, and is, only
too common in the East. The brethren would be a prey to the
sickening dread either of being brought out only to be executed, or
of being prevented from returning to their homes.

Joseph himself had endured a long experience of captive life in Egypt.

18—26. The second Interview.

18. *for I fear God*] See notes on xx. 3, 11, xxii. 12, xxxix. 9. Cf.
Lev. xxv. 43; Neh. v. 15. Joseph reassures his brethren by representing to them that the potentate of Egypt is one who recognizes the
universal Divine law of right and wrong. He fears God, who protects
the stranger and the defenceless. Perhaps there is a reference to his
brothers' disregard of this fear of God in their former treatment of himself. He, in his treatment of them, has before his eyes the fear of God.

19. *let one of your brethren*] Joseph's previous sentence in v. 16, by
which one brother should be sent back, while the remainder should
be kept in prison, is here reversed. The three days' interval had
moderated Joseph's threat and his first appearance of indignation.
The change to a more generous treatment is part of his whole policy:
see note on v. 6.

21. *We are verily guilty*] The words of Joseph's brethren represent
the vitality of conscience after a long interval of years. They have the
traditional belief that calamity will overtake the guilty. Cf. the words
of Elihu, Job xxxvi. 6—14.

his soul] See note on xii. 13. Cf. xxvii. 4, 25.

this distress] The same word is used by them to denote their present
state of trouble and Joseph's former agony of mind, when they threw
him into the cistern to die. It is the law of retaliation, "distress" for
"distress," cf. Ex. xxi. 24. Joseph's treatment works well; cf.
Isai. xxvi. 16; Hos. v. 15.

386 GENESIS XLII. 22—27

E answered them, saying, Spake I not unto you, saying, Do not sin against the child; and ye would not hear? therefore 23 also, behold, his blood is required. And they knew not that Joseph understood them; for there was an interpreter 24 between them. And he turned himself about from them, and wept; and he returned to them, and spake to them, and took Simeon from among them, and bound him before 25 their eyes. Then Joseph commanded to fill their vessels with corn, and to restore every man's money into his sack, and to give them provision for the way: and thus was it 26 done unto them. And they laded their asses with their J 27 corn, and departed thence. | And as one of them opened

22. *And Reuben answered*] See xxxvii. 21, 22. Reuben, according to E, believed Joseph to have been killed (xxxvii. 30), and had no knowledge of his being "kidnapped." He can appeal to good intentions, but not to courageous action.

his blood is required] For this phrase see note on ix. 5. Cf. 2 Chron. xxiv. 22. His disappearance meant to his brethren his death. Reuben's interference had prevented them from shedding Joseph's blood (xxxvii. 22), but they were morally guilty of his life.

23. *an interpreter*] The services of interpreters would be necessary for the maintenance of intercourse between Egyptian rulers and the inhabitants of Canaan. The Tel el-Amarna tablets shew that between the kings of Canaanite cities and the court of Egypt, communications were carried on in the Assyrian language, as a kind of *lingua franca*. For other examples in the O.T., illustrating difficulties of communication between nationalities speaking different languages, see 2 Kings xviii. 26; Ezra iv. 7.

24. *wept*] Cf. xliii. 30. Joseph's feelings are deeply stirred by overhearing words that indicate his brethren's contrition for their inhuman conduct towards himself.

Simeon] Simeon was selected to be retained in prison as the next oldest after Reuben. Reuben may have been spared, either for his previous kindness, or because, as the eldest, he would be responsible for carrying the report to Jacob. That Simeon was also the most cruel is an inference from xxxiv. 25 and xlix. 5—7, taken in conjunction with the present passage. The retention of Simeon provided a pledge for the return of the others; which otherwise might be rendered improbable through fear of further harshness from "the lord of the land." The return of their money and the gift of "provision" are meant also to stir their feelings.

27—38. THE RETURN TO CANAAN.

27. *one of them*] Anticipating *v.* 35. Lit. "the one," i.e. the others followed. This verse and *v.* 28 are from J, according to which

his sack to give his ass provender in the lodging place, he J
espied his money; and, behold, it was in the mouth of his
sack. And he said unto his brethren, My money is restored; 28
and, lo, it is even in my sack: and their heart failed them,
and they turned trembling one to another, saying, What is
this that God hath done unto us? | And they came unto 29
Jacob their father unto the land of Canaan, and told him
all that had befallen them; saying, The man, the lord of the 30
land, spake roughly with us, and took us for spies of the
country. And we said unto him, We are true men; we are 31
no spies: we be twelve brethren, sons of our father; one is 32
not, and the youngest is this day with our father in the land
of Canaan. And the man, the lord of the land, said unto 33
us, Hereby shall I know that ye are true men; leave one
of your brethren with me, and take *corn for* the famine of
your houses. and go your way: and bring your youngest 34

the money is found in the sacks at their first lodging place; see
xliii. 21. According to E, the money is found in their sacks, when
they reach their home (see *v.* 35). A word for "sack," *'amtâhath*,
a very unusual one, occurs twice in *vv.* 27 (end), 28, and thirteen
times in chs. xliii.,˙xliv. (J), but not in *v.* 35 or elsewhere in the O.T.

the lodging place] i.e. "the shelter," or wayside quarters, where
they could rest during the night. Cf. Ex. iv. 24; Jer. ix. 2. There
is, perhaps, scarcely sufficient warrant for us to assume that this was
a *khan*, or road-side inn. Such places hardly existed. A rough
shelter, a meagre encampment of black tents, with a scanty protection of a few sticks, brushwood, and blankets, behind which the
men and asses would rest, is perhaps all that is meant.

28. *their heart failed them*] J's account, as we see in xliii. 21,
must originally have represented the opening of all the sacks, and
the finding of all the money, at the "lodging place." As, however,
in E this general discovery is not made until their return to their father,
J's narrative is here restricted to the experience of one of the brethren,
and to the consternation it produced amongst them.

God hath done] They are conscious (1) that the thing is mysterious;
(2) that they might be accused of robbery; (3) that their secret guiltiness
is somehow being visited by a Power which knew all.

30. *took us for spies*] Lit. "put us as spies." Probably the words
"in ward" should be supplied, as LXX ἔθετο ἡμᾶς ἐν φυλακῇ; the
Lat. *putavit nos* renders as the English versions.

33. corn for *the famine of your houses*] The expression "take the
famine of your houses" is so strange, that probably the word for "corn"
is to be supplied, as in the parallel passage in *v.* 19. It is supplied in

E brother unto me: then shall I know that ye are no spies, but that ye are true men: so will I deliver you your brother, 35 and ye shall traffick in the land. And it came to pass as they emptied their sacks, that, behold, every man's bundle of money was in his sack: and when they and their father 36 saw their bundles of money, they were afraid. And Jacob their father said unto them, Me have ye bereaved of my children: Joseph is not, and Simeon is not, and ye will take 37 Benjamin away: all these things are ¹against me. And Reuben spake unto his father, saying, Slay my two sons, if I bring him not to thee: deliver him into my hand, and I J 38 will bring him to thee again. | And he said, My son shall not go down with you; for his brother is dead, and he only is left: if mischief befall him by the way in the which ye go,

¹ Or, *upon*

the versions, LXX, Syr. Pesh. and Targ. Onk.: LXX τὸν δὲ ἀγορασμὸν τῆς σιτοδοσίας τοῦ οἴκου ὑμῶν = "the purchase of food for your house"; Lat. *cibaria domibus vestris necessaria*.

34. *shall traffick in the land*] The Vulg. paraphrases *ac deinceps quae vultis emendi habeatis licentiam*.

35. *And it came to pass*, &c.] This verse, interposed between the brethren's report and their father's reply, seems to emphasize the difficulty of their position; the money has been returned, and Simeon is a prisoner.

36. *have ye bereaved*] Jacob, in his distress of mind, accuses his sons of being the cause of the loss, first of Joseph, and then of Simeon. Unwittingly he enforces the reproaches of their own conscience.

against me] or, as R.V. marg., *upon*. Cf. xvi. 5, xxvii. 12. Jacob is the sufferer. The Heb. preposition admits of either rendering. Cf. Lat. *in me haec omnia mala reciderunt*; LXX ἐπ' ἐμὲ ἐγένετο ταῦτα πάντα.

37. *Reuben*] Reuben is here again prominent; cf. *v.* 22. His words, offering his two sons as a pledge for the safe return of Benjamin, imply that a second journey to Egypt is regarded as a necessity and as a peril. Notice that here Reuben has two sons; in xlvi. 9 (P) four are mentioned.

Reuben here, as elsewhere in the E narrative, acts as leader; in the J narrative, it is Judah who makes a similar offer (xliii. 2). Reuben acknowledges the patriarchal authority of the head of the family over the lives of his children. Cf. xxxi. 32.

38. *he only is left*] i.e. of the sons of Rachel.

mischief] Cf. *v.* 4; Ex. xxi. 22, 23.

bring down my gray hairs, &c.] See note on xxxvii. 35; cf. xliv. 31. Jacob's prediction in these passages is probably intended to heighten

then shall ye bring down my gray hairs with sorrow to ¹the grave.   J

And the famine was sore in the land. And it came to 43 pass, when they had eaten up the corn which they had 2 brought out of Egypt, their father said unto them, Go again, buy us a little food. And Judah spake unto him, saying, 3 The man did solemnly protest unto us, saying, Ye shall not see my face, except your brother be with you. If 4 thou wilt send our brother with us, we will go down and buy thee food: but if thou wilt not send him, we will not 5 go down: for the man said unto us, Ye shall not see my 6 face, except your brother be with you. And Israel said,

¹ Heb. *Sheol*. See ch. xxxvii. 35.

the contrast presented by the dignity and happiness of his end as recorded in chaps. xlviii.—l.

the grave] Heb. *Sheol*. See ch. xxxvii. 35.

CH. XLIII. (J.) JOSEPH'S BRETHREN IN EGYPT. THE SECOND VISIT.

This chapter is taken from the J narrative, which the Compiler harmonizes with E in *vv.* 14 and 23. This and the following chapter form a continuous story, which falls into the following divisions:

xliii. 1—14.   The resolve to return to Egypt.
     15—34.   The reception in Joseph's house.
xliv. 1—17.   The divining cup.
    18—34.   Judah's Intercession.

1—14. THE RETURN TO EGYPT.

2. *Go again*] That Jacob seems to forget about Simeon, is due to the change from the E to the J narrative.

3. *Judah*] Judah is prominent throughout the J narrative. Cf. *v.* 8, xxxvii. 26, xliv. 14—34, xlvi. 28.

except your brother be with you] Admission to Joseph's presence and permission to buy corn were to depend on Benjamin's accompanying them. The other two objects mentioned in xlii. 34, (1) to disprove the charge of being spies, and (2) to obtain the release of Simeon, are not mentioned.

5. *we will not go down*] They know that corn must be got. They are forcing Jacob to give way. The J narrative is not cognisant of the Simeon incident.

6. *Israel*] Observe the change from "Jacob" (xlii. 36) to "Israel" here and *vv.* 8, 11. Jacob seems here for the first time to realize that Benjamin is a condition for the next journey to Egypt. It slowly dawns upon the old man that he must accept the conditions.

GENESIS XLIII. 6—11

J Wherefore dealt ye so ill with me, as to tell the man
7 whether ye had yet a brother? And they said, The man
asked straitly concerning ourselves, and concerning our
kindred, saying, Is your father yet alive? have ye *another*
brother? and we told him according to the tenor of these
words: could we in any wise know that he would say,
8 Bring your brother down? And Judah said unto Israel his
father, Send the lad with me, and we will arise and go; that
we may live, and not die, both we, and thou, and also our
9 little ones. I will be surety for him; of my hand shalt
thou require him: if I bring him not unto thee, and set him
10 before thee, then ¹let me bear the blame for ever: for
except we had lingered, surely we had now returned a
11 second time. And their father Israel said unto them, If it
be so now, do this; take of the choice fruits of the land in

¹ Heb. *I shall have sinned against thee for ever.*

7. *The man asked straitly*] The word "straitly" (i.e. "strictly, closely," cf. Jos. vi. 1), like "solemnly" in *v.* 3, simply emphasizes the force of the verb in Heb. Shakespeare, *Rich. III*, I. 3:
"His majesty hath *straitly* given in charge
That no man shall have private conference
......with his brother."
This verse is evidently independent of xlii. 13 (E), where the information was voluntarily given by the brethren in proof of their sincerity.

9. *I will be surety*] i.e. I will guarantee to bring him back. In xlii. 37 Reuben had been ready to pledge the lives of his two sons for Benjamin's safety. Here Judah is ready to pledge his own life; see xliv. 32. The versions fairly reproduce the original: LXX ἐκδέχομαι αὐτόν; Lat. *suscipio puerum*.

let me bear the blame for ever] R.V. marg. gives the literal rendering *I shall have sinned against thee for ever*, LXX ἡμαρτηκὼς ἔσομαι, Lat. *peccati reus ero*. Compare the same idiom in xxxi. 39, "I bare the loss," and 1 Kings i. 21, "I and my son Solomon shall be counted offenders" (Heb. sinners). The penalty will be proportioned to the failure.

10. *lingered*] Judah implies that, if it had not been for their father's feelings, by this time they would have gone down to Egypt, and returned.

11. *do this*] Jacob yields, but, true to the character of a shrewd man of the world, he advises that the formidable Grand Vizier should be propitiated with a suitable present.

choice fruits] The Hebrew word, *zimrah*, occurs only in this passage in the Pent. (cf. Amos v. 23): LXX καρποί = "fruits"; Lat. *optimi fructus*. The meaning is probable, though only conjectural.

your vessels, and carry down the man a present, a little   J
balm, and a little honey, spicery and myrrh, ¹nuts, and
almonds: and take double money in your hand; and the 12
money that was returned in the mouth of your sacks carry
again in your hand; peradventure it was an oversight: take 13
also your brother, and arise, go again unto the man: | and 14 E
²God Almighty give you mercy before the man, that he
may release unto you your other brother and Benjamin.
And if I be bereaved of my children, I am bereaved.

And the men took that present, and they took double 15 J

¹ That is, *pistachio nuts*. ² Heb. *El Shaddai*.

Some think that it may be from the Hebrew root *zmr*, "to make melody," cf. *mizmôr*, "a psalm": hence Targ. Onkelos, "What is praiseworthy in the land." It has been suggested that "the melody of the land" would mean "the produce of the land celebrated in song." Cf. Jer. li. 41.

vessels] i.e. baggage, receptacles of various kinds, e.g. "sacks" (xlii. 25); cf. 1 Sam. ix. 7.

balm] See xxxvii. 25.

honey] Possibly the material known in Syria and Palestine as *dibs*, which is the Arabian word for "grape juice boiled down to a syrup." The Hebrew word *d'bash*, however, means real "honey," and it is natural to suppose that a gift of real honey from the country would be a more acceptable offering to the Egyptian ruler. Cf. 1 Kings xiv. 3.

spicery and myrrh] See xxxvii. 25.

nuts] That is, *pistachio nuts*. The fruit of the *pistacia vera*, a rare tree in Palestine, regarded as a delicacy.

12. *double money*] Jacob recommends a double restitution (Ex. xxii. 4) for the money that had been mysteriously returned, on the improbable supposition that the affair had been an "oversight." LXX ἀγνόημα = "accidental error." Cf. the sin done "unwittingly" in Lev. iv. 13, 22; Num. xxii. 24.

14. *God Almighty*] Heb. *El Shaddai*. See note on xvii. 1. Unless inserted by the Compiler, this is the only occurrence of this Sacred Name in JE (see note on xlix. 23, which is earlier than JE). Jacob gives his parting blessing. Notice the emphasis on Benjamin's name, and the reference to Simeon (E).

give you mercy] Cf. the parallel expression in Neh. i. 11. Lat. *faciat vobis eum placabilem* gives the general meaning.

if I be bereaved] or, "according as I am bereaved." Jacob is resigned, he is ready mournfully to acquiesce in the Divine will. His forebodings are gloomy. Cf. xlii. 36. His expectation of the worst result heightens the interest of the story, as the crisis is evidently approaching.

J money in their hand, and Benjamin; and rose up, and went
16 down to Egypt, and stood before Joseph. And when
Joseph saw Benjamin with them, he said to the steward of
his house, Bring the men into the house, and slay, and
17 make ready; for the men shall dine with me at noon. And
the man did as Joseph bade; and the man brought the men
18 into Joseph's house. And the men were afraid, because
they were brought into Joseph's house; and they said,
Because of the money that was returned in our sacks at the
first time are we brought in; that he may ¹seek occasion
against us, and fall upon us, and take us for bondmen, and
19 our asses. And they came near to the steward of Joseph's
house, and they spake unto him at the door of the house,
20 and said, Oh my lord, we came indeed down at the first
21 time to buy food: and it came to pass, when we came to the

¹ Heb. *roll himself upon us.*

15—34. THE RECEPTION IN JOSEPH'S HOUSE.

15. *stood before Joseph*] The story is condensed. The men on arrival in Egypt are required to present themselves for purposes of trade before Joseph.

16. *the steward of his house*] See *v.* 19 and xliv. 1, 4. The steward of Joseph's house was the "major domo" of the establishment. Joseph himself had occupied that position. Cf. xxxix. 5.

slay] The slaying of animals indicated a banquet. It was a sign of special honour. Meat food was not usual for the Bedouin. But it was probably regularly eaten by kings and their officials, and by dwellers in towns in Egypt.

at noon] Observe the hour for a banquet. In Palestine the chief meal was in the evening. Cf. xxxi. 54; 1 Sam. ix. 19.

18. *seek occasion*] Heb. *roll himself upon us.* Cf. Job xxx. 14. Joseph's brethren suspect that this act of favour is part of a trap to put them off their guard, and then suddenly seize them on a false charge. Cf. LXX τοῦ συκοφαντῆσαι ἡμᾶς = "to bring false charges against us"; Lat. *ut devolvat in nos calumniam*. The special mention of the "asses" is a lifelike touch.

19. *at the door of the house*] Before crossing the threshold they wished to explain their innocence about the money.

According to the old Hebrew law, a thief who failed to make restitution might be seized and sold for a slave (Ex. xxii. 3).

20. *Oh my lord*] Cf. xliv. 18. The expression introduces an appeal. The word for "my lord" (*adoni*) is rendered by LXX κύριε, and by the Lat. *domine*. See Num. xii. 11; Judges vi. 13; 1 Sam. i. 26; 1 Kings iii. 17, 26.

lodging place, that we opened our sacks, and, behold, every   J
man's money was in the mouth of his sack, our money in
full weight: and we have brought it again in our hand.
And other money have we brought down in our hand to 22
buy food: we know not who put our money in our sacks.
And he said, Peace be to you, fear not: your God, and the 23
God of your father, hath given you treasure in your sacks:
I had your money. | And he brought Simeon out unto them. | (R)
And the man brought the men into Joseph's house, and 24 J
gave them water, and they washed their feet; and he gave
their asses provender. And they made ready the present 25
against Joseph came at noon: for they heard that they
should eat bread there. And when Joseph came home, 26
they brought him the present which was in their hand into

21. *the lodging place*] Cf. xlii. 27 (J).

every man's money] According to E, every man's bundle of money was found, when they emptied their sacks at their journey's end. Cf. xlii. 35.

in full weight] Lit. "in its weight." The money was not in coins, but in metal, probably bars, rings, or ingots, which had to be weighed.

23. *Peace be to you*] A formula of encouragement and reassurance, as in Jud. vi. 23; 1 Sam. xx. 21; Dan. x. 19.

the God of your father] The steward reverently ascribes their good fortune to the influence of the God of their family, concerning whom he himself could have had no knowledge. Their God had put their money in their sacks. It was mysterious. Their payments had duly been made; he had received them. They were innocent. Joseph had evidently instructed his steward what to say.

I had your money] Lit. "your money came unto me." The versions introduce a paraphrase. LXX τὸ ἀργύριον ὑμῶν εὐδοκιμοῦν ἀπέχω; Lat. *pecuniam quam dedistis mihi probatam ego habeo*.

he brought Simeon out] This clause harmonizes the narrative of J with that of E; see notes on *vv.* 3, 5, 14.

24. *water*] Cf. xviii. 4. The washing of the feet, before reclining at a meal, was customary in Palestine; cf. Luke vii. 44, "I entered into thine house, thou gavest me no water for my feet," and 1 Tim. v. 10.

25. *the present*] Cf. *v.* 11.

against Joseph came] i.e. so as to be ready when Joseph arrived. For this use of "against"="in readiness for the time when," cf. 2 Kings xvi. 12, "So did Urijah the priest make it against king Ahaz came from Damascus."

eat bread] A good instance of the use of this phrase in the sense of "to take a meal," cf. *v.* 16, xxxi. 54, xxxvii. 25.

GENESIS XLIII. 26—32

J the house, and bowed down themselves to him to the earth.
26 And he asked them of their welfare, and said, Is your father
27 well, the old man of whom ye spake? Is he yet alive?
28 And they said, Thy servant our father is well, he is yet alive.
29 And they bowed the head, and made obeisance. And he
lifted up his eyes, and saw Benjamin his brother, his
mother's son, and said, Is this your youngest brother, of
whom ye spake unto me? And he said, God be gracious
30 unto thee, my son. And Joseph made haste; for his bowels
did yearn upon his brother: and he sought where to weep;
31 and he entered into his chamber, and wept there. And he
washed his face, and came out; and he refrained himself,
32 and said, Set on bread. And they set on for him by himself,
and for them by themselves, and for the Egyptians, which
did eat with him, by themselves: because the Egyptians
might not eat bread with the Hebrews; for that is an

26. *bowed down themselves*] A second fulfilment of Joseph's dreams: see xlii. 6, xliv. 14; cf. xxxvii. 5—11.

27. *of their welfare*] Lit. "as to their peace."

Is your father well] Lit. "is there peace [to] your father." 2 Sam. xx. 9, "Is it well with thee," lit. = "Art thou peace, my brother?" Ps. cxx. 7, "I am [for] peace." The word *shâlôm* in these passages is a substantive, i.e. "peace," "health," "welfare": cf. xxix. 6, xxxvii. 4.

29. *his mother's son*] The words are added to augment the pathos of the situation. Joseph and Benjamin are the only two children of Rachel, the favourite wife of Jacob.

God be gracious] Joseph, in his dignified greeting of benediction, is made to use the word *Elohim* in its general sense of "the Divine Being," as it would be used by an Egyptian. Cf. xxxix. 9. The Sacred Name, Jehovah, is avoided.

my son] Indicating the great disparity of age between Joseph and Benjamin. Possibly J regarded Benjamin as having been born since Joseph's disappearance.

30. *his bowels did yearn*] For this phrase denoting strong feelings cf. 1 Kings iii. 26; Jer. xxxi. 20. Joseph's emotion is recorded here, as in xlii. 24, in proof of his tenderness and sympathy. The same simplicity may be found in the description of Homeric heroes.

31. *he refrained himself*] Joseph's effort of self-constraint broke down in xlv. 1.

Set on bread] As we should say, "serve up dinner."

32. *because the Egyptians...with the Hebrews*] Egyptian exclusiveness was proverbial. Their priests were not allowed to eat or drink

abomination unto the Egyptians. And they sat before him, 33 J
the firstborn according to his birthright, and the youngest
according to his youth: and the men marvelled one with
another. And ¹he took *and sent* messes unto them from 34
before him: but Benjamin's mess was five times so much
as any of theirs. And they drank, and ²were merry with
him.

And he commanded the steward of his house, saying, 44

¹ Or, *messes were taken* ² Heb. *drank largely.*

anything that had come from a foreign country (Porph. iv. 7).
Herodotus (ii. 41) mentions that no Egyptian would use any utensil
belonging to a Greek. It is noticeable in this passage that Joseph did
not eat with the Egyptians. The natural reason for this is not, as some
have supposed, because Joseph was a member of the family of a priest
(xli. 45), or even because he was a Hebrew, but on account of his
position as the Grand Vizier.

an abomination] The technical term expressing that which was
abhorrent and a source of ceremonial pollution. Cf. xlvi. 34; Ex. viii.
26. LXX βδέλυγμα; Lat. *profanum*.

33. *marvelled*] The men were mystified by their arrangement in
order of birth. It suggested magic. It was one of the uncanny things
that they could not account for.

34. *he took* and sent *messes*] R.V. marg. *messes were taken*. The
word "mess" is used here in the sense of "portion" of food. Cf.
2 Sam. xi. 8, "and there followed him a mess *of meat* from [marg.
present from] the king." The word "messmate" preserves the Old
English use. *Mess*, food, Old Fr. *mes* (*mets*), Lat. *missum*, e.g.:

"At their savoury dinner set
Of herbs and other country messes."
            Milton, *L'Allegro*, 85.

five times] Lit. "five hands"; cf. xlvii. 24. Attention has been
called to the frequent use of the number "five" in Egyptian matters
recorded in the O.T. Cf. xli. 34, xlv. 22, xlvii. 2, 24; Isa. xix. 18.
Some have connected it with the five Egyptian planets.

If an explanation is at all required, counting on one's fingers is
presumably the origin of a natural preference for the use of the numbers
"five" and "ten."

were merry] Heb. *drank largely*. This expression need not be
interpreted too literally. The men were "festive," not necessarily
"intoxicated," as LXX ἐμεθύσθησαν; Lat. *inebriati sunt*.

Compare Song of Songs v. 1, "drink abundantly"; Hag. i. 6, "ye
drink, but ye are not filled with drink."

For a special dish for the most honoured guest, cf. 1 Sam. ix. 23, 24.

J Fill the men's sacks with food, as much as they can carry,
2 and put every man's money in his sack's mouth. And put
my cup, the silver cup, in the sack's mouth of the youngest,
and his corn money. And he did according to the word
3 that Joseph had spoken. As soon as the morning was
4 light, the men were sent away, they and their asses. *And*
when they were gone out of the city, and were not yet far
off, Joseph said unto his steward, Up, follow after the men;
and when thou dost overtake them, say unto them, Where-
5 fore have ye rewarded evil for good? Is not this it in which
my lord drinketh, and whereby he indeed divineth? ye have

Ch. XLIV. (J.) Joseph and his Brethren.

1—17. The divining cup.
18—34. Judah's intercession.

1—17. The Divining Cup.

1. *with food, as much as they can carry*] The "food" means corn; and by special favour the corn is not given them by price, but on a more generous scale; as much as they could carry.

every man's money] This detail is not again referred to. It is overshadowed by the incident of the cup.

2. *the silver cup*] i.e. a well-known, or favourite, goblet. The word for "cup," the same as in Ex. xxv. 31, Jer. xxxv. 5 (where it is rendered "bowl"), seems to denote a vessel shaped like the calyx of a flower. LXX renders κόνδυ; Lat. *scyphum*.

Observe that Joseph does not reveal his intention to the steward. He plays upon his brethren the same trick as in chap. xlii.; but brings matters to a point by associating Benjamin with the loss of the cup.

4. *the city*] The name of the city is most unfortunately not given. Memphis would be suitable: cf. xlv. 10. The moment of the men's arrest is well timed. Everything had gone off well. They had got their corn; they had been acquitted of any complicity in the return of the money; they had been hospitably treated by the "lord"; they were well on their way homeward.

Wherefore have ye rewarded] The guilt of Joseph's brethren is presented in an ascending scale of enormity: (1) it was theft; (2) by guests from their host's table; (3) of an article of special sanctity. The LXX, in order to supply the connexion between *vv.* 4 and 5, inserts at the end of *v.* 4, "Ἵνα τί ἐκλέψατέ μου τὸ κόνδυ τὸ ἀργυροῦν;" = "Wherefore have ye stolen my silver cup?"

5. *whereby he indeed divineth*] "Divineth," Heb. *naḥash*: see xxx. 27; Deut. xviii. 10, "useth divination"; 1 Kings xx. 33 marg. The word shews that the silver cup was a sacred one, by means of

done evil in so doing. And he overtook them, and he 6 J
spake unto them these words. And they said unto him, 7
Wherefore speaketh my lord such words as these? God
forbid that thy servants should do such a thing. Behold, 8
the money, which we found in our sacks' mouths, we brought
again unto thee out of the land of Canaan: how then should
we steal out of thy lord's house silver or gold? With 9
whomsoever of thy servants it be found, let him die, and we
also will be my lord's bondmen. And he said, Now also 10
let it be according unto your words: he with whom it is
found shall be my bondman; and ye shall be blameless.
Then they hasted, and took down every man his sack to 11
the ground, and opened every man his sack. And he 12
searched, *and* began at the eldest, and left at the youngest:
and the cup was found in Benjamin's sack. Then they 13

which Joseph sought and obtained oracles. Some have inferred that
he must have been admitted into the priests' guild, in order to be able
to practise divination. It appears that water having been poured
into a vessel or cup, gold or silver or precious stones were thrown
into it, and the oracle or divination was derived from the rings,
ripples, or sparkles, which appeared. The name given to this class of
magic was "hydromancy," ὑδρομαντεία, or κυλικομαντεία (Jamblichus,
De Myst. iii. 14; Varro in August., *De Civ. Dei*, vii. 35). LXX renders
αὐτὸς δὲ οἰωνισμῷ οἰωνίζεται ἐν αὐτῷ.

Driver quotes from the *Travels of Norden* (circ. 1750 A.D.) a passage
in which a Nubian Sheikh says: "I have consulted my cup, and I find
that you are Franks in disguise, who have come to spy out the land."

7. *God forbid*] Lit. "far be it"=μὴ γένοιτο. The Heb. has no
appeal to the Deity; cf. Jos. xxii. 29.

They are convinced of their innocence, and indignantly repel the
insinuation that they have rewarded the "lord's" hospitality so basely.

9. *With whomsoever*] Joseph's brethren propose the harshest possible penalty, death for the thief, and slavery for all the company. Cf.
Jacob's proposal in xxxi. 32.

10. *my bondman*] Joseph's steward, while accepting the terms,
mitigates their severity. He proposes that the offender, if apprehended,
shall alone be punished, not with death, but with slavery. Joseph's
brethren readily accept the terms.

12. *searched*] There is no mention of the money in the sacks' mouths
(*v.* 1). The interest centres on the cup. That the search is made in
order of age is a dramatic touch adding to the excitement of the scene
described, and probably carried out by the directions of Joseph himself,
as if it might be assumed that the youngest was the least likely to be
the thief. Cf. xliii. 33.

J rent their clothes, and laded every man his ass, and
14 returned to the city. And Judah and his brethren came
to Joseph's house; and he was yet there: and they fell
15 before him on the ground. And Joseph said unto them,
What deed is this that ye have done? know ye not that
16 such a man as I can indeed divine? And Judah said,
What shall we say unto my lord? what shall we speak?
or how shall we clear ourselves? God hath found out
the iniquity of thy servants: behold, we are my lord's bondmen,
17 both we, and he also in whose hand the cup is found. And
he said, God forbid that I should do so: the man in whose
hand the cup is found, he shall be my bondman; but as for
you, get you up in peace unto your father.
18 Then Judah came near unto him, and said, Oh my lord,

13. *rent their clothes*] See xxxvii. 29.

14. *he was yet there*] Joseph had not yet left his official dwelling.
fell before him] The third and last fulfilment of the dreams (xxxvii. 7, 9, 10). See *v.* 26.

15. *such a man as I*] The Grand Vizier, second only to Pharaoh (see *v.* 18), married into the family of the Priest of On, and one "in whom the spirit of God is" (xli. 38).

16. *God hath found out*] Judah confesses the wrong-doing of himself and his brothers (xlii. 21). So mysterious a misfortune could only be explained as a Divine recompense for secret guilt. Cf. Num. xxxii. 23, "be sure your sin will find you out."
"God," *Elohim*, is spoken of in address to a foreigner, as Judah supposes Joseph to be. See notes on xxxix. 9, xliii. 29.

17. *God forbid*] As *v.* 7. Joseph deprecates Judah's proposal, and insists on the milder sentence already proposed by his steward. Benjamin should be kept as a slave.

18—34. JUDAH'S INTERCESSION.

This is one of the most beautiful and pathetic passages in Hebrew narrative. Judah's speech falls into two unequal divisions: (1) *vv.* 18—31 a simple recapitulation of the story, (2) *vv.* 31—34 his self-sacrificing offer of himself as a substitute for Benjamin. The points emphasized are (*a*) Joseph's previous demand to see Benjamin, (*b*) the aged father's unwillingness to let him go, (*c*) the certainty that the loss of Benjamin would be Jacob's death, (*d*) the offer to stay in Benjamin's place.

18. *Then Judah*] The prominence of Judah has been noticeable in xliii. 3, 8 and in *vv.* 14, 16 of this chapter. Benjamin, though present, is silent; Reuben takes no part.
Oh my lord] See xliii. 20.

GENESIS XLIV. 18—29   399

let thy servant, I pray thee, speak a word in my lord's ears, J
and let not thine anger burn against thy servant: for thou
art even as Pharaoh. My lord asked his servants, saying, 19
Have ye a father, or a brother? And we said unto my 20
lord, We have a father, an old man, and a child of his old
age, a little one; and his brother is dead, and he alone is
left of his mother, and his father loveth him. And thou 21
saidst unto thy servants, Bring him down unto me, that
I may set mine eyes upon him. And we said unto my lord, 22
The lad cannot leave his father: for if he should leave his
father, his father would die. And thou saidst unto thy 23
servants, Except your youngest brother come down with
you, ye shall see my face no more. And it came to pass 24
when we came up unto thy servant my father, we told him
the words of my lord. And our father said, Go again, buy 25
us a little food. And we said, We cannot go down: if our 26
youngest brother be with us, then will we go down: for we
may not see the man's face, except our youngest brother be
with us. And thy servant my father said unto us, Ye know 27
that my wife bare me two sons: and the one went out from 28
me, and I said, Surely he is torn in pieces; and I have not
seen him since: and if ye take this one also from me, and 29
mischief befall him, ye shall bring down my gray hairs with

thou art even as Pharaoh] Judah's opening words are those of graceful deference, referring to Joseph's enquiry in v. 15.

19. *My lord asked*] Cf. xliii. 7.

20. *a child of his old age*] Cf. xxxvii. 3, where the words are applied to Joseph.

his brother is dead] See v. 28, xlii. 38 (J). According to the J narrative, his brothers thought him dead. In xlii. 13 (E) Joseph's fate is referred to in vaguer terms, "one is not." This allusion to the "dead" brother in addressing Joseph adds a most effective touch to the story.

of his mother] Lit. "to his mother," i.e. of Rachel's children.

21. *that I may...upon him*] The phrase probably means something more than merely seeing Benjamin. It may indicate favourable protection, as in Ps. xxxiii. 18, xxxiv. 15.

22. *And we said, &c.*] The substance of this verse expresses more than xlii. 20 (E). The expostulation here mentioned is not there recorded.

28. *and I have not seen him since*] The unconscious pathos in the words which Judah uses must have struck Joseph to the heart.

29. *mischief befall him*] Cf. xlii. 4, 38.

J 30 ¹sorrow to ²the grave. Now therefore when I come to thy servant my father, and the lad be not with us; seeing that 31 ³his life is bound up in the lad's life; it shall come to pass, when he seeth that the lad is not *with us*, that he will die: and thy servants shall bring down the gray hairs of thy 32 servant our father with sorrow to ²the grave. For thy servant became surety for the lad unto my father, saying, If I bring him not unto thee, then shall I bear the blame to 33 my father for ever. Now therefore, let thy servant, I pray thee, abide instead of the lad a bondman to my lord; and 34 let the lad go up with his brethren. For how shall I go up to my father, and the lad be not with me? lest I see the evil that shall come on my father.

¹ Heb. *evil*.   ² Heb. *Sheol*. See ch. xxxvii. 35.
³ Or, *his soul is knit with the lad's soul* See 1 Sam. xviii. 1.

with sorrow] Heb. *evil*. "Evil" in the sense of "trouble," as in Ps. cvii. 26, or "calamity," as in Prov. xxiv. 16, a different word from "sorrow" in xlii. 38.

the grave] Heb. *Sheol*. See ch. xxxvii. 35, xlii. 38.

30. *his life...the lad's life*] Better, as R.V. marg., *his soul is knit with the lad's soul*. See 1 Sam. xviii. 1, "the soul of Jonathan was knit with the soul of David, and Jonathan loved him as his own soul." It is the affections, not the lives, of two loving persons which are intertwined.

31. *with us*] These words, which are not in the Heb., are added in the Sam., LXX, and Pesh. versions as essential to the meaning.

with sorrow] i.e. "with grief," as in xlii. 38; not "with evil," as in *v*. 29.

32. *surety*] Cf. xliii. 9.

33. *instead of the lad*] This offer on the part of Judah to remain in Egypt in the bond-service of Joseph, as substitute for Benjamin (LXX ἀντὶ τοῦ παιδίου), forms the noble climax of the generous appeal to Joseph's feelings. The unconscious irony of the situation is heightened by the fact that Judah is unaware of Joseph's personality, and yet has succeeded in making his appeal hinge upon the reference (*a*) to the old age and affectionate feelings of Jacob, and (*b*) to the loss which he has already sustained in the death of Benjamin's elder brother.

CH. XLV. (E (J).) JOSEPH REVEALS HIMSELF.

1—15. Joseph makes himself known to his brethren.
16—28. Joseph's brethren bring the news to Jacob.

The chapter, except for harmonizing insertions, e.g. in *vv*. 4, 5, is from E.

GENESIS XLV. 1—6

Then Joseph could not refrain himself before all them 45
that stood by him; and he cried, Cause every man to go out
from me. And there stood no man with him, while Joseph
made himself known unto his brethren. And he ¹wept 2
aloud: and the Egyptians heard, and the house of Pharaoh
heard. And Joseph said unto his brethren, I am Joseph; 3
doth my father yet live? And his brethren could not
answer him; for they were troubled at his presence. And 4
Joseph said unto his brethren, Come near to me, I pray
you. And they came near. And he said, I am Joseph
your brother, | whom ye sold into Egypt. | And now be not 5
grieved, nor angry with yourselves, | that ye sold me hither: |
for God did send me before you to preserve life. For these 6
two years hath the famine been in the land: and there are

¹ Heb. *gave forth his voice in weeping.*

1—15. JOSEPH MAKES HIMSELF KNOWN TO HIS BRETHREN.

1. *refrain himself*] As in xliii. 31. The vehemence of Joseph's emotion forms a trait in his character and a feature in the narrative. Cf. *vv.* 2, 14, 15; xlii. 24; xliii. 30; xlvi. 29.

2. *wept aloud*] Heb. *gave forth his voice in weeping.*

heard] We must make allowance for an Oriental hyperbole of speech, by which it is intended to convey the rapidity with which the sound of Joseph's broken exclamations, and the news of the recognition of his brethren, were heard and reported.

3. *doth my father yet live?*] This question has seemed to some a strange one after the interviews which Joseph has already had (xliii. 27, 28). But the thought of his father is uppermost in his mind, and in the agitation of the moment the turn which he gives to this first question seems to imply a desire to forget the last occasion on which they had met as brothers. He does not wait for an answer, or expect one.

they were troubled, &c.] Cf. l. 15—21. No wonder that confusion and consternation made them speechless.

4. *whom ye sold*] The narrative of J is here, as in *v.* 5, followed, according to which Joseph was sold by his brethren.

5. *nor angry with yourselves*] The Heb. is "let there not be burning in your eyes," "do not look angry, or vexed," i.e. with yourselves.

to preserve life] i.e. to preserve the life both of his brethren and father, and also of the people of Egypt. The word is rendered "reviving" in Ezra ix. 8, 9. LXX εἰς ζωήν; Lat. *pro salute vestra*. Joseph, with warm-hearted impetuosity, urges them not to take to heart their share in the past. God had overruled it all for good. Cf. Ps. cv. 17, "he sent a man before them."

E yet five years, in the which there shall be neither plowing
7 nor harvest. And God sent me before you to preserve you
   a remnant in the earth, and to save you alive ¹by a great
8 deliverance. So now it was not you that sent me hither,
   but God: and he hath made me a father to Pharaoh, and
   lord of all his house, and ruler over all the land of Egypt.
9 Haste ye, and go up to my father, and say unto him, Thus
   saith thy son Joseph, God hath made me lord of all Egypt:
J 10 come down unto me, tarry not: | and thou shalt dwell in the
E land of Goshen, | and thou shalt be near unto me, thou, and

¹ Or, *to be a great company that escape*

6. *yet five years*] Cf. xli. 30.

neither plowing nor harvest] A general phrase for agricultural operations, as in Ex. xxxiv. 21; Deut. xxi. 4; 1 Sam. viii. 12. There was not even corn enough for sowing purposes. The drought made the ground too hard for ploughing. A.V. has the Old English "earing" = "plowing." Cf. A.V. Ex. xxxiv. 21, "in earing time and in harvest." "Let them go to ear the land," Shakespeare, *Rich. II*, III. 2.

7. *to preserve you a remnant*] Lit. "to set for you a remnant," i.e. descendants; cf. Jer. xliv. 7.

by a great deliverance] R.V. marg. *to be a great company that escape*. The two clauses are very nearly identical. In the first the emphasis is on the fact of survival; in the second, on the act of preservation.

8. *not you...but God*] Notice how Joseph here for the third time ascribes his presence in Egypt to the act of God; cf. *vv.* 5 and 7.

a father to Pharaoh] According to some scholars, the word "father" was in use among Egyptians as a technical title of honour and position; cf. the use of the word in a more general sense, 2 Kings ii. 12; 1 Macc. xi. 32; and Add. Esth. xvi. 11. Observe the three phrases, "father," "lord," and "ruler," corresponding to Joseph's position, personal, social, and national, i.e. towards Pharaoh, towards the people, towards the kingdom.

10. *the land of Goshen*] Goshen mentioned only in J, xlvi. 28, 29, 34; xlvii. 1, 4, 6, 27; l. 8; Ex. viii. 22; ix. 26. By this term seems to be understood a district corresponding to the present *Wady-el-Tumilat*, a stretch of low ground extending from the eastern arm of the Delta to the Valley of Suez and the Salt Lakes. To the north and south of this district the country was barren and desert. Its identification with "Goshen" was the result of the researches carried out by M. Naville. The region has become more familiar in modern times as the country of the brief campaign terminated by the battle of Tel el-Kebir (1882). LXX here and xlvi. 34 translates Goshen, Γέσεμ Ἀραβίας = "Gesem of Arabia." "Arabia" was one of the 23 "nomes" into which the Delta was divided; and the capital of the "nome" Arabia,

thy children, and thy children's children, and thy flocks, E
and thy herds, and all that thou hast: and there will I
nourish thee; for there are yet five years of famine; lest 11
thou come to poverty, thou, and thy household, and all
that thou hast. And, behold, your eyes see, and the eyes 12
of my brother Benjamin, that it is my mouth that speaketh
unto you. And ye shall tell my father of all my glory in 13
Egypt, and of all that ye have seen; and ye shall haste and
bring down my father hither. And he fell upon his brother 14
Benjamin's neck, and wept; and Benjamin wept upon his
neck. And he kissed all his brethren, and wept upon them: 15
and after that his brethren talked with him.

And the fame thereof was heard in Pharaoh's house, 16
saying, Joseph's brethren are come: and it pleased Pharaoh
well, and his servants. And Pharaoh said unto Joseph, Say 17
unto thy brethren, This do ye; lade your beasts, and go,
get you unto the land of Canaan; and take your father and 18
your households, and come unto me: and I will give you
the good of the land of Egypt, and ye shall eat the fat of
the land. Now thou art commanded, this do ye; take you 19
wagons out of the land of Egypt for your little ones, and for

called Phakussa, has been conjecturally identified with the ancient
locality, *Kes*, with the article *pa* prefixed.

near unto me] If Joseph lived at On (xli. 45) or at Memphis,
Goshen would be near at hand.

15. *kissed*] See note on *v.* 2.

after that] Joseph's brethren were evidently slow to believe that
they might rely upon his sincerity.

16—28. JOSEPH'S BRETHREN BRING THE NEWS TO JACOB.

16. *the fame*] Lit. "the voice." It is not the sound of Joseph's
weeping, but the news of the discovery of his brethren.

18. *the good of the land*] Cf. *vv.* 20 and 23; 2 Kings viii. 9, with
the meaning of "the best produce." The second clause repeats the
same thought, in different imagery. Joseph promises the best that
Egypt can give. Cf. Num. xviii. 12, 30, 32, "best," Heb. "fat."

19. *thou art commanded*] The versions render "Command thou
them"; and this rendering avoids the awkwardness of the sudden
transition from sing. to plural, "Thou art commanded, this do ye."
As it stands, Pharaoh turns from Joseph to Joseph's brethren; but
they would hardly be present at such an interview.

wagons] Wheeled conveyances for carrying baggage: a different

E 20 your wives, and bring your father, and come. Also regard
not your stuff; for the good of all the land of Egypt is
21 yours. And the sons of Israel did so: and Joseph gave
them wagons, according to the commandment of Pharaoh,
22 and gave them provision for the way. To all of them he
gave each man changes of raiment; but to Benjamin he
gave three hundred pieces of silver, and five changes of
23 raiment. And to his father he sent after this manner; ten
asses laden with the good things of Egypt, and ten she-
asses laden with corn and bread and victual for his father
24 by the way. So he sent his brethren away, and they
departed: and he said unto them, See that ye fall not out
25 by the way. And they went up out of Egypt, and came

word from that which is rendered "chariots." The wagon is for
transport, the chariot for purposes of war or state. The Egyptian
wagon '*agolt'e* is called by a Semitic name, possibly derived from the
same form as the Hebrew '*agâlah*. See 1 Sam. vi. 7 ff.; 2 Sam. vi. 3.

20. *regard not*] Lit. "let not your eye be sparing," i.e. have no
compunction at leaving things behind

your stuff] Lit. "your vessels." LXX σκεύη; Lat. *supellex*. For
the word "stuff," cf. 1 Sam. x. 22. It is Old English for "baggage";
cf. Shakespeare, *Com. of Errors*, IV. 4: "Therefore away, to get our
stuff on board."

22. *changes of raiment*] i.e. costly robes which would be worn
instead of workday apparel on special occasions. Cf. xxvii. 15; Judg.
xiv. 12, 13, 19; 2 Kings v. 5, 22, 23. The versions LXX δισσὰς
στολάς = "double robes," and Lat. *binas stolas*, have misunderstood
the meaning.

three hundred pieces of silver] i.e. 300 shekels. See notes on xx. 16,
and xxiii. 16.

five changes] See note on xliii. 34.

24. *See that ye fall not out*] The precise meaning of Joseph's
parting words has sometimes been misunderstood. The Heb. word
which he uses is not common. It occurs in Ps. iv. 4, "Stand in awe"
(R.V. marg. *be ye angry*). So here LXX μὴ ὀργίζεσθε; Lat. *ne
irascamini*. The meaning then will be, "do not get excited, quarrel
not, and dispute not" with one another about the degree of your
guilt in your treatment of me. Cf. Reuben's reproaches in xlii. 22.
The suggestion that he warns them against being indignant at the
especial favours and gifts lavished upon Benjamin is not probable. A
different rendering, "be not alarmed," in the sense of "do not give
way to the fear that I am nursing my revenge and am meditating an out-
break of wrath against you at a later time," is hardly warranted, either
by the use of the verb or by the context. But see l. 15—21.

into the land of Canaan unto Jacob their father. And they 26 E
told him, saying, Joseph is yet alive, and he is ruler over all
the land of Egypt. And his heart fainted, for he believed
them not. And they told him all the words of Joseph, 27
which he had said unto them: and when he saw the wagons
which Joseph had sent to carry him, the spirit of Jacob
their father revived: and Israel said, It is enough; Joseph 28
my son is yet alive: I will go and see him before I die.

And Israel took his journey with all that he had, and 46
came to Beer-sheba, and offered sacrifices unto the God of
his father Isaac. And God spake unto Israel in the visions 2

26. *his heart fainted*] Lit. "became numb or cold"; as we should say, "his heart stood still' at the news. It was too good to be true.

27. *and when he saw the wagons*] He did not believe, until he had some ocular proof of the truth of the statement.

the spirit of Jacob...revived] "The spirit" (*ruah*) here,· as in Isa. lvii. 15, "to revive the spirit of the humble," simply denotes the vital powers. Cf. 1 Kings x. 5, "there was no more spirit in her," i.e. the Queen of Sheba, on seeing the glory of Solomon.

28. *It is enough*] Lat. *sufficit mihi*. Jacob's conviction is expressed in brief simple words.

It is left to our imagination to consider how his sons succeeded in satisfactorily explaining to Jacob Joseph's return to life. Did they confess all? or did they keep back part of the truth?

CH. XLVI. (J, E, P.) JACOB'S DESCENT INTO EGYPT, AND
THE GENEALOGY OF HIS FAMILY.

1—5.   Jacob at Beer-sheba (E).
6, 7.   Jacob's entry into Egypt (P).
8—27. The genealogy of Jacob (probably according to a list
        preserved by P).
28—34. Jacob's meeting with Joseph (J, E).

1—5. JACOB AT BEER-SHEBA.

1. *Beer-sheba*] Cf. xxi. 31, 33; xxvi. 33; xxviii. 10. Jacob, in xxxvii. 14 (J), is described as dwelling at Hebron.

the God of his father Isaac] For this reference to the God of the father, cf. xxvi. 24; xxviii. 13; xxxi. 53.

It is natural that Jacob would not leave his home without sacrificing to his God. He offers sacrifices at Beer-sheba, with which sanctuary Isaac had been especially connected; cf. xxvi. 23—25. Either, therefore, according to E, Jacob resided at Beer-sheba, or he had left his home at Hebron (J) and was now on his way south, seeking at Beer-sheba to obtain Divine approval for the descent into Egypt.

E 3 of the night, and said, Jacob, Jacob. And he said, Here am I. And he said, I am God, the God of thy father: fear not to go down into Egypt; for I will there make of thee
4 a great nation: I will go down with thee into Egypt; and I will also surely bring thee up again: and Joseph shall put
5 his hand upon thine eyes. And Jacob rose up from Beersheba: and the sons of Israel carried Jacob their father, and

Isaac had been forbidden to go down into Egypt (xxvi. 2). Other reasons have been suggested, e.g. thanksgiving for the life of Joseph, and fear of Joseph's anger against his brethren; cf. l. 15.

2. *in the visions of the night*] A generic plural for the phenomena of dreams. The versions give the sing. For the word, cf. Num. xii. 6; 1 Sam. iii. 15; Dan. x. 7, 8. For revelations granted at night, cf. xx. 3, xxviii. 12 ff.

Jacob, Jacob] The sentence, as it stands, is striking: "God said to Israel, 'Jacob, Jacob.'" The juxtaposition of the two names "Israel" and "Jacob" may indicate the fusion of the two narratives— J, which prefers "Israel," and E, which prefers "Jacob."

3. *I am God*] Lit. "I am the *Êl*," the name occurring in xxxi. 13; xxxiii. 20; xxxv. 1; cf. xvi. 13. LXX does not translate it. The Lat. gives *fortissimus*. It seems especially to be used of the Divine Being, the true God of Revelation, who had manifested Himself to Abraham and to Isaac.

fear not] These and the following words seem to indicate the reason of Jacob's prayer and sacrifice at Beer-sheba. He needed reassurance at the thought of leaving his home and settling in Egypt in his old age.

there] Jacob's family was to grow into a great people while they were still in Egypt (cf. xv. 13—16).

4. *I will go down*] The promise of the Divine presence is the assurance of safety and blessing. God is no mere local god of Canaan. He will be with His people, where they are; whether in Mesopotamia (xxxi. 13), in Palestine (xxxv. 3), or in Egypt.

bring thee up again] i.e. from Egypt back into Canaan. The pronoun "thee" must surely be understood of the people descended from, and personified by, Jacob, and identified with his name. It does not predict his burial in Canaanite land. The words may best be illustrated from l. 24, and not from l. 13. They foretell the Exodus of the Israelites, not the burial of Jacob.

put his hand...eyes] The last tender office performed by the nearest relative. The promise is fulfilled; see l. 1.

5. *Beer-sheba*] Jacob's home, as of his fathers, according to E (xxi. 31, xxii. 19).

the sons of Israel...Jacob their father] It is not often that the two names are found in such close collocation in the same clause; see note on *v.* 2. In all probability it betokens the work of editing and compiling the parallel narratives, of which J uses "Israel," and E and P prefer "Jacob."

their little ones, and their wives, in the wagons which   E
Pharaoh had sent to carry him. | And they took their cattle, 6   P
and their goods, which they had gotten in the land of
Canaan, and came into Egypt, Jacob, and all his seed with
him: his sons, and his sons' sons with him, his daughters, 7
and his sons' daughters, and all his seed brought he with
him into Egypt.

And these are the names of the children of Israel, 8
which came into Egypt, Jacob and his sons: Reuben,
Jacob's firstborn. And the sons of Reuben; Hanoch, 9
and Pallu, and Hezron, and Carmi. And the sons of 10

6, 7 (P). P's summarized account of the descent into Egypt. Observe the characteristic words "their goods which they had gotten"; "his seed"; "sons' sons" and "sons' daughters"; and the marked redundancy in style, similar to what is found in xii. 5; xxxi. 18; xxxvi. 6; which are all from the P narrative.

8—27 (P). We have here a list of "the names of the children of Israel which came into Egypt."

(*a*) With certain variations and expansions, the list appears also in Num. xxvi. 5—51 (with the omission of Levi), and in 1 Chron. ii.—viii. Moreover in Ex. vi. 14—16 we find the same list, so far as relates to Reuben, Simeon, and Levi (*vv.* 9—11).

(*b*) It cannot accurately be described either as a list of Jacob's descendants, for it includes Jacob himself: or as a list of those who went down into Egypt, for it includes the names of Joseph and his sons, and the names of Benjamin's sons.

(*c*) There is an element of artificiality in the computation of the list. Thus the names of Er and Onan are only mentioned to be excluded from the total (*v.* 12). Dinah, the daughter of Jacob, is included in the list of thirty and three "souls of his sons and his daughters," her name being the only female name up to that point. And Jacob himself is reckoned in the thirty-three.

(*d*) It should be noted, in the same connexion, that Leah's sons are 32, and Zilpah's 16; Rachel's are 14, and Bilhah's 7. Each concubine thus is credited with just half the number of sons that the real wife has. This arrangement is probably designed to assist the memory.

(*e*) The order which is followed in the list is that of the wives: (1) the sons of Leah (*vv.* 8—15); (2) the sons of Zilpah (*vv.* 16—18); (3) the sons of Rachel (*vv.* 19—22); (4) the sons of Bilhah (*vv.* 23—25).

9. = Ex. vi. 14; Num. xxvi. 5, 6.

Hanoch] See xxv. 4, the name of a Midianite. Reuben took possession of Midianite land; see Jos. xiii. 21.

Hezron, and Carmi] The name of Hezron (= "enclosure") occurs again *v.* 12. The town of Hezron is in S. Judah, Jos. xv. 3, 25 (?).

P Simeon; ¹Jemuel, and Jamin, and Ohad, and ²Jachin, and ³Zohar, and Shaul the son of a Canaanitish woman. ¹¹,¹² And the sons of Levi; ⁴Gershon, Kohath, and Merari. And the sons of Judah; Er, and Onan, and Shelah, and Perez, and Zerah: but Er and Onan died in the land of Canaan. 13 And the sons of Perez were Hezron and Hamul. And the sons of Issachar; Tola, and ⁵Puvah, and Iob, and Shimron.

---

¹ In Num. xxvi. 12, 1 Chr. iv. 24, *Nemuel*. ² In 1 Chr. iv. 24, *Jarib*. ³ In Num. xxvi. 13, 1 Chr. iv. 24, *Zerah*. ⁴ In 1 Chr. vi. 16, *Gershom*. ⁵ In 1 Chr. vii. 1, *Puah, Jashub*. See Num. xxvi. 23, 24.

Hezron as grandson of Judah, 1 Chron. ii. 5. Carmi (*cerem* = "vineyard"), the name of a clan; note termination in *-i*. "Beth-haccherem" occurs in Neh. iii. 14, Jer. vi. 1 as the name of a district in Judah. Compare LXX in Jos. xv. 59, where Carem is one of several names added by LXX. Carmi as (?) grandson of Judah, 1 Chron. ii. 7.

10. The same as Ex. vi. 15. In Num. xxvi. 12 ff., and in 1 Chron., Ohad is omitted, possibly through similarity to Zohar.

Jamin] In 1 Chron. ii. 27 Jamin is a descendant of Hezron, the son of Judah. "Jamin" = "right hand" (cf. xxxv. 18), and the name indicates a Simeonite clan in the south of Judah.

Zohar] In Num. xxvi. 13, 1 Chron. iv. 24, *Zerah*. See xxiii. 8, the father of Ephron, and xxxvi. 17.

the son of a Canaanitish woman] A note recording the tradition of a well-known case, in which the tribe of Simeon had assimilated a Canaanite clan. See xxxvi. 37.

11. *Gershon*] In 1 Chron. vi. 16, *Gershom*. In Ex. ii. 22 Gershom is the son of Moses. In Num. iii. 17, 38, the family of Gershon, and the families of Kohath and Merari, were entrusted with the care of the sanctuary.

12. As in Num. xxvi. 20 f.

Er...Onan] See xxxviii. 3—10. The note, in this verse, on their death is probably a later insertion for the purpose of harmonizing the numerical computation in *v.* 15.

Shelah] See xxxviii. 5.

Perez...Zerah] See xxxviii. 29, 30.

Hezron] See note on *v.* 9.

13. As in Num. xxvi. 20 f.

Tola] The judge of this name in Judg. x. 1 is also "the son of Puah," and of the tribe of Issachar, a resemblance which can hardly be accidental.

Puvah...Iob] In 1 Chron. vii. 1, *Puah, Jashub*. See Num. xxvi. 23, 24. Observe that Iob (= *Yôb*) is a different name from Job (= *'Iyyôb*) in Job i. 1 ff.

And the sons of Zebulun; Sered, and Elon, and Jahleel. 14 P
These are the sons of Leah, which she bare unto Jacob in 15
Paddan-aram, with his daughter Dinah: all the souls of his
sons and his daughters were thirty and three. And the 16
sons of Gad; ¹Ziphion, and Haggi, Shuni, and ²Ezbon, Eri,
and ³Arodi, and Areli. And the sons of Asher; Imnah, 17
and Ishvah, and Ishvi, and Beriah, and Serah their sister:
and the sons of Beriah; Heber, and Malchiel. These are 18
the sons of Zilpah, which Laban gave to Leah his daughter,
and these she bare unto Jacob, even sixteen souls. The 19
sons of Rachel Jacob's wife; Joseph and Benjamin. And 20
unto Joseph in the land of Egypt were born Manasseh and

¹ In Num. xxvi. 15, *Zephon*.   ² In Num. xxvi. 16, *Ozni*.
³ In Num. xxvi. 17, *Arod*.

14   As in Num. xxvi. 26.
Elon] The judge of this name in Judg. xii. 11 is also of the tribe of Zebulon.

15. *in Paddan-aram*] The statement that the foregoing were the names of those born in Paddan-aram (i.e. before Jacob's return into Canaan) cannot be understood literally. It illustrates the artificial lines upon which the genealogies were drawn up in the P narrative.

his daughter Dinah] The mention of Dinah is very probably due to an interpolation.

thirty and three] The names of the *male* descendants in *vv.* 9—14 give a total of *thirty-three*, in which apparently Er and Onan were, at first, reckoned, but not Dinah. The mention of "his daughters" is therefore superfluous, and possibly a gloss. Later, however, Er and Onan were excluded, and the names of Jacob himself and Dinah added, in order to make up the figure.

16. *sons of Gad*] A different enumeration is found in 1 Chron. v. 11—17.

Ziphion] In Num. xxvi. 15, *Zephon*. Zaphon a Gadite city, Jos. xiii. 27.

17. *Ishvi*] This name, omitted in Num., is probably due to the erroneous repetition of "Ishvah."

Serah their sister] Notice the solitary mention of a female descendant in the younger generation.

Heber, and Malchiel] It is tempting to compare *Ḥeber*="confederate" (1 Chron. iv. 18), with the *Ḥabiri*, and Malchiel with *Milkili*, the name of a prince of Southern Canaan in the Tel-el-Amarna tablets.

20. *unto Joseph*] Cf. xli. 50—52. LXX adds to this verse "and

GENESIS XLVI. 20—25

P Ephraim, which Asenath the daughter of Poti-phera priest of
21 On bare unto him. And the sons of Benjamin; Bela, and
Becher, and Ashbel, Gera, and Naaman, ¹Ehi, and Rosh,
22 ²Muppim, and ³Huppim, and Ard. These are the sons of
Rachel, which were born to Jacob: all the souls were
23 fourteen. And the sons of Dan; ⁴Hushim. And the sons
24 of Naphtali; ⁵Jahzeel, and Guni, and Jezer, and ⁶Shillem.
25 These are the sons of Bilhah, which Laban gave unto
Rachel his daughter, and these she bare unto Jacob: all

---

¹ In Num. xxvi. 38, *Ahiram*. ² In Num. xxvi. 39, *Shephupham* in 1 Chr. vii. 12, *Shuppim*. ³ In Num. xxvi. 39, *Hupham*. ⁴ In Num. xxvi. 42, *Shuham*. ⁵ In 1 Chr. vii. 13, *Jahziel*. ⁶ In 1 Chr. vii. 13, *Shallum*.

---

there were born the sons of Manasseh which the concubine, the Syrian, bare unto him, Machir; and Machir begat Gilead. And the sons of Ephraim the brother of Manasseh were Soutalaam and Taam, and the sons of Soutalaam Edem." LXX, therefore, here records five additional names.

21. *the sons of Benjamin*] The mention of Benjamin's *sons* in a list purporting to be a record of those who came with Jacob into Egypt is of course irreconcilable with the narrative. But it illustrates the separate origin of these lists of names (connected with P) from the general narrative preserved by J and E. The difficulty experienced by the ordinary reader was possibly felt in very early times. The LXX gives Benjamin three sons, Bela, Chobor, and Ashbel; six grandsons, sons of Bela, viz. Gera, Naaman, Ehi, Rosh, Muppim, and Huppim; and one great-grandson, Ard, the son of Gera. If this list was the original form of the genealogy, it may have been modified, in order to get rid of the strange statement, that Benjamin's grandsons and great-grandsons went down with Jacob into Egypt. Another version is given in Num. xxvi. 38—40.

Becher] In LXX Χόβωρ. Cf. 2 Sam. xx. 1, Sheba, the Bichrite.

Gera] Omitted in Num. xxvi. In Judg. iii. 15 the "judge" Ehud, the Benjamite, is the son of Gera; and in 2 Sam. xvi. 5 Shimei, of the family of Saul, the Benjamite, is the son of Gera.

Ehi] In Num. xxvi. 38, *Ahiram*, omitting Rosh.

Muppim] In Num. xxvi. 39, *Shephupham*; in 1 Chron. vii. 12, *Shuppim*. Ehi, Rosh, Muppim are probably textual variations of Ahiram and Shephupham.

Ard] = 1 Chron. viii. 3, Addar. In Num. xxvi. 40 Naaman and Ard are "sons of Bela."

23. *sons*] Only one name is given. No list of Danites appears in 1 Chron. ii.—viii.

Hushim] In Num. xxvi. 42, *Shuham*. Hushim in 1 Chron. viii. 8 belongs to Benjamin.

the souls were seven. All the [1]souls that came with Jacob 26 P
into Egypt, which came out of his loins, besides Jacob's
sons' wives, all the souls were threescore and six; and the 27
sons of Joseph, which were born to him in Egypt, were two
souls: all the souls of the house of Jacob, which came into
Egypt, were threescore and ten.

And he sent Judah before him unto Joseph, to shew the 28 J
way before him unto Goshen; and they came into the land

[1] Or, *souls belonging to Jacob that came*

26. *souls that came with Jacob*] The rendering of the margin, *souls belonging to Jacob that came*, is preferable. "With Jacob" (as LXX and Lat.) follows *v.* 7, but does not translate the Heb.

threescore and six] These and the words in the following verse before "threescore and ten" have the appearance of a gloss. In the preceding list the sons and daughters of Leah were thirty-three (*v.* 15), the sons of Zilpah sixteen (*v.* 18), the sons of Rachel fourteen (*v.* 22), and the sons of Bilhah seven (*v.* 25); the total of these is seventy. The number, therefore, of sixty-six must be regarded as the result of deducting four persons, presumably Er and Onan, and the "two souls born to Joseph in Egypt" (*v.* 20).

Note that "sixty-six" is just double that of Leah's children, thirty-three. Another computation, excluding Er and Onan, and including Dinah, would make Leah's children "thirty-two," just double Zilpah's.

27. *threescore and ten*] LXX gives "threescore and fifteen," which is followed in Acts vii. 14. The additional five persons were the three grandsons and two great-grandsons born to Joseph in Egypt. Cf. l. 23; Num. xxvi. 28 ff.

The number "seventy" being a sacred number is secured, though at the cost of some adjustment.

28—34. JACOB'S MEETING WITH JOSEPH (J, E).

This passage follows upon *vv.* 1—5.

28. *Judah*] Jacob selects Judah as the brother who would be most certain to have secured the affection of Joseph.

to shew the way...Goshen] The meaning is obscure. According to the English version, Judah was to act as an outrider, or advanced guard, to shew Jacob the route into Goshen. Another interpretation is "that he, Joseph, might give instructions to him, Judah," before Jacob's arrival. The versions represent a slightly different reading: Judah is sent ahead to arrange "that he (Joseph) should appear before (Sam., Syr. Pesh.), or 'come to meet' (LXX συναντῆσαι) him" (Jacob).

Goshen] See note on xlv. 10. The LXX here expands "Goshen" into "at Heroopolis into the land of Rameses" (καθ' Ἡρώων πόλιν εἰς γῆν Ῥαμεσσῆ), probably a duplicate rendering; cf. xlvii. 11.

J 29 of Goshen. And Joseph made ready his chariot, and went up to meet Israel his father, to Goshen; and he presented himself unto him, and fell on his neck, and wept on his 30 neck a good while. And Israel said unto Joseph, Now let me die, since I have seen thy face, that thou art yet alive. 31 And Joseph said unto his brethren, and unto his father's house, I will go up, and tell Pharaoh, and will say unto him, My brethren, and my father's house, which were in the land 32 of Canaan, are come unto me; and the men are shepherds, for they have been keepers of cattle; and they have brought 33 their flocks, and their herds, and all that they have. And it shall come to pass, when Pharaoh shall call you, and shall 34 say, What is your occupation? that ye shall say, Thy servants have been keepers of cattle from our youth even until now, both we, and our fathers: that ye may dwell in the land of Goshen; for every shepherd is an abomination unto the Egyptians.

Heroopolis (modern Tel el-Maskhuta) is the same as "Pithom," a town at the eastern extremity of the *Wady-el-Tumilat*, built by the Israelites (Ex. i. 11) for the Pharaoh of the oppression, Rameses II.

29. *wept*] The description of the meeting between Joseph and Jacob is in accord with the general representation of Joseph's warm and emotional nature. Cf. xlv. 1, 14. "A good while," i.e. at first neither of them can speak.

31. *go up*] Joseph speaks of the residence of Pharaoh as a place to which he must "go up." The metaphor is probably taken from the idea of ascent to the residence of royalty; cf. "high station," "people of eminence." The words contain no geographical significance in the sense of "up the Nile."

32. *the men are shepherds*] These words are followed by what may be a gloss, "for they have been keepers of cattle" (probably drawn from *v.* 34). If not a gloss, "shepherds" must include herdsmen, and "cattle" be used here quite generally of flocks and herds. In xlvii. 3 "thy servants are shepherds": but in xlvii. 6 Pharaoh makes them "rulers over my cattle."

34. *that ye may dwell*] Joseph's purpose is thus somewhat elaborately explained in these verses (31—34), in order to place on record how the Israelites came to occupy the fertile district on the eastern frontier of Egypt, most suitable for their own development, and most favourable to them at the crisis of the Exodus. The shrewdness and wisdom of Joseph are made to account for their occupation of Goshen.

Goshen] LXX ἐν γῇ Γέσεμ Ἀραβίᾳ, as in xlv. 10.

every shepherd is an abomination...Egyptians] This statement seems

Then Joseph went in and told Pharaoh, and said, My **47 J**
father and my brethren, and their flocks, and their herds,
and all that they have, are come out of the land of Canaan;
and, behold, they are in the land of Goshen. And from 2
among his brethren he took five men, and presented them
unto Pharaoh. And Pharaoh said unto his brethren, What 3
is your occupation? And they said unto Pharaoh, Thy 4
servants are shepherds, both we, and our fathers. And
they said unto Pharaoh, To sojourn in the land are we come;

hardly to be justified by what we know of the ancient Egyptians. Probably the word "shepherd" here, as in *v.* 32, is used loosely so as to include "herdsman." Moreover, the strong dislike of the Egyptians for the Asiatic nomads on their eastern frontier may well have contributed to this feeling. The tending of cattle and swine in Egypt was associated with a low class of people dwelling in the swampy northern regions of the Delta. For the word "abomination," cf. xliii. 32 and Ex. viii. 26. The writer's note, contained in this verse, may have been inaccurate, and yet have faithfully recorded his impression as to the cause which would account for the sons of Jacob being assigned to a fertile region on the east of the Delta.

CH. XLVII.

1—11. JOSEPH'S BRETHREN AND JACOB BEFORE PHARAOH.
12—27. THE FAMINE IN EGYPT AND JOSEPH'S POLICY.
28—31. JACOB'S DEATHBED.

1—12. *vv.* 1—4, 6^b, 12—27^a, 29—31 J; 5, 6^a, 7—11, 27^b, 28 P.

1. *Then Joseph went in*] Joseph seems to address Pharaoh as if the latter had been unaware of the coming of Joseph's family. The passage (*vv.* 1—4) seems to ignore, or to be independent of, xlv. 17—20 (E), in which Pharaoh himself offers a home in Egypt to Joseph's brethren.

the land of Goshen] Cf. xlv. 10. Joseph reports of their arrival at Goshen, as if his brothers had reached that place accidentally.

2. *five men*] How the five were selected we are not told. On the number "5" in connexion with Egypt, see note on xliii. 34. Cf. *v.* 24, xli. 34, xliii. 34, xlv. 22; Isa. xix. 18.

3. *And Pharaoh said*] Pharaoh's question and the men's answer follow the outline given by Joseph in xlvi. 34, but, instead of saying, "thy servants have been keepers of cattle," they say, "thy servants are shepherds."

4. *And they said unto Pharaoh*] Joseph's brethren were the speakers in the last clause of *v.* 3: it is natural to suppose that a question from Pharaoh has dropped out, to which they now give answer. They would hardly make the request in this verse without some invitation.

J	for there is no pasture for thy servants' flocks; for the famine is sore in the land of Canaan: now therefore, we pray thee, let thy servants dwell in the land of Goshen.
P	5 And Pharaoh spake unto Joseph, saying, Thy father and 6 thy brethren are come unto thee: the land of Egypt is before thee; in the best of the land make thy father and
J	thy brethren to dwell; in the land of Goshen let them dwell: and if thou knowest any ¹able men among them,
P	7 then make them rulers over my cattle. And Joseph brought in Jacob his father, and set him before Pharaoh: 8 and Jacob blessed Pharaoh. And Pharaoh said unto Jacob, 9 How many are the days of the years of thy life? And Jacob said unto Pharaoh, The days of the years of my ²pilgrimage are an hundred and thirty years: few and evil

¹ Or, *men of activity*   ² Or, *sojournings*

5, 6 (P). These verses interrupt the sequence of the narrative. They represent the account in P of the occupation of Goshen. The structure of the verses is a little different in LXX, where 5ᵃ is followed by 6ᵇ. 5ᵃ (J) "And Pharaoh said unto Joseph, Let them dwell in the land of Goshen, 6ᵇ and if thou knowest any able men among them, then make them rulers over my cattle. 5ᵇ (P) And Jacob and his sons came into Egypt unto Joseph. And Pharaoh king of Egypt heard of it. And Pharaoh spake unto Joseph, saying, Thy father and thy brethren are come unto thee...to dwell. 7 And Joseph brought in Jacob, &c." This probably represents an earlier text, combining J and P; and the obvious discrepancy between the accounts was subsequently modified.

6. *in the best*] Cf. Ex. xxii. 4. The land of Goshen was fertile and good for grazing: but only by Oriental courtesy could it be called "the best" land in Egypt.

able men] So LXX ἄνδρες δυνατοί. Cf. Ex. xviii. 21, 25. R.V. marg. *men of activity* as Lat. *viri industrii*.

rulers over my cattle] Pharaoh is ready to confer positions of authority, without further enquiry, upon the most capable of Joseph's brothers. The mention of the royal herds shews us that the position of herdsmen was fully recognized among the Egyptians: see note on xlvi. 34.

7. *Jacob blessed Pharaoh*] Here and in *v.* 10 Jacob is said to "bless" Pharaoh. We should understand by this the solemn and benevolent benediction which is the privilege of aged persons in addressing those of much higher rank. According to another interpretation, the word should be rendered "saluted"; cf. 1 Sam. xiii. 10; 2 Kings iv. 29.

9. *pilgrimage*] R.V. marg. *sojournings*. See xvii. 8, xxviii. 4, xxxvi. 7, xxxvii. 1 (P). The two renderings depend upon the metaphorical, or literal, explanation of Jacob's words. Is it the metaphorical

have been the days of the years of my life, and they have P
not attained unto the days of the years of the life of my
fathers in the days of their ¹pilgrimage. And Jacob blessed 10
Pharaoh, and went out from the presence of Pharaoh. And 11
Joseph placed his father and his brethren, and gave them a
possession in the land of Egypt, in the best of the land, in
the land of Rameses, as Pharaoh had commanded. | And 12 J
Joseph nourished his father, and his brethren, and all his
father's household, with bread, ²according to their families.
And there was no bread in all the land; for the famine 13

¹ Or, *sojournings*   ² Or, *according to* the number of *their little ones*

pilgrimage of life? or is it the frequent change of Jacob's abode to which he makes reference? The latter is perhaps preferable, (1) on account of the allusion to the lives of his fathers, and (2) because this metaphor in the Bible seems to be based on the experience of the patriarchs themselves. Cf. 1 Chron. xxix. 15; Ps. xxxix. 12, cxix. 19, 54; Heb. xi. 9, 13.

few] i.e. by comparison with the traditional days of old (v. 1 ff., xi. 10 ff.) according to P.

evil] Alluding to the flight from home, the hardships of the service in Haran, the loss of Joseph, the death of Rachel, the violence of Simeon and Levi (chap. xxxiv.).

they have not attained] Jacob's life of 130 years at this juncture seemed short in comparison with the 175 years of Abraham (xxv. 7) and the 180 years of Isaac (xxxv. 28).

11. *placed*] Lit. "caused to dwell"; as we should say, "settled."

the land of Rameses] This description of the land of Goshen appears only here, and in the LXX of ch. xlvi. 28. A town named Rameses is mentioned in Ex. i. 11, xii. 37; Num. xxxiii. 3, 5. In Ex. i. 11 Rameses is the name of one of the two store cities built by the children of Israel on the east of the Delta, according to Petrie = *Tel er-Retabeh*. The name given to it was probably that of the Pharaoh of the oppression, Rameses II. If so, the description of this region, where Joseph's brethren are settled, by the name of "the land of Rameses," is, strictly speaking, an anachronism, i.e. a chronological anticipation of facts, the country being denoted by a name which it came to bear two centuries later. It is a very natural thing for the Israelite writer to do; and can hardly be regarded in the light of a literary error.

12. *according to their families*] The margin, *according to* the number of *their little ones*, gives the literal rendering. Delitzsch comments, "little children being mentioned because they would require much food, and also because people would be less willing to see them in want." Cf. xlv. 11.

13—27ᵃ (J (?)). The Famine in Egypt, and Joseph's Policy.

13. *in all the land*] or "in all the earth." LXX πάσῃ τῇ γῇ;

was very sore, so that the land of Egypt and the land of
14 Canaan fainted by reason of the famine. And Joseph
gathered up all the money that was found in the land
of Egypt, and in the land of Canaan, for the corn which
they bought: and Joseph brought the money into Pharaoh's
15 house. And when the money was all spent in the land
of Egypt, and in the land of Canaan, all the Egyptians
came unto Joseph, and said, Give us bread: for why
should we die in thy presence? for *our* money faileth.
16 And Joseph said, Give your cattle; and I will give you for
17 your cattle, if money fail. And they brought their cattle
unto Joseph: and Joseph gave them bread in exchange for
the horses, and for the ¹flocks, and for the herds, and for

---

¹ Heb. *cattle of the flocks, and for the cattle of the herds*.

Lat. *in toto orbe*. Cf. xli. 54, 57; Acts xi. 28, "a great famine over all the world." "Very sore": cf. xii. 10, xli. 31, 56, xliii. 1.

fainted] A striking metaphor (the Heb. word not occurring again in O.T.) to express the complete collapse of the inhabitants of Egypt and Canaan: LXX ἐξέλιπε. Notice the association of Canaan with Egypt in these three verses 13, 14, 15. Afterwards only Egypt is spoken of.

14. *gathered up*] Joseph's policy of State granaries was completely successful. He accumulated vast wealth for his master, the King of Egypt.

Pharaoh's house] i.e. the royal treasury, "the White House," as it was known in Egypt. Cf. xli. 40.

15. *And when the money*] The inhabitants of Egypt, finding that their money was expended, voluntarily proposed the surrender, firstly, of their cattle, and secondly, in the following year (*vv.* 18, 19), of their persons and their land. There is no mention of murmuring or uprising among the people. Private ownership, except in the case of the priests (*v.* 22), was surrendered. The whole people became Pharaoh's servants, practically serfs, paying him a land tax of 20 per cent. annually (*v.* 26).

16. *I will give you*] The word "bread" is evidently understood; and is found supplied in the Sam., LXX and Vulg. versions.

17. *horses...flocks, and for the herds*] Heb. *cattle of the flocks, and for the cattle of the herds*. Observe here the mention of horses first in the list, followed by sheep, cattle, and asses. Compare the list of the live stock belonging to the nomad Abraham in xii. 16, "sheep, oxen, he-asses, men-servants, maid-servants, she-asses, camels." Camels are not mentioned here. Egyptologists inform us that the inscriptions do not record the mention of horses before the New Monarchy, circa 1530 B.C.: see note on xii. 16. The Egyptians owed to the Hyksos the introduction of horses and chariots.

GENESIS XLVII. 17—21 417

the asses: and he [1]fed them with bread in exchange for all their cattle for that year. And when that year was ended, they came unto him the second year, and said unto him, We will not hide from my lord, how that our money is all spent; and the herds of cattle are my lord's; there is nought left in the sight of my lord, but our bodies, and our lands: wherefore should we die before thine eyes, both we and our land? buy us and our land for bread, and we and our land will be servants unto Pharaoh: and give us seed, that we may live, and not die, and that the land be not desolate. So Joseph bought all the land of Egypt for Pharaoh; for the Egyptians sold every man his field, because the famine was sore upon them: and the land became Pharaoh's. And as for the people, [2]he removed them [3]to the cities from one end of the border of Egypt

[1] Heb. *led them as a shepherd*.   [2] According to Samar., Sept. and Vulg., *he made bondmen of them, from &c.*   [3] Or, *according to their cities*

fed them] Heb. *led them as a shepherd*. The same word as in xxxiii. 14, "lead on softly," and in Ps. xxiii. 2, "he leadeth me beside the still waters."

18. *We will not hide*] The LXX μή ποτε ἐκτριβῶμεν = "lest we be utterly ruined," misunderstood the Hebrew.

our bodies, and our lands] The inhabitants propose that Pharaoh should become the feudal lord of all Egypt, with complete possession of the land and absolute control over the lives of the people. The proposal is represented as emanating from the people themselves. Joseph's authority is unquestioned; his popularity never in doubt.

20. *Joseph bought all the land*] This transaction, by which, at a single stroke of business, Joseph, the Hebrew, was said to have purchased for Pharaoh the whole land of Egypt, and all the people to be Pharaoh's slaves, as the price of seed corn (cf. 23), probably sounded in the ears of an ancient Oriental people a masterpiece of cleverness. In our days it would rank as an outrageous piece of tyranny, that the king's Grand Vizier, taking advantage of his own monopoly in corn and of the people's destitution, should deprive them of the last shreds of their independence.

21. *he removed them*] Better, as Samar., Sept. and Vulg., *he made bondmen of them, from &c.* The reading in the text, followed by the R.V., is in all probability due to the recollection of Joseph's policy of storing the grain in the cities, xli. 35, 48. The reading of R.V. marg., which is that of the versions, differs extremely slightly from that of the Massoretic text. The verb "he removed" only differs from the verb "he enslaved" by one letter; the former having

27

J 22 even to the other end thereof. Only the land of the priests bought he not: for the priests had a portion from Pharaoh, and did eat their portion which Pharaoh gave them;
23 wherefore they sold not their land. Then Joseph said unto the people, Behold, I have bought you this day and your land for Pharaoh: lo, here is seed for you, and ye shall sow
24 the land. And it shall come to pass at the ingatherings, that ye shall give a fifth unto Pharaoh, and four parts shall be your own, for seed of the field, and for your food, and for them of your households, and for food for your little
25 ones. And they said, Thou hast saved our lives: let us find grace in the sight of my lord, and we will be Pharaoh's
26 servants. And Joseph made it a statute concerning the

"R" (ר) and the latter "D" (ד); cf. x. 3, 4. The latter gives a distinctly better sense. Verse 20 has already described the sale of the land, and now *v.* 21 describes how the people became servants, or serfs, to Pharaoh. Thus *vv.* 20 and 21 describe the carrying out of both parts of the people's proposal in *v.* 19.

to the cities] R.V. marg. *according to their cities*. The rendering "to the cities" agrees with the verb "he removed." But, with the preferable reading "he made bondmen," we should here read "for slaves or serfs," as LXX εἰς παῖδας. The difference in the Hebrew text, between "to the cities" and "for slaves," is very slight.

There would have been no advantage to be derived from the redistribution of the people in the cities except for convenience in feeding them. They were needed to work the soil which now belonged to Pharaoh.

22. *Only the land of the priests*] The priests of Egypt enjoyed special privileges. They were greatly enriched by the kings of the 18th Dynasty (B.C. 1587—1328). It is doubtful whether their position was so favourable under the Hyksos (see Appendix E). But they were not under the necessity of selling their land. Erman quotes an inscription from which it appears that 185,000 sacks of corn were given annually by Rameses III (B.C. 1202—1171) to the Egyptian temples (*Life in Ancient Egypt*, p. 129).

a portion] Cf. the use of this word in the sense of a fixed rate or "due," Lev. x. 13; Prov. xxx. 8 (marg.).

24. *a fifth*] Cf. xli. 34. This seems an immense impost. But it is said to compare favourably with the ruthless standard of taxation by Oriental governments, in which corruption was rife and liberty did not exist: cf. the letter of King Demetrius, 1 Macc. x. 30, "the third part of the seed," "the half of the fruit of the trees which falleth to me to receive."

26. *a statute*] The Israelites preserved this tradition concerning the origin of the system of land-tenure which prevailed in Egypt at a later time. For the expression "unto this day," cf. xxii. 14. Unfortunately it does not supply us with the date at which this section was written.

land of Egypt unto this day, that Pharaoh should have the J
fifth; only the land of the priests alone became not
Pharaoh's. And Israel dwelt in the land of Egypt, in the 27
land of Goshen; | and they gat them possessions therein, P
and were fruitful, and multiplied exceedingly.

And Jacob lived in the land of Egypt seventeen years: 28
so the days of Jacob, the years of his life, were an hundred
forty and seven years. | And the time drew near that Israel 29 J
must die: and he called his son Joseph, and said unto him,
If now I have found grace in thy sight, put, I pray thee,
thy hand under my thigh, and deal kindly and truly with
me; bury me not, I pray thee, in Egypt: but when I sleep 30
with my fathers, thou shalt carry me out of Egypt, and bury
me in their buryingplace. And he said, I will do as thou 31
hast said. And he said, Swear unto me: and he sware
unto him. And Israel bowed himself upon the bed's head.

27. *and they gat them*, &c.] This clause concludes P's narrative of the settlement of Jacob and his sons in Egypt.

28. *seventeen years*] This verse, giving the years of Jacob's life, comes from P: see *v.* 9. Note that $147 = 7 \times 7 \times 3$, sacred numbers.

29—31 (J). JACOB MAKES JOSEPH SWEAR TO BURY HIM IN CANAAN.

29. *And the time drew near*] The description of Jacob's dying moments may be compared with those of Moses (Deut. xxxi.—xxxiv.) and of David (1 Kings ii. 1).

I have found grace] Cf. vi. 9, xviii. 3, xxxii. 5, xxxiii. 8, 15 (J).

put...thy hand...thigh] See note on xxiv. 2 (J).

30. *when I sleep with my fathers*] See note on xxv. 8. When his spirit is in Sheôl, his body is to rest at Machpelah.

bury me in their buryingplace] This charge of Jacob that he should be carried out of Egypt and buried in the burying-place of his fathers, viz. in the cave of Machpelah, is repeated in xlix. 29, 30 (P). See for its execution l. 13 (P). For the burial of Isaac, see xxxv. 29 (P); and of Abraham, xxv. 9 (P).

In l. 5 Jacob speaks of the grave he had digged for himself: see note.

31. *Israel bowed himself*] Cf. 1 Kings i. 47, "and the king (David) bowed himself upon the bed." Here Jacob "bows himself" upon the bed's head, presumably in silent thanksgiving to God for the promise made to him by Joseph. So the Lat. *adoravit Israel Deum conversus ad lectuli caput*. Joseph's promise was no slight undertaking (see chap. l.). Jacob is full of gratitude.

the bed's head] The LXX following a different vocalization of the

GENESIS XLVIII. 1—3

E 48 And it came to pass after these things, that one said to Joseph, Behold, thy father is sick: and he took with him 2 his two sons, Manasseh and Ephraim. And one told Jacob, and said, Behold, thy son Joseph cometh unto thee: and
P 3 Israel strengthened himself, and sat upon the bed. | And Jacob said unto Joseph, [1] God Almighty appeared unto me at Luz in the land of Canaan, and blessed me, and said

[1] Heb. *El Shaddai*.

same Hebrew consonants, and reading *hammatteh* instead of *hammittah*, gives the rendering followed in Heb. xi. 21, "and worshipped leaning upon the top of his staff," ἐπὶ τὸ ἄκρον τῆς ῥάβδου αὐτοῦ. The staff would be his own staff, not as some have suggested, Joseph's staff of office. This reading is found also in the *Vetus Itala* and in Syr. Pesh. But the reading of the Hebrew text, "upon the bed's head," is probably the original one. The obscurity of the words led to the reading of the LXX. How should we explain "upon the bed's head"? The simplest explanation seems the most probable. The words should be connected closely with the verb "bowed himself." Ordinarily, the phrase "to bow oneself" was followed by some such expression as "to the ground," cf. xviii. 2, xxiv. 52, xxxiii. 3, xlii. 6, xliii. 26. The prostration was then made by those who were standing. Here, Jacob is recumbent. He bows himself in worship; and it was natural to express the inclination of his obeisance by some such word, as in David's case, "upon the bed" (1 Kings i. 47); or, more picturesquely, as here, "upon the bed's head." He was too weak to move much.

The suggestion that a figure of the household god, or Teraphim (cf. xxxi. 19), was at the bed's head, and that Jacob in worship turned to it, has been ingeniously supported from the narrative of 1 Sam. xix. 13. But, except as an example of conjectural ingenuity, it can hardly be considered worthy of more than a passing mention.

CH. XLVIII. (E (J, P).) JACOB'S BLESSING OF EPHRAIM AND MANASSEH.

This narrative is chiefly taken from E; but *vv*. 3—7 are from P.

1. *after these things*] A vague description of time, as in xv. 1, xxii. 1, xxxix. 7, xl. 1.

Manasseh and Ephraim] Observe the order of the names. Manasseh is put first as the elder.

3. *God Almighty*] Heb. *El Shaddai*: see note on xvii. 1. This title for the Deity and the phrases "make fruitful and multiply" (cf. i. 28), "a company of peoples" (cf. xxviii. 3, xxxv. 11), "an everlasting possession" (cf. xvii. 8), are characteristic of the style of P. "Appeared": the appearance referred to is that of xxxv. 9—13.

Luz] See xxviii. 19, xxxv. 6, 9.

unto me, Behold, I will make thee fruitful, and multiply 4   P
thee, and I will make of thee a company of peoples; and
will give this land to thy seed after thee for an everlasting
possession. And now thy two sons, which were born unto 5
thee in the land of Egypt before I came unto thee into
Egypt, are mine; Ephraim and Manasseh, even as Reuben
and Simeon, shall be mine. And thy issue, which thou 6
¹begettest after them, shall be thine; they shall be called
after the name of their brethren in their inheritance. And 7
as for me, when I came from Paddan, Rachel died ²by me
in the land of Canaan in the way, when there was still some
way to come unto Ephrath: and I buried her there in the

¹ Or, *hast begotten*   ² Or, *to my sorrow*

5. *are mine*] Joseph's sons are adopted into the family of Jacob (cf. Josh. xiv. 4); and the account records their acknowledgment to be full tribes in the parent stock of Israel.

Ephraim and Manasseh] Observe the change in order. The writer of P here, as E in *v*. 20, gives the precedent to the recipient of the greater blessing. But, while this order is found in Num. i. 10, Josh. xvii. 17, the other is the more usual; cf. Josh. xiv. 4, xvi. 4.

6. *begettest*] Better, as R.V. marg., *hast begotten*.

they shall be called] The meaning is that any other children of Joseph, and their descendants, shall be attached to the tribes of Ephraim and Manasseh, and shall be called Ephraimites or Manassites.

7. *And as for me*] This verse, with its reference to xxxv. 16—19, is introduced very abruptly. The mention of Rachel's grave is not followed by any further statement, and, standing by itself, it comes in strangely. It hardly admits of explanation as an old man's wandering soliloquy. Such an explanation is too modern in character. Possibly the passage originally contained the tradition of Jacob's request, that he might be buried in the same grave with his beloved wife, Rachel. But the entreaty to be buried at Machpelah having already (xlvii. 30) been inserted from J, it was necessary to drop the concluding portion of Jacob's utterance, i.e. the request to be buried with Rachel, to which the allusion to Rachel's death and burial at Ephrath was leading up. This theory accounts for the introduction of the touching allusion to Rachel and her burial-place, and for the sudden dropping of the subject.

Paddan] For "Paddan-aram," as in LXX. See xxv. 20.

by me] R.V. marg. *to my sorrow*, lit. "upon me," expresses the full meaning. Compare "against me" in xlii. 36; see note.

when there was still some way] See note on xxxv. 16. The Heb. gives a measure of distance; cf. 2 Kings v. 19; and the LXX gives the strange rendering κατὰ τὸν ἱππόδρομον χαβραθὰ τῆς γῆς, where χαβραθὰ

PE 8 way to Ephrath (the same is Beth-lehem). | And Israel
9 beheld Joseph's sons, and said, Who are these? And
Joseph said unto his father, They are my sons, whom God
hath given me here. And he said, Bring them, I pray thee,
10 unto me, and I will bless them. Now the eyes of Israel
were dim for age, so that he could not see. And he brought
them near unto him; and he kissed them, and embraced
11 them. And Israel said unto Joseph, I had not thought to
see thy face: and, lo, God hath let me see thy seed also.
12 And Joseph brought them out from between his knees; and
13 he bowed himself with his face to the earth. And Joseph

transliterates the Heb., and κατὰ τὸν ἱππόδρομον, "according to the race-course," reproduces the tradition that the race-course at Alexandria was the length of this Hebrew measure; cf. Schleusner, *s.v.* The Vulg. has *eratque vernum tempus* (!). "On the way to Ephrath," LXX ἐν τῇ ὁδῷ τοῦ ἱπποδρόμου.

8. *And Israel*] The narrative resumes the thread which was interrupted at *v.* 3 by the insertion of the P version. The incident about to be described was regarded as of national significance. Of the two divisions of Joseph, the younger one became the more powerful. The blessing of Jacob implies the ratification of the relation of the two new tribes to the older ones and to each other.

beheld...Who are these?] Jacob enquires as if he had not before seen the sons of Joseph. Jacob was in Goshen: Joseph and his sons lived not far off. It is possible the question is due to the old man's blindness (*v.* 10). He discerned faintly that there were two other persons with Joseph. But it is more probable that this story stands by itself, and that it assumes that Jacob had not before met Joseph's sons.

10. *the eyes of Israel*] Cf. the similar account of Isaac, xxvii. 1.

11. *thy seed also*] This expression, like the question in *v.* 8, seems to imply that Jacob had not before set eyes upon the sons of Joseph.

12. *Joseph brought...his knees*] To set a child upon the knees was to symbolize reception or adoption into the family: see note on xxx. 3. From this passage it would appear that Joseph had set Ephraim and Manasseh upon, or against, the knees of their grandfather, so that they might receive the formal symbol (not here described) of adoption. This being done, he then removes them from between the knees of Jacob.

he bowed himself] For "bowed himself," see note on xlvii. 31. Who bowed himself? (1) Either Joseph, who thus threw himself on the ground to receive the blessing described in *v.* 15. (2) Or Jacob, who thus rendered thanks to God for enabling him to adopt into his family the children of Joseph. According to (2), Jacob would be represented as able to prostrate himself with his face to the earth (see note on xlvii. 31). According to (1), *vv.* 13, 14 are interposed between Joseph's prostration in *v.* 12 and the imposition of Jacob's blessing in *v.* 15. But, if

took them both, Ephraim in his right hand toward Israel's left hand, and Manasseh in his left hand toward Israel's right hand, and brought them near unto him. And Israel 14 stretched out his right hand, and laid it upon Ephraim's head, who was the younger, and his left hand upon Manasseh's head, ¹guiding his hands wittingly; for Manasseh was the firstborn. And he blessed Joseph, and said, The God 15 before whom my fathers Abraham and Isaac did walk, the God which hath fed me all my life long unto this day, the 16 angel which hath redeemed me from all evil, bless the lads;

¹ Or, *crossing his hands*

we may regard this story as independent of xlvii. 29—31 (J), it seems simplest to refer the act to Jacob.

13. *Ephraim in his right hand*] i.e. so that the *right* hand of Jacob might rest on Manasseh the *elder*. The gesture of benediction, by the laying on of hands, signified the communication of rights and privileges. As in the story of Isaac (ch. xxvii.), the blessing by the head of the house, on his deathbed, was irrevocable. The person who received it could not be deprived of it.

14. *guiding his hands wittingly*] Better, as R.V. marg., *crossing his hands*. So LXX ἐναλλὰξ τὰς χεῖρας = "the hands crosswise"; Lat. *commutans manus*.

The aged Jacob is moved by a supernatural impulse to cross his hands as he blesses the two boys; and their destinies are determined accordingly.

15. *And he blessed Joseph*] While his hands were resting on the lads' heads, Jacob blessed Joseph by uttering his benediction upon Ephraim and Manasseh. LXX εὐλόγησεν αὐτούς = "blessed them," and Vulg. *benedixit filiis Joseph*, avoid the difficulty.

The God] Observe the threefold invocation: (1) ancestral—"the God of the fathers"; (2) personal—"the Shepherd of Israel"; (3) redemptive—"the angel of deliverance." Compare the threefold Aaronic benediction of Num. vi. 24 ff.

before whom...did walk] See xvii. 1, xxiv. 40.

fed me] Lit. "who shepherded me," Lat. *qui pascit me*. For the metaphor of the shepherd as applied to the God of Jacob, cf. xlix. 24; Ps. lxxvii. 20, lxxx. 1. The metaphor is more applicable to the leading of a multitude, or of a nation, than of an individual. But there is, as we know from Ps. xxiii. 1 and St John x. 11—16, a pathetic tenderness in the simile, even as applied to personal experience; and Jacob himself had from early times led the life of a shepherd.

The English rendering "fed" fails to reproduce the metaphor: see Isa. xl. 11, "feed like a shepherd," and compare John xxi. 15—17.

16. *the angel*] "The angel" is here indistinguishable from the

E and let my name be named on them, and the name of my fathers Abraham and Isaac; and let them grow into a
17 multitude in the midst of the earth. And when Joseph saw that his father laid his right hand upon the head of Ephraim, it displeased him: and he held up his father's hand, to remove it from Ephraim's head unto Manasseh's head.
18 And Joseph said unto his father, Not so, my father: for this is the firstborn; put thy right hand upon his head.
19 And his father refused, and said, I know *it*, my son, I know *it*: he also shall become a people, and he also shall be great: howbeit his younger brother shall be greater than he,
20 and his seed shall become [1]a multitude of nations. And

---

[1] Heb. *fulness*.

"God of Jacob." As in xvi. 7, 10, 13, it was the impersonation of the Divine Being as an Angel, whom Jacob had met and acknowledged as his God in the crises of his life, xxviii. 12—16, xxxi. 11, 13, 24, xxxii. 1, 24—31. The reference here is to the manifestation at Peniel (xxxii. 30, where see note).

hath redeemed me] "To redeem" is to play the kinsman's part, Lev. xxv. 48, 49; Ruth iii. 13, iv. 6. Jacob acknowledges that the manifestations of the Angel had been the fulfilment of a Divine goodness of purpose towards him. The idea of "redemption," the deliverance by the *Goêl*, or kinsman-Redeemer, is a favourite one in the religious teaching of the O.T., e.g. Ps. ciii. 4. Cf. Isa. xliv. 22, 23, xlix. 7, and lxiii. 9. Here the deliverance is from calamity, as in 2 Sam. iv. 9; 1 Kings i. 29. It is different from the more common word for "redeem," *pâdah* = "deliver," "ransom," e.g. in Ps. xxv. 22.

16. *let my name be named on them*] This is the formula of adoption according to E, corresponding to that in *v*. 5 according to P. The meaning seems to be, "let my name be given to them," in other words, "let them be counted as the children of Israel."

grow into a multitude] For the fulfilment of the blessing, see the numbers of the tribes, Ephraim and Manasseh, in Num. i. 33, 35, xxvi. 34, 37. Compare Deut. xxxiii. 17, "they are the ten thousands of Ephraim, and they are the thousands of Manasseh."

19. *his younger...greater*] The preference given to the younger reminds us of the blessing of Jacob himself. Cf. xxv. 23, xxvii. 29, 40. See also the story of Perez and Zerah in xxxviii. 29, 30. For the superiority of Ephraim over Manasseh, the history of Israel affords the fullest testimony. Cf. Num. i. 33, 35, ii. 19, 21.

a multitude] Lit. *fulness*, as Isai. xxxi. 4, "a multitude (lit. fulness) of shepherds." To become "the fulness of the nations" is to be as full of population as all the nations of the world; a strong hyperbole.

GENESIS XLVIII. 20—22

he blessed them that day, saying, ¹In thee shall Israel bless, saying, God make thee as Ephraim and as Manasseh: and he set Ephraim before Manasseh. And Israel said unto Joseph, Behold, I die: but God shall be with you, and bring you again unto the land of your fathers. Moreover I have given to thee one ²portion above thy brethren, which I took out of the hand of the Amorite with my sword and with my bow.

¹ Or, *By*
² Or, *mountain slope* Heb. *shechem*, shoulder.

20. *In*] Better, as marg., *By*. The meaning is that the blessing upon Ephraim and Manasseh shall be quoted as a formula for the invocation of Divine favour. Compare the blessing in Ruth iv. 11, 12.

bless] The versions, LXX, Vulg., and Syriac, give the passive "shall be blessed."

21. *bring you again*] Jacob predicts the restoration of his descendants to Canaan. This was the Divine promise. Cf. xv. 16, xlvi. 4, l. 24.

22. *portion*] Heb. *shechem*, "shoulder," i.e. *mountain slope*. This unusual expression (not elsewhere used in O.T.) for a "ridge," "saddle," or "shoulder," of a hill, is here employed as a play upon the proper name "Shechem." LXX σίκιμα ἐξαίρετον; Lat. *unam partem*. The allusion may no longer be clear; but it evidently refers to the city of Shechem, and has some bearing upon its subsequent position as a principal city in the tribe of Ephraim, and as the site of Joseph's burial-place.

above thy brethren] As if the distribution of other portions had already been made.

which I took...Amorite] This allusion to a conquest of Shechem by Jacob has nothing to correspond with it in the earlier narrative. In xxxiii. 19 Jacob purchases a parcel of ground at Shechem. In ch. xxxiv. his sons massacre the Shechemites; but on that occasion Jacob condemns their action (cf. xxxiv. 30), and departs to dwell elsewhere. Probably we have here some quite distinct tradition of a conquest of Shechem by Jacob, which is connected with a feat of arms. In Josh. xxiv. 32 it is combined with the purchase of ground in xxxiii. 19. The survival of that tradition appears in St John iv. 5.

with my sword and with my bow] In order to avoid the appearance of warlike activity on the part of the peaceful patriarchs, Targ. Onkelos renders "with my prayer and entreaty." We may compare the strange paraphrase of Jerome, "dabo tibi Sicimam quam emi in fortitudine mea, hoc est, in pecunia quam multo labore et sudore quaesivi" (*Quaest.* ed. Lagarde, p. 66). For Abraham as a warrior, see chap. xiv.

PJ 49 And Jacob called unto his sons, | and said: Gather yourselves together, that I may tell you that which shall befall you in the latter days.

2 Assemble yourselves, and hear, ye sons of Jacob;
And hearken unto Israel your father.

3 Reuben, thou art my firstborn, my might, and the ¹beginning of my strength;

¹ Or, *firstfruits*

Ch. XLIX. The Blessing of Jacob. The Death of Jacob.

The chapter falls into two divisions:
  1—27 (J). The blessing of Jacob, pronounced upon his twelve sons; derived, probably, from a very early source previous to J and E, and incorporated in J's narrative.
  28—33 (P). The death of Jacob.

1—27. The Blessing of Jacob.

1. *And Jacob called*] It is possible that this first clause may be from P, and is continued in the last clause of *v.* 28. Notice that the name "Israel," used eight times in the course of the previous 15 verses (xlviii. 8—22), here makes way for "Jacob."

in the latter days] Lit. "in the after part of days," denoting the period which is present to the vision of the Prophet. Cf. Num. xxiv. 14, "I will advertise thee what this people shall do to thy people *in the latter days*"; Isai. ii. 2; Mic. iv. 1. See Deut. iv. 30, xxxi. 29; Jer. xxiii. 20; Hos. iii. 5; Dan. ii. 28, x. 14. Cf. Heb. i. 2, "at the end of these days"; 1 Pet. i. 20, "at the end of the times"; 2 Esdr. ii. 34, "at the end of the world."

2. *Assemble yourselves*] This verse forms a kind of introduction to the main subject of the song.

and hear] The occurrence of the same Hebrew word for "hear" in the first clause, and for "hearken" in the second, is metrically a violation of the parallelism of Hebrew poetry. In English it is not apparent, as our rendering "hearken" avoids the repetition. Either "and hear" is a gloss, or another Hebrew word stood for "hearken." Cf. Deut. xxxii. 1; Isa. i. 10.

Jacob...Israel] The use of these proper names concurrently is frequent in Israelite poetry. Here it is evidence of the somewhat formal poetical prelude to the main song. Cf. Ps. cv. 23. The names emphasize the national character of the oracle, which is put into the mouth of the patriarch, and has reference to the fortunes of the twelve tribes.

3. *Reuben*] Reuben's early pre-eminence is forfeited. The tribe's loss of power is here ascribed to the curse of Jacob for an act of incest (see xxxv. 22; 1 Chron. v. 1). The territory of the tribe of Reuben

The excellency of dignity, and the excellency of power. J
¹Unstable as water, ²thou shalt not have the excellency; 4
Because thou wentest up to thy father's bed:
Then defiledst thou it: he went up to my couch.
Simeon and Levi are brethren; 5

¹ Or, *Bubbling over*   ² Or, *have not thou*

lay on the east side of the Dead Sea. In Biblical history, the Reubenites are practically unknown, except for one successful campaign against the Hagarenes (1 Chron. v. 8—10). In the Song of Deborah (Jud. v. 16), Reuben is denounced for apathy.

beginning] Better, as R.V. marg., *firstfruits*. The firstborn was expected to inherit the full strength of the parent. Cf. Deut. xxi. 17; Ps. lxxviii. 51, cv. 36. The versions follow a different text. LXX ἀρχὴ τέκνων μου; Lat. *principium doloris mei*; Aquila κεφάλαιον λύπης μου; Symmachus ἀρχὴ ὀδύνης.

The excellency] This word in Early English had the meaning of "superiority," owing to its derivation from "excel." But this has now been lost sight of.

Vulg. *major in donis, major in imperio*; Targ. Onk. paraphrases "for thee it was provided to receive three portions, the right of first-born, the priesthood, and the kingdom."

LXX must here follow a different text, σκληρὸς φέρεσθαι καὶ σκληρὸς αὐθάδης.

4. *Unstable*] The metaphor from water, *bubbling over*, is intended to express wanton or reckless vehemence. Reuben is as water without restraint pouring down in a foaming torrent. This is the thought of the renderings of LXX ἐξύβρισας; Lat. *effusus es*.

thou shalt not have] Read as R.V. marg. the imperative of de-nunciation, *have not thou*. Observe the recurrence of the note of "excelling." LXX μὴ ἐκζέσῃς.

he went up] Notice the change from the second to the third person, as if the speaker had turned away in loathing (LXX, however, ἀνέβης) from Reuben. In the Song of Moses (Deut. xxxiii. 6) the denunciation of Reuben is brief and stern, but unexplained; "let Reuben live, and not die; yet let his men be few."

It is a possible conjecture that the legend (cf. xxxv. 22) concerning Reuben embodied a cause of ancient Israelite prejudice against the Reubenites. Conceivably some marriage custom, like that of the heir receiving the concubines of his deceased father, may have been abandoned by the rest of Israel and been maintained by Reuben. (See Robertson Smith, *Kinship and Marriage*, p. 109, n. 2).

Another conjecture is that Reuben, in some treacherous way, en-croached upon the rights of the Bilhah clans, and in an isolated position wasted his strength in fierce and futile conflict with the neighbouring nomads.

5. *Simeon and Levi*] These two brothers were associated in the

428 GENESIS XLIX. 5—7

J
  Weapons of violence are their ¹swords.
6 O my soul, come not thou into their ²council;
  Unto their assembly, my glory, be not thou united;
  For in their anger they slew ³a man,
  And in their selfwill they houghed ⁴an ox.
7 Cursed be their anger, for it was fierce;
  And their wrath, for it was cruel:

¹ Or, *compacts*   ² Or, *secret*
³ Or, *men*   ⁴ Or, *oxen*

massacre of the Shechemites, to which reference is possibly here made in language of indignation. (See ch. xxxiv. 25, 30.)

swords] The Hebrew word (*m'khêrâh*) occurs only here. Its similarity in sound to the Greek μάχαιρα, "a sword," has suggested the English rendering. If it be rightly derived from a root meaning "to dig," possibly the traditional rendering denoting "a weapon" is correct. The R.V. marg., *compacts*, gives another conjecture. Driver (Add. xl.) says the word "must come from *karar*, prob. to *turn round*; hence Dillm. suggests a *curved knife*, or *sabre*." The obscurity accounts for the following variant renderings: LXX συνετέλεσαν ἀδικίαν ἐξ αἱρέσεως αὐτῶν; Lat. *vasa iniquitatis bellantia*; Targ. Onkelos, "mighty men in the land they dwelled in, they did a mighty deed"; Spurrell, "weapons of violence are their shepherds' staves"; Gunkel, "deceit and violence are their pitfalls."

6. *council*] or, as R.V. marg., *secret*. The word means either a secret confederacy, or its secret purpose. The parallelism of the clauses rather favours the former rendering.

The true spirit of Israel will have nothing to do with the savage policy hatched in the secret conclaves of these two tribes.

my glory] The word "glory" is used to denote the "soul," or the "spirit," as man's most glorious possession. Cf. Ps. xvi. 9, "my heart is glad and my glory rejoiceth"; Ps. xxx. 12, lvii. 8, cviii. 2. The LXX, reading the same Hebrew consonants with different vowels, translates "my liver" = "my affections," and, instead of "united," renders a slightly different text "contend," μὴ ἐρίσαι τὰ ἥπατά μου.

a man] or, as R.V. marg., *men*.

houghed] i.e. "mutilated," by cutting the sinews of the leg. Cf. Josh. xi. 6, 9; 2 Sam. viii. 4. LXX gives an exact rendering ἐνευροκόπησαν. The Old English "hox" is the form found in Shakespeare: *Wint. Tale*, I. 2, "thou art a coward, Which *hoxes* honesty behind."

an ox] or, as R.V. marg., *oxen*: so A.V. Instead of the Heb. *shor*, another reading, *shur*, "a wall," is followed by Lat. *suffoderunt murum*, and by Targ. Onk., Syr. Pesh., Symmachus, and Jerome; probably on account of the apparent contradiction in xxxiv. 28, 29, where the sheep and oxen are not mutilated, but carried off as booty.

7. In the curse here pronounced upon Simeon and Levi, no mention

> I will divide them in Jacob,
> And scatter them in Israel.
>
> Judah, thee shall thy brethren praise: 8
> Thy hand shall be on the neck of thine enemies;
> Thy father's sons shall bow down before thee.
>
> Judah is a lion's whelp; 9
> From the prey, my son, thou art gone up:
> He stooped down, he couched as a lion,

is made of the Levitical priesthood. Nevertheless, the patriarch's curse is evidently assumed to have produced its effect upon the two tribes. One (Levi) was scattered up and down Palestine without territorial possession; and the other (Simeon) occupied territory in a limited area, enclosed within the tribe of Judah. Cf. Josh. xix. 1—9; 1 Chron. iv. 24—39. In the Song of Moses, Simeon is not even mentioned. Levi, on the other hand, is blessed, as the tribe of the priesthood, Deut. xxxiii. 8—11.

in Jacob...Israel] See note on *v*. 2.

8—12. Judah is the recipient of a special blessing, which is distributed as follows: (1) he is the object of national eulogy, *v*. 8; (2) he is strong as a lion, and has won success, *v*. 9; (3) to him belong the monarchy and the ideal king, *v*. 10; (4) his territory is blessed with fertility, *vv*. 11 and 12.

8. *praise*] The word contains a play on the name Judah, which cannot be reproduced in a translation. See note on xxix. 35.

The transition from the sombre oracles concerning the previous three tribes to the outburst of the eulogy upon Judah is very marked.

Thy hand...neck] i.e. as Judah pursues the fleeing foe, he shall grasp them by the neck (cf. Job xvi. 12). The point of this clause lies in the geographical position of the tribe of Judah. Their territory was beset on the west and south-west by the Philistines, and on the south and south-east by the Edomites and the Amalekites. The Philistines and the Edomites were the bitterest and most persistent of Israel's foes. But they were within reach; and in their flight and retreat they are overtaken and smitten down by the victorious tribe.

bow down before thee] A reference to the Davidic monarchy which united the tribes of Israel.

9. *a lion's whelp*] For the comparison of Judah with a lion, which through this verse became its historic symbol, cf. 2 Esdras xii. 31, 32; Rev. v. 5. The metaphor of a lion is applied to Gad (Deut. xxxiii. 20) and to Dan (Deut. xxxiii. 22). For its use in poetical description, cf. Num. xxiii. 24, xxiv. 9; Micah v. 8; 1 Macc. iii. 4.

gone up] The lion, having seized and devoured its prey, returns to its fastness in the hills, secure and inaccessible.

stooped down...couched] A description of the movements of a lion (cf. Num. xxiv. 9) stalking its prey, running swiftly and secretly, and

J And as a lioness; who shall rouse him up?
10 The sceptre shall not depart from Judah,
   Nor ¹the ruler's staff from between his feet,
   ²Until Shiloh come;

¹ Or, *a lawgiver* ² Or, *Till he come to Shiloh, having the obedience of the peoples* Or, as read by the Sept., *Until that which is his shall come &c.* Another ancient rendering is, *Till he come whose it is &c.*

gathering itself for a final spring. The verb describes the habitual swiftness and force in the movements of the tribe.

10. *The sceptre*] Lit. "rod." Either a king's sceptre, or a general's baton. LXX ἄρχων = "ruler"; Lat. *sceptrum*. The rendering of the LXX, which gives a personal explanation, is unsupported by any evidence.

the ruler's staff] R.V. marg., as A.V., *a lawgiver*. The same word is found in Num. xxi. 18 ("the sceptre," marg. "the lawgiver") and Ps. lx. 7, "Judah is my sceptre" (marg. "lawgiver"). LXX ἡγούμενος = "leader"; Lat. *dux*; Syr. Pesh. "an interpreter"; Targ. Jerus. "scribe." The parallelism of the clauses makes it almost certain, that we have in this clause "the lawgiver's staff" corresponding to "the ruler's sceptre" in the previous clause.

Whether the "sceptre" and the "staff" are the insignia of national monarchy or tribal government, has been much debated. The picture of a person bearing these emblems is most suitable to the Oriental conception of a king.

from between his feet] The literal explanation is the simplest and the most picturesque. The lawgiver seated on his throne holds the wand emblematical of his office between his feet. Another explanation, illustrated by Deut. xxviii. 57, makes the expression refer to the descendants of Judah. So LXX ἐκ τῶν μηρῶν αὐτοῦ; Lat. *de femore ejus*.

Until Shiloh come] These are among the most difficult and controverted words in the book. The alternative renderings in the R.V. text and marg. represent the different lines of interpretation which have been followed. (1) "Until Shiloh come." This rendering was not known until A.D. 1534, when it was first suggested by Sebastian Münster, possibly on the strength of a Talmudic tradition. There is no allusion elsewhere in the O.T. to "Shiloh" either as a personal name, or as a Messianic title. Except for this passage, the use of "Shiloh" as indicating a person would be devoid of meaning to the Hebrew reader. True, the song is full of obscurities. But the improbability of this late interpretation is so great, that it may be dismissed from consideration. (2) "Till he come to Shiloh," i.e. "till he, Judah, comes to Shiloh." Shiloh was the resting-place of the Ark, in the centre of the tribe of Ephraim, e.g. 1 Sam. i. 24. It was destroyed by the Philistines, and its sanctuary desolated; see Jer. vii.

> And unto him shall the obedience of the peoples be.
> Binding his foal unto the vine,
> And his ass's colt unto the choice vine;
> He hath washed his garments in wine,
> And his vesture in the blood of grapes:

12—15. The theory, that the prediction in this verse received its fulfilment in Josh. xviii. 1, 8—10, is difficult to comprehend. The Davidic monarchy began after the days of Shiloh. The reference to a place in the tribe of Ephraim is quite unsuitable in this context. (3) LXX ἕως ἂν ἔλθῃ τὰ ἀποκείμενα αὐτῷ, *until that which is his shall come*, and Old Latin *donec veniant quae reposita sunt ei*. This rendering gets rid of the difficulty of a proper name. It assumes that the disputed word represents a dialect form of Hebrew words meaning "that which to him." The sense may then be Messianic. The rule of Judah shall continue until "that which is reserved for him," i.e. the age of perfect prosperity, shall come to him. (4) "Till he comes whose it is" (so Syr. Pesh.). This is also supported by Targ. Onk., "Until Messiah comes, whose is the kingdom"; cf. Symmachus ᾧ ἀπόκειται = "he for whom it is reserved." This rendering may be illustrated from Ezek. xxi. 27, "Until he come whose right it is." This last seems the most probable interpretation. Like many other passages in the song, the clause is obscure and oracular. No proper name is given[1]. The objection, that in such early days the Messianic hope did not exist, is a *petitio principii*. If this rendering be correct, the Messianic hope is here indicated in its earliest and simplest form, although its primary application may be to the dynasty of David. Many scholars, in perplexity as to the right meaning of the words, are of opinion that there is some corruption of the original Hebrew text, and that the restoration of the true text cannot be expected. There have been many emendations proposed, e.g. *môsh'lôh*, "his ruler" (Giesebrecht). Lat. *qui mittendus est* follows another reading (?).

the obedience of the peoples] The domination over foreign nations was to be the sign of Judah's ideal sovereignty. LXX προσδοκία, Lat. *expectatio*, have missed the meaning.

11. *Binding...vine*] Judah is represented as having so fruitful a soil that the vines grew richly by the wayside. The vine stem which would usually be protected from animals is used by Judah for fastening up the animal on which he rides.

The "ass" is the universal beast of burden in the East for all classes. See Judg. v. 10, x. 4; 2 Sam. xvi. 1, 2; Zech. ix. 9.

washed] The same hyperbolical description is maintained in this and the following couplet. Grapes in the land of Judah are to be so plentiful that he will wash garments in their juice.

---

[1] The suggestion that "Shelah," Judah's third son (xxxviii. 5), is intended obscurely to indicate the future hope, is most improbable.

J 12 His eyes shall be red with wine,
And his teeth white with milk.

13 Zebulun shall dwell at the ¹haven of the sea:
And he shall be for an ¹haven of ships;
And his border shall be ²upon Zidon.

14 Issachar is a strong ass,
Couching down between the sheepfolds:

¹ Heb. beach.   ² Or, by

12. *His eyes*] It may be doubted whether our rendering "red" gives the right meaning. The passage is usually illustrated from Prov. xxiii. 29, "who hath redness of eyes?" But, surely, the poet would hardly eulogize Judah by attributing to his eyes the redness of continuous drinking! It will be better to assume that the writer meant "sparkling." The versions, LXX and Vulg., give another rendering, which is probably to be preferred, "his eyes are more sparkling than wine, and his teeth whiter than milk." In this case, the verse will symbolically describe the beauty of his personal appearance, rather than the productiveness of his territory.

13. *shall dwell*] For the play probably intended on one of the meanings of Zebulun, see note on xxx. 20.

haven] Rather, as R.V. marg., Heb. *beach* or *shore*. The same word is used to describe the beach washed by the sea (Josh. ix. 1), and the shore which is sought by the ships. Zebulun's territory evidently at one time included the coast line. In Josh. xix. 10—16 the tribe of Asher comes in between Zebulun and the Mediterranean. In Jud. v. 17 it is Asher who is abiding by "the haven of the sea." But, in Deut. xxxiii. 18, 19, Zebulun is joined with Issachar in sucking "the treasure of the seas and the hidden treasures of the sand."

upon] or, *by*. See note on xlviii. 7. Delitzsch understood the preposition to mean "towards." The versions, Sam., LXX, Vulg., Syr. Pesh., render "up to," "as far as," following a different reading ('*ad*, for '*al*). "Border," better "flank," or "further side."

Zidon] The famous Phoenician capital whose neighbourhood must have been a source of wealth to the nearest Israelite tribe. See note on x. 15.

14. *a strong ass*] Lit. "a bony ass," as Aquila ὄνος ὀστώδης; Lat. *asinus fortis*. Issachar is compared, not to the wild ass, high spirited and swift, but to the strong domestic beast of burden. The territory of Issachar included the southern part of Galilee and the Valley of Jezreel. Slightly different readings are represented by the Sam. *gêrim* (instead of *gerem*), i.e. "the ass of strangers," "bearing the burdens imposed by foreigners," "a tributary." The LXX τὸ καλὸν ἐπεθύμησεν = "he desired the beautiful," gives an entirely different turn to the sense.

between the sheepfolds] For this word, see Jud. v. 16, "why satest thou among the sheepfolds?," and Ps. lxviii. 13. Issachar is represented

GENESIS XLIX. 15, 16

And he saw [1]a resting place that it was good,   15 J
And the land that it was pleasant;
And he bowed his shoulder to bear,
And became a servant under taskwork.
    Dan shall judge his people,   16
As one of the tribes of Israel.

[1] Or, *rest*

as lying contentedly among his flocks, regardless of his brethren. Instead of "sheepfolds," the versions give "boundaries." Thus LXX ἀνὰ μέσον τῶν κλήρων = "between the lots"; Lat. *inter terminos*. Another proposed rendering is "dung-heaps" or "ash-heaps." Skinner conjectures "panniers," which would be more appropriate to the metaphor.

15. *a resting place*] Better, as R.V. marg., *rest*. "Rest," as opposed to the wandering life of nomads. Cf. Deut. xii. 9; Ps. xcv. 11.

pleasant] Vulg. *optima*. LXX πίων = "fat," possibly following a slightly different reading.

bowed his shoulder] Issachar was ready to kneel, and bear any heavy burden, for the sake of a quiet life in a fertile land.

a servant under taskwork] Cf. Josh. xvi. 10, "became servants to do taskwork." Issachar is reproached for being ready to undertake forced labour, and so to acknowledge the Canaanites as his overlords. The phrase is the regular one for becoming tributary; cf. Deut. xx. 11; Jud. i. 30; Isa. xxxi. 8. In all probability there is a play upon the name "Issachar" and its derivation in the sense of "a man of hire," *îsh* and *sâchar*; cf. xxx. 18. LXX, apparently seeking to mitigate the severity of the reproach, ἐγενήθη ἀνὴρ γεωργός = "became a labourer." Targ. Onk. "he will subdue the provinces of the peoples, destroy their inhabitants, and those who are left among them shall be servants unto him and bringers of tribute."

16. *Dan*] In this and the following verse we have two independent oracles concerning the tribe of Dan. (1) *v.* 16 deals with its position in Israel; (2) *v.* 17, with its attitude towards its foes.

judge] For the play on the name Dan, see xxx. 6. The word "judge" carries with it the sense of "pleading the cause of" and "helping." Cf. Jer. xxii. 16, "he judged the cause of the poor and needy." Targum of Onkelos understood a reference to Samson to be contained in the word "judge" (Judg. xiii.—xvi.).

his people] The people of his tribe; not the people of Israel generally. The tribe possessed independence, not supremacy.

As one of the tribes] Dan, though smaller than other tribes (cf. Josh. xix. 47, 48; Jud. i. 34, 35; xviii. 11), will not be inferior in position and power, within its own domains, to the other tribes. It seems probable that Dan, standing here after Zebulun and Issachar, represents only the small northern portion of the tribe. Cf. Jud. xviii. 1, 29.

J 17 Dan shall be a serpent in the way,
An ¹adder in the path,
That biteth the horse's heels,
So that his rider falleth backward.

18 I have waited for thy salvation, O Lord.

19 Gad, ²a troop ³shall press upon him:
But he shall press upon their heel.

20 ⁴Out of Asher his bread shall be fat,

¹ Or, *horned snake*   ² Heb. *gedud*, a marauding band.   ³ Heb. *gad*, to press.   ⁴ According to some ancient versions, *Asher, his bread &c.*

17. *shall be*] Rather, "let Dan become."

adder] or, *horned snake*. The horned snake, or κεράστης, is a small, dangerous, and venomous serpent. The simile is that of a small serpent disturbed, and suddenly with deadly fangs striking a horse from behind. Dan is dangerous to his foes by ambuscades, secret raids, and guerilla warfare; cf. Judg. xviii. 27. The mention of the horse and horseman indicates the more wealthy, warrior class of the enemy.

18. *I have waited*] This parenthetical ejaculation of prayer is thought by many scholars to be a gloss. But all authorities contain the verse. There is no obvious reason for inserting such a gloss at this particular point. (*a*) The ejaculation has by some been thought to shew that, at the time of the composition of this song, Dan was engaged in a long conflict with his foes, and the issue was still doubtful. (*b*) By others it has been explained as a cry of physical weakness by Jacob. It is very possible that the verse is intended to mark the point at which the song is half finished; but it is not necessarily, therefore, an interpolation.

thy salvation] i.e. deliverance wrought by Thee. For the thought of the prayer, cf. Ps. xxv. 5, xxvii. 14, cxix. 81, 166, 174; Isa. xxv. 9.

19. *a troop*] Heb. *gedud*, "a marauding band."

shall press] Heb. *gad*, to press. These words furnish a double play upon the name of the tribe Gad. *Gad...gedud yegudennu...yagud 'ekēbām* = "Gad, raiders shall raid him, but he shall raid their rear (lit. heel)." LXX πειρατήριον πειρατεύσει αὐτόν· αὐτὸς δὲ πειρατεύσει αὐτῷ κατὰ πόδας. This warlike and independent tribe seem to have been successful in repelling the bands of marauders, Ammonites, Moabites, and Aramaeans, who threatened the eastern border of Gilead. Cf. Jud. x. 7—12; 1 Chron. v. 18—22. Later on, however, the tribe seems to have succumbed. Jer. xlix. 1.

upon their heel] i.e. he will repulse and pursue them closely, and hang upon their rear.

20. *Out of Asher*] Almost certainly the marg. gives the right reading, *Asher, his bread &c.* The preposition rendered "out of"

> And he shall yield royal dainties.
> Naphtali is a hind let loose: 21
> He giveth goodly words.
> Joseph is [1]a fruitful bough, 22

1 Heb. *the son of a fruitful* tree.

is the letter *m*, which is superfluous here, but is required for the pronoun "their," in the words "their heel" at the close of the preceding verse. The name of the tribe will then open the verse as a kind of *nominativus pendens*, i.e. "As for Asher, his bread, &c." Cf. Deut. xxxii. 4, "The Rock, his work is perfect." So the versions, LXX, Lat., Syr.

bread shall be fat] Cf. Deut. xxxiii. 24, "Blessed be Asher...and let him dip his foot in oil."

yield royal dainties] The fertility of Asher's land will supply the wants of the kings of Tyre and Sidon. In Judg. v. 17 Asher rests on the sea coast. There is a play intended on the name of the tribe Asher, and the Hebrew word for "happy" (cf. xxx. 13), referring to the "happiness" of its fertility. Cf. Arabia Felix.

21. *Naphtali*] It is doubtful whether the simile applied to this tribe is that of "a hind" or "a terebinth tree." The comparisons in the song are for the most part taken from animals, e.g. the lion of Judah, the ass of Issachar, the serpent of Dan, the wolf of Benjamin. On the other hand, Joseph is compared to a vine.

a hind let loose] Lat. *cervus emissus*, an image of swiftness and grace in movement, associated with the thought of open and extensive country. For the idea of freedom expressed in "let loose," cf. Job xxxix. 5, "who hath sent out the wild ass free, or who hath loosed the bands of the wild ass?"

He giveth goodly words] A sudden change in the description, referring apparently to the tribe's reputation for eloquence; but the transition to such a subject seems scarcely probable. The rendering "goodly lambs" is suggested, but the translation "lambs" cannot be supported from the O.T., and gives, at the best, a very prosaic sense.

By a different vocalization an entirely different turn is given to the verse. "Naphtali is a tall shoot of terebinth, one that putteth forth goodly topmost branches." "Topmost branches" would then be metaphorical for "leaders" like Barak (Judg. iv. 5), but this rendering is very questionable; though it may explain LXX Νεφθαλεὶ στέλεχος ἀνειμένον ἐπιδιδοὺς ἐν τῷ γεννήματι κάλλος.

22. *Joseph*] The blessing of Joseph extends over *vv.* 22—26. Its subject matter falls into four divisions: (1) Joseph's prosperity under the simile of a vine (*v.* 22); (2) his contest with bitter foes (*v.* 23); (3) the invocation for aid from the God of Jacob (*vv.* 24, 25[a]); (4) the blessing from heaven, sea, and earth, pronounced upon Joseph (25[b], 26).

The elaborate eulogy pronounced on Joseph reflects the predominance

GENESIS XLIX. 22—24

J   A fruitful bough by a fountain;
          His ¹branches run over the wall.
23   The archers have sorely grieved him,
          And shot at him, and persecuted him:
24   But his bow abode in strength,

¹ Heb. *daughters*.

of Ephraim and Manasseh among the tribes of Israel, in virtue both of their central position in Canaan and of their power and wealth. The impression we derive from this description of Joseph is that of 1 Chron. v. 1, 2, "his (Reuben's) birthright was given unto the sons of Joseph... Judah prevailed above his brethren, and of him came the prince; but the birthright was Joseph's."

The text in the following verses has in several places suffered from corruption. The meaning is often very obscure, and no certainty of translation is to be looked for.

A fruitful bough] Heb. *the son of a fruitful tree*. The word "fruitful" in the original contains a play upon the name "Ephraim"; see note on xli. 52; cf. Josh. xvii. 14 ff. "Bough" is probably that of a vine. Cf. Ps. cxxviii. 3; Isa. xxxii. 12, "the fruitful vine." The simile is that of a young fruitful tree, planted near a spring, whose tendrils trail down over the wall.

by a fountain] i.e. in a fertile spot. In Canaan, wherever there was moisture, there was fertility.

The versions give an entirely different rendering.

run over the wall] The branches and tendrils of the strongly growing vine throw themselves over the wall, which has been built for their protection and training. They hang down in graceful luxuriance, a pretty metaphor from nature.

23. *The archers*] The simile changes. Joseph's prosperity has attracted the attacks of jealous foes. He is beset by the archers. This verse used to be explained as containing a reference to the persecution of Joseph by his brethren. But, apart from the question whether such a topic would here be suitably introduced, the allusions throughout the song are tribal, and not personal. The enemies of Ephraim and Manasseh may have been the Canaanites (Josh. xvii. 16), or the Midianites (Jud. vi.), or the nomad Arab tribes (1 Chron. v. 19). Or, if Joseph be identified with the tribes of the northern kingdom, and a later date be possible, the reference may be to the attacks delivered from the north by the Syrians, e.g. 1 Kings xx. "Grieved" = Old English for "harassed by hostile action."

24. *his bow abode in strength*] Cf. Job xxix. 20, "my bow is renewed in my hand." Joseph was able by God's help to resist. He overthrew his assailants. His strength was unshaken. LXX καὶ συνετρίβη μετὰ κράτους τὰ τόξα αὐτῶν = "and their bows with might were broken," follows a variety of reading.

> And the arms of his hands were made ¹strong,
> By the hands of the Mighty One of Jacob,
> (²From thence is the shepherd, the stone of Israel,)
> Even by the God of thy father, who shall help thee,   25

J

¹ Or, *active* ² Or, *From thence, from the shepherd* Or, as otherwise read, *By the name of the shepherd*

the arms of his hands] Probably meaning "the strength of his hands," which held and drew the bow.

were made strong] Better, as R.V. marg., *active*. The idea is nimbleness rather than strength.

By the hands] More lit. "from the hands." The source of the deliverance of Joseph, rather than the instrumentality of it, is expressed.

the Mighty One of Jacob] A Divine title, *âbîr* = "the Strong One," which appears elsewhere, Ps. cxxxii. 2, 5; Isa. i. 24, xlix. 26, lx. 16.

From thence] No rendering gives an entirely satisfactory sense. The text is probably corrupt. (1) According to the R.V. text, the clause is a parenthesis; "from thence" means "from the Mighty One of Jacob." "The shepherd," and "the stone of Israel," are appellations of Joseph. (2) According to the R.V. marg. "from thence from the shepherd," the clause continues the thought of the previous words, and expands "by the hands of." "The shepherd," and "the stone of Israel," are then Divine titles, in apposition to "the Mighty One of Jacob." (3) "By the name of the shepherd." This is a variety of the last rendering, with the reading *shêm* = "name," instead of *shâm* = "there."

The rendering (1) seems to be improbable, since it applies to Joseph the titles of "shepherd" and "stone of Israel," which certainly we should not expect to see applied to the son of Jacob. Between (2) and (3) it is difficult to make a selection, and the text cannot be relied on. But the word *mis-shâm* (= "from thence") seems more prosaic and less impressive than *mis-shêm* (= "from the Name"); and on the whole (3) seems more probable. For the "Shepherd," as a Divine title, cf. xlviii. 15; Ps. xxiii. 1, lxxx. 1.

Prof. G. F. Moore conjectures "By the arms of the stone of Israel," which would supply a parallel to "By the hands of the Mighty One of Jacob," and would expand the thought of the previous clause ("the arms of his hands"). *Encycl. Bibl.* III. 2977, n. 14.

the stone of Israel] If used as a Divine title, the "stone" (*'eben*) is here substituted for the more usual "rock" (*ṣûr*). Cf. Deut. xxxii. 4; 1 Sam. ii. 2; 2 Sam. xxii. 2; Ps. xviii. 2, 31. It is very possible that the allusion may be to the stone (*'eben*) of Bethel (xxviii. 18), or even to the great stone of Shechem (Jos. xxiv. 26, 27), the sanctuary of the tribe and the burial-place of Joseph.

"The Name of the Shepherd of the Stone of Israel" is thus a possible, though a cumbrous title with a reference to the stone of Bethel (xxxi. 13).

25. *Even by the God of thy father*] This verse continues the subject

J

And by the Almighty, who shall bless thee,
With blessings of heaven above,
Blessings of the deep that coucheth beneath,
Blessings of the breasts, and of the womb.

26 The blessings of thy father
Have prevailed above [1] the blessings of my progenitors

---

[1] According to some ancient authorities, *the blessings of the ancient mountains, the desire* (or, *desirable things*) *of the everlasting hills*.

---

of the two previous clauses, the Divine source of help for Joseph. For "the God of thy father," cf. xxxi. 5, l. 17.

And by the Almighty] Lit. "and with (*êth*='with the help of,' see iv. 2) the Almighty." The Hebrew, however, for "by" is most probably due to an error in the transcription of one letter (*êth* for *êl*). Read "and God Almighty." "*Êl*" was read by LXX, Sam., and Syr. Pesh.

"Almighty," i.e. Shaddai, see note on xvii. 1, xxxv. 11.

who shall bless thee] Rather a prayer, = "and may he bless thee." The next words should be compared with the blessing of Joseph in Deut. xxxiii. 13, "blessed of the LORD be his land; for the precious things of heaven, for the dew, and for the deep that coucheth beneath, &c." Here three types of blessing are invoked, those of the sky, the waters, and the human race, as three sources of fruitfulness.

blessings of] Either continuing the sentence, "May he bless thee with blessings," or beginning a new sentence, "May there be to thee, &c."

heaven above] The blessings of rain and dew. Cf. xxvii. 28.

the deep that coucheth beneath] Cf. the identical words of Deut. quoted above. For "the deep that coucheth beneath" (Lat. *abyssi iacentis deorsum*), see note on i. 9. "The deep," Heb. *tehôm* (i. 2), the great subterranean reservoir of water from which, according to Israelite ideas, the springs, fountains, and rivers welled up, and gave fertility to the soil.

the breasts] For the converse of this blessing, see Hos. ix. 14. The fruitfulness of a family was deemed a proof of Divine blessing.

26. *The blessings of thy father*] i.e. the blessings invoked by Jacob, thy father, when fulfilled in the greatness and influence of the people that shall spring from thee.

Have prevailed above] i.e. have ranked higher, are of greater excellence, than the material blessings of the fair country assigned to Joseph.

the blessings of my progenitors] Better, as R.V. marg., according to some ancient authorities, *the blessings of the ancient mountains, the desire* (or *desirable things*) *of the everlasting hills*. The rendering of the R.V. text in this difficult passage depends upon a practically impossible translation, i.e. "my progenitors" (Lat. *patrum ejus*), where the Hebrew literally means "my conceivers." It is better to

Unto the utmost bound of the everlasting hills:
They shall be on the head of Joseph,
And on the crown of the head of him ¹that was separate
from his brethren.
Benjamin is a wolf that ravineth:

¹ Or, *that is prince among*

follow the rendering in the marg., which requires a very slight change in the text. Instead of "my progenitors," read "the mountains of"; and, instead of "unto," read "eternity." This has the support of LXX, ὀρέων μονίμων; and it is supported also by the parallelism of the clauses. "The everlasting hills," in the next clause, will then balance "the ancient mountains" of this clause; as is the case in the blessing of Joseph, Deut. xxxiii. 15, "and for the chief things of the ancient mountains, and for the precious things of the everlasting hills." Cf. also Hab. iii. 6.

Unto the utmost bound] A doubtful rendering, required by the translation of the previous word, '*ad*="unto." According to the better reading, this word, '*ad*, should be rendered "eternity." Instead of "bound," we should render "desire" (which is the ordinary translation of the Heb. word), in the sense of "the desirable things," thus balancing the words "the blessings" in the previous clause.

They shall be] Better, "may they be," a prayer, as in the very similar passage in Deut. xxxiii. 16, with which these two clauses should be compared; "let the blessing come upon the head of Joseph, and upon the crown of the head of him that was separate from his brethren."

on the head...crown] Words implying a benediction, with the hand resting upon the head.

that was separate from] In Hebrew the *Nazir* is "one set apart," or "consecrated," by a vow, or otherwise, for high duties. Thus Samson was a "Nazirite," separated to be the champion of his people's liberties. Perhaps, but not probably, the mention of "the crown of the head" has an allusion to the Naziritic vow. Lat. *Nazaraei inter fratres suos*. Some connect *nazir* with *nezer*="a diadem," and render by "prince"; so R.V. marg. *that is prince among* (cf. LXX ὧν ἡγήσατο ἀδελφῶν), a possible allusion to the Ephraimite kingdom.

27. *Benjamin*] The fierce and warlike qualities of Benjamin, here described under the simile of a wolf, appear in Judg. v. 14, xix., xx. 21—25.

a wolf that ravineth] i.e. a wolf that seizes and rends his prey. Cf. Ezek. xxii. 27. Elsewhere in the O.T. the simile of a wolf is used only in a bad sense.

To "ravin" is Old English for "to prey with rapacity": cf. Shakespeare, *Cymb.*, I. 6, "The cloy'd will,...ravening first The lamb."

J
> In the morning he shall devour the prey,
> And at even he shall divide the spoil.

28 All these are the twelve tribes of Israel: and this is it
P that their father spake unto them | and blessed them; every
29 one according to his blessing he blessed them. And he
charged them, and said unto them, I am to be gathered
unto my people: bury me with my fathers in the cave that
30 is in the field of Ephron the Hittite, in the cave that is in
the field of Machpelah, which is before Mamre, in the land
of Canaan, which Abraham bought with the field from
31 Ephron the Hittite for a possession of a buryingplace: there
they buried Abraham and Sarah his wife; there they buried
32 Isaac and Rebekah his wife; and there I buried Leah: the
field and the cave that is therein, which was purchased from
33 the children of Heth. And when Jacob made an end of
charging his sons, he gathered up his feet into the bed, and
yielded up the ghost, and was gathered unto his people.

at even] Compare the expression "evening wolves," i.e. those which "at even" are most terrible and savage; Jer. v. 6; Hab. i. 8; Zeph. iii. 3. It is noteworthy that there is no certain reference to the reign of Saul as conferring distinction upon the tribe. But "shall divide the spoil" recalls the description of the Benjamite monarch, who "clothed the daughters of Israel in scarlet, and put ornaments of gold on their apparel" (2 Sam. i. 24).

28—33. Verse 28^a is the editorial conclusion to Jacob's blessing. *Vv.* 28^b—33 resume from *v.* 1^a, and record Jacob's death according to P.

28. *All these are the twelve tribes of Israel*] In the enumeration of the twelve tribes, in this song, Joseph is reckoned as one; in Deut. xxxiii., Simeon is omitted, and Ephraim and Manasseh take the place of Joseph. In Num. ii., Simeon is retained; Levi is omitted; Ephraim and Manasseh replace Joseph.

29. *gathered unto my people*] See note on xxv. 8 (P).

bury me] Cf. xlvii. 29—31 (J).

30. *the cave*, &c.] See xxiii. 16—18.

31. *there they buried*, &c.] See, for the burial of Sarah, xxiii. 19; of Abraham, xxv. 9, 10; of Isaac, xxxv. 29. The burials of Rebekah and Leah are not recorded.

33. *gathered up his feet*] Jacob now lay down; he had been sitting. See xlviii. 2 (E).

yielded up the ghost] Cf. xxv. 8 (P). The phrase is an English one. The Hebrew has simply "and expired." LXX ἐξέλιπε; Lat. *obiit*.

unto his people] See note on xxv. 8. The present passage shews

And Joseph fell upon his father's face, and wept upon 50 him, and kissed him. And Joseph commanded his servants 2 the physicians to embalm his father: and the physicians embalmed Israel. And forty days were fulfilled for him; 3 for so are fulfilled the days of embalming: and the Egyptians wept for him threescore and ten days.

And when the days of weeping for him were past, Joseph 4 spake unto the house of Pharaoh, saying, If now I have

clearly that "to be gathered unto one's people" is not burial in the ancestral place of sepulture (for the account of Jacob's burial seventy days later comes in the next chapter); but the soul's departure to the gathering-place of the deceased members of the family, i.e. *Sheôl*.

CH. L. (J, P, E.)

1—13. The mourning for Jacob and his burial.
14—21. Joseph and his brethren.
22—26. Joseph's death.

With the exception of *vv.* 12, 13, which are from P, this chapter contains the narrative of J and E. *Vv.* 1—11, and 14 (J) follow upon xlvii. 29—31 (Joseph being the prominent person); *vv.* 12, 13 (P) follow upon xlix. 29—33 (Jacob's sons collectively acting together); *vv.* 15—26, from E.

1. *And Joseph*] For Joseph's strong affection for his father, cf. xlv. 3, xlvi. 29.

2. *the physicians*] LXX οἱ ἐνταφιασταί; Lat. *medici*. By this expression we should probably understand "the guild of embalmers" (ταριχευταί, Herod. II. 86), a large and influential class in Egypt, who, with an expert knowledge of the body and of drugs, practised embalming almost as a fine art.

to embalm] Embalming was carried out to great perfection in Egypt. It was supposed that the soul, or *ka*, would return to inhabit the body. The mummy was the body ready for occupation. See Budge, *The Mummy* (1893).

3. *forty days*] Herod. II. 86 mentions 70 days, and Diodorus (I. 72) mentions 72 days as the time required for the process of embalming.

threescore and ten days] It is here specially mentioned in honour of Jacob, that the Egyptian nation mourned him for 70 days.

The period of mourning for Aaron and for Moses was 30 days (Num. xx. 29; Deut. xxxiv. 8). In later historic times the period of mourning for the dead was seven days (cf. 1 Sam. xxxi. 13; Job ii. 13; Ecclus. xxii. 12; Judith xvi. 24).

4. *unto the house of Pharaoh*] Joseph does not speak to Pharaoh personally, but to the court officials. As a mourner, he is unclean and would not be permitted to approach Pharaoh.

GENESIS L. 4—9

J found grace in your eyes, speak, I pray you, in the ears of
5 Pharaoh, saying, My father made me swear, saying, Lo, I
die: in my grave which I ¹have digged for me in the land
of Canaan, there shalt thou bury me. Now therefore let me
go up, I pray thee, and bury my father, and I will come
6 again. And Pharaoh said, Go up, and bury thy father,
7 according as he made thee swear. And Joseph went up to
bury his father: and with him went up all the servants of
Pharaoh, the elders of his house, and all the elders of the
8 land of Egypt, and all the house of Joseph, and his brethren,
and his father's house: only their little ones, and their flocks,
9 and their herds, they left in the land of Goshen. And there
went up with him both chariots and horsemen: and it was a

¹ Or, *bought*

5. *have digged*] or, *bought*. Both meanings are possible. LXX and Lat. favour "digged." Syr. Pesh. and Targ. Onk. favour "bought." The word in the Hebrew appears for "to buy" in Deut. ii. 6, and for "to dig" in Gen. xxvi. 25. It has been objected that, in the case of Jacob, neither meaning is appropriate to Machpelah (xlvii. 30), and that this passage refers to some other grave, e.g. that of Rachel (see note on xlviii. 7). But it is unreasonable to press this objection. Joseph's report of Jacob's words might well imply, that either Jacob or his forefathers had thus provided a burial-place. Moreover, he might possibly have hewn out a burial-place for himself in the rock of the cave. On the whole, "digged" seems more appropriate than "bought." The language is not explicit enough to throw light upon the possibly independent legend of a burial-place, where Rachel was buried (xlviii. 7). The tradition of a "purchase" of ground by Jacob is connected with Shechem (see xxxiii. 19; cf. Acts vii. 16), but not with a burial-place.

I will come again] Joseph is anxious to assure his master, Pharaoh, that he is not going treacherously to leave the Egyptian service.

7. *all the servants of Pharaoh*] The very ample description of the Egyptian attendants at the funeral of Jacob is evidently intended (cf. *v.* 3) to impress the Israelite reader with the thought that Jacob, the father of their people, had been buried with royal honours by the Egyptians. "Went up," cf. *vv.* 5, 6, 9. See xii. 6, xlii. 38, "go down" to Egypt.

9. *chariots and horsemen*] A strange element in a burial procession, and one which it would be hard to illustrate from the records of Egypt. Possibly, we are intended to consider them in the light of a guard for the protection of the procession travelling into Canaan.

On "chariots" and "horses" in Egypt, see xlvii. 17.

GENESIS L. 9—13

very great company. And they came to the threshing-floor 10 J
of Atad, which is beyond Jordan, and there they lamented
with a very great and sore lamentation: and he made a
mourning for his father seven days. And when the inhabit- 11
ants of the land, the Canaanites, saw the mourning in the
floor of Atad, they said, This is a grievous ¹mourning to the
Egyptians: wherefore the name of it was called Abel-
mizraim, which is beyond Jordan. | And his sons did unto 12 P
him according as he commanded them: for his sons carried 13

¹ Heb. *ebel*.

10. *the threshing-floor of Atad*] *Goren-ha-Atad*, a threshing-floor of "the thornbush," or "bramble" (Judg. ix. 14, 15). The place is nowhere else referred to.

beyond Jordan] By this expression is generally meant "on the east side of Jordan." If so, we must suppose that for some reason the burial company leaving Egypt travelled round the southern extremity of the Dead Sea. But this appears extremely improbable. The traditional burial-place of Jacob was at Machpelah. No Israelite could suppose that, even for the purpose of doing honour to Jacob, it would have been necessary to go round into trans-Jordanic territory. Winckler conjectures that the original reading was "on the other side of the river" (viz. "the River of Egypt," or '*El-Arîsh*, the boundary of Egypt and Canaan, cf. Num. xxxiv. 5; 1 Kings viii. 65), and that this was carelessly altered by the error of a scribe to the more familiar phrase "beyond Jordan." Whether this conjecture be accepted or not, the present text is unintelligible. It is very unlikely that any legend would have arisen connecting Jacob's burial-place with the eastern bank of the Jordan.

seven days] See note on *v*. 3. "Lamentation" (cf. xxiii. 2), i.e. the Oriental custom of "wailing" for the dead.

11. *Abel-mizraim*] This was popularly rendered "Egypt mourns," cf. LXX πένθος Αἰγύπτου; Lat. *planctus Egypti*, but its true meaning would be "the meadow of Egypt, or "of the Egyptians." In all probability, this name recalled some incident in the days of the Egyptian sovereignty over Palestine; and, when that had faded out of recollection, the name was popularly connected with the traditional mourning of the Egyptians for Jacob, on account of the similarity in sound between '*âbêl*= "field" and '*êbel*= "mourning." For other place-names beginning with Abel, cf. Abel-cheramim (Judg. xi. 33), Abel of Beth-maacah (2 Sam. xx. 15).

beyond Jordan] The place was identified by Jerome with "Beth-Hoglah," the modern *Ain Haglah*, south of Jericho. But the identification rests on no proof. The mention of the trans-Jordanic region presents the same difficulty here as in *v*. 10.

12, 13 (P). *And his sons*] The account of Jacob's burial, according

444 GENESIS L. 13—19

P   him into the land of Canaan, and buried him in the cave of the field of Machpelah, which Abraham bought with the field, for a possession of a buryingplace, of Ephron the Hittite, before Mamre.

J 14   And Joseph returned into Egypt, he, and his brethren, and all that went up with him to bury his father, after he
E 15 had buried his father. | And when Joseph's brethren saw that their father was dead, they said, It may be that Joseph will hate us, and will fully requite us all the evil which we
16 did unto him. And they sent a message unto Joseph, saying, Thy father did command before he died, saying,
17 So shall ye say unto Joseph, Forgive, I pray thee now, the transgression of thy brethren, and their sin, for that they did unto thee evil: and now, we pray thee, forgive the transgression of the servants of the God of thy father. And
18 Joseph wept when they spake unto him. And his brethren also went and fell down before his face; and they said,
19 Behold, we be thy servants. And Joseph said unto them,

to P, is given in these two verses. They are quite distinct from the preceding narrative, and follow directly upon xlix. 33. Observe that, in P, no Egyptians, but only Jacob's sons, carried him to the burying-place of Machpelah.

14—21. JOSEPH AND HIS BRETHREN.

15. *It may be...hate us*] Lit. "supposing Joseph were to hate us." LXX μή ποτε μνησικακήσῃ ἡμῖν Ἰωσήφ. Joseph's brethren fear lest, Jacob being dead, Joseph will no longer restrain his desire for revenge.

requite] Their conscience cannot leave them alone. Cf. their fear in xlii. 28, xliv. 16, xlv. 3.

16. *sent a message*] Lit. "charged" (Lat. *mandaverunt*), the same word as in xlix. 29, in the sense of "commissioned," persons to go to Joseph. LXX παρεγένοντο and Syr. Pesh. follow a different reading, "they drew near unto." Perhaps the original text contained the delegation of two or three brothers to go unto Joseph.

Thy father did command] An unrecorded dying charge.

17. *the God of thy father*] Cf. xlix. 26. They call themselves "the servants of the God of thy father," as if it constituted a stronger appeal than "the sons of thy father." They and Joseph serve one God.

Joseph wept] Cf. note on xlv. 1.

18. *his brethren also went*] These words agree with the sending of a message (*v.* 16), but hardly with the words of *v.* 17, "when they spake unto him."

fell down] A final reminiscence of Joseph's dreams, xxxvii. 7, 10.

Fear not: for am I in the place of God? And as for you, ye meant evil against me; but God meant it for good, to bring to pass, as it is this day, to save much people alive. Now therefore fear ye not: I will nourish you, and your little ones. And he comforted them, and spake ¹kindly unto them.

And Joseph dwelt in Egypt, he, and his father's house: and Joseph lived an hundred and ten years. And Joseph saw Ephraim's children of the third generation: the children also of Machir the son of Manasseh were born upon

¹ Heb. *to their heart.*

19. *am I in the place of God*] i.e. "am I the person to punish for wrongdoing? God alone knows the hearts." LXX mistakes the meaning, τοῦ γὰρ θεοῦ ἐγώ εἰμι = "for do I belong to God"; Lat. *num Dei possumus resistere voluntati.* Symmachus is correct, μὴ γὰρ ἀντὶ θεοῦ εἰμι ἐγώ. Cf. the occurrence of the same words in xxx. 2 and 2 Kings v. 7.

20. *meant*] i.e. devised or purposed. Joseph here, as in xlv. 7, points to the Divine purpose behind the petty schemes and wrong-doings of men.

as it is this day] According to P's chronology (xlvii. 28) the famine was long past. Here, however, in E's narrative, it is evidently still raging; as is shewn also, in the next verse, by the words "I will nourish you." The E narrative, therefore, must have recorded Jacob's death as occurring not long after his arrival in Egypt.

21. *nourish you*] Cf. xlv. 11, xlvii. 12.

kindly] Heb. *to their heart.* So LXX: cf. xxxiv. 3. The Latin gives the sense *blande ac leniter*.

22—26. DEATH OF JOSEPH.

22. *an hundred and ten years*] See Josh. xxiv. 29. Attention has been called to passages in Egyptian records, in which this age is described as the ideal span of life.

23. *of the third generation*] Ephraim's children "of the third generation" might mean his great-grandchildren; cf. Ex. xxxiv. 7. But in Ex. xx. 5, Num. xiv. 18, the third generation are the grand-children, the grandparents being reckoned as the first. If this way of reckoning be here followed, Ephraim represents the first generation, and his grandchildren the third. This is also favoured by the next clause, which mentions Manasseh's *grand*-children. Joseph, therefore, lived to see his great-grandchildren. On this token of blessing, see Ps. cxxviii. 6; Prov. xiii. 22, xvii. 6.

Machir] The name of one of the leading branches of the tribe of Manasseh; cf. Num. xxxii. 39; Deut. iii. 15; Josh. xiii. 31, xvii. 1;

GENESIS L. 23—26

E 24 Joseph's knees. And Joseph said unto his brethren, I die: but God will surely visit you, and bring you up out of this land unto the land which he sware to Abraham, to Isaac, 25 and to Jacob. And Joseph took an oath of the children of Israel, saying, God will surely visit you, and ye shall carry 26 up my bones from hence. So Joseph died, being an hundred and ten years old: and they embalmed him, and he was put in a coffin in Egypt.

1 Chron. vii. 14. From these passages it appears that the family of Machir occupied Gilead: while in Judg. v. 14 Machir takes rank with the tribes of Israel.

upon Joseph's knees] A phrase denoting that Joseph, as head of the family, acknowledged and adopted the children. See note on xxx. 3, and cf. Job iii. 12, Isai. lxvi. 12, and Homer, *Od*. XIX. 401.

24. *will surely visit you*] The visitation of God in a gracious and merciful sense, as in Ex. iii. 16, iv. 31; cf. Luke i. 68, "He hath visited and redeemed his people." "Bring you up," cf. xv. 16, xxviii. 15, xlvi. 4.

which he sware, &c.] Cf. xxii. 16, xxvi. 3, xxviii. 13.

Observe how the patriarchal narrative is closing with the promise of redemption, and with the renewal of the oath to Abraham, Isaac, and Jacob.

25. *Joseph took an oath*] The fulfilment of this oath and Joseph's burial at Shechem, in the land of Ephraim, are duly recorded in Ex. xiii. 19; Josh. xxiv. 32. For these dying words of Joseph, cf. Heb. xi. 22, "by faith Joseph, when his end was nigh, made mention of the departure of the children of Israel; and gave commandment concerning his bones." As Jacob, his father, had done, Joseph forewarns his kindred that the day of the Exodus would come.

26. *they embalmed him*] See *v.* 2. Lat. *conditus aromatibus*.

in a coffin] LXX ἐν τῇ σορῷ; Lat. *in loculo*. The Hebrew word *ârôn* is the same as that rendered "ark" (of the covenant). Here it undoubtedly means the mummy case, or sarcophagus, in which the body, having been embalmed, was deposited. Joseph's mummy was carried up out of Egypt by Moses, Ex. xiii. 19.

The peaceful death of Joseph and the preparation of his body for removal to Canaan close the Narrative of the Patriarchs.

APPENDIX

A

Babylonian Myths of Creation

(from Gordon's *Early Traditions of Genesis*, pp. 325 ff.)

1. The Version of Damascius (*De primis Principiis*, ed. Kopp, cap. 125).

"Of the barbarians, the Babylonians have chosen to disregard the idea of one principial origin of all things, and assume two, Tauthe and Apason, representing Apason as the husband of Tauthe, and calling her 'the mother of the gods.' Of these two, they relate, was born an only son, Moysis, whom I conceive to be the intelligible universe, which is composed of two principal elements. Of the same parents arose another generation, Lache and Lachos; then of the same a third generation, Kissare and Asoros, of whom were born three sons, Anos, Illinos, and Aos. The son of Aos and Dauke was Belos, who, they say, was the creator of the world."

2. The Version of Berosus (Müller, *Frag. Hist. Græc.* II. 497).

"There was a time, he says, when all was darkness and water, in which existed living creatures of monstrous kinds and wondrous shapes: for men were brought to birth with two wings, and some even with four wings and two faces, some also with one body but two heads, a man's and a woman's, and double secret parts, male and female. There were other men with goats' legs and horns, others with horses' feet, and others with the hinder parts of a horse, but the fore parts those of a man, like centaurs. Bulls also were generated with the heads of men, and dogs with four bodies ending in fishes' tails, and horses and men with dogs' heads; other living creatures with horses' heads and bodies but fishes' tails, and others with the shapes of all sorts of animals. Besides these were fishes and creeping things, and snakes and other wonderful creatures with strangely intermingled shapes, representations of which are found in the temple of Bel. And over all these reigned a woman named Omorka, i.e. in Chaldean Thamte[1], which translated into Greek is θάλασσα (the sea), in numerical value equivalent to σελήνη.

"When all things were in this condition, Bel came and split the woman through the middle, and of the one half made earth and of the other heaven, and destroyed the creatures that were within her.

---

[1] Read Θαμτε for Θαλατθ (Robertson Smith).

"And this, he says, is an allegorical account of the processes of Nature. For when all was a watery mass, and living creatures of shapes like these were brought to life in it, Bel, as they call Zeus, split the darkness in two, and thus divided earth and heaven from one another, and put the Cosmos in order. The living creatures, being unable to endure the power of the light, were destroyed.

"Then Bel, seeing the ground waste, though capable of bearing fruit[1], bade one of the gods cut off his head[2], and then mix earth with the flowing blood, and so fashion men and animals that should be able to endure the air[3]. Bel also made the stars, and the sun and moon, and the five planets.

"This is the account which, according to Alexander Polyhistor, Berosus gives in his first book."

3. The Seven Tables of Creation (*KB.* vi. 3 ff.; King, *Seven Tables*, &c.).

i. 1. When above the heaven had not received its name[4],
   2. And the solid earth below was not yet called by name[4],
   3. While Apsu, the primordial, that begat them,
   4. And Chaos[5] Tiamat, that bare them all,
   5. Had their waters mingled together,
   6. When as yet no field was formed, nor marsh was to be seen[6],
   7. When none of the gods had yet come into being,
   8. And none bare a name[4], and no destinies (were fixed),
   9. Then were created the first gods in the midst (of heaven):
   10. Lachmu and Lachamu came into being...
   11. Ages increased...
   12. Then Anshar and Kishar were created...
   13. Long days passed, then came forth...
   14. Anu their son...[7].

Lines 22 ff. describe the hatred of Apsu and Mummu, his son, against the "new gods," and their plot to destroy them; the fragmentary ll. 60 ff. seem to shew how the plot was circumvented by the cunning god Ea, who laid waste Apsu and took Mummu captive (97 ff.). Tiamat resolves on vengeance.

Lines 109 ff. describe the battle-array of monstrous beings that followed her to the fight, the deadly serpents, vipers and dragons, "the hurricanes, and raging hounds, and scorpion-men, and mighty

---

[1] But Gunkel proposes ἀκαρποφόρον, i.e. "seeing the ground waste and barren," which yields a better sense.
[2] i.e. Bel's own head (cf. *Seven Tables*, vi. 5).
[3] We have omitted from the body of the text the sentence which has long been recognized as an intrusion, and was originally a marginal gloss or variant, viz. "This god cut off his head, and the other gods mixed the flowing blood with earth, and fashioned men. Therefore men are possessed of wisdom and Divine understanding."
[4] i.e. "was not yet in existence."
[5] The meaning of Mummu here is much disputed. Usually it is understood as "Chaos." Jeremias, however, omits the word, as falsely inserted from ll. 30 ff. (*Das A.T.* &c. p. 52, n. 3).
[6] Others, however, render "reed" and "thicket of reeds."
[7] The Version of Damascius helps to supply the missing links: Bel and Ea.

Marduk and Tiâmat.

From Mr P. S. Handcock's *Latest Light on Bible Lands*, by kind permission of the S.P.C.K.

APPENDIX

tempests, and fish-men and rams," spawned and armed by Ummu-Chubur[1], "who formed all things," with Kiagu as leader. Tablet ii. relates how Ea learned of their array and reported to Anshar, his father, who sent first Anu and then Ea to appease Tiamat's wrath. They are afraid, and return to Anshar. Then Marduk volunteers to go and subdue the enemy. Tablet iii. describes the gathering of the great gods in council. The first part of Tablet iv. describes the elevation of Marduk to supremacy over the gods, his army for the battle, his going forth to meet Tiamat, and the fight, ending in Marduk's complete victory.

95. The lord spread out his net, and enclosed her,
96. And the tempest that was behind him he let loose;
97. As Tiamat opened her mouth to its full extent,
98. He drove in the tempest, ere she could close her lips.
99. With terrible winds he filled her belly.
100. Her courage was taken from her, and her mouth she opened wide.
101. He seized the spear, and burst her belly,
102. Severed her inward parts, and pierced her heart.
103. He overpowered her, and cut off her life,
104. Threw down her corpse, and stood upon it.

The next lines describe the conquest of Tiamat's army. This accomplished,

128. He returned to Tiamat, whom he had conquered.
129. The lord stood upon Tiamat's body,
130. And with his merciless club he crushed her skull.
131. He cut through the channels of her blood,
132. And he made the north wind to bear it away to secret places.
133. And his fathers saw it, they rejoiced and were glad;
134. Gifts and presents they brought him.
135. Then the lord rested, and eagerly examined her corpse.
136. Then with cunning art he divided her trunk (?).
137. He split her like a flat (?) fish into two halves.
138. One half of her he set up, and made a covering for the heavens;
139. He drove in a bolt, and stationed a watch,
140. And bade them not allow her waters to issue forth.
141. Then he established the heavens as counterpart to the world below,
142. And set it over against the Ocean, the dwelling of Nudimmud.
143. Then the lord measured the shape of the Ocean[2],
144. And as a palace after its model he built Esharra,
145. The great palace Esharra, which he built as a dome of heaven,

---
[1] Ummu-Chabur (perhaps the *Omorka* of Berosus): another title for **Tiamat**.
[2] i.e. "of the palace of the Deep," the dwelling of Nudimmud (Ea).

146. And made Anu, Bel, and Ea take up their several abodes[1].
v. 1. He prepared also the stations for the great gods;
2. The Stars, their images, he set up as signs.
3. He arranged the year, and divided off its quarters.
4. For the twelve months he assigned each three stars.
5. After he had (distinguished) the days of the year by their images,
6. He founded the station of Nibir (Jupiter) to determine their bounds,
7. That none might fail, or go astray.
. . . .
11. In the midst he fixed the zenith of heaven.
12. He made the moon-god to shine forth, setting the night under him.
13. He marked him out as a body of light, to determine the days.
14. Every month, perpetually, he crowned him with a royal crown, and said:
15. "At the begininng of the month, when thou shinest on the land,
16. Shine out with thy horns, determining six days;
17. And on the seventh day halve the crown."
18. On the fourteenth day...
 (The broken lines evidently explain the connexion of the moon-god with Shamash, the sun-god.)
vi. 1. When Marduk heard the speech of the gods,
2. His heart moved him, and he devised a cunning plan.
3. He opened his mouth, and spake to Ea,
4. Even that which he had devised in his heart, he imparted to him:
5. My blood will I take, and bone will I (fashion),
6. I will make man, that...
7. I will create man, who shall inhabit the earth,
8. That the service of the gods may be established, and their shrines (be built).
9. But I will alter the ways of the gods, and I will change the paths.
10. Together shall they be oppressed, and unto evil shall they....

Another Myth of Creation (*KB*, vi. 39 ff.).

1. A holy house, a house of the gods, on holy ground had not yet been made;
2. No reed had yet sprung up, nor tree been fashioned;
3. No brick had been laid, nor brick foundation built;
4. No house erected, nor city built;

---

[1] We have here followed Jeremias' rendering (*Das A.T.* &c. p. 55), which preserves the usual significance of Esharra (the palace of heaven), while securing a satisfactory relation of the three spheres.

APPENDIX

5. No city had been made, nor population placed therein;
6. Nippur not made, nor Ekur (the sanctuary of Bel) built,
7. Uruk not made, nor Eana (the sanctuary of Anu) built;
8. The deep (Apsu) not made, nor Eridu (the sanctuary of Ea) built.
9. For a holy house, the house of the gods, the site had not been made.
10. The lands were altogether sea,
11. The soil of the islands was overflowing waters.
12. Then was Eridu made, and Esagila built,
13. Esagila, where in mid-deep the god Lugal-dul-azaga (Marduk) dwelleth,
[14. Babel was made, and Esagil was finished.]
15. And the gods, the Anunnaki, were created all together.
16. The holy city, the dwelling that delights their heart, they proclaimed on high.
17. Then Marduk laid a tress-work of reeds on the surface of the waters,
18. He made a heap of earth, and poured it out beside the reeds.
19. In order that the gods might dwell with pleasure in their house,
20. He built man:
21. With him the goddess Aruru built mankind.
22. The beasts of the field also, and the living creatures in the field he built.
23. The Tigris and the Euphrates he built, and set them in their place.
24. Their names he named in goodly style.
25. The grass, the rush of the marsh, the reed and the shrubs he built,
26. The green herb of the field he built,
27. The lands, the marshes, and the swamps,
28. The wild cow and her young, the wild calf, the ewe and her young, the lamb of the fold,
29. Plantations and forests;
30. The he-goat and the mountain-goat...
31. Marduk, the lord, filled up a dam on the margin of the sea,
32. He...a swamp, and made a bed of marsh.
33. He made...to come.
34. He built (reeds and) trees,
35. He built...on the place.
36. (He laid brick), and built a structure of brick;
37. (Houses he made), cities he built.
38. (Cities he made), a population he placed in them.
39. (Nippur he made), Ekur he built.
40. (Uruk he made), Eana he built.

APPENDIX B

A Legend of Lamech

A good illustration of Jewish *Haggadah*, i.e. Tradition which employs legend or story to interpret or supplement passages of Scripture, is furnished by the narrative explanatory of Gen. iv. 23.

"I have slain a man to my wounding, a young man to my hurt."

"Nothing is said in explanation of this; we are not told whom Lamech had killed. So a story was made up [by Jewish Tradition] —no-one knows when—which gives this explanation; Lamech was blind, and he used to amuse himself by shooting birds and beasts with a bow and arrow. When he went out shooting, he used to take with him his young nephew Tubal; and Tubal used to spy the game for him and guide his hands that he might aim his arrow right. One day, when they were out together, Tubal saw, as he thought, a beast moving in the thicket, and he told Lamech, and made aim at it, and Lamech's arrow smote the beast and killed it. But when Tubal ran to see what kind of beast it was, he found that it was not a wild beast at all. It was his ancestor Cain. For after Cain had killed Abel, and God had pronounced the curse upon him, he wandered about the earth, never able to remain in one place; and a great horn grew out of his head, and his body was covered with hair; so that Tubal seeing him in the distance among the branches of the trees and the brushwood, was deceived, and mistook him for a beast of chase. But when Tubal saw what had happened, he was terrified, and ran back to Lamech, crying out, 'You have slain our forefather Cain!' And Lamech also was struck with horror, and raised his hands and smote them together with a mighty blow. And in so doing he struck the head of Tubal with his full strength, and Tubal fell down dead. Then Lamech returned to his house, and spoke to his wives the words that are written in the Book of Genesis. This story, a very ancient one, as I said, was invented by the Jews to explain the difficult passage in Genesis; and the early Christian writers learnt it from the Jews, and it passed into many commentaries which were written in later time: so that you may still see representations of it carved in stone in churches both in England and elsewhere. In England it may be seen on the inside of the stone roof of Norwich Cathedral, and on the west front of Wells Cathedral; but you have to look carefully before you can find it."

(*Old Testament Legends* (1913), pp. xii—xiv.
By M. R. James, Litt. D.)

APPENDIX C

THE DUPLICATE ACCOUNT OF THE FLOOD

(From Chapman's *Introduction to the Pentateuch*, pp. 74—81)

Gen. vi. 5—ix. 17

Comparing vi. 5—8 and 9—13, it will be noticed that the *same facts* are recorded in both passages. There is a favourable notice about Noah, a statement that God saw the wickedness that was in the earth, and announced His determination to destroy all that was therein. This *repetition* of facts is made in very different language. Though in the English versions the word *destroy* occurs in both passages two different Hebrew words are used. The one in vi. 7, vii. 4, 23 may be rendered literally as in R.V. marg. *blot out*. The other in vi. 13, 17, ix. 11, 15 is a common word for *destroy*.

In *vv*. 5—8 it is twice stated that the Lord repented that He had made man; but in *vv*. 9—13 this is not recorded.

In *vv*. 5—8 *Jehovah*, in *vv*. 9—13 *Elohim* is the name employed to denote the Divine Being. Verse 9 commences with the words "These are the generations of Noah"...this is one of P's phrases, as also are "perfect," "Noah walked with God" (cf. Gen. v. 24; and xvii. 1, "walk before me and be thou perfect"). The same phenomena which have been observed in the accounts of Creation again present themselves in these verses which serve as an introduction to the story of the Flood. Two versions of the same facts follow one after the other; the first, by using *Jehovah*[1], and representing the Lord as "repenting," recalls the characteristics of Gen. ii. 4—25; the second uses *God*, and expressions found in ch. v. and ch. xvii. (parts of the document which has been denoted by the symbol P). The first has *blot out*, the second *destroy*. The words "from the face of the *ground*," following "blot out" in vi. 7, vii. 4 R.V., are like ii. 5, 6, 7, 9, 19 (J). P uses generally "earth." These two versions are clearly from different sources.

Do these two sources furnish material for the rest of the narrative? Further examination will shew that they do, and will also supply additional tests for distinguishing between the two sources. It will assist the reader if the results are given in a tabular form.

In the central column C a summary of the narrative is given; those facts and statements which are *repeated* are in ordinary type, those which are recorded *only once* are in *italics*. The columns on either side contain the Scripture references; the outer columns to the right and left contain selections from the passages—words and expressions which serve to distinguish between the sources. The portions in italics are placed on that side of C which is nearer to the column to which they are assigned. Italics in the *outer* columns indicate words and expressions characteristic of J and P respectively.

---

[1] Note that "GOD" in vi. 5 (A.V.) should be "the LORD" (*Jehovah*) as in R.V.

J		C		P
Noah found grace in the eyes of the Lord.	vi. 8	Noah approved by God.	vi. 9	These are the *generations of Noah*. Noah was a righteous man and *perfect* in his generations: Noah *walked with God*.
	vi. 5	God saw the wickedness of man,		
	vi. 6	*and repented that he had made man*,		
And the Lord said, *I will blot out man...from off the face of the ground*.	vi. 7	and said, I will destroy all flesh.	vi. 11, 12	
[command to make an ark.]		*Noah is commanded to make an ark*,	vi. 13	And God said unto Noah, The end of all flesh is come before me;... I will *destroy them*...
			vi. 14—16	
For *yet seven days* and *I will cause it to rain...will I blot out from off the face of the ground*.	vii. 4	for a flood will come and destroy everything,	vi. 17	I bring a flood of waters upon the earth to *destroy* all flesh...and everything that is in the earth shall *expire*.
Come thou and *all thy house*. Of every *clean* beast shalt take to thee *seven and seven*... and of beasts that are *not clean two*...each and his mate.	vii. 1—3	but Noah and his family must come into the ark with pairs of all living creatures.	vi. 18—21	I will *establish my covenant* with thee, thou and thy sons...; of *every living thing two of every sort*...they shall be *made and female*.
And Noah did according to all that the Lord commanded him.	vii. 5	Noah was obedient.	vi. 22	Thus did Noah, according to all that God commanded him, so did he.
		Noah's age at the flood.	vii. 6	600 years.
After the seven days...the waters of the flood were upon the earth.	vii. 10	The flood came.	vii. 11	In the 6ooth yr. and mo. 17th d., on the same day were all the fountains of the great deep broken up and the windows of heaven were opened.
Of *clean* beasts, and of **beasts** that are *not clean*...	(vii. 7—9)	Noah went into the ark with his family, and all living creatures.	vii. 13—16	In *the selfsame day* entered Noah ...*two and two* of all flesh as God **had** commanded him.
...and the Lord shut him in.	vii. 16			

And the waters increased, and bare up the ark...	vii. 17	The waters increase and bear up the ark.	vii. 18–20	And the waters prevailed and were increased greatly upon the earth; and the ark went upon the face of the waters. *Fifteen cubits upward* did the waters prevail, and all flesh *expired*.
All...that was in the dry land *died*, and every living thing *was blotted out* which was *upon the face of the ground*...and they *were blotted out*...	vii. 22, 23	And all flesh died.	vii. 21	
And the rain was upon the earth 40 days and 40 nights.	vii. 12	Duration of the flood.	vii. 24	And the waters prevailed upon the earth 150 days.
And the flood was 40 days upon the earth.	vii. 17			
The *rain* from heaven was restrained.	viii. 2	The flood abated.	viii. 1–3	And God *remembered* Noah...the fountains of the *deep* and the windows of heaven were stopped ...and after the end of 150 days the waters decreased.
			viii. 4	7th m. 17th day, the ark rested,
			viii. 5	10th m. 1st day, tops of the mountains were seen.
At the end of 40 days Noah opened the window...yet other seven days and again he sent forth the dove...and he stayed yet other seven days...	viii. 6–12	*Noah sends out the raven and the dove.*		
And Noah removed the covering of the ark and looked, and, behold, the *face of the ground* was dry.	viii. 13	The waters were **dried up**.	viii. 13	601st yr. 1st m. 1st day, the waters were dried up,
[departure from the ark.]			viii. 14	and in 2nd m. 27th day **was the** earth dry.
		At God's command Noah went forth from the ark.	viii. 15–19	
Noah builds an altar and offers sacrifice.	viii. 20			
		God blesses Noah	ix. 1–7	Be *fruitful* and *multiply* and *fill* the earth, as i. 28. I *establish my covenant*...neither shall all flesh be cut off...a flood to destroy *the earth*...the token of the covenant.
I will not curse *the ground...* neither will I again smite,	viii. 21, 22	and promises not to destroy all living things again.	ix. 8–17	

A glance at column C of the table is sufficient to shew the great preponderance of matter in ordinary type, i.e. of incidents which are *repeated* in these chapters. Nearly the whole of the narrative is duplicated. If the passages contained in each of the columns P and J be read consecutively, it will be seen that each of them furnishes an almost complete story. Where repetition is the rule and single record the exception (as column C shews), it will be necessary to examine the latter more closely, to see whether a reason can be given why only one account has been preserved.

Two Hebrew words occur in the narrative, which are both translated "die." In vii. 22 (J) the ordinary Heb. word is used; in vi. 17, vii. 21 a less common word (like "*expire*" in English), which outside the Hexateuch is found only in poetry, and in the Hexateuch is found only in P.

According to one account the flood is the result of prolonged rain (vii. 4; where note "blot out from off the face of the ground," R.V. [marg.]; vii. 12. Cf. "the rain from heaven was restrained," viii. 2). According to the other account waters from beneath, "the fountains of the great deep" ("deep" as in Gen. i. 2), join with those from above to produce the catastrophe (vii. 11; viii. 2).

A distinction is made between clean and unclean animals in vii. 2, 8. Seven pairs of the former but only one pair of the latter are to be taken. No such distinction is made in vi. 19, 20, vii. 15.

Two expressions are used to denote male and female: (1) *zākhār ūn^{e}ķēbhāh*, vi. 19, vii. 16, as in Gen. i. 27 (P). (2) *'īsh v^{e}ishtō* (lit. "a man and his wife[1]," here it might be rendered, "each and his mate"), vii. 2 (twice) (J).

From vii. 7 compared with vii. 10 it seems that Noah and his family came into the ark before the flood; in vii. 13 they entered "on the selfsame day."...Noah's family are described as "all thy house" in vii. 1: but in vi. 18, vii. 7, 13, viii. 15, 18 a more detailed description, "thou and thy sons and thy wife and thy sons' wives with thee," is given after the manner of P.

The indications of time are different in the two narratives. Seven days and 40 days are mentioned in vii. 4, 10, 12, 17, viii. 6, 10, 12.

A complete chronology is supplied as follows:

	Year	Month	Day
vii. 6	600th of Noah		
11		2	17
viii. 4		7	17
5		10	1
13	601st of Noah	1	1
14		2	27

According to this the complete duration was a lunar year and 10 days, i.e. a solar year, and the period of the waters prevailing

---

[1] In Hebrew, "man" and "woman" are used in the sense of "each"; of animals, and even of inanimate objects: see Gen. xv. 10; Zech. xi. 9.

APPENDIX

was 5 months, i.e. the 150 days of vii. 24 and viii. 3. This dating by the year, month and day is a characteristic of P (cf. Exod. xl. 17; Num. i. 1; ix. 1; x. 11; xxxiii. 3, 38). Other indications of his style are "in the selfsame day," vii. 13; "I will establish my covenant," vi. 18, ix. 9, 11; "the token of the covenant," ix. 12, 17.

The words and expressions which have been noted in the preceding paragraphs appear in the outer columns of the table in *italics*. The table may serve to remind the reader of the arguments, and help him to estimate their force....An account which is in form single indicates diversity of source in the same manner as the separate accounts of the Creation in the first two chapters of Genesis.

One more point remains to be considered: Does the narrative in its present form afford any evidence of the manner in which it has been put together?

The table shews that the portions which are found in J only are:
(1) The Lord repented that He had made man.
(2) The distinction between clean and unclean.
(3) The story of the raven and the dove.
(4) Noah's sacrifice.

The omission of (2) and (4) by P is in accord with his treatment of the whole patriarchal history. He abstains from recording any act of sacrifice or ceremonial distinction between clean and unclean before the establishment of a priesthood in the time of Moses.

The representation of God in P is less *anthropomorphic*...than those in other writers. This explains why the expression "the Lord *repented* that He had made man" finds no place in his narrative. It appears then that P omits *designedly*; and this accounts for his omission of (1), (2), and (4). As regards (3), P *may* have mentioned the sending forth of the raven and the dove; a compiler would not relate an incident like this in duplicate. The account of P supplies the framework of the whole narrative, and has been preserved almost, if not altogether, entire.

The portions found in P only are:
(1) The command to build the ark.
(2) The exact dates—year, month and day.
(3) The departure from the ark.
(4) The blessing of Noah.

Now (2) is quite in P's style; he alone gives the exact dates which are found in the Pentateuch. Also (4) is very similar to Gen. i. 28....
These are probably given by P only, but J's account is sufficiently complete and independent to justify the conjecture that some notices corresponding to (1) and (3) were originally contained in it. The probable position of these presumed original contents of J are indicated in the table in brackets.

Some parts of J have been expanded by a redactor (or editor) who incorporated phrases from P. The evidence in favour of this statement is most clearly furnished by vii. 7—9. Here we should expect to find J's version of the entry into the ark, parallel to P's account in vii. 13—

16. The distinction between clean and unclean points to J, but there is much in these verses that resembles P, e.g. "his sons and his wife and his sons' wives with him," vii. 7 (cf. vi. 18 and vii. 13), P's expression for "male and female" (cf. p. 78), "two and two" of all sorts, and "God" (vii. 9).

Other probable additions to the J narrative are "whom I have created" (vi. 7), "male and female," as in P (vii. 3). The preceding remarks render the following statement probable:

The material in J has been expanded by a redactor who has combined the sources. He shews affinity with P, and not with J.

APPENDIX D

(I) THE TEL EL-AMARNA TABLETS

In the year 1887, several hundred clay tablets, covered with cuneiform inscriptions, were discovered during excavations near the modern Tel el-Amarna, a place about 170 miles south of Cairo. It was the site of the new capital selected by Amenophis IV, when he abandoned Thebes and set up the worship of the Sun-god.

These tablets proved to consist of a mass of official correspondence received at the Egyptian court during the reigns of Amenophis III and his son Amenophis IV. The majority belong to the latter reign, and consist of letters addressed to the Egyptian king by foreign kings, vassal princes, and provincial governors. The importance of this correspondence can hardly be exaggerated. It throws unexpected light upon the condition of Western Asia during the two reigns of Amenophis III (1411—1375 B.C.) and Amenophis IV (1375—1358 B.C.)[1]. It includes interesting letters addressed by Burnaburiash, king of Babylonia, and by the king of Alashia (Cyprus) to Amenhotep IV. But, unquestionably, the most valuable part of the whole collection is represented by the letters and despatches sent by the vassal princes and the Egyptian provincial governors in Phoenicia and Palestine. Thus there are letters from Yapakhi, governor of Gezer; Widya, governor of Askelon; Abdi-Ḫiba, king of Jerusalem; Rib-Adda, governor of Byblos; and Abi-Milki, governor of Tyre. From Rib-Adda, who seems to have been a faithful official, no less than sixty-two letters are preserved. There are six from the king of Jerusalem.

The general tenour of these letters from governors in Palestine is the same. The Egyptian king is losing his control over Palestine and Phoenicia. His rule, for some reason, is no longer forcible and

---

[1] So Breasted: Petrie's dates are for Amenophis III, 1414—1383, and for Amenophis IV, 1383—1365. N.B. Amenophis is often transliterated as Amenhotep.

efficient. He is either indifferent, or he is not able to part with troops out of Egypt for the purpose of assisting the provinces. The Hittites are pressing from the North. A people, called by the king of Jerusalem the *Ḥabiri* and by others "robbers," are a formidable menace. The governors themselves are untrustworthy and are intriguing against one another. What with foreign foes and disloyal princes and a disaffected population, the prospect is evidently as unsatisfactory as possible. We are not surprised to learn that the Egyptian government not long afterwards lost the whole of its Phoenician and Palestinian provinces.

Abdi-Ḫiba, king of Jerusalem, seems to have maintained his loyalty as long as it was possible. The following passages illustrate his appeals for assistance, his protestations of fidelity, and the growing power of the enemy:

(*a*) "To the king, my lord, say also thus: It is Abdi-Ḫiba, thy servant. At the feet of my lord, the king, twice seven times, and thrice seven times I fall. What have I done against the king, my lord? They backbite—they slander me before the king, my lord, saying: Abdi-Ḫiba has fallen away from the king his lord."

(*b*) "Let the king take counsel with regard to his land—the land of the king, all of it, has revolted; it has set itself against me. Behold, (as for) the lands of Shêri (Seir), as far as Guti-Kirmil (Gath-Carmel), the governors have allied themselves, and there is hostility against me. Even though one be a seer, one wishes not to see the tears of the king, my lord; open enmity exists against me. As long as ships were in the midst of the sea, the power of the mighty took Nakhrina (Naharaim) and the land of Kashsi, but now the Ḥabiri have taken the cities of the king. There is not one governor for the king, my lord—all have rebelled."

(*c*) "The men of the city of Gazri, the men of the city of Gimti, and the men of the city of Kîlti have been captured. The land of the city of Rubute has revolted. The land of the king (belongs to) the Ḥabiri, and now, moreover, a city of the land of Jerusalem, the city Beth-Ninip—(this is) its name—has revolted to the people of Kîlti. Let the king...send hired soldiers.... And if there be no hired soldiers, the land of the king will go over to the men, the Ḥabiri. This deed (is the deed of) Suardatum (and) Milki-îli."

(*d*) "The Ḥabiri are capturing the fortresses of the king. Not a single governor remains among them to the king, my lord: all have perished. May the king, my lord, send help to his country. If no troops come this year, all the countries of the king, my lord, will be utterly destroyed."

Besides other political information which the Tel el-Amarna correspondence furnishes, we learn from it what from other sources could not have been expected:

(1) that Palestine, between 1420 and 1360 B.C., was an Egyptian province;

(2) that not only the kings of Babylonia, but the Egyptian

governors in Palestine, corresponded with the court of Egypt, using the Babylonian language and cuneiform writing;

(3) that the scribes, in order to avoid misunderstanding, often inserted Canaanite words to explain or interpret the Babylonian; and, that, as these Canaanite words are generally indistinguishable from later Hebrew words, we may infer that the Canaanite language, before the Exodus, was practically identical with the Hebrew;

(4) that Jerusalem (*Urusalim*) was the original name of that city, which was already an important place in the 14th century B.C. (The name "Jebus" was probably erroneously ascribed to it on account of its being occupied by the Jebusite tribe at the time of the Israelite invasion, cf. Jos. xv. 8, 63; xviii. 28; Judg. xix. 10; 1 Chron. xi. 4.)

On the Tel el-Amarna Tablets, see Driver's *Schweich Lectures*, Chap. 2; Professor Flinders Petrie's *Syria and Egypt from the Tell el-Amarna Letters* (1898); Pinches' *Old Testament*, pp. 249—300; Handcock's *Latest Light on Bible Lands* (1913); Jeremias' *O.T. in the light of the Ancient East*, 1. pp. 335 ff.

(II) The Ḥabiri

"There *may* be some connexion," says Driver, "between the 'Ḥabiri' and the 'Hebrews': the two cannot be identical, but the Hebrews may, for instance, have been a branch of them" (*Schweich Lectures*, p. 34, n. 2). "The names are certainly identical," says Jeremias. "It is, however, quite another question what relation the Ḥabiri of the Amarna letters bear to the Biblical 'Hebrews'" (*O.T. in the light of the Ancient East*, 1. p. 341).

The student may be pardoned, if he finds himself somewhat at a loss, when he reads these apparently conflicting statements by eminent authorities.

There are in reality two questions; and it is important they should be kept distinct. (*a*) The one is philological: are the words "Hebrew" and "Ḥabiri" identical? (*b*) The other is historical: are the Ḥabiri, mentioned in the Tel el-Amarna Tablets, to be identified with the Israelites who conquered Canaan?

(*a*) *Philological.* This side of the problem has been carefully discussed by scholars who arrive at very different conclusions. Thus we find Ed. Meyer asserting: "the name '*ibrim* cannot be reproduced in cuneiform in any other way" (der Name '*ibrim* kann in Keilschrift gar nicht anders wiedergegeben werden), *Die Israeliten u. ihre N.* p. 225. Skinner, referring to "the still disputed, but now widely accepted, theory that Ḥabiri in the T.A. letters is the cuneiform equivalent of the O.T. עִבְרִים ['*ibrim*]," contends that "The equation presents no philological difficulty: Ass. *ḫ* often represents a foreign ע; and *Ḥa-za-ḳi-ya-u* = יְחִזְקִיָּהוּ shows that Ass. *a* may become O.T. *i*" (p. 218).

APPENDIX 461

The opposite view is very carefully stated by Handcock in a passage which, for its clear and simple explanation, may here be quoted *in extenso*: "The crucial point is whether the initial guttural in the Hebrew word for 'Hebrew' can be equated with the 'Kh' in the Assyrian 'Khabiri.' *Ayin*, the guttural with which the word 'Hebrew' commences, has two distinct sounds, differentiated in Arabic writing, but not in Hebrew writing. Fortunately, the Septuagint, or Greek Version of the Old Testament, made by order of Ptolemy II, Philadelphus, king of Egypt from 287 B.C. or 286 to 246 B.C., generally preserves this distinction. Now the *ayin* in 'Hebrew' is represented in the Septuagint by a smooth breathing, which indicates that in this word it had a soft sound. It is perfectly true that the Hebrew *ayin* sometimes corresponds to the Assyrian *kh*, but in the cases cited by Schrader (*The Cuneiform Inscriptions and the O.T.* 1. p. 179, 2nd ed.) and Professor Clay (*Light on the O.T. from Babel*, pp. 265 ff.) the *ayin* (from a comparison with the Septuagint) probably had a hard, and not a soft, sound, as in the word 'Hebrew[1].'

"Probably the best example that can be cited in support of the theory that the Assyrian *kh* can correspond with a *soft* Hebrew *ayin* is afforded by the proper name Canaan, which, in Assyrian, is Kinnakhkhi. The *ayin* in the Hebrew word for Canaan would appear to be soft, as it is not represented in the Septuagint at all, only the vowel which accompanied it being represented in the Greek. The possibility of such an interchange may therefore be fairly argued, but not its probability, especially at the beginning of a word.

"But admitting the possibility of such an interchange, there is another consideration which renders it highly improbable in the present instance. As stated above, Sayce associates the *Khabiri-ki* of the Tell el-Amarna Letters with the Biblical Hebron. Unlike the word 'Hebrew,' the initial guttural of the Biblical word 'Hebron' is a *heth*, or hard 'h,' and the Assyrian equivalent for the Hebrew *heth* is 'kh.' It is therefore probable that the Biblical 'Hebron' and the Assyrian 'Khabiri' are *philologically* related. But the words 'Hebron' and 'Hebrew' are entirely distinct, and can under no conceivable circumstances be brought into relationship. It therefore follows that if we identify the 'Khabiri' with the 'Hebrews,' we must *ipso facto* entirely dissociate 'Khabiri' from 'Hebron.' In short, such an identification involves the rejection of a proposition which strictly conforms to the *ordinary* rules of philological transmutation in favour of one which is totally at variance with those rules, but at the same time it should be noted that though the *words* 'Khabiri' and 'Hebron' are *radically connected*, the identification of the *place* 'Khabiri-ki' with 'Hebron' is entirely hypothetical." (*The Latest Light on Bible Lands*, pp. 79—81.)

(*b*) Historical. "The historical objections vanish," says Skinner,

---

[1] The two cases cited are Gaza and Omri; in the former the initial Hebrew *ayin* is represented by "G" in the Greek, while the initial guttural of "Omri" is represented by a "Z" [=Ζαμβρεί], which implies that the *ayin* had a hard sound.

"if the Ḥabiri be identified, not with the Israelitish invaders after the Exodus, but with an earlier immigration of Semitic nomads into Palestine, among whom the ancestors of Israel were included. The chief uncertainty arises from the fact that the phonetic writing *Ḫa-bi-ri* occurs only in a limited group of letters, those of '*Abd-ḫiba* of Jerusalem.... The ideogram SA-GAS ('robbers') in other letters is conjectured to have the same value, but this is not absolutely demonstrated. Assuming that Winckler and others are right in equating the two, the Ḥabiri are in evidence over the whole country, occasionally as auxiliaries of the Egyptian government, but chiefly as its foes. The inference is very plausible that they were the roving Bedouin element of the population, as opposed to the settled inhabitants,—presumably a branch of the great Aramaean invasion which was then overflowing Mesopotamia and Syria. There is thus a strong probability that עברים [*'ibrim*] was originally the name of a group of tribes which invaded Palestine in the 15th century B.C., and that it was afterwards applied to the Israelites as the sole historic survivors of the immigrants. Etymologically, the word has usually been interpreted as meaning 'those from beyond' the river (cf. Jos. xxiv. 2 f., 14 f.); and, on that assumption, the river is certainly not the Tigris, and almost certainly not the Jordan, but *the* נהר [*nahar*] of the O.T., the Euphrates, 'beyond' which lay Ḥarran whence Abraham set out" (p. 218).

The foregoing explanation is far more probable than that which supposes the Ḥabiri, mentioned in the letters of 'Abdi-Ḫiba, king of Jerusalem, to have been the invading Israelites led by Joshua. But there seems to be no sufficient reason to call in question the statement of Ex. i. 11 that the store cities of Pithom and Raamses were built by the Hebrews, or the conclusion drawn from Naville's excavations that these cities were built in the reign of Ramses II (1292—1225 B.C.). For the present, we may conclude that the Exodus occurred during the reign of Merenptah (1225—1215 B.C.), and that the Ḥabiri who were attacking the towns of Palestine in the reign of Amenophis IV (1375—1358) may racially have been members of the same Semitic wave of invasion, Hebrew forerunners of the Israelite movement led a century and a half later by Moses and Joshua.

(III) THE APURIU

The French Egyptologist, M. Chabas, maintained half a century ago, that a foreign people, denoted *Apuriu*, or *Aperu*, or *Apriu*, and mentioned in the Inscriptions of Thothmes III (1501—1447 B.C.), Ramses II (1292—1225 B.C.) and Ramses IV (1167—1161 B.C.)[1], could

---

[1] So Breasted: Petrie's dates are Thothmes III, 1503—1449; Ramses II, 1300—1234; Merenptah, 1234—1214; Seti II, 1214—1209; Ramses III, 1202—1171; Ramses IV, 1171—1165. See Breasted's *Hist. of Ancient Egyptians* (1908), and Petrie's *Hist. of Eg.* vol. III.

be no other than the Israelites in Egypt. This view, which was at first discredited, has recently been revived. And there is to be said in favour of it (1) that, philologically, the Egyptian *'Apuriu* and the Hebrew *'Ibrim* ("Hebrews") may reasonably be held to be identical names: and (2) that the *Apuriu* are spoken of as engaged in forced labour in the quarries, &c. Those mentioned in the reign of Ramses IV must then be regarded as the descendants of those Israelites, who for one reason or another had been unable to make their escape from Egypt with the main body (see Driver's *Exodus*, pp. xli f.).

APPENDIX E

ISRAELITES IN EGYPT

I

Chronology

The Book of Genesis makes no mention of person, place, or event which enables us to say for certain under what king, or in what dynasty, Joseph was carried into Egypt, and after his elevation to be Vizier of the country was joined by his father and his brethren.

Two questions of chronology are raised: (1) what was the date of the descent into Egypt? (2) what was the date of the Exodus from Egypt?

A. *Archaeological data.*

In order to answer these questions, we are compelled, in the absence of any more direct evidence, to employ conjectures based upon *archaeological* data.

(*a*) It is a quite probable conjecture that the Amraphel of Gen. xiv. 1 is to be identified with Ḥammurabi, king of Babylon (*circ.* 2100 B.C.). Assuming the historicity of Gen. xiv., the period of Abraham, subsequent to his call, thus synchronizes with the reign of Ḥammurabi.

(*b*) M. Naville's excavations at Tel el-Maskhuta have shewn that a town of Pithom (P'etom) was founded by Ramses II (1300—1234 B.C., Petrie; 1292—1225 B.C., Breasted). It is a reasonable conjecture that this was one of the two towns Pithom and Raamses which the Israelites "built for Pharaoh" as store cities (Ex. i. 11); that Ramses II was the Pharaoh of the Oppression; and that the Pharaoh of the Exodus was his son and successor (cf. Ex. ii. 23), Merenptah, or Merneptah (1234—1214 B.C., Petrie; 1225—1215 B.C., Breasted).

(*c*) As the Tel el-Amarna letters shew that in the 15th cent. B.C. Canaan was subject to Egyptian rule, it is a reasonable conjecture that the invasion of the land by the Israelites under Joshua did not take place before 1400 B.C.; in other words, that the Exodus was later than that date.

According to these conjectures, based upon archaeological data, the conclusions are

(1) that the whole period from the call of Abraham to the Exodus extends from *circ.* 2100 B.C. to *circ.* 1230 B.C.;

(2) that the Exodus took place in the reign of Merenptah, or Merneptah, about 1230—1220 B.C.

Moreover, there is fair ground for assuming that the elevation of a young Hebrew to be Vizier of Egypt and the donation of the pasture-lands of Goshen to Hebrew clans would be less likely to have occurred under a native dynasty than under the Semitic Hyksos kings; and that "the new king over Egypt which knew not Joseph" (Ex. i. 8) may possibly represent the change from the Hyksos to the XVIIIth dynasty. Accordingly, as the expulsion of the Hyksos occurred in 1587 B.C., it has been conjectured

(3) that the elevation of Joseph and the descent of the Israelites into Egypt took place before *circ.* 1600 B.C.

The approximate dates, according to these conjectures, are as follows:

(1) The Call of Abraham, 2100 B.C.
(2) The Descent into Egypt, 1600 B.C.
(3) The Exodus, 1230 B.C.

B. *Biblical dates.*

In juxtaposition with these dates it will be convenient to put the traditional Biblical dates:

		Heb.	Sam. and LXX
(1)	The Call of Abraham	2136 B.C.	1921 B.C.
(2)	The Descent into Egypt	1921 ,,	1706 ,,
(3)	The Exodus	1491 ,,	1491 ,,
(4)	The Foundation of the Temple (4th year of Solomon)	1011 ,,	1011 ,,

(4) There are 480 years from the Exodus to the Foundation of the Temple; cf. 1 Kings vi. 1.

(3) There are 430 years' sojourn in Egypt; cf. Ex. xii. 40[1] (Sam. and LXX by adding "and in the land of Canaan" halve this period; cf. Gal. iii. 17; Jos. *Ant.* ii. 15. 2).

(1), (2) There are 215 years of the Patriarchs' sojourn in Canaan:

From the Call of Abraham (xii. 4) to the birth of Isaac (xxi. 5),	25 years
From the birth of Isaac to the birth of Jacob and Esau (xxv. 26),	60 years
From the birth of Jacob to his descent into Egypt (xlvii. 9),	130 years
	215 years

---

[1] The sojourn in Egypt appears as 400 years in Gen. xv. 13 (J), cf. Acts vii. 6; "four generations" in Gen. xv. 16 (J), cf. Ex. ii. 13 (E), vi. 16, 18, 20 (P).

APPENDIX

It will be seen that the traditional Biblical dates are not in agreement with those which are derived from Archaeology. The discrepancy is in respect of (*a*) the interval between the Call of Abraham and the Exodus; (*b*) the interval between the Exodus and the age of Solomon.

		(A) *Archaeological*	(B) *Biblical*
(1)	The Call of Abraham	circ. 2100 B.C.	2136 B.C.
(2)	The Descent into Egypt	circ. 1600 ,,	1921 ,,
(3)	The Exodus	circ. 1230 ,,	1491 ,,
(4)	The 4th year of Solomon	circ. 965 ,,	1011 ,,

According to A, the Exodus took place 870 years after the Call of Abraham, and 265 years before the founding of Solomon's Temple.

According to B, it took place 645 years after the Call of Abraham, and 480 years before the founding of Solomon's Temple.

According to A there are 500, according to B 215, years between the Call of Abraham and the Descent into Egypt.

At present, there seems to be no prospect of harmonizing the two groups of figures.

There is little reason to doubt that the P chronology, as incorporated in the books of Genesis and Exodus, and represented in 1 Kings vi. 1, is at the best an artificial system; and one to which too much importance ought not to be attached. For instance, it is probable that the 480 years between the Exodus and the building of the Temple represent a conventional period, symbolized by 12 generations of 40 years each.

On the other hand, it may well be considered doubtful whether the interval between Abraham and the Exodus extended over so long a period as 870 years (from 2100 B.C. to 1230 B.C.). (See Driver's *Genesis*, pp. xxvi—xxx; *Exodus*, pp. xxx f., xlv f.; Skinner's *Genesis*, pp. xiv—xvii; cf. article on "Chronology" in Hastings' *D.B.*)

NOTE. The P chronology, which reckoned the period from the Creation to the Exodus as 2666 years, was probably based on the tradition that 4000 years were to elapse between the Creation and the coming of the Messiah, and two-thirds of this period, i.e. 2666 years, were completed at the Exodus.

		Heb. text	Sam.	LXX
(1)	From the Creation to the Flood (Gen. v., vii. 11)	1656	1307	2262
(2)	From the Flood to the Call of Abraham (Gen. xi. 10—26, xii. 4)	365	1015	1145
(3)	From the Call of Abraham to the Exodus (as above)	645	430	430
		2666	2752	3837

II

Chronology of principal Egyptian Kings from the Thirteenth to the Nineteenth Dynasty

(With the dates given by Petrie and Breasted)

Egyptian Kings	Petrie	Breasted	Summary of events based on Breasted's Tables
Thirteenth to Seventeenth Dynasty	2565–1587	1788–1580	
Hyksos kings	2098–1587	1680–1580	Conquest and domination of Egypt by Semitic invaders
Eighteenth Dynasty	1587–1328	1580–1350	Expulsion of Hyksos: restoration of native Monarchy
Thothmes I	1541–1516	1547?–1501	Conquest of Cush, and of all Syria and Canaan
Thothmes III	1503–1449	1501–1447	Frequent Asiatic campaigns · Egyptian Empire extends to Euphrates
Amenophis III	1414–1383	1411–1375	Alliance with kings of Mitanni and Babylon: gigantic commercial connexions. Commencement of Semitic migration into Syria
Amenophis IV (Ikhnaton, or Khu-n-aten)	1383–1365	1375–1358	Religious reform or revolution: Thebes forsaken; new capital: Amarna correspondence; Canaan threatened by Habiri hordes on E. and by Hittites on N. Asiatic vassal princes, some conquered by Hittites, others regain independence
Nineteenth Dynasty	1328–1202	1350–1205	
Seti I	1326–1300	1313–1292	Canaan recovered by Egypt: great war with Hittites.
Ramses II	1300–1234	1292–1225	Great Egyptian prosperity. War in Asia. Oppression of Hebrews
Merenptah (or Merneptah)	1234–1214	1225–1215	Repulse of Libyans. Probable period of Exodus. First mention of Israel on monuments

III

The Hyksos

Assuming that the Pharaoh in the days of Joseph was one of the Hyksos, we have next to enquire what is known about these foreign conquerors of Egypt.

The Twelfth Dynasty had closed with a period of weakness and confusion. There swept into the Delta a horde of Asiatic invaders, apparently of Semitic origin, who overcame all resistance and took possession of the entire country of Egypt. Their capital was a stronghold in the Delta named Avaris, the site of which has not yet been discovered.

A Fragment of the History of Manetho, quoted by Josephus in his *Contra Apionem* (I. 14) has preserved the tradition of later times. "Its statements may be summarized as follows: In the reign of a king named Timaios the gods were angry with Egypt, and there came up from the East a race of ignoble men who conquered the country without a battle. They treated the native population with great cruelty, burned the cities, and demolished the temples. Thereafter they made one Salatis their king, and he established a great fortified camp at a place called Avaris (Ḥēt-uārt) on an arm of the Nile near Bubastis. Here he kept a garrison of 240,000 men. The Hyksos domination lasted for 511 years. Six kings are named—Salatis, 19 years; Beon, 44; Apakhnas, 36; Apophis, 61; Iannas, 50; Assis, 49. Eventually the kings of the Thebaid made insurrection against the oppressors, and under a king named Misfragmouthosis drove them into Avaris, and blockaded them there. Finally an arrangement was reached whereby the Hyksos were allowed to depart from Egypt into Syria, where they built the fortress called Jerusalem. They were called *Hyksos*, or 'Shepherd kings,' because *Hyk* in the sacred language of Egypt signifies a 'king,' and *sos* in the vulgar dialect a 'shepherd.' Some say that they were Arabians....

"An Inscription of Queen Hatshepsut, dating from only two generations after the expulsion of the invaders, says:

> 'I have restored that which was in ruins,
> I have raised up that which was unfinished,
> Since the Asiatics were in the midst of Avaris of the North land,
> And the barbarians were in the midst of them,
> Overthrowing that which had been made,
> While they ruled in ignorance of Râ.'

. . . .

"As to the duration of the period of oppression there is no certainty. Manetho's six named kings account for 260 years, and he states that these were the first kings, leaving others unnamed to fill up the 511 years. Petrie accepts the estimate of Manetho, allowing a century for the period of invasion and gradual conquest—260 years of more or less stable rule under the named kings, and the remaining century and a half for the struggle ending in the expulsion of the invaders. Breasted, on the other hand, who, following Meyer, allows only 208 years for the dynasties from the XIIth to the XVIIIth, maintains that 100 years is ample for the Hyksos period.... Material relics of the Hyksos kings are scanty.... Two Apepas can be identified.... One or other of these Apepas may be the 'Apophis' of the Manethonian fragment.... More important are the relics of Khyan who may, perhaps, be identified with the 'Iannas' of the fragment. Traces of his rule have been found in both Upper and Lower Egypt, while a granite lion bearing his cartouche was found at Baghdad, and an alabastron with his name was discovered by Evans at Knossos. One of the titles used by Khyan upon his scarabs and cylinders is *anq adebu*, 'embracer of the lands.' These facts have inspired Breasted's imagination to the reconstruction of a vanished Hyksos empire, embracing all the territory from the Euphrates to the first cataract of the Nile, and governed during part of its history by a ruler of the Jacob tribes of Israel in the person of that Pharaoh whose scarabs give his name as Jacob-her or Jacob-el....

"As to the name of the invaders, the first syllable is obviously the Egyptian *Ḥeq*, 'ruler,' the second may conceivably be *Shasu*, which was the generic Egyptian title for the pastoral races of the Eastern deserts. Khyan names himself *Ḥeq Setu*, 'chief of the deserts,' and perhaps the derivation may lie here...there is no reason to doubt the tradition that they were of Arabian, or at least of Semitic, origin. Their existing relics suggest that, while the beginning of their rule may have been marked by harshness and oppression, the tradition of their unbounded cruelty and destructiveness is exaggerated. As in so many other cases, the land conquered its conquerors, and the Apepas and Khyans became in all essentials Egyptian Pharaohs. Their influence upon the native Egyptian race was probably beneficial, and its results may be traced in the wider outlook and renewed vigour of the nation under the XVIIIth dynasty. In all probability the introduction of the horse and chariot as instruments of warfare was due to them, and may have been the chief cause of their easy conquest of the land."

James Baikie in Hastings' *Encycl. Religion and Ethics*, vol. VI. (1913), *s.v.* Hyksos.

See also Flinders Petrie, *History of Egypt*, I. 233 ff., II. 1—24; Breasted's *History of the Ancient Egyptians* (1908), chap. xii.

IV

Illustrations of Narratives in Genesis from Egyptian Antiquities

(*a*) The Patriarchs' entrance into Egypt; cf. Gen. xiii., xlii., xlvii.
In the Tombs at Beni-Hassan in Upper Egypt, about midway between Memphis and Thebes, there is preserved a vivid representation

of a family of the Aamu going down into Egypt. The monument on which this scene is depicted belongs to the reign of Usertesen II of the XIIth dynasty, *circ.* 2684—2660 B.C. (Petrie). Aamu is probably a general word for nomad Asiatics. The type of face is Semitic. The family consists of thirty-seven persons. Their possessions are fastened upon the backs of asses. The leader of the party is *ḥeq setu Absha* (or Absha, prince of the deserts), and he is bringing a present to the king of Egypt. The scene illustrates the reception of Asiatics, and affords a representation of the influx into Egypt which had already begun in the 3rd millennium B.C. (Petrie, *Hist. Eg.* I. 172).

(*b*) Seven years' famine in Egypt; cf. Gen. xli.

On a rock upon an island in the Nile, between Elephantiné and the first Cataract, there is a hieroglyphic inscription dating from the reign of Ptolemy Soter II which relates how certain lands in the neighbourhood had been given as an offering to Chnum the god of Elephantiné by the king Zoser (*circ.* 2800 B.C.) because of a seven years' famine: "my heart is in sore grief because of misfortune; seeing that, in my time, for the space of seven years the Nile has failed to come (i.e. there has been no proper Nile flood). The fruits of the field are lacking: there is a scarcity of herbage; there is nothing to eat; the children are crying, the young people can only just creep about."

Hugo Gressmann, *Altorientalische Texte u. Bilder*, Bd I. p. 233.

(*c*) The king's Vizier interrogates a messenger; cf. Gen. xlii. 9.

Assuming that Joseph was raised to be Vizier under one of the Hyksos kings, there is especial interest in the following extract from the Sallier II papyrus describing the relations between Apepa (Apophis) and the vassal king of Thebes, Seqenen-Ra: "Egypt was in the hands of enemies, and nobody was lord in that day. There was indeed a king, Seqenen-Ra; but he was a chief in the City of the South (Thebes), while enemies abode in the Town of the Aamu, and Apepa was king in Avaris....The messenger of king Apepa betook himself to the governor of the city of the South, and was brought before the governor of the city of the South country. He spoke thus, when he spoke to the messenger of king Apepa: 'Who hath sent thee hither to the city of the South? art thou come in order to spy out?'" (See Ball, *Light from the East*, p. 81; and Petrie, *Hist. Eg.* II. pp. 19—21.)

The eminent Orientalist, C. J. Ball, is strongly of opinion that the Hyksos king, Apepa I, is to be identified with the Pharaoh of the Book of Genesis. Cf. Gen. xlii. 23, xliii. 32, xliv. 5. "The Sallier papyrus also records that the court of Apepa was famous for its magicians....The tradition preserved by the Byzantine writer George Syncellus or Chancellor (fl. A.D. 800), that the Pharaoh of Joseph's days was named Aphophis, is one which is now found to agree exactly with the testimony of the monuments. There were two Hyksos kings named Apepa or Aphophis; but it was probably during the reign of Apepa I of the 15th dynasty that Joseph rose to power. During this period the court of Lower Egypt was at Zoan, in the field of Zoan." See Ps. lxxviii. 12, 43.

(*d*) The Tale of the Two Brothers, in the d'Orbiney papyrus, which was written for Seti II, of the XIXth dynasty (*circ.* 1214—1209 B.C., Petrie), illustrates Gen. xxxix. The following is a brief epitome from Petrie's *Egyptian Tales* (ii. 36 ff.).

There were two brothers, Anpu and Bata, living together in one house. The elder one, Anpu, one day sends Bata back from the field, in which they are working, to fetch some seed from the house. In the house Anpu's wife makes an immoral proposal to Bata, which Bata rejects. In the evening, on Anpu's return to the house, his wife accuses Bata on the false charge of wrongful advances. Anpu in rage seeks out his brother to slay him. But the story ends with Anpu's being persuaded of his brother's innocency: and he puts his wife to death for her wickedness.

V

The Egyptian Grand-Vizier
(From Breasted's *History of the Ancient Egyptians*, chap. xiii.)

"§ 184. The supreme position occupied by the Pharaoh meant a very active participation in the affairs of government. He was accustomed every morning to meet the vizier...to consult with him on all the interests of the country, and all the current business which necessarily came under his eye....Early in the Eighteenth Dynasty...the business of government and the duties of the Pharaoh had so increased that he appointed a second vizier. One resided at Thebes, for the administration of the South, from the cataract as far as the nome of Siut; while the other, who had charge of all the region north of the latter point, lived at Heliopolis. For administrative purposes the country was divided into irregular districts, of which there were at least twenty-seven between Siut and the cataract, and the country as a whole must have been divided into over twice that number. The head of the government in the old towns still bore the feudal title 'count,' but it now indicated solely administrative duties and might better be translated 'mayor' or 'governor.' Each of the smaller towns had a 'town-ruler,' but in the other districts there were only recorders and scribes, with one of their number at their head.

"§ 185. ...For purposes of taxation all lands and other property of the crown, except that held by the temples, were recorded in the tax-registers of the White House, as the treasury was still called....On the basis of these, taxes were assessed. They were still collected in naturalia: cattle, grain, wine, oil, honey, textiles and the like. Besides the cattle-yards, the 'granary' was the chief sub-department of the White House, and there were innumerable other magazines for the storage of its receipts. If we may accept Hebrew tradition as transmitted in the story of Joseph, such taxes comprised one-fifth of the produce of the land (Gen. xlvii. 23—27). The chief treasurer, through the local officials above noticed, collected all such taxes; he was, however, under the authority of the vizier, to whom he made a report every morning, after which he received permission to open the offices and magazines for the day's business....

"§ 186. In the administration of justice the southern vizier played even a greater rôle than in the treasury. Here he was supreme....Every morning the people crowded into the 'hall of the vizier,' where the ushers and bailiffs jostled them into line that they might 'be heard,' in order of arrival, one after another. All crimes in the capital city were denounced and tried before him, and he maintained a criminal docket of prisoners awaiting trial or punishment, which strikingly suggests modern documents of the same sort....

"§ 188. The southern vizier was the motive power behind the organization and operation of this ancient state. We recall that he went in every morning and took counsel with the Pharaoh on the affairs of the country; and the only other check upon his untrammelled control of the state was a law constraining him to report the condition of his office to the chief treasurer. His office was the Pharaoh's means of communication with the local authorities, who reported to him in writing on the first day of each season, that is, three times a year. It is in his office that we discern with unmistakable clearness the complete centralization of all local government in all its functions. He was minister of war for both army and navy, and in the Eighteenth Dynasty at least, 'when the king was with the army,' he conducted the administration at home. He had legal control of the temples throughout the country, or, as the Egyptian put it, 'he established laws in the temples of the gods of the South and the North,' so that he was minister of ecclesiastical affairs. He exercised advisory functions in all the offices of the state; so long as his office was undivided with a vizier of the North he was grand steward of all Egypt, and there was no prime function of the state which did not operate immediately or secondarily through his office. He was a veritable Joseph and it must have been this office which the Hebrew narrator had in mind as that to which Joseph was appointed. He was regarded by the people as their great protector, and no higher praise could be proffered to Amon when addressed by a worshipper than to call him 'the poor man's vizier who does not accept the bribe of the guilty.'...Several of [the viziers of the Eighteenth Dynasty] have left a record of their installation, with a long list of the duties of the office, engraved and painted upon the walls of their Theban tombs, and it is from these that we have drawn our account of the vizier."

VI

Special Note on the Egyptians in the Time of Joseph
The Hyksos: Joseph as Grand Vizier, etc.

I. We have no certain means of deciding the period of Egyptian History to which is to be assigned the Episode of Joseph and of the descent of Jacob into Egypt.

In all probability, it belongs to the time at which Egypt was overrun and subjugated by Asiatic invaders who are known by the name of the Hyksos.

According to Flinders Petrie, "the whole duration of the foreign dominion of this people and their descendants was 511 years" (*Hist. of Eg.* I. p. 236, 1895), from the Fifteenth to the Seventeenth Dynasty, about 2098—1587 B.C. Unfortunately there is great uncertainty concerning the length of this period. The available materials relating to it are scanty in the extreme. More recently, Professor J. H. Breasted has given reasons for assigning a much shorter duration to the domination of the Asiatics. His Chronological Summary is as follows: "Thirteenth to Seventeenth Dynasties, 208 years (1788—1580). Great confusion, usurpation, civil war. Hyksos rule about 100 years (1675—1575 B.C.?)" (*A Hist. of the Ancient Egyptians*, p. 425, 1908).

Unquestionably, it is natural to assume that the time of an Asiatic domination over Egypt would have been most favourable (1) to the advancement of a Semite, like Joseph, to the position of Vizier; and (2) to the generous reception of nomad Asiatics, like Jacob and his sons, by the Pharaoh. It is also natural to assume, that the accession of an Egyptian king "which knew not Joseph" (Ex. i. 8) denoted the expulsion of the Hyksos, and the renewal of a native Egyptian monarchy. (See Driver's *Exodus*.)

II. The data which have been employed for calculating this period are as follows:

1. The identification of Amraphel in Gen. xiv. 1 with Hammurabi, King of Babylon. If this be correct, it determines the date of Abraham as about 2100 B.C.

2. The store-cities Pithom and Raamses were built in the reign of the Pharaoh of the Oppression (Ex. i. 11). The builder of Pithom was Ramses II, as has been shewn by the excavations of Pithom (*Tell el Mashkuta*) by M. Naville. The reign of Ramses II lasted either from 1300 to 1234 (Petrie), or from 1292 to 1225 (Breasted).

3. The successor of Ramses II was Merenptah (or Mernephtah), to whose reign the Exodus has generally been assigned; and in whose Inscriptions occurs the first mention of Israel in the Ancient Monuments: "Ysirraal is desolated, its seed (or fruit) is not."

4. According to the tradition preserved in Ex. xii. 40, 41 (Heb.

text), the Israelites were 430 years in Egypt; compare the mention of 400 years in Gen. xv. 13.

5. Assuming that the Exodus occurred about 1230 B.C., the Israelites arrival in Egypt, 430 years previously, would have been about 1660 B.C., which synchronizes with the period of the dominion of the Hyksos.

6. In general agreement with this conclusion would be the evidence furnished by the Tel el-Amarna Letters, according to which at the time of Amenhotep III (1414—1383) and Amenhotep IV of Egypt (1383 —1365), Canaan was a province, held by vassal-kings under the rule of the Egyptian king. The Exodus could not well have taken place previous to that date.

These *data* are not in agreement with the Chronology of the Hebrew tradition, acccording to which the Exodus occurred in 1491 (1 Kings vi. 1), the descent of Jacob into Egypt 1921, and the call of Abraham 2136.

The Hebrew tradition (P), however, in assigning only 215 years to the lives of the Patriarchs in Canaan, is following a highly artificial system of chronology.

From the call of Abraham (xii. 4) to the birth of Isaac (xxi. 5)	= 25 years
From the birth of Isaac to the birth of Jacob (xxv. 26)	= 60 ,,
From the birth of Jacob to Jacob's descent into Egypt (xlvii. 9, 28)	= 130 ,,
	= 215 years

III. The Hyksos. Professor Breasted gives the following summary of the history of the Hyksos:

"About 1657 B.C., before the close of the Thirteenth Dynasty, there now poured into the Delta from Asia a possibly Semitic invasion such as that which in prehistoric times had stamped the language with its unmistakable form; and again in our own era, under the influence of Mohammed's teaching, had overwhelmed the land....These invaders, now generally called the Hyksos, after the designation applied to them by Josephus (quoting Manetho), themselves left so few monuments in Egypt that even their nationality is still the subject of much difference of opinion; while the exact length and character of their supremacy, for the same reason, are equally obscure matters.... The late tradition regarding the Hyksos, recorded by Manetho and preserved to us in the essay of Josephus against Apion, is but the substance of a folk-tale...." (Breasted, *A Hist. of the Anc. Egyptians*, pp. 174 f.).

"Two generations after the Hyksos had been expelled from the country, the great queen Hatshepsut, narrating her restoration of the temples they had desecrated, calls them 'Asiatics' and 'barbarians' dwelling in Avaris and ruling 'in ignorance of Re.'

"The still earlier evidence of a soldier in the Egyptian army that expelled the Hyksos shows that a siege of Avaris was necessary to drive them from the country; and, further, that the pursuit of them was continued into southern Palestine, and ultimately into Phoenicia or Coelesyria....From these earlier documents it is evident that the Hyksos were an Asiatic people who ruled Egypt from their stronghold of Avaris in the Delta. The exact site is still undetermined.... The later tradition as quoted from Manetho by Josephus is as follows:

"'There was a king of ours whose name was Timaios, in whose reign it came to pass, I know not why, that God was displeased with us, and there came unexpectedly men of ignoble birth out of the eastern parts, who had boldness enough to make an expedition into our country, and easily subdued it by force without a battle. And when they had got our rulers under their power, they afterwards savagely burnt down our cities and demolished the temples of the gods, and used all the inhabitants in a most hostile manner, for they slew some and led the children and wives of others into slavery. At length they made one of themselves king, whose name was Salatis, and he lived at Memphis and made both Upper and Lower Egypt pay tribute, and left garrisons in places that were most suitable for them. And he made the eastern part especially strong, as he foresaw that the Assyrians who had then the greatest power, would covet their kingdom and invade them. And as he found in the Saite [read Sethroite] nome a city very fit for his purpose—which lay east of the arm of the Nile near Bubastis, and with regard to a certain theological notion was called Avaris—he rebuilt it and made it very strong by the walls he built around it and by a numerous garrison of two hundred and forty thousand armed men, whom he put into it to keep it' (*Contr. Apion.* i. 14).

"If we eliminate the absurd reference to the Assyrians and the preposterous number of the garrison at Avaris, the tale may be credited as in general a probable narrative....Still quoting from Manetho, Josephus says: 'All this nation was styled Hyksos, that is, Shepherd Kings: for the first syllable "hyk" in the sacred dialect denotes a king, and "sos" signifies a shepherd, but this is only according to the vulgar tongue: and of these was compounded the term Hyksos. Some say, they were Arabians.' According to his epitomizers, Manetho also called them Phoenicians.

"Turning to the designations of Asiatic rulers as preserved on the Middle Kingdom and Hyksos monuments, there is no such term to be found as 'ruler of shepherds,' and Manetho wisely adds that the word 'sos' only means shepherd in the late vulgar dialect. There is no such word known in the older language of the monuments. 'Hyk' (Egyptian Ḥḳ '), however, is a common word for ruler, as Manetho says, and Khian, one of the Hyksos kings, often gives himself this title upon his monuments, followed by a word for 'countries' which by slight and very common phonetic changes might become 'sos';

so that 'Hyksos' is a not improbable Greek spelling for the Egyptian title 'Ruler of Countries'" (Breasted, pp. 176-178).

..."The influence upon Egypt of such a foreign dominion, including both Syria-Palestine and the lower Nile valley, was epoch-making....It brought the horse into the Nile valley and taught the Egyptians warfare on a large scale. Whatever they may have suffered, the Egyptians owed an incalculable debt to their conquerors" (*ibid.* p. 184).

"After the expulsion of the Hyksos from the Delta frontier, the victorious Egyptian king Ahmose reigned supreme. The old landed nobility had almost become extinct. 'All Egypt was now the personal estate of the Pharaoh just as it was after the destruction of the Mamlukes by Mohammed Ali early in the nineteenth century. It is this state of affairs which in Hebrew tradition was represented as the direct result of Joseph's sagacity' (Gen. xlvii. 19, 20)" (*ibid.* p. 189).

"The supreme position occupied by the Pharaoh meant a very active participation in the affairs of government. He was accustomed every morning to meet the vizier, still the mainspring of the administration....Early in the Eighteenth Dynasty...the business of government and the duties of the Pharaoh had so increased that he appointed a second vizier. One resided at Thebes, for the administration of the South, from the cataract as far as the nome of Siut; while the other, who had charge of all the region north of the latter point, lived at Heliopolis....For purposes of taxation all lands and other property of the Crown, except that held by the temples, were recorded in the tax-registers of the White House, as the treasury was still called....On the basis of these taxes were assesed. They were still collected in naturalia : cattle, grain, wine, oil, honey, textiles, and the like. Besides the cattle-yards, the 'granary' was the chief sub-department of the White House, and there were innumerable other magazines for the storage of its receipts. If we may accept Hebrew tradition as transmitted in the story of Joseph, such taxes comprised one-fifth of the produce of the land (Gen. xlvii. 23-27)" (*ibid.* pp. 196, 197).

V. The position of Joseph as Vizier. "The southern vizier was the motive power behind the organization and operation of this ancient state. We recall that he went in every morning and took council with the Pharaoh on the affairs of the country ; and the only other check upon his untrammelled control of the state was a law constraining him to report the condition of his office to the chief treasurer. His office was the Pharaoh's means of communication with the local authorities, who reported to him in writing on the first day of each season, that is, three times a year. It is in his office that we discern with unmistakeable clearness the complete centralization of all local government in all its functions. He was minister of war for both army and navy, and in the Eighteenth Dynasty at least, 'when the King was with the army,' he conducted the administration at home.

He had legal control of the temples throughout the country, or, as the Egyptian put it 'he established laws in the temples of the gods of the South and the North,' so that he was minister of ecclesiastical affairs. He exercised advisory functions in all the offices of the state; so long as his office was undivided with a vizier of the North he was grand steward of all Egypt, and there was no prime function of the state which did not operate immediately or secondarily through his office. He was a veritable Joseph, and it must have been this office which the Hebrew narrator had in mind as that to which Joseph was appointed. He was regarded by the people as their great protector, and no higher praise could be proffered to Amon when addressed by a worshipper than to call him 'the poor man's vizier who does not accept the bribe of the guilty'" (Breasted, pp. 200 f.).

VI. SUMMARY OF EGYPTIAN HISTORY FROM THIRTEENTH TO NINETEENTH DYNASTY (1788—1215 C.).

(Based on Breasted, *History of Anc. Egypt*, pp. 425—430.)

Thirteenth to Seventeenth Dynasties Great confusion, usurpation, civil war. Hyksos rule about 100 years	1788–1580	Hyksos consolidate Syrian power, probably at Kadesh, and absorb Egypt.
EMPIRE, FIRST PERIOD	1580—1350	Assyrian and Babylonian power in decline.
Eighteenth Dynasty Thebes 1 Ahmose I	1580—1557	Expulsion of Hyksos: Syria-Palestine tributary to Egypt.
2 Amenhotep I 3 Thutmose I	1557—1501	
4 Thutmose II 5 Hatshepsut 6 Thutmose III	1501—1447	All states of Syria-Palestine Egyptian vassals. Power of Kadesh, leading Syrian state, centre of Hyksos power, now broken.
7 Amenhotep II	1448—1420	
8 Thutmose IV	1420—1411	
9 Amenhotep III	1411—1375	Greatest splendour of Empire.... Kheta (Hittites) begin absorption of Syria, Amarna letters.
10 Ikhnaton (Amenhotep IV)	1375—1358	Khabiri Semites begin migration into Syria and Palestine Monotheist: religious revolution. Thebes forsaken. Amarna Letters. Hittites seize Syria to Amor: Khabiri Semites invade Palestine, Hebrews with them.
11—13	1358—1350	Complete dissolution of Egyptian Empire in Asia.

APPENDIX

EMPIRE SECOND PERIOD			1350 1—150	Former Asiatic vassal-kingdoms of Egypt gain independence, or are absorbed by Hittites.
Nineteenth Dynasty			1350—1205	
1 Harmhab	..	.. ..	1350—1315	Reorganization: Thebes restored.
2 Ramses I	..	.. ..	1315—1314	
3 Seti I	..	.. ..	1313—1292	Palestine recovered: first conflict with Hittites.
4 Ramses II	..	.. ..	1292—1225	War with Hittites, 16 years: treaty with Hittites 1271. Oppression of Hebrews (?)
5 Merenptah	..	.. ..	1225—1215	Asiatic campaign; "Israel" among defeated. "Israel" first mentioned on the monuments "Exodus" of Israelites (?)

INDEX

Abel 69
Abel-mizraim 443
'âbîr 437
Abraham, Abram (names) xliv, 151, 198
abrech 379
'abyss' 5, 438
Accad 137
Adam, *âdâm* 29, 37, 84, 98
'adder' 434
agriculture xlv, 56, 58
'akêdah 243
alliteration 4, 75, 211
altar 114, 158, 236, 337
Amalek 171, 345
Amorites 139, 190
Amraphel xiii, 167, 170, 179, 463
angel 230, 293
'angel of the LORD' 194
anthropomorphisms xx, 98, 108, 114
'aprons' 52
'Apuriu 462 f.
Aquinas, St Thomas 24, 44, 65
Arabia 143
Aram 141 f.
Ararat 111
archaeology xliii
ark 101 f.
Asher xliii, 304, 434 f.
astral myth xli, 174
astronomy 12, 46, 352
Augustine, St 65, 245

Babel 136, 144 ff.
Babylon xxv, 136
Babylonian legends, &c. xxxviii, 60 ff., 115 ff., 447 ff.

'bakemeats' 370
'bdellium' 33
'beasts' 17
'bed's head' 420
be'êr 277
Beer-lahai-roi 196
Beer-sheba 232, 279
'before the LORD' 136
beka 255
Bela 168, 348
'believe' 187
Benjamin xvii, 340, 380, 439
Berossus xxxvi, 101, 118, 447
Bethel 295, 336
Bethlehem 340
'betimes' 279
Birs Nimrud 147
bitumen 146, 172
'bless oneself' 156, 208, 239, 274; 'blessing' 16, 155, 423; of Isaac 283; of Jacob 426
blood 74 f., 122, 354
blood-revenge 77, 289
'bottle' 229
'bowels' 394
'brass' 80
'brother' = relative 163, 173, 313
Browning, Robert 29
'butler' 367
'butter' 206

Cain 68
'call upon' xxi, 83
Calneh 137
Calvin 235, 236, 242, 259
'camels' 253, 255
Canaanite, the 158

INDEX

'cattle' 17, 103
Chaldees 152 f.
Chapman's *Pentateuch* x, xiv, xvi, 453 ff.
chariots 378 f.
Charles, Dr 63, 183
Chedorlaomer 167
Cherubim 59
'choice' 246
'choice fruits' 390
chronology xxvii f., 90 f., 463 f.,
circumcision 199 f., 334 [476 f.
'clean', 'unclean' 104
'coat of many colours' 351
'coffin' 446
'comfort' 87, 205, 289
'commune' 211, 247
Cook, Dr S. A. 193, 228
Cosmogonies of Genesis 42 ff.
covenant 103, 124, 126, 188 f., 199
'covering of the eyes' 225
'create' 2, 15
Creation, Babylonian myths of 447 ff.
'cursed' 53, 56, 156, 285
Cush 134 f.
'cut off' 201

'D' xix
Damascus 175, 186
Dan (place) xv, xlv, 174; (tribe) 303, 433 f.
Davidson, Prof. A. B. 23, 59, 98, 211, 362, 365
'days' 7 f.
Dead Sea 209, 217
'deep, the' 5, 107, 438
'deep sleep' 38, 189
Delitzsch, Prof. F. 47
development 16
Dillmann x, 288, 338
Dinah xxxiv, 305, 331 f.
'divine' 306, 396
Documents (J, E, P) xviii ff.
Dothan 353
'dowry' 333
'dreadful' 294
dreams xxii, 351, 369

Driver, Dr xxvii, lxiii, 53, 139, 167, 273, 288, 397, 428

'E' xix, xxi f.
'east, children of the' 296; 'east country' 264
'eastward' 30, 146
'eat bread' 319, 355, 393
Eber 141
Eden 30 f., 47
Eder, tower of 341
Edom 271, 344 ff.
Egypt 119, 134, 159, 365, 371, 379 f., 395, 413, 416, 418, 472 ff.
Egyptian Kings 466
'Êl lviii

    Êl Elyon lix, 176 f.

    Êl Shaddai lix, 197, 290, 391, 438

    Êl 'Olam 233

Elam 141, 167
Elath 171
election xlvi, xlix f.
Elohim lvi
embalming 441
Engedi 171
Enoch 78, 86
'entreat' 161
ephah 206
Ephraim and Manasseh xxxiv, 381, 420 ff.
Erech 136
Erman 380, 418
Esau 270; Esau's wives 279, 343
etymology, popular 38, 68, 82
Euphrates 35, 191
Eve 57

faith, Abraham's lii, 155 f., 242
Fall, Note on the 60 ff.
famine 159, 273, 381, 469
'father's kin' 201
'find grace, favour, &c.' xxi, 99, 321
'firmament' 8 f.
Flood, the 96 ff., 453 ff.; date of, xxxvi

INDEX

folk-lore xxiii, xxxii, xxxviii
'folly' xv, 333
'forasmuch as' xxi, 206, 213, 328
'Fortunate' 304
'fountain' 254
Frazer, J. G. 162
'furniture' 315

Gad 304, 434
'gate' 212, 248
'gathered to one's people' 265
Genealogies xxxv ff., 79, 89, 132 ff., 149 ff., 152, 154, 239, 265, 407
'generations' xi, xxviii, 26, 83
Genesis, Book of, name ix
geology 4, 10
Gerar 222, 276
'gift' 328
Gihon 33
Gilead 304, 313, 446
'glory' = soul 428
God, Names of lvi ff.
'God forbid' 397 f.
'good' 22
Gordon 75, 82, 447 ff.
Goshen 402, 411
'governor' 383
'grain overseers' 376
'grave' = *Sheôl* 357, 400
'grisled' 311
'guard, captain of the' 358

Ḥabiri 173, 370, 460 ff.
Hadad 348
Hagar 192 f., 227 ff., 266
haggadah 243, 452
Ham 126 ff.
Hamath 140
Ḥammurabi xliii, 136, 167, 179 f.
Havilah 33, 135, 267
Hebrew 173, 366, 370, 461 f.
Hebron 166, 245, 461
'help meet' 36
Heth 139; children of, 246
Hiddekel 34
historical value of Genesis xxxviii ff.
'honey' 391
Horites 171, 346

horses 416
hospitality 205
'hough' 428
human sacrifice 241
'hundredfold' 276
Hyksos 379, 416, 418, 467 ff., 474

'image of God' 20, 84, 123
'imagination' 98
individual, rights of liv, 243
inspiration xlvi f.
intercession 211
'interpreter' 386
Isaac lii, 202, 207, 227
'isles' 133 f.
Israel 325, 339
Issachar 305, 432

'J' xix ff.
Jabbok 323 f.
Jacob, name of 270, 272 f.; character lii
Japheth 129
Jastrow, Dr 61 f.
Javan 132
Jehovah lvii
'Jehovah-jireh' 237
Jeremias, Prof. xli, 120
Jerome, St 184, 370
'jewels' 260
'Jordan, beyond' 443
Joseph 306, 350 ff., 435 ff.
Jubilees, Book of xlii, 342
Judah 302, 359 ff., 429 ff.
'judge' 210

Kedar 266
kedêshah 360 f.
ḳesitah 330
Keturah 263
Kikkar, the 164
Kiriath-arba 245, 342
'knees, to bear upon the' 303, 446

'ladder' 292
Lamech, Songs of xxxv, 81 f.; Legend of 452

languages, diversity of 145 f.
Lankester, Ray 21
'latter days' 426
'lentils' 272
Levi 302, 331 ff., 427 f.
levirate marriage 359 f.
light 7
'lightly' 275
'lights' 12
'linen, fine' 378
lion 429
longevity of patriarchs 91
Lot 151, 172, 212 ff.; Lot's wife 218

Macalister 138
Machir 445 f.
Machpelah 247 f.
'magicians' 373
Mahanaim 320
'male and female' 20, 103
Mamre 166, 173, 249
man, nature of xlviii, 20, 29; prehistoric xxxviii
'mandrakes' 304
marriage customs 300
Martensen 62
'meat' 22, 257
'meditate' 262
Melchizedek xlvi, 175, 182 ff.
'mercy and truth' 256
Meredith, Geo. 73
Merenptah lxviii, 463, 466
'merry' 395
'mess of pottage' 271; 'messes' 395
Messiah 1, 55, 156, 430 f.
Midianites 263, 356
Milton 6, 94, 395
'mist' 29
Mizpah 318
Mizraim 134, 138, 192
Moab and Ammon xxxiv, 220
moral difficulties liii ff.
'Moriah, land of' 234
mourning 44
mummy 441
myth xxxii

nabî xv, 223
'nakedness of the land' 384
names 37, 301
Names of God xviii, lvi ff.
Naphtali 303, 435
Natural Religion 177
Negeb, the xv, 158, 162
nephesh 15, 30, 124, 340
Nephilim 95
nezem 255
Nile, River 372
Nimrod 135 f.
Noah 87 ff.; Song of 130 f.
Nod, land of 78

'oak of Moreh' 157
'oaks of Mamre' 173
'officer' 358
'olive-leaf' 112
On 379
'onyx' 33
Ophir 143
Origen 127

'P' xxvi ff.
Paddan-aram 268, 290
Paradise 30, 47
'parcel' 330
Patriarchal Narratives xiii, xxxix ff.
Patriarchs, antediluvian 88 f.
Peniel, Penuel 325 f.
Pentateuch ix, xiv; compilation of xvi
Perez 363
Perizzite 163, 191
Peters 293
Pharaoh 160, 384
Phicol 231, 278
Philistines xv, 138, 233, 273
Philo 183
'pilgrimage' 414
'pillar' xxvi, 295, 317, 339
'place' 10, 157, 235, 292
'plague' 161
'Plain, the' (of Jordan) 164
'plain man' 270
'plane' 308
polytheism xii, 2, 18

INDEX

'poplar' 308
Potiphar xxxi, 358, 363
'princes' 266
promises, the xlix, 155
Prophets, Hebrew xiii, xxiv
Protevangelium 54

races, dispersion of 132 ff., 144 f.
Rachel's grave 340
rainbow, the 125
Rameses 415
Ramses II lxviii, 412, 463
Rashi 24
'ravin' 439
'red' 269, 271
'reed-grass' 373
religious teaching of Gen. xlvi ff.
Reuben xxiv, 301, 341, 354, 388, 426
'ring' 255
River, the 313
'river of Egypt' 191

Sabbath, the xxvii, 25, 40 f.
sacrifice 57, 70; of Cain 71; of Isaac 240 ff.
'saith the LORD' 238
Salem 175
Sanday and Headlam 66
Sarah xvii, 152, 160, 201
Sayce, Prof. 33 f., 47, 143, 340
science 45 f.
'sea'=West xv, 158
Sea, the Salt 169
'sea-monsters' 15
'self-same day' 108, 203
Seir 320, 344
'set' 14
Sethites, the 83 f., 89 f.
Shakespeare 207, 309, 324, 368, 404
Sheba 135, 264
Shechem 425
shekel 248
Shem 129, 141 f., 154
shepherds xlv, 413
Shiloh l, 430 f.
Shinar 137, 146

'signs' 13
sin xlviii
'sinew' 326
Six Days, the 44
Skinner, Dr 116, 164, 332
Sodom and Gomorrah 209, 217 f.
'sojourner' 246; 'sojournings' 199, 414
'sons of God' 93
'souls' 157
South, the 158
'spicery' 355
'spies' 384, 387
spirit, the 5; 'spirit of God' 377
'sporting' 275
'stink, make to' 336
'straitly' 390
'stranger' 246
'stuff' 404
Succoth 329
'supplant' 286
'sweet savour' 114
'Sword, Song of the' 81
'Syrian' 291

'tabret' 314
'Tale of Two Brothers' 365, 470
Talmud 64
'tamarisk tree' 233
Targum 24, 69, 327, 353, 431
Tarshish 133
Tel el-Amarna Tablets xliii, 139, 458 ff.
'tell' 187
'tender' 299
Tennant, Dr F. R. 66
Tennyson 73
tenth, tithe 177, 296
Terah xxxvi
teraphim xiii, 313
terebinth 157, 166, 337
'to this day' xiv, 238
Tiamat 5, 43, 448 f.
Tigris 34
tōhû va-bhōhû 4
Tōrah ix, xlvi
'tree of life,' the 31

INDEX

'unawares' 335
Ur of the Chaldees 152, 188
Uru-salim (=Jerusalem) 176
Uz 142

'vessels' 391
vizier 383, 470 f.
vow 295

'walk with God, to,' 85, 197
'ward' 368
'weigh, to' 249
'well-stricken' 207, 250
Wesley, Charles 323

'west' 158
Westcott, Bp xxxii, 184
Wiclif, 345
'wild ass' 195
'windows of heaven' 107
word of God 6, 155

Xisuthros xxxvi

Zaphenath-paneah 379
Zebulun 305, 432
Ziggurat 145 f.
Zoar 164, 217